PUBLICATION UPDATE

Route to: ☐_____ ☐_____ ☐_____ ☐_____
          ☐_____ ☐_____ ☐_____ ☐_____

Thompson on Real Property, Second Thomas Edition

Publication 67261   Release 10   June 2010

HIGHLIGHTS

Updates

- *New* **Second Thomas Edition of Volume 13**. Updates throughout Volume 13 by Professor David Thomas include analysis of new case law and statutes of national importance.

- **7 NEW CHAPTERS**

- The treatise now contains 14 volumes in the Second Thomas Edition: 1, 2, 3, 4, 5, 6, 7, 8, 9, 10, 11, 12, 13 and 15.

EXPANDED COVERAGE IN-CLUDES NEW CHAPTERS ON REAL PROPERTY LAW IN THE FOLLOWING COUNTRIES:

- **Canada;**
- **Kazakhstan;**
- **Korea;**
- **India;**
- **Poland;**
- **Philippines;** and
- **Romania.**

Matthew Bender provides continuing customer support for all its products:

- Editorial assistance—please consult the "Questions About This Publication" directory printed on the copyright page;

- Customer Service—missing pages, shipments, billing or other customer service matters (1-800-833-9844).

- Outside the United States and Canada, (518) 487-3000, or fax (518) 487-3584;

- Toll-free ordering (1-800-223-1940).

www.lexis.com

THOMPSON ON REAL PROPERTY

SECOND THOMAS EDITION

DAVID A. THOMAS

Editor-in-Chief

Volume 13

 LexisNexis

QUESTIONS ABOUT THIS PUBLICATION?

For questions about the **Editorial Content** appearing in these volumes or reprint permission, please call:

Nancy Greening, J.D. at 1-908-673-3361
Email: .... nancy.h.greening@lexisnexis.com
Kelly Prichett, J.D. at .... 1-800-424-0651 Ext. 3361
Email: .... kelly.a.prichett@lexisnexis.com

For assistance with replacement pages, shipments, billing or other customer service matters, please call:

Customer Services Department at . . . . (800) 833-9844
Outside the United States and Canada, please call . . . . (518) 487-3000
Fax Number . . . . (518) 487-3584
Customer Service Website . . . . http://www.lexisnexis.com/custserv/

For information on other Matthew Bender publications, please call

Your account manager or . . . . (800) 223-1940
Outside the United States and Canada, please call . . . . (518) 487-3000

Library of Congress Card Number: 98-85590

ISBN: 978-1-5583-4156-2

Cite this volume of the treatise as 13 Thompson on Real Property, Second Thomas Edition (David A. Thomas, ed. LexisNexis).

Editorial Offices
121 Chanlon Rd., New Providence, NJ 07974 (908) 464-6800
201 Mission St., San Francisco, CA 94105-1831 (415) 908-3200
www.lexisnexis.com

MATTHEW◆BENDER

CONTRIBUTORS TO VOLUME 13

JOHN JA BURKE
Professor of Law, and Director of the Law School at the Kazakhstan Institute of
Management, Economics and Strategic Research
Chapter 106KZ (Kazakhstan)

C. DAVID DEBENEDETTI
DeBenedetti Majewski Szczesniak
Poland
Chapter 106PL (Poland)

NICHOLAS S. HAMMOND
Hammond, Bogaru & Associates
Chapter 106RO (Romania)

PROFESSOR GEORGE LEFCOE
The Law Center
University of Southern California
Chapters 102 and 104

ROMAN NURPEISSOV
Salans Almaty
Kazakhstan
Chapter 106KZ (Kazakhstan)

PROFESSOR DAVID A. THOMAS
J. Reuben Clark Law School
Brigham Young University
Chapters 103, 105, and 106AT (Austria), 106BR (Brazil), 106CA (Canada), 106CH
(Switzerland), 106CL (Chile), 106CN (China), 106DE (Germany), 106DK
(Denmark), 106EG (Egypt), 106EU (European Union), 106FR (France), 106GB
(Great Britain), 106IN (India), 106JP (Japan), 106KE (Kenya), 106KR (South
Korea), 106MX (Mexico), 106PH (Philippines), 106RU (Russia)

AUTHOR BIOGRAPHIES

David A. Thomas

David A. Thomas is the Rex E. Lee Endowed Chair and Professor of Law at Brigham Young University's J. Reuben Clark Law School, where he has taught since 1974. He was born in Los Angeles, California, in 1944, and was educated in Utah schools after 1950. He earned his B.A. and M.L.S. degrees at Brigham Young University (1967, 1977) and his J.D. at Duke University Law School (1972), after an interruption for military service in Vietnam. Following law school graduation, he completed a federal judicial clerkship and practiced law in Salt Lake City, before joining the law school faculty at Brigham Young University. As a teacher and author in both property and civil procedure areas, he has effectively combined theory and practice in conducting real property transactions, dispute resolution, and expert witness assignments. He proposed and drafted Utah first statutory changes in common law easement rules, which were enacted as the state's enabling legislation for historic preservation easement; he also drafted Utah's long range highway corridor preservation legislation. Professor Thomas has been admitted to practice before the Utah Supreme Court, the U.S. District Court for the District of Utah, the U.S. Tenth Circuit Court of Appeals, and the United States Supreme Court. He has been a bar examiner for Utah and has prepared bar examination questions for Utah and several other states. He has also served on numerous law school accreditation site inspection teams. He is a member of the real property section of the American Bar Association, where he has held numerous leadership positions. He is also a founding member of the Real Estate Transactions Section of the Association of American Law Schools.

Professor Thomas has published extensively on real property, civil procedure and common law legal history topics, including chapters in several treatises and articles in professional journals. He is the author (with Backman) of *A Practical Guide to Disputes Between Adjoining Landowners*, *Utah Civil Practice*, *Utah Civil Procedure*, and (with Backman) Utah Real Property Law. He is fluent in German and has been active in research and scholarly affairs in the United Kingdom and continental Europe.

John JA Burke

John JA Burke, B.A., J.D. PhD, is Professor of Law, and Director of the Law School at the Kazakhstan Institute of Management, Economics and Strategic Research. He also is Professor of Law, Department of Law, at the Riga International School of Economics and Business Administration, Latvia. Professor Burke revises the European Union Law Digest for LexisNexis, and serves as Counsel to the Legislature of the State of New Jersey. His areas of expertise include international trade law, EU financial services law, and private international law. He has practiced law in the public and private sectors in the United States and Europe, and is a member of the bars of New York and New Jersey. He is the former Rector of International University Audentes, and of the Riga Graduate School of Law, Riga. He has a substantial publication record. He is under contract to write manuscripts on the Financial Services Law of the European Union, and the Business Law of the People's Republic of China. Professor Burke is obtaining his Msc. in Finance and Management, Switzerland, and his certification in Financial Modeling, New York City.

C. David DeBenedetti, Esq.
NY Attorney, Partner

David DeBenedetti specializes in issues related to investment funds, hedge funds, as well as venture capital transactions, mergers and acquisitions. Moreover, he deals with planning and implementation of investments, specifically in their cross-border aspects. He graduated from

AUTHOR BIOGRAPHIES

the University of Toledo (B.A. cum laude 1991) and from Georgetown University Law School (J.D. 1996). Between 1997 - 2004 he co-operated with the Warsaw and New York offices of an international law firm. He has spoken at numerous conferences and meetings on investing in Poland, bankruptcy and recovery, Polish securities law, structuring real estate deals, and intellectual property in Warsaw, New York, London, Tokyo, Los Angeles and Miami. Mr. DeBenedetti co-authored a White Paper published by the Polish Association of Financial Investors in 2004 concerning the legal aspects of structuring leveraged buyout in Poland. As of October 2008, he has joined the Lazarski School of Commerce and Law. He teaches a seminar on mergers & acquisitions. He is an Attorney of the State of Ohio (1997, currently inactive) and the State of New York (2001). He is a member of American Bar Association, New York State Bar Association and Rotary Club. Languages: English (native) and Polish.

Nicholas S. Hammond

Nicholas S. Hammond is a founder and a managing partner of Hammond, Bogaru and Associates and has been practising law and working in Romania since 1990. He was born in Cambridge England and qualified as a solicitor in 1971. He worked in the City of London both as a partner and owner of a number of law firms. In 1990 he moved to Bucharest Romania firstly with his own law firm Hicks Arnold, and latterly consulting with a number of major international law firms in relation to their offices and development of their business until he set up his own independent practise with Cristian Bogaru. He is registered with the Law Society as a practising solicitor as well as Romanian bar as a foreign lawyer practising in Romania. He has worked on a number of EU funded assignments in Romania including the harmonisation of Romanian laws to EU laws and also provided input into the drafting of legislation. He has worked on a number of PHARE projects as well as other institutional funded projects. He has counsel many international companies in respect of their business in Romania as well as advising on the impact and effect of Romanian law. He has written a number of articles in relation to Romanian law and its application from the view point of a foreign investor.

George Lefcoe

Professor **George Lefcoe** has been a Professor of Law at the University of Southern California since 1962, and is currently the Florine and Ervin Yoder Professor of Real Estate Law. He has also taught at Yale University Law School, Boston University Law School, and the University of Utah College of Law. He has served on Los Angeles city and county commissions: the county Regional Planning Commission, the county High Technology Council, and the city's Board of Convention Center Commissioners. As a land use and real estate finance consultant he has worked with federal, state and local governments, and with firms and foundations in the United States, the United Kingdom and Japan. His most recent publication is the text from which the material in this treatise was adapted, *Real Estate Transactions* (Michie Company, 1993).

Appreciation is expressed to Kadi Kurgpold, administrative assistant and accomplice.

Roman Nurpeissov

Roman Nurpeissov is an associate in the Almaty office of Salans. He is also an Adjunct Senior Lecturer at the Kazakh Institute of Management, Economics and Strategic Research. Roman was admitted to practice in Kazakhstan in 2002, and successfully passed the New York Bar Examination in July 2009. Roman received his LL.B. from the Kazakh-American University, his LL.M. from Vanderbilt University, and his J.D. from the University of Michigan, where he was the Articles Editor of the Michigan Journal of International Law. He also was a summer clerk to the Honorable Eugene E. Siler Jr., Senior U.S. Circuit Judge (U.S. Court of Appeals for the Sixth Circuit), and the Honorable Thomas A. Wiseman Jr.,

AUTHOR BIOGRAPHIES

Senior U.S. District Judge (U.S. District Court, Middle District of Tennessee). Prior to joining Salans, Roman used to work as a tax consultant at Deloitte's Almaty office.

Note About Reorganization of Chapter 106 in this Second Thomas Edition

This second Thomas edition of Volume 13 of Thompson on Real Property changes the chapter numbering convention for the international coverage in Chapter 106. Chapter numbers now incorporate the ISO two-digit numbering code so that the country code is now part of the chapter number. For example, the Chapter 106 coverage of Austria is now named Chapter 106AT, since the two-digit country code for Austria is AT (formerly, the Austria coverage was designated Chapter 106-B). Countries covered in this chapter are now arranged in alphabetical sequence according to their ISO codes.

Volume 13 Table of Contents

See **Volume 15 for a complete Publication Table of Contents.**

Volume 13 Table of Contents

Volume 13 Table of Contents

Volume 13 Table of Contents

Volume 13 Table of Contents

Volume 13 Table of Contents

CHAPTER 106RO PROPERTY LAW IN ROMANIA

CHAPTER 106RU PROPERTY LAW IN RUSSIA

CHAPTER 103

FEDERAL AND STATE SECURITIES REGULATION OF REAL ESTATE TRANSACTIONS

Professor David A. Thomas
J. Reuben Clark Law School
Brigham Young University

SYNOPSIS

§ 103.01   Introduction to the Chapter.

This chapter describes how federal and state governments affect certain real estate transactions through securities laws and regulations. The chapter identifies those real estate transactions that are subject to securities laws and regulations and then describes in some detail the usual processes required for compliance with those laws and regulations. The most significant of these requirements are imposed by federal law. States have similar and complementary laws and regulations and also impose licensing requirements on those who regularly deal in securities, including securities affecting real estate transactions.

§ 103.02   Brief History of Federal Securities Regulation.

The Transportation Act of 1920 contained provisions for the first permanent federal regulation of securities.[1] That act regulated securities by requiring railroad common carriers to obtain authorization from the Interstate Commerce Commission before issuing their own securities or accepting obligations with respect to securities from any other entity. Because the main objective of the act was to insure adequate rail transportation service, achieving investor protection through securities regulation was only one of

---

[1] Now codified as 49 U.S.C. § 11,301.

several ways to accomplish that objective.[2]

In March, 1933, President Franklin D. Roosevelt called for legislation to regulate securities as part of a broader program to restore the nation's financial health. Congress reacted swiftly, and the Securities Act of 1933 became effective in May, 1933.[3] The act reflected a policy decision favoring greater disclosure over heavier direct regulation, and to implement this policy required use of registration statements and prospectuses as prerequisites to offering securities to the public. Under the act, material misrepresentations or omissions in the disclosures required during the registration process or in prospectuses could result in civil liabilities and criminal penalties. The focus of the 1933 securities legislation was the initial distribution or offering of securities in the stream of interstate commerce. As for subsequent trading of such securities, the main regulation was left to the 1934 Securities Exchange Act.[4]

Specifically, the Securities Exchange Act of 1934 sought to generate more and better information on behalf of and from those who traded in securities, to regulate the securities markets, and to prevent and remedy fraud in securities trading. To accomplish this, the 1934 Act required stock exchanges to register with the Securities Exchange Commission (SEC), and the SEC was empowered to regulate certain practices of the stock exchanges, as well as to require current information from companies issuing securities, and to enforce margin rules. As the act has been amended in subsequent years, its regulatory reach has extended to a broader group of issuing companies, to associations of securities broker-dealers, to takeover bids, and to processes for clearance and settlement.

The depression decade of the 1930's saw enactment of other major securities acts following the basic acts of 1933 and 1934. These subsequent securities acts included the Public Utilities Holding Company Act of 1935, the Trust Indenture Act of 1939, the Investment Company Act of 1940, and the Investment Advisers Act of 1940. Since that decade there has been virtually no major securities legislation except for the Securities Investors Protection Act of 1970 and portions of the Bankruptcy Reform Act of 1978.

The objective of the Public Utilities Holding Company Act of 1935[5] was to reform several of the worst accounting and securities manipulation

---

[2] The relationship of investor protection to the main purpose of the 1920 Transportation Act was expressed by the U.S. Supreme Court as "the establishment of a new federal railway policy to insure adequate transportation service by means of securing a fair return on capital devoted to the service, restoration of impaired railroad credit, and regulation of rates, security issues, consolidations and mergers in the interest of the public." Schwabacher v. United States, 334 U.S. 182, 191–192 (1948).

[3] 15 U.S.C. § 77a *et seq.*

[4] 15 U.S.C § 78 *et seq.*

[5] 16 U.S.C. §§ 791a-825r.

practices in the public utilities companies. By this act, a scheme of direct regulatory intervention was introduced into the public utilities sector; this intervention was a more heavy-handed approach than the less onerous disclosure schemes featured in the earlier securities acts.

The next securities regulation act was the 1939 Trust Indenture Act,[6] which incorporated both regulatory and disclosure approaches. This act requires the appointment of independent trustees to protect the rights of those who purchase securities issued under trust indentures. These securities are often bonds or other debt securities issued by a pension trust or a trust created as security for a bond issue, and they may be issued only under indentures approved or qualified by the SEC; as part of the process of becoming so qualified, the issuers must meet disclosure requirements which are similar to those in other SEC registration procedures.

The regulatory approach, as opposed to the disclosure approach, was also a part of the Investment Company Act of 1940.[7] This act regulated investment companies, which, as defined in the act, are securities issuers that are engaged primarily in the business of investing, reinvesting or trading in securities. Investment companies are also issuers that are in the business of issuing face-amount securities of the installment type or acquiring investment securities having a value of more than 40% of the acquirer's total assets.[8] Following amendments under the Investment Company Amendments Act of 1970[9] and the Small Business Investment Incentive Act of 1980,[10] the present Investment Company Act seeks to correct abuses in sales practices, to regulate investment advisers' fees, to enable greater shareholder participation in management, to strengthen capital structures, and to improve the quality of available accounting information.

The Investment Advisers Act was also promulgated in 1940. This act requires investment advisers to register with the SEC and identifies certain fraudulent and deceptive practices which are made illegal under the act.[11]

The Securities Investor Protection Act of 1970 is intended to provide protection against broker insolvency.[12] To accomplish this, brokers and dealers must pay annual assessments for an investor protection fund, which

---

[6] 15 U.S.C. § 77aaa *et seq.*

[7] 15 U.S.C. § 80a-1 *et seq.*

[8] 15 U.S.C § 80a-3(a). "Face-amount certificates of the installment type" are securities which obligate the issuer to pay a certain amount on specific dates after the investor makes a series of required installment payments." *Id.* at §§ 80a-2(a)(15), 80a-4(1).

[9] 84 Stat. 1413.

[10] 94 Stat. 2275.

[11] 15 U.S.C. § 80b-6 *et seq.*

[12] 15 U.S.C. § 78aaa *et seq.* The act was amended in 1978, 92 Stat. 249, and in 1982, 96 Stat. 1409.

fund is also backed by the federal government.

Of concurrent authority with the federal regulation of securities and of those who deal in securities are similar securities regulations in each of the states, commonly under the heading "blue sky laws." The major federal enactments recognize the concurrent jurisdiction and usefulness of state regulation, specifically preserving "all other rights and remedies that may exist at law or in equity."[13] Common law rights of action under state law have been recognized in cases involving the federal securities laws and those common law rights are preserved unless explicitly rejected.[14]

The Private Securities Litigation Reform Act of 1995, intended to reduce abusive litigation and coercive settlements, imposed new regulations and requirements on private plaintiff class actions.[15]

§ 103.03   Real Estate Transactions Subject to Federal Securities Regulation.

§ 103.03(a)   Definitions of Securities in Various Real Estate Transactions.

It is important to identify those real estate transactions that involve securities subject to federal or state regulation, but what constitutes a security in a normal financial context might not constitute a security in the context of a real estate transaction. Therefore, the objective of this section is to identify those types of real estate transactions that are likely to involve or generate securities subject to federal or state regulation. Even if it is determined that certain real estate transactions and their securities instruments are subject to such regulation, it may also be ultimately determined that broad exemptions in those federal and state acts apply in the context of real estate transactions and may diminish or even eliminate the need for following the normal registration or other procedures that are part of securities regulation.

The extremely broad definition of "security" in the federal securities acts was intended to encompass the instruments then known to be securities and also to anticipate instruments that might be devised in the future that could

---

[13] 15 U.S.C. § 77p (Securities Act of 1933), § 78bb(a) (Securities Exchange Act of 1934), § 77zzz (Trust Indenture Act of 1939).

[14] *See* 1 Louis Loss & Joel Seligman, Securities Regulation 420, and cases cited in n.146 (4th ed. 2006).

[15] P.L. 10467 (Dec. 22, 1995); Mathews v. Kidder, Peabody & Co., Inc., 161 F.3d 156 (3d Cir. 1998) (securities litigation reform act removes fraud in the sale of securities as a predicate act for a private cause of action under RICO); Santiago Gonzalez v. Santiago, 141 F. Supp. 2d 202 (D. P. R. 2001) (defendants not entitled to attorney fees and costs under the Private Securities Litigation Reform Act); Burton v. Ken-Crest Services, Inc., 127 F. Supp. 2d 673 (E.D. Pa. 2001) (Private Securities Litigation Reform Act bars an action arising from an alleged conspiracy to mislead employees about pension plan investments).

also function as securities. A "security" is defined in the 1933 Securities Act as follows:

> The term "security" means any note, stock, treasury stock, bond, debenture, evidence of indebtedness, certificate of interest or participation in any profit-sharing agreement, collateral-trust certificate, preorganization certificate or subscription, transferable share, investment contract, voting-trust certificate, certificate of deposit for a security, fractional undivided interest in oil, gas, or other mineral rights, any put, call, straddle, option or privilege on any security, certificate of deposit, or group or index of securities (including any interest therein or based on the value thereof), or any put, call, straddle, option, or privilege entered into on a national securities exchange relating to foreign currency, or, in general, any interest or instrument commonly known as a "security", or any certificate of interest or participation in, temporary or interim certificate for, receipt for, guarantee of, or warrant or right to subscribe to or purchase, any of the foregoing.[16]

In the 1934 Securities Exchange Act is another definition of "security," which differs from the 1933 act definition somewhat in its structure but as a definition is quite equivalent in its coverage:

> The term "security" means any note, stock, treasury stock, bond, debenture, certificate of interest or participation in any profit-sharing agreement or in any oil, gas, or other mineral royalty or lease, any collateral-trust certificate, preorganization certificate or subscription, transferable share, investment contract, voting-trust certificate, certificate of deposit, for a security, any put, call, straddle, option, or privilege on any security, certificate of deposit, or group or index of securities (including any interest therein or based on the value thereof), or any put, call, straddle, option, or privilege entered into on a national securities exchange relating to foreign currency, or in general, any instrument commonly known as a "security"; or any certificate of interest or participation in, temporary or interim certificate for, receipt for, or warrant or right to subscribe to or purchase, any of the foregoing; but shall not include currency or any note, draft, bill of exchange, or banker's acceptance which has a maturity at the time of issuance of not exceeding nine months, exclusive of days of grace, or any renewal thereof the maturity of which is likewise limited.[17]

The U.S. Supreme Court has attempted to minimize the technical differences in wording between the two definitions and has "repeatedly ruled that the definitions . . . are virtually identical and will be treated as such in

---

[16] 15 U.S.C. § 77b(1); Securities and Exchange Commission v. TLC Investments and Trade Co., 179 F. Supp. 2d 1149 (C.D. Cal. 2001) (real estate investments treated as securities); Jacob v. Schlichtman, 622 N.W.2d 852 (Neb. 2001) (a bond necessary for transfer of property in a replevin action is not a security in a state action under an in forma pauperis statute).

[17] 15 U.S.C. § 78c(a)(10).

our decisions dealing with the scope of the term."[18]

These definitions in some cases go too far and in some cases not far enough. The types of securities listed in the definitions are neither exhaustive nor can they be taken too literally. For instance, not every note is a security. In recognition of this, the preface to both of the securities definitions declares that the listed examples in the definitions apply only in the context of when they are "used in this chapter," and they do not apply if "the context otherwise requires—."[19] With this warning, therefore, it is possible that a particular instrument is not a security even if it fits into one of the types listed in the definitions; or an instrument may be a security even if it does not appear in the listed types of definitions.

More essential to characterizing an instrument or a transaction as a security is the economic substance of the instrument or transaction. No comprehensive definition of the substantive economic characteristics commonly found in a security are given in the federal securities acts, but in examining the judicial interpretations of the various types of securities listed in the definitions, certain characteristics emerge as especially important.

The extended discussion of particular types of securities in the following pages focuses on those types of securities most likely to appear in real estate transactions. These include notes; evidences of indebtedness; stock; oil, gas and other mineral rights; investment contracts; interests in trusts; and equipment trust certificates.

§ 103.03(a)(1)   Notes.

Although the federal securities definitions make reference to "any note" as being a security, obviously some types of notes, such as a personal note given as part of a consumer credit transaction, are not treated as securities for purposes of federal securities regulation.[20] Determining which kinds of notes *are* considered securities has occupied much judicial attention. The U.S. Supreme Court decision in *Reves v. Ernst & Young*[21] made an attempt to resolve that question with a four-part test. According to *Reves*, a note is considered a security if it meets each of the four criteria described in the opinion:

1. A note is likely to be considered a security

   if the seller's purpose is to raise money for the general use of a business enterprise or to finance substantial investments and the buyer is interested

---

[18] Landreth Timber Co. v. Landreth, 471 U.S. 681 (1985).

[19] 15 U.S.C. §§ 77b, 78c(a).

[20] *See, e.g.,* Hunssinger v. Rockford Bus. Credits, Inc., 745 F.2d 484, 492 (7th Cir. 1984) (to give a note when purchasing consumer goods is not to participate in a securities transaction).

[21] 494 U.S. 56 (1990).

primarily in the profit the note is expected to generate. . .[22]

The note is probably not a security if it

is exchanged to facilitate the purchase and sale of a minor asset or consumer good, to correct for the seller's cash-flow difficulties, or to advance some other commercial or consumer purpose . . .[23]

2. The note is probably a security if the court, in examining the plan for distributing the notes, determines that there is "common trading [in the notes] for speculation or investment."[24]

3. A note will probably be considered a security if the public perception of the note is that it is a security. It was significant that the notes in the *Reves* case were advertised as "investments."

4. If "some other factor such as the existence of another regulatory scheme significantly reduces the risk of the instrument, thereby rendering application of the Securities Acts unnecessary,"[25] the note will probably not be considered a security subject to federal regulation.

One scholar has pointed out that the criteria are essentially the same as the criteria in *SEC v. W.J. Howey Co.*,[26] a decision the *Reves* court explicitly rejected.[27]

---

[22] *Id.* at 66. Plains Electric Generation and Transmission Cooperative, Inc. v. New Mexico Public Utility Commission, 967 P.2d 827 (N.M. 1998) (a cooperative's agreement with a company is not a security within the meaning of the Public Utility Act).Pollack v. Laidlaw Holdings, Inc., 27 F.3d 808 (2d Cir. 1994), *cert. denied*, 513 U.S. 963 (1995) (under the "family resemblance" test a note is presumed to be a security unless it resembles one of the categories statutorily defined as not a security).

[23] *Id.* at 66. Smidt v. Drobny, 1997 U.S. Dist. LEXIS 20746 (N.D. Ill. 1997) (Defendant refused to deliver securities pursuant to promissory note made to plaintiff after the value of the securities went up on the ground the note was intended as a loan); United States v. G & T Enters., 978 F. Supp. 1232 (N.D. Iowa 1997) (Assignment is given as security for the payment of and the performance of all covenants and agreements of assignor in that certain note), *aff'd*, 149 F.3d 1188 (8th Cir. Iowa 1998).

[24] *Id. at 66.* Trust Co. v. N.N.P., Inc., 104 F.3d 1478 (5th Cir. 1997) (National Mortgage Association Certificates were investment instruments because of their inherent risk, and defendant cannot get around it by UCC filing); Ausa Life Ins. Co v. Ernst & Young, 1997 U.S. Dist. LEXIS 21357 (S.D.N.Y. 1997) (Plaintiffs justifiably relied on JWP's financial statements and Ernst & Young's unqualified reports on those financial statements to analyze the investment quality of JWP's Notes). *See*, James W. Everett, Jr., "Are Promissory Notes Securities?" 40 *UCC L.J.* 1 (Fall 2007).

[25] *Id.* Local 875 I.B.T. Pension Fund v. Pollack, 992 F. Supp. 545 (E.D.N.Y. 1998) (Defendant failed to properly monitor the investment of the $9.3 million in the note which had been made by ignoring the SEC bulletin regarding prime note bank fraud forwarded to the Trustees by Prudential Securities).

[26] 328 U.S. 293 (1946).

[27] James D. Gordon III, *Interplanetary Intelligence About Promissory Notes as Securities,* 69 Tex. L. Rev. 383, 403 (1990); Countryside, L.P. v. Comm'r, T.C. Memo 2008-3 (T.C. 2008) (privately issued promissory notes included in a liquidation distribution were not

§ 103.03(a)(2)   Evidences of Indebtedness.

According to the 1933 Securities Act, but not to the 1934 Securities Exchange Act, "any evidence of indebtedness" is included in the definition of a security. As declared by one court, an evidence of indebtedness includes "all contractual obligations to pay in the future for consideration presently received";[28] as a definition of a security, however, this description is a bit too broad. For instance, a promissory note could be an evidence of indebtedness, just as it could be a note within the definition of the preceding section, but it is probably not the type of interest intended to come under the coverage of the definition of evidence of indebtedness as a security. More likely the term "evidence of indebtedness" refers to instruments such as loan commitments and guarantees[29] and investment certificates.[30] Most loan commitments, however, are obtained from lenders in the ordinary course of business and do not fall under the definition of "evidence of indebtedness" as a security.[31] An evidence of indebtedness that is considered a security subject to federal regulation probably meets the same criteria as for notes in the preceding section.

Because of judicial decisions, the absence of "evidence of indebtedness" from the section of securities definitions in the 1934 Securities Exchange Act probably is not significant. In a decision under the 1934 Act, the U.S. Supreme Court held that a bank certificate of deposit was not a security, but did not rely on the absence of the "evidence of indebtedness" wording from the 1934 Act's definition in reaching its decision.[32] However, several years earlier, a lower federal court had held an open-account loan to be not a security under the 1934 Act, precisely because the "evidence of indebtedness" wording was not in the Act.[33]

§ 103.03(a)(3)   Stock.

The federal definition of a security includes "any" stock, but not all shares corresponding to interests in an enterprise or entity are considered stock for securities regulation purposes. To be a security within the federal definitions, the stock must be part of an arrangement involving

> an investment of money in a common enterprise with profits to come solely

---

considered marketable securities); State v. McGuire, 735 N.W.2d 555 (Wis. App. 2007) (a promissory note issued by the defendant to the sole investor qualified as a security).

[28] United States v. Austin, 462 F.2d 724 (10th Cir.), *cert. denied,* 409 U.S. 1048 (1972).

[29] *Id.*

[30] B. K. Med. Sys. v. Clesh, 770 F.2d 1067 (3d Cir. 1985).

[31] McGovern Plaza Joint Venture v. First of Denver Mtg. Investors, 562 F.2d 645 (10th Cir. 1977).

[32] Marine Bank v. Weaver, 455 U.S. 551 (1982).

[33] Zeller v. Bogue Elec. Mfg. Corp., 476 F.2d 795 (2d Cir.), *cert. denied,* 414 U.S. 908 (1973).

from the efforts of others . . . The touchstone is the presence of an investment in a common venture premised on a reasonable expectation of profits to be derived from the entrepreneurial or managerial efforts of others . . . By contrast, when a purchaser is motivated by a desire to use or consume the item purchased—to occupy the land or to develop it themselves—. . . the securities laws do not apply.[34]

§ 103.03(a)(4)   Oil, Gas and Other Mineral Rights.

Securities regulation may be imposed on "any . . . fractional undivided interest in oil, gas, or other mineral rights . . . ."[35] Such fractional undivided interests may arise when exploration and production companies, in seeking access to oil, gas and other mineral resources, obtain leasehold interests from owners of the land that they consider most promising. These leaseholds are for the mineral rights only and are given in return for consideration composed of cash, periodic rental payments, and fractional shares, or royalty interests, of the value of minerals actually produced from the leased land. If the lessor, as consideration for the lease, actually obtains an interest in the value of production, that interest is almost always a fractional share of the entire royalty, with the balance of the fraction being held by the lessee, and that is also a fractional share.

Even though the definition of a security includes a "fractional interest," it has been held that the royalty interest held by a landowner/lessor is not a fractional interest, despite the fact that such an interest is itself a fraction of the entire royalty. Only if the royalty right held by the lessor is further divided for sale to others is a "fractional interest" created that is a security subject to federal regulation. Without being so divided, the lessor's royalty right is considered a mere leasehold interest that was not intended for regulation as a security.[36] Sometimes the lessor's royalty interest is not divided, but is repackaged and sold to the public in ways that subject it to securities regulation under some other portion of the definition. For example, a security is formed if royalty rights are offered in the form of contracts for delivery of the mineral production or its value,[37] or if the royalty rights are conveyed to a trustee, who then issues participating trust certificates for beneficial interests in the royalties.[38] Offerings of mineral rights may be considered securities under investment contract criteria.[39]

---

[34] United Housing Found., Inc. v. Forman, 421 U.S. 837 (1975). *See also* Landreth Timber Co. v. Landreth, 471 U.S. 681 (1985).

[35] 15 U.S.C. § 77b(1).

[36] SEC v. C.M. Joiner Leasing Corp., 320 U.S. 344 (1943); Penturelli v. Spector, Cohen, Gadon & Rosen, P.C., 779 F.2d 160 (3d Cir. 1985) (coal leases).

[37] SEC v. Crude Oil Corp. of Am., 93 F.2d 844 (7th Cir. 1937).

[38] SEC v. Jones, 12 F. Supp. 210 (S.D.N.Y.), *aff'd,* 79 F.2d 617 (2d Cir. 1935), *rev'd on other grounds sub nom.* Jones v. SEC, 298 U.S. 1 (1936).

[39] SEC v. Goldfield Deep Mines Co., 758 F.2d 459 (9th Cir. 1985).

It is perhaps in consideration of these variants that the 1934 Act defines mineral rights as securities in terms even more broad than those of the 1933 Act, referring to "any . . . certificate of interest or participation in any profit-sharing agreement or in any oil, gas, or other mineral royalty or lease."[40] This wording is broad enough that the issue of whether a landowner's royalty interest remains whole or has become fractional may be avoided.

§ 103.03(a)(5) Investment Contracts.

"[A]ny . . . investment contract" is included in the definitions of a security found in both the 1933 and the 1934 Acts. A judicial definition of investment contract was delivered in a U.S. Supreme Court case involving an offering of units of a citrus grove development, combined with a contract for managing the property and distributing the proceeds to investors. The Court directly addressed the definition of investment contract by declaring that

> an investment contract for purposes of the Securities Act means a contract, transaction or scheme whereby a person invests his money in a common enterprise and is led to expect profits solely from the efforts of the promoter or a third party, it being immaterial whether the shares in the enterprise are evidenced by formal certificates or by nominal interests in the physical assets employed in the enterprise.[41]

Before this case, holdings in other courts had treated the various segments of such schemes as separate transactions, one for the sale and the other for the management of real property. This position was rejected in the *Howey* case, whose holding took into account the overall effect of the land sales contract, warranty deed and service contract, concluding that all of these elements in combination constituted an investment contract.

The definition of investment contract in *Howey* has been subsequently refined in other cases, and now it is not required that the consideration for the investment contract consist only of money;[42] a variety of concepts of "common enterprise" have arisen;[43] the profits that are expected by the investors may consist either of income earnings or of capital appreciation;[44] and it is only required that expected profits come "significantly" from the

---

[40] 15 U.S.C. § 78c(a)(10).

[41] SEC v. W.J. Howey Co., 328 U.S. 293 (1946).

[42] International Bhd. of Teamsters v. Daniel, 439 U.S. 551 (1979).

[43] *See, e.g.,* Milnarik v. M-S Commodities, Inc., 457 F.2d 274 (7th Cir.), *cert. denied,* 409 U.S. 887 (1972); SEC v. Koscot Interplanetary, Inc., 497 F.2d 473 (5th Cir. 1974); SEC v. Glenn W. Turner Enters., Inc., 474 F.2d 476 (9th Cir.), *cert. denied,* 414 U.S. 821 (1973).

[44] Tcherepnin v. Knight, 389 U.S. 332 (1967).

efforts of others, rather than "solely" from the efforts of others.[45] Even under this expanded definition, a mere real estate investment which may possibly produce profit from general increases of land values in the area does not render the investment a security under the definition of investment contract. Only if the project relies on the efforts of others to develop or manage the property would the scheme include the additional elements required for such an investment to be treated as a security.[46]

It is, of course, common for the sale of real or personal property to be coupled with retention and management of the property by the seller, and if that is the case the arrangement is treated as an investment contract or some other form of security. Such schemes that have involved real property have included cemetery plots,[47] orchards and vineyards,[48] other farm land,[49] and mortgage servicing plans.[50] Some of these arrangements have been conducted under the partnership form of business organization. If such a partnership entity is a limited partnership, with limited partners being the passive investors, most likely the investment will be considered a security, especially if the interests are transferable and are offered to the public.[51]

---

[45] SEC v. Glenn Turner Enters., Inc., 474 F.2d 476 (9th Cir.), *cert. denied,* 414 U.S. 821 (1973).

[46] United Housing Found., Inc. v. Forman, 421 U.S. 837 (1975); McCown v. Heidler, 527 F.2d 204 (10th Cir. 1975); Contract Buyers League v. F & F Inv., 300 F. Supp. 210, 224 (N.D. Ill. 1969), *aff'd sub nom.* Baker v. F & F Inv., 420 F.2d 1191 (7th Cir.), *cert. denied,* 400 U.S. 821 (1970).

S.E.C. v. Current Financial Services, Inc., 100 F. Supp. 2d 1 (D.D.C. 2000) ("investment agreements" were securities); Steinhardt Group Inc. v. Citicorp, 126 F.3d 144 (3d Cir. 1997) (a "securitization" transaction involving a pool of delinquent residential mortgage loans was not an investment contract).

People v. Destro, 2008 Colo. App. LEXIS 896 (Colo. Ct. App. May 29, 2008) (unpublished case) (a scheme of buying real estate and selling it to investors qualified as an investment contract and thus as a security); S.E.C. v. Merrill Scott & Associates, Ltd., 505 F. Supp. 2d 1193 (D. Utah 2007) (foreign investment schemes promoted for tax advantages, asset protection or profits were considered investment contracts and therefore securities); Majors v. South Carolina Securities Com'n, 644 S.E.2d 710 (S.C. 2007) (an investment opportunity in tax lien certificates was considered an investment contract and therefore a security); S.E.C. v. Merchant Capital, LLC, 483 F.3d 747 (11th Cir. 2007) (interests in registered limited liability partnerships were investment contracts and therefore securities).

[47] SEC v. Kaanehe Litig. Rels., 3756 (D. Haw. 1967); SEC v. Mount Vernon Mem. Park, 664 F.2d 1358 (9th Cir.), *cert. denied,* 456 U.S. 961 (1982) (decided under the Investment Company Act).

[48] SEC v. Tung Corp. of Am., 32 F. Supp. 371 (N.D. Ill. 1940) (trees); State v. Agey, 88 S.E. 726 (N.C. 1916) (orchards); Kerst v. Nelson, 213 N.W. 904 (Minn. 1927) (vineyards).

[49] Prohaska v. Hemmer-Miller Dev. Co., 256 Ill. App. 331 (1930).

[50] Los Angeles Trust Deed & Mtg. Exch. v. SEC, 285 F.2d 162 (9th Cir. 1960), *cert. denied,* 366 U.S. 919 (1961).

[51] SEC v. Murphy, 626 F.2d 633 (9th Cir. 1980).

However, if some responsibility for managing the enterprise has been delegated to the limited partners, quite likely the arrangement will not be found to be a security.[52]

No security is at issue when the transaction consists only of the sale of real property, without management or other agreements attached; the arrangement is still not a security even when the property is transferred in the form of shares, such as stock in a cooperative or in some condominium arrangement.[53] Among those arrangements, however, resort condominiums or time-share properties that are sold with emphasis on profits to be expected from the units being rented out during certain times of the year will be treated as securities.[54] Even the sale of an undeveloped lot will be treated as a security if the sale is clearly for investment rather than for the buyer's use, and if the promotion heavily emphasizes the economic inducements.[55]

§ 103.03(a)(6)   Interests in Trusts.

Interests in trusts are subject to federal securities regulation, but only in a very narrow sense. Trusts are not even directly mentioned in the federal securities definitions, but in the 1933 Act's definition of a person, a trust is included.[56] In this context trusts are subject to securities regulation only "where the interest or interests of the beneficiary or beneficiaries are evidenced by a security."[57] Thus, federal securities regulation is limited to Massachusetts or business trusts, a form of business organization used when property is conveyed to a trustee who manages it on behalf of beneficiaries, and the interests of the beneficiaries are evidenced by transferable certificates. Therefore, the interests in real estate investment trusts are considered securities,[58] and interests in other forms of real estate enterprises which have the purpose of holding interests in real estate for investment purposes are also considered securities. These forms of enterprise include syndicates, partnerships, joint ventures and other incorporated or unincorporated issuers of securities.[59]

---

[52] Rodeo v. Gillman, 787 F.2d 1175 (7th Cir. 1986).

[53] United Housing Found. v. Forman, 421 U.S. 837 (1975); SEC v. W.J. Howey Co., 328 U.S. 293 (1946); SEC v. C.M. Joiner Leasing Corp., 320 U.S. 344 (1943).

[54] Sec. Act Rel. No. 5347 (1973).

[55] Aldrich v. McCulloch Props., Inc., 627 F.2d 1036 (10th Cir. 1980); McCown v. Heidler, 527 F.2d 204 (10th Cir. 1975); Firth v. Lu, 12 P.3d 618 (Wash. App. 2000) (a purchase motivated by a desire to use or consume the products of the land is not an investment premised on a reasonable expectation of profits and is not a security under federal securities law).

[56] 15 U.S.C. § 77b(2).

[57] *Id.*

[58] Sec. Act Rel. 4422 (1961).

[59] *See* SEC Form S-11, which is used for registration of real estate investment trusts and the other forms of business entities for holding real estate investments.

§ 103.03(a)(7)   Equipment Trust Certificates.

One of the ways in which securities regulation is applied is by identifying certain issuers that are subject to such regulation. An issuer of an equipment trust certificate is subject to federal securities regulation, an issuer meaning "the person by whom the equipment or property is or is to be used."[60] In one important respect the treatment of equipment trust certificates as securities touches upon real estate transactions: a conveyance of land and buildings to a trustee who then issues a long-term lease to the grantor and further issues certificates of shares in the trustee/lessor's interest in equipment to beneficiaries, is considered a security.[61]

§ 103.03(b)   Real Estate Securities and Transactions Subject to Federal Securities Regulation.

In the preceding sections are discussions of certain instruments that can be considered as securities subject to federal regulation when involved in real estate transactions. From those sections it may be perceived that certain common forms of business organization that are used for acquiring and holding real estate investments are typically subject to federal securities regulation. These forms of business organization or activity include real estate investment trusts (in which parties pool capital in a trust that is formed to invest in real estate), real estate syndications (which is a more general term for any organization in which members pool funds to invest in real estate),[62] partnerships (which are entities in which participants pool their funds and sometimes their efforts for real estate investments, agreeing to function in various roles such as a general partner or a limited partner), and joint ventures, a general term for enterprises in which participants pool their resources for a single business enterprise without forming either a partnership or a corporation, and in which they have equal rights and duties).

Also apparent from the preceding sections is the perspective that certain types of real estate activities and real estate instruments are subject to securities regulation. These activities or instruments include activities in which a loan is given in return for a note or some other evidence of indebtedness, and the surrounding circumstances reinforce the suggestion that the loan is actually an investment rather than a lending transaction;

United States Securities and Exchange Commission v. Infinity Group Company, 212 F.3d 180 (3d Cir. 2000) (property transfer contracts under which investors contributed money to a trust were considered securities).

[60] 15 U.S.C. § 77b(4).

[61] *See* 2 Louis Loss & Joel Seligman, Securities Regulation 1056 (3d ed. 1989); S.E.C. v. ETS Payphones, Inc., 123 F. Supp. 2d 1349 (N.D. Ga. 2000) (a sale and leaseback arrangement was a security when all profit expectations were dependent upon the ability of the seller to generate revenue).

[62] Real estate syndications generally take the form of limited partnership interests or interests in joint or profit-sharing ventures. Sec. Act Rel. No. 4877 (1967).

shares of stock representing an investment in a common enterprise which is based on the investor's expectation of profits resulting from the efforts of others, rather than shares representing interest in real property which is to be used or occupied by the shareholders; any activities in which fractional shares of landowner mineral royalty interests are transferred to others; investment contracts whose provisions call for profits to be realized not only from appreciation in property value but also from agreements by issuers to retain possession of the realty and to develop or manage property; and certain sale/lease-back arrangements by which a trust is a lessor of equipment and issues certificates of interest to the trust beneficiaries.

COMPUTER-ASSISTED RESEARCH

LEXIS: real estate w/2 securit! or transaction! w/30 federal w/2 securit! w/2 regulat!

§ 103.04 How to Comply with Federal Securities Regulation Requirements for Real Estate Transactions.

The federal government's method of securities regulation is to present to potential securities investors full disclosure of accurate information related to the investment. With such full and accurate information, an investor who is also attempting to assess market forces is theoretically able to make more sound investment decisions. In addition to promoting and facilitating full and accurate disclosure, the various federal securities regulations also attempt to prevent or at least make more difficult the kinds of fraudulent conduct which have traditionally occurred in the processes of offering and selling securities. The rather straightforward method for achieving both of these purposes is to require that those who offer securities register the securities with the Securities and Exchange Commission, and, in the course of registration, to submit the information necessary to inform investors and put them in a better position to avoid being victimized by fraudulent conduct. In certain typical situations where avoiding fraudulent conduct or obtaining the full information seems less important for investor protection, broad exemptions from the registration and other securities requirements have developed, which exemptions apply either to particular types of securities or to particular types of securities transactions. Even where an exemption exists, however, some other less onerous filing and information requirements may be imposed and, in any event, the prohibitions against fraud still apply in full force. All of these provisions that apply to securities generally also apply fully to securities that emerge from various real estate transactions. In the sections to follow, various compliance requirements and exemptions provisions are described as they apply to securities generally, and those also apply fully to securities connected with real estate transactions.

§ 103.04(a)   Registration of Securities in Real Estate Transactions.

§ 103.04(a)(1)   When Registration Is Required.

Once an instrument has been identified as a security according to the various statutory definitions discussed in the preceding paragraphs, as interpreted by various cases, then usually the issuer of that security must go through a process of registration before issuance may occur. Any security that is to be offered or sold through interstate commerce or mail, and which is not otherwise exempt, must be registered. Moreover, any security *may* be registered even if it is not *required* to be registered.[63]

The constitutional basis for the 1933 Securities Act is the federal government's power to regulate interstate commerce, and the 1933 Act prohibits using means of interstate commerce, communication, transportation, or the mails to sell, offer to sell, carry, buy, or offer to buy any security, or even to carry a prospectus relating to a security, unless certain registration requirements have been met.[64] Some of those restrictions are lifted when a registration statement is filed; other restrictions are removed when the filed registration statement becomes effective. Stated in another way, it is unlawful to use interstate means in selling or transporting a security, unless a registration statement for the security is in effect.[65] It is unlawful to use interstate means for transporting a prospectus relating to a security or for transporting a security for sale or delivery after sale, unless that security is accompanied by a prospectus and the prospectus contains certain information required in the registration process.[66] It is unlawful to use interstate means for offering to sell or buy a security, with a prospectus or by some other means, unless a registration statement has been filed and the filing is not at the time subject to a refusal order or a stop order.[67]

§ 103.04(a)(2)   The Process of Registration: Filing.

To register a security an issuer must file a registration statement in triplicate; one of the three copies must be signed by the

> issuer, its principal executive officer or officers, its principal financial officer, its comptroller or principal accounting officer, and the majority of its board of directors or persons performing similar functions.[68]

When the registration statement and the required fee are received by the SEC, the registration statement is deemed filed:[69] the registration fee is an

---

[63] 15 U.S.C. § 77f(a).

[64] 15 U.S.C. § 77e.

[65] 15 U.S.C. § 77e(a).

[66] 15 U.S.C. §§ 77e(b), 77j.

[67] 15 U.S.C. § 77e(c).

[68] 15 U.S.C. § 77f(a).

[69] 15 U.S.C. § 77f(c).

amount equal to 10th of one percent of the maximum proposed offering price of the securities, and not less than $100.[70]

Once a registration statement has been filed, it is open to public inspection and copying.[71] After the filing of the registration statement has occurred, issuers may make offers to sell securities, but these offers may be made only by writing and by proper prospectus.

§ 103.04(a)(3)   Determination of the Date of Effectiveness.

Once the filing date of the registration statement has been established, the next important date is the effective date. A registration statement (or an amendment to a filed registration statement) becomes effective on the twentieth day after filing, unless the SEC has agreed to an earlier effective date,[72] or has delayed the effective date because of problems with the statement or amendment.[73] From and after the effective date of the registration statement, sales may be made when the sale transaction is accompanied by a proper prospectus.[74]

§ 103.04(a)(4)   Summary of Information Required for Securities Filings.

The registration statement is in essence a statement of certain required information, and the basic information requirements are described in Schedule A of 15 U.S.C. § 77aa; if a security issued by a foreign government or one of its political subdivisions is to be registered, the registration statement must meet the information requirements set out in Schedule B of 15 U.S.C. § 77aa.[75]

Schedule A is reproduced in Appendix 1 of this chapter. The main categories of the information required under Schedule A are summarized as follows:

    a.   names and addresses of the issuers and all principal parties associated with or having an interest in the issuer;

    b.   a description of the issuer's business organization and activities and financial structure, including copies of such fundamental instruments as corporate articles and bylaws, trust instruments and partnership agreements;

    c.   a description of the securities to be offered, including proposed uses for the funds raised, compensation of principal officers, and

---

[70] 15 U.S.C. § 77f(b).

[71] 15 U.S.C. § 77f(d).

[72] 15 U.S.C. § 77h(a).

[73] 15 U.S.C. §§ 77h(b), (d) and (e).

[74] 15 U.S.C. § 77e.

[75] 15 U.S.C. § 77g.

commissions and other expenses related to the offering;

d.   a description of the issuer's contracts and transactions that are not in the ordinary course of business; and

e.   a current balance sheet and a current profit and loss statement for the issuer and for any business to be acquired with proceeds from the offering.

§ 103.04(a)(5)   Summaries of Forms Most Frequently Used in Securities Filings for Real Estate Transactions.

Because various types of securities or the transactions in which they are used can be substantively quite different, the SEC has promulgated several different registration forms for use with certain types of securities or with transactions in which securities are a part. Those different forms each indicate which items of the Schedule A requirements described above are needed for that particular transaction or security. A list of the registration statement forms currently in use is found in Appendix 2.

Three of those specialized forms relate to real estate transactions and are summarized below to give a general understanding of the scope and depth of information required to register securities connected with real estate transactions. The first form thus described is Form S-1, which is the general form of registration statement; this form is reproduced in Appendix 3. The other form is Form S-11, which is for securities of certain real estate companies; this form is reproduced in Appendix 4. Form S-18, formerly used for securities whose offering price is $7,500,000 or less, was rescinded in 1992. One other specialized form, Form S-10 for registering oil and gas interests or rights, was rescinded in 1982.

§ 103.04(a)(5)(i)   Summary of Form S-1, Registration Statement Under the Securities Act of 1933.

Form S-1 is the general registration form used for most transactions and is used if none of the specialized forms are appropriate. The instructions for Form S-1 combine the instructions from two extensive regulations, Regulation C (which contains the general requirements for registration statements)[76] and Regulation S-K (which contains requirements relating to the non-financial portions of registration statements).[77] The provisions of Regulation C are reproduced in Appendix 5 and those of Regulation S-K are contained in 17 C.F.R. Sections 229.10 to .915.

In part I of Form S-1 the registrant is required to provide the types of information which should appear in the prospectus that is prepared as part of

---

[76] 17 C.F.R. §§ 230.400 to 230.499.

[77] 17 C.F.R. §§ 229.1 to 229.802.

the securities offering. The detailed information requirements for part I are found in various provisions of Regulation S-K, as noted in the parenthetical statements below, and those requirements may be summarized as follows:

a. information for the covers of the prospectus (Reg. S-K Items 501 and 502);

b. information on risk factors connected with the offering (Reg. S-K Item 503);

c. how the proceeds will be used (Reg. S-K Item 504);

d. determining the offering price (Reg. S-K Item 505);

e. dilution by insider purchasing (Reg. S-K Item 506);

f. selling by security holders (Reg. S-K Item 507);

g. the plan of distribution (Reg. S-K Item 508);

h. characteristics of securities being registered (Reg. S-K Item 202);

i. interests held by named experts and counsel (Reg. S-K Item 509);

j. information about the issuer (Reg. S-K Items 101–201, 301–404, 510); and

k. the SEC position on indemnification for Securities Act liabilities (Reg. S-K Item 510).

In Part II of Form S-1 the applicant must provide types of information other than the information that would be required in the prospectus. The details of these requirements are found in various provisions of Regulation S-K, are noted in the parenthetical statements below, and may be summarized as follows:

a. other expenses of issuance and distribution (Reg. S-K Item 511);

b. provisions for indemnifying officers and directors (Reg. S-K Item 702);

c. details of recent sales of unregistered securities (Reg. S-K Item 701);

d. exhibit and financial statement schedules (Reg. S-K Item 601); and

e. a description of the undertakings (Reg. S-K Item 512).

The format, handling and other procedural rules for registration statements generally, including for registrations using Form S-1, are found in Regulation C.

§ 103.04(a)(5)(ii)   Summary of Form S-11, for Registration Under the Securities Act of Securities of Certain Real Estate Companies.

One who wishes to register securities that are issued by a real estate investment trust would use Form S-11. Form S-11 would also be used by any other issuer

> whose business is primarily that of acquiring and holding for investment real estate or interests in real estate or interests in other issuers whose business is primarily that of acquiring and holding real estate or interests in real estate for investment.[78]

Form S-11 and the general requirements of the 1933 Act are usually not applicable to an investment company that is covered by the Investment Company Act of 1940.

In Part I of Form S-11, the applicant must provide the types of information that are required to appear in the prospectus which is prepared as part of the offering. Details of those requirements are found in various provisions of Regulation S-K and are summarized as follows:

    a.   information for the covers of the prospectus (Reg. S-K Items 501 and 502);

    b.   information on the risk factors and earnings ratio (Reg. S-K Item 503);

    c.   determining the offering price (Reg. S-K Item 505);

    d.   dilution by insider purchasing (Reg. S-K Item 506);

    e.   selling by security holders (Reg. S-K Item 507);

    f.   the plan of distribution (Reg. S-K Item 508);

    g.   how the proceeds will be used (Reg. S-K Item 504);

    h.   selected financial data (Reg. S-K Item 301);

    i.   management's discussion and analysis of the issuer's financial condition and the results of operations (Reg. S-K Item 303);

    j.   information about the registrant;

    k.   the registrant's policies with respect to certain debt and securities transactions;

    l.   the investment policies of the registrant in real estate or real estate interests, in real estate mortgages, in securities of or interests in persons primarily engaged in real estate activities, and in investments in other securities;

    m.   descriptions of real properties held or to be acquired by registrant;

    n.   certain operating data pertaining to registrant's real properties;

    o.   tax treatment of registrant and its security holders;

    p.   market price of and dividends on the registrant's common equity and related stockholder matters (Reg. S-K Item 201);

---

[78] SEC Form S-11, A.

q.   description of registrant's securities (Reg. S-K Item 202);

r.   description of pending legal proceedings involving registrant (Reg. S-K Item 103);

s.   security ownership held by management and certain beneficial owners (Reg. S-K Item 403);

t.   directors and officers (Reg. S-K Item 401);

u.   executive compensation (Reg. S-K Item 402);

v.   description of certain insider transactions and relationships (Reg. S-K Item 404);

w.   information about the selection, management and custody of the registrant's investments;

x.   the registrant's policies with respect to certain insider transactions or activities;

y.   limitations of insider liability;

z.   financial statements and information (Reg. S-K Items 302 and 304); and

aa. the interests of the named experts and counsel (Reg. S-K Items 302 and 304).

In Part II of Form S-11, the applicant must provide information other than the information that should appear in the prospectus. Details of those requirements are found in various provisions of Regulation S-K and may be summarized as follows:

a.   other expenses of issuance and distribution (Reg. S-K Item 511);

b.   sales to special parties;

c.   recent sales of unregistered securities (Reg. S-K Item 701);

d.   provisions for indemnifying officers and directors (Reg. S-K Item 702);

e.   how the proceeds from the stock being registered are to be treated;

f.   financial statements and exhibits (Reg. S-K Item 601); and

g.   undertakings (Reg. S-K Item 512).

Instructions for the format, handling and other procedural rules for this registration statement are drawn from Regulation C and are incorporated into the instructions for this form.

§ 103.04(a)(6)   Procedures for Filing; Summary of Post-Filing Requirements.

In addition to the substantive information requirements contained in the instructions for the various registrations statements, additional procedural requirements are imposed by Regulation C. By way of example, the basic requirements of registration statements specify that the statement must be filed in triplicate;[79] at the same time Regulation C requires an additional ten copies to be filed with the Commission for use in the examination process.[80]

When the document preparation is complete, then the registration material and the appropriate fee are received by the SEC and the date of this receipt is designated as the filing date.[81] Usually the registration materials are deposited with or sent to the principal office of the SEC in Washington, D.C.,[82] but in some cases it is possible to file the materials in a different location. For instance, the registration statement for securities to be offered at a competitive bidding may be filed at any regional or branch office of the SEC.[83]

It is very important to determine the precise filing date, because usually the "effective date" of the filing is entirely dependent upon the filing date. In most registrations, the effective date of the registration occurs exactly twenty days after the filing date. The filing date is also important because it is the time at which an issuer may begin the offering processes,[84] and the effective date is important because that marks the time at which an issuer may begin sales and deliveries.[85] The effective dates that routinely arise exactly twenty days after the filing date have been defined as beginning at the expiration of nineteen 24-hour periods following 5:30 p.m. Eastern Time on the date of filing.[86] For applicants using specialized registration forms, occasionally the time of the effective date differs from the usual twenty-day period. For instance, when an applicant uses Form S-8, which is to be used for securities offered to employees under an employee benefit plan, registrations are effective automatically and immediately upon filing.[87]

Other circumstances may arise which delay the effective date beyond the period of twenty days after the filing date. When the SEC determines that the registration materials are inaccurate or deficient in some respect, it may issue an order that delays the effective date until those deficiencies have been corrected as required by the order.[88] Before it issues such an order, the SEC gives notice by personal service to the registrant within ten days of the filing date, and the notice must state that the registrant has opportunity for a

---

[79] 15 U.S.C. § 77f(a).

[80] 17 C.F.R. § 230.402(b).

[81] 15 U.S.C. § 77f(c).

[82] 17 C.F.R. § 230.455.

[83] 17 C.F.R. § 230.445(b).

[84] 15 U.S.C. § 77e(a).

[85] 15 U.S.C. § 77e(c).

[86] 17 C.F.R. § 230.459.

[87] 17 C.F.R. §§ 230.456, 230.462.

[88] 15 U.S.C. § 77h(b).

hearing within ten days after service.[89] When the applicant amends the registration as required, the SEC then issues a statement or declaration to that effect, and the registration statement, as amended, becomes effective upon the original effective date or upon the date of the declaration, whichever is later.[90]

Occasionally, an applicant will submit an amendment to a registration statement without waiting for an SEC notice. Such an amendment is deemed filed when it is actually received by the SEC.[91] The filing of an amendment, either upon the applicant's own initiative or upon SEC order, alters the effective date in one of two ways. If the amendment is filed before the basic registration statement has reached its effective date, the basic registration statement is considered as having been filed on the date when the amendment was filed, and the effective date for the amended registration statement then normally occurs twenty days after the amended filing date.[92] If the amendment is filed after the basic registration statement has already reached its effective date, the amended registration statement is assigned an effective date as determined by the SEC, "having due regard to the public interest and the protection of investors."[93]

An applicant may also request that the SEC accelerate the effective date of a registration statement, and in considering such requests the SEC invokes the same standard of due regard to the public interest and protection of investors.[94] It is also possible for an applicant to file an amendment for the express purpose of delaying the effective date of a registration statement. For such an amendment, a filing date is assigned as necessary to achieve the desired delay in the effective date of the registration statement.[95]

In addition to the process by which the SEC issues an order resulting in an amendment to registration materials, the SEC may also issue a stop order suspending the effectiveness of the registration statement, any time it finds an omission or misstatement of material fact in the registration materials.[96] It should be remembered that in none of these SEC actions, whether delaying or stopping a registration or permitting a registration to go on to effective date, is the SEC issuing judgments about the merits of the securities, and it must be especially emphasized that acceptance of a filing is not an approval

---

[89] *Id.*

[90] *Id.*

[91] 17 C.F.R. § 230.474.

[92] 15 U.S.C. § 77h(a).

[93] 15 U.S.C. § 77h(c).

[94] 17 C.F.R. § 230.461.

[95] 17 C.F.R. § 230.473.

[96] 15 U.S.C. § 77h(d).

or endorsement of the securities by the SEC.[97]

One further post-registration procedural requirement is imposed on issuers. After a registration is accepted and sales have taken place, most issuers must file with the SEC four copies of Form SR, Report of Sales of Securities and Use of Proceeds Therefrom, at the end of the first three-month period following the effective date and every six months thereafter, until the proceeds from the offering have been used or the offering itself has come to a conclusion.[98]

§ 103.04(a)(7)   Registration Exemptions and Alternative Offering Procedures for Real Estate Transactions.

§ 103.04(a)(7)(i)   Overview of Securities Exemptions.

Even if the arrangements of a particular real estate transaction fit the definition of a security, and even if it is determined that the security is subject to the securities regulation provisions of federal or state law, it is still possible that complete compliance with those provisions is not required because of exemptions that may apply. Exemptions may apply either to types of securities or to types of transactions. Of the several types of securities that are exempted from federal registration requirements, most are not of the types that would be involved in real estate transactions. However, among the statutorily exempted securities that could be found in real estate transactions are "certificates issued by a receiver or by a trustee or debtor in possession in a case under Title 11, with approval of the court";[99] securities exchanged by an issuer exclusively among its existing security holders (except under Title 11);[100] securities exchanged for securities for claims or for property interests (or partly for cash, which exchanges typically take place in reorganizations), if the statutory fairness requirements are met;[101] and securities offered or sold only to persons residing within a single state or territory, and sold by an issuer that is resident in or incorporated and doing business in that particular jurisdiction, which is the so-called intrastate issues exemption.[102] The statutory exemption provisions are found in 15 U.S.C. § 77c.

The statutory exemptions for certain types of securities exist side by side with certain regulatory exemptions resulting from the statutory authority given to the SEC to prescribe by regulation certain other exemptions for

---

[97] 17 C.F.R. § 231.3115.

[98] 17 C.F.R. § 230.463.

[99] 15 U.S.C. § 77c(a)(7).

[100] 15 U.S.C. § 77c(a)(9).

[101] 15 U.S.C. § 77c(a)(10).

[102] 15 U.S.C. § 77c(a)(11).

small issues and issues of limited character. In exercise of this regulatory authority, the SEC has fashioned some exemptions that do relate to real estate transactions, including exemptions for qualified issues amounting to no more than $1,500,000; for fractional undivided interests in oil or gas rights that do not exceed $250,000; and for shares of stock offered or sold in the so-called private offerings.

The statutory and regulatory exemptions for securities described in the preceding paragraphs must also be considered in connection with statutory and regulatory exemptions for certain securities transactions. Among the exempt transactions are several that likely pertain to real estate transactions, including transactions by a person who is not an issuer, certain private offerings, large sales of real estate mortgage notes, and sales to accredited investors.

When securities are under any form statutory exemptions, whether the exemption relates to specific securities or to transactions, the issuer does not need to submit information to the SEC and the prospectus or other offering literature may have form and content as chosen by the issuer.[103] If, on the other hand, the exemption is a regulatory rather than a statutory exemption, then the issuer must observe any auxiliary or additional requirements or substitute requirements imposed by the regulation.[104]

In the following paragraphs the principal securities exemptions and transactions exemptions that may pertain to real estate transactions are discussed.

§ 103.04(a)(7)(ii)   Intrastate Issues as Exempted Securities.

The Securities Act of 1933 is generally not applied to issues that are offered or sold to residents in a single state or territory, if the issuer is a person resident or doing business or is a corporation doing business in that state or territory.[105] This exemption is a statutory exemption and is described in the statutory language as an exemption for securities based on the statute. In practice, the exemption ostensibly for securities is treated as an exemption for transactions, because what is being exempted is the manner of offering and selling the securities rather than the securities themselves. Also there is a regulatory counterpart to this statutory exemption, found in Rule 147, under which the SEC attempts to provide some objective criteria for determining eligibility for the statutory exemption.[106] However, the statu-

---

[103] It should be noted that the statutory exemption for intrastate offerings provides exemption only from the registration requirements of the 1933 Securities Act. Registration requirements of the 1934 Securities and Exchange Act and all anti-fraud provisions still apply even to securities offered under the intrastate exemption.

[104] Sec. Act Rel. No. 217 (1934).

[105] 15 U.S.C. § 77c(a)(11).

[106] 17 C.F.R. § 230.147.

tory exemption may stand on its own and if the issuer does not meet the specific criteria for eligibility found in the regulations of Rule 147, the issuer may still qualify directly under the terms of the statute.[107] An example of how the regulation's requirements go beyond the statute is the explicit and objective standard in Rule 147 that an issuer must have derived at least 80% of its gross revenues from the state or territory in which it seeks to place its intrastate issue under the exemption.[108] As already stated, if an issuer does not meet the 80% standard, it may still qualify for the intrastate exemption directly under the terms of the statute. Rule 147 also requires that resales be deferred until nine months after the initial offering closes,[109] and that in the written materials describing the offer, the resale limitation must be disclosed.[110] Rule 147 is available from the SEC on the Internet at http://www.sec.gov.

COMPUTER-ASSISTED RESEARCH

LEXIS: intrastate w/5 issue! w/30 exempt! w/5 securit! w/30 real estate

§ 103.04(a)(7)(iii)   Small Issues as Exempted Securities (Regulation A).

Another statutory exemption pertaining to securities is the SEC authority to exempt from registration certain offerings that are so small in value or otherwise limited in character that the need for protection of investors and the public generally does not require invoking registration provisions.[111] The statutory limit for this exemption is for offerings that do not exceed $5,000,000 in value.

The SEC has also promulgated regulations explaining the details of this exemption, known as Regulation A,[112] and under this regulation, despite the $5,000,000 statutory ceiling, the small issue exemption is extended only to issues of not more than $1,500,000 in value.[113] Regulation A is available from the SEC on the Internet at http://www.sec.gov.

An issuer who has its principal place of business operations in the U.S. or Canada is eligible for exemption under Regulation A.[114] The exemption may not be available if the principals or underwriters of the issuer have had their securities-related conduct questioned during the recent past under proceed-

---

[107] 17 C.F.R. § 230.147, Preliminary Note 1.

[108] 17 C.F.R. § 230.147(c).

[109] 17 C.F.R. § 230.147(e).

[110] 17 C.F.R. § 230.147(f)(3).

[111] 15 U.S.C. § 77c(b)

[112] 17 C.F.R. §§ 230.251 to 230.263.

[113] 17 C.F.R. § 230.251(b).

[114] 17 C.F.R. §§ 230.252(a)(1) and (2).

ings that are still pending or that were resolved unfavorably.[115] When an offering seeks to invoke the exemption of Regulation A, a statement based on Form 1-A must be prepared and submitted.[116] Form 1-A is available from the SEC on the Internet at http://www.sec.gov. That statement must usually be filed in the SEC regional office in the region where the issuer conducts its principal business operations.[117] That offering statement should also include the offering circular (copies of which are also to be provided to offerees or purchasers,) and the content of that offering circular as it pertains to offers and sales is also prescribed by regulation.[118] This exemption is an example of a statutory exemption that is rather severely altered by regulation, and, even if the exemption applies, there are additional filing requirements imposed by regulation. Reports of sales under this exemption must be submitted within 30 days after the end of each six-month period following the date of the original offering.[119]

COMPUTER-ASSISTED RESEARCH

LEXIS: small w/5 issue! w/30 exempt! w/5 securit! w/30 real estate

§ 103.04(a)(7)(iv)   Certain Fractional Oil and Gas Issues as Exempted Securities (Regulation B).

Another exemption that may apply to real estate transactions is for certain fractional undivided interests in oil and gas rights offered for less than $250,000.[120] This exemption is described in Regulation B, and Regulation B is available from the SEC on the Internet at http://www.sec.gov.

The fractional undivided interests in oil and gas rights to which this exemption may apply include landowners' royalty interests, overriding royalty interests, working interests, participating interests, and certain oil and gas payments, such as rights to participate in the proceeds from the sale of oil and gas.[121] This exemption is not available to an offeror if the offeror or one of its principals has committed securities violations or other similar misconduct during the past several years.[122]

Although this exemption excuses the offeror from meeting the standard securities requirements, the regulation imposes alternative requirements. For instance, at least ten days before the offering begins, the offeror must file with the SEC four copies of an offering sheet that contains certain

---

[115] 17 C.F.R. 230.251(a)(1).

[116] 17 C.F.R. § 230.251(d).

[117] *Id.*

[118] 17. C.F.R. §§ 230.253, 230.255.

[119] 17 C.F.R. § 230.257.

[120] 17 C.F.R. §§ 230.300 to 230.346.

[121] 17 C.F.R. § 230.300(a)(1).

[122] 17 C.F.R. § 230.306.

information required in the regulation. The required information is contained on one of four schedules and the schedule to be used is determined by the type of interest being offered.[123] The appropriate offering sheet must be in the hands of the offeree before an offer may be made and at least 48 hours before a sale may be made.[124] Not more than 15 days after an offering sheet has expired, the offeror must file a report on Form 1-G (Report of Sales of Oil or Gas Interests Pursuant to Regulation B);[125] and not more than three months after the conclusion of the offering, the offeror must file with the SEC and send to securities purchasers a report on Form 3-G (Report of Results of Offering).[126] Form 3-G is available from the SEC on the Internet at http://www.sec.gov.

COMPUTER-ASSISTED RESEARCH

LEXIS: fractional w/5 (oil or gas) w/5 (issue! or interest!) w/30 exempt! w/5 securit! w/30 real estate

§ 103.04(a)(7)(v)   Transactions by a Non-Issuer as Exempted Transactions.

When securities transactions are conducted by a non-issuer, a statutory exemption is available,[127] but an accompanying regulation, Rule 144,[128] sets out additional criteria and standards for determining if the exemption is available. Where the basic statutory exemption extends to "transactions by any person other than an issuer, underwriter, or dealer," but such transactions are not normally part of a securities distribution, Rule 144 imposes conditions designed to insure that those who invoke the exemption are not underwriters engaged in a distribution. The text of Rule 144 is available from the SEC on the Internet at http://www.sec.gov.

Rule 144 is not exclusive and does not limit the availability of any other applicable exemption.[129] If an offeror does not meet the qualifications of Rule 144, some other regulatory or even statutory exemption may be available.

Because the exemptions under Rule 144 usually pertain to transactions conducted by a non-issuer, the exemption may be conditioned upon making adequate disclosure about the issuer. One way in which adequate disclosure occurs is if the issuer is subject to the reporting requirements imposed by the 1934 Securities Exchange Act, and has been so for at least 90 days prior to

---

[123] 17 C.F.R. § 230.326.

[124] 17 C.F.R. §§ 230.310(b) and (d).

[125] 17 C.F.R. § 230.316(a).

[126] 17 C.F.R. § 230.316(b).

[127] 15 U.S.C. § 77d(1).

[128] 17 C.F.R. § 230.144.

[129] 17 C.F.R. § 230.144(j).

the transaction to be exempted. Normally, the Rule 144 public disclosure standards are met by the Securities Exchange Act reporting requirements.[130] For issuers, Rule 144 may be satisfied if the offeror has made available to the public certain information equivalent to that specified in Rule 15c2-11(a)(5).[131] The provisions of Rule 15c2-11 is available from the SEC on the Internet at http://www.sec.gov.

For the exemption based on Rule 144, several important restrictions are in effect. For instance, under this exemption, the securities to be sold must have been held for at least two years before sale;[132] Rule 144 imposes various limitations on the amount of securities that may be sold during any three-month period;[133] and Rule 144 also imposes limitations on the manner of sale.[134] The offeror also must file an additional form if the sales as proposed during any three-month period are in excess of either 500 shares or an aggregate sale price of $10,000. Form 144 (Notice of Proposed Sale of Securities Pursuant to Rule 144)[135] is available from the SEC on the Internet at http://www.sec.gov.

COMPUTER-ASSISTED RESEARCH

LEXIS: transaction! w/5 non-issue! w/30 exempt! w/5 securit! w/30 real estate

§ 103.04(a)(7)(vi)   Private Offerings as Exempted Transactions (Regulation D).

An important statutory exemption for transactions is found in the language of the 1933 Securities Act stating that the act "shall not apply to . . . transactions by an issuer not involving any public offering."[136] The SEC has taken a rather narrow view of this exemption, permitting it to apply to banks in their lending activities and to larger institutional purchasers of securities and to small groups of related persons in business ventures. But if the exemption is sought for transactions involving speculative securities offered to uninformed and unrelated persons, the SEC believes that the

---

[130] 17 C.F.R. § 230.144(c).

[131] 17 C.F.R. § 230.144(c)(2).

[132] 17 C.F.R. § 230.144(d).

[133] 17 C.F.R. § 230.144(e).

[134] 17 C.F.R. § 230.144(f). These limitations generally require that Rule 144 transactions be conducted either through a broker or through a "market maker" as defined in the 1934 Securities Exchange Act. "Market maker" is there defined as "any specialist permitted to act as a dealer, any dealer acting in the capacity of block positioner, and any dealer who, with respect to a security, holds himself out (by entering quotations in an inter-dealer communications system or otherwise) as being willing to buy and sell such security for his own account on a regular or continuous basis." 15 U.S.C. § 78c(a)(38).

[135] 17 C.F.R. § 230.144(h).

[136] 15 U.S.C. § 77d(2).

exemption will not serve the public policies of the securities statutes. Therefore, the private offering exemption would not apply when a company offers shares of its stock to certain "key" employees.[137]

Even though this exemption is a statutory exemption, the SEC has again promulgated regulations to accompany the statute, which regulations are more detailed and specific in defining how to qualify for and apply the exemption. The principal regulation accompanying this statutory exemption for private offerings is Regulation D, which is available from the SEC on the Internet at http://www.sec.gov.[138] Under the terms of Regulation D, the exemption for private offerings applies to issuers only and is an exemption for transactions rather than for securities.[139]

In Regulation D are found general rules applied to all of the types of exemptions authorized under Regulation D (which general requirements are contained in Rule 502),[140] and Regulation D also has specific rules for different types of private offering exemptions. A common question is whether separate sales are a part of the same offering. In an offering consisting of separate sales, it must be determined whether integration rules apply so that the eligibility of the entire offering can be determined.[141] Regulation D also has rules determining whether particular purchasers are entitled to receive information about the securities before they make the purchase. No such requirement is applied to sales to certain sophisticated investors, but the requirement of prior information must be met for certain other investors.[142] In general, for an offering governed by the provisions of Regulation D, it is not permissible to advertise for or recruit purchasers from among the general public.[143]

Sales that do occur under the exemption of Regulation D are usually considered restricted, which means that those securities may be resold only after certain time and registration requirements have been met.[144] As with other exempt offerings, a post-offering reporting requirement is imposed; within 15 days after the first sale, an issuer must file with the SEC a completed Form D (Notice of Sales of Securities Pursuant to Regulation D or Section 4(6)). The provisions of Form D is available from the SEC on the Internet at http://www.sec.gov.

One of the important specific exemptions under Regulation D is found in

---

[137] 17 C.F.R. § 231.4552; SEC v. Ralston Purina Co., 346 U.S. 119 (1953).

[138] 17 C.F.R. §§ 230.501 to 230.508.

[139] 17 C.F.R. § 230.501(g); Preliminary Note 4 to Regulation D.

[140] 17 C.F.R. § 230.502.

[141] 17 C.F.R. § 230.502(a).

[142] 17 C.F.R. § 230.502(b).

[143] 17 C.F.R. § 230.502(c).

[144] 17 C.F.R. § 230.502(d).

Rule 504,[145] which rule eliminates registration requirements for offerings of $1,000,000 or less. Another important exemption is in Rule 505, which exempts offerings of up to $5,000,000 if not more than 35 investors are participating in the offering.[146] Even this restriction of the number of the purchasers is removed, under the exemption described in Rule 506, if all the purchasers are either accredited investors or are otherwise experienced and knowledgeable in finance and business matters.[147]

Any of these exemptions in Regulation D can apply to real estate transactions. For example, an undivided equity interest in a land syndication or a participation interest in a real estate joint venture may qualify as a private offering, but only if the issuers comply fully with the applicable information and disclosure requirements.[148] An intrastate issue exemption has also been applied to a partnership interest in a real estate syndicate which was formed to complete the purchase and lease back of a motel.[149]

COMPUTER-ASSISTED RESEARCH

LEXIS: private w/5 offering! w/30 exempt w/5 securit! w/5 transaction! w/30 real estate

§ 103.04(a)(7)(vii)   Large Sales of Real Estate Mortgage Notes as Exempted Transactions.

One exemption that applies exclusively to real estate transactions is the statutory exemption for large sales of real estate mortgage notes.[150] This extremely detailed exemption was added to the Securities Act in 1975 and, because of its detail, no further elaboration has been provided through additional rules or regulations. The exemption applies to promissory notes secured by first liens on real estate with structures, and to "participation interests in such notes."[151] If the notes are originated by a federally supervised or state supervised financial institution, then no sale may be for less than $250,000, the purchase price must be paid in cash not more than 60 days after the time of sale, and each purchaser must buy for its own account only, in order for the exemption to apply.[152] Notes originated by a federally approved mortgagee are subject to the same restrictions and also may be sold

---

[145] 17 C.F.R. § 230.504.

[146] 17 C.F.R. § 230.505.

[147] 17 C.F.R. § 230.506.

[148] Andrews v. Blue, 489 F.2d 367 (10th Cir. 1973); SEC v. Royal Hawaiian Mgt. Corp. & Ryan, 1966–1967 CCH Dec. § 91,982 (C.D. Cal. 1967).

[149] Pawgan v. Silverstein, 265 F. Supp. 898 (S.D.N.Y. 1967).

[150] 15 U.S.C. § 77d(5).

[151] 15 U.S.C. § 77d(5)(A).

[152] 15 U.S.C. §§ 77d(5)(A)(i)(a), (b) and (c).

to a qualified lending institution or insurance company.[153] These parties may also enter into non-assignable contracts to buy or sell such notes, and, if the contract will be completed within two years, such transactions are also exempt. If the restrictions as to qualified purchasers and sellers and as to minimum value of purchases are observed, certain resales of these notes are also permitted under this exemption.

§ 103.04(a)(7)(viii)   Sales to Accredited Investors as Exempted Transactions.

A new exemption for offers or sales to accredited investors was added in 1980 by the Small Business Issuers' Simplification Act.[154] This statutory exemption has no accompanying rules or regulations, although the statute does require the issuer to file "such notice with the Commission as the Commission shall prescribe."[155] Of particular interest in this statutory exemption is a legislative definition of "accredited investor," which refers to several kinds of institutional investors and to

> any person who, on the basis of such factors as financial sophistication, net worth, knowledge and experience in financial matters, or amount of assets under management qualifies as an accredited investor under rules and regulations which the Commission shall prescribe.[156]

It is also required under this exemption that the offering not exceed $5,000,000 in value and that there be no advertising or public solicitation in connection with the transaction.[157]

§ 103.04(b)   Penalties for Violations of Registration Requirements.

§ 103.04(b)(1)   False Registration Statements.

A registration statement is materially false if it omits a material fact or contains an untrue statement of a material fact, and any person whose acquisition of a security is affected by such false information has a cause of action against various parties responsible for the false registration statement. Such defendants are jointly and severally liable and include any persons who signed the statement, directors or partners of the issuer (either present or named with consent as future directors or partners), and underwriters. To some of these parties certain defenses are available that invoke the defendant's good faith and reasonable belief in the truth of the contents of the statements.[158] However, these defenses based on good faith are not

---

[153] 15 U.S.C. § 77d(5)(A)(ii).

[154] 15 U.S.C. § 77d(6).

[155] *Id.*

[156] 15 U.S.C. § 77b(a)(15).

[157] 15 U.S.C. § 77d(6).

[158] 15 U.S.C. §§ 77k(b), (c), and (f). State v. Fashion Place Assocs., 638 N.Y.S.2d 26 (1996).

available to the issuer. Actions brought for such claims must be commenced within one year after the omission or untrue statement is discovered or should have been discovered, but in no event more than three years after the public offering occurred.[159]

Damages, will vary according to whether the original purchaser still holds the security or has transferred it, but the damages may not exceed the original public offering price of the security plus appropriate costs and fees.[160]

§ 103.04(b)(2) Violations in Registration and Prospectus Procedures; Penalties for False Prospectus Contents and False Communications.

Apart from the consequences of making offerings with false registration statements, civil liability can result from offering or selling a security in violation of any of the Securities Act requirements for registration and for the prospectus.[161] Liability can also result from engaging in such offering or selling of a security when using any interstate means of transportation or communication.[162] In those actions, only the party who actually offers or sells a security is liable to the purchaser, and, if the purchaser knew that the items were false and misleading, or knew that the defendant did not know that, the defendant will escape liability.

If the successful plaintiff in such an action still owns the security, the measure of damages is the purchase price plus interest, less income received.[163]

If the legal action is based upon such false communications and false prospectus contents, it must be commenced within one year after the omission or untrue statement was discovered or should have been discovered, but in no event more than three years after the public offering was conducted.[164] Actions based on registration and prospectus violations must be brought within one year after the violation occurs and, if discovery is delayed, in no event more than three years after the sale.[165]

§ 103.04(b)(3) Summary of the Anti-Fraud Provisions.

Making offerings of securities that are subject to the requirements of

---

[159] 15 U.S.C. § 77m.

[160] 15 U.S.C. § 77k(e).

[161] 15 U.S.C. § 77l(a)(1). First Presbyterian Church of Mankato, Minn. v. John G. Kinnaird & Co., 881 F. Supp. 441 (D. Minn. 1995) (intentional and negligent misrepresentation).

[162] 15 U.S.C. § 77l(a)(2).

[163] *Id.*

[164] 15 U.S.C. § 77m.

[165] *Id.*

federal regulations is often expensive and time consuming, and issuers and offerors often make great efforts to fit within one of the exemptions. Even then, alternative reporting requirements are often imposed by the exemptions. Whether securities being offered are fully subject to regulation or are exempt from some of the requirements, certain restrictions imposed by federal law apply in every case, inasmuch as all securities offerings under the jurisdiction of federal securities regulation must comply with the anti-fraud provisions of the securities acts.[166]

In general, these anti-fraud provisions prohibit any person or entity connected with the offer or sale of securities from using any means or instruments to defraud, from obtaining money or property by misrepresenting or omitting statements of material fact, or from engaging in any activity that operates as a fraud or deceit, especially if the mails or other means of interstate commerce or communication are used.[167] The anti-fraud provisions also impose requirements on those who endorse securities for consideration, principally that the endorsers must disclose the fact and the amount of consideration they receive for their endorsements.[168]

Noted below are summary descriptions of illegal activities in connection with securities that have commonly been held to violate the anti-fraud provisions:

   a.   churning or artificially stimulating activity in accounts to create the impression of an active market;[169]

   b.   cross-trading for profit between customer accounts by a broker which does not disclose its true capacity;[170]

   c.   selling stock in a fictitious corporation;[171]

   d.   delivering forged imitations of genuine bonds;[172]

---

[166] 15 U.S.C. § 77q(c).

[167] 15 U.S.C. § 77q(a); McMahan Securities Co. L.P. v. Aviator Master Fund, Ltd., 868 N.Y.S.2d 669 (2008) (broker-dealer's alleged fraud by negligent misrepresentation).Gray v. First Winthrop Corp., 82 F.3d 877 (9th Cir. 1996); In re JDN Realty Corp. Securities Litigation, 182 F. Supp. 2d 1230 (N.D. Ga. 2002) (real estate counsel for corporation not held primarily liable for securities fraud).

S.E.C. v. Kirkland, 533 F.3d 1323 (11th Cir. 2008) (complaint alleging that defendant fraudulently enticed investors to buy unregistered securities).

[168] 15 U.S.C. § 77q(b).

[169] Newkirk v. Hayden, Stone & Co., 1964–1966 CCH Dec. § 91,621 (S.D. Cal. 1965).

[170] Norris & Hirschberg, Inc. v. SEC, 177 F.2d 228 (D.C. Cir. 1949).

[171] Sherwood v. United States, 300 F.2d 603 (5th Cir. 1962).

[172] Seeman v. United States, 90 F.2d 88 (5th Cir. 1937).

e. use of advantageous inside information;[173]

f. receiving kickbacks on sales induced by failure to disclose;[174]

g. excessive or unfair mark-ups and mark-downs;[175]

h. manipulating market price through artificial stimulation of apparent market activity;[176]

i. making purported payments to purported investors to create the impression of return on investments;[177]

j. selling unregistered securities as part of a public offering;[178]

k. operating as issuers corporations whose purpose is to promote pyramid sales and multi-level distributorship plans, in which recruitment rather than sales is the function;[179]

l. use of misleading sales literature;[180]

m. depriving the issuer of part of the proceeds from sales of the offering;[181]

n. inadequate supervision of salesmen or others involved in the offering;[182] and

o. withholding shares from the public offering in order to make private sales.[183]

Also prohibited by the anti-fraud provisions of the securities acts are certain failures to disclose material items of information. Examples of material matters whose non-disclosure has been held fraudulent include

---

[173] In the Matter of Jack Schaefer, 1975–1976 CCH Dec. § 80,322 (Admin. Proc. File No. 3-2783, 1975).

[174] United States v. Fields, 592 F.2d 638 (2d Cir. 1978), *cert. denied,* 442 U.S. 917 (1979).

[175] *In re* Blumenfeld, 1979–1980 CCH Dec. § 82,396 (Admin. Proc. File No. 3-5282, 1979).

[176] SEC v. Scott Taylor & Co., 183 F. Supp. 904 (S.D.N.Y. 1959).

[177] SEC v. Universal Serv. Ass'n, 106 F.2d 232 (7th Cir. 1939).

[178] In the Matter of Benjamin, 1957–1961 CCH Dec. § 76,616 (1958).

[179] SEC v. Steed Indus., 1974–1975 CCH Dec. § 94,917 (N.D. Ill. 1974).

[180] In the Matter of First Maine Corp., 1957–1961 CCH Dec. § 76,642 (1959); Las Campanas Ltd. P'ship v. Pribble, 943 P.2d 554 (N.M. App. 1997) (Minor technical violation didn't give purchaser right to rescind the contract); Securities and Exchange Commission v. Kings Real Estate Investment Trust, 222 F.R.D. 660 (D. Kan. 2004) (individual investor, seeking to recover a $1 million-dollar investment was permitted to intervene in an SEC civil enforcement action against a real estate investment trust).

[181] In the Matter of Bankers Sec. Co., 6 S.E.C. 631 (1940).

[182] In the Matter of Shearson, Hammill & Co., 1964–1966 CCH Dec. § 77,306 (1965).

[183] In the Matter of H. Hentz & Co., 1969–1970 CCH Dec. § 77,853 (1970).

insolvency of the broker,[184] financial information about the issuer,[185] accurate information about the market history of the stock,[186] information about a merger involving the issuer,[187] purchaser charges,[188] seller's profits or commissions,[189] authorship of published materials,[190] changes in investment advice,[191] and failure to disclose that sales were short sales (in which the seller does not yet actually own or possess the securities at the time of sale).[192]

Even a party not directly participating in fraudulent conduct can still be held liable or guilty for various forms of conduct which are deemed to be aiding and abetting the fraudulent conduct. Aiding and abetting was established when it was shown that the fraud that was committed by the primary party was known of by the alleged aider and abetter, who also gave substantial assistance to the commission of the fraud.[193] Sometimes attorneys and accountants who advise issuers are charged as aiders and abetters.[194]

By way of summary, it can be said that fraud as an element in offering or selling any security is prohibited by statute whenever the mails or interstate transportation or communication are used. The statute prohibits the persons from using "any device, scheme, or artifice to defraud," from obtaining "money or property by means of any untrue statement of a material fact or any omission to state a material fact," or from engaging "in any transaction, practice, or course of business which operates or would operate as a fraud or deceit upon the purchaser."[195]

---

[184] In the Matter of Leo G. MacLaughlin Sec. Co., 1964–1966 CCH Dec. § 77,317 (1966).

[185] Danser v. United States, 281 F.2d 492 (1st Cir. 1960).

[186] SEC v. R.A. Holman & Co., 1964–1966 CCH Dec. § 91,554 (S.D.N.Y. 1965).

[187] SEC v. National Student Mktg. Corp., 538 F.2d 404 (D.C. Cir. 1976) *cert. denied,* White and Case v. SEC, 429 U.S. 1073 (1977).

[188] In the Matter of Peoples Sec. Co., 1957–1961 CCH Dec. § 76,687 (1960).

[189] SEC v. Torr, 15 F. Supp. 315 (S.D.N.Y. 1936), *rev'd on other grounds,* 87 F.2d 446 (2d Cir. 1937).

[190] In the Matter of Axe Sec. Corp., 1964–1966 CCH Dec. § 77,148 (1964).

[191] Butcher v. Sherrerd, 1971–1972 CCH Dec. § 78,466 (1971).

[192] United States v. Naftalin, 441 U.S. 768 (1979).

[193] Fund of Funds, Ltd. v. Arthur Andersen & Co., 567 F.2d 225 (2d Cir. (1977).

[194] Parquitex Partners v. Registered Fin. Planning Servs., 1987 CCH Dec. § 93,255 (D. Or. 1987) (attorney; dictum); Ackerman, Jablonski, Porterfield & De Ture v. Alhadeff, 1986–1987 CCH Dec. § 92,756 (W.D. Wash. 1986) (accounting firm; motion to dismiss denied).

[195] 15 U.S.C. § 77q(a). *In re* Impac Mortg. Holdings, Inc. Securities Litigation, 554 F. Supp. 2d 1083 (C.D. Cal. 2008) (mortgage securities fraud class action based on officers' statements).

As mentioned before, the anti-fraud provisions apply to all securities under federal jurisdiction, including those that are exempted,[196] and they also apply to the transactional exemptions.[197]

Enforcement of the anti-fraud provisions is typically accomplished by the SEC, which usually seeks either injunctive measures or refers the matter to the Attorney General for criminal prosecution.[198] The federal anti-fraud provisions make no specific reference to a private right of action and federal courts continue to be divided over whether a private right of action should be implied in the federal law.[199]

Likewise, there is no indication in the statute whether a private right of action to enforce anti-fraud provisions applies in state courts, which are given concurrent jurisdiction over enforcement actions under the 1933 Securities Act.[200]

COMPUTER-ASSISTED RESEARCH

LEXIS: anti-fraud w/5 provision! w/30 securit! w/2 act! w/50 real estate

§ 103.05   Federal Regulation of Broker-Dealers in Real Estate Transactions.

§ 103.05(a)   Definitions of Securities Brokers and Dealers.

In addition to regulation of securities and securities transactions and issuers of securities, much attention in the federal securities regulation scheme has focused on brokers and dealers, who usually are the parties offering and selling the securities to the general public. Regulation of securities at point of sale is believed to be very effective in eliminating much potential misconduct from securities transactions.

In the context of federal securities regulation, a broker means "any person engaged in the business of effecting transactions in securities for the account of others, but does not include a bank."[201] The closely related concept of dealer

> means any person engaged in the business of buying and selling securities for his own account, through a broker or otherwise, but does not include a

---

[196] 15 U.S.C. § 77q(c).

[197] *See, e.g.,* United States v. Roylance, 690 F.2d 164 (10th Cir. 1982); Spatz v. Borenstein, 513 F. Supp. 571 (N.D. Ill. 1981).

[198] 15 U.S.C. § 77t(b).

[199] *See, e.g.,* Herman & MacLean v. Huddleston, 459 U.S. 375 (1983) (reserving decision on whether a private right of action is implied in the anti-fraud decisions); Kirshner v. United States, 603 F.2d 234 (2d Cir. 1978), *cert. denied,* 442 U.S. 909 (1979) (implying a private right of action); Newman v. Prior, 518 F.2d 97 (4th Cir. 1975) (holding no private right of action is implied).

[200] 15 U.S.C. § 77v(a).

[201] 15 U.S.C. § 78c(a)(4).

bank, or any person insofar as he buys or sells securities for his own account, either individually or in some fiduciary capacity, but not as part of a regular business.[202]

§ 103.05(b)   Securities Brokers and Dealers Who Are Subject to Federal Securities Registration Requirements.

When brokers and dealers are determined to be subject to federal jurisdiction, the basic requirement they must meet is to be registered according to the provisions of the 1934 Securities Exchange Act. This requirement applies to all brokers and dealers which are not natural persons; or who are natural persons not associated with a broker or dealer which is not a natural person (unless the natural person broker or dealer deals exclusively in intrastate commerce and does not use any facility of a national securities exchange); and who use the mails or any means or instrumentality of interstate commerce "to effect any transactions in, or to induce or attempt to induce the purchase or sale of, any security" (except exempt securities, commercial paper, bankers' acceptances, or commercial bills).[203]

Some brokers and dealers are exempt from registration requirements because they are conducting business entirely within a state or in connection with certain banking instruments, but the SEC has also created other exemptions by rule or order.[204] Under this rulemaking authority of the SEC, brokers and dealers enjoy exemptions for transactions in corporate shares that represent ownership in corporate apartment developments,[205] for transactions involving certain foreign brokers and dealers,[206] for transactions involving foreign underwriters participating in certain foreign distributions of American securities,[207] for transactions in variable annuities of insurance companies,[208] and for certain transactions by certain non-bank lenders under Small Business Administration approval, if the lender does not engage in transactions for its own account;[209] brokers and dealers also enjoy a limited exemption for a natural person who is a member of a national securities exchange, extending for 45 days after termination of the person's association with a registered broker or dealer.[210]

---

[202] 15 U.S.C. § 78c(5).

[203] 15 U.S.C. § 78o(a)(1).

[204] 15 U.S.C. § 78o(a)(2).

[205] 17 C.F.R. § 240.15a-2.

[206] 17 C.F.R. § 240.15a-6.

[207] 17 C.F.R. § 241, Interpretive Release No. 7366 (July 9, 1964).

[208] 17 C.F.R. § 241, Interpretive Release No. 8389 (Aug. 29, 1968).

[209] 17 C.F.R. § 240.15a-5.

[210] 17 C.F.R. § 240.15a-4.

§ 103.05(c)   Summary of Federal Registration Requirements for Securities Brokers and Dealers.

§ 103.05(c)(1)   How to Apply for Registration.

At the federal level, a broker or dealer registers by filing with the SEC an application on Form BD, which is available from the SEC on the Internet at http://www.sec.gov.[211] Form BD requires that information be provided about the organizational and financial relationships and background of the broker or dealer. The regulation governing this registration further requires that

> Every broker or dealer who files an application for registration on Form BD . . . shall file with such application, in duplicate original, a statement of financial condition as of a date within 30 days of the date in which such statement is filed . . .[212]

In the statement of financial condition, the instructions for which is available from the SEC on the Internet at http://www.sec.gov, the applicant is required to disclose the nature and amount of assets and liabilities and net worth of the applicant, a computation of the applicant's aggregate indebtedness and net capital, which computation shall comply with the requirements pertaining to the applicant's business or national securities exchange.[213]

Within 45 days after submission of the application, the SEC must act,[214] and upon SEC action the application will either be granted or will become the subject of further administrative proceedings to determine whether it should be denied. The applicant is given notice and opportunity for hearing in connection with these proceedings. Any proceedings for denial must be concluded within 120 days from when the application was submitted.[215]

Occasionally a broker or dealer will apply to register another broker or dealer which is yet to be formed or organized and is to be a successor to the applicant, or in fact a successor will have already been formed or organized shortly after the application is submitted. If the SEC grants the application of the initial registrant, but in the meantime, a successor has been created, the successor may accept the original registration as its own any time within 45 days after the application was granted.[216] If that occurs, then the successor must file its own follow-up application on Form BD within 30 days after becoming the successor, and then the SEC may take up to an

---

[211] The registration requirement is statutorily imposed by 15 U.S.C. § 78o(b)(1). The regulatory requirement to use Form B-D is in 17 C.F.R. § 240.15b1-1, and the authority to promulgate the form is in 17 C.F.R. § 249.501.

[212] 17 C.F.R. § 240.15b1-2.

[213] 17 C.F.R. § 240.15b1-2(a).

[214] 15 U.S.C. § 78o(b)(1).

[215] 15 U.S.C. § 78o(b)(1)(B).

[216] 15 U.S.C. § 78o(b)(2)(A).

additional 45 days to act on the application from the successor. Under some circumstances, when an unregistered broker-dealer succeeds a registered broker-dealer and then files a Form BD, the later application will be deemed filed by the predecessor.[217] In that case, the original registration could remain in effect for a successor for up to 75 days.[218]

If the successor-applicant is a fiduciary such as an executor, a trustee in bankruptcy, or a receiver, that fiduciary has 30 days after beginning the fiduciary duties in which to file a Form BD with the required fiduciary information.[219]

§ 103.05(c)(2)   Conduct That May Lead to Denial, Suspension or Revocation of Applications and Registrations.

A broker-dealer application for registration can be denied on the same grounds that the registration itself can be denied,[220] and those prohibitions also apply to "persons associated" with the broker or dealer. Those associated persons are statutorily defined as follows:

> the term "person associated with a broker or dealer" or "associated person of a broker or dealer" means any partner, officer, director, or branch manager of such broker or dealer (or any person occupying a similar status or performing similar functions), any person directly or indirectly controlling, controlled by, or under common control with such broker or dealer, or any employee of such broker or dealer, except that any person associated with a broker or dealer whose functions are solely clerical or ministerial shall not be included in the meaning of such term for purposes of section 78o(b) of this title (other than paragraph (6) thereof).[221]

Of course, it is statutorily prohibited to engage in activities as a broker or dealer without being registered.[222] It is also prohibited wilfully to make a false or misleading statement in an application for registration. The SEC can deny an application for registration or revoke the registration itself when it discovers such false and misleading statements. Revocations have been considered or issued for misleading statements about the location of the applicant's principal office,[223] about whether the applicant engaged in prior

---

[217] 17 C.F.R. § 240.15b1-3(b).

[218] 17 C.F.R. § 240.15b1-3(a).

[219] 17 C.F.R. § 240.15b1-4.

[220] 15 U.S.C. §§ 78o(b)(1) and (4); First Presbyterian Church of Mankato, Minn. v. John G. Kinnaird & Co., 881 F. Supp. 441 (D. Minn. 1995) (intentional and negligent misrepresentation).

[221] 15 U.S.C. § 78c(a)(18).

[222] 15 U.S.C. § 78o(a)(1).

[223] In the Matter of Phillips, 5 S.E.C. 634 (1939).

sales in a prohibited capacity,[224] about a prior broker-dealer relationship and conducting transactions while insolvent,[225] about a listing of capital,[226] about a balance sheet,[227] and about prior violations of restrictions on aggregate indebtedness.[228]

Revocations in other cases have been issued for failure to disclose. Failures to disclose resulting in revocation or denials of registration have included failures to disclose change of address,[229] a connection with another firm,[230] a control person,[231] registrant's majority stockholder as a beneficial owner,[232] a felony conviction,[233] an injunction,[234] and a prior broker-dealer relationship.[235]

Revocations have also occurred for the following types of misconduct: artificially depressing and otherwise manipulating the price of a security or the market;[236] conducting boiler-room operations;[237] converting customer funds and securities;[238] failure to carry out a customer order;[239] failure to file annual reports of financial condition;[240] felony conviction of one of the registrant's controlling persons;[241] fraudulent conduct in offering and selling securities;[242] fraudulent intent to distribute securities;[243] issuing a false

---

[224] Holman & Co., Inc., 42 S.E.C. 866 (1965).

[225] Fliederbaum, Mooradian & Co., 1961–1964 CCH Dec. § 76,951 (1963).

[226] Associated Underwriters, Inc., 1961–1964 CCH Dec. § 76,916 (1963).

[227] Maine Corp., 38 S.E.C. 882 (1959).

[228] Lando-Host & Co., 5 S.E.C. 572 (1939).

[229] Security Serv., Inc., 1961–1964 CCH Dec. § 76,230 (1963).

[230] Walston & Co., 7 S.E.C. 937 (1940).

[231] Financial Counsellors, Inc. v. S.E.C., 339 F.2d 196 (2d Cir. 1964).

[232] Maine Corp., 38 S.E.C. 882 (1959).

[233] Kent, dba Ralph C. Kent & Co., 4 S.E.C. 204 (1938).

[234] Marks, dba Monroe Marks Company, 9 S.E.C. 669 (1941).

[235] Fliederbaum, Mooradian & Co., 1961–1964 CCH Dec. § 76,951 (1963); Associated Underwriters, Inc., 1961–1964 CCH Dec. § 76,916 (1963).

[236] Thomas L. McGhee, 1984 CCH Dec. 77,198 (1984); Abrahams, 18 S.E.C. 61 (1945); Scone Invs., L.P. v. American Third Mkt. Corp., 1998 U.S. Dist. LEXIS 5903 (S.D.N.Y. 1998) (Brokers and control persons conspired together to devise and implement an unlawful scheme to manipulate the market prices of thinly traded "penny stock" securities).

[237] B. Fennekohl & Co., 41 S.E.C. 210 (1962).

[238] James E. Scott & Co., 28 S.E.C. 30 (1948).

[239] Investment Serv. Co., 41 S.E.C. 148 (1962).

[240] Samson, Roberts & Co., 42 S.E.C. 612 (1965).

[241] Lockaby, dba J. S. Lockaby & Co., 29 S.E.C. 271 (1949).

[242] Holman & Co., 42 S.E.C. 866 (1965); Primavera Familienstiftung v. Askin, 173 F.R.D. 115 (S.D.N.Y. 1997) (alleging defendant misrepresented mortgage-backed securities as "risk balanced," "market neutral"); National Western Life Ins. Co. v. Merrill Lynch, 1997

offering circular;[244] making false entries in books and records;[245] making an improper inducement to purchase;[246] misapplying sales proceeds;[247] misrepresentations in making sales;[248] not disclosing client costs;[249] not disclosing market control;[250] paying operating expenses with client funds;[251] previous SEC restrictions and conditions not met;[252] record-keeping violations;[253] selling registrant's own stock improperly;[254] selling unregistered securities;[255] and violating capital requirements.[256]

Registration suspensions or denials have been issued for the following offenses: failure to control employees' unlawful activities;[257] failure to file an address change;[258] failure to file an annual report;[259] failure to notify the SEC of a license suspension by the state;[260] and selling unregistered securities.[261]

COMPUTER-ASSISTED RESEARCH

LEXIS: securit! broker! or dealer! w/15 den! or suspen! or revo! w/5

U.S. Dist. LEXIS 9706 (S.D.N.Y. 1997) (alleging Merrill Lynch fraudulently concealed the fact that the sponsor of cooperative housing had no assets of its own).

[243] In the Matter of Reinhardt & Co., 4 S.E.C. 749 (1939).

[244] American Sec. Assocs., 41 S.E.C. 624 (1963).

[245] Armstrong, Jones & Co., 42 S.E.C. 888 (1968).

[246] Siesfeld, dba Leo G. Siesfeld & Co., 11 S.E.C. 746 (1942); Potter v. American Medicare Corp., 484 S.E.2d 43 (Ga. App. 1997) (falsely inducing plaintiff to purchase its stock).

[247] Kahn & Co., 42 S.E.C. 671 (1965).

[248] Billings Assocs., Inc., 43 S.E.C. 641 (1967). *In re* Newbridge Networks Sec. Litig., 962 F. Supp. 166 (D.D.C. 1997) (Statements about product sale are misleading in light of declining sales); Meadows v. SEC, 119 F.3d 1219 (5th Cir. 1997) (Registered broker-dealer misrepresented the operation of venture and its financial situation to investors and kept silence in return for payment), *reh'g denied*, 1997 U.S. App. LEXIS 31093 (5th Cir. 1997).

[249] Hughes v. S.E.C., 174 F.2d 969 (D.C. Cir. 1949).

[250] Sterling Sec. Co., 39 S.E.C. 487 (1959).

[251] Jay Morton & Co., 1961–1964 CCH Dec. § 76,909 (1963).

[252] Leeby, dba Lawrence R. Leeby & Co., 32 S.E.C. 307 (1951).

[253] Security Planners Assocs., Inc., 44 S.E.C. 738 (1971).

[254] Investment Registry of Am., Inc., 21 S.E.C. 745 (1946).

[255] Shaw, 26 S.E.C. 538 (1947); SEC v. Parkersburg Wireless L.L.C., et al., 991 F. Supp. 6 (D.D.C. 1997) (Defendant sold unregistered securities to unemployed and retired and old investors through high-pressure phone solicitations).

[256] Whitney & Co., Inc., 40 S.E.C. 1100 (1962).

[257] Reynolds & Co., 39 S.E.C. 902 (1960).

[258] In the Matter of Farnick, dba Kellogg Brokerage Co., 5 S.E.C. 570 (1939).

[259] Winterhalter, dba Harold E. Winterhalter Co., 42 S.E.C. 774 (1965).

[260] In the Matter of Duncan Collins & Co., 4 S.E.C. 27 (1938).

[261] Lloyd, Miller & Co., 41 S.E.C. 200 (1962).

application! or registration! w/50 real estate

§ 103.05(d)   Rules for Brokers and Dealers to Ensure Financial Responsibility and Customer Protection.

In addition to the prohibitions against broker-dealer conduct involving deceit, other regulations attempt to insure the financial reliability of brokers and dealers, again as a means of protection for investors. Thus the SEC imposes certain rules regarding financial responsibility and customer protection, which rules apply to brokers and dealers who use the mail or some other instrumentality in interstate commerce in offering and selling securities.[262] These rules, which are very technical, impose requirements relating to net capital,[263] the conditions under which a broker or dealer may use a customer's free credit balance,[264] and certain other standards for customer protection, including physical control of securities and maintenance of reserves when using customer funds.[265] These rules are available from the SEC on the Internet at http://www.sec.gov.

§ 103.05(e)   Standards of Conduct for Securities Brokers and Dealers.

Brokers and dealers are also subject to the prohibitions contained in the 1934 Securities Exchange Act, which require them to refrain from offering or selling securities "by means of any manipulative, deceptive, or other fraudulent device or contrivance,"[266] or from engaging "in any fraudulent, deceptive, or manipulative act or practice," or from making any fictitious quotation.[267]

The regulations issued in connection with these statutory prohibitions describe several practices deemed to be "manipulative, deceptive, or other fraudulent device or contrivance." These prohibited practices include any act which operates as a fraud or deceit upon any person, untrue and omitted statements of material fact, misrepresentations as to the merits of a security implied by broker-dealer registration, failure to disclose issuer control of a broker-dealer, failure to disclose a broker-dealer's interest in the distribution, excessive purchases from discretionary accounts, representations that sales are at "market" prices without substantiating grounds or information, and use of pro forma balance sheets.[268]

---

[262] 15 U.S.C. § 78o(c)(3).

[263] 17 C.F.R. § 240.15c3-1.

[264] 17 C.F.R. § 240.15c3-2.

[265] 17 C.F.R. § 240.15c3-3.

[266] 15 U.S.C. § 78o(c)(2).

[267] *Id.* First Presbyterian Church of Mankato, Minn. v. John G. Kinnaird & Co., 881 F. Supp. 441 (D. Minn. 1995) (intentional and negligent misrepresentation).

[268] 17 C.F.R. §§ 240.15c1-2-240.15c1-9.

Other fraudulent practices are identified in Commission rules, and these include hypothecation of customers' securities under certain circumstances, accepting a sale price for securities without prompt transmission of the consideration, not making certain disclosures when extending credit in connection with a securities transaction, and distributing securities without complying with prospectus requirements.[269] Other rules prohibit fictitious quotes[270] and certain sales practices for low-priced securities.[271]

§ 103.05(f)   Rules for Transactions in Penny Stocks.

The Penny Stock Reform Act of 1990 prohibits brokers and dealers from using the mails or other means of interstate commerce for offering or selling penny stock unless they have complied with the requirements of the Act. The requirements, to be supplemented by regulation, went into effect on April 15, 1992.[272]

§ 103.05(g)   The Requirement of Securities Association Membership.

Even after the procedures and burdens of registration are met, a broker or dealer must comply with substantial reporting requirements and is also required either to become a member of a registered securities association or to conduct business solely on a national securities exchange of which it is a member.[273] The National Association of Securities Dealers, Inc. (NASD) is the only securities association which has been registered by the SEC.

If a broker or dealer wishes to join the NASD, the applicant must first send to the NASD district office where the broker or dealer has its principal place of business:

(1)   a copy of its current submission to the Securities and Exchange Commission pursuant to Rule 15b1-2(c) under the Securities Exchange Act of 1934;

(2)   its most recent trial balance, balance sheet, supporting schedules and computation of net capital;

(3)   a copy of its written supervisory procedures;

(4)   a list of all officers, directors, general partners, employees and other persons who will be associated with it at the time of admission to membership;

(5)   a description of business activities in which it intends to engage; and

---

[269]   17 C.F.R. §§ 240.15c2-1–240.15c2-5, 240.15c2-8.

[270]   17 C.F.R. §§ 240.15c2-6, 240.15c2-7.

[271]   17 C.F.R. § 240.15c2-6.

[272]   15 U.S.C. § 78o(g). *See* Pub. L. 101-429, 104 Stat. 931 (1990).

[273]   15 U.S.C. § 78o(b)(8).

(6)   such other relevant information and documents as may be requested by the District Office.[274]

After the information has been submitted, a representative of the applicant must appear in a "pre-membership interview," where the following points will be covered:

(1)   the nature, adequacy, source and permanence of applicant's capital and its arrangements for additional capital should a business need arise;

(2)   the applicant's proposed recordkeeping system;

(3)   the applicant's proposed internal procedures, including compliance procedures;

(4)   the applicant's familiarity with applicable NASD rules and federal securities laws;

(5)   the applicant's capability to properly conduct the type of business intended in view of the:

    A.   number, experience and qualifications of the persons to be associated with it at the time of its admission to membership;

    B.   its planned facilities;

    C.   arrangements, if any, with banks, clearing corporations and others, to assist it in the conduct of its securities business;

    D.   supervisory personnel, methods and procedures; and

(6)   other factors relevant to the scope and operation of its business.[275]

After the interview, the district office has 30 days to notify the applicant whether the application has been granted, denied, or granted subject to restrictions or modifications. If the applicant is dissatisfied, a review can be conducted by the district committee, if a request is made within fifteen days after notification of the determination from the district office. At this review the applicant may appear and present evidence and the review committee's determination shall be made "within a reasonable time."[276]

A further review is available if the district committee determination is not acceptable to the applicant, and this review is conducted by the Board of Governors if the applicant so requests within fifteen days after being notified of the committee's determination. The Board of Governors also is required to issue its determination within a reasonable time.[277]

The determination from the Board of Governors is subject to review by

---

[274] NASD Manual, By-laws Schedule C, Part I, § (1)(a).

[275] NASD Manual, By-laws Schedule C, Part I, § (1)(c).

[276] NASD Manual, By-laws Schedule C, Part I, § (2)(a) through (c).

[277] NASD Manual, By-laws Schedule C, Part I, § (2)(d) through (g).

the Securities and Exchange Commission upon request by the applicant.[278] Each of these review proceedings is an independent review and is not bound to any extent by any of the preceding actions.

As part of the membership application process for the broker or dealer, certain persons within the brokership or dealership are required to be registered. Among these persons are all of the broker's or dealer's principals,[279] all representatives,[280] and all assistant representatives for order processing.[281] Each of these persons must pass a qualification examination which is appropriate to the duties and category of registration for such person.

COMPUTER-ASSISTED RESEARCH

LEXIS: (national association w/1 securities dealers) or nasd w/15 membership w/5 requir! w/50 real estate

§ 103.06   The Complementary Relationship of Federal and State Securities Regulation of Real Estate Transactions.

At the federal level, the major attempt to correct abuses in the quality of securities offered and sold throughout the country was embodied in the 1933 Securities Act, which imposed various disclosure and registration requirements in securities issues. The Securities Exchange Act of 1934, on the other hand, attempted to correct abuses in the securities distribution process by imposing registration and qualification requirements on parties who were involved in offering or selling securities.

The respective requirements of the 1933 and 1934 federal securities acts impact independently. Thus instruments may need to be registered as securities under the 1933 Act, and the broker-dealers who distribute those interests may also need to be registered under the 1934 Act. Or a securities issue that is exempt from registration under the 1933 Act may nevertheless need to be distributed by broker-dealers who are required to be registered under the 1934 Act. Together the basic federal securities laws are intended to enhance the integrity of the offering and the integrity of the distribution process.

Most states also adhere to this view, requiring—in addition to registration of securities issues—the registration of broker-dealers, as well as of persons who function as salespersons or agents for broker-dealers.[282] All states

---

[278] NASD Manual, By-laws Schedule C, Part I, § (2)(f).

[279] NASD Manual, By-laws Schedule C, Part II.

[280] NASD Manual, By-laws Schedule C, Part III.

[281] NASD Manual, By-laws Schedule C, Part IV.

[282] Section 201(a) of the *Uniform Securities Act* requires that broker-dealers and sales representatives be licensed or exempted from licensing, and Section 201(b) prohibits a broker-dealer from employing a salesperson who is not licensed or not exempt. State v. 7040

impose some regulation of securities activities through their so-called "blue sky" laws, and federal legislators have refrained from pre-empting the securities regulation field for federal regulation alone. Certainly the intrastate exemption for securities offered and sold solely within a single jurisdiction is at least partially justified on the assumption that such offerings are subject to statute regulation. Another example of federal accommodation of state regulation is the federal recognition of concurrent state court jurisdiction over Securities Act enforcement actions.[283] State law influence may also be seen in those cases "borrowing" state blue sky law limitation of actions periods to apply in federal securities law enforcement cases.[284]

The combined effect of federal and state regulation of the securities distribution processes is to enhance the reliability and fairness of securities distribution in the following ways:

1. Persons who play a role in the distribution process should be registered and found to be qualified.

2. Standards of suitability are established for prospective investors.

3. Restrictions are imposed on how long an offer can be outstanding, how investment commitments may be made, and how payments may be made.

4. Limits are established for imposing and administering the offering expenses and marketing fees.

5. Impermissible marketing techniques are identified.

6. Certain reports, to both investors and regulatory officials, are required.

Colonial Road Associates Co., 671 N.Y.S.2d 938 (1998) (state attorney general action against a cooperative corporation which had offered real estate securities for sale); State v. Metz, 671 N.Y.S.2d 79 (1998) (action to enjoin sponsors from selling real estate securities in connection with sponsorship of cooperative apartment complexes).

[283] 15 U.S.C. § 77v(a).

[284] *See, e.g.,* Herm v. Stafford, 663 F.2d 669 (6th Cir. 1981); Parrent v. Midwest Rug Mills, 455 F.2d 123 (7th Cir. 1972); Hudson v. Capital Mgt. Int'l, Inc., 1982–1983 CCH Dec. § 99,222 (N.D. Cal. 1982); SEC v. T & D Management Co., 1981–1982 CCH Dec. § 98,266 (D. Utah 1981); Reid v. Madison, 438 F. Supp. 332 (E.D. Va. 1977); Corey v. Bache & Co., Inc., 355 F. Supp. 1123 (S.D. W. Va. 1973); Eureka Homestead Soc. v. Zirinsky, 1997 U.S. Dist. LEXIS 6343 (E.D. La. May 7, 1997) (Eureka's Blue Sky Law claims are not viable; it cannot show that it did not know or should not have known of the "untruth[s] or omission[s]"); Cooperativa De Ahorro Y Credito Aguada v. Kidder, Peabody & Co., 129 F.3d 222, Fed. Sec. L. Rep. (1st Cir. 1997) (Federal courts applied the local statute of limitations to claims under section 10(b), but thereafter the Supreme Court adopted a one-and three-year limitations period for such claims. Congress then passed a new statute providing that local statutes of limitations should continue to govern suits filed prior to the Supreme Court decision, and allowing reinstatement of claims that had already been dismissed under the new Supreme Court rule).

§ 103.07 State Regulation of Securities Broker-Dealers in Real Estate Transactions.

The activities of states in regulating securities and those who distribute them fall with particular force in real estate transactions. Added to the substantial federal registration requirements for broker-dealers are separate sets of broker-dealer registration requirements in each of the states. Broker-dealers who engage in securities transactions are subject to these diverse regulations, and one type of real estate transaction—the real estate "syndicate" or "syndication"—has been peculiarly susceptible to the jurisdiction of state and federal securities regulation. In the remainder of this section, the concept of syndicates will be explained and their characteristics as securities clarified. In the following section will be found summaries of state licensing and registration requirements for securities broker-dealers, including those whose securities activities extend to real estate transactions, such as syndications.

§ 103.07(a) "Syndicate" and "Syndication" Defined.

The terms "syndicate" and "syndication" have achieved such broad and common usage that modern writers on the subject seem to not bother to define them. Yet the very breadth of the terms makes it difficult for the novice to comprehend the precise concepts embodied in the words. In its most basic and simplistic sense, a syndicate is a group, and a syndication is the activity undertaken by the group, an activity which for purposes of this chapter is a real estate investment. The terms "syndicate" and "syndication" are, however, used interchangeably, so that the definition is stated by one author as follows:

> A syndication is, most simply, a group form of investment. This group has been assembled to make and operate a specific business enterprise. The most common form of group real estate investment is the limited partnership. Ownership interests in limited partnerships are considered to be securities. Securities must be registered pursuant to Section 5(a) of the Securities Act of 1933 unless an exemption from registration is available.[285]

While a syndicate may be formed for many purposes other than real estate investments, in fact, almost all syndications are real estate syndications. The real estate syndication has been specifically defined as "a direct participation investment in an entity organized to engage in the acquisition, development and/or management and sale of real estate."[286] Embodied in this definitional statement are several unique characteristics of real estate syndicates and syndications:

---

[285] Jay B. Berstein, The Professional Syndicator: A Guide for Creating Limited Partnerships 1 (1981).

[286] Lewis G. Mosburg, Jr., Real Estate Syndicate Offerings Law & Practice 3 (1974).

1. They are "direct participation" investments, and the syndicate (although not the individual investors) frequently participates actively in the development and management of the property. The direct control over the investment is an attractive feature of a syndication.

2. Investment benefits—cash flow, equity accrual, and tax advantages, if any—accrue directly to the syndicate participants, rather than being subject to the rather more fickle fluctuations of the securities markets.

3. The group aspect of the syndicate both opens a wider range of investments to the combined invested assets and permits the risk to be spread among a larger number of investors.

4. Even though the syndicate is active in managing the investment, the individual investors are passive limited partners, needing no special expertise or other resources in order to realize a return on their investment. This division of responsibility is a key to understanding the appeal of the real estate syndicate:

> Real estate syndication represents the combination of the capital of the passive investors and the entrepreneurial contributions and managerial skills of the promoter. The latter, usually in the role of the general partner in a limited partnership, performs the entrepreneurial function of bringing together the many elements necessary to make a real estate deal. He orchestrates the regulatory issues, the tax factors, the financial questions, the economic forces, the managerial problems, the legal considerations, the money sources. The syndicator packages the investment and his is a multi-faceted task whose responsibilities are continuing and changing over time. He makes available to investors a collection of professional talent that few could afford on an individual basis.[287]

The appeal of the limited partnership form for real estate syndicates thus lies in its limited liability for the limited partner investors, direct "flow-through" tax benefits, and centralized professional management.

A distinction may be drawn between private and public syndications. The private syndicate is a limited partnership with a relatively small group of affluent investors whose investments are obtained under private offering rules, rather than the more complex public offering rules. The public syndicate raises money from a larger number of small investors through fully regulated public offerings.

COMPUTER-ASSISTED RESEARCH

LEXIS: syndicat! w/5 real estate w/30 securit!

---

[287] Stephen E. Roulac, Real Estate Syndication Digest, 1972; *Principles and Applications* 1 (1972).

§ 103.07(b)   Real Estate Investment Syndications as Securities.

Investments in real estate syndications are almost always considered securities under both federal and state securities laws. This does not mean that all syndications investments are regulated in the same way by securities laws, but it does mean that they are within regulatory jurisdiction. Under the 1933 Federal Securities Act,

> The term security means any note, . . . evidence of indebtedness, certificate of interest or participation in any profit-sharing agreement, . . . preorganization certificate or subscription, transferable share, investment contract, . . . or, in general, any interest or instrument commonly known as a "security", or any certificate of interest in or participation in, temporary or interim certificate for, receipt for, guarantee of, or warrant or right to subscribe to or purchase, any of the foregoing.[288]

The definition of a security in the various states is essentially the same, because most states have adopted a version of the Uniform Securities Act, which defines a security with the same language as the federal act.[289]

Thus, the typical real estate syndication in which "the non-promoting co-venturers [i.e., investors who are limited partners] are simply furnishing money, with the hope of profiting from the skill with which the syndicator puts their money to use,"[290] is clearly a security under federal[291] and state law.

The determination that investors' interests in real estate syndications are securities is of enormous legal importance. It means that the full range of regulatory apparatus is invoked for many ventures, and those ventures that do not come under the various disclosure and registration requirements enjoy that circumstance only because they have qualified for one or more exemptions created under securities law.[292] Moreover, an intriguing interplay between federal and state securities laws has emerged, so that in certain situations federal regulation is relaxed if state regulation is vigorous.

---

[288] 15 U.S.C. § 77b(a)(1).

[289] *Uniform Securities Act* § 401(l). The following American jurisdictions have adopted some version of the Uniform Securities Act, including its definition of a security: Alabama, Alaska, Arkansas, Colorado, Connecticut, Delaware, District of Columbia, Georgia, Hawaii, Idaho, Indiana, Iowa, Kansas, Kentucky, Maine, Maryland, Massachusetts, Michigan, Minnesota, Mississippi, Missouri, Montana, Nebraska, Nevada, New Hampshire, New Jersey, New Mexico, North Carolina, Oklahoma, Oregon, Pennsylvania, Rhode Island, South Carolina, South Dakota, Tennessee, Utah, Virginia, Washington, West Virginia, Wisconsin, and Wyoming.

[290] Lewis G. Mosburg, Jr., Real Estate Syndicate Offerings Law & Practice 13 (1974).

[291] S.E.C. v. W.J. Howey Co., 328 U.S. 293 (1946); S.E.C. v. C.M. Joiner Leasing Corp., 320 U.S. 344 (1943).

[292] Adler v. William Blair & Co., 648 N.E.2d 226 (Ill. App. 1995), *app. denied*, 657 N.E.2d 615 (Ill. 1995) (fraud, misrepresentation and breach of fiduciary duty alleged by investors who purchased limited partnership interests in a real estate syndication).

COMPUTER-ASSISTED RESEARCH

LEXIS: real estate w/2 invest! w/5 syndicat! w/30 securit!

§ 103.08   Summary of State Registration and Licensing Requirements for Securities Brokers and Dealers.

In this section is provided a summary of each state's licensing and registration requirements applicable to brokers, dealers and associated persons under that state's "blue sky" securities regulation laws. Of course, these requirements apply to any broker-dealers who are participating in real estate transactions, including syndications, that are deemed to be securities under state law and regulation. This information is shown in a somewhat uniform format for each state.

§ 103.08(a)   Alabama.

Dealers and salespersons must register.

Principals must register upon dealer registration.

The term of registrations is one year ending December 31.

An examination is required.

Fees: $200 for a dealer; $50 for an agent.

Statutory reference: Ala. Code § 8-6-3.

§ 103.08(b)   Alaska.

Broker-dealers and agents must register.

An examination is required unless the applicant is exempt.

As established by regulation.

Statutory reference: Alaska Stat. §§ 45.55.030 to .060.

§ 103.08(c)   Arizona.

Dealers and salespersons must register.

The term of registration is one year.

An examination may be required of prospective dealers and salespersons.

Fees: $300 for dealer; $40 for salespersons.

Statutory reference: Ariz. Rev. Stat. Ann. §§ 44-1941 to-1981.

§ 103.08(d)   Arkansas.

Broker-dealers and agents must register.

The term of registration is one year.

An examination is required unless the applicant is exempt.

$ 300 for broker-dealers; $75 for agent.

Statutory reference: Ark. Stat. Ann. §§ 23-42-301 to-308.

§ 103.08(e)   California.

Broker-dealers and agents must be licensed.

The term of the license is one year.

An examination is required.

Fees: $300 for broker-dealers, plus the broker-dealer's share of costs and expenses, based on the number of the broker-dealers' agents and offices.

Statutory reference: Cal. Corp. Code §§ 25200–25402; Cal. Bus. & Prof. Code §§ 10131.3, 10153.9.

§ 103.08(f)   Colorado.

Broker-dealers and sales representatives must be licensed.

The term of the license is one year.

An examination is required if applicant is not federally registered.

Fees: For a broker-dealer, $145 for the application and $130 for the annual fee; for a sales representative, $15 for the application and $25 for the annual fee.

Statutory reference: Colo. Rev. Stat. §§ 11-51-401 to -708.

§ 103.08(g)   Connecticut.

Broker-dealers and agents must be registered.

The term of registration is one year.

An examination is required.

Fees: Broker-dealer registration is $250, and renewal is $150; agent registration is $50, and renewal is $50.

Statutory reference: Conn. Gen. Stat. Ann. 36-474 to 36-482 transferred to Conn. Gen. Stat. Ann. 36b-2 to 36b-14; 36-483 repealed; 36-484 transferred to Conn. Gen. Stat. Ann. 36b-15 to 36b-33.

§ 103.08(h)   Delaware.

Broker-dealers and agents must be registered.

The term of registration is one year.

An examination is required.

Fees: $250 for broker-dealer; $50 for an agent.

Statutory reference: Del. Code Ann. tit. 6, §§ 7313-7329.

§ 103.08(i)   District of Columbia.

Broker-dealers and agents must be licensed.

The term of the license is one year.

An examination is required for agents and sole-proprietor broker-dealers.

Fees: $250 for initial or renewal license for a broker-dealer; $25 for initial or renewal license for an agent. Examination fee is $25.

Statutory reference: D.C. Code Ann. §§ 2-2603 to 2-2614.

§ 103.08(j)   Florida.

Dealers and associated persons must register; registration with the S.E.C. is also required, except for dealer-issuers.

The term of registration is one year.

An examination may be required of applicant and one or more principals or general partners.

Fee: $200 for a dealer, plus $100 for each branch office in the state; $40 for associated persons.

Statutory reference: Fla. Stat. Ann. §§ 517.12 to 517.241.

§ 103.08(k)   Georgia.

Dealers, limited dealers, salespersons, limited salespersons must register.

The term of registration is one year.

An examination is required.

Fees: $250 for initial registration of dealers and limited dealers, $100 for annual renewal; $50 for initial registration of salespersons and limited salespersons, $40 for annual renewal.

Statutory reference: Ga. Code Ann. §§ 10-5-3, 10-5-4.

§ 103.08(l)   Hawaii.

Dealers and salespersons must register.

The term of registration is one year.

An examination may be required.

Fees: $200 for dealers; $50 for salespersons.

Statutory reference: Hawaii Rev. Stat. §§ 485A-410.

§ 103.08(m)   Idaho.

Broker-dealers and salespersons must register.

The term of registration is one year.

An examination is required.

Fees: $100 for a broker-dealer; $20 for a salesperson.

Statutory reference: Fee is in Idaho Code § 30-1437.

§ 103.08(n)   Illinois.

Dealers and salespersons must register.

The term of registration is one year.

An examination is required unless waived.

Fees: $300 for dealers; $40 for salespersons.

Statutory reference: Ill. Rev. Stat. ch. 1211/2, §§ 137.1 to .2-12b.

§ 103.08(o) Indiana.

Broker-dealers and agents must register.

The term of registration is one year.

An examination is required unless exempt.

Fees: $250 for broker-dealer initial registration, $125 for renewal; $100 for investment advisor initial registration; $50 for renewal. $25 for agent initial registration, $25 for renewal.

Statutory reference: Ind. Code Ann. §§ 23-2-1-8 to-14.

§ 103.08(p) Iowa.

Broker-dealers and agents must register.

The term of registration is one year.

An examination is required for agents.

Fees: $200 for broker-dealers, registration and renewals; $30 for agents, registration and renewals.

Statutory reference: Iowa Code Ann. §§ 502.301 to .304.

§ 103.08(q) Kansas.

Broker-dealers and agents must register.

The term of registration is one year.

An examination may be required.

Fees: $300 for broker-dealers, initial and renewal; $50 for agents, initial and renewal.

Statutory reference: Kan. Stat. Ann. § 17-1254.

§ 103.08(r) Kentucky.

Broker-dealers and agents must register.

The term of registration is one year.

An examination may be required.

Fees: $120 for broker-dealers, initial and renewal; $100 for investment advisors, initial and renewal. $50 for agents, initial and renewal.

Statutory reference: Ky. Rev. Stat. § 292.330.

§ 103.08(s) Louisiana.

Dealers and salespersons must register.

The term of registration is one year.

An examination is required.

Fees: $250 for dealers; $60 for salespersons.

Statutory reference: La. Rev. Stat. Ann. §§ 51.703 to .704.

§ 103.08(t)   Maine.

Broker-dealers and sales representatives must be licensed.

The term of the license is one year.

An examination may be required.

Fees: $200 initial fee for broker-dealers plus $50 for each branch office in this State, $200 renewal fee for broker-dealer plus $30 for each branch; $200 initial fee for investment advisor, $100 renewal; $40 sales representatives, initial and renewal.

Statutory reference: Me. Rev. Stat. Ann. tit. 32, §§ 10301 to 10314.

§ 103.08(u)   Maryland.

Broker-dealers and agents must register.

The term of registration is one year.

An examination is required.

Fees: $250 for broker-dealers, initial and renewal; $35 for agents, initial and renewal.

Statutory reference: Md. Ann. Code §§ 11-401 to -417.

§ 103.08(v)   Massachusetts.

Broker-dealers and agents must register.

The term of registration is one year.

An examination is required.

Fees: $300 for broker-dealers, original and renewal; $40 for agents, original and renewal.

Statutory reference: Mass. Gen. Laws Ann. ch. 110A, §§ 201 to 204.

§ 103.08(w)   Michigan.

Broker-dealers and agents must register.

The term of registration is one year.

An examination is required.

Fees: $250 annual fee for broker-dealers; $30 annual fee for agents. An examination fee may be required.

Statutory reference: Mich. Comp. Laws. Ann. §§ 451.601 to .604.

§ 103.08(x)   Minnesota.

Broker-dealers and agents must be licensed.

The term of the license is one year.

An examination may be required.

Fees: $200 for broker-dealers, initial and renewal; $50 for agents, initial and renewal.

Statutory reference: (fees in 80A.28).

§ 103.08(y)   Mississippi.

Broker-dealers and agents must register.

The term of registration is one year.

An examination is not required.

Fees: $200 for broker-dealers, initial and renewal; $50 for agents, initial and renewal.

Statutory reference: Miss. Code Ann. §§ 75-71-301 to -333.

§ 103.08(z)   Missouri.

Broker-dealers and agents must register.

The term of registration is one year.

An examination is required unless exempted.

Fees: $200 initial and $100 renewal for broker-dealers; $50 initial and renewal, agents.

Fees: As required by the Secretary of State.

§ 103.08(aa)   Montana.

Broker-dealers and salespersons must register.

The term of registration is one year.

An examination is required.

Fees: $200 for broker-dealers, initial and renewal; $50 for salespersons, initial and renewal.

Statutory reference: Mont. Code Ann. 30-10-201 to -210.

§ 103.08(bb)   Nebraska.

Broker-dealers, issuer-dealers, and agents must register.

The term of registration is one year.

An examination is required for issuer-dealers and agents.

Fees: $250 for broker-dealers, $100 for issuer-dealers, $40 for agents.

Statutory reference: Neb. Rev. Stat. §§ 8-1103, 8-1108.01.

§ 103.08(cc)   Nevada.

Broker-dealers and sales representatives must be licensed.

The term of the license is one year.

An examination is required.

Fees: $55 for sales representatives, initial and annual.

Statutory reference: Nev. Rev. Stat. §§ 90.310 to .440.

§ 103.08(dd)   New Hampshire.

Broker-dealers, issuer-dealers and agents must be licensed.

The term of the license is one year.

An examination may be required.

Fees: $200 for license, $50 for application, $100 for amendment broker-dealers; $50 for issuer-dealers; $25 for application in case of issuer-dealers' agents; $25 for amended license in case of agents.

Statutory reference: (fees are in N.H. Rev. Stat. Ann. § 421-B:31).

§ 103.08(ee)   New Jersey.

Broker-dealers, agents, and issuers must register.

The term of registration is two years.

An examination is required.

Fees: as set by rule of the bureau chief.

Statutory reference: N.J. Stat. Ann. §§ 49:3-56 to -65.

§ 103.08(ff)   New Mexico.

Broker-dealers and sales representatives must be licensed.

The term of the license is one year.

An examination is required.

Fees: $300 for broker-dealers; $35 for sales representatives.

Statutory reference: N.M. Stat. Ann. §§ 58-13B-3 to -19.

§ 103.08(gg)   New York.

Dealers, brokers and salespersons must register (issuers must register as broker-dealers).

The term of registration is four years.

An examination is required.

Fees: $800 for brokers and dealers; $800 for issuers for offerings over $500,000 and $200 for issuers for offerings under $500,000; $100 for salespersons. The fee for real estate broker-dealers is $200, plus $10 for each partner, officer, director or principal.

Statutory reference: N.Y. Gen. Bus. L. §§ 359-e to 359-f.

§ 103.08(hh)   North Carolina.

Dealers and salespersons must register.

The term of registration is one year.

An examination is required for salespersons.

Fees: $200 for dealers, initial and renewal; $55 for sales persons, initial and renewal.

Statutory reference: N.C. Gen. Stat. §§ 78A-36 to -40.

§ 103.08(ii)   North Dakota.

Dealers and salespersons must register.

The term of registration is one year.

An examination is required.

Fees: $200 for dealers, registration and renewal; $50 for sales representatives.

Statutory reference: N.D. Cent. Code §§ 10-04-10 to -19.

§ 103.08(jj)   Ohio.

Dealers and salespersons must be licensed.

The term of the license is one year.

An examination is required unless waived.

Fees: The initial and renewal fee for dealers is computed at $30 for each salesperson employed, with a minimum of $150 and a maximum of $5,000; $50 for salespersons, initial and renewal; $75 examination fee for each dealer applicant; $50 examination fee for each salesperson applicant.

Statutory reference: Ohio Rev. Code Ann. §§ 1707.14 to .19.

§ 103.08(kk)   Oklahoma.

Broker-dealers and agents must register.

The term of registration is one year.

A written and/or oral examination may be required.

Fees: $300 for broker-dealers, initial and renewal; $50 for broker-dealer agent, issuer agent, or broker-dealer principal, initial and renewal.

Statutory reference: (fees are in Okla. Stat. tit. § 412).

§ 103.08(ll)   Oregon.

Broker-dealers, salespersons, and mortgage brokers must register.

The term of registration is one year.

An examination may be required.

Fees: $100 initial fee and $50 renewal fee for broker-dealers and mortgage brokers; $15 initial fee and a renewal fee of $15 plus a $5.

Statutory reference: Or. Rev. Stat. §§ 59.165 to .225.

§ 103.08(mm)   Pennsylvania.

Broker-dealers and agents must register.

The term of registration is one year.

An examination is required.

Fees: Not specified in the statute.

Statutory reference: Pa. Stat. Ann. tit. 70, §§ 1-301 to -306.

§ 103.08(nn)   Rhode Island.

Brokers, salespersons, and limited salespersons must be licensed.

The term of the license is effective until expiration, revocation, or withdrawal.

An examination is required.

Fees: $250 for broker-dealers, plus $50 for each branch office; $50 for sales representatives.

Statutory reference: R.I. Gen. Laws §§ 7-11-101 to -215.

§ 103.08(oo)   South Carolina.

Broker-dealers and agents must register.

The term of registration is one year.

An examination is required.

Fees: $300 for broker-dealers; $100 for agents.

Statutory reference: S.C. Code Ann. §§ 35-1-410 to -620.

§ 103.08(pp)   South Dakota.

Broker-dealers and agents must register.

The term of registration is one year.

An examination may be required.

Fees: $150 for broker-dealers, initial and renewal; $125 for agents, initial and renewal.

Statutory reference: S.D. Codified Laws Ann. §§ 47-31A-201 to -204.

§ 103.08(qq)   Tennessee.

Broker-dealers, issuer-dealers, and agents must register.

The term of registration is one year.

An examination may be required.

Fees: $200 for broker-dealers, initial and renewal; $50 for agents, initial and renewal.

Statutory reference: Tenn. Code Ann. §§ 48-2-109 to -124.

§ 103.08(rr)   Texas.

Dealers, agents, and salespersons must register.

The term of registration is one year.

An examination is required.

Fees: $75 for dealers' original application, $40 for renewal; $35 for salesperson's original application, $20 for renewal.

Statutory reference: (fees are in Tex. Rev. Civ. Stat. Ann. ch. 269, art. 581-35).

§ 103.08(ss)   Utah.

Broker-dealers and agents must register.

The term of registration is one year.

An examination is required.

Fees: Not specified in the statute.

Statutory reference: Utah Code Ann. §§ 61-1-1 to -6.

§ 103.08(tt)   Vermont.

Broker-dealers and sales representatives must register.

The term of registration is one year.

An examination is not required.

Fees: $250 for dealers; $45 for sales representatives.

Statutory reference: Vt. Stat. Tit. 9 §§ 4213 to 4219.

§ 103.08(uu)   Virginia.

Broker-dealers and agents must register.

The term of registration is one year.

An examination may be required.

Fees: $200 for broker-dealers, initial and renewal; $30 for agents, initial and renewal.

Statutory reference: Va. Code §§ 13.1-504 to -506.

§ 103.08(vv)   Washington.

Broker-dealers and salespersons must register.

The term of registration is one year.

An examination is required unless exempt.

Fees: $150 for broker-dealers' original registration, $75 for renewals; $40 for salespersons' original registration, $20 for renewals.

Statutory reference: (fees are in Wash. Rev. Code § 21.20.340).

§ 103.08(ww)   West Virginia.

Broker-dealers and agents must register.

The term of registration is one year.

An examination is required for agents.

Fees: $250 for broker-dealers; $55 for agents.

Statutory reference: W. Va. Code §§ 32-2-201 to -204.

§ 103.08(xx)   Wisconsin.

Broker-dealers and agents must be licensed.

The term of the license is one year.

An examination is required.

Fees: $200 for broker-dealers, initial and renewal; $30 for agents, initial and renewal. Broker-dealers pay an additional $30 for each office in Wisconsin.

Statutory reference: (fees are in Wis. Stat. § 551.52).

§ 103.08(yy)   Wyoming.

Broker-dealers and agents must register.

The term of registration is one year.

An examination is required for agents, unless exempted.

Fees: $200 for broker-dealers; $35 for agents.

Statutory reference: Wyo. Stat. §§ 17-4-103 to-106.

§ 103.09   Appendices.

Appendix 1

Schedule A of 15 U.S.C. § 77aa.

77aa.   Schedule of information required in registration statement
SCHEDULE A

(1) The name under which the issuer is doing or intends to do business;

(2) the name of the state or other sovereign power under which the issuer is organized;

(3) the location of the issuer's principal business office, and, if the issuer is a foreign or territorial person, the name and address of its agent in the United States authorized to receive notice;

(4) the names and addresses of the directors or persons performing similar functions, and the chief executive, financial and accounting officers, chosen or to be chosen if the issuer be a corporation, association, trust, or other entity; of all partners, if the issuer be a partnership; and of the issuer, if the issuer be an individual; and of the promoters in the case of a business to be formed, or formed within two years prior to the filing of the registration statement;

(5) the names and addresses of the underwriters;

(6) the names and addresses of all persons, if any, owning of record or beneficially, if known, more than 10 per centum of any class of stock of the issuer, or more than 10 per centum in the aggregate of the outstanding stock of the issuer as of a date within twenty days prior to the filing of the registration statement;

(7) the amount of securities of the issuer held by any person specified in paragraphs (4), (5) and (6) of this schedule, as of a date within twenty days prior to the filing of the registration statement, and, if possible, as of one year prior thereto, and the amount of the securities, for which the registration statement is filed, to which such persons have indicated their intention to subscribe;

(8) the general character of the business actually transacted or to be transacted by the issuer;

(9) a statement of the capitalization of the issuer, including the authorized and outstanding amounts of its capital stock and the proportion thereof paid up, the number and classes of shares in which such capital stock is divided, par value thereof, or if it has no par value, the stated or assigned value thereof, a description of the respective voting rights, preferences, conversion and exchange rights, rights to dividends, profits, or capital of each class, with respect to each other class, including the retirement and liquidation rights or values thereof;

(10) a statement of the securities, if any, covered by options outstanding

or to be created in connection with the security to be offered, together with the names and addresses of all persons, if any, to be allotted more than 10 per centum in the aggregate of such options;

(11) the amount of capital stock of each class issued or included in the shares of stock to be offered;

(12) the amount of the funded debt outstanding and to be created by the security to be offered, with a brief description of the date, maturity, and character of such debt, rate of interest, character of amortization provisions, and the security, if any, therefor. If substitution of any security is permissible, a summarized statement of the conditions under which such substitution is permitted. If substitution is permissible without notice, a specific statement to that effect;

(13) the specific purposes in detail and the approximate amounts to be devoted to such purposes, so far as determinable, for which the security to be offered is to supply funds, and if the funds are to be raised in part from other sources, the amounts thereof and the sources thereof, shall be stated;

(14) the remuneration, paid or estimated to be paid, by the issuer or its predecessor, directly or indirectly, during the put year and ensuing year to (a) the directors or persons performing similar functions, and (b) its officers and other persons, naming them wherever such remuneration exceeded $25,000 during any such year;

(15) the estimated net proceeds to be derived from the security to be offered;

(16) the price at which it is proposed that the security shall be offered to the public, or the method by which such price is computed, and any variation therefrom at which any portion of such security is proposed to be offered to any persons or classes of persons, other than the underwriters, naming them or specifying the class. A variation in price may be proposed prior to the date of the public offering of the security, but the Commission shall immediately be notified of such variation;

(17) all commissions or discounts paid or to be paid, directly or indirectly, by the issuer to the underwriters in respect of the sale of the security to be offered. Commissions shall include all cash, securities, contracts, or anything else of value, paid, to be set aside, disposed of, or understandings with or for the benefit of any other persons in which any underwriter is interested, made, in connection with the sale of such security. A commission paid or to be paid in connection with the sale of such security by a person in which the issuer has an interest or which is controlled or directed by, or under common control with, the issuer shall be deemed to have been paid by the issuer. Where any such commission is paid the amount of such commission paid to each underwriter shall be stated;

(18) the amount or estimated amounts, itemized in reasonable detail, of expenses, other than commissions specified in paragraph (17) of this schedule, incurred or borne by or for the account of the issuer in connection with the sale of the security to be offered or properly chargeable thereto,

including legal, engineering, certification, authentication, and other charges;

(19) the net proceeds derived from any security sold by the issuer during the two years preceding the filing of the registration statement, the price at which such security was offered to the public, and the names of the principal underwriters of such security;

(20) any amount paid within two years preceding the filing of the registration statement or intended to be paid to any promoter and the consideration for any such payment;

(21) the names and addresses of the vendors and the purchase price of any property, or good will, acquired or to be acquired, not in the ordinary course of business, which is to be defrayed in whole or in part from the proceeds of the security to be offered, the amount of any commission payable to any person in connection with such acquisition, and the name or names of such person or persons, together with any expense incurred or to be incurred in connection with such acquisition, including the cost of borrowing money to finance such acquisition;

(22) full particulars of the nature and extent of the interest, if any, of every director, principal executive officer, and of every stockholder holding more than 10 per centum of any class of stock or more than 10 per centum in the aggregate of the stock of the issuer, in any property acquired, not in the ordinary course of business of the issuer, within two years preceding the filing of the registration statement or proposed to be acquired at such date;

(23) the names and addresses of counsel who have passed on the legality of the issue;

(24) dates of and parties to, and the general effect concisely stated of every material contract made, not in the ordinary course of business, which contract is to be executed in whole or in part at or after the filing of the registration statement or which contract has been made not more than two years before such filing. Any management contract or contract providing for special bonuses or profit-sharing arrangements, and every material patent or contract for a material patent right, and every contract by or with a public utility company or an affiliate thereof, providing for the giving or receiving of technical or financial advice or service (if such contract may involve a charge to any party thereto at a rate in excess of $2,500 per year in cash or securities or anything else of value), shall be deemed a material contract;

(25) a balance sheet as of a date not more than ninety days prior to the date of the filing of the registration statement showing all of the assets of the issuer, the nature and cost thereof, whenever determinable, in such detail and in such form as the Commission shall prescribe (with intangible items segregated), including any loan in excess of $20,000 to any officer, director, stockholder or person directly or indirectly controlling or controlled by the issuer, or person under direct or indirect common control with the issuer. All the liabilities of the issuer in such detail and such form

as the Commission shall prescribe, including surplus of the issuer showing how and from what sources such surplus was created, all as of a date not more than ninety days prior to the filing of the registration statement. If such statement be not certified by an independent public or certified accountant, in addition to the balance sheet required to be submitted under this schedule, a similar detailed balance sheet of the assets and liabilities of the issuer, certified by an independent public or certified accountant, of a date not more than one year prior to the filing of the registration statement, shall be submitted;

(26) a profit and loss statement of the issuer showing earnings and income, the nature and source thereof, and the expenses and fixed charges in such detail and such form as the Commission shall prescribe for the latest fiscal year for which such statement is available and for the two preceding fiscal years, year by year, or, if such issuer has been in actual business for less than three years, then for such time as the issuer has been in actual business, year by year. If the date of the filing of the registration statement is more than six months after the close of the last fiscal year, a statement from such closing date to the latest practicable date. Such statement shall show what the practice of the issuer has been during the three years or lesser period as to the character of the charges, dividends or other distributions made against its various surplus accounts, and as to depreciation, depletion, and maintenance charges, in such detail and form as the Commission shall prescribe, and if stock dividends or avails from the sale of rights have been credited to income, they shall be shown separately with a statement of the basis upon which the credit is computed. Such statement shall also differentiate between any recurring and nonrecurring income and between any investment and operating income. Such statement shall be certified by an independent public or certified accountant;

(27) If the proceeds, or any part of the proceeds, of the security to be issued is to be applied directly or indirectly to the purchase of any business, a profit and loss statement of such business certified by an independent public or certified accountant, meeting the requirements of paragraph (26) of this schedule, for the three preceding fiscal years, together with a balance sheet, similarly certified, of such business, meeting the requirements of paragraph (25) of this schedule of a date not more than ninety days prior to the filing of the registration statement or at the date such business was acquired by the issuer if the business was acquired by the issuer more than ninety days prior to the filing of the registration statement;

(28) a copy of any agreement or agreements (or, if identical agreements are used, the forms thereof) made with any underwriter, including all contracts and agreements referred to in paragraph (17) of this schedule;

(29) a copy of the opinion or opinions of counsel in respect to the legality of the issue, with a translation of such opinion, when necessary, into the English language;

(30) a copy of all material contracts referred to in paragraph (24) of this schedule, but no disclosure shall be required of any portion of any such contract if the Commission determines that disclosure of such portion

would impair the value of the contract and would not be necessary for the protection of the investors;

(31) unless previously filed and registered under the provisions of this subchapter, and brought up to date, (a) a copy of its articles of incorporation, with all amendments thereof and of its existing bylaws or instruments corresponding thereto, whatever the name, if the issuer be a corporation; (b) copy of all instruments by which the trust is created or declared, if the issuer is a trust; (c) a copy of its articles of partnership or association and all other papers pertaining to its organization, if the issuer is a partnership, unincorporated association, joint-stock company, or any other form of organization; and

(32) a copy of the underlying agreements or indentures affecting any stock, bonds, or debentures offered or to be offered.

In case of certificates of deposit, voting trust certificates, collateral trust certificates, certificates of interest or shares in unincorporated investment trusts, equipment trust certificates, interim or other receipts for certificates, and like securities, the Commission shall establish rules and regulations requiring the submission of information of a like character applicable to such cases, together with such other information as it may deem appropriate and necessary regarding the character, financial or otherwise, of the actual issuer of the securities and/or the person performing the acts and assuming the duties of depositor or manager.

Appendix 2

Availability of SEC Forms Currently in Use.

A complete and current list of forms is found on the SEC's website (http://www.sec.gov/about/forms/secforms.htm). The website also provides the forms themselves. Registrants may be required to file electronically, either via EDGAR (corporate and fund registrants) or via IARD (investment advisers), rather than on printouts of the forms.

Appendix 3

Form S-1.

**UNITED STATES
SECURITIES AND EXCHANGE COMMISSION
Washington, D.C. 20549**

OMB APPROVAL
OMB Number: 3235-0065
Expires: December 31, 2012
Estimated average burden
hours per response 833.00

FORM S-1

REGISTRATION STATEMENT UNDER THE SECURITIES ACT OF 1933

_____

(Exact name of registrant as specified in its charter)

_____

(State or other jurisdiction of incorporation or organization)

_____

(Primary Standard Industrial Classification Code Number)

_____

(I.R.S. Employer Identification Number)

_____

(Address, including zip code, and telephone number,
including area code, of registrant's principal executive offices)

_____

(Name, address, including zip code, and telephone number,
including area code, of agent for service)

_____

(Approximate date of commencement of proposed sale to the public)

If any of the securities being registered on this Form are to be offered on a delayed or continuous basis pursuant to Rule 415 under the Securities Act of 1933 check the following box: ☐

If this Form is filed to register additional securities for an offering pursuant to Rule 462(b) under the Securities Act, please check the following box and list the Securities Act registration statement number of the earlier effective registration statement for the same offering. ☐

If this Form is a post-effective amendment filed pursuant to Rule 462(c) under the Securities Act, check the following box and list the Securities Act registration statement number of the earlier effective registration statement for the same offering. ☐

If this Form is a post-effective amendment filed pursuant to Rule 462(d) under the Securities Act, check the following box and list the Securities Act registration statement number of the earlier effective registration statement for the same offering. ☐

Indicate by check mark whether the registrant is a large accelerated filer, an accelerated filer, a non-accelerated filer, or a smaller reporting company. See the definitions of "large accelerated filer," "accelerated filer" and "smaller reporting company" in Rule 12b-2 of the Exchange Act.

Large accelerated filer ☐   Accelerated filer ☐

Non-accelerated filer ☐ (Do not check if a smaller reporting company)   Smaller reporting company ☐

SEC 870 (02-08)   **Persons who are to respond to the collection of information contained in this form are not required to respond unless the form displays a currently valid OMB control number.**

Calculation of Registration Fee

Title of Each Class of Securities to be Registered	Amount to be Registered	Proposed Maximum Offering Price Per Unit	Proposed Maximum Aggregate Offering Price	Amount of Registration Fee

Note: Specific details relating to the fee calculation shall be furnished in notes to the table, including references to provisions of Rule 457 (§230.457 of this chapter) relied upon, if the basis of the calculation is not otherwise evident from the information presented in the table. If the filing fee is calculated pursuant to Rule 457(o) under the Securities Act, only the title of the class of securities to be registered, the proposed maximum aggregate offering price for that class of securities and the amount of registration fee need to appear in the Calculation of Registration Fee table. Any difference between the dollar amount of securities registered for such offerings and the dollar amount of securities sold may be carried forward on a future registration statement pursuant to Rule 429 under the Securities Act.

GENERAL INSTRUCTIONS

I. Eligibility Requirements for Use of Form S-1

This Form shall be used for the registration under the Securities Act of 1933 ("Securities Act") of securities of all registrants for which no other form is authorized or prescribed, except that this Form shall not be used for securities of foreign governments or political subdivisions thereof.

II. Application of General Rules and Regulations

A. Attention is directed to the General Rules and Regulations under the Securities Act, particularly those comprising Regulation C (17 CFR 230.400 to 230.494) thereunder. That Regulation contains general requirements regarding the preparation and filing of the registration statement.

B. Attention is directed to Regulation S-K (17 CFR Part 229) for the requirements applicable to the content of the non-financial statement portions of registration statements under the Securities Act. Where this Form directs the registrant to furnish information required by Regulation S-K and the item of Regulation S-K so provides, information need only be furnished to the extent appropriate.

III. Exchange Offers

If any of the securities being registered are to be offered in exchange for securities of any other issuer, the prospectus shall also include the information which would be required by item 11 if the securities of such other issuer were registered on this Form. There shall also be included the information concerning such securities of such other issuer which would be called for by Item 9 if such securities were being registered. In connection with this instruction, reference is made to Rule 409.

IV. Roll-up Transactions

If the securities to be registered on this Form will be isued in a roll-up transction as defined in Item 901(c) of Regulation S-K (17 CFR 229.901(c)), attention is directed to the requirements of Form S-4 applicable to roll-up transactions, including, but not limited to, General Instruction I.

V. Registration of Additional Securities

With respect to the registration of additional securities for an offering pursuant to Rule 462(b) under the Securities Act, the registrant may file a registration statement consisting only of the following: the facing page; a statement that the contents of the earlier registration statement, identified by file number, are incorporated by reference; required opinions and consents; the signature page; and any price-related information omitted from the earlier registration statement in reliance on Rule 430A that the registrant chooses to include in the new registration statement. The information contained in such a Rule 462(b) registration statement shall be deemed to be a part of the earlier registration statement as of the date of effectiveness of the Rule 462(b) registration statement. Any opinion or consent required in the Rule 462(b) registration statement may be incorporated by reference from the earlier registration statement with respect to the offering, if: (i) such opinion or consent expressly provides for such incorporation; and (ii) such opinion relates to the securities registered pursuant to Rule 462(b). *See* Rule 411(c) and Rule 439(b) under the Securities Act.

VI. Offerings of Asset-Backed Securities.

The following applies if a registration statement on this Form S-1 is being used to register an offering of asset-backed securities. Terms used in this General Instruction VI. have the same meaning as in Item 1101 of Regulation AB (17 CFR 229.1101).

A. *Items that may be Omitted.*

Such registrants may omit the information called for by Item 11, Information with Respect to the Registrant.

B. *Substitute Information to be Included.*

In addition to the Items that are otherwise required by this Form, the registrant must furnish in the prospectus the information required by Items 1102 through 1120 of Regulation AB (17 CFR 229.1102 through 229.1120).

C. *Signatures.*

The registration statement must be signed by the depositor, the depositor's principal executive officer or officers, principal financial officer and controller or principal accounting officer, and by at least a majority of the depositor's board of directors or persons performing similar functions.

VII. Eligibility to Use Incorporation by Reference

If a registrant meets the following requirements immediately prior to the time of filing a registration statement on this Form, it may elect to provide information required by Items 3 through 11 of this Form in accordance with Item 11A and Item 12 of this Form:

A. The registrant is subject to the requirement to file reports pursuant to Section 13 or Section 15(d) of the Securities Exchange Act of 1934 ("Exchange Act").

B. The registrant has filed all reports and other materials required to be filed by Sections 13(a), 14, or 15(d) of the Exchange Act during the preceding 12 months (or for such shorter period that the registrant was required to file such reports and materials).

C. The registrant has filed an annual report required under Section 13(a) or Section 15(d) of the Exchange Act for its most recently completed fiscal year.

D. The registrant is not:

    1. And during the past three years neither the registrant nor any of its predecessors was:

        (a) A blank check company as defined in Rule 419(a)(2) (§230.419(a)(2));

        (b) A shell company, other than a business combination related shell company, each as defined in Rule 405 (§230.405); or

        (c) A registrant for an offering of penny stock as defined in Rule 3a51-1 of the Exchange Act (§240.3a51-1 of this chapter).

    2. Registering an offering that effectuates a business combination transaction as defined in Rule 165(f)(1) (§230.165(f)(1) of this chapter).

E. If a registrant is a successor registrant it shall be deemed to have satisfied conditions A., B., C., and D.2 above if:

    1. Its predecessor and it, taken together, do so, provided that the succession was primarily for the purpose of changing the state of incorporation of the predecessor or forming a holding company and that the assets and liabilities of the successor at the time of succession were substantially the same as those of the predecessor; or

    2. All predecessors met the conditions at the time of succession and the registrant has continued to do so since the succession.

F. The registrant makes its periodic and current reports filed pursuant to Section 13 or Section 15(d) of the Exchange Act that are incorporated by reference pursuant to Item 11A or Item 12 of this Form readily available and accessible on a Web site maintained by or for the registrant and containing information about the registrant.

PART I—INFORMATION REQUIRED IN PROSPECTUS

Item 1.   Forepart of the Registration Statement and Outside Front Cover Page of Prospectus.

Set forth in the forepart of the registration statement and on the outside front cover page of the prospectus the information required by Item 501 of Regulation S-K (§229.501 of this chapter).

Item 2.   Inside Front and Outside Back Cover Pages of Prospectus.

Set forth on the inside front cover page of the prospectus or, where permitted, on the outside back cover page, the information required by Item 502 of Regulation S-K (§229.502 of this chapter).

Item 3.   Summary Information, Risk Factors and Ratio of Earnings to Fixed Charges.

Furnish the information required by Item 503 of Regulation S-K (§229.503 of this chapter).

Item 4.   Use of Proceeds.

Furnish the information required by Item 504 of Regulation S-K (§229.504 of this chapter).

Item 5.   Determination of Offering Price.

Furnish the information required by Item 505 of Regulation S-K (§229.505 of this chapter).

Item 6.   Dilution.

Furnish the information required by Item 506 of Regulation S-K (§229.506 of this chapter).

Item 7.   Selling Security Holders.

Furnish the information required by Item 507 of Regulation S-K (§229.507 of this chapter).

Item 8.   Plan of Distribution.

Furnish the information required by Item 508 of Regulation S-K (§229.508 of this chapter).

Item 9.   Description of Securities to be Registered.

Furnish the information required by Item 202 of Regulation S-K (§229.202 of this chapter).

Item 10.   Interests of Named Experts and Counsel.

Furnish the information required by Item 509 of Regulation S-K (§229.509 of this chapter).

Item 11.   Information with Respect to the Registrant.

Furnish the following information with respect to the registrant:

(a)   Information required by Item 101 of Regulation S-K (§229.101 of this chapter), description of business;

(b)   Information required by Item 102 of Regulation S-K (§229.102 of this chapter), description of property;

(c)   Information required by Item 103 of Regulation S-K (§229.103 of this chapter), legal proceedings;

(d) Where common equity securities are being offered, information required by Item 201 of Regulation S-K (§229.201 of this chapter), market price of and dividends on the registrant's common equity and related stockholder matters;

(e) Financial statements meeting the requirements of Regulation S-X (17 CFR Part 210) (Schedules required under Regulation S-X shall be filed as "Financial Statement Schedules" pursuant to Item 15, Exhibits and Financial Statement Schedules, of this Form), as well as any financial information required by Rule 3-05 and Article 11 of Regulation S-X. A smaller reporting company may provide the information in Rule 8-04 and 8-05 of Regulation S-X in lieu of the financial information required by Rule 3-05 and Article 11 of Regulation S-X;

(f) Information required by Item 301 of Regulation S-K (§229.301 of this chapter), selected financial data;

(g) Information required by Item 302 of Regulation S-K (§229.302 of this chapter), supplementary financial information;

(h) Information required by Item 303 of Regulation S-K (§229.303 of this chapter), management's discussion and analysis of financial condition and results of operations;

(i) Information required by Item 304 of Regulation S-K (§229.304 of this chapter), changes in and disagreements with accountants on accounting and financial disclosure;

(j) Information required by Item 305 of Regulation S-K (§229.305 of this chapter), quantitative and qualitative disclosures about market risk.

(k) Information required by Item 401 of Regulation S-K (§229.401 of this chapter), directors and executive officers;

(l) (I) Information required by Item 402 of Regulation S-K (§229.402 of this chapter), executive compensation, and information required by paragraph (e)(4) of Item 407 of Regulation S-K (§229.407 of this chapter), corporate governance;

(m) Information required by Item 403 of Regulation S-K (§229.403 of this chapter), security ownership of certain beneficial owners and management; and

(n) Information required by Item 404 of Regulation S-K (§229.404 of this chapter), transactions with related persons, promoters and certain control persons, and Item 407(a) of Regulation S-K (§229.407(a) of this chapter), corporate governance.

Item 11A. Material Changes.

If the registrant elects to incorporate information by reference pursuant to General Instruction VII., describe any and all material changes in the registrant's affairs which have occurred since the end of the latest fiscal year for which audited financial statements were included in the latest Form 10-K and that have not been described in a Form 10-Q or Form 8-K filed under the Exchange Act.

Item 12. Incorporation of Certain Information by Reference.

If the registrant elects to incorporate information by reference pursuant to General Instruction VII.:

(a) It must specifically incorporate by reference into the prospectus contained in the registration statement the following documents by means of a statement to that effect in the prospectus listing all such documents:

(1) The registrant's latest annual report on Form 10-K filed pursuant to Section 13(a) or Section 15(d) of the Exchange Act that contains financial statements for the registrant's latest fiscal year for which a Form 10-K was required to have been filed; and

(2) All other reports filed pursuant to Section 13(a) or 15(d) of the Exchange Act or proxy or information statements filed pursuant to Section 14 of the Exchange Act since the end of the fiscal year covered by the annual report referred to in paragraph (a)(1) above.

Note to Item 12(a). Attention is directed to Rule 439 (§230.439) regarding consent to use of material incorporated by reference.
(b)(1) The registrant must state:

(i) That it will provide to each person, including any beneficial owner, to whom a prospectus is delivered, a copy of any or all of the reports or documents that have been incorporated by reference in the prospectus contained in the registration statement but not delivered with the prospectus;

(ii) That it will provide these reports or documents upon written or oral request;

(iii) That it will provide these reports or documents at no cost to the requester;

(iv) The name, address, telephone number, and e-mail address, if any, to which the request for these reports or documents must be made; and

(v) The registrant's Web site address, including the uniform resource locator (URL) where the incorporated reports and other documents may be accessed.

Note to Item 12(b)(1). If the registrant sends any of the information that is incorporated by reference in the prospectus contained in the registration statement to security holders, it also must send any exhibits that are specifically incorporated by reference in that information.

(2) The registrant must:

(i) Identify the reports and other information that it files with the SEC; and

(ii) State that the public may read and copy any materials it files with the SEC at the SEC's Public Reference Room at 100 F Street, N.E., Washington, DC 20549. State that the public may obtain information on the operation of the Public Reference Room by calling the SEC at 1-800-SEC-0330. If the registrant is an electronic filer, state that the SEC maintains an Internet site that contains reports, proxy and information statements, and other information regarding issuers that file electronically with the SEC and state the address of that site (http://www.sec.gov).

Item 12A. Disclosure of Commission Position on Indemnification for Securities Act Liabilities.

Furnish the information required by Item 510 of Regulation S-K (§229.510 of this chapter).

PART II—INFORMATION NOT REQUIRED IN PROSPECTUS

Item 13. Other Expenses of Issuance and Distribution.

Furnish the information required by Item 511 of Regulation S-K (§229.511 of this chapter).

Item 14. Indemnification of Directors and Officers.

Furnish the information required by Item 702 of Regulation S-K (§229.702 of this chapter).

Item 15. Recent Sales of Unregistered Securities.

Furnish the information required by Item 701 of Regulation S-K (§229.701 of this chapter).

Item 16. Exhibits and Financial Statement Schedules.

(a) Subject to the rules regarding incorporation by reference, furnish the exhibits as required by Item 601 of Regulation S-K (§229.601 of this chapter).

(b) Furnish the financial statement schedules required by Regulation S-X (17 CFR Part 210) and Item 11(e) of this Form. These schedules shall be lettered or numbered in the manner described for exhibits in paragraph (a).

Item 17.   Undertakings.

Furnish the undertakings required by Item 512 of Regulation S-K (§229.512 of this chapter).

SIGNATURES

Pursuant to the requirements of the Securities Act of 1933, the registrant has duly caused this registration statement to be signed on its behalf by the undersigned, thereunto duly authorized in the City of _____,
State of _____, on_____ , 20___.

_____
(Registrant)

_____
By (Signature and Title)

Pursuant to the requirements of the Securities Act of 1933, this registration statement has been signed by the following persons in the capacities and on the dates indicated.

_____
(Signature)

_____
(Title)

_____
(Date)

Instructions.

1.   The registration statement shall be signed by the registrant, its principal executive officer or officers, its principal financial officer, its controller or principal accounting officer and by at least a majority of the board of directors or persons performing similar functions. If the registrant is a foreign person, the registration statement shall also be signed by its authorized representative in the United States. Where the registrant is a limited partnership, the registration statement shall be signed by a majority of the board of directors of any corporate general partner signing the registration statement.

2.   The name of each person who signs the registration statement shall be typed or printed beneath his signature. Any person who occupies more than one of the specified positions shall indicate each capacity in which he signs the registration statement. Attention is directed to Rule 402 concerning manual signatures and to Item 601 of Regulation S-K concerning signatures pursuant to powers of attorney.

INSTRUCTIONS AS TO SUMMARY PROSPECTUSES

1.   A summary prospectus used pursuant to Rule 431 (§230.431 of this chapter), shall at the time of its use contain much of the information specified below as is then included in the registration statement. All other information and documents contained in the registration statement may be omitted.

   (a)   As to Item 1, the aggregate offering price to the public, the aggregate underwriting discounts and commissions and the offering price per unit to the public;

   (b)   As to Item 4, a brief statement of the principal purposes   for which the proceeds are to be used;

   (c)   As to Item 7, a statement as to the amount of the offering, if any, to be made for the account of security holders;

   (d)   As to Item 8, the name of the managing underwriter or underwriters and a brief statement as to the nature of the underwriter's obligation to take the securities; if any securities to be registered are to be offered otherwise than through underwriters, a brief statement as to the manner of distribution; and, if securities are to be offered otherwise than for cash. a brief statement as to the general purposes of the distribution, the basis upon which the securities are to be offered, the amount of compensation and other expenses of distribution, and by whom they are to be borne;

   (e)   As to Item 9, a brief statement as to dividend rights, voting rights, conversion rights, interest, maturity;

7

(f)   As to Item 11, a brief statement of the general character of the business done and intended to be done, the selected financial data (Item 301 of Regulation S-K (§229.301 of this chapter)) and a brief statement of the nature and present status of any material pending legal proceedings; and

(g)   A tabular presentation of notes payable, long term debt, deferred credits, minority interests, if material, and the equity section of the latest balance sheet filed, as may be appropriate.

2.   The summary prospectus shall not contain a summary or condensation of any other required financial information except as provided above.

3.   Where securities being registered are to be offered in exchange for securities of any other issuer, the summary prospectus also shall contain that information as to Items 9 and 11 specified in paragraphs (e) and (f) above which would be required if the securities of such other issuer were registered on this Form.

4.   The Commission may, upon the request of the registrant, and where consistent with the protection of investors, permit the omission of any of the information herein required or the furnishing in substitution therefor of appropriate information of comparable character. The Commission may also require the inclusion of other information in addition to, or in substitution for, the information herein required in any case where such information is necessary or appropriate for the protection of investors.

Appendix 4

Form S-11.

UNITED STATES
SECURITIES AND EXCHANGE COMMISSION
Washington, D.C. 20549

OMB APPROVAL	
OMB Number:	3235-0067
Expires:	June 30, 2011
Estimated average burden	
hours per response. 763	

FORM S-11

FOR REGISTRATION UNDER THE SECURITIES ACT OF 1933
OF SECURITIES OF CERTAIN REAL ESTATE COMPANIES

GENERAL INSTRUCTIONS

A. Rule as to Use of Form S-11.

This form shall be used for registration under the Securities Act of 1933 of (i) securities issued by real estate investment trust, as defined in Section 856 of the Internal Revenue Code, or (ii) securities issued by other issuers whose business is primarily that of acquiring and holding for investment real estate or interests in real estate or interests in other issuers whose business is primarily that of acquiring and holding real estate or interest in real estate for investment. This form shall not be used, however, by any issuer which is an investment company registered or required to register under the Investment Company Act of 1940. In addition, this form shall not be used for an offering of asset-backed securities, as defined in 17 CFR 229.1101.

B. Application of General Rules and Regulations

(a) Attention is directed to the General Rules and Regulations under the Securities Act, particularly those comprising Regulation C thereunder (17 CFR 230.400 to 230.494). That Regulation contains general requirements regarding the preparation and filing of registration statements.

(b) Attention is directed to Regulation S-K (17 CFR Part 229) for the requirements applicable to the content of the nonfinancial statement portions of registration statements under the Securities Act. Where this Form directs the registrant to furnish information required by Regulation S-K and the item of Regulation S-K so provides, information need only be furnished to the extent appropriate.

C. Exchange Offers

If any of the securities being registered are to be offered in exchange for securities of any other issuer, the prospectus also shall include the information which would be required by Items 9 to 16, and Item 18 if securities of such other issuer were being registered on this form. Item 26 also shall be answered as to any promoter, director, officer or security holder of such other issuer who is an affiliated person of the registrant.

D. Definitions.

Unless the context clearly indicates the contrary, the following definitions apply:

Affiliated person. The term affiliated person means any of the following persons: (i) any director or officer of the registrant; (ii) any person directly or indirectly controlling or under direct or indirect common control with the registrant; (iii) any person owning of record or known by the registrant to own beneficially 10 percent or more of any class of equity securities or the registrant; (iv) any promoter of the registrant directly or indirectly connected with the registrant in any capacity; (v) any principal underwriter of the securities being registered; (vi) any person performing general management or advisory services for the registrant; and (vii) any associate of any of the foregoing persons.

Director. The term director means any director of a corporation, trustee of a trust, general partner of a partnership, or any person who performs for an organization functions similar to those performed by the foregoing persons.

Governing instruments. The term governing instruments means the Charter, trust agreement, partnership agreement, bylaws or other instruments under which the registrant was organized or created or under which it will operate.

Mortgage. The term mortgage means any mortgage, deed of trust or other evidence of indebtedness secured by a lien upon real estate or upon any interest in real estate.

Share. The term share means a share of stock in a corporation, a share or other unit of beneficial interest in a trust or unincorporated association, a limited partnership interest, or any similar equity interest in any other type of organization.

E. Foreign Issuers

A foreign private issuer may comply with Items 19, 20, 21, 22 and 26 of this Form by furnishing the information specified it Items 6, 7.A, 8.A.7, and 18 of Form 20-F (§249.220f of this chapter).

F. Roll-up Transactions

If the securities to be registered on this Form will be issued in a roll-up transaction as defined in Item 901(c) of Regulation S-K (17 CFR 229.901(c)), attention is directed to the requirements of Form S-4 applicable to roll-up transactions, including, but not limited to, General Instruction I.

G. Registration of Additional Securities

With respect to the registration of additional securities for an offering pursuant to Rule 462(b) under the Securities Act, the registrant may file a registration statement consisting only of the following: the facing page; a statement that the contents of the earlier registration statement, identified by file number, are incorporated by reference; required opinions and consents; the signature page; and any price-related information omitted from the earlier registration statement in reliance on Rule 430A that the registrant chooses to include in the new registration statement. The information contained in such a Rule 462(b) registration statement shall be deemed to be a part of the earlier registration statement as of the date of effectiveness of the Rule 462(b) registration statement. Any opinion or consent required in the Rule 462(b) registration statement may be incorporated by reference from the earlier registration statement with respect to the offering, if: (i) such opinion or consent expressly provides for such incorporation; and (ii) such opinion relates to the securities registered pursuant to Rule 462(b). See Rule 411(c) and Rule 439(b) under the Securities Act.

H. Eligibility to Use Incorporation by Reference

If a registrant meets the following requirements immediately prior to the time of filing a registration statement on this Form, it may elect to provide information required by Items 3 through 28 of this Form in accordance with Item 28A and Item 29 of this Form:

1. The registrant is subject to the requirement to file reports pursuant to Section 13 or Section 15(d) of the Securities Exchange Act of 1934.

2. The registrant has filed all reports and other materials required to be filed by Section 13(a), 14, or 15(d) of the Exchange Act during the preceding 12 months (or for such shorter period that the registrant was required to file such reports and materials).

3. The registrant has filed an annual report required under Section 13(a) or Section 15(d) of the Exchange Act for its most recently completed fiscal year.

4. The registrant is not:
(a) And during the past three years neither the registrant nor any of its predecessors was:
(i) A blank check company as defined in Rule 419(a)(2) (§230.419(a)(2) of this chapter);

(ii) A shell company, other than a business combination related shell company, each as defined in Rule 405 (§230.405 of this chapter); or
(iii) A registrant for an offering of penny stock as defined in Rule 3a51-1 of the Exchange Act (§240.3a51-1 of this chapter).
(b) Registering an offering that effectuates a business combination transaction as defined in Rule 165(f)(1) (§230.165(f)(1) of this chapter).

5. If a registrant is a successor registrant it shall be deemed to have satisfied conditions 1, 2, 3, and 4(b) above if:

(a) Its predecessor and it, taken together, do so, provided that the succession was primarily for the purpose of changing the state of incorporation of the predecessor or forming a holding company and that the assets and liabilities of the successor at the time of succession were substantially the same as those of the predecessor; or

(b) All predecessors met the conditions at the time of succession and the registrant has continued to do so since the succession.

6. The registrant makes its periodic and current reports filed pursuant to Section 13 or Section 15(d) of the Exchange Act that are incorporated by reference pursuant to Item 28A or Item 29 of this Form readily available and accessible on a Web site maintained by or for the registrant and containing information about the registrant.

UNITED STATES
SECURITIES AND EXCHANGE COMMISSION
Washington, D.C. 20549

FORM S-11

FOR REGISTRATION UNDER THE SECURITIES ACT OF 1933
OF SECURITIES OF CERTAIN REAL ESTATE COMPANIES

(Exact name of registrant as specified in governing instruments)

(Address, including zip code, and telephone number,
including area code, of registrant's principal executive offices)

(Name, address, including zip code, and telephone number, including area code, of agent for service)

Approximate date of commencement of proposed sale to the public _____

If any of the Securities being registered on this Form are to be offered on a delayed or continuous basis pursuant to Rule 415 under the Securities Act, check the following box: ☐

If this Form is filed to register additional securities for an offering pursuant to Rule 462(b) under the Securities Act, check the following box and list the Securities Act registration statement number of the earlier effective registration statement for the same offering.   ☐

If this Form is a post-effective amendment filed pursuant to Rule 462(c) under the Securities Act, check the following box and list the Securities Act registration statement number of the earlier effective registration statement for the same offering.   ☐

If this Form is a post-effective amendment filed pursuant to Rule 462(d) under the Securities Act, check the following box and list the Securities Act registration statement number of the earlier effective registration statement for the same offering.   ☐

If delivery of the prospectus is expected to be made pursuant to Rule 434, check the following box.   ☐

Indicate by check mark whether the registrant is a large accelerated filer, an accelerated filer, a non-accelerated filer, or a smaller reporting company. See the definitions of "large accelerated filer," "accelerated filer" and "smaller reporting company" in Rule 12b-2 of the Exchange Act.

Large accelerated filer ☐   Accelerated filer ☐
Non-accelerated filer ☐ (Do not check if a smaller reporting company)   Smaller reporting company ☐

CALCULATION OF REGISTRATION FEE

Title of Securites to be registered	Amount to be registered	Proposed maximum offering price per unit	Proposed maximum aggregate offering price	Amount of registration fee

Note: Specific details relating to the fee calculation shall be furnished in notes to the table, including references to provisions

*Inclusion of this paragraph is optional. See Rule 473.

SEC 907 (02-08)   **Persons who to respond to the collection of information contained in this form are not required to respond unless the form displays a currently valid OMB control number.**

of Rule 457 (§230.457 of this chapter) relied upon, if the basis of the calculation is not otherwise evident from the information presented in the table.

If the filing fee is calculated pursuant to Rule 457(o) under the Securities Act, only the title of the class of securities to be registered, the proposed maximum aggregate offering price for that class of securities and the amount of registration fee need to appear in the Calculation of Registration Fee table. Any difference between the dollar amount of securities registered for such offerings and the dollar amount of securities sold may be carried forward on a future registration statement pursuant to Rule 429 under the Securities Act.

The registrant hereby amends this registration statement on such date or dates as may be necessary to delay its effective date until the registrant shall file a further amendment which specifically states that this registration statement shall thereafter become effective in accordance with Section 8(a) of the Securities Act of 1933 or until the registration statement shall become effective on such date as the Commission, acting pursuant to said Section 8(a), may determine.*

PART I. INFORMATION REQUIRED IN PROSPECTUS

Item 1. Forepart of Registration Statement and Outside Front Cover Page of Prospectus.

(a) Set forth on the outside front cover page of the prospectus the information required by Item 501 of Regulation S-K (§229.501 of this chapter).

(b) If there are any limitations on the transferability of the securities being registered, so state on the outside front cover page of the prospectus and refer to a statement elsewhere in the prospectus as to the nature of such limitations. If there is no market for securities of the same class as those being registered, so state on the outside front cover page of the prospectus; otherwise, state elsewhere in the prospectus the nature of the market for such securities and the market price thereof as of the latest practicable date prior to the filing of the registration statement or amendment thereto.

Item 2. Inside Front and Outside Back Cover Pages of Prospectus.

Set forth on the inside front cover page of the prospectus or, where permitted, on the outside back cover page, the information required by Item 502 of Regulation S-K (§229.502 of this chapter).

Item 3. Summary Information, Risk Factors and Ratio of Earnings to Fixed Charges.

(a) Furnish the information required by Item 503 of Regulation S-K (§229.503 of this chapter).

(b) Where appropriate to a clear understanding by investors, an introductory statement shall be made in the forepart of the prospectus, in a series of short, concise paragraphs, summarizing the principal factors which make the offering speculative. Where appropriate, statements with respect to the following shall also be set forth:

    (1) A comparison in percentages of the securities being offered to the public and those issued or to be issued to affiliated persons;

    (2) The extent to which security holders may be liable for the acts or obligations of the registrant;

    (3) Allocation of cash distributions between the public security holders and security holders who are affiliated persons;

    (4) The compensation and other forms of compensation and benefits to be received, directly or indirectly, by affiliated persons, including in the case of underwriters a comparison of the aggregate compensation to be received by them with the aggregate net proceeds from the sale of the securities being registered.

Item 4. Determination of Offering Price.

Furnish the information required by Item 505 of Regulation S-K (§229.505 of this chapter).

Item 5. Dilution.

Furnish the information required by Item 506 of Regulation S-K (§229.506 of this chapter).

Item 6. Selling Security Holders.

Furnish the information required by Item 507 of Regulation S-K (§229.507 of this chapter).

Item 7. Plan of Distribution.

Furnish the information required by Item 508 of Regulation S-K (§229.508 of this chapter).

Item 8. Use of Proceeds.

Furnish the information required by Item 504 of Regulation S-K (§229.504 of this chapter).

Item 9. Selected Financial Data.

Furnish the information required by Item 301 of Regulation S-K (§229.301 of this chapter).

Instruction. If, pursuant to this Item, a statement showing the pro forma taxable operating results of the registrant is included in the registration statement, the Commission or its staff may request as supplemental information, which the registrant should be prepared to furnish promptly upon request, a schedule reconciling such pro forma results with the historical operating results (see Rule 3-14 of Regulation S-X).

Item 10. Management's Discussion and Analysis of Financial Condition and Results of Operations.

Furnish the information required by Item 303 of Regulation S-K (§229.303 of this chapter).

Item 11. General Information as to Registrant.

    (a) State the name and form of organization of the registrant and the name of the State or other jurisdiction the laws of which govern with respect to the organization of the registrant.

    (b) State the date on which the governing instruments became operative and the date on which they will expire. If the duration of the registrant may be sooner terminated or may be extended, outline briefly the pertinent provisions.

    (c) If the registrant is not a corporation state briefly the provisions of the governing instruments with respect to the holding of annual or other meetings of security holders. If the governing instruments do not provide for such meetings state the policy or proposed policy of the registrant with respect to holding annual or other meetings of security holders.

    (d) If the registrant was organized within the last five years, give the full names of all promoters and indicate all positions and offices with the registrant now held or intended to be held by each such promoter.

Instruction. If any person named as a promoter is no longer connected with the registrant in any capacity, so state.

Item 12. Policy with Respect to Certain Activities

Describe the policy of the registrant with respect to each of the following types of activities, indicating whether such policy may be changed by the officers and directors without a vote of security holders.

Indicate the extent to which the registrant proposes to engage in such activities and the extent to which it has engaged in such activities during the past three years.

(a) To issue senior securities.

(b) To borrow money.

(c) To make loans to other persons.

(d) To invest in the securities of other issuers for the purpose of exercising control.

(e) To underwrite securities of other issuers.

(f) To engage in the purchase and sale (or turnover) of investments.

(g) To offer securities in exchange for property.

(h) To repurchase or otherwise reacquire its shares or other securities.

(i) To make annual or other reports to security holders, indicating the nature and scope of such reports and whether they will contain financial statements certified by independent public accountants.

Instructions.

1. The policy or proposed policy of the registrant with respect to each activity shall be described separately. If the registrant does not propose to engage in a particular activity, a specific statement to that effect shall be made. The information shall be given in such manner and detail as will be meaningful to investors.

2. For the purpose of (c), the purchasing of a portion of publicly distributed bonds, debentures or other securities, whether or not the purchase was made upon the original issuance of the securities, is not to be considered the making of a loan by the registrant.

Item 13. Investment Policies of Registrant.

Describe the policy of the registrant with respect to investing in each of the following types of investments, indicating whether such policy may be changed by the directors without a vote of security holders, the percentage of assets which the registrant may invest in any one type of investment and, in the case of securities, the percentage of securities of any one issuer which the registrant may acquire and the principles and procedures the registrant will employ in connection with the acquisition of assets.

(a) *Investments in real estate or interests in real estate.*

Instructions.

1. Indicate the geographic area or areas in which the registrant proposes to acquire real estate or interests in real estate.

2. The types of real estate and interests in real estate in which the registrant may invest shall be indicated; for example, office buildings, apartment buildings, shopping centers, industrial and commercial properties, special purpose buildings and undeveloped acreage.

3. The method or proposed method of operating and financing the registrant's real estate shall be briefly described. Indicate any limitations on the number or amount of mortgages which may be placed on any one piece of property.

4. The answer to this item shall be such as will be appropriate in view of the nature of the registrant's business, its history and its experience and the proposed nature of its business and activities.

5. Include a specific statement as to whether or not it is the registrant's policy to acquire assets primarily for possible capital gain or primarily for income.

6. State the registrant's policy as to the amount or percentage of assets which will be invested in any specific property.

7. Include a statement with respect to any other material policy with respect to real estate activities.

(b) *Investments in real estate mortgages.*

Instructions.

1. Indicate the types of mortgages; for example, first or second mortgages and whether such mortgages are to be insured by the Federal Housing Administration or guaranteed by the Veterans Administration or otherwise guaranteed or insured, and the proportion of assets which may be invested in each type of mortgage or in any single mortgage.

2. Include a description of each type of mortgage activity in which the registrant intends to engage such as originating, servicing and warehousing of mortgages and its portfolio turnover policy.

3. Indicate the types of properties subject to mortgages in which the registrant invests or proposes to invest; for example, single family dwellings, apartment buildings, office buildings, bowling alleys, commercial properties and unimproved land.

(c) Securities of or interests in persons primarily engaged in real estate activities.

Instructions.

1. Indicate separately the types of securities of or interest in persons engaged in real estate activities (for example, common stock, interests in real estate investment trusts, partnership interests, joint venture interests) in which the registrant may invest and the proportion of its assets which may be invested in each such type of security or interest.

2. Indicate the primary activities of persons in which the registrant will invest such as mortgage sales, investment in office buildings or investments in undeveloped acreage And the investment policies of such persons.

3. State the criteria followed in the purchase of such securities and interests (for example, securities listed on a national securities exchange, minimum net income requirements, period of operation of issuer).

(d) *Investments in other securities.*

Instructions.

1. Indicate the type of securities (for example, bonds, preferred stocks, common stocks) and the industry groups in which the registrant may invest and the percentage of its assets which it may invest in each such type or industry group.

2. Instruction 3 to paragraph (c) shall also apply to this paragraph.

Item 14. Description of Real Estate.

(a) State the location and describe the general character of all materially important real properties now held or intended to be acquired by or leased to the registrant or its subsidiaries. Include information as to the present or proposed use of such properties and their suitability and adequacy for such use. Properties not yet acquired shall be identified as such.

(b) State the nature of the registrant's or subsidiary's title to, or other interest in, such properties and the nature and amount of all material mortgages, or other liens or encumbrances against such properties. Set forth briefly the current principal amount of each such material encumbrance, its interest and amortization provisions, its pre-payment provisions and its maturity date and balance to be due at maturity assuming no payment has been made on principal in advance of its due date.

(c) Outline briefly the principal terms of any lease of any of such properties or any option or contract to purchase or sell any of such properties.

(d) Outline briefly any proposed program for the renovation, improvement or development of such properties, including the estimated cost thereof and the method of financing to be used. If there are no present plans for the improvement or development of any unimproved or undeveloped property, so state and indicate the purpose for which the property is to be held or acquired.

(e) Describe the general competitive conditions to which the properties described above are or may be subject.

Instructions.

1. What is required is information essential to an investor's understanding of the securities being registered. Detailed descriptions of the physical characteristics of individual properties or legal descriptions by metes and bounds are not required and should not be given. If the registrant has a number of properties, the information may be given in tabular form to the extent that it is practicable to do so.

2. The information shall be furnished separately as to each property the book value of which amounts to ten percent or more of the total assets of the registrant and its consolidated subsidiaries or the gross revenue from which for the last fiscal year amounted to ten percent or more of the aggregate gross revenues of the registrant and its consolidated subsidiaries for the registrant's last fiscal year. With respect to other properties the information shall be given by such classes or groups and in such detail as will reasonably convey the information required.

3. Include a statement as to whether, in the opinion of the management of the registrant the properties are adequately covered by insurance.

Item 15. Operating Data.

Furnish the following information with respect to each improved property which is separately described in answer to Item 14.

(a) Occupancy rate expressed as a percentage for each of the last five years.

(b) Number of tenants occupying ten percent or more of the rentable square footage and principal nature of business of such tenant.

(c) Principal business, occupations and professions carried on in, or from the building.

(d) The principal provisions of the leases between the tenants referred to in (b) above including, but not limited to: rental per annum, expiration date, and renewal options.

(e) The average effective annual rental per square foot or unit for each of the last five years prior to the date of filing.

(f) Schedule of the lease expirations for each of the ten years starting with the year in which the registration statement is filed, stating (i) the number of tenants whose leases will expire, (ii) the total area in square feet covered by such leases, (iii) the annual rental represented by such leases, and (iv) the percentage of gross annual rental represented by such leases.

(g) Each of the properties and components thereof upon which depreciation is taken, setting forth the (i) Federal tax basis, (ii) rate, (iii) method, and (iv) life claimed with respect to such property or component thereof for purposes of depreciation.

(h) The realty tax rate, annual realty taxes and estimated taxes on any proposed improvements.

Instruction. Instruction 3 to Item 14 shall apply to this Item.

Item 16. Tax Treatment of Registrant and Its Security Holders.

(a) Briefly describe the material aspects of the tax treatment of registrant under Federal income tax laws and the Federal tax treatment of registrant's security holders with respect to distributions by registrant, including the tax treatment of gains from the sale of securities or property and distributions in excess of annual net income.

(b) If any of the securities being registered are to be offered in exchange for other securities or property indicate the tax effect upon such exchanges of the Federal income tax laws.

Item 17. Market Price of and Dividends on the Registrant's Common Equity and Related Stockholder Matters.

Furnish the information required by Item 201 of Regulation S-K (§229.201 of this chapter).

Item 18. Description of Registrant's Securities.

Furnish the information required by Item 202 of Regulation S-K (§229.202 of this chapter).

Item 19. Legal Proceedings.

Furnish the information required by Item 103 of Regulation S-K (§229.103 of this chapter).

Item 20. Security Ownership of Certain Beneficial Owners and Management.

Furnish the information required by Item 403 of Regulation S-K (§229.403 of this chapter).

Item 21. Directors and Executive Officers.

Furnish the information required by Item 401 of Regulation S-K (§229.401 of this chapter).

Item 22. Executive Compensation.

Furnish the information required by Item 402 of Regulation S-K (§229.402 of this chapter), and the information required by paragraph (e)(4) of Item 407 of Regulation S-K (§229.407(e)(4) of this chapter).

Item 23. Certain Relationships and Related Transactions and Director Independence.

Furnish the information required by Items 404 and 407(a) of Regulation S-K (§§229.404 and 229.407(a) of this chapter). If a transaction involves the purchase or sale of assets by or to the registrant, otherwise than in the ordinary course of business, state the cost of the assets to the purchaser and, if acquired by the seller within two years prior to the transaction, the cost thereof to the seller. Furthermore, if the assets have been acquired by the seller within five years prior to the transaction, disclose the aggregate depreciation claimed by the seller for federal income tax purposes. Indicate the principle followed in determining the registrant's purchase or sale price and the name of the person making such determination.

Item 24. Selection, Management and Custody of Registrant's Investments.

(a) Describe the arrangements made or proposed to be made by the registrant with respect to the following:

(1) Management of the registrant's real estate, including arranging for purchases, sales, leases, maintenance and insurance.

    (2) The purchase, sale and servicing of mortgages for the registrant.

    (3) Investment advisory services.

  (b) If any of the services specified in paragraph (a) are performed or to be performed by any affiliated person, furnish the following information as to such person:

    (1) Name and address.
    (2) Nature of principal business.
    (3) Principal occupations during the last five years.

    (4) Nature of all existing direct or indirect material interests in or business connections with the registrant or any of its other affiliated persons.
    (5) Nature of all services rendered to the registrant and its subsidiaries.
    (6) Aggregate compensation received from the registrant and its subsidiaries, directly or indirectly, during the registrant's last fiscal year and the capacities in which such remuneration was received.

Instructions.

1.   If any person whose principal occupations during the last-five years are described in answer to paragraph (b)(3) is a corporation or other organization, include the name and principal occupations during the last five years of each principal executive officer of such corporation or other organization.

2.   The information required by paragraph (b) need not be furnished with respect to any director or officer of the registrant who performs the services specified solely in his capacity as such director or officer and who receives no additional compensation directly or indirectly for such services.

Item 25. Policies with Respect to Certain Transactions.

    Outline briefly any provisions of the governing instruments limiting any director, officer, security holder or affiliate of the registrant, or any other person in the following respects. If the governing instruments contain no such provisions, describe the policy of the registrant with respect to such matters.

  (a) Having any direct or indirect pecuniary interest in any investment to be acquired or disposed of by the registrant or any of its subsidiaries or in any transaction to which the registrant or any of its subsidiaries is a party or has an interest.

  (b) Engaging for their own account in business activities of the types conducted or to be conducted by the registrant and its subsidiaries.

Item 26. Limitations of Liability.

    Outline briefly the principal provisions of the governing instruments or of any contract or arrangement to which the registrant or a subsidiary is a party with respect to limitations on the liability of affiliated persons or any of their directors, officers or employees.

Instructions. If any of such provisions are broad enough to cover liability arising under the Securities Act of 1933, the effect of Section 14 of that Act upon such provisions should be indicated.

Item 27. Financial Statements and Information.

    Include in the prospectus the financial statements required by Regulation S-X, the supplementary financial information required by Item 302 of Regulation S-K (§229.302 of this chapter) and the information concerning changes in and disagreements with accountants on accounting and financial disclosure required by Item 304 of Regulation S-K (§229.304 of this chapter). Although all schedules required by Regulation S-X are to be included in the registration statement, all such schedules other than those prepared in accordance with Rules 12-12, 12-28 and 12-29 of the Regulation S-X may be omitted from the prospectus. Asmaller reporting company may provide the information in Article 8 of Regulation S-X (§210.8 of this chapter) in lieu of the financial information required by other parts of Regulation S-X, and need not provide the supplementary financial information required in Item 302 of Regulation S-K.

Item 28. Interests of Named Experts and Counsel.

Furnish the information required by Item 509 of Regulation S-K (§229.509 of this chapter).

Item 28A. Material Changes.

If the registrant elects to incorporate information by reference pursuant to General Instruction H, describe any and all material changes in the registrant's affairs which have occurred since the end of the latest fiscal year for which audited financial statements were included in the latest Form 10-K and which have not been described in a Form 10-Q or Form 8K filed under the Exchange Act.

Item 29. Incorporation of Certain Information by Reference.

If the registrant elects to incorporate information by reference pursuant to General Instruction H:

(a) It must specifically incorporate by reference into the prospectus contained in the registration statement the following documents by means of a statement to that effect in the prospectus listing all such documents:

(1) The registrant's latest annual report on Form 10-K filed pursuant to Section 13(a) or Section 15(d) of the Exchange Act which contains financial statements for the registrant's latest fiscal year for which a Form 10-K was required to have been filed; and

(2) All other reports filed pursuant to Section 13(a) or Section 15(d) of the Exchange Act or proxy or information statements filed pursuant to Section 14 of the Exchange Act since the end of the fiscal year covered by the annual report referred to in paragraph (a)(1) of this Item.

Note to Item 29(a). Attention is directed to Rule 439 (§230.439 of this chapter) regarding consent to use of material incorporated by reference.

(b)(1) The registrant must state:

(i) That it will provide to each person, including any beneficial owner, to whom a prospectus is delivered, a copy of any or all of the reports or documents that have been incorporated by reference in the prospectus contained in the registration statement but not delivered with the prospectus;

(ii) That it will provide these reports or documents upon written or oral request;

(iii) That it will provide these reports or documents at no cost to the requester;

(iv) The name, address, telephone number, and e-mail address, if any, to which the request for these reports or documents must be made; and

(v) The registrant's Web site address, including the uniform resource locator (URL) where the incorporated reports and other documents may be accessed.

Note to Item 29(b)(1). If the registrant sends any of the information that is incorporated by reference in the prospectus contained in the registration statement to security holders, it also must send any exhibits that are specifically incorporated by reference in that information.

(2) The registrant must:

(i) Identify the reports and other information that it files with the SEC; and

(ii) State that the public may read and copy any materials it files with the SEC at the SEC's Public Reference Room at 100 F Street, NE, Washington, DC 20549. State that the public may obtain information on the operation of the Public Reference Room by calling the SEC at 1800-SEC-0330. If the registrant is an electronic filer, state that the SEC maintains an Internet site that contains reports, proxy and information statements, and other information regarding issuers that file electronically with the SEC and state the address of that site (http://www.sec.gov).

Item 29A. Disclosure of Commission Position on Indemnification for Securities Act Liabilities.

Furnish the information required by Item 510 of Regulation S-K (§229.510 of this chapter).

PART II. INFORMATION NOT REQUIRED IN PROSPECTUS

Item 30. Quantitative and Qualitative Disclosures About Market Risk.

Furnish the information required by Item 305 of Regulation S-K (§ 229.305 of this chapter).

Item 31. Other Expenses of Issuance and Distribution.

Furnish the information required by Item 511 of Regulation S-K (§229.511 of this chapter).

Item 32. Sales to Special Parties.

Name each person or specify each class of persons (other than underwriters or dealers, as such) to whom any securities have been sold within the past six months, or are to be sold, by the registrant or any security holder for whose account any of the securities being registered are to be offered, at a price varying from that at which securities of the same class are to be offered to the general public pursuant to this registration. State the consideration given or to be given by each such person or class.

Item 33. Recent Sales of Unregistered Securities.

Furnish the information required by Item 701 of Regulation S-K (§229.701 of this chapter).

Item 34. Indemnification of Directors and Officers.

Furnish the information required by Item 702 of Regulation S-K (§229.702 of this chapter).

Item 35. Treatment of Proceeds from Stock Being Registered.

If the capital shares are being registered hereunder and any portion of the consideration to be received by the registrant for such shares is to be credited to an account other than the appropriate capital share account, state to what other account such portion is to be credited and the estimated amount per share. If the consideration from the sale of par value shares is less than par value, state the amount per share involved and its treatment in the accounts.

Item 36. Financial Statements and Exhibits.

    (a) List all financial statements filed as part of the registration statement, indicating those included in the prospectus.

    (b) Furnish the exhibits required by Item 601 of Regulation S-K (§229.601 of this chapter).

Item 37. Undertakings.

Furnish the information required by Item 512 of Regulation S-K (§229.512 of this chapter).

SIGNATURES

Pursuant to the requirements of the Securities Act of 1933, the registrant certifies that it has reasonable grounds to believe that it meets all of the requirements for filing on Form S-11 and has duly caused this registration statement to be signed on its behalf by the undersigned, thereunto duly authorized, in the City of _____, State of _____, on

_____.

_____

(Date)

_____

(Issuer)

By

_____

(Signature and Title)

Pursuant to the requirements of the Securities Act of 1933, this registration statement has been signed by the following. persons in the capacities and on the dates indicated.

_____

(Signature)

_____

(Title)

_____

(Date)

Instructions.

1. The registration statement shall be signed by the registrant, its principal executive officer or officers, its principal financial officer, its controller or principal accounting officer, and by at least a majority of the board of directors or persons performing similar functions. If the registrant is a foreign person, the registration statement shall also be signed by its authorized representative in the United States. Where the registrant is a limited partnership, the registration statement shall be signed by a majority of the board of directors of any corporate general partner signing the registration statement.

2. The name of each person who signs the registration statement shall be typed or printed beneath his signature. Any person who occupies more than one of the specified positions shall indicate each capacity in which he signs the registration statement. Attention is directed to Rule 402 concerning manual signatures and Item 601 of Regulation S-K concerning signatures pursuant to powers of attorney.

CHAPTER 104

THE PROMISSORY NOTE IN REAL ESTATE TRANSACTIONS[1]

Professor George Lefcoe
The Law Center
University of Southern California

SYNOPSIS

---

[1] Parts of this chapter have been adapted from George Lefcoe, Real Estate Transactions (Michie 1993).

§ 104.01   Note Formalities.

§ 104.01(a)   The Difference Between the Note and the Deed of Trust.

Few first-time homebuyers can afford Polonius' captious advice, "Neither a borrower nor a lender be." They buy their homes on credit, signing promissory notes (I.O.U.s) in the process. However, by themselves, these promises to repay don't offer lenders sufficient assurance of repayment, especially for the considerable sums needed to buy a house. Borrowers could easily overcommit themselves later with additional borrowings, lose their jobs, or just become careless in paying on their I.O.U.s. So lenders almost always insist that buyers pledge their newly-bought homes as security for their loan. In this case, the financing document which secures the collateral is known as a mortgage. Other types of security interests include deeds of trust, ground leases, and installment land contracts.

There are several differences between notes and security instruments. The former is a promise to repay a debt and evidences that money was loaned to the borrower, while the latter pledges specific property that the lender can seize and sell to repay the underlying debt if the borrower reneges on his promise to pay.

Another difference is that "the obligation is more important than the security."[2] Valid notes can exist unsecured. Banks customarily lend money without demanding collateral or other security. That's what credit card financing is. On the other hand, the validity and enforceability of a security interest depends entirely on the existence of an underlying, outstanding obligation. No obligation, no mortgage.

The primacy of the obligation is evidenced in many legal rules. Inconsistencies between the note and the mortgage are resolved in favor of the note's provisions.[3] When a lender assigns a note, the purchaser of the note also gets the mortgage along with it, even if the lender hadn't meant to transfer the mortgage.[4] If a mortgage lender assigns a mortgage without

---

[2] Roger Bernhardt, California Mortgage and Deed of Trust Practice 15 (2d ed. 1990). Vernor v. Southwest Federal Land Bank Association, 77 S.W.3d 364 (Tex. App. 2002) (a promissory note was not void for lack of a co signature); ABN Amro Mortgage Group, Inc. v. Stantz, 2004 Ohio 2089 (Ohio Ct. App. 2004) (a mortgagor who did not execute a promissory note did not owe money to the mortgagee pursuant to a note).

[3] Pacific Fruit Exch. v. Duke, 284 P. 729 (Cal. App. 1930). *See* Ann M. Burkhart, Third Party Defenses to Mortgages, 1998 B.Y.U. L. Rev. 1003; R. Wilson Freyermuth, Enforcement of Acceleration Provisions and the Rhetoric of Good Faith, 1998 B.Y.U. L. Rev. 1035.

[4] Kernohan v. Manss, 41 N.E. 258 (Ohio 1895). The holder of a note and mortgage sold the mortgage along with a forged copy of the note. Then it sold the genuine note to a subsequent purchaser. The court held that the subsequent purchaser had priority to the underlying debt upon foreclosure of the mortgage. Lewis v. Hare, 275 B.R. 586, 591 (Bankr. D. Colo. 2002) (At common law the security attaches to the deed of trust).

assigning the underlying note, the assignee cannot foreclose the mortgage.[5] If the originating lender sells the loan first to A and then to B but delivers the note to lender A and only a copy of the note to lender B, A's interest is superior to B's. A prevails even though B knows nothing of A's interest and A doesn't record the assignment of the mortgage until after B records its assignment. The law of negotiable instruments, and not the recording acts, determines the outcome. A wins because A has possession of the note.[6]

Once the debt is repaid, the lender is absolutely bound to release the security instrument. If a lender or trustee fails to execute a reconveyance or satisfaction on demand when the debt is paid, he can be held liable for any damage the buyer suffers as a result—including lost sales or financing opportunities.[7]

§ 104.01(b)   Contents of the Note and the Deed of Trust.

Provisions regarding repayment of the debt appear in the note, such as: (1) the amount of the loan principal, (2) the rate of interest, (3) the term to maturity (length of time you have to repay the debt), (4) whether the borrower can pay early (prepayment), (5) the penalty for making payments late, and so on. Provisions about preservation of the security property appear in the deed of trust, such as the pledgor's promises to maintain the property in good condition, keep it adequately insured for the benefit of the lender, and pay all property taxes and special assessments when due to avoid liens.

Some provisions surface both in the note and the deed of trust. One such provision is a "due-on-sale" clause which gives the lender the option of declaring all debt immediately due if the borrower sells the property without the lender's prior approval of the buyer.[8] These clauses are included in notes because a sale could affect the lender's exposure on the debt if the new buyer takes over payments on the debt and is a poor credit risk. They are included in security instruments because a sale could also affect the value of the security property if the new borrower is a property destroyer, or lets property tax and insurance bills slide.

§ 104.01(c)   Secured Promises Need Not Be for Money.

Say your neighbor promises to let you share her new tennis court if you

---

[5] Kluge v. Fugazy, 536 N.Y.S.2d 92 (1988).

[6] American Bank of the South v. Rothenberg, 598 So. 2d 289 (Fla. App. 1992).

[7] Satine v. Koier, 164 A.2d 913 (Md. 1960). The mortgagor was entitled to additional construction costs incurred as a result of a delay in obtaining financing, which was itself caused by the mortgagor's refusal to reconvey title. *See generally* Warden in 55 Am. Jur. 2d *Mortgages* 491 (1971): "In addition to the statutory penalty, a mortgagor is generally permitted to recover for losses which proximately result from the refusal of the mortgagee to discharge the mortgage." Kiowa Tribe of Oklahoma v. Manufacturing Technologies, Inc., 523 U.S. 751 (1998) (Indian tribe entitled to sovereign immunity on note which it had signed, even though the note related to the tribe's commercial activities).

[8] "Due-on-sale" clauses are discussed in § 104.08(a), *infra*.

waive your rights under the local zoning code to a five-foot separation between where her court begins and your lot line ends. Could your right to use the court be secured by a deed of trust on it? What if your law firm's new landlord promises to pay your rent on the lease you're abandoning in order to move into his building. Can the landlord's obligation be secured by a mortgage on the new building? (Assuming these mortgages are valid, why might you prefer them to an easement to use the tennis court or a promise by your landlord to pay rent on your former space?)

Most secured obligations are for the repayment of money, but a mortgage can be valid even if it doesn't secure an obligation to repay money. It can secure the "performance of an act,"[9] such as a promise by the mortgagor to furnish water and sewer facilities,[10] to build a driveway,[11] to construct an apartment house,[12] to use property for church purposes,[13] or to supply the property owner with food, shelter, and "the necessities of life" for the rest of her days.[14] To be mortgageable, though, these promises must be "readily translatable into money, albeit without precision."[15]

There are two reasons that mortgage obligations must be readily reducible to cash. One is simply to facilitate a court-ordered assessment of damages.

The second is more complicated. Defaulting mortgagors are protected against forfeitures of the "equity" value in their properties. They owe their lenders a repayment of debt, plus interest and costs. But no more. Once the lender forecloses and pockets a sum sufficient to pay off the loan, any surplus from the foreclosure sale belongs to the property owner. To determine the surplus, an estimate has to be made of the value of the debtor's performance. The creditor's right to foreclose becomes problematic if the obligation lacks liquidity.[16] That is why smart creditors stipulate liquidated damages for the performance of promises not already reduced to a dollar amount.

---

[9] Cal. Civ. Code §§ 2872, 2920.

[10] Valley Vista Land Co. v. Nipomo Water & Sewer Co., 72 Cal. Rptr. 181 (1968).

[11] Jeffrey Towers, Inc. v. Straus, 297 N.Y.S.2d 450 (1969).

[12] Pawtucket Inst. for Sav. v. Gagnon, 475 A.2d 1028 (R.I. 1984).

[13] Congregational Church Bldg. Soc. v. Osborn, 94 P. 881 (Cal. 1908).

[14] Thompson v. Glidden, 445 A.2d 676 (Me. 1982).

[15] Application of Jeffrey Towers, Inc., 291 N.Y.S.2d 41, 45 (1968). The court upheld the validity of a mortgage securing the borrower's promise to install a sewer main, construct a driveway, and complete an apartment house, but held that the mortgage could not secure the borrower's promise to consent to zoning applications because the monetary value of the borrower's cooperation was too speculative. Kissinger v. Genetic Evaluation Center, Inc., 618 N.W.2d 429 (Neb. 2000) (promissory note held supported by adequate consideration).

[16] Grant S. Nelson & Dale A. Whitman, Real Estate Finance Law § 2.2, at 20–23 (5th ed. 2007).

§ 104.01(d)   Oral Promises to Make Loans.

The English Statute of Frauds requires that certain types of contracts be written in order to be enforceable, among which are contracts for interests in land. But what about promises to make loans secured by a mortgage or deed of trust? Are they promises regarding an "interest in land?" The borrower's promise to convey to the lender a security interest in real property definitely involves an "interest in land" and needs written confirmation to satisfy the Statute of Frauds.[17] But the lender's loan commitment is a promise to lend money. Nonetheless, some courts have thought the Statute of Frauds applies to both.[18] Even the lender's promise contemplates a security interest. Other courts have been receptive to plaintiff borrowers and granted damages for the lender's breach of an oral promise to make a loan even though the borrower's promise to convey a mortgage was unenforceable because it was also oral only. These cases hold the lender's promise not within the Statute of Frauds.[19]

In reality, the lender will almost always require the borrower to sign a note evidencing the loan well before the lender actually advances funds. Some lenders give borrowers written and enforceable loan commitments, by which they obligate themselves to make the loan. Loan commitments are more readily available to commercial borrowers than to homebuyers.

Many loans are not subject to the Statute of Frauds, so lenders have convinced the legislatures of 35 states to adopt some form of the American Banker's Association's model statute requiring that credit agreements be written in order to be enforceable.[20] However, these statutes do not apply to real estate mortgages and other security agreements.

§ 104.02   How Much to Borrow.

§ 104.02(a)   Underwriting Standards; Qualifying the Borrower.

Every prudent lender is trying to unearth answers to the big question: Will the borrower be able and willing to repay the debt on schedule? Mortgage

---

[17] *See* Sleeth v. Sampson, 142 N.E. 355 (N.Y. 1923).

[18] *See* Bozzi v. Greater Delaware Valley Sav. & Loan Ass'n, 389 A.2d 122 (Pa. 1978), holding that oral agreements to lend money in consideration for a mortgage must be in writing pursuant to the Statute of Frauds. *See also* Philips Credit Corp. v. Regent Health Group, Inc., 953 F. Supp. 482, 517 (S.D.N.Y. 1997) (In New York a mortgage on real property is governed by the statute of frauds and must be in writing to be enforceable); George A. Nation, III, The Clardy Case: Lessons for Lenders Concerning Commitment Letters And Other Pre-Loan Contracts, 114 Banking L.J. 347, 365 n.3 (1997).

[19] *See* Sleeth v. Sampson, 142 N.E. 355 (N.Y. 1923). *See* Landes Constr. Co. v. Royal Bank of Canada, 833 F.2d 1365 (9th Cir. 1987) (judgment against bank for $18.5 million upheld).

[20] 1989 Joint Task Force of the Committee on Consumer and Commercial Financial Services.

lenders refer to the four "Cs" of underwriting: collateral, capacity, character, capital.

Collateral is the value of the security property.

Capacity is the borrower's income. Lenders commonly utilize two ratios to aid them in determining whether a buyer is a good credit risk.[21] One is the ratio of a borrower's income to her fixed installment debt (car loans, credit card balances, student loans), called a "total debt ratio" (TDR). The TDR includes mortgage payments. If the lender's cutoff was 38%, a borrower whose income was $100,000 would not be given a loan if her total debts exceeded $38,000 a year.

This concern may be warranted since research conducted by a high-volume insurer of low downpayment home loans indicates that borrowers with ratios higher than 33% and total debt ratios in excess of 38% have a 60% higher delinquency rate than standard borrowers.[22]

The second ratio is the borrower's net income to the borrower's total housing costs (the mortgage repayment, taxes, insurance and, perhaps, maintenance). Presently, ratios higher than 32% are worrisome to most mortgage lenders.

The formulas and ratios change from time to time, with richer households generally paying smaller shares of their net income for housing than poorer ones. U.S. households actually spend between 15 and 40% of their income for housing.

Character is the borrower's past credit history, including bankruptcies or foreclosures. Even though a loan applicant may not have huge credit card or personal debts before buying a house, the borrower could always go on a binge after getting the mortgage. On the other hand, behavior is usually patterned so credit histories are taken as reliable indicators of creditworthiness.

Capital is cash or liquid assets at the borrower's disposal to make the down payment and tough out a temporary health set back or job loss. Thus, net worth is taken into account and is defined as the total of the borrower's assets minus liabilities.

All in all, the mortgage underwriter will need the following mass of data to process a loan:

- ID numbers for savings and checking accounts;
- signed forms authorizing institutions to release account information

---

[21] Kenneth R. Harney, Relaxed Standards for Home Loans Bring Surge in Mortgage Defaults, Daily Record, June 30, 1995, at 7.

[22] Kenneth R. Harney, Relaxed Standards for Home Loans Bring Surge in Mortgage Defaults, Daily Record, June 30, 1995, at 7.

so the borrower's claimed assets can be verified;

- account numbers for money market funds;
- credit card balances;
- loan documents on outstanding debt;
- retirement fund verifications;
- a list of assets and outstanding mortgages or other liens against them;
- the borrower's last two years' tax returns;
- verifications of employment;
- appraisals of property that the borrower owns;
- a credit report;
- written explanations for any blemishes in the applicant's credit history.

With increased computerization, this costly and annoying process is streamlined.

§ 104.02(a)(1)   Pre-approved Mortgages.

Some prospective homebuyers want to enter the marketplace armed with more than a vague idea of their borrowing ability. They seek commitments by lenders or mortgage brokers to make a loan of a certain amount, contingent on the appraised value of the property selected. Not many lenders issue these commitments, which are also known as "pre-approved" mortgages.

On the other hand, obtaining advance commitments isn't necessarily in the borrowers' best interests. They must pay an up-front fee for them, and one-third of the pre-approved mortgages are never used because the borrowers find better loans elsewhere. But in a tight housing market when values are rising swiftly, borrowers with a financing commitment have an edge when bidding against buyers who insist on "financing contingency" loopholes in any contract they sign.[23]

Some borrowers just meet with a friendly loan officer at a bank or mortgage broker before commencing their house search, disclose their financial situation, and obtain the loan officer's informal estimate of how much money they could expect to borrow.

§ 104.02(a)(2)   Filing False Loan Applications.

"Where fraudulent loan applications were once an immeasurably tiny portion of total loans, they now account for between 4% and 10% of all applications taken nationwide."[24]

---

[23] *See* Sing, *Preapproved Mortgage Has Advantages,* L.A. Times, Aug. 20, 1988, at D3.

[24] Greg Benson, retail banking expert at a Washington trade association, *quoted in* Kathy

Lenders aren't universally cautious in their underwriting standards—the procedures they use to qualify borrowers. Lately, in a rush to cut expenses and increase business volume, lenders have employed loan brokers on a pure commission basis. No loan means no commission for the broker. Although this incentive system rewards efficient brokers, it also encourages reckless underwriting practices. Sometimes, commission-dependent brokers are tempted to encourage borrowers to misstate the facts: "Forget about the alimony, automobile, and student loan payments," they may urge. "It will only slow down the approval." Striving to be competitive, lenders only compound the problem by offering loan applicants quick approvals. They churn out speedy reviews of a loan applications by not bothering to closely verify what the applicant reports. These loans are sometimes called "E-Z qualifiers." Loan brokers can often get questionable applicants qualified when they know that the borrower's application won't be thoroughly scrutinized.[25]

Don't fall into the trap. Filing false statements on bank loan documents is a federal offense.[26] The U.S. Government can seize your house if you bought it with proceeds from a loan you got by making false statements in your loan application, and your lender is F.D.I.C.-insured.[27] The legal standard for forfeiture is similar to that required for a search warrant, probable cause. Anthony Paul Feher lost his house at 4031/2 Skyline Drive, La Habra Heights, California, because he claimed to have been employed at Action Garage Door 1984–86 and the owner of the company declared Mr. Feher had never been employed there.[28]

M. Kristof, *The Pinocchi Papers,* L.A. Times, July 21, 1993 at D1, col. 2.

[25] For a description of how overanxious borrowers falsify loan application information, *see* Kuhn v. Spatial Design, Inc., 585 A.2d 967 (N.J. Super. A.D. 1991). The trial court found that the borrowers "were encouraged to submit such an application by Prudential's dependably credulous way of dealing with income and asset information submitted to it." 585 A.2d at 969. This was a "no documentation" loan. Prudential never made the loan because the borrowers got cold feet and decided to kill the deal by "coming clean" with the lender, prompting the lender to cancel its loan commitment. The buyers' obligation to purchase was contingent on the commitment.

[26] 18 U.S.C. § 1014.

[27] United States v. Platenburg, 657 F.2d 797 (5th Cir. 1981) (the financial institution must be F.D.I.C. insured for criminal prosecution under 18 U.S.C. § 1014).

[28] United States v. 4031/2 Skyline Dr., 797 F. Supp. 796 (C.D. Cal. 1992). In this case, the loan was not in default and the lender did not initiate the seizure. This was an "easy-qualifier" loan with a 25% down payment so the lender didn't verify employment. The case is not being appealed. The Robert Bruss Cal. Real Est. L. Newsl., January 1993, at 1. The proceedings were in rem, civil. There is an innocent owner exception to civil forfeiture under the law, but Mr. Feher did not plead it. *See generally* Gregory Pulles et al., FIRREA: A Legislative History and Section-by-Section Analysis 1424–26 (1992).

The Case of Mr. Jones:[29] Real Estate Fraud
and Lending as Underwriting Practices in Laguna Beach

by Diane D. Stalder

Mr. Jones was a fairly competent and successful licensed real estate broker. In the early 1980s, however, Mr. Jones fell on hard times as interest rates rose above 20% and, according to Mr. Jones, you couldn't give real estate away.

Jones decided to take matters into his own hands and create deals, even without a buyer. He established the Irvine Corporation, which he advertised as a relocation service for people whose jobs caused them to move into and out of homes in the Orange County area. The fact that the sellers would immediately move out of the area helped Jones in several ways. They were anxious to sell their homes in a bad market and it would be much more difficult for them to check him out.

Jones advertised to find sellers in this position, saying that he had buyers from out-of-town looking for homes. He said that he was a broker and would broker the deal. Jones actually became the broker *and* the buyer by assuming a number of false identities. Jones would offer the legitimate sellers a very reasonable (good) price for their home with two conditions:

1. Sellers accept 90% of the price from a bank loan and the other 10% on what Jones termed a 2nd Trust Deed, which was actually a promissory note from the buyer. No money down.

2. Sellers pay the points on the loan and commission to Jones, usually 6% of the purchase price. Jones obtained the loan from the bank (at the historically high rates of interest), paid the sellers 90% of the purchase price, and collected the commission and points. Sellers left town with the assurance that the buyers would be paying off the balance.

Jones did this for some 29 properties, all private homes, assuming seven different identities and acting as buyer and broker in the process. At times, his wife or a friend would appear as the buyer.

Jones would take over each property and then lease it out, again for a reasonable price. He pocketed the rent money. Jones never made any interest or principal payments on the bank loans. He was hoping interest rates would go down and property prices would rise. He would then be able to refinance and sell to legitimate buyers, pay back the banks and make a profit. Rates did not fall quickly enough.

It wasn't long before banks foreclosed and, discovering that the buyers did not really exist, uncovered Jones's scam. Jones was arrested. Jones was convicted on mail and real estate fraud and received five years. 18 U.S.C. §§ 1341, 1342. He was ordered to pay $210,000 in restitution upon release. Jones escaped from Lompoc after 13 months of service. Eighteen months later, he was apprehended as a fugitive and returned to incarceration at Terminal Island, where he got an additional 60 days for escape, and another

---

[29] Name changed for privacy purposes.

eight months of parole time denied. He will spend over forty months in prison.

In calculating his parole, the fraud offense was rated according to the amount of loans, which added up to some $4 million, even though the lenders' actual loss was under $500,000. The significant "real loss" was the default of the promissory notes to the sellers for 10% and the approximately $40,000 the banks claimed they forfeited, mostly in administrative costs. Since houses were so difficult to sell at the time, with interest rates approaching 20%, sellers wouldn't have agreed to take back notes if they could have sold for cash instead. The 10% represented, for most sellers, a calculated gamble, one where the dice were loaded against them, as it turns out.

Jones's monetary gains were the commissions and rents he collected totalling less than $150,000. The parole commission seemed fixated on the $4 million figure and had a hard time understanding "where the money went." Most of it went, of course, to the sellers. Jones is convinced he did his sellers a service and that morally he is not particularly culpable, although he realizes the false identities and escape were not bright moves. He really blames the whole affair on bad market conditions at the time and still probably thinks about the money he lost out on and the prison term he could have avoided "had the market taken an upswing in time. . .."

For prospective borrowers, there is a message here about lender underwriting standards. Lenders may not be as meticulous when they originate loans as they become once a default occurs. But the penalties for "fudging" the loan application can put borrowers behind bars.

Penalties can also involve professionals—lawyers, accountants, appraisers—having their licenses suspended or revoked.

§ 104.02(b)　How Much Is Enough: Leverage and the Down Payment.

Should you borrow as much as a lender is willing to lend, or should you accumulate a larger down payment before jumping into home ownership?[30] Borrowing money is known as "leveraging" because it magnifies the effect of gains and losses that come from investing with the use of borrowed funds.

The advantage of leveraging to the max is that you enhance your financial

---

[30] Or should you keep your downpayment and pledge assets as collateral for the downpayment? With a pledged asset mortgage, the lender accepts assets, typically certificates of deposit (C.D.s), equivalent to the amount of the downpayment as collateral for the mortgage. The interest on the pledged C.D.s continues to accrue to the owner during the pledge period. When the mortgagor achieves the agreed-upon minimum equity in the property, the lender releases its interest in the collateral. Although the borrower may pay a slightly higher interest rate for this variation of a zero-down loan, the borrower has the advantage of earning interest on the collateral, whereas no interest is earned on the traditional cash downpayment. Kenneth R. Harney, *More Lenders Now OK Collateral in Place of a Down Payment*, Los Angeles Times, Feb. 18, 1996, at K4.

return if the value of the property increases at a rate greater than your after-tax cost of borrowing. This is known as "positive leverage." Conversely, if values lag, your losses will be even larger because you leveraged yourself. This is known as "negative leverage."

Cautious homebuyers worry about another aspect of "leveraging"—whether they can comfortably shoulder their debt in the event of a temporary wage loss. Statistically, default and foreclosure rates are the highest when borrowers only make small down payments.

LEVERAGE DEFINED[31]

[Leverage is the relationship between net operating income (NOI) and debt service (D/S). Net operating income is gross income minus all expenses except debt service. Expenses include taxes, insurance, and maintenance. Debt service is principal plus interest. When NOI > D/S, leverage is positive. When D/S < NOI, leverage is negative.]

To explain how leverage works, let us start with an investor who buys a $10 million apartment house that yields $1,500,000 after expenses. On an all-cash purchase, he will earn a 15 percent cash yield on his investment. Suppose instead that he borrows to make the purchase: first, $5,000,000, then $9,000,000. If the mortgages bear 12 percent interest, and if the annual debt service (that is, the combined amount of interest and principal reduction) is designed to pay off the mortgages in 25 years, the cash flow and cash yield appear below:

(a) *$5,000,000 mortgage, $5,000,000 cash down payment*

Cash flow before debt service	$1,500,000
Less debt service	$633,000
Cash flow after debt service	$867,000
Cash yield on $5,000,000 down payment	17.34%

(b) *$9,000,000 mortgage, $1,000,000 cash down payment*

Cash flow before debt service	$1,500,000
Less debt service	$1,139,400
Cash flow after debt service	$360,600
Cash yield on $1,000,000 down payment	36.06%

If we were to continue to project cash yield based on ever-shrinking down payments, the investment return would approach infinity. And by placing elsewhere the cash that mortgaging replaces, the investor can expand and diversify his holdings.

[The easiest way to appreciate the impact of leverage is to imagine the investor is able to put the original $10 million into one project all cash, two projects with 50% down, or 10 projects at $1,000,000 each.]

It is useful to understand how leverage can bring a geometric increase in investment return. Note that it depends upon the investor turning a profit on

---

[31] Allan Axelrod et al., Land Transfer and Finance 133–35 (3d ed. 1986). Copyright © 1986 by Little, Brown & Company Reprinted with permission.

the borrowed funds; this, in turn, depends upon a favorable spread between the "points" (points equal percentage) of debt service and the "free and clear" rate of return on the investment. To illustrate this principle with the $5,000,000 mortgage:

(1)	Free and clear return (at 15%) on $5,000,000 of borrowed funds	$750,000
(2)	Debt service (at 12.66 points) on $5,000,000 mortgage	$633,000
(3)	Profit on the borrowed funds (1 minus 2)	$117,000
(4)	Profit on the equity or down payment funds	$750,000
(5)	Overall cash flows (3 plus 4)	$867,000

Thus our investor has enhanced his rate of return by adding to the regular 15 percent yield that his down payment generates, the $117,000 profit on the borrowed moneys. By increasing the spread between free-and-clear return and debt service costs, or by increasing the ratio of borrowed to equity capital, the investor will improve his leverage advantage. To test your understanding, repeat this calculation for a $9,000,000 mortgage.

It follows, inevitably, that leverage will produce negative results if the assumptions above are reversed and the mortgage debt service costs exceed the free-and-clear rate of investment return. Suppose, in our example, that the free-and-clear return on an all-cash investment is only $1,300,000 (13 percent) and that the investor can only obtain a 15-year mortgage on any moneys that he borrows. If we assume the same 12 percent interest rate, the annual debt service for each $1,000,000 of mortgage comes to $144,600 (14.46 points). We now have an unfavorable spread between the "points" of debt service and the "free and clear" rate of investment return. The impact on cash yield, assuming a $5,000,000 mortgage, appears below:

$5,000,000 mortgage, $5,000,000 cash down payment

Cash flow before debt service	$1,300,000
Less debt service	$723,000
Cash flow after debt service	$577,000
Cash yield on $5,000,000 down payment	11.54%

And, as the borrowed funds increase, the disadvantage grows geometrically. You might work out the figures for a $6,000,000 mortgage, a $7,000,000 mortgage, etc.

With medicine, one dose may be restorative, five doses fatal. So, too, with leverage. If it is too great, it may ruin. The investor (and the lender) gamble that operating income will be enough to carry the debt. In the first example, where $5,000,000 was borrowed, $867,000 was left after debt service; when $9,000,000 was borrowed, only $360,000 remained. These amounts, $867,000 and $360,000, are the margin of solvency. If the margin disappears (rentals down, expenses up), the investor faces the uninviting options of finding cash elsewhere or defaulting on his loan, unless he is able to refinance the debt so as to reduce or postpone the debt service requirements. Needless to say, the slimmer the margin of solvency, the shakier the investment. History records more than one real estate empire that was leveraged into oblivion.

Note: (1) The False Promise of Positive Leverage Analysis. Rents may sink below projected levels. Expenses may float far above gross income. But D/S remains stubbornly at the level promised in the note. The false promise of positive leverage analysis is that despite present NOI exceeding D/S by comfortable margins, it may not always. The more highly leveraged the project, the greater the chance that the debtor will lose the project if what begins as a positive relationship of NOI to D/S turns negative.

(2) Cash Flow vs. Net Return as Measures of Leverage. The above analysis rests on "cash in" and "cash out" as the basis for determining whether taking on debt is a good idea or a bad one. On the expense side, the authors include payments of both principal *and* interest—not interest alone. Some investors exclude repayments of principal in their "cost of funds" calculation, regarding principal repayments as a build-up of equity and not part of the price of borrowed funds.

On the earnings side, the authors count only net income (rent minus taxes, insurance, and maintenance). They exclude unrealized appreciation, even if the property's value is taking off. This is understandable, since what goes up can come down and investors with appreciating property don't actually pocket their profits until they sell or refinance. Nonetheless, some methods for calculating returns on real estate (or other) investments take into account property appreciation. Also, investors who don't plan to sell quickly may be able to borrow against appreciated value.

One danger of including unrealized appreciation is that investors may wind up borrowing heavily and happily in deals that produce negative cash flows. They think that they are leveraging positively because they have a positive sum after subtracting interest costs from net annual returns (income after expenses + appreciation). The fallacy of this calculus is readily seen when unrealized appreciation disappears in a real estate market downturn.

Among the people who used this errant method of calculating investment returns were many southern California homebuyers in 1987 and 1988. Who could have faulted them in 1988, when house prices rose 30% while interest rates fluctuated between 9.5–10.5%? Unfortunately, in 1989, home prices remained steady in some places and declined as much as 10% in others. Buyers who were paying interest rates of 10–11% experienced the pitfalls of negative leverage. By 1992, some California home prices had plummeted 20–33% from their 1989 highs, the dangers of negative leverage became ever more apparent, and the rate of foreclosures increased.

The owners of highly leveraged commercial properties suffered too, as office and shopping center rents plunged below the owners' "break even" line. Owners were forced to dig into their own pockets to meet mortgage payments or lose their properties through foreclosure.

§ 104.02(c)   Where Homebuyers Go for Financing.[32]

There are several types of lending institutions which fund mortgage loans. Among them are: mortgage brokers, mortgage bankers, savings banks, commercial banks and consumer finance lenders.

Originations of Residential Mortgages
by Type of Lender (1990)[33]

Mortgage Brokers. Mortgage brokers don't lend money. Rather, they help borrowers get loans by locating lenders and "packaging" applications so that loans can be processed quickly. Once the borrower has been approved and the funds disbursed, the mortgage broker's job is done. Mortgage brokers earn their money by charging part of the loan origination fee as commission, and by charging application and other service fees.

The major drawback with using mortgage brokers is that they have no control over the funding of the loan or the loan terms. Lenders are free to change the loan terms at any time before the loan closes and can also delay the loan by requesting for additional information. The advantage to using mortgage brokers is that they have quick and efficient access to a vast number of lenders. With so many lenders to choose from, chances are the borrower will get better loan terms than he could on his own.

Mortgage bankers borrow money from lenders to make their own loans. Because they are in a position to place billions of dollars of impound accounts with commercial banks at low interest rates, they enjoy the benefit of open lines of credit at bargain rates. Mortgage bankers then package and sell groups of their loans to investors in the secondary market. Unlike mortgage brokers, mortgage bankers also service mortgages for the investors and handle defaults on payments.

Mortgage bankers have four sources of income:

(1)   Loan origination fees, usually one percent of the loan amount, paid by the borrower;

(2)   The difference between what they pay for bank credit and what they earn in interest on mortgages held during 30–90 days before selling them in the secondary market;

(3)   The sale premium they earn when interest rates fall during the 30–90 days they are holding for sale the loans they have originated;

---

[32] Significant portions of this section have been based on information from Robert Kratovil & Raymond J. Werner, Real Estate Law 327 (9th ed. 1988).

[33] Grant S. Nelson & Dale A. Whitman, Real Estate Transfer, Finance, and Development 908 (4th ed. 1992).

(4)   Servicing fees, ranging from 25 to 50 basic points % to % of loan principal, plus late fees and prepayment penalties. The loan servicer usually pockets late charges and prepayment fees. These are seldom passed along to the mortgage purchaser.

They then package and sell groups of their loans to investors in the secondary market. Unlike mortgage brokers, mortgage bankers also service mortgages for the investors and handle defaults on payments. They make their money by charging loan origination fees to borrowers and servicing fees to investors. They also make money on the spread between the interest rates accepted by their borrowers and the rates specified by their investors.

Mortgage banks differ from banks in that they are not chartered by either the state or federal governments. Some states do regulate mortgage banks, but they are not members of the Federal Reserve System. The accounts of their investors, unlike bank depositors, aren't insured by the Federal Deposit Insurance Corporation (F.D.I.C.). Mortgage bankers are often called "noninstitutional" or "nonregulated" lenders. Except for minimal state regulation, the only real "requirements" placed upon them are by their investors and insurers who specify limits on mortgage sizes, ratios, lending areas and types of loans.

Consumer Finance Lenders. Consumer finance lenders make credit card loans, auto loans, home equity loans, and purchase money loans, among others.

Life Insurance Companies. Life insurance companies often work with mortgage brokers who find loans for them. In 1950, life insurance companies held about 19% of all single-family mortgages, especially F.H.A.-insured loans, and were content with the moderate yields and great safety of these loans. Competition for yields forced them to cut down their home mortgage lending so that they accounted for less than 2% of all home loans originated in 1990. Chasing higher yields, they invested in commercial real estate and are now experiencing the inevitable corollary between risk and return.

Savings and Loans (now called Savings Banks). Savings and loan institutions pool the savings of individuals for investment in residential mortgages. They hold more mortgage debts and originate more mortgages than any other institutions. In fact, over 80% of S&L assets are held in one- to four-family mortgage loans and 30–40% of all residential mortgages are originated by S.&L.'s.

Originally, S.&.L.s only financed homes within their local lending area.

Recently, savings banks have also participated in the secondary market as both buyers and sellers. Some have even formed mortgage banking subsidiaries to originate loans for sale in the secondary market.

Savings banks must be chartered either by a state or by the federal government. If they are federal institutions, they must also meet certain federal lending standards promulgated by the Federal Savings and Loan Insurance Corporation and the Federal Home Loan Bank Board. Because the F.S.L.I.C. and the F.H.L.B.B. have been dissolved, lending standards are now enforced by the F.D.I.C.

In the 1980s, regulators encouraged savings associations to try to increase their yields by investing in acquisition and development loans to homebuilders, construction loans for all types of projects, including office buildings, shopping centers and resorts, and "joint ventures" with developers. Some of these projects failed to sell or rent at the prices which savings association underwriters had anticipated.

Because savings associations were capitalized very thinly, losses on portfolio loans meant insolvency in some instances.

Congress created the Resolution Trust Corporation to "resolve" these troubled institutions through liquidation, merger with stronger institutions or acquisition by investors who could improve management and provide more capital. Furthermore, federal regulations have increased the capital requirements for savings and commercial banks. The amount of capital an institution must retain depends on how risky its loan portfolio is. Regulators require less capital to support portfolios of residential mortgage loans than portfolios of commercial properties or construction loans.

Commercial Banks. Commercial banks also accumulate funds and reloan them, but they generally use shorter-term, time- and demand-deposit accounts to fund their loans. Historically, commercial banks preferred short-term loans, especially construction loans. Now they are becoming significant lenders for single-family home loans and participate actively in the secondary mortgage markets, sometimes organizing mortgage pools of loans they originate.

Some commercial bank holding companies own mortgage banks. Commercial banks loan mortgage bankers money to originate loans and then are paid back when the mortgage bankers sell those loans in the secondary market. Commercial banks are also the largest income-property lenders, and the largest lenders for construction loans.

Commercial banks are chartered by either a state or the federal government. All federally-chartered and some state-chartered banks belong to the Federal Reserve System. Congress has given the Federal Reserve some authority to regulate all banks. All state and federally chartered banks insured by the FDIC are subject to its rules.

§ 104.02(d)   Is There Mortgage Broker or Lender Liability for Aggressive Loans? Fiduciary Duty Contrasted with Duty to Counsel.

If your lender is overly optimistic about your future earnings prospects and the buoyancy of local property markets and allows you to borrow far more than you can repay and maybe more than the property is worth, do you have a possible defense to nonpayment?

Court opinions are divided on whether lenders generally owe borrowers a fiduciary duty.[34] Such a duty is created when one person undertakes to act "primarily for another's benefit. . .".[35] From a distance, in the lender-borrower relationship one seems to be on one's own, which is why banks are not usually thought to owe depositors or borrowers a fiduciary duty.[36] However, special circumstances could create a fiduciary duty for the lender.[37] For instance, a bank could hold itself out as an advisor and evolve a connection with a customer, inducing the customer to believe that the lender had the customer's best interests in mind and not its own:

> . . . a bank whose officer strongly suggests that a borrower buy a particular enterprise or property would run a high risk of owing a fiduciary responsibility to that borrower, particularly if the borrower had dealt with the bank for a long time and trusted the officer.[38] In one case, a widow was advised by her banker to sell her ranch to repay the $200,000 she owed the bank—a bank she had dealt with for 24 years and had often received financial advice from. A bank vice-president who assisted her with the sale had entered a partnership agreement with the ranch purchasers a few days before the sale. The court held that the bank owed the widow a fiduciary duty which was breached when the vice-president failed to disclose his interest in the transaction.[39] As a result, the widow was allowed to rescind

---

[34] *Compare* Barrett v. Bank of America, 183 Cal. App. 3d 1362 (1986) (where the court found that a fiduciary duty existed between a bank and its borrower) with Bloomfield v. Nebraska State Bank, 465 N.W.2d 144 (Neb. 1991) (where the court refused to impose a fiduciary duty on the bank). *See also* Price v. Wells Fargo Bank, 213 Cal. App. 3d. 465 (Cal. App. 1989) (stating that Barret was inconsistent with both past authority and current trends in the law); see Cecil J. Hunt III, The Price of Trust: An Examination of Fiduciary Duty and the Lender-Borrower Relationship, 29 Wake Forest L. Rev. 719 (1994); *see also* Travel Serv. Network, Inc. v. Presidential Fin. Corp. of Mass., 959 F. Supp. 135, 144 (D. Conn. 1997) (Lender-debtor relationship generally does not give rise to fiduciary relationship under Massachusetts law); ADT Operations, Inc. v. Chase Manhattan Bank, 662 N.Y.S.2d 190, 195 (1997) (Fiduciary duty is not created between bank and its customer by mere communication of confidential information from customer to bank, which is a necessary incident of virtually any extension of credit). Compare Klein v. First Edina National Bank, 196 N.W.2d 619 (Minn. 1972) (fiduciary duty may exist in "special circumstances").

[35] Black's Law Dictionary 625 (6th ed. 1990).

[36] *See* Comment, *Recent Lender Liability Decisions in Nebraska: A Rational Approach,* 25 Creighton L. Rev. 631, 656 (1992); Comment, *The Fiduciary Controversy: Injection of Fiduciary Principles into the Bank-Depositor and Bank-Borrower Relationship,* 20 Loy. L.A. L. Rev. 795, 810 (1987).

[37] Kim v. Sumitomo Bank, 17 Cal. App. 4th 974 (Cal. App. 1993) (In California, a lender normally does not owe a fiduciary duty to the borrower. In this case, the court discusses and rejects the argument that lenders who effectively "control" the borrowers may cause a fiduciary duty to arise); *In re* King Street Investments, Inc., 219 B.R. 848 (B.A.P 9th Cir. 1998) (A mortgage broker engaged in constructive fraud in breach of his fiduciary duty to the lenders by making misrepresentations to the lenders).

[38] Rosse, Comment, *Recent Lender Liability Decisions in Nebraska: A Rational Approach,* 25 Creighton L. Rev. at 631, 661 (1992).

[39] Deist v. Wachholz, 678 P.2d 188 (Mont. 1984).

the sale.

One author has made the case that the lender becoming the borrower's fiduciary arises far more commonly than cases like the widow's would imply. Whenever the relationship transcends the bargained-for attributes of an arm's length contract and becomes one of trust as the borrower comes to rely on the lender, often to the lender's pecuniary benefit the lender is often characterized as a fiduciary. The borrower's claim to damages for breach of that relationship depends on whether the borrower can show "a causal link between the lender's breach of its corresponding fiduciary duty." If so, all that remains is to measure damage.[40]

However, the fiduciary characterization is more likely to materialize after a loan agreement is concluded than while lender and borrower are negotiating loan terms. The "contract" model usually describes accurately the loan origination relationship. Once the loan is entered, the lender then processes the loan, services it, and reviews requests for forbearance or extensions. During these stages of the lender-borrower relationship (processing, servicing, recasting), a fiduciary situation may evolve.

In comparison to whatever obligation banks owe their borrowers, do mortgage brokers owe their borrowers more? Mortgage brokers aren't lenders; rather, they are the borrower's agent and are paid to find the best lending source for the borrower. So courts have sometimes imposed an additional duty on mortgage brokers—not a fiduciary duty, but a duty of disclosure.

In one case, two pensioners used the services of a mortgage broker who aided them in obtaining a loan that required a $400 monthly payment when the borrowers' total monthly income, all from social security, was $500. The court gave this instruction to the jury:

> As a fiduciary, First Alliance Mortgage Company had a duty to disclose in writing and orally explain the material facts of the transaction to the [borrowers]. In addition, *it had a duty to counsel* and to draw to the attention of the Rogers' unfavorable material terms of the loans.[41]

The loan was for $28,500. The jury found for the plaintiffs in the sum of $1 million. On appeal, the case was remanded for retrial on the issue of punitive damages.[42]

Counsel for the borrowers had relied on *Wyatt v. Union Mortgage*[43] for the proposition that:

---

[40] Cecil J. Hunt III, The Price of Trust: An Examination of Fiduciary Duty and the Lender-Borrower Relationship, 29 Wake Forest L. Rev. 719, 726 (1994).

[41] The appellate opinion is unpublished. Wright v. First Alliance Mortgage Co., appealing Case No. SOC 75629.

[42] 598 P.2d 45 (Cal. 1979).

[43] Harris, *The Effect of Real Rates of Interest on Housing Prices*, 2 J. Real Est. Fin. & Econ. 47 (1989). There is a sizeable amount of finance literature on this theme. *See* Patric H.

. . . the mortgage broker's obligation to make disclosure extends beyond bare written disclosure of the terms of a transaction to duties of oral disclosure and counseling regarding the unfavorable material term of the loan. It does not mean that [the lender] had a duty to decide for the [borrowers] whether or not the loan should be taken.

What, exactly, is meant by a "duty of oral disclosure *and counseling*"? Is it enough for the mortgage broker to explain the terms of the loan or must he also offer advice to the borrower on whether the loan is a good one and whether the borrower will be able to repay, given her income and other obligations? Mortgage brokers hope disclosure will suffice. Borrowers sometimes expect more, especially when they rely on mortgage brokers or lenders for advice.

§ 104.03   The Rate of Interest and Monthly Payment Levels.

§ 104.03(a)   The Effect of Interest Rates on Potential Homebuyers.

Lenders and borrowers see interest rates from different angles. Interest is income to the lender; without it, there can be no profits. Repayment of principal alone would leave the lender in a hole since the lender's cost of doing business is roughly 2–4% per annum for each dollar of loans processed and serviced. ("Service" means to collect monthly payments, monitor defaults and, if necessary, foreclose.)

Most homebuyers are sensitive to interest rates. That is why home sales can be dramatically affected by interest rate levels. Nonetheless, even at times when rates reached historic highs (the late 1970s), home prices climbed rapidly and buyers just kept coming, while in 1990–91 with rates at historic lows—below 10%—home sales were sluggish.

Professor Jack C. Harris offers this explanation:

> Buyers off-set the rate of interest against their expectations of inflation, after-tax mortgage costs, and annual appreciation in home prices. Buyers who believe interest rates could get lower and house prices might fall still further stay out of the market even when rates are historically low. Buyer who believe interest rates driven by inflation are going to rise and house prices are also likely to go up, are likely to buy even when rate are at historic highs.[44]

So, although interest rates are important, their effect is also hedged by buyer expectations about both money and housing market futures.

Hendershott, *Real User Costs and the Demand for Single-Family Housing,* 2 Brookings Papers on Econ. Activity 401 (1980); Patric H. Hendershott, *Home Ownership and Real House Prices: Sources of Change, 1965–1985,* 7 Housing Fin. Rev. 1 (1988).

[44] Harris, *The Effect of Real Rates of Interest on Housing Prices,* 2 J. Real Est. Fin. & Econ. 47 (1989). There is a sizeable amount of finance literature on this theme. *See* Patric H. Hendershott, *Real User Costs and the Demand for Single-Family Housing,* 2 Brookings Papers on Econ. Activity 401 (1980); Patric H. Hendershott, *Home Ownership and Real House Prices: Sources of Change, 1965–1985,* 7 Housing Fin. Rev. 1 (1988).

§ 104.03(b)   "Affordability": The Factors That Determine Monthly Payment Levels.

Besides interest rates, borrowers are also concerned about "affordability," as measured by monthly payment levels. The borrower's ability to pay depends on the down payment and the monthly costs of the mortgage, not just the nominal after-tax rate of interest. The monthly payment is a composite of: (1) the amount borrowed, (2) the arrangements for the repayment of principal, (3) the maturity or length of the loan, and (4) the interest rate. Only a formula which accounts for all four variables can adequately show how the monthly payment is derived.

The monthly payment level will depend in part on how the principal amount borrowed is to be repaid. One option (now prohibited by statute in many states) allows the borrower to defer making any principal repayments until the end of the term. This was common in the U.S. until the Great Depression. Up to that time, lenders had allowed borrowers to refinance when the loan expired, but the credit crunch of the Depression left many lenders squeezed for cash. They couldn't afford to refinance, so borrowers defaulted in record numbers when lenders called in their loans. There was nowhere borrowers could turn for refinancing.

If the loan principal isn't amortized (paid off) during the term of the loan, the big final payment is called a balloon payment. A "balloon" is a lump-sum repayment of principal to make up for principal deferred during the life of the loan. The advantage of the balloon is that, to the extent the principal repayment is deferred, monthly payments are lower. The drawback is that the balloon, when it descends, can crush the borrower, causing foreclosure and loss of the property. Optimistic borrowers often expect to refinance their loans as balloons float their way. They are depending on money being available on terms they can afford in the distant future. They are also taking a big risk—predicting the weather is a lot easier than guessing which way the winds of mortgage finance will blow.

Nearly all home loans provide for self-amortization during the loan term so that all the principal will have been repaid at the end of the term.

> The more typical form of self-amortizing mortgage involves *level payment* debt service, that is, equal (usually monthly) debt service installments. Given this objective, the calculation of the (monthly) installment derives from a formula with three variables: original principal balance, the length of the loan, and the rate of interest. Tables that aid in the computation are readily available, for example, from banks and mortgage brokers.

> You should be aware of the changing relationship between interest and principal in the level payment mortgage; with each installment the interest component gets smaller while the amortization grows. Take, for example, a $50,000, 12 percent, 30-year mortgage, carrying monthly debt service of $514.50. Each installment of debt service goes first toward the payment of interest on the unpaid loan; whatever sum remains goes then into principal

reduction. Allocation of interest and principal for the first three months and the final month appears in Table 2-8.

Notice also, how slowly amortization proceeds via the level payment mortgage. Table 2-9 shows the percent of unpaid debt remaining at 5-year intervals on this hypothetical loan.

The usual alternative to a *level payment* self-amortizing mortgage is the so-called *constant amortization* (declining payment) loan, which one sees more often in investment situations. This method of amortization requires equal amounts of principal reduction in each installment. Again using the example of a $50,000, 12 percent, 30-year mortgage, the schedule of debt service appears in Table 2-10.

Over the thirty years, if the hypothetical mortgages go to term, the level payment mortgage will be far more costly. Why is that?[45]

TABLE 2-7

Monthly Level Payments (Dollars) to Amortize $1000
Various Amortization Periods and Interest Rates

Term in Years				
14.0	15.53	13.32	12.44	12.04	11.85
13.0	14.93	12.65	11.72	11.28	11.06
12.0	14.35	12.00	11.01	10.53	10.29
11.0	13.77	11.37	10.32	9.80	9.52
10.0	13.22	10.75	9.65	9.09	8.78
9.0	12.67	10.14	9.00	8.39	8.07
8.0	12.13	9.56	8.36	7.72	7.34

TABLE 2-8

1	$514.50	$500.00	$14.50	$49,985.50
2	514.50	499.86	14.64	49,970.86
3	514.60	499.71	14.79	49,956.07
—	—	—	—	—
—	—	—	—	—
360	514.50	5.00	509.50	0

TABLE 2-9

5	$48,830	97.66
10	46,710	93.42
15	42,855	85.71
20	35,845	71.69
25	23,120	46.24
30	0	0

---

[45] Allan Axelrod et al., Land Transfer and Finance 178–80 (3d ed. 1986).

TABLE 2-10

1	$638.88	$500.00	$138.88	$49,861.12
2	637.49	498.61	138.88	49,722.24
3	636.10	497.22	138.88	49,583.36
—	—	—	—	—
—	—	—	—	—
360	140.27	1.39	138.88	0

The combination of interest and principal repayment, stated as a percentage of the total loan obligation, is called the *constant*. For instance, if your interest rate is 10% but your monthly payments are 11.5% of the amount borrowed, your constant would be 11.5%. The extra 1.5% above the interest rate isn't an error on the part of your lender; it is explained by the fact that you are repaying some principal each month, in addition to interest. Most homebuyers are less concerned about the interest rate than the constant the total amount of the monthly payment.

If repayment of principal was the same each month and the interest rate was fixed, then monthly payments would decline to reflect the fact that as the principal was being progressively repaid, the interest on the unpaid balance was being reduced proportionately. With *constant amortization of principal* there is no uniform *constant* monthly payment. No two monthly payments are the same. Most first-time buyers would hate this because their biggest mortgage payment burdens would occur early in the borrowing cycle, when they can least afford them.

§ 104.03(c)   Fixed vs. Adjustable Rate Mortgages (F.R.M.s vs. A.R.M.s).

§ 104.03(c)(1)   The Rationale for A.R.M.s.

Conceptually, the nominal or contract rate of interest can be divided into two separate parts. One part is the "real" rate of interest. The other part accounts for the fact that the underlying value of the principal is subject to inflation. Without this second component of interest, the lender would get back in *real* dollars less than he loaned, even if the debt was fully repaid in *nominal* dollars.

Lenders making fixed-rate loans have no choice but to estimate what the inflation rate will be over the life of the loan, which can be especially difficult for long-term obligations. The lender must build the inflation assumption into the rate. If the lender has guessed too low a number, it loses. For long-term obligations, this loss can be significant. On the other hand, if the lender over-estimates the rate of inflation and interest rates fall below the contracted fixed rate, borrowers will prepay their loans in order to refinance at the lower rates

Complicating the fixed-rate lender's dilemma is the fact that they must compete in open markets where their competitors may have made guesses different from theirs about future inflation. Since most institutional lenders are highly leveraged and must pay their savers competitive yields, they don't enjoy the luxury of staying out of the market when they believe that current interest rates underestimate future inflation risks.

As a vivid example of the risks of making fixed-rate loans, consider what happened in the early 1980s. Fixed mortgage interest rates on long-term mortgage loans written in the 1960s and early 1970s were lower than the rates of inflation in the 1978–82 period. Borrowers were delighted to repay deflated debts, but lenders got caught in the squeeze between the rising costs of funds (rates on deposits) and low yielding, long-term fixed-rate mortgage loans. Many institutions have yet to recover.

In response, Congress enacted a law in 1982 authorizing all lenders to make residential mortgage loans at fluctuating interest rates.[46] These loans are called adjustable rate loans (A.R.M.s). An adjustable rate loan removes the lender's guesswork about inflation by tying the rate to an index which will ride with inflation. As inflation and market competition for savings push up the rates lenders must pay to keep deposits, mortgage borrowers with ARMs absorb these increases in the form of higher mortgage interest rates.

Borrowers also benefit from adjustable rate loans because they generally carry initial contract rates of interest well below those of equivalent fixed-rate loans. The lower starting rates of interest allow many first-time homebuyers to qualify for the loan they need, whereas they would have been priced out of the fixed-rate loan market. In addition, some lenders lure borrowers by offering special first-year rates on A.R.M.s well below current fixed-rate loans. These are called "teaser" rates. There has been some regulatory pressure to limit these teaser rates because they can fool inattentive borrowers into underestimating how high their payments will rise as soon as the "teaser" period ends, usually in six months or a year.[47] Also, some bank regulators are insisting that banks consider only the permanent rate, and not the "teaser" rate, when qualifying borrowers.

§ 104.03(c)(2)   Truth-in-Lending.

The Federal Consumer Protection Act of 1968 (Truth-in-Lending)[48] imposes special disclosure obligations on lenders originating ARMS, in

---

[46] 12 U.S.C. § 3801 *et seq.* The statute also allowed other alternative mortgage instruments, such as the shared appreciation mortgage, the reverse annuity mortgage and the graduated payment loan described in Chapter 15, *infra.*

[47] This has been done by secondary market makers who insist that monthly payments on the loans they purchase not rise by more than 7.5% in any year. *See* William N. Eskridge, Jr., *One Hundred Years of Ineptitude: The Need for Mortgage Rules Consonant with the Economic and Psychological Dynamics of the Home Sale and Loan Transaction,* 70 Va. L. Rev. 1083, 1171 n.276 (1984).

[48] 15 U.S.C. § 1601 *et seq.*

addition to the mandatory loan disclosures of amount financed, finance charges and the borrower's three-day right to cancel.[49] Implementation of Truth-in-Lending is entrusted to the Federal Reserve Board through a regulation known as Regulation Z, which was revised in 1980 by the Truth-in-Lending Simplification Act.

The error tolerance in finance charge disclosures has been increased by the Truth in Lending Amendments of 1995.[50] Home mortgage lenders will be protected from excessive penalties and liability for small technical and calculation errors in the finance charge and annual percentage rate disclosures. The disclosure on a home equity loan is treated as accurate if it does not vary from the actual finance charge by $100 (the prior limit was $10). A variance that equals ½ to 1 percent of the loan amount on a non-purchase money mortgage is allowed; up to 1 percent on refinance loans.

The impetus for this legislation was the 1994 Eleventh Circuit ruling in *Rodash v. AIB Mortgage Co.*, in which rescission of a home equity mortgage was upheld because the lender failed to "clearly and conspicuously disclose" the borrower's three-day right to cancel and erroneously included $226 in charges and tax in the amount financed instead of the finance charge.[51] After the *Rodash* ruling, numerous class action and individual lawsuits were subsequently filed by borrowers attempting to get out of their loan obligations on the basis of the TILA violations with rescission penalties. Retroactive lender relief is provided for *Rodas*-based class actions that were still pending certification on January 1, 1995, and individual actions filed after June 1, 1995.

---

[49] Beach v. Ocwen Fed. Bank, 523 U.S. 410 (U.S. 1998) (The borrowers obtained a load in 1986. In 1991 they stopped making mortgage payments, and in 1992 the lender commenced a foreclosure action. The borrowers hoped to rescind the mortgage based on the lender's violation fo the Truth in Lending Act (TILA). The Supreme Court held that the TILA allows borrowers to sue for damages within 1 year of closing, and allows borrowers to allege damages in defense even if the 1-year time period has expired. However, borrowers cannot ask for rescission fo the mortgage after the 3-year time period regardless of their procedural posture in the litigation. The 3-year time period is not a statue of limitation. The 3-year time limit on rescission is based on the very clear Congressional intent that borrowers should not be able to rescind based on TILA after 3 years have passed since closing.); Green Tree Acceptance, Inc. v. Anderson, 981 P.2d 804 (Okla. Ap. 1999) (The lender brought suit to foreclose a mortgage. The borrower claimed he did not understand the nature of the transaction and the legal implications of mortgaging his house. Borrowers was allowed to counter-claim seeking damages under the Truth in Lending Act and asserting that he was never told of his rights to rescind); Berkeley Federal Bank & Trust v. Siegel, 669 N.Y.S.2d 334 (N. Y. App. Div 1998) (The lender commenced foreclosure proceedings and the borrower asserted TILA and demanded rescission. The court determined that the foreclosure proceeding could continue, if the borrower failed to tender the loan principal in a timely manner); *Truth in Lending-Recession, Consumer Remedies and Creditor Defenses in closed-End Transactions*, 19 U. Tol. L. Rev. 491, (1988).

[50] 15 U.S.C. § 1605(F).

[51] 16 F.3d 1142.

The Home Ownership and Equity Protection Act of 1994 has expanded Truth-in-Lending to include high-interest "home improvement and remodeling" loans.[52] Additional disclosure requirements and restrictions have been added for "high-rate" home equity and mortgage refinance loans, whether used for home improvement or general purposes, that are secured by a principal dwelling. Home equity lines of credit and principal residence purchase loans are exempt.

A loan is "high rate" if the APR exceeds the yield on Treasury securities by more than 10% or the borrower's total points and fees exceed the greater of 8% of the loan or $400.[53] Credit cannot be extended without a determination of the borrower's ability to repay the loan.[54] Negative amortization is prohibited.[55] Loans of five years or less must be fully amortized because balloon payments are not allowed.[56] Prepayment penalties are generally prohibited and the rate of interest after default may not be increased.[57]

§ 104.03(c)(3)   Computing the Rate; Choosing the Index.

Adjustable rate obligations are computed by adding the indexed rate, say, the six-month or one-year Treasury bill, to a margin, between 2–3% usually. The combined total is the interest rate the borrower pays. (Index + margin = interest rate.)[58]

---

[52] 12 C.F.R. 226.32(a).

[53] 12 C.F.R. 226.32(a).

[54] 15 U.S.C. § 1639(h).

[55] 15 U.S.C. § 1639(f).

[56] 15 U.S.C. § 1639(e).

[57] 15 U.S.C. § 1639(c), (d).

[58] Some researchers have suggested that the margin depends on how tight the caps are on the loan, the length of the rate adjustment frequency, the type of index used, the contract rate, the loan size, the up-front fees, and the call for prepayment and other options (*e.g.,* "due-on-sale" features). *See, e.g.,* Jarjisu Sa-aadu & Clemon F. Sirmans, *The Pricing of Adjustable Rate Mortgage Contracts,* 2 J. Real Est. Fin. & Econ. 253 (1989); Bastin v. First Indiana Bank, 694 N.E.2d 740 (Ind. App. 1998) (Borrower had taken an adjustable rate mortgage and sued the lender claiming that the lender had improperly calculated the interest rate. The rate was to be based on the average rate of 6 month U.S. Treasury bills and could be adjusted every 6 months. The lender initially obtained the rate information from the Federal Reserve Board statistical report and later began obtaining the rates from the Wall Street Journal. The borrower argued that in a period of increasing rates, the one week timing difference between the publication of the rates from the 2 sources hurt the borrower. The court held that the lender was required to use the Federal Reserve Board statistical report); Hubbard v. Fidelity Federal Bank, 91 F.3d 75 (9th Cir. 1996) (The lender was supposed to send notice of the annual payment adjustment between 30 and 45 days before the payment adjustment took place. The lender began to send the notices 65 days before the change and the borrower alleged that the lender was therefore improperly calculating the interest rate. The borrowers were allowed a breach of contract claim, but it was limited by the statute of limitations);

The chosen index must be regularly published on a recognized financial instrument. The borrower's interest rate is revised from time to time as the chosen index moves up or down with inflation. Since the index chosen will never be zero and may itself incorporate a premium above the rate of inflation, the lender receives that inflation-proof "kicker" as an additional "real" return above the margin.

There are several indexes to which variable rates are keyed. They don't move identically, a factor borrowers rarely consider, but should in choosing a loan.[59]

Each lender has its favorite index. Some lenders feel comfortable with indexes based on the cost of funds from depositors, the Office of Thrift Supervision (O.T.S.)[60] or the Federal Reserve System. Because these indices reflect the lenders' cost of funds, they offer the lender protection against a mismatch between income and expenses.

Many key institutional investors care only about the spread between mortgage yields and the other investments available to them measured against U.S. Treasury obligations. So "T-bill" rates are also sometimes used as the base rate against which "adjustables" are played. Short-term (three and six months) "T-bill" rates are more volatile than one year "T-bill" rates, and all "T-bill" rates are more volatile than the "cost of funds" indices.

As capital flows have become global, an international measure, L.I.B.O.R., is frequently seen in U.S. mortgages. L.I.B.O.R. stands for the London Interbank Offered Rates.[61]

> The push for L.I.B.O.R. mortgages comes mainly from foreign banks and thrifts that buy mortgages in bulk. L L.I.B.O.R. is the benchmark interest rate at which many of these institutions raise money, so they are

---

Circle Mortg. Corp. v. Kline, 645 So.2d 75 (Fla. Dist. Ct. App. 1994) (The borrower claimed diminution in the value of his loan caused by the lender's breach in failing to execute new documents that stated the interest rate for his adjustable rate mortgage. The court held that the damages would be too speculative considering the borrower had not sold his home, and there was evidence that the loan wouldn't lose much value if it were refinanced).

[59] Several articles have been written on how consumers can compare fixed vs. adjustable rates. James Alm & James R. Follain, *Consumer Demand for Adjustable Rate Mortgages,* 6 Housing Fin. Rev. 1 (1987); Michael R. Asay, *Pricing and Analysis of Adjustable Rate Mortgages,* 45 Mortgage Banking 61 (Dec. 1984); Upinder S. Dhillon et al., *Choosing Between Fixed and Adjustable Rate Mortgages,* 19 J. Money, Credit and Banking 260 (1987); Statman, *Fixed Rate or Index-Linked Mortgages from the Borrower's Point of View: A Note,* 17 J. Fin. & Quantitative Analysis 451 (1982).

[60] The O.T.S. has taken the place of the Federal Home Loan Bank Boards, and maintains Federal Home Loan A.R.M. (Adjustable Rate Mortgage) Indexes, including the widely used 11th O.T.S. (formerly F.H.L.B.) index.

[61] This index is the average of interbank offered rates for dollar deposits in the London market based on quotations at five major banks.

eager to have L.I.B.O.R.-linked assets on the other side of the balance sheets, too.[62]

While "T-bill" rates are sometimes vulnerable to domestic policy manipulation, L.I.B.O.R. is relatively free of government interference because the U.K. keeps its hands off private bank transactions in non-U.K. currency.

A.R.M.s must state an adjustment period between one rate change and the next. A loan with an annual adjustment is called a one-year A.R.M. Lenders using the one-year Treasury bill rate as an index usually adjust the interest rate annually.

Borrowers have a harder time figuring out their liability on adjustable-rate loans than they do on fixed-rate loans. So do lenders.

> Federal regulators have growing concerns that savings and loans may be erroneously overcharging many holders of adjustable-rate mortgages and have asked all thrifts to check their method of calculating the payments.

> Private consultants said the over-charges in most cases aren't huge in the range of $500 to $1,000 over the life of the loan but one consultant estimated in testimony on Capitol Hill that the total amount thrifts owe customers could be $8 billion to $15 billion.[63]

§ 104.03(d)   "Caps" on Adjustables.

At first, borrowers weren't receptive to adjustable rates because they could envision those indexes taking off and leaving them in the dust, with no way to keep up their monthly payments. The challenge of luring borrowers into accepting adjustable rate mortgages was met by placing "caps" or limits on how variable the rate would be.[64] The use of "caps" is so widespread now that an American Bar Association committee guide to homebuying advises: "If an adjustable rate mortgage does not contain rate caps, you should not accept that mortgage."[65]

---

[62] Anders, *U.S. Lenders Tie Mortgages to London Interbank Rate,* Wall St. J., Aug. 3, 1988, at B1.

[63] Duke, *Adjustable-Rate Mortgage Errors Spark Concerns,* Wall St. J., Oct. 26, 1990, at A16.

[64] Jan K. Brueckner, *The Pricing of Interest Rate Caps and Consumer Choice in the Market for Adjustable-Rate Mortgages,* 5 Housing Fin. Rev. 119 (1986); Christopher L. Peterson, *Truth, Understanding, and High-Cost Consumer Credit: The Historical Context of the Truth in Lending Act,* 55 Fla. L. Rev. 807 (2003).

[65] A.B.A. Standing Comm. on Lawyers' Title Guaranty Funds, Buying or Selling Your Home 14 (1991); Preston v. First Bank of Marietta, 473 N.E.2d 1210 (Ohio App. 1983) (Borrowers brought suit against their lender, challenging the lender's ability to raise interest rates according to the variable rate mortgage agreement. The court held for the borrowers, determining that the terms of the variable rate mortgage were too vague to be valid. The agreement put no limits on the interest rate or the amount the borrowers must pay. The lenders could enforce an interest rate increase, but the borrowers could not enforce an interest rate decrease); *but see* Murello Constr. Co. v. Citizens Home Sav. Co., 505 N.E.2d 637 (Ohio

The three types of adjustable rate caps are: (1) payment, (2) annual, and (3) life-of-loan. "Annual" and "life-of-loan" caps are usually ceilings on the chargeable rate of interest. The borrower pays the full allowable rate up to the cap limit. The "payment" cap pertains to the combined principal and interest due, assuring the concerned borrower that next month's payment will never exceed this month's by more than a fixed percentage.

Annual caps restrict the amount by which the *interest* rate levied in any subsequent year can exceed the *rate* that existed in the first (or base) year. A 2-point cap means that if the rate in year one was 9%, the rate in the following year can't be greater than 11%, even if the underlying index increased by more than 2%. The borrower under an annual cap can't be liable for a rate greater than what the lender is able to charge in that year. The unpaid obligation is just carried forward to future years. For instance, if the index actually rises by 3 points to 12% in year two, the 3rd point can be carried forward into the next year in a loan with a 2-point annual cap.

Anticipating the possibility that cumulative liability under annual caps could eventually drive rates beyond the borrower's reach, life-of-loan caps guarantee that the interest rate won't ever surpass a certain figure. A 5% life-of-loan cap on a loan that began at 10% ensures that the interest rate will never exceed 15%.

A loan with a cap on monthly payments but no life-of-loan or annual cap on interest can result in "negative amortization." "Negative amortization" means that the borrower's debt may be growing over time, not shrinking, as it would with each payment on a fixed-rate loan.

The following provides an example of negative amortization: Suppose you take out a 30-year, $150,000 ARM with a starting rate of 9% and a payment cap of 7.5%. Your monthly payments for principal and interest would start at about $1,207.

One year later, rates have increased to 13%, which would make the monthly amount due about $1,664. But your payment cap of 7.5% means that your monthly payment can't be more than $1,298, which is $366 short of the amount due.

What happens to this deficiency? Even though you don't have to pay it now, don't think that you are getting off easy. The lender simply adds it to the outstanding balance of your loan, meaning that you'd owe *more* money, not less, with each passing month.

Negative amortization isn't too bad if your property value is increasing quickly or if you are getting big pay increases. In these cases, your equity is

App. 1985) (variable rate loans are valid despite the lack of an ascertainable standard for computing the interest payments, at least in commercial settings. The court distinguished this case from Preston by stating that the borrowers in Preston were "unsophisticated consumers," whereas the borrowers in this case were "astute businessmen and their attorneys").

growing at a much faster rate than your loan balance is rising. Moreover, there are some benefits to loans that have the potential of negative amortization.

Most of these loans have lower introductory rates that make mortgages easier to get. The borrower's income can support more debt because the beginning payments will be relatively low. Also, most lenders allow their borrowers to pay a little bit extra each month to avoid negative amortization. Therefore, these loans offer more flexibility than fixed-rate loans, which require a fixed monthly payment.[66]

Of course, the very life-of-loan or annual interest cap that assures borrowers that they aren't getting in over their heads also defines the boundary above which the lender is no longer able to match its cost of deposits with the interest charged to borrowers.

Still, lenders are at least partially benefitted by "caps" on the borrower's obligations. When rates are adjusted upward with no limits, borrowers tend to default if their personal incomes don't track interest rates very well. Defaults mean losses to the lender, not only of interest, but sometimes of principal as well. So, while a "cap" does leave the lender open to the risk of wild interest rate fluctuations above the cap, it also helps lenders avoid the deadly default rates that "uncapped" loans could trigger. Even with caps, defaults on adjustable rate loans are higher than on fixed-rate loans.[67]

Choosing between Fixed and Adjustable-rate Mortgages

Lower initial rates	Borrower may be financially strapped when the full rate kicks in
If rates decline, the borrower's goes down automatically without refinancing	If interest rates arise, A.R.M. rates go up too
A.R.M.s are easier to assume whereas fixed-rate loans are generally not assumable	Traditionally, home buyers don't want A.R.M.s
Loan points and fees are usually lower than for fixed-rate loans	Points and fees are deductible in the year they are paid by homebuyer
Some A.R.M.s allow conversion to fixed rates sometime in the future	Some fixed-rate loans allow later conversion to an A.R.M.

---

[66] Myers, *Negative-Amortization Stirs Unease*, L.A. Times, Oct. 21, 1990, at K8.

[67] Jarjisu Sa-aadu, *Legal Restrictions, Credit Allocation and Default Risk under Fixed and Adjustable Rate Mortgages*, 7 Housing Fin. Rev. 225 (1988). The author studied defaults for 1979–1985 at First Federal Savings and Loan Association, Davenport, Iowa. Among his conclusions: A.R.M. defaults are the same regardless of the index used, and "the practice of capping may not be effective in reducing default risk and/or the reduction achieved through capping may not completely offset the risk of negative amortization engendered by capping." *Id.* at 245.

"Caps" limit how much loan payments can increase in any year or over the life of the loan

Caps can lead to negative amortization

§ 104.03(e)   Note Fixed for Five Years, Adjustable Thereafter.

Some loan programs combine fixed and variable rates in different combinations. In the loan excerpted below, the rate is fixed for the first five years and then switches to an adjustable rate with caps.

1. BORROWER'S PROMISE TO PAY

In return for a loan that I have received, I promise to pay U.S. $558,400.00, plus interest, to the order of the Lender. The Lender is California Federal Bank, a Federal Savings Bank.

I understand that the Lender may transfer this Note. The Lender or anyone who takes this Note by transfer and who is entitled to receive payments under this Note is called the "Note Holder."

2. INTEREST

Interest shall be charged on unpaid principal beginning on the date I receive principal and continuing until the full amount of principal has been paid. I will pay interest initially at a yearly interest rate of 10.250%. The interest rate I pay shall be changed in accordance with Section 4 of this Note.[68]

The interest rate required by Section 2 and Section 4 of this Note is the rate I will pay both before and after any default described in Section 8.2 of this Note.

3. PAYMENTS

    3.1 Time and Place of Payments

I will pay principal and interest by making payments every month.

I will make my monthly payments on the first day of each month beginning on November 01, 1990. I will make these payments every month until I have paid all of the principal and interest and any other charges described below that I may owe under this Note. My monthly payments shall be applied first to interest and other charges then due and the remainder to principal. If, on October 01, 2020, I still owe amounts under this Note, I will pay those amounts in full on that date, which is called the "Maturity Date."

I will make monthly payments at Lender's principal office, any of Lender's branches, or at any other location that the Note Holder may designate.

    3.2 Initial Amount of My Monthly Payments

The initial amount of each of my monthly payments shall be U.S. $5,003.84. This amount may change.

4. INTEREST RATE CHANGES

---

[68] *See* Harris v. Coles, 60 S.W.3d 848 (Tenn. App. 2001) (maker of promissory note is required to pay only simple interest).

4.1 Change Dates

My interest rate may change on the first day of October, 1995, and on the first day of the month every 1 month(s) thereafter. Each date on which my interest rate could change is called a "Change Date."

4.2 The Index

Any changes of the interest shall be based upon an index. The "Index" is

"Monthly weighted average cost of funds for the 11th District Savings Institutions," as computed monthly by the Federal Home Loan Bank of San Francisco and made available in their information bulletin "Monthly Weighted Average Cost of Funds for the 11th District Savings & Loans."

The Index figure which is used to calculate the interest rate is called the "Index Value." If the Index is no longer available, the Note Holder will choose a new index that is based upon comparable information. The Note Holder will give me notice of this choice.

4.3 Calculation of Interest Rate Changes

On or before each Change Date, the Note Holder will calculate my new interest by adding 2.500% to the most recent Index Value available as of the date 15 days before the Change Date. The Note Holder will then round the result of this addition to the nearest one-eighth of one percentage point (0.125%). Subject to the limits stated in Section 4.4 of this Note, this rounded amount shall be my new interest rate until the next Change Date.

4.4 Limitations on Interest Rate Changes

THE SECTIONS BELOW WHICH APPLY TO MY LOAN ARE: (C), (D).

(c) My interest rate shall never be greater than 13.950% as long as I do not sell or transfer the property which is subject to the Security Instrument described in Section 12. After any sale or transfer of that property, the interest rate shall never be greater than 13.950% or an interest rate that is more than 3.7000% greater than the interest rate at the time of such sale or transfer (whichever is higher).

(d) In no event shall my interest rate be less than 7.0000%.

5. MONTHLY PAYMENT CHANGES

THE SECTIONS BELOW WHICH APPLY TO MY LOAN ARE:

5.1, 5.2, 5.3, 5.4.

5.1 Payment Change Dates

My monthly payment may change beginning on the first day of November, 1995, and on that day every 12 month(s) thereafter. Each of these dates is called a "Payment Change Date." I will pay the amount of my new monthly payment each month beginning on each Payment Change Date.

5.2 Calculation of Monthly Payment Changes

Before each Payment Change Date, the Note Holder will calculate the amount of the monthly payment that would be sufficient to repay the unpaid principal that I am expected to owe at the Payment Change Date in full on the maturity date in substantially equal installments at the interest rate effective during the month preceding the Payment Change Date. The result of this calculation is called the "Full Payment." Unless Section 5.3 below requires me to pay a different amount, my new monthly payment will be in the amount of the Full Payment.

5.3 Limitations on Monthly Payment Changes

Any increase or decrease in my monthly payment, calculated as described in Section 5.2 of this Note, shall be limited to an amount that is no more than 7.5000% of the amount of my monthly payment immediately before such increase or decrease, except on the 6th Payment Change Date and on each succeeding 5th Payment Change Date thereafter. On those Change Dates, I will begin paying the Full Payment as my monthly payment until my monthly payment changes again. I also will begin paying the Full Payment as my monthly payment on the final Payment Change Date.

5.4 Additions to My Unpaid Principal

My monthly payment, as required by this Section 5, could be less than the amount of the interest portion of the Full Payment. If so, each month that my monthly payment is less than the interest portion, the Note Holder will subtract the amount of my monthly payment from the amount of the interest portion and will add the difference to my unpaid principal. The Note Holder also will add on the amount of this difference to my unpaid principal each month. The interest rate on the interest added to principal will be the rate required by Section 4 of the Note.

7. EXTENSION AND DECREASE OF TERM

If at any Change Date my monthly payment is to be increased, the notice I receive will show what extension of the term of this Note, if any, would result in Amortization at a monthly payment substantially the same as that I am then paying. I will have an option to extend the term as shown in that notice. I may exercise that option by giving notice to the Note Holder of my intent to do so, on a form which Note Holder provides, within the time the Note Holder states in the Notice. In no event, however, shall the total term of this Note exceed 480 months. At any time that I have extended the term of this Note, my monthly payment will not be decreased. On any Change Date on which my payment amount is subject to change, if the calculation of a monthly payment described in Section 5 of this Note would result in a decrease in my monthly payment, the Note Holder will reduce the term of this Note to the term at which the unchanged monthly payment would result in Amortization. When my monthly payment is an amount which would result in Amortization over a term ending at the Maturity Date, future monthly payments will be changed as described in Section 5 of this Note.

9. BORROWER'S RIGHT TO PREPAY

I have the right to make payments of principal at any time before they are due. A payment of principal only is known as "Prepayment." When I make a Prepayment, I will tell the Note Holder in writing that I am doing so. I may make a full Prepayment or Partial Prepayments without paying any

Prepayment charge. The Note Holder will use all of my Prepayments to reduce the amount of principal that I owe under this Note. If I make a partial Prepayment, there will be no changes in the due dates or in the amount of my monthly payment unless the Note Holder agrees in writing to those changes. My partial Prepayment may reduce the amount of my monthly payments after the first monthly payment change in accordance with Section 5.1 of this Note following my partial Prepayment. However, any reduction due to my partial Prepayment may be offset by an interest rate increase.

THIS NOTE CONTAINS PROVISIONS FOR INTEREST RATE CHANGES WITHOUT CORRESPONDING PAYMENT CHANGES AND MAY ALLOW DEFERRED INTEREST TO BE ADDED TO MY UNPAID PRINCIPAL. THE PRINCIPAL AMOUNT I MUST REPAY COULD BE GREATER THAN THE AMOUNT ORIGINALLY BOR-ROWED. THIS IS SOMETIMES CALLED "NEGATIVE AMORTIZA-TION."

§ 104.03(f) Usury Laws.

§ 104.03(f)(1) History and Policy.

Legal limits on the amount of interest a lender may charge are on the statute books in all states but two, Massachusetts and New Hampshire. The antecedents of these laws, repugnant to free market principles, can be traced to the Old Testament,[69] the New Testament (St. Luke 6:35),[70] the writings of Plato and Aristotle, ancient Roman law (Tacitus, The Annals, Book VI, ch. 16), and Eighteenth Century English Law (12 Annals 2, ch. 16 (1713)).

> In the course of its history the concept of usury has covered a variety of meanings. Originally it referred to all returns derived from the lending of capital and carried no moral opprobrium. With the growing condemnation of the financial abuses of the moneylenders the term came to be confined to credit transactions carrying excessive charges and thus acquired a distinct ethical connotation. In the Middle Ages all direct payments for loans were deemed usurious and condemned as sinful. In modern times the term was again narrowed down and now it refers only to excessive loan charges, while the payment of moderate rates is covered by the more neutral term interest. . ..

> The ethical nature of the concept of usury renders it impossible to formulate permanent and definite criteria of what constitutes a usurious transaction. As long as freedom of contract remains the corner stone of economic organization, it is not the economist but the legislator who must decide at what point a voluntary economic transaction constitutes an abuse

---

[69] *Deuteronomy* 23:19: "Thou shalt not lend upon usury to thy brother. . .."; 23:20: "Unto a stranger thou mayest lend upon usury. . .." (King James).

[70] "But love your enemies, and do good, and lend, expecting nothing in return. . .." (New American Standard).

of economic freedom and thus an act of usury.[71]

Like all forms of price control, usury laws have their defenders who want to shield hapless consumers from overreaching lenders, and critics who argue that these laws force the least creditworthy borrowers into the arms of the most lawless lenders. In a classic analysis of U.S. usury laws, Professor Marion Benfield concluded that usury laws, as applied to home mortgage loans, only worked to disadvantage consumers and housing producers.[72] When market interest rates, buoyed by inflation, floated above usury ceilings, mortgage lenders either withdrew, risked making loans at illegal rates, or invented ways around the usury limits that courts would not interfere with. These evasive devices always cost borrowers a premium to cover the transaction cost.[73]

§ 104.03(f)(2)   An Example of a Usury Law.

As a specific example, here is a California usury law enacted by popular initiative in 1919, and amended by voter initiative in 1976.[74]

CALIFORNIA CONSTITUTION, ARTICLE XV. USURY

§ 1.   Interest rates

Section 1. The rate of interest upon the loan or forbearance of any money, goods, or things in action, or on accounts after demand, shall be 7 percent per annum but it shall be competent for the parties to any loan or forbearance of any money, goods or things in action to contract in writing for a rate of interest:

(1) For any loan or forbearance of any money, goods, or

---

[71] Pascal Salin, *Usury,* 15 Encyclopedia of the Social Sciences, 193–94 (Edwin Robert Anderson Seligman ed. 1934). *See generally* Guyora Binder & Robert Weisberg, *Cultural Criticism of Law*, 49 Stan. L. Rev. 1149, 120106 (1997); Cindy T. Beal, Note & Comment, *Recent Changes in the Texas Usury Statutes—Do They Affect Common Law Usury Claims?* 3 Tex. Wesleyan L. Rev. 421, 424 (1997).

[72] Marion Benfield, *Money, Mortgages, and Migraine—The Usury Headache,* 19 Case W. Res. L. Rev. 819 (1968). Professor Benfield did see great advantages, however, in legislation which limited interest rates on small loans to consumers. "The enactment of small loan laws substantially improved the position of the consumer-borrower of small sums by supplanting low usury rates which provided a reasonable profit for credit suppliers. Social science researchers have made it clear that such laws do lower interest rates to consumers and that, in their absence, in more recent times, rates have been five or six times higher than the small loan rates." *Id.* at 840 n.108. *See also* Richard Lewis Peterson & Gregory, A. Falls, Impact of a Ten Percent Usury Ceiling: Empirical Evidence (Credit Research Center, Purdue Univ. 1981) (Credit was more available to low income borrowers in Little Rock, Arkansas, with a 10% usury ceiling, than in most states permitting higher rates)

[73] *Id.*

[74] *See* Section 104.03(f)(3) *below.*

things in action, if the money, goods, or things in action are for use primarily for personal, family, or household purposes, at a rate not exceeding 10 percent per annum; provided, however, that any loan or forbearance of any money, goods or things in action the proceeds of which are used primarily for the purchase, construction or improvement of real property shall not be deemed to be a use primarily for personal, family or household purposes; or

(2) For any loan or forbearance of any money, goods, or things in action for any use other than specified in paragraph (1), at a rate not exceeding the higher of (a) 10 percent per annum or (b) 5 percent per annum plus the rate prevailing on the 25th day of the month preceding the earlier of (i) the date of execution of the contract to make the loan or forbearance, or (ii) the date of making the loan or forbearance established by the Federal Reserve Bank of San Francisco on advances to member banks under Sections 13 and 13a of the Federal Reserve Act as now in effect or hereafter from time to time amended (or if there is no such single determinable rate of advances, the closest counterpart of such rate as shall be designated by the Superintendent of Banks of the State of California unless some other person or agency is delegated such authority by the Legislature).

No person, association, copartnership or corporation shall by charging any fee, bonus, commission, discount or other compensation receive from a borrower more than the interest authorized by this section upon any loan or forbearance of any money, goods or things in action.

However, none of the above restrictions shall apply to any obligations of, loans made by, or forbearances of, any building and loan association . . . or to any corporation . . . or any credit unions . . . or any duly licensed pawnbroker or personal property broker, or any loans made or arranged by any person licensed as a real estate broker by the State of California and secured in whole or in part by liens on real property, or any bank . . . or any nonprofit cooperative association . . . or credit from any federal intermediate credit bank . . . or to any successor in interest to any loan or forebearance exempted under this article. . . .. The Legislature may from time to time prescribe the maximum rate per annum of, or provide for the supervision, or the filing of a schedule of, or in any manner fix, regulate or limit, the fees, bonuses, commissions, discounts or other compensation which all or any of the said exempted classes of persons may charge or receive from a borrower in connection with any loan or forbearance of any money, goods or things in action.

The rate of interest upon a judgment rendered in any court of this state shall be set by the Legislature at not more than 10 percent per annum. Such rate may be variable and based upon interest rates charged by federal agencies or economic indicators, or both.

In the absence of the setting of such rate by the Legislature, the rate of interest on any judgment rendered in any court of the state shall be 7 percent per annum.

The provisions of this section shall supersede all provisions of this Constitution and laws enacted thereunder in conflict therewith.

§ 104.03(f)(3)   The Federal Preemption of State Usury Laws.

Federal law, namely the Depository Institutions Deregulation and Monetary Control Act of 1980,[75] preempts state usury laws, at first only as to certain loans those secured by first liens on residential real estate, and made by certain "federally related" lenders. It was later expanded to cover state-chartered residential lenders and most residential mortgages.[76] There is

---

[75] 12 U.S.C. § 1735-5.

[76] 12 U.S.C. § 1735-5. The primary usury preemption was contained in the Alternative Mortgage Transactions Parity Act, 12 U.S.C. § 3801 et seq., and now applies to any loan that is: (1) Secured by residential real property, stock in a residential housing corporation, or a first lien on a manufactured home; and (2) *Made by a lender insured or* regulated by an agency of the federal government, approved by the Secretary of Housing and Urban Development for participation in a mortgage insurance program under the National Housing Act, or who is an individual financing the sale or exchange of the individual's principal residence [emphasis added]; or (3) Made, insured, guaranteed, supplemented, or assisted in any way by an officer or agency of the federal government or under or in connection with a housing, urban development or related program administered by a federal officer or agency; or (4) Eligible for purchase by the Federal National Mortgage Association, the Government National Mortgage Association, or the Federal Home Loan Mortgage Corporation or is from a financial institution from which it could be purchased by the Federal Home Loan Mortgage Corporation; or (5) Made by a creditor who makes or invests in residential loans including loans or credit sales secured by first liens on manufactured homes, aggregating more than $1,000,000 per year; or (6) Made by any creditor who sells manufactured homes financed by loans or credit sales, if the creditor has an arrangement to sell or does sell the loans or credit sales to another lender, institution, or creditor that does not make or invest in residential real estate loans or credit sales secured by first liens on manufactured homes aggregating more than $1,000,000 per year. Many states have adopted usury laws governing retail installment

no requirement that the borrower live in the house or that the funds be used to purchase it.

The law was a comprehensive banking regulation overhaul. It permitted banks to pay interest on checking accounts and liberalized savings association investment rules. Before that, regulated lenders were only allowed to pay interest on time or savings accounts. This had given savings associations an edge in competing with banks for savings dollars. Also, other intermediaries were offering money-market-based investments to savers, threatening both banks and savings associations with liquidity problems.

Congress saw that banks and S.& L.s (now called savings banks) would have to pay savers more in order to retain deposits, and could do so only if their revenues from interest charges rose to cover the increased cost of deposits. State usury ceilings would break the chain of rising interest rates necessitated by the then-rampant inflation. Hence, the Act. It was aimed at helping savings associations and banks survive in the early 1980s when double-digit inflation was driving many of them into the ground.

Excluded from the federal usury preemption are second mortgages, commercial loans[77] (other than those secured by first liens on residential real estate) and loans made by institutions not defined in the act as "federally related." All commercial and savings banks and credit unions insured by the federal government are "federally related." Pension funds, non-banking corporations, and individual lenders are not.

The federal preemption only protects lenders on loans made after December 22, 1979. Moreover, states had the option of reinstating their usury laws, by statute or vote of the people, if they did so within 3 years. Fifteen states and Puerto Rico did.[78] Twelve of these jurisdictions permit any rate of interest as long as it is disclosed.[79]

---

sales, small loans, second mortgages, and pawnbrokers. *See* National Consumer Law Center, Usury and Consumer Credit Regulation (1987 & Supp.) 37. *See also* Varr v. Olimpia, 53 Cal. Rptr. 2d 106 (1996).

[77] *In re* Stipetich, 294 B.R. 635 (W.D. Pa. 2003) (the investment loan constituted a commercial loan because it was used for an investment in a commercial enterprise and therefore was excludable from Maryland's usury laws.

[78] The fifteen states are Alaska, Colorado, Georgia, Idaho, Iowa, Kansas, Maine, Massachusetts, Minnesota, Nebraska, Nevada, North Carolina, South Carolina, South Dakota, and Wisconsin. *See* William N. Eskridge, Jr., *One Hundred Years of Ineptitude: The Need for Mortgage Rules Consonant with the Economic and Psychological Dynamics of the Home Sale and Loan Transaction,* 70 Va. L. Rev. 1083, 1109 n.92 (1984). California didn't opt to retain its usury law over the federal preemption. Thus, in California the buyer of a shopping center or office building would be protected under the California usury law, but a homebuyer would not be, since the federal statute preempts the state usury law on residential, but not commercial transactions.

[79] Charles L. Edson & Barry G. Jacobs, Secondary Mortgage Market Guide, App. C, at 10–15 n.7 (1991).

§ 104.03(f)(4)   The Four Elements Necessary to Establish Usury Under State Law.

For a loan to be usurious, four elements must be present. It must be: (a) a loan; (b) made above the legal interest limit; (c) with intent to violate the law; (d) of funds absolutely, not contingently repayable.

§ 104.03(f)(4)(i)   What Is a Loan: Distinguishing "Sales" from "Loans."

Usury laws limit the rate of interest on loans, but these laws don't attempt to set limits on rents or sales prices. This tempts lenders desiring rates of interest above the usury ceiling to avoid labelling the loan as a loan. Sometimes the lender "buys" the security property from the borrower, allows the borrower to lease it back and at the end of the lease term to exercise an option to repurchase the property. The lease payments and option price substitute for interest. The "lender" pegs the option at a price so far below the property's true value, the "borrower" is sure to exercise it.

The Equitable Mortgage. Leases and contracts are forms often used to disguise what are really secured loans in order to evade usury laws because usury laws don't apply to sales prices or rents. Just because the parties to a transaction call their deal a sale and leaseback, or a sale with a lease and option to purchase, doesn't mean that courts are bound to that characterization. Courts can be persuaded to reclassify a transaction and call it a mortgage when they have been convinced it was really a security interest disguised as something else.

When courts re-classify a transaction as a mortgage loan, the resulting legal estate or interest is called an *equitable* mortgage. An equitable mortgage is a transaction in some other form that one of the parties can persuade a court to recast as if it had been a mortgage all along.

> A mortgage can be equitable because either the form of transfer does not create a lien—rather, it creates less (as, for example, where a contract of sale is executed) or creates more (as, for example, where a deed, absolute on its fee, is used)—or because the alleged mortgagor has himself only an equitable interest in the property.[80]

The Typical Loan Disguised as a Sale Transaction. Many attempts to evade usury laws by disguising loans as sales take this form: the owner, who is really the borrower, sells property worth $75,000 to the lender at a discounted price of $50,000. The owner/borrower retains the right to repurchase the property at the end of one year for $70,000. Courts have had little trouble piercing these veiled sales to unfurl the underlying loan. In effect, the "lender" has loaned the owner $50,000, secured by property worth

---

[80] D. Barlow Burke, Jr., Real Estate Transactions 222 (1993).

$75,000, for an interest charge of $20,000 (70,000—50,000).[81]

There is a special irony in the loan-disguised-as-a-sale. Many early mortgage loans took this form. The borrower deeded property to the lender on the condition that the borrower could regain title by repaying the debt on its due date. If a borrower was even a day late, he lost the security property. It was precisely to prevent such forfeitures of title that English equity courts gave borrowers time extensions before allowing lenders to close out (foreclose) the borrower's title. The right to pay late was called the "equity" of redemption because it was courts of equity which first bestowed this redemption right on borrowers. So the loan-disguised-as-a-sale has an ancient lineage. Originally deployed to deprive the borrower of her equity of redemption, it is widely used in attempts to evade usury laws.

The Sale Accompanied by a True Purchase Money Loan. One class of creditors has been excused from observing usury limits because the loan element was lacking: sellers of homes or goods who take back credit for part of the purchase price. When the seller of goods or a house takes back an I.O.U., the seller is "forbearing" to collect the full purchase price. Technically, the seller is making a loan to the buyer. It makes little difference to the buyer to be making periodic payments to the seller instead of a third-party lender.

Yet, in the nineteenth century, courts started protecting sellers against usury claims. They reasoned that the seller's primary intent was not to make a loan, but rather to make a sale. The loan was "incidental" to the seller's main objective. Courts also saw no point in subjecting sellers to usury laws which they could easily evade by jacking up the price of a credit sale proportionately. These transactions have been regarded as:

> [n]ot a subterfuge devised to conceal what was in fact a loan . . . the sale of one's own property is not a loan whatever by the terms or conditions of the purchase. . . .. He [the owner] may offer to sell at a designated price for cash or at a much higher price on credit, and a credit sale will not constitute usury however great the difference between the two prices, unless the buying and selling was a mere pretense.[82]

---

[81] *See, e.g.,* Golden State Lanes v. Fox, 42 Cal. Rptr. 568 (1965). In this case, the "buy back" was mandatory. But even if it had taken the form of an "option," and the value of the "security" property greatly exceeded the option price, the "borrower" would be under pressure to exercise the option; Crim v. E.F. Hutton, Inc., 381 S.E.2d 492 (S.C. 1989) (A customer loaned money to his stockbroker. When the stockbroker defaulted, the customer sued the stockbroker's company. The court concluded that the advance was a loan and not a sale of a security, the broker was not acting in the scope of his employment, and therefore the company could not be liable. The court held that a security is "an investment in a common venture premised on a reasonable expectation of profits to be derived from the entrepreneurial or managerial efforts of others").

[82] Verbeck v. Clymer, 261 P. 1017, 1019 (Cal. 1927); Mandelino v. Fribourg, 242 N.E.2d 823 (N.Y. 1968).

We can only guess why courts never regarded the premium a seller might charge for goods bought on credit as a form of disguised interest.[83] Professor Benfield suggests that this is just another example of how the judiciary sanctioned legitimate, arm's-length transactions, despite the usury laws.

The seller later may modify the loan, perhaps agreeing to defer payment in exchange for a higher interest rate. If the court regards the change as a modification, the seller preserves the "purchase money" status of the loan.[84] If the court sees the change as having created a new loan, the new loan lacks "purchase money" status and the lender becomes susceptible to usury sanctions if the interest rate exceeds usury limits.[85] The new loan could be usurious even though the original loan being purchase money was exempted from usury laws by federal preemption and common law. Consider the case of the good-hearted seller who answers her buyer's plea for reduced monthly payments by knocking down the interest on a purchase money loan from 12% to 11%, in a state where 10% is the usury cap. When she magnanimously consents to enter a refinancing at 11%, she could inadvertently fall into the usury trap. Courts eager to avoid tripping up the generous seller, classify the transaction as a modification and hold the modified reduced rate not usurious. In this way, they to avoid producing "a somewhat absurd and clearly inequitable result."[86] To facilitate this result, the seller should document the change as a modification and never cancel the old note to substitute a new one in its place.

The absurdity of the "new loan"/"modification" distinction can be seen by this example: Suppose purchase money borrowers fall behind in their payments. The loan is overdue. The borrowers want to extend the loan maturity date because they can't repay the loan on time. The seller agrees to extend the maturity date of the loan, in exchange for an increase in the interest rate from 10% to 15% (a rate above the usury ceiling, but comparable to market rates at the time). The lender could refuse, insist the overburdened borrower pay on time, let the borrower default, and then

---

[83] If the seller were subject to the Truth in Lending Act (TILA), it might violate the TILA to include the premium a seller charges for buying on credit as part of the "amount financed" instead of including it in the "finance charge." Further, the time price doctrine has been abolished in many Retail Installment Sales Acts and other statutes regulating credit sales. *See* National Consumer Law Center, Usury and Consumer Credit Regulation 12426 (1987).

[84] Lakeview Meadows Ranch v. Bintliff, 111 Cal. Rptr. 414 (1973).

[85] If the buyer and seller agree to a *new* loan taking the place of the vendor's original purchase money loan, the seller is susceptible to a usury challenge on the new loan. Ghirardo v. Antonioli, 17 Cal. Rptr. 2d 664(1993), *overruled by* Ghirardo v. Antonioli, 924 P.2d 996 (Cal. 1996).

[86] D.C.M. Partners v. Smith, 278 Cal. Rptr. 778, 781 (1991). Modifications of the original purchase money loan aren't usurious. If the buyer and seller agree to a new loan taking the place of the vendor's original purchase money loan, the seller is susceptible to a usury challenge on the new loan. Ghirardo v. Antonioli, 17 Cal. Rptr. 2d 664 (1993).

foreclose. The purchase money lender would purchase the security property at foreclosure. Then the lender could resell the home subject to a new 15% loan. This loan would clearly be "purchase money." As such, it would enjoy an automatic usury exemption. But if the lender had simply substituted a new loan for the old one and saved the borrower the costs and distress of foreclosure, the substituted loan would probably have been usurious. Some courts have thought this anomaly absurd. "If the parties could lawfully avoid the usury laws indirectly by going through the foregoing convoluted process, there should be no reason why they should not be able to do so *directly*."[87]

Distinguishing a Joint Venture from a Loan. If L advances funds to B for investment on the understanding that L is to receive half the profits, the fact that the anticipated profit level could yield L a return far above 10% doesn't necessarily mean L has committed usury. For usury laws to apply, the transaction needs to be a loan, not a joint venture or partnership. The criteria distinguishing a loan from a joint venture include: whether B is unconditionally obligated to repay L; whether repayment is entirely contingent on the venture's generating profits; whether L and B share losses as well as gains; and whether L and B share responsibility for making investment decisions.

Selling the Loan. Another important "sale or loan" question arises when the original lender sells the loan. Suppose a bank, having made a loan of $1,000 at 10%, sells the note to an investor for $500. The result is that the investor who bought the note is collecting interest at a rate greater than 10%–20% in this case.

These transactions aren't regarded as usurious; they are "sales" of notes in the secondary mortgage market. The borrower is paying only the legal rate of interest on the $1,000 actually borrowed. It is the originating lender who loses $500 by selling the loan at a discount. Usury laws are dedicated to protecting borrowers, not lenders, from "excessive" charges.[88]

A deviously clever lender, seizing upon the distinction between originating a loan and buying an existing loan, might try to disguise an origination as a sale. The lender would do this by setting up a "straw" lender who would make the loan and immediately sell it to the "true" and "usurious" lender at

---

[87] DCM Partners v. Smith, 278 Cal. Rptr. 778, 782 (1991). *See also* Ferrigno v. Cromwell Dev. Assoc., 689 A.2d 1150, 115354 (Conn. App. 1997) (Rights and obligations of parties are fixed at time that mortgage note is executed, so that an obligation that is not usurious at its inception will not become usurious as result of subsequent events).

[88] Federal tax law requires lenders' "original issue discounts" to be spread over the life of the loan in computing their income for tax liability purposes. 26 U.S.C. § 1272. But the rules are limited to the "original issue" discount. The lender *selling* a loan at a discount is in quite a different position than one who made the loan originally with "points" or at a discount. The lender selling at a loss is then allowed to deduct it against "like kind" gains. 26 U.S.C. § 163(e).

a deep discount. The borrower *who receives only the discounted sum* has a good claim of usury against the "straw." The borrower can reach the true lender only by proving that the straw was acting for the lender all along.[89]

It is sometimes difficult to tell whether an originating lender is selling a loan or just borrowing against it. If the primary lender merely borrows money from a secondary lender, pledging the deeds of trust obtained from the borrowers as collateral for the loan, the lender might be subject to usury limits. In one example of an obvious sale, Lender 1 sells a loan or group of loans to Lender 2 for a fixed sum. This transaction would not fall under the ambit of usury laws. But suppose Lender 1 guarantees Lender 2 against losses, retains the right to service the loans and even enjoys a right to repurchase them. Suppose as well that Lender 2 only paid 70–80% of the loans' fair market value. This "sale" may well be recharacterized as a "loan." Furthermore, not only might it be usurious, if Lender 1 went bankrupt, Lender 2 could be classified a general, unsecured creditor, not the owner of the loans.[90]

§ 104.03(f)(4)(ii)   What Is "Interest"?[91]

In determining whether a particular payment is "interest" for usury purposes, courts are not as concerned about what the borrower pays, as they are with what the lender receives as a charge for the use of money. But an informed borrower who is comparative shopping for a loan will consider the total costs of the loan. To the borrower, it doesn't matter whether the money paid is classified as "interest" or just "fees." Instead of waiting for the loan closing documents to see what the loan finally costs, she will ask in advance about all the charges she will have to pay to close the loan, which may include more than just the face amount of interest on the note and origination fees such as points and discounts.

(1) *Lender Fees*: Lenders charge fees for originating loans, committing themselves to make a loan at a fixed future date, getting appraisals, credit reports, surveys, and title insurance, administering loan escrows, preparing mortgages, recording and processing loans, and paying for underwriters' fees and legal work (possibly on the high side, since lawyers know their

---

[89] Janisse v. Winston Inv. Co., 317 P.2d 48 (Cal. App. 1957). *See* Eugene E. Glushon, *The California Usury Law: The Lender's Trap and the Borrower's Windfall?,* 43 Cal. St. B.J. 56 (1968). *But see* White v. Seitzman, 230 Cal. App.2d 756 (Cal. App. 1964).

[90] *See, e.g., In re* Lemons and Assocs., 67 B.R. 198 (Bankr. D. Nev. 1986); Major's Furniture Mart, Inc. v. Castle Credit Corp., 602 F.2d 538 (3d Cir. 1979). *See also* Robert D. Aicher & William J. Fellerhoff, *Characterization of a Transfer of Receivables as a Sale or a Secured Loan upon Bankruptcy of the Transferor,* 65 Am. Bankr. L.J. 181 (1991); Homer Kripke, *Conceptual Obsolescence in Law and Accounting—Finance Relations Between Retailer and Assignee of Retail Receivables,* 1 B.C. Indus. & Com. L. Rev. 55, 60–61 (1959).

[91] For useful background on various ways of calculating interest, *see* National Consumer Law Center, Usury and Consumer Credit Regulation 63 *et seq.* (1987).

clients are passing these costs along to borrowers who desperately want the loans and probably won't question the fees).[92] Fees are not treated as interest if they are charges for something other than the use of money, especially if the fee is paid to a third party—lawyer, appraiser, or escrow agent.[93]

Here is one law professor's critique of the general rule that fees aren't counted as interest for usury purposes:

> The common-law rule was that closing costs paid out immediately to third parties (e.g., survey fees, title charges, and taxes) are not includable as interest because they are not compensation to the lender. Although some of the charges are incurred at the lender's insistence, courts reasoned that it is ultimately in the borrower's self-interest to be certain of boundaries and the title's validity. This theory fails to justify not allocating at least part of those lender-required fees to the interest rate; nor is it persuasive when applied to payments for property appraisal, credit checks, and attorney review of loan agreements. The benefit of these latter tasks inures almost entirely to the lender. Despite these objections, state legislatures ratified the common law when they drafted detailed usury law definitions of interest after 1966.

> Under the common law, charges that the lender retains to pay for its own performance of loan-related services are also not interest, as long as these charges are "reasonable." Because courts rarely found lender charges unreasonable, this rule effectively excluded lender-retained closing costs from classification as interest. Nevertheless, this rule was followed by legislative codifications in the 1960's and 1970's.[94]

(2) *Points and Discounts*: What about "points" and discounts from the amount borrowed? "Points" refer to the percentage of the loaned amount which the borrower pays the lender for the loan. "Discounts" are deductions from the face amount of the loan. A loan of $100,000 at two points costs the borrower $2,000. A loan discounted by two points will net the borrower $98,000, although her repayment will be calculated as if she had received the full $100,000.

For usury purposes, courts treat "points" and discounts as interest if they are paid by the *buyer*.[95] They are then amortized over the estimated or actual

---

[92] For lenders regulated as real estate brokers, California has enacted dollar limits for some of these fees and charges, *e.g.,* capping appraisal, credit report, and other loan processing fees at 5% of the principal loan amount or $390, whichever is greater, but not to exceed $700 in any event. Cal. Bus. & Prof. Code §§ 10241(a), 10242.

[93] Phipps v. Guar. National Bank of Tallahassee, 2003 U.S. Dist. LEXIS 16984 (No. 03-420-CV-W-GAF, W.D. Mo., Sep. 17, 2003) (origination and discount fees were considered "interest").

[94] William N. Eskridge, Jr., *One Hundred Years of Ineptitude: The Need for Mortgage Rules Consonant with the Economic and Psychological Dynamics of the Home Sale and Loan Transaction,* 70 Va. L. Rev. 1083, 1092–93 (1984). Reprinted with permission.

[95] Fausett & Co. v. G & P Real Estate, Inc., 602 S.W.2d 669 (Ark. 1980) (discounting loans can violate usury law where the effective rate of interest would exceed the usury limit).

life of the loan when making usury calculations. "Seller-paid points were not often challenged because homebuyers were not aware that they were paid. When they were challenged, they posed difficult questions."[96]

Incidentally, a lender's preference for "point" v. "interest" income depends quite a lot on federal tax and accounting practice. Lenders whose stock is actively traded on securities markets are eager for "income now" to boost their current reported earnings and thus push up the value of their stock. When conventional accounting practice allowed lenders to count points as earnings in the year the loan was made, they got as many "points" "up front" as they could. Current accounting practice requires that points and "original issue" discounts be amortized over the life of the loan. Most loans are paid before maturity. Since "points" are amortized over the stated life of the loan and are not recognizable as income sooner than the stated maturity unless the loan is prepaid, income from point-taking or discount-charging is understated. As a reult, you will see ads offering "no-point" loans. When loans are prepaid before maturity, the lender can then count as income the revenue from points or discounts not already booked.

Sometimes lenders charge borrowers a commitment fee in exchange for the lender's promise to make a loan at a later date. The lender's commitment letter gives the borrower the option of taking the loan or not. Is the commitment fee "interest" for usury calculations?

The common-law authorities generally agreed that bona fide commitment fees are not interest because the fee is not paid for the use of money, but only for the option of later using it. In the integrated home sale and loan transaction, however, this "option" is almost always exercised, as the homebuyers will use most or all of the precommitted mortgage money. After 1966, a few states did redefine interest to include mortgage commitment fees under some circumstances.[97]

(3) *Late Charges and Prepayment Penalties*: Late charges and prepayment penalties are legitimate costs of doing business and are deductible as interest paid by the borrower if otherwise qualified under the Internal Revenue Code.[98] They are also taxable income for lenders. But they aren't interest for usury calculations because the borrower has the option of avoiding the charges by paying on the scheduled due date.[99]

Similarly, even though borrowers may deduct interest on purchase money loans made by sellers and the sellers are taxed on the income they receive

---

[96] Eskridge, 70 Va. L. Rev. at 1093.

[97] *Id.* at 1093–94.

[98] 26 U.S.C. § 163.

[99] *See Lazzareschi Inv. Co. v. San Francisco Fed. Sav. & Loan Ass'n*, § 104D(4), *infra*. Garcia v. Tex. Cable Partners, 114 S.W.3d 561 (Tex. App. 2003) (late fee was not usurious because it did not constitute interest).

from the loan, the loans are treated as part of a sale and thus escape the usury net. Moreover, sellers who take back notes for part of the purchase price and charge interest at less than 9% risk having some of the principal recharacterized as interest for federal income tax purposes.[100]

§ 104.03(f)(4)(iii)   Intent.

"Intent" to make a usurious loan is a question of fact, not law.[101] That means the trial court's determination will usually be upheld. "A review of the plethora of decisions involving the issue of usury indicates a great deal of apparent inconsistency. Different cases with similar facts reach opposite conclusions."[102] An unspoken premise is that usury laws are intended to penalize lenders for exploiting the necessitous and unwary. So the comparative sophistication of the parties matters. Once a court decides to treat a transaction as a usurious loan, the element of intent is readily overcome. Lenders are presumed to know the law. Usually, all the borrower needs to prove is that the lender voluntarily and consciously accepted interest at more than the legal maximum.

The "intent" element gives courts a chance to uphold deals that seem reasonable, even though they could be analyzed as disguised, usurious loans. Say a film or TV producer runs short of cash and promises a financial angel the right to buy stock in the production company or project at a favorable price, with a repurchase option or even a repurchase obligation. The investor's return on the cash put up might exceed the usury limit, but the risks of film production are great, the investor's return was justified by the risk, and the borrower initiated the deal and even suggested using purchase options to skirt the usury laws. Later, the borrower invokes the usury law and seeks treble damages. California courts, in several cases like this, have found no "intent" to commit usury and have enforced the deals as agreed upon.[103]

In other situations, California courts found the requisite intent where the lender contracted for "disguised" interest in sums that seemed excessive in light of the risk. In one case, the plaintiff owned 182 acres that it was trying to develop for a golf course (120 acres) and some houses (62 acres). A teamsters union pension fund had agreed to lend $500,000 to finance the project in two years, but couldn't advance the funds before that time. The plaintiff ran short of cash while developing the golf course and tried to borrow against the teamster loan commitment.

The defendants agreed to loan $500,000 at 91/2%, ostensibly. But in

---

[100] 26 U.S.C. § 1274 (1992).

[101] Janisse v. Winston Inv. Co., 317 P.2d 48 (Cal. App. 1957). *But see* White v. Seitzman, 230 Cal. App.2d 756 (Cal. App. 1964).

[102] Harry D. Miller and Marvin B. Starr California Real Estate 646 (2d ed. 1989).

[103] Lindsey v. Campbell, 282 P.2d 948 (Cal. App. 1955); Martyn v. Leslie, 290 P.2d 58 (Cal. App. 1955).

reality, the defendant-lender wanted 10% on top of that, so the plaintiff-borrower was persuaded to grant the defendant an option to buy the residential acreage (62 acres) at $3,000 per acre—a price well below its market value. As part of the deal, the defendant gave the plaintiff a reciprocal option to repurchase the 62 acres and thereby erase the lender's bargain deal. Under the option, the plaintiffs could repurchase the land at $800 per acre in the first year of the loan, $1,600 in the second, $3,200 in the third, $4,000 in the fourth, and $4,800 in the fifth year, but not until the $500,000 had been repaid.

The plaintiff breached, but won a judgment that the loan terms were usurious. He didn't have to pay interest on the $500,000 note, and got back the interest he had already paid.

The defendant-lender appealed and lost. At trial, it came out that the lender and developer had agreed to a 91/2% loan with 10 "points." The lender felt that he couldn't make a decent profit on any less of a return than that. The repurchase option had been set to yield about $50,000 per year ($800 x 62 acres) to the lender, in addition to its fixed 91/2% return. Thus, lender received an effective return of nearly 20% per year. The court found the evidence sufficient to show usurious intent.[104]

§ 104.03(f)(4)(iv) "Absolutely, Not Contingently, Repayable."

This criterion denotes the difference between equity and debt. The classic formulation appears in the *Restatement of Contracts* § 527 (1932). It excepts any repayment obligation from usury, ". . . if the repayment promised on failure of the condition to occur is materially less than the amount of the loan or debt with the highest permissible interest. . .." Comment a:

> If the probability of the occurrence of the contingency on which the diminished payment is promised is remote, or if the diminution should the contingency occur is slight as compared with the possible profit to be obtained if the contingency does not occur, the transaction is presumedly usurious.

Hence, the contingent interest feature escapes usury on the Restatement's terms if: (1) the borrower's promise to pay is conditional, (2) the portion of the repayment at a fixed rate is "materially" below the usury ceiling, (3) the contingency that could cause the lender to lose the right to the interest above the usury limit is more than remote, and (4) the lender's loss if the contingency failed would be more than "slight."

Bondholders and mortgagees are usually guaranteed repayments in the sense that the borrower promises repayment absolutely. By contrast, shareholders have no right to dividends; these are discretionary or "contingent" and depend entirely on profits and corporate practice. In fact, you

---

[104] Mission Hills Dev. Corp. v. Western Small Business Inv. Co., 260 Cal. App. 2d 923 (1968).

might have to sell your stock at a loss. Therefore, equity interests with no guarantee of repayment do not count as loans.

> Contingent yields on loans are also exempt.

> It is the general rule that a loan in consideration of a share of profits, income, or earnings, in lieu of, in addition to, interest, is not usurious, in the absence of certainty that the arrangement would produce a return in excess of the legal rate of interest, *even though the principal is to be repaid in any event.* [Emphasis added][105]

Consider three cases:

(1) A creditor is promised a full return of principal at the highest legal rate of interest *plus* a share in the debtors' profits. This deal oversteps the Restatement's bounds of the "contingency" rule. First, the creditor gets the highest legal rate of interest no matter what happens. Any debtor profit—a dime's worth—will push the creditor's yield over the usury limit line. Second, there is only a slight chance that the enterprise will never make a profit. Why would anyone invest if they thought otherwise?

(2) A lender agrees to forego *any* fixed and definite return in exchange for a percentage of net (i.e., after expenses) profit. Even if that percentage eventually yields the lender a sum greatly exceeding the usury limit, the lender isn't violating usury laws. The lender isn't receiving any interest, you might say, or, alternately, all of the return is totally contingent because none of it is absolutely repayable.[106]

(3) The debtor guarantees the lender a partial return of principal and a very high interest rate—but lower than the usury limit—plus an equity "kicker" based on the debtor's profit. This case is a close one. The contingency exemption might or might not save the lender. You can see the determining factors by reviewing the first two examples.

§ 104.03(f)(5)   Exempt Lenders.

Many types of lenders are exempt from usury laws, either by federal or state law. Most lenders, including banks, are exempt from state usury laws under the Depository Institutions Deregulation and Monetary Control Act of 1980,[107] but not all lenders are covered by the federal preemption. For instance, pension funds do not enjoy the benefit of the preemption. Moreover, if a nonexempt lender arranges a loan through a bank which is

---

[105] Concord Realty v. Continental Funding, 776 P.2d 1114, 1122 (Colo. 1989), *citing* Annotation, *Agreement for Share in Earnings of or Income from Property in lieu of, or in Addition to, Interest as Usurious,* 16 A.L.R.3d 475 (1967). *But see* Dikeou v. Dikeou, 928 P.2d 1286 (Colo. 1997).

[106] Thomassen v. Carr, 58 Cal. Rptr. 297 (Cal. App. 1967) (where the lender received 30% of the developer's sale profits, the transaction was not usurious).

[107] 12 U.S.C. § 1735f-7 exempts "federally related" lenders.

exempt, this won't protect the nonexempt lender from otherwise being subject to a state's usury law.

Equally significant, the federal law only applies to lenders whose loans are "secured by a first lien on residential real property."[108] On loans secured by commercial property or home equity loans, lenders are still potentially subject to state usury laws. California, Connecticut, Colorado and Delaware exempt banks. Savings banks are exempt in California, Colorado, Connecticut, Florida, Illinois, Louisiana, Minnesota, Ohio, South Dakota, and West Virginia.[109]

To see how subtle some lender exemptions are, consider the real estate broker's exception in California. Loans made or "arranged" by real estate brokers are exempt under Article XV of the California Constitution. To *make* a loan, the broker must actually be supplying the loan funds. To *arrange* a loan, the broker must act as an intermediary and collect fees for arranging the loan, in order for the lender to rest assured that the transaction will be exempt from usury laws.

In *Jones v. Kallman*,[110] a loan qualified for exemption because it was "arranged" by a licensed real estate broker, even though the broker had only "minimal participation" in arranging it. The court held that some "compensation" to the broker would be necessary to exempt the loan from the state usury law. "Points" were paid to a partner of the broker, who put a portion of the points into the partnership business, thereby "compensating" the broker.[111]

This is an important case since many real estate brokers facilitate the closing of deals by seeking financing for their clients. Under *Jones*, real estate brokers can now claim exemptions as "arrangers" and cite fees received as proof of it. *Any* California lender working with a real estate broker can provide funding under the broker's "arranging" exemption, and probably be free of usury constraints.

---

[108] *Id.*

[109] This list comes from Marion Benfield, *Money, Mortgages, and Migraine—The Usury Headache,* 19 Case W. Res. L. Rev. 819, 851 (1968). Since the article was written in 1968, anyone needing current information needs to check his or her state's current usury law.

[110] 244 Cal. Rptr. 609 (Cal. App. 1988).

[111] The broker's right to collect a fee for this service was challenged as a "kickback" from the lender. "Kickbacks" in real estate settlements or closings are prohibited by the federal Real Estate Settlement and Procedures Act (R.E.S.P.A.). 12 U.S.C. § 2607. The court, in McCarrick v. Polonia Fed. Sav. & Loan Ass'n, 502 F. Supp. 654 (D. Pa. 1980) ruled that such fees aren't kickbacks.

§ 104.03(f)(6)   The Corporate Borrower Exemption.

The usury laws in about thirty states exempt corporate borrowers.[112] In other states, usury rate limits for corporate borrowers are above those for noncorporate borrowers.

> The corporate exception statutes fix differing qualifications for the exemption. Many of them provide blanket corporate exemptions, but in some states there are special limitations. In New York, for example, the exemption does not apply to a corporation whose principal asset is a one- or two-family dwelling if it was organized within 6 months prior to the execution of any notes or security instruments issued in connection with the loan. The Washington statute makes a corporate borrower subject to the usury law on obligations on which an individual is also liable.

> There has been a split of authority as to whether the exemption statutes apply to a corporation organized specially for the purpose of taking advantage of them. In New York it is permissible to form a corporation for the express purpose of avoiding the usury laws, and the same result has been reached in Maryland and Illinois on an estoppel theory.

> On the other hand, New Jersey has taken a very hard line, holding that the defense of usury is available where a corporation is formed in an attempt to avoid the usury statutes. In 1956, the New Jersey Supreme Court suspended from practice for a year a lawyer who had arranged an incorporation for the purpose of avoiding the usury statute. Florida also has decisions inferring that general usury statutes apply where the incorporation is for the sole purpose of avoiding them. Even in New York, there are limits to the corporate exemption rule. In a case where the husband and wife, owners of a small incorporated retail hardware business, borrowed money through the corporation for the purpose of making a down payment on a home they were purchasing, the court held that the corporate exemption did not apply.

> The effect of the corporate usury exemption, in spite of the cases holding that it cannot be used for the sole purpose of avoiding the usury statutes and in spite of exclusions from the corporation exceptions like those in New York and Washington, is to provide a vehicle by which borrowers for a business purpose can escape the general usury laws. Incorporation may be inconvenient and may increase the total cost of the loan, but the incorporation method can be and is used to provide financing which would not otherwise be available.[113]

§ 104.03(f)(7)   Penalties.

State usury laws vary hugely in their penalties for breach. Some work a

---

[112] Where corporate borrowers are denied the usury defense, they are denied it against national banks as well. 12 C.F.R. § 7.7310.

[113] Benfield, *Money, Mortgages, and Migraine—The Usury Headache,* 19 Case W. Res. L. Rev. 819, 849–51 (1968).

forfeiture of principal and interest.[114] Others relieve the debtor of the obligation to pay any interest at all.[115] Some disallow only the collection of that amount of interest which exceeds the usury limit and impose no other penalty.[116] Some laws discharge the borrower from paying any interest, allow the borrower to offset interest paid against the principal due, and provide damages for treble the amount of excess interest actually paid.[117] Willful usury is a felony in some states, punishable by up to five years in state prison,[118] and a misdemeanor in nearly a dozen others.[119] There are relatively short statutes of limitations, though.

Lenders retain the right to foreclose on a deed of trust even if the underlying note was usurious; however, the debt may be reduced because of the usury violation.

§ 104.03(f)(8)   Savings Clauses.

Some lenders try to limit their usury damage exposure by using savings clauses. Usury savings clauses are designed to negate the intent element, i.e., that the lender voluntarily and consciously accepted interest exceeding the legal maximum. They reduce charges to legal limits, with no refunds for past overcharges. However, courts have found loans usurious, notwithstanding the inclusion of such clauses.[120]

Whether the inclusion of a usury savings clause negates per se a lender's intent to charge usurious interest was the subject of a recent decision of the

---

[114] Ark. Const. art. XIX, § 13; Conn. Gen. Stat. § 37-8. *See also* Ferrigno v. Cromwell Dev. Assoc., 689 A.2d 1150, 1152 (Conn. App. 1997) (As usury penalty, no action may be brought to collect principal or interest on any loan with interest rate in excess of 12%).

[115] Neb. Rev. Stat. § 45-105. *See also* Barton v. Moore, 558 N.W.2d 746, 748 (Minn. 1997) (Court held that loan found to be usurious under state law subjected lender to loss of the interest).

[116] Pa. Stat. Ann. tit. 41 § 501.

[117] Cal. Uncod. Init. Meas. & Stat. 1919, Act 1919-1 § 3(a). The borrower may be denied the treble damage remedy if he was the guiding hand and had initiated the transaction. White v. Seitzman, 41 Cal. Rptr. 359 (1964).

[118] Cal. Uncod. Init. Meas. & Stat. 1919, Act 1919-1 § 3(b).

[119] *See, e.g.,* N.Y. Penal Law § 190.40.

[120] Ronald Friend, *Shared Appreciation Mortgages,* 34 Hastings L.J. 329, 348 (1982). Two cases finding the loans usurious anyway are: Oklahoma Preferred Fin. & Loan Corp. v. Morrow, 497 P.2d 221 (Okla. 1972) and Southwestern Investment Co. v. Hockley County Seed & Delinting, Inc., 511 S.W.2d 724 (Tex. 1974). Compare Imperial Corporation of America v. Frenchman's Creek Corp., 453 F.2d 1338 (5th Cir. 1972), where the interest exceeded the legal limit by $3,835, but the entire amount of interest was not forfeited because of the clause. Instead, the excess interest was applied to the principal balance. *See also* Coastal Cement Sand Inc. v. First Interstate Credit Alliance Inc., 956 S.W.2d 562, 572 (Tex. App. 1997) (Savings clause is ineffective against usury claim if it directly contradicts explicit terms of contract).

Florida Supreme Court in Jersey Palm-Gross, Inc. v. Paper.[121] The plaintiff real estate partnership, faced with a purchase money loan that was almost due, urgently needed a $200,000 bridge loan for construction of an office building. The defendant real estate developer declined their offer of an equity partner interest upon investment of $200,000, but agreed to an 18-month loan of $200,000 at 15% interest (total interest of $45,000). Shortly before closing, the defendant insisted on a 15% equity interest as additional consideration. The equity interest, valued at $90,000, effectively raised the interest rate to 45%. The legal interest limit in Florida is 25%, with forfeiture of the principal as a penalty for usury.[122]When the developer sued the borrowers for repayment of the loan that was in default, the borrowers defended on the basis that the loan was an unenforceable debt because it was usurious. The developer appealed the trial court's order of forfeiture, arguing that the court had failed to consider a usury savings clause in the promissory note when the issue of intent was determined.

The Supreme Court approved and adopted the appellate ruling that a usury savings clause was only "one factor to be considered in the overall determination of whether the lender intended to exact a usurious interest rate. Such a standard strikes a balance between the legislative policy of protecting borrowers from overreaching creditors and the need to preserve otherwise good faith, albeit complex, transactions which may inadvertently exact an unlawful interest rate."[123] Holding that a usury savings clause cannot by itself preclude a usury finding, the court reasoned that a contrary holding would permit a lender to circumvent the usury laws by merely including a disclaimer of usurious intent in a contract with a clearly usurious interest rate.

Borrowers have no right to waive their protection under the usury law. So savings clauses aren't exculpatory per se. A "savings" clause did rescue the lender in *Arneill Ranch v. Petit.*[124] California's usury law provides for floating rates capped at 5% above the Federal Reserve Bank, San Francisco, discount rate. The rate in *Arneill Ranch* was tied to prime, and below the usury ceiling on the day the loan was entered. The prime rate increased faster than the discount rate and the lender found itself with a loan earning interest above the usury ceiling. The court invoked a savings clause in the note to justify its conclusion that the lender hadn't intended to make a usurious loan.

A lender also successfully invoked a savings clause in a more doubtful

---

[121] 658 So. 2d 531, 535 (Fla. 1995).

[122] Fla. Stat. ch. 687.071(7).

[123] Jersey Palm-Gross, Inc. v. Paper, 658 So. 2d 531, 535 (Fla. 1995).

[124] Arneill Ranch v. Petit, 134 Cal. Rptr. 456 (Cal. App. 1976). *See also* Parhms v. B & B Ventures, Inc., 938 S.W.2d 199 (Tex. App. 1997) (Late payment provision of land contract did not unequivocally call for usurious interest and usury savings clause was effective).

situation in *In re Dominquez*.[125] The maximum allowable rate under the usury law at the time of the loan was 16.5%. The contract interest rate was 17% and thus above the usury ceiling on the day the note was written. Nonetheless, the court invoked the savings clause as evidence the lender lacked intent to make a usurious loan.

§ 104.03(f)(9)   Choice of Laws.

Suppose a lender doing business in New York agrees to lend money to a California corporation for a development project in California. The loan is executed and funds are disbursed and repaid in New York. The loan agreement specifies that New York law is to govern the transaction.

The borrower defaults and the lender sues in California. The borrower contends that California law should apply, under which corporations enjoy the protection of the usury law. In New York, they don't. Which state's usury law will the courts apply to the contract?

The governing standard is the *Restatement (Second) of Conflict of Laws* § 203 (1971):

> The validity of a contract will be sustained against the charge of usury if it provides for a rate of interest that is permissible in a state to which the contract has a substantial relationship and is not greatly in excess of the rate permitted by the general usury law of the state of the otherwise applicable law. . ..

"Substantial relationship" is defined as a "normal and natural relationship to the contract and the parties." Comment C, § 203.

Many cases on conflict of laws and usury have ruled that states do not have such an overwhelming public policy concern in its usury laws as to override the contracting parties' decision to choose the law of another state, as long as there was some nexus between the parties, the transaction and the other state.[126]

In this case, California courts will honor the New York choice-of-law agreement. They see support for their view that the state doesn't have an uncompromising public policy preference for its own usury laws, because the law itself exempts most institutional lenders. Further, California was one of those states that elected *not* to opt out of the federal usury preemption statute. Therefore, we shouldn't expect California courts to set aside a

---

[125] *In re* Dominquez, 995 F. 2d 883 (9th Cir. 1993).

[126] Ury v. Jewlers Acceptance Corp., 38 Cal. Rptr. 376 (1964); Gamer v. Forgan, 135 Cal. Rptr. 230 (1976). In Continental Mortgage Investors v. Sailboat Key, Inc., 395 So. 2d 507 (Fla. 1981), the lender was in Massachusetts and the loan was made and repaid there. The agreement specified that Massachusetts law was to apply. The borrower and property were in Florida. The court upheld the parties' choice-of-law provision because the provision was agreed upon by both parties in good faith, wasn't devised to evade usury laws, and Massachusetts had a "normal relation" with the transaction.

"choice of law" provision merely because it frees the lender from California's usury law.

Nonetheless, the parties still must demonstrate that their contract has a reasonable relationship to the state whose law they have chosen. Practically, this means that usury disputes concerning contracts with choice of law provisions can't be readily resolved on the pleadings. An evidentiary trial is usually going to be necessary.[127]

One way a lender might avoid the ordeal of an evidentiary trial is to add a choice-of-jurisdiction provision to its documentation, requiring that the case be tried in a state which is more friendly to the parties' choice of law rules.[128]

§ 104.04 The Length of the Term: Is Shorter Better?

Mortgage loans are typically long-term; twenty- to thirty-year lengths are common. For the borrower, the trade-off in the length of the loan is apparent: lower monthly payments vs. greater interest payments over the life of the loan.

The borrower's monthly payment burden can be eased by detaching the loan's due date from the amortization of principal schedule. In Canada, for instance, most home loans are amortized as if they had been written for 25 years, yet all the principal becomes due and payable every five years. Canadian lenders allow refinancing every five years as a matter of course, but at prevailing market rates. If they didn't, borrowers would face big balloon payments. Here is an example of the borrower's trade-off:

Monthly Mortgage Payments[129]

Suppose Mr. Matthews buys a home for $106,250. He puts down $21,250 in cash and gets a 30-year, fixed-rate mortgage for $85,000 at 10 percent interest—in other words, a "conventional" loan at market rates and terms. Monthly payments for principal and interest total $745.94.

At the end of 30 years, Matthews has made 360 mortgage payments and spent a total of $268,537. Of the money paid to the lender, $85,000 was principal and $183,537 was interest—an amount substantially greater than the apparent acquisition price of the property.

But a 30-year loan is not the only way to organize a mortgage. Within the bounds of a 10 percent interest rate, Matthews—or you or I—could easily cut the interest bill for an $85,000 loan by $100,000—or more. Suppose,

---

[127] Mencor Enters. v. H.E.T.S. Equities Corp., 235 Cal. Rptr. 464 (1987).

[128] *See* Note, *Choice-of-Law, Venue, and Consent-to-Jurisdiction Provisions in California Commercial Lending Agreements: Can Good Draftsmanship Overcome Bad Choice-of-Law Doctrine?*, 23 Loy. L.A. L. Rev. 1337 (1990).

[129] Peter G. Miller, The Common-Sense Mortgage 2-3 (3d ed. 1987). Excerpt and Table following copyright © 1985, 1986, 1987 by Peter G. Miller. Reprinted by permission of Harper Collins Publishers Inc.

for example, that Matthews decides to increase his mortgage payment by $5.09 a day—not an unreasonable expense in the context of a $100,000 home or an era when a good hamburger costs five dollars anyway. Let's look at what happens:

— Monthly payments rise to $898.73.

— The debt to the lender is reduced at a far faster rate than would have been possible with payments of $745.94 per month.

— Because principal payments have been increased, the length of the loan is shortened from 360 months to 187 months. In other words, the loan term is now 15.58 years rather than 30 years.

— Interest costs are slashed by just over $100,000.

(See Table 1).

Loan size	$85,000	$85,000
Interest rate	10 percent	10 percent
Monthly payment	$745.94	$898.73
Extra monthly cost	None	$152.79
Number of payments	360	187
Potential interest cost	$183,536.90	$83,062.37
Potential cash saving	None	$100,474.53

Ask yourself: If you were Matthews, would you set aside $38.20 a week—hardly the cost of a meal for two at many restaurants—to cut your mortgage bill by $100,000? Is it worth spending $152.79 a month to knock out almost 15 years of mortgage payments?

Raising monthly mortgage payments is only one path to lower financing costs.

Many homeowners with 30-year fixed rate mortgages are refinancing them with 15-year fixed rate loans.[130]

For the lender the 30-year vs. 15-year amortization trade-off is also complicated. Longer loan terms give the lenders more interest over the life of the loan, but shorter loan maturities give lenders the chance to reevaluate the credit risk periodically and to refinance if they are satisfied with it or cash out if they aren't. Shorter maturities also enable lenders to re-lend prepaid funds at prevailing market rates.

Some borrowers justify the higher cumulative interest they pay on longer term loans because: (1) they don't plan to hold the property for anywhere near as long as the loan maturity; (2) they itemize their deductions and

---

[130] *See* Lucinda Harper, *Mortgage Refinancings Bring Increase in Payments as 15-year Term Spreads,* Wall St. J., Oct. 7, 1992, at A2, col. 2. "There's a mix of people opting for shorter mortgages. Some are baby-boomers who want to have enough equity in the house to borrow against by the time the kids go to college. Others are nearing retirement and don't want the continued burden of monthly mortgage payments." *Id.*

consider the *after*-tax costs of mortgage interest; and (3) they are discounting the absolute amounts to present value.[131]

Another reason why borrowers may not be too concerned about paying more cumulative interest is that stretching payments over a longer period of time lowers the loan's monthly payments. Cash-strapped borrowers can more easily qualify for loans and wealthier buyers get bigger loans for nicer houses. Reducing the monthly payment by just $37 could lower the annual income needed to qualify for a loan by more than $1,200.[132] In high-cost areas where larger loans are needed, the savings can have an even more dramatic impact.

§ 104.05   Prepayment.

§ 104.05(a)   Why Borrowers Prepay.

Once a borrower has carefully chosen a loan of ideal length why would such a borrower ever have a change of heart and want to pay it off before maturity?

§ 104.05(a)(1)   Refinancing for Lower Rates, to Cash Out, to Reduce Risks, to Simplify Their Lives.

The borrower may want to refinance to take advantage of lower market rates of interest or convert the rising equity value into cash by increasing the size of her loan. Homeowners also pay off debts ahead of maturity either because they want to decrease the amount of risk in their lives by reducing their leverage (debt/equity ratios), or because they don't want to be bothered by having to keep track of monthly payments.

§ 104.05(a)(2)   Tax-Motivated Refinancing.

Some refinancings are tax-motivated. Before 1986, all interest payments were deductible, whether on home loans, car loans, or unsecured borrowings. Since then, only *consumers* can deduct only interest on home loans. Rather complex rules circumscribe the interest deductions allowed on funds borrowed for use in a trade, business or passive investment activity, to acquire investment property or to produce portfolio income.[133] As interest deductions for personal consumption were being phased out, tax-conscious homeowners shifted as much of their borrowing as they could to home loans. For some, this meant borrowing on the "equity" by taking out a new junior loan. For others, it meant refinancing by paying off present loans and obtaining newer, larger ones.

Congress tried to limit homeowners converting non-deductible interest to

---

[131] Allan Axelrod et al., Land Transfer and Finance 136 (3rd ed. 1986).

[132] From Myers, *Some Lenders Now Offering 40-Year Loans,* L.A. Times, Feb. 5, 1989, at H1. The calculation was done for a 40-year mortgage as compared to a 30-year mortgage.

[133] 26 U.S.C. §§ 163, 469.

deductible by refinancing their mortgages. Congress "capped" the deductibility of home mortgage and home equity interest payments.[134] No tax-motivated homeowner refinances without first checking with an accountant to determine the extent to which interest on the refinanced loan will be deductible under present (and ever-changing) rules.

A second category of tax-motivated refinancing occurs as a borrower's loan repayments shift from being mostly deductible interest in the early years of the loan to mostly non-deductible repayments of principal in the later years.[135] Refinancing, say, a 30-year loan in the 20th year of its life, restores the borrower's ability to benefit from the mortgage interest deduction.

§ 104.05(a)(3)   Sale-Triggered Refinancing.

Many prepayments are triggered when homeowners sell. Their lenders may "call" their loans or their buyers may insist that the old loans be paid off because they are paying all cash, or because they want a new and bigger loan, a more favorable interest rate, a lender they like better, or a fixed instead of an adjustable rate.

§ 104.05(a)(4)   Default-Induced Refinancing.

Prepayments may also be forced on borrowers if they default. Should the lender foreclose, the mortgage will be prepaid out of foreclosure sale proceeds.

§ 104.05(b)   Why Lenders Care About Prepayments.

Lender attitudes about prepayment vary.

§ 104.05(b)(1)   Protecting Portfolio Matches.

Pension funds and insurance companies generally disfavor prepayment. They often hold long-term mortgages in their portfolios to match accrual on long-term obligations and prepayments could upset this balance.

§ 104.05(b)(2)   Minimizing the Interest Risk.

Some lenders which raise their capital in short-term money markets

---

[134] There is a $1,000,000 cap on acquisition indebtedness. Debt incurred in a refinancing is acquisition indebtedness up to the balance of the acquisition debt just prior to the refinancing. For example, say a homeowner takes out a $200,000 loan to buy a house. The homeowner pays the loan down to $180,000 and refinances. The homeowner can deduct mortgage interest on the refinancing only up to $180,000. But the homeowner will probably be able to treat the sum above $180,000 as a "home equity" loan and deduct up to $100,000 of it. 26 U.S.C. § 163(h).

[135] In the early stages of repayment, most of the debt service goes towards paying interest on the loan. As the loan nears maturity, most of the principal has been repaid, so that the interest portion of the debt service becomes minimal; most of the debt service goes towards principal repayment. Because only interest is tax-deductible, a borrower starts to lose this deduction as the loan matures.

welcome prepayments. The shorter loan maturities prevent them from getting squeezed between rising short-term costs of funds and declining long-term mortgage rates.

Some lenders are indifferent to prepayment because they have hedged their interest rate risks by selling their loans immediately after originating them.

§ 104.05(b)(3)   Minimizing the Credit Risk.

Prepayments can be heaven-sent for lenders who have made risky loans on thin borrower equities. They are joyful to greet returning principal they weren't sure they would ever see again.

§ 104.05(b)(4)   Estimating the Premiums and Discounts Attributable to Interest Rate Fluctuations.

To see the connection between interest rate fluctuations and the right to prepay, consider this example: in January, 1990, a borrower gets a 30-year $150,000 mortgage loan, with a fixed interest rate at 12%, the going rate at the time. Monthly payment: $1,542.92. Two years later, interest rates have fallen to 10%. What is the then-present value of the right to receive payments under this 2-year-old loan? The principal balance will have been reduced to $148,842.42, but the loan will be worth $173,760—only if the borrower can't prepay. A 12% loan sells for a premium in a 10% market. Conversely, if rates rose to 14%, the loan would be worth $129,566.08, a discount of $19,276.34.

§ 104.05(b)(5)   Keeping the Premium and Avoiding the Discount Caused by Rate Fluctuations.

Some lenders don't like prepayment because they want to lock in rates on mortgages to prevent cost-conscious borrowers from refinancing when long-term rates fall.

§ 104.05(b)(6)   Speculating On High-Risk Loans Being Prepaid at Full Face Value.

Prepayments are a boon to certain loan investors who bought the loans at a discount, hoping that they would later be paid off at full face value. Say a trust deed investor buys a loan in default on a rundown but well-located property. He gets a deep discount for the loan because it is in default. Later, a developer comes along to buy and rehab the property; however, he needs to refinance in order to obtain the necessary construction funds. To do so, the developer must clear the record of the outstanding mortgage debt by paying it off at par. The loan purchaser then pockets a whopping gain equal to the discount at which he bought the loan.

§ 104.05(b)(7)   Prepayment: The Secondary Market Challenge.

Unpredictable prepayments can pose a serious risk to individual and institutional investors who buy mortgage loans in the secondary market.

These mortgage buyers are eager to pocket the margins above Treasury yields that government-insured (F.H.A., V.A.) loans offer when packaged into bonds issued by the Federal National Mortgage Association and other similar institutions.

Prepayment privileges are analogous to a bond issuer's right to call the obligation and prepay it before the scheduled maturity date. When such a right exists, it puts the investor on notice not to rely on the premium yield because it can be lost if the entire investment is suddenly repaid.

A stockbroker quoted in the Wall Street Journal explained it very well when he said that the biggest problem for mortgage investors is: "[Y]ou don't know when you're going to get paid."[136] The frequency of prepayments fluctuates with changes in the economy, interest rates, and the housing market. Purchasers of mortgage-backed securities are particularly worried when rates go down and prepayments speed up; this scenario is exactly the opposite of what the mortgage holder wants. One analyst figures that bullish investors expecting a steady stream of income over, say, seven years at today's prepayment rates, could find their investment paid off in as little as 2½ years if interest fell just 1.5%.[137] They would find the mortgage game a losing one since mortgage bonds would "shorten up" just when they wanted them to stay long. "Similarly, if rates rose substantially, prepayments would slow down, so the mortgage security would transform itself into a very long-term bond just when it was best to do the opposite."[138]

Prepayment patterns are so important that guessing them right can bring instant riches while guessing them wrong can bring ruin. Therefore, trying to predict prepayment patterns has become a major enterprise for academic researchers. None have been hugely successful to date, even though reams of pages have been filled with mathematical models attempting to do the trick.

Michael Lewis, in *Liar's Poker*,[139] an account of life at Salomon Brothers, describes how the firm tried to guess which homeowners "with 4, 6 and 8 percent home mortgages were irrationally insisting on paying down their home loans when the prevailing mortgage rate was 16 percent." To analysts at Salomon "The American homeowner became . . . a sort of laboratory rat. The researchers charted how previously sedentary homeowners jumped and started in response to the shock of changes in the rate of interest."[140] Once

---

[136] Donnelly, *Mortgage Bonds: Safe but Not Risk Free,* Wall St. J., Mar. 14, 1990, at C1. Lenders without clauses barring prepayment for at least a few years see their investments in long-term loans as a "heads we lose, tails you win" game.

[137] *Id.*

[138] *Id.*

[139] Michael M. Lewis, Liar's Poker 118 (1989).

[140] Kevin W. Brown Usury and Consumer Credit Regulation 148 (1987).

researchers were satisfied that one group of homeowners was more likely than another to pay off low-interest loans, Salomon would buy them—at steep discounts, of course, and reap windfall gains when they were paid in full.

§ 104.05(c)   Prepayment: A Right or a Privilege.

In its simplest form, a prepayment penalty is a fee that a borrower is contractually obligated to pay if he or she chooses to pay off a debt prior to its scheduled retirement date.[141]

Few mortgage notes omit references to prepayment. They either allow it (with or without an accompanying fee), or prohibit it (typically, for a period of years shorter than the stated maturity of the loan). The simplest way of the note signaling that the maker has a right to prepay is for the promise to pay a specified sum to be followed by the words "or more." The maker who has the option of paying a specified sum "or more" may discharge the note by prepayment.[142] Prepayment prohibitions are typically referred to as "lock-in" clauses, graphic enough. What about when the note omits reference to prepayment privileges? Does the law presume that the borrower has the right to prepay in the absence of a note clause barring it? Here is the surprising answer:

> Contrary to what is probably pervasive popular belief, a mortgagee has a common law right to refuse an early tender or "prepayment" of principal or interest. This rule is derived from the classic case of Brown v. Cole, 14 L.J. (N.S.) Ch. 167, Chancery, 1845, where the court stated that if mortgagors "were allowed to pay off their mortgage money any time after the execution of the mortgage, it might be attended with extreme inconvenience to mortgagees, who generally advance their money as an investment."[143]

Certainly the right to prepay is worth something to the borrower. It also makes a loan less valuable to a lender than if the borrower were locked in. One researcher recently estimated the value of prepayment at 1.4% per year per dollar of loan. A borrower for whom prepayment without penalty is

---

[141] National Consumer Law Center, Usury and Consumer Credit Regulation 148 (1987).

[142] Harry D. Miller & Marvin B. Starr, California Real Estate 222 (2d ed. 1989).

[143] Grant S. Nelson & Dale A. Whitman, Real Estate Transfer, Finance, and Development 521 (4th ed. 1992). California follows the majority rule presumptively barring prepayment. Smiddy v. Grafton, 124 P. 433 (1912). Brannon v. McGowan, 683 So.2d 994 (Ala. 1996); George v. Fowler, 978 P.2d 565 (Wash. App. 1999) (Holding that prepayment was a privilege, and lenders were entitled to earn a fee for prepayment by the borrower. Even an absolute prohibition of prepayment is not unduly restrictive, because the lender is merely guaranteeing a rate of return.); Prudential Ins. Co. of America v. Rand & Reed Powers Partnership, 141 F.3d 834 (8th Cir. 1998) (An Iowa statute prohibited penalties charged by the lender on prepayment of a loan used to purchase agricultural land. However, completely barring prepayment is allowed, because completely barring prepayment is not a penalty).

important can shop for a form that allows it. Since form notes invariably treat the issue explicitly, there isn't much current litigation on whether prepayment is a right or a privilege. When the promissory note or mortgage is silent on the issue, many jurisdictions follow the common law. In *Patterson v. Tirollo*, the New Hampshire Supreme Court reaffirmed state laws on negotiable instruments, holding that absent an express prepayment right in the promissory note, a mortgagor has no legal right to pay a debt in advance of the maturity date.

However, several courts and one state legislature now allow homeowners a right to prepay unless the note expressly disallows it. For example, the Pennsylvania Supreme Court in *Mahoney v. Furches* held that a rebuttable presumption of a prepayment right exists where the mortgage note is silent. The court reasoned promotion of the policy against restraints on alienation outweighed the policy of protecting a mortgagee's investment interest from anticipation.

The legislatures of California[144] and New Mexico[145] have given home-buyers more than the benefit of a default rule. Here is the California statute:

> . . . where the original principal obligation is a loan for residential property of four units or less, the borrower under any note or evidence of indebtedness secured by a deed of trust or mortgage or any other lien on real property shall be entitled to prepay the whole or any part of the balance due, together with accrued interest, at any time.[146]

California's statute doesn't apply to buyers of *commercial* property or apartments of more than four units.[147] Presumably, their greater ability to negotiate specific loan conditions leaves them with less need of legislative protection in their dealings with lenders.

The California legislature could have chosen a less intrusive route by reversing the common-law presumption against prepayment. It could have put the drafting burden on lenders by legislating, as Florida and Indiana have done, that borrowers have the right to prepay, absent express language in the note to the contrary.[148] This might have been sensible since lenders are in a better position than borrowers to appreciate that silence on prepayment doesn't imply acquiescence. Under a presumption-only rule, lenders could block prepayment simply by spelling out in their mortgage or deed of trust forms, "the borrower has no right to pay off this loan early." The California

---

[144] Cal. Civ. Code § 2954.9(a)(1).

[145] N.M. Stat. Ann. § 56-8-30.

[146] Cal. Civ. Code § 2954.9(a)(1). A similar provision enacted by the New Mexico legislature was enforced in favor of the buyer of a "recreational" (second) residence in Naumburg v. Pattison, 711 P.2d 1387 (N.M. 1985).

[147] Cal. Civ. Code § 2954.9(a)(3).

[148] Ind. Code Ann. § 28-1-21-23(b)(7); Fla. Stat. Ann. § 697.06.

legislature went further, giving owner-occupiers of one-to-four unit residential property the absolute right to prepay without penalty after five years. Before then, the lender may charge no more than six months interest on the amount prepaid which exceeds 20% of the original principal amount.[149] California also bars charges on prepayments which occur after rate increases in variable rate mortgages.[150]

The legislature did carve out an exception for noncommercial sellers taking back purchase money loans where prepayment could trigger dire tax consequences.[151] These lenders can lawfully prohibit prepayment, but only in the year of sale.

State and national banks may impose prepayment penalties on adjustable-rate mortgage loans,[152] and federally chartered savings banks may impose prepayment penalties on fixed and adjustable rate mortgage loans.[153] These rights must be reserved by contract. However, the U.S. Department of Housing and Urban Development (HUD), which regulates all FHA-insured and VA-guaranteed home mortgages, allows mortgagors to prepay at any time without penalty.[154] These are home loan and apartment loan programs.

§ 104.05(c)(1)   Involuntary Prepayment.

A prepayment provision is usually invoked by the lender when the mortgagee takes voluntary action to pay the principal balance on the mortgage in advance of the maturity date. But, what if the mortgage indebtedness is paid prior to term through an involuntary action such as a condemnation proceeding to take the encumbered property by eminent

---

[149] Cal. Civ. Code § 2954.9(b).

[150] Cal. Civ. Code § 1916.5(a)(5).

[151] A vendor who desires installment sale reporting of gain under § 453 of the Internal Revenue Code could lose the benefit of that provision if the purchaser-borrower prepaid. The installment sale provisions allow sellers to match their gains for tax purposes with their actual receipt of payment, instead of having to pay up on the paper profit in the year of sale. Case and statutory law is sympathetic to these vendor-lenders. *See, e.g.,* Williams v. Fassler, 167 Cal. Rptr. 545, 549 (1980), which upheld a prepayment penalty of 50% as valid, "if the penalty is reasonably related to the obligee's anticipated risk of incurring increased tax liability upon the occurrence of the prepayment."

California allows a seller taking back a loan secured by a deed of trust to prohibit prepayment during the calendar year in which the sale and loan take place, as long as the seller does not take back four or more such deeds of trust during such calendar year. Cal. Civ. Code § 2954.9(a)(3). However, the legislature hasn't directly addressed the question of whether a seller wanting more than a one-year deferral of capital gains taxes on the sale can reserve the right to a prepayment penalty equal to his accelerated tax liability if the borrower prepays.

[152] *See* 12 C.F.R. 29.6, 29.9.

[153] 12 C.F.R. 545.34(c); 12 C.F.R. 545.33(f)(2).

[154] *See, e.g.,* 24 C.F.R. 203.22(b), 234.37(b).

domain? Can the lender enforce the prepayment provision?

Some jurisdictions consider prepayment provisions to be applicable only to a voluntary decision by the borrower to prepay the mortgage. In *Jala Corp. v. Berkeley Sav. & Loan Ass'n*, a New Jersey appellate court held that a prepayment provision that was silent on condemnation only contemplated a voluntary exercise by the mortgagor of the right to prepay, not an involuntary exercise of the right by reason of a taking in eminent domain. An Ohio district court quoted *Jala* extensively in holding that absent an express agreement, a mortgagor who sold the encumbered property under direct threat of condemnation was not liable for payment of the prepayment penalty. The trial court in a New York case held that an express provision for payment of a prepayment penalty in the event of condemnation would be enforceable when apportioning a condemnation award

The lesson here is clear. A well-drafted prepayment provision should include an express provision that the parties to the agreement have contemplated the possibility of condemnation and agreed that the prepayment penalty is payable in the event of condemnation of the encumbered property by eminent domain.

§ 104.05(d)   Prepayment Charges: Is the Sky the Limit?

§ 104.05(d)(1)   The Six Months' Interest Charge.

Notes often allow prepayment for a price. The overwhelming majority of prepayment fees in home mortgages allow the borrower to prepay up to 20% of the principal in any one year, above which the lender may levy a charge of six months unpaid interest on the prepaid balance.[155]

§ 104.05(d)(2)   Legislative and Regulatory Curbs on Prepayment Fees.

Many states prohibit or limit entirely prepayment fees in residential mortgages.[156] Prepayment fees in Veterans Administration (V.A.) guaranteed or Federal Housing Administration (F.H.A.) insured loans are prohibited and these loans may be prepaid at any time.[157] The Federal National Mortgage

---

[155] Frank S. Alexander, *Mortgage Prepayment: The Trial of Common Sense,* 72 Cornell L. Rev. 288, 316 (1987).

[156] 41 Pa. Cons. Stat. § 405; N.J. Stat. Ann. 46:10B-2, 10B-3; Ill. Ann. Stat. ch. 17, para. 6404(2)(a) (see now 815 ILCS 205/4(2)(a)) (for loans with interest rates of more than 8%); Mo. Ann. Stat. § 408.036 (no fee if mortgage is paid off after five years); Mich. Comp. Laws § 438.31c(c) (no penalty if home loan is paid off after three years, 1% of prepaid amount collectible as fee before that); N.Y. Gen. Oblig. Law § 5-501(3)(b) (owner-occupied 1-6-unit dwelling penalties only available for prepayment in first year of loan not to exceed three months' interest); Cal. Civ. Code § 2954-9 (20% prepayable free in any year, maximum charge of six months' interest in excess of 20% prepaid in a 12-month period); Glukowsky v. Equity One, Inc., 821 A.2d 485 (N.J. Super. 2003).

[157] 38 C.F.R. § 36.4310, 24 C.F.R. § 203.22(b).

Association (F.N.M.A.) and the Federal Home Loan Mortgage Corporation (F.H.L.M.C.) do not enforce prepayment clauses in the home mortgages they own.

§ 104.05(d)(3)   What Are the Lender's Actual Damages When a Loan Is Prepaid?

The Cost of Replacing the Funds. When their prepayments are challenged, in court and out, articulate lenders assert that it costs something to replace an old loan with a new one. They should be able to charge the prepaying borrower the costs of finding and making a new loan.

Consumer advocates regard this claim as preposterous, a "double" tax, because lenders are well compensated for refinancing costs by the fees they charge the new borrower. The old borrower pays the cost of the reconveyance. The cost of originating the new loan is assessed against new borrowers in the form of processing fees, document preparation charges, appraisal and credit checking fees, loan escrow fees, and origination fees. Any borrower who has actually paid these charges and fees can readily attest that lenders have overlooked nothing in making sure that all their expenses are reimbursed.

Loss of Interest on Prepaid Funds Between the Time the Old Loan Is Paid and a New Loan Is Made. Lenders also contend that they lose interest during the time it takes to reloan prepaid monies.

Consumer advocates rejoin, "In the dark ages before mass lending and computerized fund placement systems, this may have been true. But today money in vast quantities can be shifted around the globe with the punch of a key. Within a matter of hours, a day or two if the lender is badly managed, redeposited funds are back in play."

The Lender Needs Protection Against the Borrower Prepaying When Rates Fall. One argument supporting prepayment charges relates to interest rate fluctuations. When rates rise, borrowers clutch their below-market loans like umbrellas in a downpour. When rates fall, they drop them fast.[158] Lenders take a drubbing come rain or shine in the money market, and prepayment charges are their only protection against getting washed out.

In response, prepayment fee opponents contend that: (1) interest rate fluctuations are part of what the lender already charges the borrower in setting rates; (2) at most, this rationale would only justify prepayment penalties when borrowers repay loans whose rates are above current market rates. Lenders don't need protection when borrowers repay loans whose rates are lower than prevailing market rates because they are actually getting a windfall; (3) the prepayment penalty commonly assessed in residential

---

[158] Jerry Green & John B. Shoven, *The Effects of Interest Rates on Mortgage Prepayments,* 18 J. Money, Credit and Banking 41 (1986).

loans—six months interest on the amount prepaid which exceeds 20% of the original balance—bears no connection to the lender's interest rate loss when loans with above-market rates are prepaid.

When the borrower voluntarily sells and pockets a substantial capital gain to boot, many courts are sympathetic to lenders, and condone their skimming off just a little of the cream that the borrower might never have enjoyed but for the initial loan. Lenders count on most long-term mortgage loans being prepaid before maturity, 7–11 years for most 30-year loans, and expect fees from prepayments.

Many bankruptcy courts have been unsympathetic to prepayment fees. Borrowers selling on the eve of, or during bankruptcy, aren't going home with full pockets. Giving secured lenders prepayment fee gravy can mean depriving hungry unsecured creditors of anything.

§ 104.05(d)(4) The Legal Challenge to Prepayment Penalties.

One of the leading challenges to prepayment penalties was brought by Mr. Lazzareschi. He thought he had a good case when he took San Francisco Savings and Loan Association to court in 1967. They wouldn't allow him to prepay a $300,000 loan on property used for commercial purposes at 5% in a 9% market unless he paid them $9,130.32 as a prepayment charge.[159] "They should thank me, not penalize me," was the thrust of his argument in *Lazzareschi Investment Co. v. San Francisco Federal Savings and Loan Association*, "They will be able to reloan this $300,000 at a rate higher than they are getting on it right now."

Mr. Lazzareschi's legal argument had three parts:

(a) *Is a Prepayment Fee a Penalty?* In real estate contracts, California courts let sellers pocket only so much of a breaching buyer's downpayment as absolutely necessary to cover the seller's actual loss from the breach. Lazzareschi didn't see why lenders shouldn't likewise get their hands slapped for trying to squeeze more from prepaying borrowers than the prepayment really cost the lender. If individual sellers aren't allowed to recover unless they experience an actual loss, why should lenders be?

The court answered: prepayment isn't a breach because it is the borrower's voluntary choice. The court in *Lazzareschi* held, as most courts do, that the fee wasn't a penalty because it was the borrower who elected to prepay. The prepayment privilege was exercisable solely at the borrower's discretion. It is like an option contract. The prepayment fee is what the borrower pays for exercising the option to prepay. Option fees aren't ever regarded as "penalties." A sensible borrower who isn't profiting from the exercise of the option won't exercise it. So prepayment fees shouldn't be treated as if they were penalties for breach.

---

[159] 99 Cal. Rptr. 417 (1971).

(b) *Should Prepayment Provisions Be Tested Against Rules Concerning Liquidated Damages?* If they were, they would probably be unenforceable. First, money damages are always easy to estimate in prepayment cases. The lender's actual loss is readily calculable. It is the present value of the differential between the contract rate and the market rate at the date of prepayment, multiplied by the repaid principal. Furthermore, the price loans bring in the secondary market can be used to determine "market value at date of breach."

Moreover, the customary penalty of six months' interest on the unpaid principal balance above 20% bears no reasonable relationship to the lender's probable loss.

In a rising market the lender has no loss. It can relend the funds at a mark-up above what the prepaying borrower had contracted to pay. In a falling market, six months' interest would give the lender too much or too little depending on the gap between the contract rate and the market rate at date of breach. Anyway, that is the borrower's case against prepayment penalties as invalid liquidated damages.

Many courts, including California's, reject the application of liquidated damages criteria to prepayments. Liquidated damages rules only apply when a contract has been breached. A borrower exercising a prepayment privilege isn't breaching the contract at all. The borrower is electing an alternate route to performance of the contract. The prepayment fee isn't meant to be an estimate of the lender's damage in the event of a breach of contract—like a late payment penalty, for instance. Rather, it is the price for the borrower deciding to go with an alternate performance.

The theory of "voluntary alternate performance" fails, of course, when the prepayment is triggered by the mortgaged property being taken by eminent domain, destroyed by a casualty, or when the lender exercises its option to accelerate upon default or a change in ownership.

Some bankruptcy courts have rejected the "voluntary alternate performance" theory. Since at common law borrowers have no right to prepay, a prepayment is a breach of the contract to borrow money for a fixed time. "[T]he charge is a liquidated damage provision inserted to compensate the lender for the breach of early payment, and is not part of an alternative performance."[160] Bankruptcy courts may regard prepayments resulting from reorganizations as involuntary, and may therefore be prepared to characterize prepayment fees as penalties for breach.

(c) *Usury.* Add the six months prepaid interest to the face interest on the loan, and it will sometimes add up to more than the state statutory interest rate maximum under usury laws. Should prepayments be regarded as

---

[160] *In re* A. J. Lane & Co., 113 B.R. 821, 825 (Bankr. D. Mass. 1990). *But see In re* Financial Center Assoc., 140 B.R. 829 (Bankr. E.D N.Y. 1992)

"interest," and subjected to usury limits?[161]

Most institutional lenders are exempt from state usury limits by federal law. But even if they weren't, the *Lazzareschi* court explained that the fee isn't a charge for the use of money. It is a charge for NOT using the money.[162]

Nonetheless, the court in *Lazzareschi* acknowledged that some prepayment penalties could be so high as to bump into the ceiling of "unconscionability." The six months' interest fee wasn't held unreasonable or unconscionable in *Lazzareschi* because it was exactly the sum allowed at the time by the Federal Home Loan Bank Board in all residential loans subject to its jurisdiction (virtually all savings associations in the U.S.) until 1984. Currently, savings banks are free to contract for any rate.[163]

§ 104.05(d)(5)   Impact of Prepayment Fee on Sellers.

Sellers are well advised to calculate the dent a prepayment charge will make in their net sale proceeds before committing themselves to a fixed selling price. To save the prepayment fee, some sellers shift this cost to the buyer by contract. Buyers who have to pay the prepayment fee may try harder to assume the existing loan and think twice before electing to refinance.

§ 104.05(d)(6)   Yield Maintenance Fees.

Commercial prepayment fees are often computed on the basis of "yield maintenance." This is the sum which, if invested at prevailing market rates, will give the lender its bargained rate of return. The formula should be constructed to take into account the unpaid balance of the loan, accrued interest, and the original loan term.[164] Here is a typical "yield maintenance" provision for a fixed-rate mortgage:

> The "Note Prepayment Fee" shall be (i) the present value of all remaining payments of principal and interest, discounted at the Treasury Rate, less (ii) the amount of principal being prepaid, but shall not be less than zero. The "Treasury Rate" shall be the annualized yield on securities issued by the United States Treasury having a maturity equal to the remaining term of the Loan, as quoted in Federal Reserve Statistical Release H. 15 (519) under the heading "U.S. Government Securities—Treasury Constant Maturities" for the date most nearly two weeks before the prepayment date (or a

---

[161] *See, also* Gulf Coast Inv. Corp. v. Prichard, 438 S.W.2d 658 (Tex. Civ. App. 1969) (Dallas 1969) *writ refused* 447 S.W.2d 676 (Tex. Sup. Ct. J. 1969).

[162] *See, also* Boyd v. Life Ins. Co. of the Southwest, 546 S.W.2d 132 (Tex. 1977) (holding that prepayment charges do not constitute interest for usury purposes). Annotation, *Usury as Affected by Repayment of, or Borrower's Option to Repay, Loan Before Maturity*, 75 A.L.R. 2d 1265 (1961).

[163] 12 C.F.R. § 545.34(c).

[164] Warrington 611 Assocs. v. Aetna Life Ins. Co., 705 F. Supp. 229 (D.N.J. 1989).

comparable rate if this rate is no longer published), adjusted to reflect a monthly payment interval. If the above rate is not available for a term equal to the remaining term of the loan, the Treasury Rate shall be determined by interpolating between the yields on securities of the next longer and the next shorter maturity.[165]

This sort of yield maintenance provision has been enforced in non-bankruptcy situations, but has been set aside in several bankruptcy cases as an "unreasonable fee, cost or charge. . .."[166] One court faulted a yield maintenance clause that had failed to credit the borrower by discounting to present value and also because it used the market rate for U.S. Treasury notes instead of the market rate for first mortgages due on the day that the loan would have been repaid.[167] The reason the Treasury note rate gives the mortgage lender too much is that the mortgage lender will be able to loan prepaid funds at a premium above the Treasury note rate. Under the yield maintenance formula the prepaying borrower receives no credit for that premium. "It would have been permissible for the parties to have chosen an index rate such as that for U.S. Treasury notes that differs from the market for long term first mortgages, provided that some appropriate adjustment to bring this note up to the first mortgage rate was included." The same note was also faulted for containing no discount for present value. The prepayment fee provision had one more flaw; it had a floor, obligating the borrower to pay 1% of the prepaid principal, even if the yield maintenance clause produced a zero net to the lender. The lender defended this as a way of recouping the costs it had incurred in originating the loan. The court rejected the argument because the lender had given the borrower no credit against transaction costs for the time the loan had been in effect. Also, the sum in the case ($150,000) exceeded any reasonable cost imputed to loan origination. Another bankruptcy court went further; the loan was prepaid at a time when interest rates were higher than the contract rate. Since the lender could have invested the loan proceeds at a higher rate, the bankruptcy court decided to credit the borrower with this windfall.[168] Lazzareschi would have been delighted, but lenders' counsel aren't pleased by these results.[169]

A yield maintenance fee provision that would protect the lender's expectations of return and protect the borrower by discounting the loss to

---

[165] James L. Lipscomb, Structuring Complex Real Estate Transactions 20 (1992 Cum. Supp.).

[166] 11 U.S.C. § 506(b).

[167] *In re* Skyler Ridge, 80 B.R. 500 (Bankr. C.D. Cal. 1987). The parties agreed that the yield maintenance clause should be regarded as a liquidated damage provision. *But see In re* Financial Center Assoc., 140 B.R. 829 (Bankr. E.D N.Y. 1992).

[168] *In re* Kroh Bros. Dev. Co., 88 B.R. 997 (Bankr. W.D. Mo. 1988).

[169] James L. Lipscomb, Structuring Complex Real Estate Transactions 22 (1992 Cum. Supp.).

present value and eliminating fixed percentage premiums might use the following calculation to determine the prepayment fee:

> Multiply the outstanding principal balance which is being prepaid by the difference between the interest rate then in effect on the note and the Reference Rate (defined as U.S. Treasury Notes, market rate on conventional first mortgages, etc.), on a monthly basis, to arrive at a Monthly Payment Differential. The present value would reflect the number of scheduled monthly payments foregone as a result of the prepayment, the size of the Monthly Payment Differential, and the Reference Rate, by discounting an annuity (using the standard formula for the present value of an annuity) equal to the Monthly Payment Differential for the number of months remaining, to an interest rate equal to the Reference Rate.[170]

§ 104.05(d)(7)   Are Partial Payments Allocated to the Final Payments Due on the Loan or to Current Payments?

Say a borrower has lots of cash in December and January, so the borrower makes six months of loan payments in advance. In February and March, the borrower runs short of cash. May the lender foreclose or must it allocate the early payments to cover the February and March deficits? Courts differ in their answers.

One California court held that the borrower was out of luck because the prepayments are applied to the last payment due,[171] but a Texas court found *for* the borrower and required the lender to apply the prepaid sums to current payments.[172]

§ 104.05(d)(8)   Lender Who Mistakenly or Inadvertently Waives a Prepayment Fee Can't Recover It Later from the Borrower.

In 1988 the borrowers borrowed $7,060,000 at 10.25% on a loan due in 1995. A year later, they wanted to refinance when rates fell to 9%. But their note called for a prepayment fee. It would have come to $653,998.74 at that time. They called their loan servicer to ask what fee it would charge if they refinanced elsewhere to take advantage of falling rates. "Nada," they were told. So they refinanced and paid off the old loan. Fifteen months later, the lender discovered its mistake and went after the borrowers for the big prepayment fee.

---

[170] Robert S. Greenbaum, *Yield Maintenance on Mortgage Prepayment—Another Trap for the Unwary*, Metro. Corp. Counsel, Feb. 1996, at 59.

[171] Smith v. Renz, 265 P.2d 160 (Cal. App. 1954).

[172] Bradford v. Thompson, 470 S.W.2d 633 (Tex. 1971). *See also* Steen v. Bump, 649 N.Y.S.2d 731 (1996). Annotation, *Excess of Payment for One Period as Applicable to Subsequent Period under Contract or Mortgage Providing for Periodic Payments*, 89 A.L.R. 3d 947 (1979).

"Get outta here," the appellate court told the lender. (The court's actual words were the judicial equivalent: "Under the circumstances, recovery by CalFed would be inequitable.") Recovery would be inequitable because: (1) the lender benefits by having the loan fully paid off 5.5 years earlier than its stated maturity, (2) the borrowers would not have refinanced to save less than $90,000 a year for 5.5 years if they had known they would have to pay $653,998.74 for the privilege; (3) the mistake was all the lender's, not the borrower's fault.[173]

§ 104.05(d)(9)   Who Benefits and Who Pays When a Form Mortgage Gives the Borrower the Right to Prepay Without Penalty?

Prepayment is a matter of right in the M.A. form note. Under such a note, the borrower, in effect, enjoys the benefit of the right to prepay without a penalty. This is like a call provision in a bond or stock where the debtor can compel the holder of the note to sell at a prearranged price the original contact price in the case of mortgage loans. The lender or the purchaser of a loan in the secondary mortgage market assumes the risk of prepayment. The risk is that the debtor will compel the lender to sell the note and mortgage at its full face value precisely when it is actually more valuable when the face interest rate is above current market rates, so that the market value of the note is greater than its original contract price. This risk has a price. Lenders who originate or trade in residential mortgages exact that price in the form of higher interest rates than they would accept on mortgage notes where the borrower assumes the prepayment risk by agreeing to pay a steep fee for the right to prepay.

Not all borrowers would place the same value on the right to prepay, given a choice, when the loan is first entered. If all borrowers were given no choice but to accept loans with prepayment provisions, homeowners who didn't expect to pay off mortgages early would be asked to subsidize those who did expect to prepay. Among the most likely to refinance are high-income borrowers with greater liquidity and big equities in their houses. They are in a better position to refinance when interest rates fall than minority and low-income borrowers. They have an easier time finding mortgage money when they desire it. They can offer refinancing lenders safer loans because they have larger equities in their houses. They are more likely to sell and to refinance in connection with a sale as they "trade up" to more expensive houses, or as they relocate for better jobs. Low-income households are less mobile,[174] less likely to find lucrative employment elsewhere, and have a harder time refinancing.

---

[173] California Fed. Bank v. Matreyek, 10 Cal. Rptr. 2d 58 (1992).

[174] *See* Peter Chinoy & Isaac F. Megbolugbe, Hedoni, *Mortgages*, 5 J. Housing Res. 1 (1994).

There is an exception to this rule. Defaulting borrowers automatically trigger an involuntary prepayment when the lender is forced to take back the property through foreclosure. Low-income borrowers are at greater risk of default since they possess thinner cash reserves to cover expenses in times of personal crisis job loss or protracted illness.

What low-income borrowers need who have limited funds for down payments is the chance to buy default insurance instead of paying higher mortgage interest rates for prepayment insurance they are not likely to use.

For this reason, two researchers concluded: "The rules of the mortgage market, with the near-total ban on prepayment penalties, amounts to more than just a subsidy of the wealthier borrowers by the poorer; it is one of the reasons that restrict poor people from getting a mortgage in the first place."[175]

They argue that low-income households would be better off putting the money they saved by agreeing to prepayment penalties towards default insurance. By purchasing extra default insurance, they would make their loans less risky, and more attractive, to lenders. Many low-income borrowers who don't qualify for loans with automatic prepayment rights but also have no borrower-purchased default insurance would qualify if only they could take that portion of the interest rate presently going to cover the lender's prepayment risk and apply it to the purchase of default insurance.

Professor Chinoy and Isaac F. Megbolugbe, the Director of Housing Research at M.A., divide the mortgage market into four groups:

(1)   Low-income borrowers are disproportionately attracted to mortgages insured by the FHA or guaranteed by the VA. VA and FHA loan principal ceilings are lower; loans are capped at the median sales price in the county. These loans also carry low down payment requirements (3% of the first $25,000, 5% of the typical average, with closing costs financeable). Therefore, government-backed loans are more attractive than other types of loans to the low-to moderate-income buyer. Almost half of African-American and Hispanic borrowers finance through the FHA and VA programs. Under these loans, the default risk is insured by mortgage insurance funded by the borrower and paid into a fund called Mutual Mortgage Insurance. Shortfalls are covered by the full faith and credit of the U.S. Treasury, in other words, federal taxpayers. The default insurance premium ranges from 3.8 to 6.5% of the present value of the loan balance.

(2)   Many savings banks and other lenders sell their mortgages to M.A. or F.H.L.M.C.government-sponsored, privately owned institu-

---

[175] *Peter Chinoy*, quoted in Michael Quint, A Mortgage Penalty, or a Plus? New York Times, Oct. 25, 1994, at C1.

tions. They promulgate form mortgages and will only buy mortgages conforming to those form instruments. Lenders originating loans with lower than 80% loan-to-equity ratios must lay off part of the default risk by having the borrower purchase private mortgage insurance.

(3) Private firms unregulated have created secondary market vehicles, buying loans from mortgage brokers and other originators and selling them in pools to investors. Units of Prudential, General Motors, General Electric, Chase Manhattan and Citicorp are among them.

(4) Finally, there are lenders who originate loans to hold in their own portfolios.

The point is that each group uses a form that treats default risk and prepayment risk uniformly throughout its portfolio. Borrowers aren't presented a choice of trading more default protection for less prepayment protection or vice versa. Mortgages are sold like cars with few options. Everyone has to buy a sunroof in some dealerships. No one can get one at any price from other manufacturers. There is no chance of trading off a sunroof for a more powerful engine or antilock brakes. This forces cross-subsidies to buyers who like the features that come with the standardized package from those who would have preferred to pay less and live without these features.

The point is that each group uses a form that treats default risk and prepayment risk uniformly throughout its portfolio. Borrowers aren't presented a choice of trading more default protection for less prepayment protection or vice versa. Mortgages are sold like cars with few options. Everyone has to buy a sunroof in some dealerships. No one can get one at any price from other manufacturers. There is no chance of trading off a sunroof for a more powerful engine or antilock brakes. This forces cross-subsidies to buyers who like the features that come with the standardized package from those who would have preferred to pay less and live without these features.

§ 104.05(d)(10)   The New Generation of Prepayment Charges.

Some lenders are offering borrowers loans with prepayment penalties but not the draconian six months' interest of yesteryear which penalized the borrower for prepaying anytime a sum often greatly in excess of the lender's actuarial loss due to prepayments, with no benefit to the borrower who agreed to it. Under one of the new generation of prepayment penalties, the borrower has the choice of agreeing to pay a charge of 2% of the outstanding loan amount for prepaying in the first three years of the loan. In exchange, the lender reduces the interest rate or closing costs by a sum comfortably exceeding the 2%. The trade-off is extremely attractive to borrowers pretty confident they won't be prepaying in the first three years.[176] Borrowers not interested in the trade-off are given mortgages prepayable without penalty, but pay a higher interest rate for it.

§ 104.05(d)(11)   Impact of Prepayment Fee on Sellers.

Sellers are well-advised to calculate the dent a prepayment charge will make in their net sale proceeds before committing themselves to a fixed selling price. To save the prepayment fee, some sellers shift this cost to the buyer by contract. Buyers who have to pay the prepayment fee may try harder to assume the existing loan and think twice before electing to finance.

§ 104.06   Late Payments.

Most notes, secured or unsecured, levy a "late payment" charge. They have two purposes: (1) to prod borrowers into making timely payments, and (2) to reimburse lenders for the costs of cajoling the tardy, and the loss of earnings on the late payment. The charge could be a fixed dollar amount, a percentage of the late installment, or a percentage of the unpaid balance of the entire debt.

§ 104.06(a)   Legal Theories: Usury and Liquidated Damage Analysis.

In a handful of court fights, challengers have argued that late charges are a form of additional interest and so should be kept within usury limits, or that late charges are a penalty for partial breach and should be evaluated against liquidated damage standards.[177]

Courts have generally rejected the usury analysis because the purchaser can avoid the charge by paying on time. Moreover, the severe penalties that accompany usury infractions also steer courts away from the usury route.[178] On the other hand, Louisiana courts view late charges as additional interest for the lender's extending the credit.[179]

---

[176] *Michael Quint, A Mortgage Penalty, or a Plus?, New York Times*, Oct. 25, 1994, at C1.

[177] *In re* Brunswick Apartments of Trumbull County, Ltd., 169 F.3d 333 (6th Cir. 1999) (The language of the promissory note which allowed the lender to assess a 5% penalty on each late installment payment did not authorize the lender to assess a 5% penalty on the final balloon payment).

[178] Grant S. Nelson & Dale A. Whitman, Real Estate Finance Law 443–47 (5th ed. 2007).

[179] Federal courts have decided late charges are interest, at the behest of out-of-state lenders seeking courts to rule that federal law preempting "interest rates" also preempted state limitations on late charges. Greenwood Trust Co. v. Massachusetts, 971 F.2d 818 (1st Cir. 1992); Hill v. Chemical Bank, 799 F. Supp. 948 (D. Minn. 1992). "While in those cases, it was consumers in states with good consumer protection laws who lost, the precedent is a double-edged sword which may on other occasions support a borrower's argument that late fees are interest." National Consumer Law Center, Usury and Consumer Regulations 69 (1993 Cum. Supp).

The liquidated damage characterization has a larger judicial following, although some courts reject it because they perceive late charges, like prepayment fees, as a contract or option for an alternate performance.[180]

Some would argue that lenders don't need liquidated damage clauses for late payments. Actual damages should suffice because the lender's loss can be readily estimated when the breach occurs by determining the earnings foregone and the costs of collection.

In a leading case on the topic, *Garrett v. Coast and Southern Federal Savings Loan Association*,[181] the California Supreme Court held that a charge of two percent of *the entire principal balance of the debt* was invalid as a penalty. The lender was only damaged by being deprived of payment actually past due. Because only a portion of the principal debt was past due, a late charge could not lawfully be a function of the balance of the entire debt. To be valid, the court held that the late payment charge had to be a function of the amount of money overdue or a fixed dollar sum based on the lender's actual cost of collection. This analysis is widely followed.

§ 104.06(b)   Statutory Limits.

Many states have enacted legal limits on late charges.[182] The limit for F.H.A. and V.A. loans is 4%.[183] Federal regulators have preempted state late

---

[180] *Id.*

[181] 511 P.2d 1197 (Cal. 1973). In 1978, the California legislature revised California Civil Code 1671 to change from establishing presumptive invalidity of liquidated damages clauses to establishing presumptive validity of liquidated damages clauses.

[182] Regulated rates typically range from 2% to 6% of the overdue sum. *See, e.g.*, U.C.C. 2.5925, 1974 (setting a 5% late charge maximum); N.C. Gen. Stat., ch. 24, art. 1 (4% of payment past due, disclosed in advance to borrower); Or. Rev. Stat., tit. 9, ch. 86 (not to exceed 5% of delinquent sum, if reserved by contract, and 15 days overdue); Va. Code Ann., tit. 6.1, ch. 7.3 (not to exceed 5% of sum overdue, free of acceleration, if reserved in contract with borrower, made later than 7 days after due date); W. Va. Code, ch. 31, art. 17 (secondary mortgage loans not to exceed 5% of payment overdue made 15 or more days later); Mass. Gen. Laws Ann. Part II, tit. 1, ch. 38 (3% of sum overdue, if more than 15 days late, applies only to residential mortgage loans, 14 dwelling units).

In California, the late payment fee on a mortgage or trust deed secured by an owner-occupied, single-family dwelling is 6% of the installment due or $5, whichever is greater. A payment is not late until ten days after the due date of the installment. The borrower has to occupy the property within 90 days of signing the deed of trust or mortgage.

If the security property is anything but a single-family, owner-occupied dwelling, the late payment fee is 10% of the installment due or $5, whichever is greater. On a balloon payment loan, the late charge is measured by the largest single monthly installment previously due, other than the balloon payment, multiplied by the sum of one plus the number of months occurring since the late payment charge began to accrue. Cal. Bus. & Prof. Code 20242.5. Bus. & Prof. Code § 10242.5(a) and (c).

[183] 24 C.F.R. § 203.25, 38 C.F.R. § 36.4212(c).

charge rules for federally chartered savings banks.[184] The Federal Housing Administration has done the same for federally insured or guaranteed mortgages.[185]

§ 104.06(c) Stay of Foreclosure During Late Charge "Grace" Period.

Most loans provide a grace period—10 or 15 days—before the late payment penalty accrues.[186] An unintended consequence of the grace period may be that the lender is barred from foreclosing on a chronically late borrower as long as the borrower brings the debt current within the late payment "grace" period.[187]

Justice Johnson, J., defended this result in *Baypoint Mtg. Corp. v. Crest Premium Real Estate Invs. Retirement Trust*[188]:

> One of the most important functions of the law is to maintain a proper balance between creditor and debtor. To this end, it attempts to match the creditor's remedy to the debtor's default. Major defaults justify drastic remedies; minor defaults only warrant lesser remedies. Thus, where the debtor is unable or unwilling to pay at all the creditor is entitled to recapture the security the debtor gave for the loan. By threatening this ultimate loss the creditor often succeeds in pressuring the recalcitrant debtor into coming up with the money to pay the debt after all. If not, the creditor is at least made whole or as nearly whole as he can be by return of the property the debtor put up to secure the loan.

> In this case, appellant Crest Premium asks this court to sanction the use of this same drastic remedy to deal with a minor and common failure of debtors—making installment payments a few days after the initial "due date." This is the functional equivalent of employing a blunderbuss to kill a gnat. Indeed, the loan papers in this case afforded the creditor a remedy more in keeping with the nature of the debtor's offense—a 10 percent "late payment fee" which is imposed after 10 days' delay when the gnat at least could be said to have turned into a fly.

> Great mischief could be visited on creditor-debtor relations in California were we to accept Crest Premium's invitation. To allow creditors to impose foreclosure—and its attendant expenses—whenever a debtor is a few days late in a monthly payment would open up thousands or perhaps millions of California homeowners and other debtors to an extraordinary additional financial burden. Moreover, the threat of such a severe penalty would place

---

[184] 12 U.S.C. § 1735f.

[185] 12 U.S.C. § 1715b.

[186] Miller v. Balcanoff, 566 So.2d 1340 (Fla. Dist. Ct. App. 1990) (The fact that there was a 10-day "grace" provision included in the promissory note did not authorize the lender to accelerate the entire obligation if payments were more than 10 days late).

[187] 214 Cal. Rptr. 531 (1985).

[188] 168 Cal. App.3d at 831–32, 214 Cal. Rptr. at 539–40.

undue pressure on debtors, thus destroying the important but delicate balance between creditors and debtors.

§ 104.06(d)   Acceleration on Default.

Mortgage notes provide that in the event of default the entire debt becomes due and payable. This is called acceleration. Without an acceleration clause, the lender would have to file a separate foreclosure suit each month the borrower missed a payment.

While "equity abhors forfeiture and penalties," an acceleration of debt on a mortgage is regarded as neither a forfeiture nor a penalty.[189] The borrower got the loan proceeds. Acceleration is the first logical step in the lender's reaching the security property for repayment.

> An action to foreclose a mortgage is equitable in nature. . .. In a suit of equitable cognizance to foreclose a real estate mortgage the trial court may refuse foreclosure where there has been a technical default due to a mistake or mere venial inattention and of no damage to the mortgage security or prejudice to the mortgagee.[190]

Courts have stayed acceleration when the borrower was one day late in making a payment because time had not been declared to be of the essence in the note or deed of trust,[191] the lender had consistently accepted late payments on a debt amply secured,[192] or the lender had accepted payments by mail and a mailed check was never received, but the mortgagor cut a new check within a week of being notified of the default.[193]

On the other hand, there are states in which lenders are allowed to accelerate even against borrowers ready to pay up, whose nonpayment or partial payment was due to an honest mistake or a clerical error. The leading case strictly enforcing an acceleration clause against a borrower ready to cure the default is *Graf v. Hope Bldg. Corp.*[194] A clerk cut a check $401.87 short of the required $6,121.56 payment. As soon as the error was caught, the lender was informed. But it never demanded the correct payment. Instead, it waited until the grace period expired and initiated foreclosure. The opinion provided an impassioned dissent by Justice Cardozo:

> When an advantage is unconscionable depends upon the circumstances. It is not unconscionable generally to insist that payment shall be made

---

[189] Jacobson v. McClanahan, 264 P.2d 253 (Wash. 1953).

[190] Beal v. Mars Larsen Ranch Corp., Inc., 586 P.2d 1378, 1382 (Idaho 1978).

[191] Bisno v. Sax, 346 P.2d 814, 818 (Cal. Dist. Ct. App. 1959). *See also* Jenkins v. U.S.A. Foods, Inc., 912 F. Supp. 969 (E.D. Mich. 1996).

[192] Kreiss Potassium Phosphate Co. v. Knight, 124 So. 751 (Fla. 1929). *See generally,* Robert R. Rosenthal, *The Role of Courts of Equity in Preventing Acceleration Predicated Upon a Mortgagor's Inadvertent Default,* 22 Syracuse L. Rev. 897 (1971).

[193] Kerin v. Udolf, 334 A.2d 434 (Conn. 1973).

[194] Graf v. Hope Bldg. Corp., 171 N.E. 884 (N.Y. 1930).

according to the letter of a contract. It may be unconscionable to insist upon adherence to the letter where the default is limited to a trifling balance, where the failure to pay the balance is the product of mistake, and where the mortgagee indicates by his conduct that he appreciates the mistake and has attempted by silence and inaction to turn it to his own advantage.[195]

Despite Justice Cardozo's words often cited outside New York to justify stays of acceleration, strict enforcement of acceleration clauses is the law in New York to this day.[196] The *Graf* rule does *not* apply in New York to payments made late but within the grace period, payments lost in the mail, or where the lender had waived tardiness.

§ 104.06(e)   "Arrears" vs. Advance Payment Schedules.

Notes secured by mortgages or deeds of trust often call for payments to fall due monthly "in arrears" at the end of the month during which the obligation accrued. This is quite a pleasant surprise to former tenants who almost always had been required to pay rent monthly in advance. The present value of the deferral over a 30-year lease equals one month's interest. Some mortgages, though, do call for payment in advance, just like leases, and others for payment in the middle of the month.

§ 104.07   Difference Between "Assuming" and Taking "Subject to."

§ 104.07(a)   When the Distinction Matters.

A buyer may elect to finance a home purchase by arranging a new loan or by keeping the existing loan in place. The buyer's rights will depend on whether the seller's note is assumable and whether it has a due-on-sale clause accelerating the total unpaid balance of the debt if the seller transfers the property without the lender's prior consent. If the buyer decides to keep the existing loan in place, the buyer can either assume it or take subject to it. Here is the difference.

A new buyer takes *subject to the deed of trust* if the deed of trust was duly recorded, or if the buyer actually knows about it and hasn't arranged for the seller to pay it off at closing. A new buyer *assumes the note* if the buyer agrees personally to repay the balance of the debt due.

The difference between a purchaser taking "subject to" the deed of trust and "assuming" the note becomes significant only when the debt exceeds the value of the security property. A buyer taking "subject to" the deed of trust risks losing the property through foreclosure if the debt goes into default. An

---

[195] 171 N.E. at 888.

[196] Bruce J. Bergman, *Strict Acceleration in New York Mortgage Foreclosure—Has the Doctrine Ended?*, 8 Pace L. Rev. 475 (1988). The author concludes: ". . . the doctrine, although sometimes criticized, has not been persuasively or effectively limited or changed." 8 Page at 534. But *Graf* did *not* apply to payments made late but within the grace period, payments lost in the mail, or where the lender had waived tardiness.

assuming grantee is at an even greater risk. Not only does the assuming grantee risk foreclosure on default but, in addition, will be personally liable to cover any deficiency between the debt and what the foreclosure sale yields.

§ 104.07(b)   Protecting the "Subject to" Buyer.

A buyer who plans to keep the existing financing in place needs to condition the obligation to purchase on the lender allowing the buyer to assume or take subject to the loan. The buyer needs to confirm the principal and interest due and whether the loan is in good standing. If tax and insurance impound accounts exist, they should be verified and prorated on closing.[197]

§ 104.07(c)   How the Buyer Becomes an Assuming Grantee.

Typically, L, the lender, has reserved the right to approve A's successors (A being the original borrower). As a condition of loan transfer approval, L will insist that B (the new buyer) sign an agreement personally *promising to repay* the balance of the debt.[198] By signing that agreement, B will become an "assuming grantee."

The formalities necessary for the buyer to become an assuming grantee vary from state to state. In most states, including New York and California, the agreement to assume must be in writing. New York also requires that the amount assumed be stated and that the writing be signed and acknowledged at the time of the conveyance.[199] In California, the assumption agreement must be in writing signed by the assuming grantee or appear in the conveyance itself (which is not signed, ordinarily, by the grantee).[200]

Pennsylvania treats a conveyance subject to a mortgage as the buyer's implied assumption of the debt. But only the seller—not the lender—can sue on the implied assumption.[201]

Parol evidence is admissible to establish that an assumption was truly intended. Some courts require that the evidence be "clear and convincing."[202]

Suppose, though, that the buyer never promises the *lender* to pay off the old debt but does promise the *seller* to pay it off. Can the lender sue the

---

[197] For a more in-depth discussion, *see* Robert Kratovil & Raymond J. Werner, Real Estate Law 363 (9th ed. 1988).

[198] Connecticut Savings Bank v. Obenauf, 758 A.2d 363 (Conn. App. 2000) (transferee of property not liable for promissory debt note owed solely by transferor).

[199] N.Y. Gen. Oblig. Law § 5-705.

[200] 171 Cal. Civ. Code 1624(f).

[201] Steinert v. Galasso, 63 A.2d 443 (Pa. 1949).

[202] Cassidy v. Bonitatibus, 497 A.2d 1018 (Conn. App. 1985).

buyer directly on the promise the buyer made to the seller if the buyer doesn't pay? Yes, on several theories. The most common theory is that the lender is a third-party beneficiary of the buyer's promise to the seller.[203] Another theory is that the buyer's assumption promise is an asset of the seller's that the lender can reach with the aid of equity, an equitable assets theory advanced by Professor Williston.[204] Other concepts have been invoked to justify giving the lender standing to sue the buyer directly.[205] Although the practical consequences of each theory vary,[206] the point is that the lender can sue the buyer on a promise the seller made to the lender to pay the debt. Some states have statutory limits barring lenders from claiming deficiency judgments against buyers. But, in the absence of these statutes, the issue of personal liability casts a shadow that few informed buyers or sellers would overlook in the overbuilt, default-riddled era of the early 1990s.

§ 104.07(d)   Effect on Seller of Buyer Assuming or Taking Subject to the Existing Loan.

Does the seller care whether the buyer meticulously continues payments to the lender once the deal closes? Isn't the seller out of the picture when the buyer moves into the house and starts paying the mortgage? Not necessarily.

Once the seller signs a promissory note to a lender, the seller can't cut the ties to the lender by later contracting to sell the property. When a grantee assumes the existing mortgage, the grantee becomes the primary obligor for the debt. The land is the primary fund for repayment, then the grantee, but the grantor remains as the lender's surety for the grantee.[207]

If the lender recovers against the original seller, the seller may seek reimbursement from her buyer if the buyer had assumed the debt. Even if the buyer only took "subject to" the debt but the lender recovers against the seller, almost all states allow the seller to stand in the lender's shoes and *foreclose* to secure reimbursement.[208] This right is called subrogation. Only in Arizona has the seller's right of subrogation been denied when the buyer took "subject to" the existing mortgage.[209]

---

[203] *See* Grant S. Nelson & Dale A. Whitman, Real Estate Finance Law 296–298 (5th ed. 2007).

[204] Samuel Williston, *Contracts for the Benefit of a Third Person,* 15 Harv. L. Rev. 766, 767 (1902).

[205] *See* Grant S. Nelson & Dale A. Whitman, Real Estate Finance Law 298–300 (5th ed. 2007).

[206] Roger Bernhardt, California Mortgage and Deed of Trust Practice 417 (2d ed. 1990).

[207] Roger A. Cunningham & Saul Tischler, *Transfer of the Real Estate Mortgagor's Interest,* 27 Rutgers L. Rev. 24 (1973).

[208] Seward v. New York Life Ins. Co., 152 S.E. 346 (Va. 1930).

[209] Best Fertilizers of Arizona, Inc. v. Burns, 570 P.2d 179 (Ariz. 1977).

The lender can excuse the original borrower from liability on the note by entering what is called a novation agreement, or a release, and thereby accept the buyer as the sole obligor on the debt. F.H.A.-approved lenders have been instructed to prepare such releases when a homeowner sells to a creditworthy purchaser who executes an agreement to assume and pay the mortgage debt.[210] Fees can be charged for the releases.[211]

The lender may inadvertently release the seller by altering the terms of the underlying obligation in ways that increase the seller's exposure. That certainly would be true if the lender and buyer agreed to raise the interest rate or increase the principal without the seller's consent.[212] It would also be true if the lender released all or part of the security property from the lien of the mortgage. Courts have differed on whether the grantor would be totally discharged[213] or discharged only to the extent of the value of the property released.[214]

States differ on whether extending the date for principal repayment discharges a surety (which is what the seller becomes). The majority rule is that the seller is discharged if the extension was made without his consent.[215] In some states, the seller remains liable despite the time extension, to the extent of the difference between the unpaid debt and the value of the property on the day the debt was originally due.[216] The reasoning for this rule is that the seller is no worse off for the extension and might be better off if the buyer eventually pays up.[217]

The case for releasing the seller is certainly compelling when the value of

---

[210] F.H.A. Mortgage Letter 90-9 (Mar. 20, 1990). The V.A. has a similar rule, 38 C.F.R. §§ 4209, 4232, 4285, as amended by Fed. Reg. 37468 (Sept. 12, 1990).

[211] The original borrower can consent to continued liability which would happen, presumably, only when the lender wasn't entirely satisfied with the successor's credit.

[212] Oellerich v. First Fed. Sav. & Loan Ass'n of Augusta, 552 F.2d 1109 (5th Cir. 1977) (interpreting Georgia law).

[213] Hughes v. Tyler, 485 So. 2d 1026 (Miss. 1986).

[214] Mann v. Bugbee, 167 A. 202 (N.J. 1933). Presumably, if the debt was reduced in proportion to the release, the surety should remain contingently liable for the balance due since she wouldn't have been injured by the release. *See also* Bissonnette v. Wylie, 693 A.2d 1050, 1056 (Vt. 1997) (Proper measure of amount surety may offset against his liability due to impairment of collateral is extent to which collateral was discharged for consideration below its actual value).

[215] Union Mut. Life Ins. Co. v. Hanford, 143 U.S. 187 (1892) (interpreting Illinois law); Antisdel v. Williamson, 59 N.E. 207 (N.Y. 1901).

[216] Feigenbaum v. Hizsnay, 175 N.Y.S. 223 (1919). *See, also* Petters v. Storm, 272 N.W. 409 (Neb. 1937), for the principle that a mortgagee cannot hold a mortgagor liable for any deficiency that the mortgagee himself caused.

[217] However, in a California case, the lender extended the due date on the loan for two years, at the new buyer's request. That alone was held sufficient to justify letting the seller, the original obligor, off the hook. Braun v. Crew, 192 P. 531 (Cal. 1920).

the security property drops like a stone during the extension period and the lender wants the seller to cover the deficiency gap.[218] When the value hasn't declined though, the seller's case for release seems less convincing. The Uniform Commercial Code, which governs negotiable notes, allows a surety to get off the hook when the lender grants a time extension or a material modification, but only to the extent the extension or modification results in the surety recovering less from the primary debtor.[219]

Lenders try to seal off all of the original obligor's escape routes. In a typical deed of trust form, you will find a clause stating that the lender can grant a later owner a time extension or other modification without releasing "the liability of the original Borrower or Borrower's successor in interest." At least one court has held that this language will allow the lender to extend the time for payment without discharging the seller (the original obligor).[220] But it isn't explicit enough to keep the seller on the hook if the lender also raises the interest rate on the debt.[221]

Provisions in the note may oblige an assuming grantee to "keep all of the promises made in this note." Also, the original borrower may waive the right to insist that the note holder demand payment first from the new buyer (presentment), and the right to notice if the new buyer has missed payments (notice of dishonor).

§ 104.08   Restrictions on the Borrower's Right to Assign or Borrow.[222]

§ 104.08(a)   Due-on-Sale.

§ 104.08(a)(1)   The Difference Between Due-on-Sale Clauses and Prohibitions Against Sale.

The borrower remains the owner of the security property even though it is encumbered. A mortgagor or trustor can sell her equity freely and without the lender's consent. The doctrine barring "restraints on alienation" would not allow lenders to restrict the borrower's *right to sell.*

Technically, the rights of the mortgagee are not impaired by the borrower selling her equity.[223] After the sale, the original mortgagor remains liable on

---

[218] George Neff Stevens, *Extension Agreements in the "Subject-To" Mortgage Situation,* 15 U. Cin. L. Rev. 58 (1941).

[219] U.C.C. § 3-605.

[220] First Fed. Sav. & Loan Ass'n of Gary v. Arena, 406 N.E.2d 1279 (Ind. 1980).

[221] *Id.*

[222] *See* Telephone Equipment Network, Inc. v. T/A Westchase Place, Ltd., No. 01-01-00650-CV, 2002 Tex. App. LEXIS 2104 (Tex. App. 2002) (a landlord may obtain a prejudgment attachment of tenant's property to prevent holder of promissory note from improperly selling that property with intent to defraud landlord).

[223] Purdy v. Irwin, 18 Cal. 350 (1861); 44 Cal. Jur. 3d 678 (1978).

the debt (unless discharged by the lender), the new owner either takes subject to the lender's security interest or assumes it, and the lien remains as good against the property as it ever was.

Lenders may nonetheless use "due-on-sale" clauses to restrict indirectly the borrower's right to sell.[224] A "due-on-sale" clause gives the lender the option of declaring all of the unpaid debt immediately due and payable if the borrower sells the security property without the lender's prior consent. In other words, before selling the security property, the borrower would have to pay off the loan, unless the lender were willing to keep the loan in place for the new buyer.

§ 104.08(a)(2)   Why Homeowners Don't Like Due-on-Sale Clauses.

Homeowners prefer having the option of passing along their existing loans to their buyers, especially if the loans are at below-market rates.

Tempers flared over the "due-on-sale" issue in the late 1970s and early 1980s, when inflation drove mortgage rates close to 20%. Homeowners with 7–10% fixed-rate loans desperately wanted to pass those loans onto their buyers as an added incentive. Many homeowners would then take back a junior purchase money loan, if necessary, to make the deal work. But lenders were equally determined to call in as many of those deeply below-market loans as they could. The rate of inflation exceeded the nominal rate of interest on many of these loans so that *real* rates of interest were negative. No wonder borrowers wanted to pass these loans along and lenders wanted to call them in.

§ 104.08(a)(3)   The Legal Battle Congress Resolved in Favor of Lenders.

About a dozen state courts and legislatures were extremely friendly to the borrowers and insisted, through case law or statutes, that buyers be allowed to assume existing loans if they proved creditworthy and the transfer wouldn't result in an impairment of the lender's security.[225]

Congress came down hard on the side of the lenders, whose deposits it was insuring for billions, and preempted the field. It enacted the Garn-St. Germain Act, under which lenders are entitled to enforce due-on-sale clauses with certain modest limitations, described later.[226]

The federal law applies to every "loan, mortgage, advance, or credit sale

---

[224] *Spanish Oaks, Inc. v. Hy-Vee, Inc.*, 655 N.W.2d 390 (Neb. 2003).

[225] *See* Grant S. Nelson & Dale A. Whitman, Real Estate Transfer, Finance, and Development 471 (8th ed. 2009); Richard C. Maxwell, *The Due-on-Sale Clause: Restraints on Alienation and Adhesion Theory in California,* 28 U.C.L.A. L. Rev. 197 (1980).

[226] 96 Stat. 1505, 12 U.S.C. § 1705-3, as amended Nov. 30, 1983, 97 Stat. 1237.

secured by a lien on real property." Every secured lender is protected by the act.

§ 104.08(a)(4)   Why Lenders Use Due-on-Sale Clauses.

Lenders use due-on-sale clauses for four reasons: (1) to make sure that the new borrower is a good credit risk, (2) to reappraise the security property to see if it is still valuable enough to justify keeping the debt in place, (3) to bring the loan interest rate and its terms in line with prevailing market rates and terms, and (4) to reduce the volume of real estate loans in their portfolios.

The third objective is so important that due-on-sale clauses are far more likely to be found in fixed rate than in adjustable rate loans. Most adjustables are "freely assumable."[227]

§ 104.08(a)(5)   Why Due-on-Sale Clauses Are Optional, Not Automatic.

Well drafted "due-on-sale" clauses avoid accelerating loans *automatically* when the mortgagor sells for three reasons: (1) lenders want to forestall clever borrowers from selling and later trying to avoid prepayment penalties by claiming that the loan was called as a result of the "due-on-sale" provision; (2) lenders often allow assumption. They are happy with the new buyer and the loan (adjusted to the prevailing market rates); and (3) the federal law protecting all lenders against state interference with the enforcement of due-on-sale clauses was written to apply only to optional acceleration clauses.[228]

§ 104.08(a)(6)   Congressional Limits on Lenders' Rights to Invoke Due-on-Sale Clauses in Residential Transactions.

The act does place some limits on the situations in which home mortgage lenders (those secured by "less than five dwelling units") are free to invoke their due-on-sale clauses. The limits described below do not apply to lenders on commercial property—anything other than properties secured by less than five dwelling units. Here is the statutory list of transactions in which home mortgage lenders are prohibited from deploying due-on-sale clauses:

(1)   the creation of a lien or other encumbrance subordinate to the

---

[227] *See* Paula C. Murreay Due-on-Sale Clauses in Adjustable Rate Mortgages, 12 Real Est. L.J. 229 (1984).

[228] Presumably, the act would not protect lenders inserting increased-interest-on-transfer clauses in their loans, allowing assumptions, but at higher rates. However, lenders wouldn't need federal protection against state courts if they were using increased interest clauses. The doctrine most cited by state courts to strike down due-on-sale clauses was that those clauses unduly restrained the borrowers' right to aliennate mortgaged property. Increased-interest clauses probably wouldn't run afoul of state court "restraint" rules as long as the rate didn't exceed market rates at the time.

lender's security instrument which does not relate to a transfer of rights of occupancy in the property;[229]

(2) the creation of a purchase money security interest for household appliances;

(3) a transfer by devise, descent, or operation of law on the death of a joint tenant or tenant by the entirety;

(4) the granting of a leasehold interest of three years or less not containing an option to purchase;

(5) a transfer to a relative resulting from the death of a borrower;

(6) a transfer where the spouse or children of the borrower become an owner of the property;

(7) a transfer resulting from a decree of a dissolution of marriage, legal separation agreement, or from an incidental property settlement agreement, by which the spouse of the borrower becomes an owner of the property;

(8) a transfer into an inter vivos trust in which the borrower is and remains a beneficiary and which does not relate to a transfer of rights of occupancy in the property; or

(9) any other transfer or disposition described in regulations prescribed by the Federal Home Loan Bank Board.[230]

Congress passed a law "encouraging" lenders utilizing "due-on-sale"

---

[229] The transactions to which due-on-sale clauses can apply include: sales of the property by installment sale contract, long-term leases with options, or other devices in which junior financing is made, usually by the vendor, to facilitate a disguised sale.

A borrower who sells and takes back a purchase money loan invites the lender's accelerating under a due-on-sale clause. Sometimes borrowers attempt to evade these provisions by entering long-term installment sale contracts. They remain the primary obligor on the existing mortgage loan. The new buyer enters a contract of sale and takes possession. The buyer makes payments on the contract sufficient to enable the seller to pay the existing debt. When the buyer has paid enough to establish an equity of her own in the property, most installment sale contracts allow the buyer to obtain a deed and a purchase money mortgage.

Is the installment sale contract a sale or transfer sufficient to justify the lender accelerating under a due-on-sale clause? Or must the lender wait until the contract is executed and the property deeded? Courts are divided. In one sense, the acceleration can be seen as unjustified because the seller, the original borrower, remains the legal owner. The federal exemption for junior financing doesn't apply "to a transfer of rights of occupancy in the property." Installment contracts usually involve a change in possession.

The typical due-on-sale clause explicitly anticipates and precludes the use of an installment sale contract as a way to evade acceleration on sale: "If all or any part of the Property OR ANY INTEREST IN IT IS SOLD OR TRANSFERRED. . . ." The sale under a contract certainly counts as the transfer of an interest in the property. *See* New Home Fed. Sav. & Loan Assn., 482 A.2d 625 (Pa. 1989).

[230] 12 U.S.C. § 1701j-3(d).

powers "to permit an assumption of a real property loan at the existing contract rate or at a rate which is at or below the average between the contract and market rate . . . and nothing in this section shall be interpreted to prohibit any such assumption."[231] The statute only encourages, it doesn't require, lenders to give assuming borrowers a rate break. Presumably, though, homebuyers will seldom be interested in assuming a loan at rates above current market.

§ 104.08(a)(7)   States Could Opt Out of the Federal Rule Favoring Due-on-Sale Clauses but Only as Applied to State Chartered Lenders.

The federal law gave states the option of applying their own rules to due-on-sale clauses appearing in the mortgages of *state-chartered and regulated* lending institutions. Maine,[232] Massachusetts,[233] New York,[234] South Carolina,[235] and Wisconsin[236] exercised their option. In these states, due-on-sale clauses are enforceable if they are written by a federally chartered lender, but they might not be if the loan is written by a state-chartered lender. State law must be consulted to determine their enforceability in those five states.

§ 104.08(b)   Due-on-Encumbrance: Restrictions on the Borrower's Right to Further Borrowing.

A due-on-encumbrance clause gives the lender the right to declare the entire unpaid balance of the debt due and payable if the borrower takes out another loan secured by the same property without the lender's consent.

§ 104.08(b)(1)   Why Senior Lenders Sometimes Benefit from Borrower's Obtaining Second Mortgages.

Why should a senior lender care if a borrower takes on junior debt? The presence of other potential payors should calm the senior creditor. The junior lender becomes a second potential source of repayment for the senior. If the senior's debt isn't paid on time and it forecloses, the junior lien will be erased if there isn't enough money from the sale to pay them all. Thus, juniors have an incentive to forestall foreclosure sales by doing their best to make sure that the debtor doesn't default, even if this means personally making payments the borrower skips.

A senior lender won't lose its lien priority to a junior creditor unless the

---

[231] 12 U.S.C. § 1201j-3(b)(3).

[232] Me. Rev. Stat. Ann. tit. 9-A, § 1-110.

[233] Mass. Gen. L. ch. 183, § 60.

[234] N.Y. Banking Law § 6-g.

[235] S.C. Code Ann. § 29-3-10.

[236] Wis. Stat. § 138.053.

senior later decides to modify its loan terms in a way that jeopardizes the junior's security interest without the junior's consent.

One advisor counsels purchasers of junior liens:

> If you are a junior lien holder, a letter should be written to the senior lender advising him of your address and telephone number and that you are also a lender on the property. Assure him that you recognize your responsibility to protect senior lenders, and state your willingness to step in to cover any defaults. Such a letter, coupled with a request that you be notified of any default, often goes a long way toward encouraging the senior's goodwill.

> Attaining the senior's goodwill can be valuable if the borrower defaults in his obligations: Unless the senior is agreeable to some other arrangement, the borrower's failure to keep up his payments will ordinarily compel you to step in and cover senior defaults. Furthermore, unless you've given the senior appropriate notice . . . an uncooperative senior may not bother informing you of a default in his loan until he gets around to commencing foreclosure—after as much as a year's past due payments have accumulated. And unless the senior is obliging enough to coordinate his efforts with you, the borrower's filing bankruptcy will trigger independent legal action by the senior, the cost of which may be deducted from your security.[237]

Senior creditors know that junior lienors are another potential source of repayment but they defend due-on-encumbrance clauses anyway.

§ 104.08(b)(2)   Why Lenders Don't Like to See Borrowers Encumber Property Too Much.

They point out that borrowers can stretch themselves too thin through subsequent borrowing. If a borrower has little or no cash in a project, the borrower may be tempted to make riskier moves. If things go badly, the lender gets stuck with the downside loss. If things go well, the borrower keeps the gravy above the loan amount. Lenders like to know the borrower has something to lose if things go badly. As one scholar puts it: "In the extreme case in which the value of the firm equals the value of outstanding debt, the firm has nothing to lose and everything to gain by adopting a 'shoot the moon' strategy."[238] Furthermore, once a project is heavily mortgaged, the borrower may decide not to invest in it even if the investment would be profitable because too much of the yield will go to pay off loans.

Lenders also fear that commercial developers, especially, would lose any incentive to "mind the store" if they were free to mortgage away all their equity. They would direct their personal attention and talents to projects in which they had substantial equities, and not to projects "owned" by their

---

[237] George Coats, Smart Trust Deed Investment in California 93 (2d ed. 1988).

[238] Daniel R. Fischel, *The Economics of Lender Liability,* 99 Yale L.J. 131, 134 (1989).

lenders. Finally, there is compelling evidence that borrowers are much more likely to default on properties with no equities or negative equities, than on properties in which they have substantial equity.

§ 104.08(b)(3)   Why Homeowners Need Home Equity Loans.

For homeowners, a due-on-encumbrance clause can work a great hardship. Many homeowners have no substantial assets except the equity values in their houses. They may need to borrow for health emergencies and tuition, or just to stay solvent. Forcing them to get their home mortgage lender's approval before taking on junior debt might result in compromising their access to a home equity loan which could be their best source of ready cash in an emergency.

A due-on-encumbrance clause doesn't prohibit the debtor from borrowing more. It only stops her from encumbering property which is already secured. The borrower can still obtain unsecured loans, and these can burden a borrower even more since unsecured financing is quite costly.

§ 104.08(b)(4)   The Congressional Word on Due-on-Encumbrance Clauses.

Congress voted to protect homeowners by prohibiting due-on-encumbrance clauses in home loans. Lenders are thus barred from calling in loans merely because their borrowers pledged their house to secure a home equity loan. (An "equity" loan is any loan secured by whatever value the debtor still has in the property after at least one secured debt.)

In contrast, Congress didn't prohibit lenders from pulling the plug on commercial developers who borrow against already encumbered property. In these situations, state law governs. Where state courts find due-on-encumbrance clauses to be "unreasonable restraints on alienation" or otherwise objectionable, such clauses are unenforceable.

§ 104.08(b)(5)   Possible State Court Responses to Commercial Lenders' Due-on-Encumbrance Clause Enforcement Practices.

Consider the circumstances under which a state court might grant or deny a lender the right to enforce a due-on-encumbrance clause:

Case One: the lender makes a first mortgage loan of $100,000 when the security property was worth $150,000. Its value is now $300,000. The borrower wants to borrow a second $100,000. The lender will refinance the existing loan but only at a rate much higher than the borrower is currently paying, and greater than what other lenders are charging for a second or "home equity" loan. If the borrower goes elsewhere for junior funding the lender threatens to call the senior loan, especially if its interest rate is below market.

The lender in this case can be said to be engaging in opportunistic behavior. The borrower will certainly contend that the lender is attempting to obtain a benefit not contemplated by the initial agreement at the borrower's expense. The lender will rejoin that it contemplated using this clause as a way to call loans in a rising market.

Case Two: The senior lender makes the same loan but this time, the borrower's financial situation has deteriorated and the value of the security property is now $125,000. The borrower seeks another $25,000 in secured debt.[239]

Here, the borrower's claim that the lender is engaging in opportunistic behavior is unpersuasive. The senior lender's fears of loss are justifiable. If the lender believes that enforcing the due-on-encumbrance clause will help preserve the security interest it had bargained for, it is easy to see why courts might agree and allow the lender to call the loan if the borrower infringes on a due-on-encumbrance provision.

§ 104.08(b)(6)   Drafting and Interpreting "Due-on" Clauses.

Even in those circumstances where a senior lienor could enforce a due-on-encumbrance clause, the lender still needs to have reserved that right in its note and mortgage. Suppose the loan only contains a "due-on-sale" clause but makes no mention of "encumbrances?" The mortgage prohibits the "sale or transfer of all or any part of the property or any interest in it." Does this encompass a "mortgage or further encumbrance?" The answer is not obvious.[240]

Lenders can argue that a "sale" includes an encumbrance since the very point of any security instrument is to give the lender the *right to sell* the property in the event of default.

Borrowers can respond that ambiguities are read against the drafter, which is generally the lender. So, if the lender had meant to prohibit further secured borrowing, it should have said so plain and clear. Thoughtful drafting keeps these types of disputes at a minimum.

If a Senior Lienor Doesn't Accelerate When the Borrower Incurs Junior Encumbrances, Is the Senior Lienor Barred from Accelerating When the Junior Lien Is Foreclosed?

The statutory exception barring home mortgage lenders from invoking due-on-sale or due-on-encumbrance clauses expressly allows lenders to

---

[239] A majority of state courts which confronted a comparable "restraints on alienation" challenge to the enforcement of due-on-sale clauses before the federal law was enacted upheld these clauses as reasonable per se when lenders invoked them just to raise rates to prevailing market levels. *See* Grant S. Nelson & Dale A. Whitman, Real Estate Transfer, Finance, and Development 460, text at n.4 (4th ed. 1992).

[240] Annotation, *Validity and Enforceability of Due-on-Sale Real-Estate Mortgage Provisions*, 61 A.L.R. 4th 1070 (1988).

accelerate when those devices are accompanied by transfers of rights to occupancy in the property.

A junior lien results in a change in the right to occupy the property only on foreclosure when the original borrower is displaced by the purchaser at the foreclosure sale. Despite this, at least two courts have held that even on foreclosure, the lender may not accelerate. The statutory "change of occupancy" language only applies at "the creation of a lien." It makes no explicit provision for lien foreclosures. ". . . [t]he lender should reasonably anticipate that the borrower could default and the second lien could be foreclosed upon."[241]

Fewer than one loan in a hundred results in foreclosure. So, arguably, it would be wrong to require the senior lienor to act as if every borrower who takes out a home equity loan is headed down the road of default.

When the lender forecloses on the junior lien, some courts have held that the senior lienor should not have to live with the purchaser at foreclosure anymore than it would have been obliged to accept any other substitute owner. Congress must not have intended that result when it enacted the "occupancy transfer" exception.

"Foreclosure of the second mortgage . . . transfer title, all incidents of ownership, and occupancy to third parties with whom the first mortgage holder has not dealt."[242]

A dissenting judge in the above case observed:

> The effect of the majority's ruling will be to limit the availability and increase the cost of equity loans, since secondary lenders must now face a new threat to their security in the event of a foreclosure. Such a ruling harms the homeowner, contradicts the deed of trust at issue, and is inconsistent with our law.[243]

§ 104.08(c) The Double Whammy: Prepayment Penalties Coupled with Due-on-Sale or Due-on-Encumbrance Clauses.

A borrower who is desperately eager to sell her house and equally anxious to avoid paying a prepayment penalty needs to find a buyer willing to take title subject to the loan in place. Her efforts can be thwarted by a lender who refuses to accept the buyer and, instead, invokes a due-on-sale clause, calling the loan and demanding a prepayment fee.

Some courts see nothing wrong with a lender including both prepayment

---

[241] Blitz v. Marion, 786 P.2d 490, 492 (Colo. App. 1989). *See also* Matter of Ruepp, 321 S.E.2d 517 (N.C. App. 1984).

[242] Unifirst Federal Sav. v. Tower Loan of Miss., 524 So. 2d 290, 293 (Miss. 1986).

[243] *Unifirst Federal Sav.*, 524 So. 2d at 295. The dissent pointed out that the phrase "sold or transferred" in a due-on-sale clause does not explicitly include the granting of a lien, or the enforcement, execution or foreclosure of such a lien.

penalty and due-on-sale clauses in the same mortgage, as long as they aren't invoked concurrently. A court which sanctioned the use of both those clauses in the same loan explained it this way:

> The two provisions, rather than working contemporaneously, are used as economic complements to one another. While the *due-on-sale clause* enables a lender to require early payment of lower than market interest rate loans, the *prepayment penalty* is used to discourage refinancing by the borrower when market interest rates fall below the rate on the borrower's existing loan. The two provisions, therefore, are used by lenders to achieve different goals. Both are at least arguably necessary to protect a lender's long term loan portfolio.[244]

Still, if the lender enforces both a steep prepayment fee and a due-on-sale clause at the same time, he puts the borrower in a tight bind. Suppose a young lawyer buys a house for $300,000, putting $60,000 down. Later, she learns that her firm is going out of business and that her services will no longer be needed. She finds a job in a city 200 miles away and decides to sell her house. Her mortgage of $240,000 calls for a prepayment penalty of six months' interest. The interest rate is 10%, fixed, and the loan is fully amortized over a 25-year term.

She lists her house for $325,000. Her best offer is $320,000. After paying a 6% brokerage commission, title and closing costs, she would be left with just enough to pay off the loan and start looking again for a comparable house where she found her new job.

But what about the prepayment penalty of nearly $12,000? Her "equity" would be reduced from $60,000 to $48,000 if she had to pay it. So instead, she shifts the prepayment fee obligation to her buyer in the purchase-and-sale contract. (Note that if the buyer decides to take subject to the existing loan, no one will have to pay the $12,000. This gives her buyers a powerful incentive—$12,000 worth—to think twice before objecting to keeping the loan in place).

What if the lender should turn down the buyer? The lender might reject the buyer because of his credit history or because interest rates have risen and the lender wants a higher rate of interest. The seller will be able to avoid the prepayment penalty only by finding a better qualified buyer or a buyer

---

[244] McCausland v. Bankers Life Ins. Co., 757 P.2d 941, 946 (Wash. 1988). While the text of the court's opinion ascribes "different goals" to prepayment and due-on-sale clauses, the paragraph itself ascribes the same goal—minimizing the lender's interest risk—to both clauses. The lender invokes due-on-sale when the market rate of interest exceeds the loan contract rate. The lender invokes prepayment when the market rate of interest is lower than the contract rate. *See generally* Annotation, *Validity and Construction of Provision of Mortgage or Other Real-Estate Financing Contract Prohibiting Prepayment for a Fixed Period of Time,* 81 A.L.R.4th 423 (1990). *But see* Warrington 611 Assoc. v. Aetna Life Ins. Co., 705 F. Supp. 229 (D. N.J. 1989); George v. Fowler, 978 P.2d 565 (Wash. App. 1999) (A prepayment penalty does not conflict with the due-on-sale clause).

willing to pay the higher interest rate.

Maybe the lender is exercising the due-on-sale clause in hopes of getting paid off because it wants to have less money invested in real estate mortgages. Perhaps its regulators have increased the lender's capital requirements and the lender is calling real estate loans like crazy to firm-up its liquidity picture. Under these circumstances, prepayment will be unavoidable if the seller still needs to sell. Will the seller be liable for the prepayment fee if the prepayment was involuntary?

The borrower may see no reason why she should have to pay a penalty for prepayment. Her only choice is to pay off the old loan or forfeit the right to sell her house. Conversely, lenders see no reason why they shouldn't collect prepayment penalties even when the buyer was willing to keep the loan in place but the lender wasn't. After all, the borrower needn't have sold. Further, if prepayment penalties weren't due on these occasions, a borrower could avoid them by threatening a sale and daring the lender to invoke the clause. The borrower could then claim that the acceleration was involuntary and that the lender's right to levy a prepayment fee was forfeited.

The borrower has the edge when the prepayment clause doesn't expressly apply to both involuntary and voluntary accelerations. In these cases, courts are likely to hold that the prepayment clause was only intended to be applied for voluntary prepayments.[245] Nowadays though, most prepayment penalty clauses are written to come into play whether the loan is paid off voluntarily or not, and even when prepayment follows the lender's rejection of a proffered potential buyer.

In some states, these clauses are enforced as written.[246] Some state legislatures[247] and courts[248] prohibit prepayment penalties when the prepay-

---

[245] Tan v. California Fed. Sav. & Loan Ass'n, 189 Cal. Rptr. 775 (1983). When the loan is prepaid out of fire insurance proceeds, or a condemnation award, courts have held that the implied covenant of good faith prohibits the lender from electing to have the funds used to pay down the loan and charging a prepayment penalty. Milstein v. Security Pac. Nat'l Bank, 103 Cal. Rptr. 16 (1972); 999 v. C.I.T. Corp., 776 F.2d 866 (9th Cir. 1985). *But see* Biancalana v. Fleming, 45 Cal. App. 4th 698 (Cal. App. 1996) (Unlike the Tan case, there was no ambiguity in the terms that could be resolved against the lender).

[246] Pacific Trust Co. T.T.E.E. v. Fidelity Fed. Sav. & Loan Ass'n, 229 Cal. Rptr. 269 (1986).

[247] *See* Cal. Civ. Code § 2954.10. California allows lenders on all nonresidential loans to enforce their borrowers' waivers of this statutory protection. But waivers after January 1, 1984, "shall be separately signed or initialed by the obligor and its enforcement shall be supported by evidence of a course of conduct by the obligee of individual weight to the consideration in that transaction for the waiver or agreement." *See also* N.Y. Real Prop. Law § 254-a; Va. Code Ann. § 6.1-330.33 (no prepayment penalty when lender accelerates under due-on-sale clause).

[248] Slevin Container Corp. v. Provident Fed. Sav. & Loan Ass'n, 424 N.E.2d 939 (Ill. 1981); Crockett v. First Fed. Sav. & Loan Ass'n, 224 S.E.2d 580 (N.C. 1976).

ment results from lenders accelerating debts under a due-on-sale clause on owner-occupied residences.

The Federal Home Loan Bank Board, under its authority to promulgate regulations under the Garn-St. Germain Act, prohibits prepayment penalties if a lender "exercises a due-on-sale clause by written notice."[249]

§ 104.08(d)   "Lock-ins" and Due-on-Sale Clauses.

The lender's simultaneous enforcement of "lock-in" *and* due-on-sale clauses can also frustrate a borrower's efforts to sell the security property. Many commercial loans contain "lock-in" clauses, barring prepayment for a period of years—usually five to seven.[250]

Suppose the owner of an office building or shopping center wants to sell, but the loan agreement has "lock-in" and "due-on-sale" clauses. The lender refuses to allow the prospective borrower to assume the loan and threatens foreclosure if the owner sells without consent.

"All right, we'll refinance," says the owner.

"No, you can't for five years," replies the lender.

Proceeding with the sale without securing the lender's approval is dangerous, unless the buyer has enough cash to repay the old loan when it is called; new lenders won't be easy to find once a notice of default has been filed.

The practical result is that the borrower can't sell during the "lock-in" period. Prospective buyers can't get the lender's approval to assume the existing loan, and the seller can't pay off the old loan because of the lock-in.

Borrowers have sometimes petitioned for court relief from this "double whammy."[251] In one decided case the borrower lost, although the court

---

[249] The Federal Home Loan Bank Board doesn't allow prepayment fees if the lender refuses to permit the purchaser of property to assume the mortgage. 50 Fed. Reg. 46749 (codified at 12 C.F.R. § 591.5(b)(2). *See also In re* LHD Realty Corp., 726 F.2d 327 (7th Cir. 1984) (prohibiting mortgagee from accelerating on a due-on-sale clause and concurrently levying a prepayment penalty).

[250] In Trident Ctr. v. Connecticut Gen. Life Ins. Co., 847 F.2d 564 (9th Cir. 1988), the note provided that the borrower was prohibited from prepaying the $56,500,000 loan for the first 12 years of its 15-year maturity. The note also gave the lender the right to accelerate if the borrower defaulted, and in that event to charge a 10% prepayment fee. The borrower wanted to prepay in order to refinance at lower rates, and argued that the 10% prepayment fee-on-default-and-acceleration gave the borrower an implicit option to escape the 12-year lock-in and to prepay early by paying the 10% penalty. The court observed that the loan documents "squarely address the precise issue that is the subject of this dispute; to all who read English, they appear to resolve the issue fully and conclusively." Nonetheless, the court allowed the borrower the chance to introduce "extrinsic evidence of possible ambiguity," applying California law.

[251] Eyde Bros. Dev. Co. v. Equitable Life Assurance Soc. of the United States, 697 F.

acknowledged that there could be "special circumstances" justifying relief. Obviously, commercial borrowers can't count on courts to release them from their loan agreements if they tie themselves up this way.

§ 104.09   Tailoring Note Provisions to Lender's Risks.

Most institutional mortgage lenders (savings and commercial banks, credit unions) are "go betweens," collecting money from savers and passing it along to borrowers.

Broadly speaking, the green goods business contains two discernible sources of risk: an interest and a credit risk. Loan applicants who appreciate the type of risk a lender has in mind may be in a better position to satisfy the lender's needs for documentation and other assurances. Lenders who appreciate the distinction between credit and interest risk should be able to draft more coherent loan provisions and apply existing provisions sensibly.

§ 104.09(a)   Interest Risk.

The interest risk is that fluctuations in interest rates will devalue a lender's loans without a corresponding decrease in its obligations. It is similar to the risk faced by any retailer whose profits depend on the spread between her cost of goods plus overhead and her sales prices. The lender's stock-in-trade are "green goods"—savings and checking accounts and funds borrowed from other sources. It sells money for a price—and earns interest and fee income. When the interest rates paid to savers plus the cost of making mortgage loans exceed what borrowers are paying in interest, the intermediary is in big trouble.

Lenders seek to avoid this risk (a) by indexing mortgage rates to savings costs so that the rates paid to savers are matched with the rates charged to borrowers; (b) by shifting the risk to others by selling their mortgage loans on origination and pocketing fees on the sale; and (c) purchasing various financial instruments to hedge against interest rate fluctuations.

§ 104.09(b)   Credit Risk.

The credit risk is that the debt won't be paid. There are two types of credit risks: security and collection. The security aspect is simply that the value of the security property on foreclosure may not be sufficient to pay off the debt. That is why loans are seldom made for more than 90% of the value of the security property, and are often considerably less. The bigger the cushion between the loan and the value of the security property, the less the security risk. Moreover, as property values are expected to fluctuate over the life of a loan, amortization of principal is essential in minimizing security risks. With each repayment of principal, the effective loan-to-value ratio declines.[252]

Supp. 1431 (W.D. Mich. 1988), *aff'd without opinion,* 888 F.2d 127 (6th Cir. 1989).

[252] St. Bernard Sav. and Loan Ass'n v. Cella, 856 F. Supp. 1166 (E.D. La. 1994) (A loan

The second aspect of the credit risk deals with collecting from the borrower. Prospective borrowers whose income and wealth are not ample enough to support their debt service are supposed to be ferreted out by credit checks and minimum ratios of income to debt service, but it isn't easy to predict when calamity will strike a region or a family. When borrowers default, lenders often ascribe it to an "improper regard for obligations," but for borrowers of modest means, defaults aren't necessarily a voluntary choice. Usually, these borrowers get caught short of cash by job layoffs or illness before they have had time to build up any equity in their homes.

The credit risk refers to the repayment of both principal and interest on the debt. Some students approaching the rather theoretical dichotomy between credit and interest risk wrongly confuse the phrase "interest risk" with whether the borrower will make timely payments of interest. That is part of the credit risk. Of course, all payments of principal and interest, whether timely or late, give the lender the opportunity to relend the funds at prevailing market rates. In this sense, the line between credit and interest risk may seem blurry. But on relending the funds, the lender still must face the challenge of placing them with creditworthy borrowers and on terms that will keep the lender from getting caught in an interest squeeze. Therefore, whether the borrower will make timely payments really falls under credit risk.

Both the "security" and "collection" aspects of the credit risk are exacerbated in markets where property values are declining rapidly. "Security" declines because loan-to-value ratios deteriorate when values slip away. "Collection" problems ensue when some borrowers decide to abandon their houses and their loans because they realize that their repayments of principal are not producing equity value.

Sometimes, in attempting to avoid one type of risk, lenders inadvertently expose themselves to the other. Consider the consequences of the lender's turning to adjustable rate loans in order to reduce their interest risk.

Two factors influence a lender's credit risk. The ratio of the monthly loan payment to the borrower's income and the ratio of the loan debt to the value of the house. On a fixed-rate loan, as long as the borrower's nominal income doesn't decrease, her payment/income level never deteriorates over the life of the loan. With each monthly payment, a little more of the principal debt is repaid. As long as the house doesn't lose its value, the lender's loan-to-value ratio gets better each month.

With an adjustable rate loan, it is quite possible for the debt service to outpace the borrower's income. The "caps" on the loan which ease the

---

was conditioned on creditworthiness, and the bank was not required to disclose its reasons for changing the terms of the loan, even though the revisions were not related to increased credit risk).

monthly payment burden may also create negative amortization, causing the loan balance actually to increase over time. If the value of the house doesn't rise proportionately, the lender's loan-to-value ratio on an adjustable loan can easily increase over time. Thus, the lender's credit risk may run amok as it attempts to curb its interest risk—to the dismay of federal agencies that pushed banks into adjustable rate lending.

> In a superficially conceived effort to reduce the deposit-insurance subsidy to interest-volatility risk, deposit insurers have encouraged thrifts to make ARMs [adjustable rate mortgages] instead of FRMs [fixed rate mortgages]. . .. They failed to adjust mortgage-insurance premiums and house-appraisal and mortgagor-qualification practices to take account of the distinctly greater dangers of default that are occasioned by the built-in graduated *payment shock* dictated by sharp first-year interest-rate buy downs and by the possibilities of negative amortization and downward trends in the future price of housing.[253]

§ 104.09(c)   Why Most Savers Are Oblivious to the Riskiness of Savings and Commercial Bank Portfolios.

Most bank *savers* are oblivious either to interest or credit risks for the simple reason that their bank accounts are insured by instrumentalities of the federal government. For them, an account of up to $100,000 is as good as a U.S. Treasury note. Given so lush a source of capital at such favorable rates, it is no wonder that many savings associations failed as a result of unwise investments. (What would you be tempted to do if you could borrow for your fantasy investments with the federal government assuring your creditors against loss?!)

§ 104.10   Secondary Markets and Negotiability.

§ 104.10(a)   The Secondary Market: Why Mortgage Notes Are Sold.[254]

Mortgage payments constitute one of the largest monthly cash flows in the U.S. However, most mortgagors neither realize nor care about the complexity of the mortgage-trading business. They send their monthly payments to a loan servicer and try to forget about the whole ordeal until next month's payment falls due.

Mortgagors may not realize that their loan payments probably don't wind

---

[253] Richard L. Kane, *Change and Progress in Contemporary Mortgage Markets,* in Housing and the New Financial Markets 270 (Richard L. Florida ed. 1986). Tania Davenport, *Note: An American Nightmare: Predatory Lending in the Subprime Home Mortgage Industry,* 36 Suffolk U. L. Rev. 531 (2003).

[254] *See* Raymond J. Anders, *A Loan's Odyssey: How a Home Mortgage Got Into a Huge Pool that Lured Investors,* Wall St. J., Aug. 17, 1988, at A1, and Kratovil & Werner, Real Estate Law 276–77 (9th ed. 1988). The Federal Home Loan Mortgage Corporation publishes a journal called *Secondary Mortgage Markets.*

up in their lender's hands; more than half of all home mortgages are sold into the "secondary" mortgage market by the lenders who originated them. Federal law does require that lenders alert their borrowers that their loans might be sold, but the significance of this disclosure is probably lost on most borrowers.[255]

On the other side of the secondary mortgage market are mortgage investors. They buy and sell mortgages and other loans. Mortgages are often pooled so that cross-country or even international investors may wind up owning a piece of the same mortgage pool. The process is called "securitization" because the ultimate investor ends up owning a security—an undivided interest in a large number of mortgages—rather than owning individual mortgages. Although the mortgage trading business didn't start until the 1970s, in 1991 the secondary mortgage market contained over $1.2 trillion worth of mortgages.

The yields on mortgage-backed securities are about one percentage point higher than on government bonds. Mortgage-backed securities usually have triple-A ratings, which make them favored investments among insurance companies and pension funds. They get those ratings because the underlying mortgage loans are government insured, government guaranteed, privately insured, or because the security instrument itself is guaranteed by a solvent quasi-governmental agency or by a solvent and respected private firm.

Mortgage-backed bonds are more secure than individual mortgage loans originated by any one local lender, because by "pooling" loans the risk of default is spread among thousands of borrowers in different parts of the country.[256] A recession in one part of the country won't hit lenders there nearly as hard if they had sold local loans and bought into pools of loans originated throughout the country.

Savings banks and other institutions which make loans can (1) keep them, (2) sell them, or (3) use them as collateral and borrow against them.

Mortgage originators like savings and commercial banks have become comfortable selling their mortgage loans. They free themselves of possible risks from interest rate fluctuations. They leverage their capital in order to make more loans. By selling the loans they originate, they multiply the total amount they can invest in loans. The income they earn from the process of originating loans is based on the volume of new lending they are able to do.

---

[255] 12 U.S.C. § 2605(a): "Each person who makes a federally related mortgage loan shall disclose to each person who applies for the loan, at the time of application for the loan, whether the servicing of the loan may be assigned, sold, or transferred to any other person at any time while the loan is outstanding."

[256] One of the reasons Congress chartered the Federal National Mortgage Association (F.N.M.A.) was to provide a geographic spread, to even out regional differences in interest rates, and to create a means of spreading the risks inherent in mortgage portfolios that were heavily concentrated in one state or region.

Quite often, the originating lenders continue to service the loans and earn fees for servicing loans. That is why mortgagors may not realize that their loan has been sold; the originating lender continues to collect monthly payments.[257]

Originating lenders don't get to pass all the credit risk to the mortgage purchaser because they are usually required to buy back bad loans and replace them with good ones, and to coinsure losses from the loans they sell. Also, it is always possible for a well managed savings bank to sell good mortgages it originated and unintentionally to buy into a portfolio of poorly secured mortgages.

Here is how the "secondary" mortgage market works. First, the lender makes the loan.

Second, the originating lender sells the loan to an entity like the Federal Home Loan Mortgage Corporation ("Freddie Mac" or "F.H.L.M.C."), the Federal National Mortgage Company ("Fannie Mae" or F.N.M.A.), the Government National Mortgage Association ("Ginnie Mae" or G.N.M.A.), or a private investment banking or securities firm. These institutions buy vast amounts of home loans from savings banks and other lenders.

Freddie Mac was created by Congress in 1970 to promote the growth of the secondary market for conventional home mortgages.[258] The funds generated by the sale of mortgage-backed securities are its primary source of money for mortgage purchases. Both Freddie Mac and Fannie Mae are private corporations with statutory authority to purchase mortgages that meet their eligibility requirements. Ginnie Mae is a federal agency that issues government-guaranteed securities backed by FHA, VA, and Farmers Home Administration ("FmHA") mortgages.

Usually, an institution will line up investors before beginning to create a pool, for fear of being stuck with millions, if not billions, of dollars in unwanted mortgages. Typical investors might include a savings bank seeking to hedge against rising interest rates and insurance companies looking for safer yields higher than they could get from government bonds.

Large institutions don't have to sell their loans to get their cash out of them. They can securitize pools of their own loans. In 1977, Bank of

---

[257] G.N.M.A., F.N.M.A., the F.H.L.M.C., and other secondary market mortgage buyers require that their loan servicers adhere to detailed rules and regulations. G.N.M.A., for instance, requires that the servicer meet certain eligibility requirements, enter a Servicing Agreement, consent in writing to service the loan, and have an office "with servicing facilities satisfactory" to G.N.M.A. within approximately 100 miles of the mortgaged property. 24 C.F.R. § 350.1.

[258] James A. Newell and Michael R. Gordon, *Electronic Commerce and Negotiable Instruments (Electronic Promissory Notes)*, 31 Idaho L. Rev. 819, 823 (1995).

America became the first private institution to do that.[259]

Third, the issuing institution may enhance the credit of the pool by guaranteeing its repayment or pledging to add other assets to the pool if some of the mortgages go into default. The secondary market maker may insist that the originating lender promise to buy back loans in default or assume some or all of the loss. It may also elect to deal only in loans insured by the F.H.A., guaranteed by the V.A., or insured by private mortgage insurers.

Fourth, the issuer resells interests in the mortgages in standardized pools, enabling investors to buy mortgages in multimillion-dollar batches without having to laboriously scrutinize each mortgage.

Fifth, the issuers make a secondary market in these securities by trading in them for their own or their clients' accounts.

The first mortgage pools were "pass-throughs." The buyer in a pass-through takes an undivided interest in the underlying mortgages. An investor in a pass-through is exposed to the full prepayment risk. The risk is that mortgagors will prepay when rates fall (called contraction risk) and slow down their prepayments when rates rise (called the extension risk).

In 1983, the Federal Home Loan Mortgage Corporation (F.H.L.M.C.) offered a new type of security called a collateralized mortgage obligation (C.M.O.). In a C.M.O., the issuer retains title to the mortgages and pledges to make payments to holders of participation certificates in the mortgage pool. The payment schedule can be quite different than what the participation certificate holder would have received in a direct pass-through. For one thing, some investors didn't want monthly mortgage payments even though most mortgages are paid monthly. The C.M.O. issuer is able to provide payments quarterly, annually, or on whatever schedule the investor prefers.

The evolution of C.M.O.s was limited only by the creativity of securities brokers and the preferences of potential investors. For instance, a $100 million mortgage pool might consist of four groups of certificates called tranches, with average lives of 3, 7, 10 and 20 years, respectively. The 3-year tranche might receive a variable yield tied to a financial index, while the 20-year tranche might receive a fixed 8% yield.

In the earliest C.M.O.s, all principal repayments on the underlying mortgages were pledged to a group of certificate holders who got back their entire investment before any principal repayments went to investors in the second group.[260]

Later, C.M.O.s allowed the prepayment risk to be split up and specifically apportioned among the tranches. The holders of the 3-year tranche might get

---

[259] Frank J. Fabozzi, The Handbook of Mortgage-Backed Securities 151 (Probus 1992).

[260] *See generally id.*

the first prepayments, the holders of the 7-year the next. Often there will be a category of bonds that pay no interest until they mature or are called. (These are called zero coupon bonds because they don't have any interest coupons the bondholder can clip and cash in.) The zero coupon bondholders get fully repaid out of the mortgage principal when all the holders of the other tranches are fully paid. Bonds in tranches are sold to investors whose financial needs are met by a particular tranche.

When a commercial bank organizes a mortgage pool it might prefer to sell its mortgage loans to the pool rather than pledging them as *collateral* because the sale reduces the banks asset and capital requirements. These are called pay-throughs.

Most of these mortgage pools are REMICs—real estate mortgage investment conduits. A REMIC is a creature of the tax code.[261] It is treated as a pass-through entity, which means that the REMIC itself is exempt from taxation and all of its income is allocated and taxed to the REMIC holders.[262]

The secondary mortgage market creates liquidity for mortgage originators and mortgage investors. Liquidity has brought investors into the mortgage market, investors who would otherwise have bought government securities or corporate bonds. By increasing the supply of mortgage capital, the secondary mortgage market has reduced home mortgage interest rates.

The benefit to borrowers can be measured by looking at the spread between Treasury bills and home mortgages of the same maturity before the secondary market existed (say, 1963) and the rate spread today. In 1963, there was a spread of 200 basis points (two percentage points) between the 30-year T-bill and 30-year mortgage rates. Today, that spread is around 100 basis points.[263]

Liquidity and volatility seem to go hand-in-hand, causing mortgage rates to become extremely sensitive to changes in the credit markets. If a Dutch pension fund can buy a share of a Des Moines home mortgage, the underlying interest rate available to Des Moines homebuyers is going to be sensitive to global interest rates, which the Dutch pension fund will see as alternatives to its buying a share in a mortgage pool.

§ 104.10(b)   Negotiability.

§ 104.10(b)(1)   The Implications of Negotiability.

A note can be negotiable or non-negotiable, but this has nothing to do with

---

[261] I.R.C. § 860A.

[262] *See* Boris I. Bittker & Lawrence Lokken, 3 Federal Taxation of Income, Estate and Gifts § 58.3.2 (rev. 3d ed. 2005, Supp. 2009).

[263] *See* The Wall Street Journal, Sept. 28, 1992, at C15, col. 2. The spread between C.M.O.s and U.S. Treasuries on that day ranged from 90 (20-year seasoned issues) to 115 (2-year new issues).

whether the lender can sell (or assign) the note. Notes and mortgages are presumed saleable absent explicit language to the contrary.

This may strike borrowers as unfair because their right to assign their mortgage debt is usually hemmed in by a due-on-sale clause. Yet, the lender's right to sell the loan isn't subject to the borrower's prior approval. The crucial difference between the debtor's and creditor's positions is that the creditor is assigning the *right* to receive money. The debtor is assigning the *obligation* to pay back a loan. Most creditors legitimately question a substitution of one debtor for another while few debtors care who pockets their monthly payments.

"Negotiability" means that the note can pass from the original creditor to a "holder in due course" free of certain defenses the debtor may have had against the original creditor. "To take free of a mortgagor's defenses, the assignee must win on both issues. He must both hold a negotiable note and be a holder in due course."[264] The theory is that negotiable notes are like money and should be freely transferable; loan purchasers shouldn't have to worry about the possible invalidity of the paper.

The lost defenses are "personal" ones, not "real." The "real" ones survive the note being negotiated.

The Uniform Commercial Code lists some of the "real" defenses.[265] They include, among others, infancy, duress, illegality of the transaction, and "fraud that induced the obligor to sign the instrument with neither knowledge nor reasonable opportunity to learn of its character or its essential terms."[266] Among the "personal" defenses: The original lender never actually made its promised loan or the debtor actually paid off the loan before her lender sold the note. The buyer of a negotiable note takes free of all "personal" defenses.

The distinction between "real" and "personal" defenses parallels the difference between contracts that are voidable and those that are void. A void contract is really no contract at all—because of a forgery, for instance, or some other defense amounting to illegality or a lack of mutual assent to form

---

[264] D. Barlow Burke, Jr., Real Estate Transactions 263 (1993), citing First Maryland Fin. Serv's Corp. v. District Realty Title Ins. Corp., 548 A.2d 787 (D.C. App. 1988) (note, negotiable, holder not in due course).

[265] U.C.C. § 3-305(a). Ann M. Burkhart, *Restatement of Mortgages Symposium: Third Party Defenses to Mortgages*, 1998 BYU L. Rev. 1003.

[266] U.C.C. § 3-305(a)(1). The "real/personal" or "void/voidable" distinction lends to inventive legal arguments. In one case, an *unlicensed* contractor did some work. The work may have been paid for by a note and second trust deed on which the borrower defaulted. The court held that the borrower's default would be excused if the borrower could prove that the note was payment for the construction work. The note would then have been illegal (void), ruled the court, because under state law, unlicensed contractors can't sue to enforce contracts for which a license is required. Wilson v. Steele, 259 Cal. Rptr. 851 (1989).

a contract. A voidable contract is one which a party can elect to invalidate because, say, she was induced to sign it by a misrepresentation or because of a failure of consideration—the original creditor never disbursed all the loan funds the debtor is now being sued to repay.

In almost all states *the holder in due course* of a negotiable note secured by a mortgage takes the mortgage as well as the note free from defenses that the mortgagor would have had against the original mortgagee.[267] Lenders have generally carried the day in establishing legal protection for mortgages identical to that of the note. If the note is negotiable, so is the accompanying mortgage.

You can see how the consequences of negotiability can be harsh to the borrower. If the borrower never got the loan proceeds, or paid off the loan after the lender had sold the note to a "holder in due course," the borrower would still be liable for the face amount of the note. Moreover, generally speaking, the mortgage "follows" the note so the present holder of the note can foreclose if the borrower doesn't pay.[268] Like bankruptcy and limited liability for corporations, negotiability sacrifices a few deceived innocents for the sake of the many in the marketplace.

In the case of home loans, the benefits of negotiability can be measurable. Two authors compared the price of adjustable rate loans in Chicago, where they are held to be non-negotiable, with comparable adjustable rate loans in the District of Columbia, where they are legally negotiable. They found that the Chicago rates were higher and attributed the differential to the non-negotiability feature, concluding that borrowers are best served, too, by negotiability.[269]

What can borrowers do to protect themselves? They could insist on seeing the note before making each payment and demand its return after making their final payment. Individual lenders might be able to comply with this request, but institutional lenders probably wouldn't. They often store notes in remote locations and don't record each payment on the back of the note as they did in days of yore. Because borrowers usually pay by check or by authorized bank account withdrawal, any borrower who asked to see the note each month would be regarded as an extremely odd duck.

Lenders sometimes ask borrowers to sign duplicate notes because they

---

[267] A few states have reversed or modified the H.D.C. doctrine. *See* Grant S. Nelson & Dale A. Whitman, Real Estate Finance Law § 5.30, at 421 n.1 (5th ed. 2007).

[268] *But see,* Johnson v. Howe, 223 N.W. 148 (Minn. 1929). The mortgagor can continue paying the mortgagee after the mortgagee has been assigned until the mortgagor receives actual notice of the assignment. The H.D.C. of the negotiable note may have a suit against the original maker despite failure to notify her of the assignment, but can't foreclose the mortgage if the debt has been repaid once.

[269] *See* Janine S. Hiller & Stephen P. Ferris, *Variable Interest Rates and Negotiability: A Response,* 94 Com. L.J. 48, 52–53 (1989).

"lost" the original. Borrowers should be wary of these requests. The lender could sell the note to someone who didn't realize it was a duplicate and the borrower could end up having to pay the same debt twice if the original note was never destroyed.

Mortgage purchasers can protect themselves against unknown infirmities between the mortgagor and the original mortgagee by obtaining a statement signed by the mortgagor stating that he has no defenses to the enforcement of the mortgage. This document is variously called a *waiver of defenses, estoppel certificate, no set-off certificate,* or *declaration of no defenses.*[270] A certificate offers better protection than the holder-in-due-course doctrine because it protects the mortgage purchaser against both real and personal defenses.

An estoppel certificate signed by the maker of the note doesn't protect the note purchaser against defenses or claims belonging to third parties. But the purchaser of the note may prevail against some third party claims if he has no notice of them and the note is non-negotiable for reasons other than the way it was negotiated.[271]

§ 104.10(b)(2)   The U.C.C. Requirements for Negotiability.

To be negotiable, the U.C.C. requires that the note: (1) contain an unconditional promise to pay a fixed amount of money and no other promise by the maker; (2) be payable on demand or at a definite time; (3) be payable to order or to the bearer at the time it is issued or first comes into possession of a holder; and (4) be for a fixed amount of money.[272]

---

[270] Robert Kratovil & Raymond J. Werner, Real Estate Law 325 (9th ed. 1988).

[271] *See* Grant S. Nelson & Dale A. Whitman, Real Estate Finance Law (2d ed. 1985) 391–92.

[272] U.C.C. 3-104 is codified in Cal. Com. Code § 3104:

Form of Negotiable Instruments; "Draft"; "Check"; "Certificate of Deposit"; "Note." (1) Any writing to be a negotiable instrument within this division must:

(a) Be signed by the maker or drawer; and

(b) Contain an unconditional promise or order to pay a sum certain in money and no other promise, order, obligation or power given by the maker or drawer except as authorized by this division; and

(c) Be payable on demand or at a definite time; and

(d) Be payable to order or to bearer.

(2) A writing which complies with the requirements of this section is

(a) A "draft" ("bill of exchange") if it is an order;

(b) A "check" if it is a draft drawn on a bank and payable on demand;

(c) A "certificate of deposit" if it is an acknowledgement by a bank of receipt of money with an engagement to repay it;

(d) A "note" if it is a promise other than a certificate of deposit.

(3) As used in other divisions of this code, and as the context may require, the terms

§ 104.10(b)(2)(i)   Unconditional Promise to Pay.

(i) Incorporating Non-Pecuniary Obligations of the Mortgagor Into the Note Jeopardizes Its Negotiability. The condition requiring an unconditional promise to pay money and no other promise would arguably be violated if the provisions of the deed of trust regarding property maintenance, covenants against illegal uses, and the like were incorporated into the note. But by statute the negotiability of the note isn't jeopardized by a "promise or power to maintain or protect collateral."[273] Negotiability would, however, be destroyed by language that "the debtor hereby grants a security interest in the property."[274] These promises involve acts other than paying money. Hence, lenders who expect to sell their notes and want them to be negotiable are careful not to incorporate by reference the terms of the deed of trust into the note.[275] The farthest they may go and still claim negotiability is to refer to the existence of the accompanying deed of trust.[276]

(ii) Adjustable Rate Notes Were Often Held Non-Negotiable Under U.C.C. Language Requiring Notes to be for a Fixed Amount of Money, but Court Opinions, Revised U.C.C. Provisions, and State Statutes Are Reinstating Their Negotiability. A section of the U.C.C. had conditioned negotiability on instruments bearing a "sum certain."[277] A U.C.C. comment specified that the "sum certain" had to be capable of being determined from "the instrument itself without reference to any outside source."[278] Early cases in the 1980s successfully challenged adjustable rates as nonnegotiable. These court opinions held that adjustable loans were not for a

---

"draft," "check," "certificate of deposit" and "note" may refer to instruments which are not negotiable within this division as well as to instruments which are so negotiable.

[273] U.C.C. 3-104. is codified in Cal. Com. Code 3104: Form of Negotiable Instruments; "Draft"; "Check"; "Certificate of Deposit"; "Note." (1) Any writing to be a negotiable instrument within this division must: (a) Be signed by the maker or drawer; and (b) Contain an unconditional promise or order to pay a sum certain in money and no other promise, order, obligation or power given by the maker or drawer except as authorized by this division; and (c) Be payable on demand or at a definite time; and(d) Be payable to order or to bearer. (2) A writing which complies with the requirements of this section is (a) A "draft" ("bill of exchange") if it is an order; (b) A "check" if it is a draft drawn on a bank and payable on demand; (c) A "certificate of deposit" if it is an acknowledgement by a bank of receipt of money with an engagement to repay it; (d) A "note" if it is a promise other than a certificate of deposit. (3) As used in other divisions of this code, and as the context may require, the terms "draft," "check," "certificate of deposit" and "note" may refer to instruments which are not negotiable within this division as well as to instruments which are so negotiable.

[274] U.C.C. § 3-112(1)(c).

[275] U.C.C. § 3-112(1).

[276] "A promise or order is not unconditional if the instrument . . . states that it is subject to or governed by any other agreement." U.C.C. § 3.105(2).

[277] U.C.C. § 3-104(1)b.

[278] U.C.C.§ 3-106 cmt. 1.

"sum certain" because the rate of interest couldn't be determined by reading the face of the note.[279]

Later courts, particularly in 1991 and 1992, realized that the overriding purposes of the U.C.C., predictability and flexibility to address new commercial realities, were being thwarted by this literal reading of the "sum certain" standard.[280] Nearly half of all mortgage loans are adjustable, and the literal reading of the U.C.C. was resulting in their being declared non-negotiable. The idea of the U.C.C. was for commercial law to track changing commercial realities, not to throw roadblocks in the way. Judges became persuaded to read the "sum certain" phrase not as requiring mathematical certainty but commercial certainty. Anyone signing an adjustable-rate loan can calculate the sum due, even if the note itself doesn't specify a fixed rate. Lenders tell borrowers anyway, when the rate changes. By 1993, eight state courts had decided the issue, five for and three against negotiability.[281]

To assure the negotiability of adjustable-rate loans in the future, almost all states have enacted statutes making them negotiable. Most of these statutes are based on a revised U.C.C. provision deleting the "sum certain" language, and substituting a "fixed amount of money" standard which applies only to the loan principle.[282] Any interest rate fixed or adjustable is sufficient. Some statutes sanction as negotiable any loan calling for "a stated rate of interest" if the rate is readily ascertainable by a publicly available index or its equivalent.[283]

---

[279] One diligent author counted ten cases decided on the subject in the past one hundred years and found eight cases against the negotiability of adjustable-rate loans, two in favor. Gary B. Tillman, Variable Interest Rates, Negotiability, and the Sum Certain Requirement, 22 U.C.C. L.J. 36 n.3 (1989). *See, e.g.,* Taylor v. Roeder, 360 S.E.2d 191 (Va. 1987). (The borrower's loan was adjustable, three points over the Chase Manhattan prime rate. Because the interest rate couldn't be determined from the face of the instrument alone, the Virginia Supreme Court held that the sum was not certain, and hence couldn't be negotiable). *See also* Doyle v. Trinity Sav. & Loan Ass'n, 869 F.2d 558 (10th Cir. 1989); Gary B. Tillman, The Effect of Variable Interest Rates on Negotiability, 48 Ia. L. Rev. 710 (1988).

[280] Note, A Call to Arms: Denial of Negotiability to Variable Rate Notes Interferes with the Secondary Mortgage Market's Ability to Price Risk Efficiently, 22 Cumberland L. Rev. 745 (1992). *See also* Rockwell, Basic Considerations in Reviewing Commercial Loan Documents, 6 Prac. Real. Est. Law 13, 1819 (Sept. 1990).

[281] *See* Janine S. Hiller, Variable Interest Rates and Negotiability: Conflict and Crisis, 46 Okla. L. Rev. 257, 260–61 (1993).

[282] U.C.C. 3-104(a); U.C.C. Rev. Art. 3, 3-112(b): Interest may be stated in an instrument as a fixed or variable amount of money or it may be expressed as a fixed or variable rate or rates. The amount or rate of interest may be stated or described in the instrument in any manner and may require reference to information not contained in the instrument. If an instrument provides for interest, but the amount of interest payable cannot be ascertained from the description, interest is payable at the judgment rate in effect at the place of payment of the instrument and at the time interest first accrues.

[283] These are based on a 1987 Discussion Draft amending U.C.C. 3-106(2).

A number of states adopted statutory language one commentator has described as "relatively unique."[284]

§ 104.10(b)(2)(ii)   Negotiation vs. Assignment.

The condition "payable to order or bearer" focuses on the process by which the note is transferred. If an instrument is payable to order it is negotiated by delivery with any necessary endorsement. If payable to bearer it may be negotiated by delivery.[285] "Notes secured by mortgages are nearly always in order rather than bearer form. Hence, both endorsement and delivery are essential elements in the negotiation."[286]

The requisite process of negotiation is violated if the note purchaser takes as an "assignee." One who obtains a payment on *the order of* the original payee *isn't bound* by the terms of the original transaction.[287] A contract assignee assumes all the rights and obligations of her assignor.[288] Those rights and obligations include the very defenses that the "holder in due course" hopes to shed.

§ 104.10(b)(3)   "Holder in Due Course" (H.D.C.) Defined.

Only holders in due course enjoy the benefits of negotiability. To be a "holder in due course," a person must be a holder[289] of a negotiable instrument "who takes the instrument (a) for value; (b) in good faith; and (c) without notice that it is overdue or has been dishonored or of any defense against or claim to it on the part of any person."[290] The "holder in due

---

[284] Janine S. Hiller, Variable Interest Rates and Negotiability: Crisis and Conflict, 46 Okla. L. Rev. 257, 272 (1993).

[285] U.C.C. § 3-201(b).

[286] Grant S. Nelson & Dale A. Whitman, Real Estate Transfer, Finance, and Development 486 (4th ed. 1992).

[287] U.C.C. § 3-305(b) subjects the assignee to all defenses of any party which would be available in an action on a simple contract.

[288] The use of the word "assignment," in California at least, doesn't necessarily affect "its character as an endorsement." Cal. Com. Code § 3202(4).

[289] A "holder" is a "person in possession of a negotiable instrument that is payable either to bearer or to the order of the person in possession," or a "person in possession of a document of title if the goods are deliverable either to bearer or to the order of the person in possession." U.C.C. 1-201(21).

[290] U.C.C. § 3-302. When the assets or liabilities of a bank or savings association are taken over by the FDIC or the FSLIC, the assets are seldom endorsed to them, so the federal regulators would not be "holders in due course" under state law. To be a "holder in due course," a person must be a holder of a negotiable instrument who takes "the instrument (i) for value, (ii) in good faith, (iii) without notice that the instrument is overdue or has been dishonored or that there is an uncured default with respect to payment of another instrument issued as part of the same series, (iv) without notice that the instrument contains an unauthorized signature or has been altered, (v) without notice of any claim to the instrument described in Section 3-306, and (vi) without notice that any party has a defense or claim in

course" is another way of describing a bona fide purchaser.

§ 104.10(b)(3)(i)   For Value.

Many notes and mortgages especially junior liens, are sold at deep discounts. Does the purchaser of a note who pays only a fraction of its face value automatically find himself outside the protected circle of H.D.C.s? Absolutely not, if the price he paid reflected the credit or interest risk inherent in the transaction. Very deep discounts have been allowed in certain cases ($7,000 for an $11,064 note, for instance).[291]

§ 104.10(b)(3)(ii)   Good Faith.

Sometimes the purchaser of a note has been so "closely connected" to the originator that borrowers were allowed to raise defenses against the note purchaser that they had against the originating lender. Most of these cases concern home improvement scams where a smooth talking salesman persuades an unsophisticated homeowner to sign a contract for, say, wood or aluminum siding, along with a mortgage and note, all at an exorbitant price. The work is never done or badly done, and the note is swiftly negotiated to a cooperating lender. Where the note-purchasing lender drafts the seller's forms, approves the seller's procedures in advance, checks the debtor's credit, buys all or most of the seller's paper, and there is common or related ownership and management, the lender has sometimes lost the benefit of its H.D.C. status.[292]

§ 104.10(b)(3)(iii)   Notice.

What counts as "notice" is illustrated by U.C.C. § 3-304. For instance, the purchaser of a note has notice that something is wrong if the purchaser knows that it is overdue, that the obligation is void, or that it has already been paid. Notice here is measured by a subjective standard (what the purchaser knew or probably knew) and not by an objective standard (what the purchaser should have known). Although U.C.C. § 1-201(25) does inculpate the purchaser of a note who has "reason to know" something is amiss, most courts accept that as long as the purchaser doesn't have actual notice of the debtor's defenses against the original creditor, she takes free of them. The debtor's only action would be against the original lender if the note had been partly or fully paid, and negotiated to a purchaser without

---

recoupment described in Section 3-305(a)." UCC 3-302(a)(2). *See* W. Robert Gray, *Limitations on the FDIC's D'Oench Doctrine of Federal Common-Law Estoppel: Congressional Preemption and Authoritative Statutory Construction,* 31 S. Tex. L.J. 245 (1990).

[291] Wilson v. Steele, 259 Cal. Rptr. 851 (1989).

[292] James J. White & Robert S. Summers, Uniform Commercial Code § 17-6 (5th ed. 2007). Some states have simply abolished the holder-in-due-course defense for some retail sales. The holder of a promissory note under these laws is subject to the same defenses as the original vendor. *See, e.g.,* Vt. Stat. Ann tit. 9, § 2455.

notice of the payment.[293]

§ 104.10(b)(4)   The Importance of Possession of a Note.

A borrower who appreciates what "negotiability" means will demand that the note be handed over in exchange for the final payment. Anticipating this, responsible lenders store notes carefully.

Here is how one investor in second deeds of trust puts it:

> Possession of the original of the note carries with it a presumption of ownership, regardless of whether the bearer is the note's named owner. Without the original note, your position in any nonjudicial foreclosure or litigation will be made more difficult. For that reason, the original of the note should be kept in a safe deposit box or similarly secure location.

> Other documents are important, but they don't need as careful safekeeping [as the note]. Deeds of trust, assignments, and other recorded papers can all be duplicated from records maintained by the county recorder, and the copies will be considered admissible as evidence in court when certified by the county recorder. Replacement title policies and escrow papers can be obtained from their places of origin; missing insurance policies and appraisals are major inconveniences when lost, but their absence is seldom fatal. A missing or lost note, however, can be more than an inconvenience.

> Before safekeeping the original note, make a photocopy, front and back, for your current files. The photocopy will save digging out the original note should a question arise (as almost invariably it does) concerning its exact wording. And if the original is somehow destroyed or misplaced, a photocopy showing all the original note's signatures will save you much inconvenience later, should foreclosure be necessary.[294]

The priority of a promissory note secured by a mortgage, a transaction that creates an interest in real estate, is established by recordation in the county real estate records and governed by the recording act statute of the jurisdiction. However, an assignment of a promissory note to a third party to secure an obligation owed to the third party, even if secured by a mortgage or other collateral, creates a security interest in the obligor's note, not the underlying collateral. Therefore, perfection of an assigned promissory note is governed by U.C.C. 9-304, which requires possession of "goods, instruments, money, negotiable documents or chattel paper" to perfect the

---

[293] For a recent case on what counts as notice, *see* Krilich v. Milliken Mtg. Co., 554 N.E.2d 422 (Ill. App. 1990). When defendant purchased the note, it was visibly altered and the rider contained different terms than the note. The discrepancy raised a fact sufficient to take the case to the jury. The disputed fact: was the defendant notified of the borrower's defense that the note had been altered without her consent?

[294] George Coats, Smart Trust Deed Investment in California 92–93 (2d ed. 1988). Markin v. Chebemma Inc., 526 F. Supp. 2d 890 (N.D. Ill. 2007) (action by bearer of promissory note undertaken in exchange for real property).

holder's interest.[295]

Consider the investors in *In re* Sprint Mortgage Bankers Corp. who loaned money to a mortgage broker in return for assignment of the notes and mortgages given to the mortgage broker by borrowers.[296] The lenders never took possession of the notes because they assumed that recordation of promissory notes secured by real estate mortgages would be sufficient to perfect their interests and secure their lien priority.When the mortgage broker filed Chapter 7 bankruptcy, a New York appellate court upheld the bankruptcy court's determination that the unperfected notes were a part of the debtor's estate and the lenders were unsecured creditors with interests subordinate to the bankruptcy trustee. The court noted that although U.C.C. 9-104 states that Article 9 generally does not apply to the transfer of an interest in or lien on real estate, the interest created in this transaction was a security interest in an instrument to which Article 9 would control, not the recording act statute. This case further demonstrates the importance of possession of a promissory note.

§ 104.10(b)(5)   Does the Borrower Have a Right to Notice of Sale or Assignment of Note?[297]

Suppose D, the debtor, prepays the note and L, the lender, writes out a receipt verifying the prepayment. But L had previously sold the note to H and no one told D that L had done so. In fact, H didn't learn about the prepayment until he initiated collection proceedings against D on the due date. Is D liable to H anyway, or does H lose out for not having notified D before purchasing the note from L? If H had notified D of its intent to purchase or had requested an estoppel certificate from D, H might have found out L's little secret, i.e., that the debt had already been paid off.

In most states, purchasers of negotiable notes don't need to notify the mortgagors that they are the new owners. Moreover, if the mortgagors continue to make payments to the original mortgagees, they cannot claim credit for those payments on the underlying debt.

If the note is negotiable, the note purchaser can force the debtor to pay off the note a second time. The debtor's only recourse would be against the original lender. This is a cheerless prospect, especially if the creditor is in bankruptcy.

The only way to protect themselves from paying twice is to demand production of the note and obtain endorsement of each payment thereon. There is no practical way to do this when the lenders are institutional. Two

---

[295] U.C.C. 9-304.

[296] note.177 B.R. 4 (E.D.N.Y. 1995).

[297] *See generally* Annotation, *Recording Assignment of Mortgage,* 89 A.L.R. 171 (1934). *See also* Robert Kratovil & Raymond J. Werner, Real Estate Law 326–27 (9th ed. 1988).

leading experts conclude: "The law should be changed to make payment to the assignor binding until notice of the assignment has been given."[298]

The rule that the H.D.C. of a negotiable note has no obligation to notify the mortgagor has also been soundly criticized for its "great potential for mischief and unfairness, since it produces far different results than most lay mortgagors would expect."[299]

When the note is *non-negotiable*, the borrower won't be liable twice for repayments she makes to the original creditor, until she has actually been notified that the note has been assigned. The general law of contracts protects the obligor if the obligator has received no notice that the debt has been assigned and doesn't know that it has. The obligator can continue paying the original lender with impunity and will be credited with all the payments made to the original lender until the obligator learns that the note has been sold.

The note purchaser who is required to notify the mortgagor of an assignment must do so personally. He can't just record the assignment. The reason is obvious: mortgagors should not have to search the public records every time they need to make a payment.[300] Moreover, it doesn't take a heroic effort for the assignee to mail personal notice to the mortgagor. Purchasers of the property from the mortgagor, though, are held responsible for recorded assignments.[301] They would have come across them anyway in searching title before they bought the property.

§ 104.10(b)(6)   Why the Lack of Notice When a Note Is Sold Doesn't Result in Massive Losses to Borrowers.

§ 104.10(b)(6)(i)   Many Loans Continue to Be Serviced by the Originating Lender.

Mortgage buyers often contract to have the originating lender continue servicing the loan. "Servicing" includes collecting monthly payments from the borrower and remitting them to the new owner of the note, keeping tax and insurance impound accounts, paying the borrower's property tax and insurance premiums when they come due, pursuing delinquent borrowers and foreclosing if instructed by the note holders.

---

[298] Robert Kratovil & Raymond J. Werner, Real Estate Law 398 (9th ed. 1988).. The authors point out that the U.C.C. has made this change in Article 9 for notes secured by chattel paper.

[299] Grant S. Nelson & Dale A. Whitman, Real Estate Finance Law 393 (2d ed. 1985). *See also* Id. At 469-449 (5th ed. 2007).

[300] *See, e.g.,* Minn. Stat. Ann. § 507.32: "The record of an assignment of a mortgage shall not in itself be notice of such assignment to the mortgagor, the mortgagor's heirs or personal representatives, so as to invalidate any payment made by either of them to the mortgagee."

[301] Erickson v. Kendall, 191 P. 842 (Wash. 1920).

Servicing fees are usually paid as a percentage of the principal debt. The servicer also keeps the "float" on the impound accounts which is the interest rate it can earn on those accumulated payments less what it pays borrowers on them.

§ 104.10(b)(6)(ii)   Federal Law Requires Both the Old and New Servicing Agent to Inform the Borrower of the Change.

Federal law requires lenders to inform prospective borrowers what the institution's servicing policies are.[302] With an actual transfer of servicing, the law prescribes that the old servicer let the borrower know the change is about to happen, fifteen days ahead of time. Then, the new servicer is supposed to notify the borrower the switch has happened, fifteen days afterwards.

§ 104.10(b)(6)(iii)   The New Owner of the Note May Be Estopped from Disclaiming Responsibility for Payments the Debtor Makes to the New Owner's Servicing Agent.

The market for servicing rights has grown rapidly because there are enormous economies of scale in the business. This means that a local lender may be induced to sell its servicing right to a large, remote institution. "Mix ups"—loan payments not properly credited or lost—are common when loan servicers change.

Once the purchaser of a note authorizes it to be serviced by the originating lender or some other institution, the note purchaser, as principal, bears responsibility for the misdeeds of its agents.

If the purchaser of the note changes servicing agents without informing the borrower, it may be estopped from denying the validity of payments the borrower made to the old servicer. The "course of dealing" has misled the borrower into believing that the servicing agent originally designated is still legally empowered to collect payments.

If the servicing agent absconds with the borrower's money, the loss would probably have to be borne by the principal, not the mortgagor.

§ 104.10(b)(6)(iv)   The New Holder of the Note May Not Have Perfected Its Status as a Holder in Due Course.

Sometimes the loan originator doesn't actually sell its loans. It pledges them as collateral in order to obtain financing for its operations. Mortgage bankers often work this way. They borrow on lines of credit from

---

[302] 12 U.S.C. § 2605.

commercial banks, originate loans with those borrowed funds, and eventually sell the loans in the secondary market. Between the time they originate a loan and find a buyer for it, they may pledge the loans they originate to the commercial bank, usually for periods of six to eight weeks.

The mortgage banker seldom actually endorses the notes over to the commercial banks. Sometimes the mortgage broker even retains possession of the documents. Even if the bank obtains possession, it may not be treated as the purchaser of the notes but rather as the originator's creditor. Without an endorsement, delivery, or intent to purchase, the commercial bank is not protected as a holder-in-due-course.

§ 104.10(b)(6)(v)   Lenders Do Usually Notify Borrowers Where They Are Supposed to Send Their Payments When Servicing Agents Are Changed.

Borrowers are usually notified when their servicing agents change. Lenders want borrowers to mail their payments to the right place. They don't relish being forced to invoke "negotiability" claims in order to get paid. Each time a new servicing agent takes over, borrowers usually can expect to receive notice of it.

§ 104.10(b)(6)(vi)   The Phony Notice Scam.

Reliance on this process has led to "loan servicing scams." Con artists write official-seeming requests to borrowers, directing loan payments to their own post office boxes, which are often out of town. Smart borrowers, on receiving a notice, ask for verification signed by an officer of the old loan servicer. They also insist that the new loan servicer provide an 800-number, payment coupons, and an authorization-to-receive-payment letter signed by a corporate officer.

The Uniform Consumer Credit Code obliterates the H.D.C. doctrine by providing that a seller "may not take a negotiable instrument other than a check . . . as evidence of the obligation of the consumer."[303] When a merchant or contractor takes back the consumer's note for payment, the transaction is called a consumer credit sale. Purchasers of consumer paper resulting from consumer credit sales under to the U.C.C.C. are responsible for overseeing their vendor's business operations, at the risk of going to court against dissatisfied consumers carrying valid defenses to payment. They can't claim H.D.C. status.

---

[303] U.C.C.C. (Uniform Commercial Credit Code) § 3.307. Other scams may involve promissory notes. *See, e.g.,* Hodges v. Swafford, 863 N.E.2d 881 (Ind. App. 2007) (in exchange for lenders paying off the mortgage, the mortgagor transferred the deed to the house to the lenders and entered into a contract to buy the house back; lenders were required to deed the house back to the mortgagor, who was ordered to execute a promissory note and mortgage in favor of the lenders).

A truly shifty and well-advised seller could try to side-step this statutory assault on the H.D.C. doctrine by separating the sale from the loan. The seller could form an independent financing corporation to make loans to consumers (consumer loans). The consumers would borrow first and buy later. The financing corporation would sell the consumers' notes, maybe even before the consumers had used the loan proceeds to buy whatever the seller was palming off. The purchasers of the note would be holders in due course from a lender, and not a seller. Hence, they would not be subject to U.C.C.C.'s injunction against sellers taking anything but checks as negotiable instruments from consumers.[304]

To catch these clever sellers, the U.C.C.C. listed various connections between sellers and lenders that would disqualify lenders from claiming H.D.C. status when the paper they were buying was consumer loans: the lender knew what the seller was up to, the lender was related to the seller, the seller guaranteed the loan, the lender supplied the seller with contract documents, the loan was conditioned on the consumer's making the particular purchase, and the lender knew about earlier complaints from the seller's customers.[305]

The U.C.C.C. is limited in application. It only protects individual debtors, not organizations, and only for purchases serving a personal, family, household or agricultural purpose.[306] The U.C.C.C. doesn't apply to most mortgages because they are given to secure the repayment of money and not to secure purchase contracts for goods or services. The U.C.C.C. would apply when a homeowner gives a home improvement contractor a note and mortgage to secure payment of the contract. The Code does not apply if the debt is secured by a mortgage and the interest rate is 12% or lower.[307] If the sale involves goods or services such as home improvements, and not an interest in land, the Code only applies if the amount financed does not exceed $25,000 adjusted according to changes in the Consumer Price Index.[308]

§ 104.10(b)(6)(vii)   Servicer Liability for Truth-in-Lending Violations.

Servicers of loans purchased by the Federal Home Loan Mortgage Corporation (F.H.L.M.C.) are required to accept a conveyance of the mortgage loan. The servicer reconveys the loan to Freddie Mac, while retaining the right to service the loan. At least one district court held that this momentary possession of legal title made the servicer an assignee of the

---

[304] *Id.*

[305] U.C.C.C. § 3.405(1).

[306] *Id.* § 1.301(12)(a)(iii).

[307] *Id.* § 1.031(12)(b)(ii).

[308] *Id.* §§ 1.01(12)(a)(v), 1.106(1).

lender who could be held liable for Truth in Lending Act (T.I.L.A.) violations committed by the original mortgagee.[309] The T.I.L.A. Amendments of 1995 clarified that a loan servicer will not be treated as an assignee if legal title is held merely for administrative convenience and the loan servicer is not or was not the mortgagee.[310]

§ 104.10(b)(6)(viii)   Electronic Promissory Notes: The Wave of the Future?

The promissory note would become a part of cyberspace if the Uniform Commercial Code (U.C.C.) were amended to permit the use of electronic promissory notes in addition to the traditional paper-based promissory notes. Article 3-104 of the U.C.C. requires a writing for a negotiable instrument. But, commentators James A. Newell and Michael R. Gordon have concluded that processing, recording, and storing promissory notes via electronic media would streamline the mortgage servicing and origination processes and increase profitability through the substantial reduction of the servicing costs associated with creating, handling, transporting and storing paper promissory notes.[311]

Considering the voluminous increase in the sale of mortgages into the secondary market, the cost savings could be significant. In 1993, mortgage lenders originated 1.01 trillion dollars in mortgages.[312] As part of this mortgage process, the mortgage industry creates millions of promissory notes.

Although this idea is novel, the shift from paper-based documents to electronic records is a growing trend in commercial transactions. Letters of credit, federal income tax returns and other traditionally paper-based documents now have electronic analogs. Most of the mortgages purchased by the Federal Home Loan Mortgage Corporation ("Freddie Mac") are pooled electronically for the issuance of participation certificates (mortgage-backed securities), which are in turn "issued" as an electronic "book entry" in the computerized records of a Federal Reserve Bank.

The hypothetical model posed by Newell and Gordon envisions an electronic promissory note that is generated as part of an electronic mortgage origination. If the mortgage is sold in the secondary market, the promissory note could be electronically transferred to a depository entity, such as a clearing corporation, that would maintain records of ownership, administer the transfer of notes, and perform other storage and negotiation duties.

---

[309] Myers v. Citicorp Mortgage, Inc., 878 F. Supp. 1553 (D. Ala. 1995).

[310] Truth in Lending Act Amendments of 1995, 7, 104 H.R. 2399 (codified at 15 U.S.C. § 1641(F)).

[311] James A. Newell & Michael R. Gordon, *Electronic Commerce and Negotiable Instruments (Electronic Promissory Notes)*, 31 Idaho L. Rev. 819 (1995).

[312] *Id.*

Signatures and endorsements for negotiation and transfer of holder-in-due-course status could be affixed electronically, using identification and security codes unique to the endorser. Delivery could be effected through electronic transmission of the note to the depository entity, which would hold the note as custodian for the note-holder.

Although possession of a promissory note is important for recognition and enforcement of the holder's ownership rights, the language in the U.C.C. with respect to physical possession and paper writings could be revised to recognize an electronic counterpart, such as a paper reproduction of the original electronic note certified by the depository entity. As the commentators put it:

> Furthermore, the Code [U.C.C.] will need to recognize that the most important attributes of a promissory note, whether paper-based or electronic-based, are the rights possessed by the holder, i.e., the contract rights and the holder-in-due-course status. For a holder, the continued legal recognition of these rights is far more important than the means by which the rights are set down and preserved. An electronic promissory note, which can be negotiated, notwithstanding the fact that the note is not represented by a paper-based memorial, should be a permissible alternative under the law of commerce.[313]

§ 104.11   Bibliography.

Books

Lefcoe, George. Real Estate Transactions, Finance, and Development (6th ed. 2009).

Grant S. Nelson & Dale A. Whitman, Real Estate Finance Law (5th ed. 2007).

Articles

Cassling, Donald R. "Bank's Action to Enforce Guaranties on Commercial Promissory Notes Not Subject to Six-Year Limitations Period Governing Actions on Negotiable Instruments, But Instead Barred by Shorter Limitations Period Regarding Guarantees Where Guarantors Did Not Qualify as Accommodation Parties to the Notes," 125 *Banking L.J.* 98 (January, 2008).

Darmstadter, Howard. "Promissory Notes," 10 *Scribes J. Legal Writing* 145 (2005–2006).

MacDonald, Duncan. "The Story of a Famous Promissory Note," 10 *Scribes J. Legal Writing* 79 (2005–2006).

Nation, George A., III. "Prepayment Fees in Commercial Promissory Notes: Applicability to Payments Made Because of Acceleration," 72 *Tenn. L. Rev.* 613 (Winter, 2005).

Annotations

Annotation, Economic duress or business compulsion in execution of promissory note, 79 *A.L.R.* 3d 598.

Annotation, Effect on bona fides of purchaser of promissory note of fact that there

---

[313] *Id.*

is interest due and unpaid upon it, 40 *A.L.R.* 832.

Annotation, Necessity of introducing evidence to show reasonableness of attorney's fees where promissory note provides for such fees, 18 *A.L.R.* 3d 733.

Annotation, Promissory notes as securities under sec. 2(1) of Securities Act of 1933 (15 U.S.C.A. sec 77b(1)), and sec. 3(a)(10) of Securities Exchange Act of 1934 (15 U.S.C.A. sec. 78c(a)(10)), 39 *A.L.R. Fed.* 357.

Annotation, Validity of provision in promissory note or other evidence of indebtedness for payment, as attorneys' fees, expenses, and costs of collection, of specified percentage of note, 17 *A.L.R.* 2d 288.

CHAPTER 105

ALTERNATIVE DISPUTE RESOLUTION IN REAL PROPERTY MATTERS

Professor David A. Thomas
J. Reuben Clark Law School
Brigham Young University

SYNOPSIS

§ 105.01   Introduction.

This chapter provides a general survey description of various methods of Alternative Dispute Resolution (ADR) and how they may be applied to real property matters. The ADR methods discussed here represent ADR in its fullest sense, which includes techniques for avoiding litigation entirely as well as processes that accelerate or shorten the litigation process. Some techniques, such as negotiation and compromise, apply in both contexts.

In real property matters, resort to the courts for dispute resolution is inexplicable and unsatisfactory to many who have experienced firsthand the frustrating delays, expenses and occasional inconsistencies of such litigation; thus, there is great and growing fervor behind the quest for alternative means of dispute resolution. This seems especially apparent when the property values at issue have not been large nor the legal issues complex.

It should be remembered, however, that access to the courts is a fundamental right and should not lightly be restricted. Therefore, state and federal legislation has arisen to encourage rather than mandate certain types of alternative dispute resolution. Such legislation may restrict or limit access to the courts in some circumstances, but usually will not foreclose it entirely. The impact of such ADR legislation is noted in the chapter.

COMPUTER-ASSISTED RESEARCH

LEXIS: alternative dispute resolution w/30 real w/1 property

§ 105.02   Devices for Settling Claims or Shortening Litigation.

§ 105.02(a)   In General.

All types of disputes, whether or not related to real property, may be resolved by one or more of the techniques discussed in this section. An infinite variety of factors may motivate a party to enter into an accord or a compromise, for example, but certainly chief among them is the desire to obtain some benefit from a claim while avoiding the time and expense of even ordinary, not to mention protracted, litigation. The mutuality of benefits derived from these arrangements depends heavily on the attorneys' skills as negotiators.

§ 105.02(b)   Mini-Trial.

To conduct a mini-trial, the parties select a qualified person to function as a private judge. Then, a short trial of issues in dispute is carried out before the judge. The trial, however, is not intended to be binding; its main purpose is to permit the parties to present the strengths of their respective cases, expose them to adversarial questioning and a thoughtful judicial response, and then attempt to reach a settlement after those views have been aired and evaluated. The usual context for the mini-trial is a dispute between corporations, and the trial is attended by corporate officers who have authority to conclude settlement agreements. Negotiations between those persons toward settlement following the mini-trial may be aided by comments from the "judge," who—while remaining impartial—may be invited to explain a judge's views of how the parties' positions will fare in the courts. The mini-trial is thus a form of structured negotiation that could even shift into a form of mediation.[1]

One variant of the mini-trial is the mini-arbitration, a proceeding in which the parties conduct the "trial" before an arbitrator and then accept the arbitrator's decision as binding.[2]

COMPUTER-ASSISTED RESEARCH

LEXIS: mini-trial w/50 property

§ 105.02(c)   Summary Jury Trial.

Another variant of the mini-trial is the summary jury trial, in which the parties present their cases before a jury of lay persons rather than before a group of corporate executives. The case presentations are oral arguments and summations only, with no examination of witnesses. The "jury" then renders a verdict, which is usually advisory only. After the presentations, the lawyers may question the "jurors," and, armed with such additional insights into the strengths and weaknesses of their positions, may enter into a settlement conference with the judge.[3]

The mini-trial and the summary jury trial are most useful in cases involving complex issues between wealthy parties. In the real property context, it is possible that litigation involving title to large tracts of land or major nuisance or mineral claims could be of such proportions as to benefit from the somewhat elaborate and expensive "dry run" represented by the mini-trial and summary jury trial methods.

COMPUTER-ASSISTED RESEARCH

LEXIS: summary w/1 jury w/1 trial w/50 property

§ 105.02(d)   Accord and Satisfaction.

If one party's conduct results in harm to another party, with a claim or cause of action based thereon, the offending party may offer to satisfy the claim with some substitute performance or consideration. This offer is the

---

[1] Eric D. Green, *Getting Out of Court—Private Resolution of Civil Disputes,* 28 Boston Bar J. 11 (May/June 1984); Eric D. Green, *Reading the Landscape of ADR—The State of the Art of Extrajudicial Forms of Dispute Resolution,* 100 F.R.D. 513 (1983).

[2] Roger Borovoy, *Alternative Dispute Resolution in Technical Litigation,* 100 F.R.D. 527 (1983); Browning v. Kelly, 1997 Conn. Super. LEXIS 3299 (unreported) (defendant's motion for summary judgment granted when plaintiff failed to rebut admissions in mini trial).

[3] *Federal Procedure Rule Service, District Court of Michigan, Western District Rule 44b; The New ADR Rules in the Western District of Michigan,* 2 Alternatives 10 (October 1984).

accord.[4] If the proffered accord is accepted, the performance of what was offered as the accord is the satisfaction.[5] When the accord is followed by the satisfaction, it bars the original claim.[6]

COMPUTER-ASSISTED RESEARCH

LEXIS: accord w/1 satisfaction w/50 property

§ 105.02(e)　Compromise and Settlement.

The process of compromise and settlement both resembles accord and satisfaction and differs from it. As with accord and satisfaction, a compromise is the offer to tender an alternative performance in response to a disputed claim, and the settlement is the actual performance of the proffered compromise.[7] However, a compromise is valid and enforceable even before settlement occurs,[8] whereas, the accord is not effective to bar the original claim, until the satisfaction occurs.[9] Furthermore, while the accord and

---

[4] Grove v. Winter, 554 N.E.2d 722 (Ill. App. 1990); International Union, United Auto., Aerospace, & Agr. Implement Workers of Am. (UAW) v. Yard-Man, Inc., 716 F.2d 1476 (6th Cir. 1983); S. Leo Harmonay, Inc. v. Binks Mfg. Co., 597 F. Supp. 1014 (S.D. N.Y. 1984); Stahl Mgt. Corp. v. Conceptions Unlimited, 554 F. Supp. 890 (S.D. N.Y. 1983); So v. 514 10th Street Associates, L.P., 834 A.2d 910 (D.C. 2003) (Part performance of an executory agreement to compromise a claim does not amount to accord and satisfaction).

[5] Polin v. Major, 502 N.E.2d 355 (Ill. App. 1986); Priem v. Shires, 697 S.W.2d 860 (Tex. Civ. App. 1985); Allan Constr. Co., Inc. v. Dahlstrom Corp., No. 03 96 00469 CV, 1997 Tex. App. LEXIS 4673 (Tex. App. 1997) (unpublished) (accord and satisfaction by transfer of title to properties resulting from dispute between highway construction contractors); Frantz v. Piccadilly Place Condominium Ass'n, Inc., 597 S.E.2d 354 (Ga. 2004) (Without a bona fide dispute or controversy as to the amount of the judgment, a condominium association's acceptance of a check from a unit owner marked "settlement in full" did not constitute an accord and satisfaction); Hollingsworth v. State Farm Fire & Cas. Co., 2005 U.S. Dist. LEXIS 3694 (E.D.Pa., 2005) (an offer for a compromise settlement is only a starting point of negotiation if the opposite party does not acknowledge or respond to it, and is therefore not binding).

[6] Seger v. Drews, 784 P.2d 133 (Or. App. 1989); Harrison v. Lucero, 525 P.2d 941 (N.M. App. 1974). Accord and satisfaction cannot be reached by the unilateral actions or claims of a party. Pueblo Bank & Trust Co. v. Steele, 110 F.3d 74 (10th Cir. 1997) (unpublished opinion); First Bank of Missouri v. Bac O'Flint Ltd., 104 F.3d 358 (4th Cir. 1996); Minnesota Chippewa Tribal Hous. Corp. v. Reese, 978 F. Supp. 1258 (D. Minn. 1997); Baums Dairy Farms, Inc. v. United States, 996 F. Supp. 705 (E.D. Mich 1998); McMahon v. New London County Mut. Ins. Co., 1999 Conn. Super. Lexis 2338, Pogge v. Department of Revenue, 703 So. 2d 523 (Fla. App. 1997).

[7] Harding v. Will, 500 P.2d 91 (Wash. 1972); Clayton v. Henry, No. 05 96 01898 CV, 1999 Tex. App. LEXIS 1305 (Tex. App. 1999) (unpublished) (failed challenge to compromise settlement agreement).

[8] Matter of Thompson's Estates, 601 P.2d 1105 (Kan. 1979); Blaylock v. Akin, 619 S.W.2d 207 (Tex. Civ. App. 1981); New York Air Brake Corp. v. General Signal Corp., 873 F. Supp. 747 (N.D.N.Y. 1995) (settlement agreement).

[9] Flagel v. Southwest Clinical Psychiatrist, P.C., 755 P.2d 1184 (Ariz. App. 1988); Goslin v. Racal Data Commun., Inc., 468 So. 2d 390 (Fla. App. 1985); Reily Elec. Supply, Inc. v.

satisfaction may relate to any claim, even undisputed or liquidated,[10] a compromise and settlement may pertain only to disputed claims. Also, an accord or satisfaction applies only to claims relating to the person or personal property,[11] whereas, a compromise and settlement may apply to all types of claims, including conflicting claims to real property.[12]

COMPUTER-ASSISTED RESEARCH

LEXIS: compromise w/1 settlement w/50 property

§ 105.02(f)   Novation and Release.

A novation and a release can result either from an accord and satisfaction or from a compromise and settlement. If either the accord or the compromise is accepted as a substitute promised performance, the original obligation of performance is extinguished and a novation results.[13] If the compromise or accord relinquishes a claim or discharge of performance, it may be termed a release.

COMPUTER-ASSISTED RESEARCH

LEXIS: novation w/1 release w/50 property

§ 105.03   Arbitration.

§ 105.03(a)   Arbitration Defined and Distinguished.

Arbitration is a nonjudicial process of investigating and resolving matters in dispute between parties.[14] Parties who resort to arbitration generally expect it to be more efficient, less expensive and less formal than litigation.[15]

Hollenberg, 535 So. 2d 1321 (La. App. 1988); Bestor v. American Nat'l Stores, Inc., 691 S.W.2d 384 (Mo. App. 1985); BancOhio Nat'l Bank v. Abbey Lane, Ltd., 13 Ohio App. 3d 446 (Ohio App. 1984); Mercury Marine Div., Brunswick Corp. v. Costas, 342 S.E.2d 632 (S.C. App. 1986); Rhea v. Marko Constr., 652 S.W.2d 332 (Tenn. 1983).

[10] Bowater North Am. Corp. v. Murray Mach., Inc., 773 F.2d 71 (6th Cir. 1985); Barry Props., Inc. v. Blanton & McCleary, 525 A.2d 248 (Md. App. 1987); Fortner v. Merrill Lynch, Pierce, Fenner & Smith, Inc., 687 S.W.2d 8 (Tex. App. 1984).

[11] Hershey v. Simpson, 725 P.2d 196 (Idaho App. 1986).

[12] *In re* Fischer, Key Bar Invs., Inc. v. Fischer, 116 F.3d 388 (9th Cir. 1997), *amended* by 127 F.3d 819 (9th Cir. 1997).

[13] Malanca v. Falstaff Brewing Co., 694 F.2d 182 (9th Cir. 1982); Malmstrom v. Kaiser Alum. & Chem. Corp., 231 Cal. Rptr. 820 (1986); Quealy v. Anderson, 714 P.2d 667 (Utah 1986); Patton v. TPI Petroleum, Inc., 356 F. Supp. 2d 921 (E.D. Ark. 2005) (a provision in a commercial tenant agreement cannot suffice as a novation of a pre-existing section of the lease, if the provision does not relate to that section).

[14] Christmas v. Cimarron Realty Co., 648 P.2d 788 (N.M. 1982).

[15] Mayflower Ins. Co. v. Pellegrino, 261 Cal. Rptr. 224 (1989); Village of Cairo v. Bodine Contr'g Co., 685 S.W.2d 253 (Mo. App. 1985); Reynolds v. Whitman, 663 N.E. 2d 867 (Mass. App. 1996), *cert. denied,* 665 N.E.2d 1004 (Mass. 1996) (Court supports arbitration for divorce cases because it is efficient, reduces court congestion, and minimizes acrimony. Needs to be reviewed by judge, particularly in the disposition of property); Cacheris v. Mayer

Like litigation, arbitration functions as both a fact-finding process, and a process for resolving the matters in dispute, and for determining an award for the prevailing party. Both the factual and remedial determinations resulting from an arbitration process are binding on the parties and are not intended merely to be submitted to a court for judicial approval. Judicial intervention in the arbitration process is appropriate only when difficulties in enforcement arise or when claims of impropriety in the arbitration proceedings are pressed.

§ 105.03(b)   The Common Law of Arbitration.

Although arbitration usually takes place because parties have agreed to arbitrate and today is subject to much statutory regulation, a common law of arbitration nevertheless exists. The common law of arbitration will not recognize a right of one party to force another to arbitrate a dispute, even under a prior agreement.[16] This means that private arbitration agreements are revocable at will by either party.

Once the parties enter arbitration, by their common consent, several principles of the common law of arbitration are applicable:

(1)   no right of jury trial and no right to resort to a court for instruction in the law is recognized;

(2)   the arbitrator is not required to explain reasons for the award; and

(3)   only limited judicial review of the award is permitted.[17]

COMPUTER-ASSISTED RESEARCH

LEXIS: arbitration w/30 common law

§ 105.03(c)   Statutory Modification of Arbitration Law.

State arbitration statutes began to appear in the early decades of the 20th century and made private arbitration agreements specifically enforceable by either party.[18] In some states the statutory provisions did not make major

---

Homes, Inc., 969 S.W.2d 876 (Mo. App. 1998) (arbitration is intended to be easier and faster than trial court determination).

[16]   Howard County Bd. of Educ. v. Howard County Educ. Ass'n, Inc., 487 A.2d 1220 (Md. App. 1985); International Union, United Auto. Aircraft, etc. v. Benton Harbor Malleable Indus., 242 F.2d 536 (6th Cir.), *cert. denied*, 355 U.S. 814 (1957); Phillips v. American Underwriters Life Insurance Co., 2002 Cal. App. Unpub. LEXIS 3268 (No. B147850, Mar. 8, 2002) (both parties' consent was required for the arbitration provision of the real estate agreement to be enforceable).But see Sheller by Sheller v. Frank's Nursery & Crafts, Inc., 957 F. Supp. 150 (N.D. Ill. 1997) (Prior agreement to arbitrate was upheld, case stayed pending arbitration); Bel Ray Co. v. Chemrite Ltd., 181 F.3d 435 (3d Cir. 1999).

[17]   Bernhardt v. Polygraphic Co. of Am., Inc., 350 U.S. 198 (1956); Valenti v. Hopkins, 926 P.2d 813, n.3 (Or. 1996); Raffaelli v. Raffaelli, 946 S.W.2d 139 (Tex. App. 1997).

[18]   Snyder v. Superior Court in and for Amador County, 74 P.2d 782 (Cal. App. 1930); Finsilver, Still & Moss v. Goldberg, Maas & Co., 171 N.E. 579 (N.Y. 1930).

changes in the common law of arbitration, but simply supplemented the common law.[19] Other state statutes, beginning with New York's arbitration act in 1921,[20] made significant changes in the common law of arbitration, but did not abolish it.[21] Comprehensive arbitration statutes in yet other states have completely abrogated the common law of arbitration in their jurisdictions.[22]

In 1956, the National Conference of Commissioners on Uniform State Laws issued a revised Uniform Arbitration Act, modeled after the New York act, which had also been followed in several other states. This uniform act has now been adopted in 28 states and the District of Columbia, and substantially similar legislation has been enacted in 14 additional states.

The constitutionality of some state arbitration statutes has been challenged by arguments that the statutes deprive parties of property without due process of law,[23] or improperly extend judicial powers to private persons,[24] and impair contract obligations.[25] All the statutes have withstood such attacks.

§ 105.03(d)   Requirements, Scope and Effect of Arbitration Agreements.

Under common law, agreements to submit present or future disputes to arbitration may be either oral or written.[26] However, common law also requires that such a submission agreement be in writing if the eventual arbitration award will achieve what the parties could do only in writing, such

---

[19] King v. Beale, 96 S.E.2d 765 (Va. 1957).

[20] N.Y. Civ. Prac. L. & R. § 7501 *et seq.*

[21] Wark & Co. v. Twelfth & Sansom Corp., 107 A.2d 856 (Pa. 1954); Britex Waste Co. v. Nathan Schwab & Sons, 12 A.2d 473 (Pa. Super. 1940).

[22] Kelso-Burnett Co. v. Zeus Dev. Corp., 437 N.E.2d 26 (Ill. App. 1982); Crofoot v. Blair Holdings Corp., 260 P.2d 156 (Cal. App. 1953); Hedges v. Carrigan, 11 Cal. Rptr. 3d 787 (2004) (United States Arbitration Act preempted compliance with certain conditions precedent in the arbitration clause of a real estate contract); Murphy v. Murphy, 2004 Tex. App. LEXIS 1420 (No. 2 02 449 CV, Feb. 12, 2004) (an agreement for the sale of two properties in Colorado was held to affect interstate commerce, so the Federal Arbitration Act and not the Texas arbitration law applied).

[23] Wenger v. Finley, 541 N.E.2d 1220 (Ill. App. 1989); Finsilver, Still & Moss v. Goldberg, Maas & Co., 171 N.E. 579 (N.Y. 1930).

[24] Moss v. Department of Mental Health, 406 N.W.2d 203 (Mich. App. 1987); Snyder v. Superior Court of Amador County, 74 P.2d 782 (Cal. App. 1930).

[25] Conejo Valley Unified Sch. Dist. v. William Blurock & Partners, Inc., 169 Cal. Rptr. 102 (1980); Berkovitz v. Arbib & Houlberg, Inc., 130 N.E. 288 (N.Y. 1921).

[26] Wetzel v. Sullivan, King & Sabom, P.C., 745 S.W.2d 78 (Tex. App. 1988); Lilley v. Tuttle, 117 P. 896 (Colo. 1911); Red Springs Presbyterian Church v. Terminix Co. of N.C., 458 S.E.2d 270 (N.C. App. 1995) (The parties' signature on the contract established a valid agreement to arbitrate a dispute).

as determine the title to land.[27] In those states where the submission agreement is governed by statute rather than the common law, such agreements almost always must be in writing, and this requirement is strictly enforced.[28] In jurisdictions where common law and statutory arbitration co-exist and the parties do not specify which set of rules they choose to follow, the choice of rules will be inferred from the parties' conduct.[29]

If agreements or contract clauses require parties to arbitrate future disputes, those agreements or clauses may, without more formalization, suffice as submission agreements if they apply to all such future disputes.[30] However, under some state arbitration statutes, such agreements do not actually achieve the submission of a dispute to arbitrations, but may be the

---

[27] *Id.*

[28] Apex Realty, Inc. v. Schick Realty, Inc., 577 A.2d 534 (N.J. Eq.), *appeal denied,* 604 A.2d 597 (N.J. 1990); Application of Downer Corp., 304 P.2d 756 (Cal. App. 1956); Marcus & Millichap Real Estate Inv. Brokerage Co. v. Hock Inv. Co., 80 Cal. Rptr.2d 147 (Cal. App. 1998) (sellers did not initial arbitration clause in purchase agreement, so there was no agreement to arbitrate); Rhode v. E & T Invs., Inc., 6 F. Supp. 2d 1322 (M.D. Ala. 1998) (statute precludes arbitration of express/written warranty claims by buyer of manufactured home, referring to Magnuson Moss Warranty Federal Trade Commission Improvement Act, 101 *et seq.*, 15 U.S.C. § 2301 et seq.); C & L Enterprises, Inc. v. Citizen Band Potawatomi Indian Tribe of Oklahoma, 532 U.S. 411 (2001) (arbitration provisions in a contract constituted a waiver of the tribe's sovereign immunity against lawsuits to enforce the arbitration award).

[29] Brennan v. General Acc., Fire & Life Assur. Corp., 574 A.2d 580 (Pa. 1990); Pick Indus., Inc. v. Gebhard-Berghammer, Inc., 56 N.W.2d 97 (Wis. 1953); Bank v. International Bus. Mach. Corp., 915 F. Supp. 491 (D. Mass. 1996), *rev'd by,* 99 F.3d 46 (1st Cir. 1996) (partner opposing mortgage purchase by partnership was not required to submit issue to arbitration); Insignia Homes, Inc. v. Hinden, 675 So. 2d 673 (Fla. App. 1996); Louise Gardens of Encino Homeowners' Association, Inc. v. Truck Insurance Exchange, Inc., 98 Cal. Rptr. 2d 378 (2000) (agreement subject to statutory contractual arbitration law).

[30] Stein v. Drake, 254 P.2d 613 (Cal. App. 1953); Ex parte Napier, 723 So. 2d 49 (Ala. 1998) (unsuccessful challenge of unconscionability to arbitration clause related to purchase of mobile home, although purchasers were in their seventies and had never completed high school); Williams v. Aetna Fin. Co., 700 N.E.2d 859 (Ohio 1998) (arbitration clause held unconscionable and unenforceable because lender and home repair pitchman conspired to defraud purchaser); Green Tree Agency, Inc. v. White, 719 So. 2d 1179 (Ala. 1998) (no duty to disclose that installment contract contains arbitration clause covering future disputes); Rogers v. Peinado, 101 Cal. Rptr. 2d 817 (2000) (arbitration clause in contract barred one party from maintaining an action for malicious prosecution against the other party); Halloran v. Buccheiri, 2003 Ohio App. LEXIS 5047 (No. 82745, Oct. 23, 2003) (an arbitration provision in an agreement between owners and an architect did not apply to the architect's subsequent services as a subcontractor); Lemmon v. Lincoln Property Co. 307 F. Supp. 2d 1352 (M.D. Fla, 2004) (Arbitration agreement containing all inclusive language is enforceable if it is not vague, even if it contains claims under civil right acts); Wolschlager v. Fidelity Nat. Title Ins. Co., 4 Cal. Rptr. 3d 179 (Cal. App. 2003) (incorporation of an arbitration clause into a contract through the incorporation of a document is valid if the incorporation is clear, unequivocal, and easily accessible).

basis for compelling a submission.[31]

Submission agreements must contain provisions that identify the issues or matters subject to arbitration, confer jurisdiction over the parties, and empower the arbitrator to resolve the dispute. If the content of submission agreements is defined by statute, the parties must strictly comply with the statutory requirements, because those requirements are usually held to be jurisdictional.[32]

Some submission agreements are self-executing, so that parties may proceed directly to the arbitration process; other agreements may contain only the commitment to arbitrate, and still require the appointment of arbitrators and submission of the matter to those appointees before further proceedings can take place.[33]

It is also possible for the parties to submit to arbitration a matter already in litigation. Under common law[34] and under some arbitration statutes, such a submission terminates the litigation and the jurisdiction of the court.[35] Under other statutes, the litigation is merely stayed pending the outcome of the arbitration.[36]

In a related issue, it has been held that merely entering into an agreement

---

[31] Newburger v. Lubell, 177 N.E. 424 (N.Y. 1931); In re Smith, 276 N.Y.S. 221 (1934); Scheele v. Justices of the Supreme Court of the State of Arizona, 257 F.3d 1082 (9th Cir. 2001) (requirements of arbitration rules do not constitute a taking); Fradella v. Seaberry, 952 So. 2d 195 (Miss. App. 2006) (an arbitration provision requiring to submit claims against the realtor to arbitration was not supported by consideration).

[32] Commercial Factors Corp. v. Kurtzman Bros., 280 P.2d 146 (Cal. App. 1955); Hill v. National Auction Group, Inc., 873 So. 2d 244 (Ala. App. 2003) (in an arbitration provision in a listing agreement between owner and auctioneer, a bidder was not subject to the provision as a third party beneficiary).

[33] Turner Constr. Co. v. H & S Forming of S. Florida, Inc., 567 So. 2d 1036 (Fla. App. 1990); Crofoot v. Blair Holdings Corp., 260 P.2d 156 (Cal. App. 1953); Ellis Constr., Inc. v. Vieux Carre Resort Properties, L.L.C., 934 So. 2d 206 (La. App. 2006) (arbitration right preserved by preliminary injunction);Abel Homes at Maranja Villas, LLC v. Hernandez, 960 So. 2d 891 (Fla. App. 2007) (right to arbitration waived by failure to submit timely demand for arbitration).

[34] Pick Indus., Inc. v. Gebhard-Berghammer, Inc., 56 N.W.2d 97 (Wis. 1953). *But see* Laur & Mack Contracting Co. Inc. v. Di Cienzo, 651 N.Y.S. 2d 831 (1996).

[35] Crofoot v. Blair Holdings Corp., 260 P.2d 156 (Cal. App. 1953); Ross Brothers Construction Co., Inc. v. International Steel Services, Inc., 383 F.3d 867 (7th Cir. 2002) (arbitration clause was valid so district court was required to transfer the affected claim to arbitration).

[36] Mountain Plains Constructors, Inc. v. Torrez, 785 P.2d 928 (Colo. 1990); Carpenter v. Bloomer, 148 A.2d 497 (N.J. Super. 1959); Sheller v. Frank's Nursery & Crafts, Inc., 957 F. Supp. 150 (N.D. Ill. 1997) (Prior agreement to arbitrate was upheld, case stayed pending arbitration); Cecala v. Moore, 982 F. Supp. 609 (N.D. Ill. 1997) (Suit for violation of Residential Real Property Disclosure Act stayed pending arbitration according to provision in realty sales agreement).

to submit a matter for arbitration, without actually undertaking the arbitration process, will not stop the running of the statute of limitations.[37] However, a party to the submission agreement may be estopped from asserting the statute of limitations as a defense if the arbitration agreement was the cause for delaying subsequent litigation.[38]

COMPUTER-ASSISTED RESEARCH

LEXIS: arbitration w/5 agreement! w/30 require! or scope! or effect!

§ 105.03(e)   The Arbitration Award.

§ 105.03(e)(1)   Technical Requirements.

The decision of an arbitrator or of arbitrators is called the award. Unless otherwise required by statute or by the parties' agreement, the award need only express the result of the arbitration, without supporting rationale.[39] Many of the state arbitration statutes also require the award to be in writing and to be signed by the arbitrators[40] and, in some instances, even acknowledged.[41]

According to the common law of arbitration, unless the parties have agreed to accept a decision by a majority of the arbitrators, the award must be based on a unanimous decision of the arbitrators.[42] Under most arbitration statutes a decision supported by a simple majority of the arbitrators suffices for a valid award.[43]

The arbitration award should consider and dispose of all the issues required to be resolved by the submission agreement.[44] Also, the award must

---

[37] Dresser v. Bindi, 271 Cal. Rptr. 137 (1990); Hornblower v. George Washington Univ., 31 App. D.C. 64 (1908).

[38] Martin v. Potashnick, 217 S.W.2d 379 (Mo. 1949).

[39] Apex Realty, Inc. v. Schick Realty, Inc., 577 A.2d 534 (N.J. Eq.), *appeal denied,* 604 A.2d 59 (N.J. 1990); Bryson v. Higdon, 21 S.E.2d 836 (N.C. 1942); Bradfordt Co. v. Hallmark Bldrs., Inc., 205 B.R. 971 (Bankr. M.D. Fla. 1996).

[40] Griffith Co. v. San Diego College for Women, 289 P.2d 476 (Cal. 1955).

[41] Griffith Co. v. San Diego College for Women, 289 P.2d 476 (Cal. 1955); Sandford Laundry v. Simon, 35 N.E.2d 182 (N.Y. 1941).

[42] Twait v. Farmers Mutual Hail Ins. Co., 91 N.W.2d 575 (Iowa 1958).

[43] Travelers Indem. Co. v. Walton, 384 So. 2d 939 (Fla. App. 1980); Clinton Water Ass'n v. Farmers Constr. Co., 254 S.E.2d 692 (W. Va. 1979).

[44] Johnston v. Johnston, 554 N.Y.S.2d 851 (1990); Mercury Oil Refining Co. v. Oil Workers Inter'l Union, 187 F.2d 980 (10th Cir. 1951), *disapproved on other grounds*, Textile Workers Union v. Lincoln Mills of Ala., 353 U.S. 448 (1957); Mehler v. The Terminix International Company L.P., 205 F.3d 44 (2nd Cir. 2000) (to be covered by the arbitration clause of the contract, the suit need only arise out of or relate to the contract); Cold Mountain Builders, Inc. v. Lewis, 746 A.2d 921 (Maine 2000) (arbitrator acted within the range of his discretion); Sweatt v. International Development Corporation, 531 S.E.2d 192 (Ga. App. 2000) (arbitrator exceeded authority); Pacific Development, L.C. v. Orton, 23 P.3d 1035

not deal with issues outside the terms of the submission agreement,[45] and an award on such matters is void.[46]

Arbitrators are required to be fair and just in their decisions,[47] but they are not required to follow rules of common law, unless that is required by the terms of the submission agreement or by statute.[48]

COMPUTER-ASSISTED RESEARCH

LEXIS: arbitration w/5 award! w/30 require!

§ 105.03(e)(2)   Enforcement of the Award.

Under common law an arbitration award is not self-enforcing.[49] Therefore, a party seeking enforcement of an arbitration award against a recalcitrant party must bring a judicial action on contract; the contract theory is appropriate, because the award is subsumed into the submission agreement.[50] Under statutory arbitration, unless common law remedies are also available, the statutory procedure for enforcement should be followed.[51]

The plaintiff in an enforcement action can establish a *prima facie* case by

---

(Utah 2001) (arbitrator exceeded authority). Nobles v. Rural Community Insurance Services, 303 F. Supp. 2d 1292 (M.D. Ala. 2004) (an arbitration decision concerning insurability of land estopped the insurer from re litigating that issue).

[45] Daley v. City of Hartford, 574 A.2d 194 (Conn. 1990), *cert. denied,* 498 U.S. 982 (1991); Carr v. Kalamazoo Vegetable Parchment Co., 92 N.W.2d 295 (Mich. 1958).

[46] Lynch v. Three Ponds Co., 656 P.2d 51 (Colo. App. 1982); Niles-Bement-Pond Co. v. Amalgamated Local 405, I. U., U. A., A. & A., 97 A.2d 898 (Conn. 1953).

[47] Jacob v. Pacific Export Lumber Co., 297 P. 848 (Or. 1931); Gerdetz v. Central Or. Irrig. Co., 163 P. 980 (Or. 1917).

[48] Johnston v. Johnston, 554 N.Y.S.2d 851 (1990); Morganti, Inc. v. Boehringer Ingelheim Pharmaceuticals, Inc., 563 A.2d 1055 (Conn. App. 1989); Zelle v. Chicago & N.W.R. Co., 65 N.W.2d 583 (Minn. 1954); Park Construction Co. v. Independent Sch. Dist. No. 32, Carver County, 11 N.W.2d 649 (Minn. 1943).

[49] Weber v. Lynch, 375 A.2d 1278 (Pa. 1977); Kennecott Utah Copper v. Becker, 195 F.3d 1201 (10th Cir. 1999).

[50] Richardson v. Harris, 818 P.2d 1209 (Nev. 1991); Lewiston-Auburn Shoeworkers Protective Ass'n v. Federal Shoe, Inc., 114 A.2d 248 (Me. 1955); Machu Pichu, Ltd. v. Massan Shipping Ind., 1997 U.S. Dist. LEXIS 20299 (E.D. La.); Lee County v. Fort Myers Airways, Inc., 688 So. 2d 389 (Fla. App. 1997); Sylvester v. Abdalla, 903 P.2d 410 (Or. App. 1995) (attorney fees awarded for successful resistance to exception to arbitrator's award); Busconi v. Dighello, 668 A.2d 716 (Conn. App. 1995), *cert. denied,* 670 A.2d 3321 (Conn. 1996) (lien foreclosure action based on federal court's judgment confirming arbitration award); Spearhead Constr. Corp. v. Bianco, 665 A.2d 86 (Conn. App. 1995), *appeal denied,* 667 A.2d 554 (Conn. 1995) (enforcement of arbitration judgment); Zelvin v. JEM Builders, Inc., 942 A.2d 455 (Conn. App. 2008) (application by vendors to vacate or modify the award; vendors failed to show that arbitrators manifestly disregarded the law in awarding money damages.).

[51] Wm. C. Blanchard Co. v. Beach Concrete Co., Inc., 297 A.2d 587 (N.J. Super. 1972); Carpenter v. North River Ins. Co., 436 S.W.2d 549 (Tex. Civ. App. 1968).

presenting evidence showing a valid award regular on its face; thereafter, the burden is on the defendant to impeach the award.[52]

COMPUTER-ASSISTED RESEARCH

LEXIS: arbitration w/5 award! w/30 enforc!

§ 105.03(e)(3)   Impeachment or Vacation of the Award.

To discredit or invalidate an arbitration award is referred to as impeachment. In general, at common law, arbitration awards will be impeached or set aside only if the arbitrators lacked jurisdiction, the arbitrators exceeded their authority, or if the arbitrators' conduct was tainted by fraud, gross negligence, or other serious misbehavior.[53] An award will be impeached for a mistake of law only if the arbitrators were required to follow substantive law in determining the award.[54]

If an arbitration award is to be vacated, it must be under one or more provisions of the applicable arbitration statute. Arbitration statutes generally list the grounds for vacating an award as they are found in the Uniform Arbitration Act:

> procurement [of the award] by corruption, fraud or other undue means;
>
> evident partiality by an arbitrator;
>
> exceeding of powers by arbitrators;
>
> refusal by arbitrators to postpone hearings or hear evidence so as to substantially prejudice the rights of a party;
>
> absence of a valid arbitration agreement or technical defects in the conduct of the proceedings.[55]

---

[52] Mork v. Eureka-Security Fire & Marine Ins. Co., 42 N.W.2d 33 (Minn. 1950).

[53] Board of Educ. of Bremen Community High Sch. Dist. No. 228, Cook County v. Bremen Dist. No. 228 Joint Faculty Ass'n, 449 N.E.2d 960 (Ill. App. 1983), *aff'd in part, rev'd in part,* 461 N.E.2d 406 (Ill. 1984); Coleman Co. v. International Union, United Auto., Aircraft and Agr. Implement Workers of Am., 317 P.2d 831 (Kan. 1957); Durkin v. Cigna Property & Casualty, 986 F. Supp. 1356 (D. Kan. 1997) (motion to vacate denied because arbitrator held not to have exceeded his authority); Cacheris v. Mayer Homes, Inc., 969 S.W.2d 876 (Mo. App. 1998) (vacation of award only under limited circumstances, referring to V.A.M.S. 435.405); Floyd Co. Bd. of Educ. v. EUA Cogenex Corp., 1999 U.S. App. Lexis 29692 (6th Cir. 1999); Conmac Corporation v. Southern Diversified Development, Inc., 539 S.E.2d 532 (Ga. App. 2000) (arbitration panel overstepped its authority in modifying an award); Sweatt v. International Development Corporation, 531 S.E.2d 192 (Ga. App. 2000) (arbitrator exceeded authority in the content of the award).

[54] Holman v. Trans World Airlines, 737 F. Supp. 527 (E.D. Mo. 1989); Board of Educ. of Bremen Community High Sch. Dist. No. 228, Cook County v. Bremen Dist. No. 228 Joint Faculty Ass'n, 449 N.E.2d 960 (Ill. App. 1983), *aff'd in part, rev'd in part,* 461 N.E.2d 406 (Ill. 1984); Moshonov v. Walsh, 94 Cal. Rptr. 2d 597 (2000) (arbitrator's decision to not award attorney's fees was final and not subject to judicial review).

[55] Uniform Arbitration Act § 12. Metrobuild Associates, Inc. v. Nahoum, 857 N.Y.S.2d 564 (2008) (trial court exceeded its authority in vacating arbitration award). Wittich v.

An arbitration award can also be set aside for a material mistake that clearly appears on the face of the award, such as an arithmetic mistake.[56] Also, an arbitrator's mistake that will cause the award to operate in a way they did not intend can be a ground for setting aside the award.[57]

COMPUTER-ASSISTED RESEARCH

LEXIS: arbitration w/5 award! w/30 impeach! or vacat!

§ 105.03(f)   Compulsory Arbitration.

In some jurisdictions, as a matter of course, civil claims below a certain amount are submitted by the court to an arbitration panel, or even to a single arbitrator. If a party disagrees with the result of the arbitration under those circumstances, a trial de novo may be held. However, if the new trial does not produce a more favorable result for the party requesting the trial, that party must pay costs to the other party and will be denied interest from the time of the award. Statutes that impose "compulsory arbitration" or that afford the parties no choice or alternative with respect to arbitration have generally been held unconstitutional, because they deprive parties of the right to trial by jury;[58] however, if a statutory "compulsory arbitration"

Wittich, 948 So. 2d 195 (La. App. 2006) (party not entitled to have arbitration award vacated); Birkey Design Group, Inc. v. Egle Nursing Home, Inc., 687 A.2d 256 (Md. App. 1997); Chen v. Chen, 688 A.2d 636 (N.J. Super. 1997); Labenski v. Kraizberg, 651 N.Y.S.2d 62 (1996); Zackiva Communications Corp. v. Milberg Weiss Bershad Spechrie & Lerach, 636 N.Y.S.2d 768 (1996) (no ground for vacating arbitration award), *abrogated by*, 666 N.Y.S.2d 985 (1997) (only regarding discovery issue); Hill v. Cloud, 648 So. 2d 1383 (La. App. 1995) (no grounds for vacating arbitration award); Gobegic Medical Care Facility v. AFSCME Local 992, AFL CIO, 531 N.W.2d 728 (Mich. App.) (arbitrator's decision vacated because it was contrary to public policy), *app. denied*, 549 N.W.2d 560 (Mich. 1995); Americrete, Inc. v. West Alabama Lime Co., 758 So. 2d 415 (Miss. 2000) (the court in affirming the award has a duty to issue its reasoning and thus must make findings of fact and conclusions of law when requested); Zelvin v. JEM Builders, Inc., 942 A.2d 455 (Conn. App. 2008) (application by vendors to vacate or modify the award; vendors failed to show that arbitrators manifestly disregarded the law in awarding money damages); Board of Managers of 225 East 57th Street Condominium v. Campaniello Real Estate, 837 N.Y.S.2d 644 (2007) (arbitration award vacated because the arbitrator exceeded her authority in determining powers of real estate company).

[56] Hough v. Osswald, 556 N.E.2d 765 (Ill. App.), *appeal denied,* 561 N.E.2d 692 (Ill. 1990); Stradinger v. City of Whitewater, 277 N.W.2d 827 (Wis. 1979); Joint School Dist. No. 10, City of Jefferson v. Jefferson Educ. Ass'n, 253 N.W.2d 536 (Wis. 1977); Trafalgar House Const., Inc. v. MSL Enters., Inc., 494 S.E.2d 613 (N.C. App. 1998) (referring to Construction Industry Arbitration Rules of American Arbitration Association (CIAR) as being consistent with state law, G.S. § 567.149(a)(3)); Connecticut Valley Sanitary Waste Disposal, Inc. v. Zielinski, 763 N.E.2d 1080 (Mass. 2002) (arbitration award could not be modified based on the receipt of additional evidence).

[57] Hoboken Manufacturers' R.R. Co. v. Hoboken R.R. Warehouse & Steamship Connecting Co., 27 A.2d 150 (N.J. Ch. 1942), *aff'd,* 31 A.2d 801 (N.J. App. 1943); Standard Constr. Co. v. Hoeschler, 14 N.W.2d 12 (Wis. 1944).

[58] Brooklyn Caledonian Hosp. v. Cintron, 557 N.Y.S.2d 842 (1990); United Farm

requirement is coupled with the right of appeal or the right to an original trial after arbitration, even with certain financial risks attached, such statutes have been upheld.[59]

COMPUTER-ASSISTED RESEARCH

LEXIS: compulsory w/2 arbitration

§ 105.03(g)   Real Property Issues Amenable to Arbitration.

Subject to any limitations imposed by an applicable arbitration statute, parties generally may have real property disputes submitted to and determined by arbitration.[60] An arbitration award cannot actually convey title (although it can authorize a conveyance),[61] or determine such issues as whether a river bank has been formed by accretion or avulsion,[62] but it can settle a boundary dispute.[63]

A party to a real property dispute has slightly different remedies under arbitration than under ordinary litigation. A real property disputant may seek to enforce the performance of the arbitration agreement itself. Under

---

Workers Nat'l Union v. Babbitt, 449 F. Supp. 449 (D. Ariz. 1978); Attorney General v. Johnson, 385 A.2d 57 (Md. 1978); Hays County Appraisal Dist. v. Mayo Kirby Springs, Inc., 903 S.W.2d 394 (Tex. App. 1995) (statute requiring binding arbitration held unconstitutional), *aff'd on appeal after remand*, 1997 Tex. App. LEXIS 5876 (No. 03 97 00029 CV, Nov. 13, 1997, Tex. App.) (unpublished); Government of Virgin Islands v. 0.459 Acres of Land, 886 F. Supp. 2 (D. V.I. 1995) (joint stipulation to enter binding arbitration was an enforceable contract), *rev'd on other grounds by*, 75 F.3d 860 (3rd. Cir. 1996).

[59] American Universal Ins. Co. v. DelGreco, 530 A.2d 171 (Conn. 1987); A. Fred Miller, Att'ys at Law, P.C. v. Purvis, 921 P.2d 610 (Alaska 1996) (compulsory arbitration over attorney's fees upheld using an "arbitrary and capricious standard" of review); Shimko v. Lobe, 706 N.E.2d 354 (Ohio App. 1997) (compulsory Arbitration upheld due to safeguards, including limited review before the Court of Common Pleas); Kedzior v. CDC Dev., 704 N.E.2d 54 (Ohio App. 1997); Desiderio v. NASD, 1999 U.S. App. Lexis 23269 (2d Cir. 1999); Segal v. Silberstein, 67 Cal. Rptr. 3d 426 (2007) (arbitration required by parties' business operating agreements).

[60] Cox v. Heuseman, 97 S.E. 778 (Va. 1919); Garrison v. Palmas Del Mar Homeowners Ass'n, Inc., 538 F. Supp. 2d 468 (D. Puerto Rico) (a claim of right to make repairs to property was subject to arbitration). JPMorgan Chase Bank v. Reibestein, 824 N.Y.S.2d 259 (2006) (landlord's breach of contract claim was arbitrable); Harris v. Green Tree Fin., 1997 U.S. Dist. LEXIS 20792 (E.D. Pa.) (motion to compel arbitration denied due to unconscionability), *rev'd and remanded by* 183 F.3d 173 (3d Cir. 1999); Baker v. Conoco Pipeline Co., 280 F. Supp. 2d 1285 (N.D. Okla. 2003 (an arbitration provision in an easement "touched and concerned" the land).

[61] Vail v. American Way Homes, Inc., 435 A.2d 993 (Conn. 1980); Fore v. Berry, 78 S.E. 706 (S.C. 1913); Kedzior v. CDC Dev., 704 N.E.2d 54 (Ohio App. 1997) (Court held lower court erred in referring case to arbitration because the statute indicated arbitrators had no jurisdiction to decide a title claim for real property).

[62] State v. Loy, 299 N.W. 908 (N.D. 1941).

[63] Fehrman v. Bissell Lumber Co., 204 N.W. 482 (Wis.), *rehearing denied*, 205 N.W. 905 (Wis. 1925).

common law arbitration, the remedy for breach of an agreement to arbitrate is only an action for breach of contract to recover whatever damages can be proved from the breach.[64] In contrast to other real property actions, specific performance will not be granted,[65] unless arbitration of certain issues was a condition precedent to commencing court action on a larger matter.[66] If the arbitration agreement is under authority of a state statute rather than common law, the performance of the agreement is usually enforceable by either specific performance or an action for damages.[67]

COMPUTER-ASSISTED RESEARCH

LEXIS: arbitration w/30 real w/1 property

§ 105.03(h)   Evaluation of Arbitration as an Alternative to Litigation.

As is evident from the statutory and case law that has grown up around the concept of arbitration, an arbitration proceeding can be complex, protracted, and often subject to major litigation after the arbitration proceeding. In the view of some, arbitration is potentially so cumbersome and expensive that, as a method of alternative dispute resolution, it has lost some appeal.[68] However, arbitration enjoys great and growing popularity for some kinds of cases, almost to the point of being the exclusive dispute resolution method.[69]

COMPUTER-ASSISTED RESEARCH

LEXIS: arbitration w/30 litigation w/15 alternative!

§ 105.04   Conciliation.

Conciliation facilitates communication between the parties by an emphasis on ensuring that the parties fully and correctly understand each other's positions and motivations by whatever sequence of conferences and consul-

---

[64] Thompson v. Phillips Pipe Line Co., 438 P.2d 146 (Kan. 1968); Goerke Kirch Co. v. Goerke Kirch Holding Co., 176 A. 902 (N.J. App. 1935).

[65] Gamble v. Sukut, 302 P.2d 553 (Or. 1956); Office & Professional Employees Int'l Union v. Brownsville Gen. Hosp., 186 F.3d 326 (3d Cir. 1999).

[66] Palmer v. Clark, 106 Mass. 373 (1871).

[67] Amalgamated Ass'n of S.E.R.M.C.E. v. Pittsburgh Ry. Co., 142 A.2d 734 (Pa.), *cert. denied,* 358 U.S. 882 (1958).

[68] Roger Borovoy, *Recent Developments in Alternative Forms of Dispute Resolutions (ADR),* 100 F.R.D. 499 (1983). *But see* Board of Managers of Courtyards at Woodlands Condo. Ass'n v. IKO Chicago, Inc., 697 N.E.2d 727, 732 (Ill. 1998) ("It is a well established principle that arbitration is a favored alternative to litigation by state, federal and common law because it is a speedy, informal, and relatively inexpensive procedure for resolving controversies arising out of commercial transactions."); Cole v. Hiller, 715 So. 2d 451 (La. App. 1998) (strong public policy favoring arbitration as alternative to litigation).

[69] Rosenberg v. Merrill Lynch, Pierce, Fenner & Smith, Inc., 170 F.3d 1 (1st Cir. 1999).

tations best accomplishes that.[70] By contrast with mediation, discussed below, conciliation lacks mediation's more formal structure of joint and separate meetings with the parties.

If a statute directs a party to attempt conciliation,[71] and conciliation is defined as the attempt to reach a reasonable, voluntary, and mutual understanding, what constitutes fulfillment of the statutory duty often depends on the intransigence of the other party.[72]

COMPUTER-ASSISTED RESEARCH

LEXIS: conciliation w/50 real w/1 proeprty

§ 105.05   Negotiation and Mediation.

Negotiation is the process whereby parties confer for the purpose of agreeing to go forward in a matter or to settle a dispute. It may be appropriately undertaken at any stage in the legal relations of parties, from the beginning to post-trial matters.[73] Parties rely on negotiation either to prevent a dispute from arising by anticipating and reaching agreement on issues of potential conflict, or to reach a settlement or accommodation after the issues have come into conflict. As a mechanism for dispute resolution, it is an alternative to litigation.

Sometimes, negotiations may be assisted by mediation, a process by which a neutral party helps the negotiating parties identify issues and possible solutions.[74] Normally, the mediator has no independent authority and serves only the functions assigned by agreement of the parties. While mediation may seem inhibited by this requirement of voluntary participation by the parties, it retains a significant advantage over negotiation as a dispute resolution device, in that the parties retain control over every aspect of the dispute.[75] The usual sequence for mediation is for the mediator to meet with

---

[70] Frank E.A. Sander, *Varieties of Dispute Processing,* 70 F.R.D. 111 (1976).

[71] *See, e.g.,* 29 U.S.C. § 626(b).

[72] Oscar Mayer Co. v. Evans, 441 U.S. 750 (1979); Marshall v. Sun Oil Co. (Delaware), 605 F.2d 1331 (5th Cir.), *rehearing denied,* 610 F.2d 818 (5th Cir. 1979); *In re* Spectrum Techs., Inc., 183 B.R. 360 (Bankr. E.D.N.Y. 1995) (request for conciliation conference and appeal of conciliation order).

[73] Roger Fisher, *What about Negotiation as a Specialty?,* 69 ABA Journal 1221 (Sept. 1983).

[74] Joseph B. Stulberg, *Negotiation Concepts and Advocacy Skills: The ADR Challenge,* 48 Albany L. Rev. 719 (1984); Note, *Protecting Confidentiality in Mediation,* 98 Harv. L. Rev. 423 (1984); Mills v. Vilas County Board of Adjustments, 660 N.W.2d 705 (Wis. App. 2003) (refusal to enforce mediation agreement).

[75] Frank E.A. Sander, *Diversifying Legal Solutions,* 35 *Harvard L. Bull.* 4 (Summer/Fall 1984); Yaekle v. Andrews, 195 P.3d 1101 (Colo. 2008) (a provision of the Dispute Resolution Act enabled the parties to convert an agreement reached during mediation into an enforceable court order); DR Lakes Inc. v. Brandsmart U.S.A. of West Palm Beach, 819 So. 2d 971 (Fla. App. 2002) (the statutory privilege of confidentiality did not apply to

all parties together and then separately with each party.[76]

COMPUTER-ASSISTED RESEARCH

LEXIS: negotiat! or mediat! w/50 real w/1 property

§ 105.06   Consensual References; Factfinders.

Some states have adopted statutes authorizing consensual references, known colloquially as "rent-a-judge." Under such statutes, the parties agree to hire a retired judge or other qualified person to conduct a private but complete trial of their dispute. After hearing the dispute, the private judge reaches a decision and the ruling has the same force as a court judgment.[77]

The obvious advantages of this procedure are the ability to choose a qualified—even an expert—person to try the case, better control over the timing of hearing and trial schedules, flexibility of procedures, confidentiality, and efficiency.

Under a wide variety of statutes, most states permit limited issues of fact or law to be referred to third parties.[78] In most of these states, however, the private judge's determinations are not accorded the weight of a regular verdict or judgment.

COMPUTER-ASSISTED RESEARCH

LEXIS: consensual w/1 reference! w/50 real w/1 property
               rent-a-judge w/50 real w/1 property

§ 105.07   Ombudsman.

An ombudsman performs functions very similar to those of a conciliator or mediator, but usually in the context of a dispute between a private person and a governmental agency.[79] The ombudsman may have a specific commission from the agency or legislature to deal with complaints from the

---

communications made during mediation); Ong v. Mike Guido Properties, 668 So. 2d 708 (Fla. App. 1996); Suarez v. Jordan, 35 S.W.3d 268 (Tex. App. 2000) (court ordered mediation).

[76] Frank E.A. Sander, *Varieties of Dispute Processing,* 70 F.R.D. 79, 111 (1976); Peacock v. Spivey, 629 S.E.2d 48 (Ga. App. 2006) (owner of allegedly contaminated property voluntarily signed a mediation agreement and was not entitled to a jury trial on the issue of whether he was under duress at the time he signed the mediation agreement).

[77] *Self-help: Extra Judicial Rights, Privileges and Remedies in Contemporary American Society,* 37 Vand. L. Rev. 845, 1015 (1984); Eric D. Green, *Getting Out of Court—Private Resolution of Civil Disputes,* 28 Boston Bar J. 11 (May/June 1984); Note, *The California Rent-A-Judge Experiment: Constitutional and Policy Considerations of Pay-As-You-Go Courts,* 94 Harv. L. Rev. 1592 (1981).

[78] Eric D. Green, *Getting Out of Court—Private Resolution of Civil Disputes,* 28 Boston Bar J. 11 (May/June 1984); Note, *The California Rent-A-Judge Experiment: Constitutional and Policy Considerations of Pay-As-You-Go Courts,* 94 Harv. L. Rev. 1592 (1981).

[79] Paul R. Verkuil, *The Ombudsman and the Limits of the Adversary System,* 75 Colum. L. Rev. 845 (1975). *See e.g.,* A.R.S. 41 1312 (Ombudsman for Private Property Rights);

public. Certain powers of investigation may also be conferred on the ombudsman, including powers to subpoena, and to obtain and examine records and other information. An ombudsman's proposed solutions are not binding, but often are influential or persuasive in dealing with the affected government agency.[80]

COMPUTER-ASSISTED RESEARCH

LEXIS: ombudsman w/50 real w/1 property

§ 105.08 Bibliography.

Books

American Arbitration Association. *ADR: A Practical Guide to Resolve Construction Disputes: Alternative Dispute Resolution in the Construction Field.* Dubuque, Iowa: Kendall/Hunt Pub., 1994.

Brazil, Wayne D. *Effective Approaches to Settlement: A Handbook for Lawyers and Judges.* Clifton: Prentice & Hall Law Business, 1988.

Freedman, Lawrence, *Legislation on Dispute Resolution.* Washington, D.C.: American Bar Assoc., 1984.

Freeman, Michael, ed. *Alternative Dispute Resolution.* New York: New York U. Press, 1995.

Nolan Haley, Jacqueline M. *Alternative Dispute Resolution in a Nutshell.* St. Paul, Minn.: West Pub. Co., 1992.

Rangarajan, L.N. *The Limitation of Conflict: A Theory of Bargaining and Negotiation.* London: Croom Helm, 1985.

Roth, Bette J., Randall W. Wulff & Charles A Cooper. *The Alternative Dispute Resolution Practice Guide.* Rochester, N.Y.: Lawyers Cooperative, 1993.

Ruben, Alan Miles. *Elkouri and Elkouri: How Arbitration Works.* Book News, Inc., Portland, Ore., 2004.

Sander, Frank E.A. *Mediation, A Select Annotated Bibliography.* Washington, D.C.: American Bar Assoc., 1984

Wall, James A. *Negotiation, Theory and Practice.* Glenview: Scott Foresman, 1985.

Articles

Alfini, James P. "Alternative Dispute Resolution and the Courts." *Judicature* Vol. 69 (1986) 252.

"Alternative Dispute Resolution: A Special Issue." *Texas B.J.* Vol. 51 (1988) 14.

"Arbitration: Deciding Scope of Arbitrator's Powers." 28 *Real Est. L. Rep.* (Dec. 1998) 6.

Borovoy, Roger. "Alternative Dispute Resolution in Technical Litigation." *F.R.D.* Vol. 100 (1983) 527.

Brandon, Douglas I., et. al. "Self-Help: Extra-Judicial Rights, Privileges and

---

O.R.S. 446.543 (Manufactured Dwelling Park Ombudsman); U.C.A. 63 34 13 (Private Property Ombudsman).

[80] *Self-help: Extra Judicial Rights, Privileges and Remedies in Contemporary American Society,* 37 Vand. L. Rev. 845, 1031 (1984).

Remedies in Contemporary American Society." *Vand. L. Rev.* Vol. 37 (1984) 845, 1015.

Brazil, Wayne D. "Protecting the Confidentiality of Settlement Negotiations." *Hastings L.J.* Vol. 39 (1988) 955.

Brunet, Edward. "Questioning the Quality of Alternate Dispute Resolution." *Tul. L. Rev.* Vol. 62 (1987) 1.

Burnett, Arthur L., Sr. "An Advisory Summary Trial Procedure as a Useful Pretrial Method to Promote Settlement of Civil Cases." *Fed. B. News & J.* Vol. 32 (1985) 290.

Burnham, Scott J. "A Primer on Accord and Satisfaction." *Montana L. Rev.* Vol. 47 (1986) 1.

Comment, "Arbitration—A Viable Alternative?" *Fordham Urb. L.J.* Vol. 3 (1974) 53.

Carr, Frank and Lester Edelman. "The Mini-Trial: An Alternative Dispute Resolution Procedure." *Arb. J.* Vol. 42 (1987) 7.

Carbone, Sasha, and Sandra Partridge. "Real Estate Industry Arbitration Rules: How Owners & Corporate Occupants Can Avoid Costly Errors," 552 *PLI/Real* 451 (April, 2008).

Christensen, Eric C. "Trends in New Mexico Law: 1994–95: Civil Procedure/Alternative Dispute Resolution-New Mexico Applies Collateral Estoppel to Issues Fully and Fairly Litigated in Arbitration Proceedings: Rex, Inc. v. Manufactured Housing Committee of New Mexico, Manufactured Housing Division." *N.M. L. Rev.* Vol. 26 (Summer 1996) 513.

Comment, "Arbitration A Viable Alternative?" *Fordham Urb. L.J.* Vol. 3 (1974) 53.

Comment, Haynes. "Private Means to Public Ends; Implications of the Private Judging Phenomenon in California." *U.C. Davis L. Rev.* Vol. 17 (1984) 611.

Comment, "Institutionalization of Alternative Dispute Resolution by the State of California." *Pepp. L. Rev.* Vol. 14 (1987) 943.

Comment, "The Mediator-Lawyer: Implications for the Practice of Law and One Argument for Professional Responsibility Guidance—A Proposal for Some Ethical Considerations." *U.C.L.A. L. Rev.* Vol. 34 (1986) 507.

Cooley, John W. "Arbitration vs. Mediation—Explaining the Differences." *Judicature* Vol. 69 (1986) 263.

Craver, Charles B. "Negotiation Techniques: How to Keep Br'er Rabbit Out of the Brier Patch." *Trial* Vol. 24 (June, 1988) 65.

Dauber, Cynthia B. "The Ties That Do Not Bind: Nonbinding Arbitration in Federal Administrative Agencies." *Admin. L.J. Am. U.* Vol. 9 (1995) 165.

Davidson, Jonathan and Susan L. Trevarthen. "Land Use Mediation: Another Smart Growth Alternative," 33 *Urb. Law.* 705 (Summer, 2001)

Davis, James F. "Recent Developments in Alternative Forms of Dispute Resolutions (ADR)." *F.R.D.* Vol. 100 (1983) 499.

Davis, Kenneth R. "When Ignorance of the Law Is No Excuse: Judicial Review of Arbitration Awards." *Buff. L. Rev.* Vol. 45 (Winter 1997) 49.

Day, Minh. "Alternative Dispute Resolution and Customary Law: Resolving Property Disputes in Post Conflict Nations, A Case Study in Rwanda," 16 *Geo. Immigr. L.J.* 235 (Fall, 2001).

Dellapa, Fred M. "Citizen Dispute Settlement: A New Look at on Old Method." *Fla. B.J.* Vol. 51 (1977) 516.

Donner, Michael F. "Litigation Avoidance 101: Thinking Through the Use of Boilerplate Provisions for Arbitration, Mediation, and Attorney Fees in Real Estate Contracts." 17 *Prob. & Prop.* 19 (May/June 2003).

Donovan, Michael D. and David A. Searles. "Preserving Judicial Recourse for Consumers: How to Combat Overreaching Arbitration Clauses." 10 *Loy. Consumer L. Rev.* (1998) 269.

Fisher, Roger. "What About Negotiation as a Specialty?" *A.B.A.J.* Vol. 69 (1983) 1221.

Fowks, Robert J. "Alternative Dispute Resolution—A Primer." *J. Kan. B.A.* Vol. 56 (1987) 12.

Fowler, Thomas L. "Court Ordered Arbitration In North Carolina: Selected Issues of Practice and Procedure." 21 *Campbell L. Rev.* 191 (Spring, 1999).

"Fraud: Can Nullify Arbitration Provision." 28 *Real Est. L. Rep.* (Aug. 1998) 3.

Galanter, Marc. "The Emergence of the Judge as a Mediator in Civil Cases." *Judicature* Vol. 69 (1986) 257.

Gislason, Adam Furlan. "Demystifying ADR Neutral Regulation in Minnesota: The Need for Uniformity and Public Trust in the Twenty First Century ADR System." 83 *Minn. L. Rev.* 1839 (June 1999).

Goldberg, George. "Agreement to Arbitrate." *Practical Lawyer* Vol. 24 (1978) 61.

Goldberg, Thomas C., Eric D. Green and Frank E.A. Sander. "Book Review: Dispute Resolution." *Willamette L. Rev.* Vol. 23 (1987) 1.

Goldfien, Jeffrey H. "Thou Shalt Love they Neighbor: RLUIPA and the Mediation of Religious Land Use Disputes," 2006 *J. Disp. Resol.* 435.

Green, Eric D. "Reading the Landscape of ADR—The State of the Art of Extra-judicial Forms of Dispute Resolution." *F.R.D.* Vol. 100 (1983) 513.

Guttell, Steven M. "Analysis of a Technique of Dispute Settlement: The Expanding Role of Arbitration." *Suffolk U.L. Rev.* Vol. 7 (1973) 618.

Hammond, Celeste. "'A Real Estate Focus: The (Pre) (As)Sumed 'Consent' of Commercial Binding Arbitration Contracts: An Empirical Study of Attitudes and Expectations of Transactional Lawyers." 36 J. *Marshall L. Rev.* 589 (Spring, 2003).

Harding, Margaret M. "The Clash Between Federal and State Arbitration Law and the Appropriateness of Arbitration as a Dispute Resolution Process." 77 *Neb. L. Rev.* (1998) 397.

Henry, James F. "Alternative Dispute Resolution: Meeting the Legal Needs of the 1980s." *Ohio St. J. Disp. Resol.* Vol. 1 (1985) 113.

Herman, Lori. "Resolving Real Estate Disputes Through Arbitration." 79 *Am. Jur. Trials* 159 (June 2004).

Imperati, Samuel J. "Alternative Dispute Resolution Symposium Issue: Mediator Practice Models: The Intersection of Ethics and Stylistic Practices in Mediation." *Willamette L. Rev.* Vol. 33 (Summer 1997) 703.

King, Donald B. "Consumer Ombudsman." *Commercial L. J.* Vol. 79 (1974) 355.

Lacher, Stephen J. "Alternative Dispute Resolution (ADR) in the 90's and Beyond:

A View from the Neutral's Seat." *N.Y. St. B.J.* Vol. 67 (Sept. Oct. 1995) 45.

Lambros, Thomas D. "Summary Jury Trials." *Litig.* Vol. 13 (1986) 52.

Lanni, Adriaan. Case Note: "Protecting Public Rights in Private Arbitration." *Yale L.J.* Vol. 107 (1998) 1157.

Levi, Edward H. "Business of the Courts, A Summary and a Sense of Perspective." *F.R.D.* Vol. 70 (1984) 212.

Lind, E. Allan and Benjamin R. Foster. "Alternative Dispute Resolution in the Federal Courts: Public and Private Options." *Fed. B. News & J.* Vol. 33 (1986) 127.

Murray, Daniel E. "A Potpourri of Recent Federal Arbitration Cases Involving Domestic and International Arbitration." 13 *BYU J. Pub. L.* 293 (1999).

Netter, Edith M. "Mediations in the Public Interest: Land Use Examples." *Colo. L. Rev.* Vol. 19 (1995) 113.

Note: "Arbitration: Shaffer v. Jeffrey. The Oklahoma Supreme Court Rejects the Separability Doctrine and Takes a Step Back in the Enforcement of Arbitration Clauses Under Oklahoma Law." *Okla. L. Rev.* Vol. 50 (Summer 1997) 243.

Note, "Compulsory Judicial Arbitration in California: Reducing the Delay and Expense of Resolving Uncomplicated Civil Disputes." *Hastings L.J.* Vol. 29 (1988) 475.

Note, "Enforceability of Mediated Agreements." *Ohio St. J. Disp. Resol* Vol. 1 (1986) 385.

Note, "Mandatory Mediation and Summary Jury Trial; Guidelines for Ensuring Fair and Effective Processes." *Harv. L. Rev.* Vol. 103 (1990) 1086.

Note, "Med-Arb An Alternative to Interest Arbitration in the Resolution of Contract Negotiation Disputes." *Ohio St. J. Disp. Resol.* Vol. 3 (1988) 385.

Oehmke, Thomas H. "Appealing Adverse Arbitration Awards." 94 *Am. Jur. Trials* 211 (November 2004).

Oehmke, Thomas H. "Arbitration Highways to the Courthouse: A Litigator's Roadmap." 86 *Am. Jur. Trials* 111 (June 2004).

Oler, Jr. "Compulsory Arbitration in Pennsylvania: Effect of an Appeal by One of Several Parties." *Penn. B. Q.* Vol. 48 (1977) 557.

Page, Reba and Frederick T. Lees. "Roles of Participants in the Mini-Trial." *Pub. Cont. L.J.* Vol. 18 (1980) 54.

Patterson, Roger T. "Dispute Resolution in a World of Alternatives." *Cath. U. L. Rev.* Vol. 37 (1988) 591.

Phillips, Barbara A. "Alternative Dispute Resolution Symposium Issue: Mediation: Did We Get it Wrong?" *Willamette L. Rev.* Vol. 33 (Summer 1997) 649.

Phillips, Barbara A. and Anthony C. Piazza. "Mediation is a Tool for Managing Litigation." *Fed. B. News & J.* Vol. 32 (1985) 240.

Policzer, Milt. "Winning Without Trial." *Litig.* Vol. 14 (1988) 43.

Posner. "The Summary Jury Trial and Other methods of Alternative Dispute Resolution: Some Cautionary Observations." *U. Chic. L. Rev.* Vol. 53 (1986) 366.

Note, "Private Judging: An Effective and Efficient Alternative to the Traditional Court System." *Val. U. L. Rev.* Vol. 21 (1987) 681.

Note, "Protecting Confidentiality in Mediation." *Harvard L. Rev.* Vol. 98 (1984) 441.

Note, "The California Rent A Judge Experiment: Constitutional and Policy Considerations of Pay As You Go Courts." *Harv. L. Rev.* Vol. 94 (1981) 1592.

Raven, Robert D. "Alternative Dispute Resolution: Expanding Opportunities." *Arb. J.* Vol. 43 (1988) 44.

Riskin, Leonard L. "Toward New Standards for the Neutral Lawyer in Mediation." *Ariz. L. Rev.* Vol. 26 (1984) 329.

Rosenberg, Maurice and Myra Shubin. "Trial by Lawyer: Compulsory Arbitration of Small Claims in Pennsylvania." *Harv. L. Rev.* Vol. 74 (1961) 448.

Ruhl, J.B. "Alternative Dispute Resolution Symposium: Thinking of Mediation As a Complex Adaptive System." *BYU L. Rev.* (1997) 777.

Said, Irene Stanley. "The Mediator's Dilemma: The Legal Requirements Exception to Confidentiality Under the Texas ADR Statute." *S. Tex. L. Rev.* Vol. 36 (1995) 579.

Sander, Frank E.A. "Diversifying Legal Solutions." *Harv. L. Sch. Bull.* Vol. 35 (1984) 4.

Sander, Frank E.A. "Varieties of Dispute Processing." *F.R.D.* Vol. 70 (1976) 79.

Schuyler, Nina. "Coercive Harmony: An Anthropologist and a Former Federal Judge Debate the Purpose of Mandatory ADR." *Cal. Law.* Vol. 15 (May 1995) 37.

Shampnoi, Elizabeth, "Arbitration Rules for the Real Estate Industry (Including a Mediation Alternative) As Amended and Effective September 15, 2005: How Owners & Corporate Occupants Can Avoid Costly Errors," 539 *PLI/Real* 477 (April 4 5, 2007)

Shapiro, David J. "Private Judging in the State of New York: A Critical Introduction." *Colum. J.L. & Soc. Probs.* Vol. 23 (1990) 275.

Smith, James E. "Don't Rush to Justice: An Argument Against Binding North Dakota Courts to Arbitration." *N. Dak. L. Rev.* Vol. 73 (1997) 459.

Sochynsky, Yaroslav. "Mediating Real Estate Disputes." 12 *Prob. & Prop.* (July Aug. 1998) 22.

Speidel, Richard E. "Consumer Arbitration of Statutory Claims: Has Pre Dispute Mandatory Arbitration Outlived Its Welcome?" 40 *Ariz. L. Rev.* 1069 (Fall 1998).

Spiegelman, Paul J. "Developments in Alternative Dispute Resolution." *J. Legal Educ.* Vol. 37 (1987) 26.

Sternlight, Jean R. "Forum Shopping for Arbitration Decisions: Federal Courts' Use of Antisuit Injunctions Against State Courts.'"147 U. *Pa. L. Rev.* (1998) 91.

Sternlight, Jean R. "Rethinking the Constitutionality of the Supreme Court's Preference for Binding Arbitration: A Fresh Assessment of Jury Trial, Separation of Powers, and Due Process Concerns." *Tul. L. Rev.* Vol. 71 (1997) 1.

Stulberg, Joseph B. "Negotiation Concepts and Advocacy Skills: The ADR Challenge." *Alb. L. Rev.* Vol. 48 (1984) 719.

"Symposium Issue on Alternative Dispute Resolution." *Pepp. L. Rev.* Vol. 14 (1987) 769-942.

Syverud, Kent D. "Symposium on Alternative Dispute Resolution: ADR and the Decline of the American Civil Jury." *UCLA L. Rev.* Vol. 44 (1997) 1935.

Yarn, Douglas. "The Death of ADR: A Cautionary Tale of Isomorphism Through Institutionalization." 108 *Penn St. L. Rev.* 929 (2003).

Thompson, Mark. "Rented Justice, Business Is Booming for Rent-A-Judges, and the Courts Could Learn from Their Success." *Cal. Law.* Vol. 8 (1988) 42.

"Trends in Alternative Dispute Resolution." *N.Y.U. Rev. L. & Soc.* Change Vol. 14 (1986) 739.

Tutterow, John T. "A Focus on Unincorporated Businesses. Note. The Constitution v. Arbitration: Rollings v. Thermodyne and a Proposal for a New Alternative to Arbitration." *Okla. City U. L. Rev.* Vol. 22 (Summer 1997) 697.

Verkuil, Paul R. "The Ombudsman and the Limits of the Adversary System." *Colum. L. Rev.* Vol. 75 (1975) 845.

Ware, Stephen J. "Default Rules from Mandatory Rules: Privatizing Law Through Arbitration." 83 *Minn. L. Rev.* 703 (February 1999).

Washington, Monica J. "Compulsory Arbitration of Statutory Employment Disputes: Judicial Review Without Judicial Reformation." 74 *N.Y.U. L. Rev.* 844 (June, 1999).

Welsh, Nancy A. "'Stepping Back Through the Looking Glass: Real Conversations with Real Disputants About Institutionalized Mediation and Its Value." 19 *Ohio St. J. on Disp. Resol.* 573 (2004).

Wickard, Joshua M. "Mandatory Arbitration in Real Estate and Related Transactions," 45 *Advocate* 18 (November, 2002).

Wissler, Roselle L. "Alternative Dispute Resolution Symposium Issue. The Effects of Mandatory Mediation: Empirical Research on the Experience of Small Claims and Common Pleas Courts." *Willamette L. Rev.* Vol. 33 (Summer 1997) 565.

Zick, Vicki. "Reshaping the Constitution to Meet the Practical Needs of the Day: The Judicial Preference for Binding Arbitration." 82 *Marq. L. Rev.* 247 (Fall 1998).

Annotations

Annotation, *Admissibility of Affidavit or Testimony of Arbitrator to Impeach or Explain Award,* 80 A.L.R.3d (1977) 155.

Annotation, *Appealability of Order or Decree Compelling or Refusing to Compel Arbitration,* 64 A.L.R. 4th (1956) 652.

Annotation, *Appealability of State Court's Order or Decree Compelling or Refusing to Compel Arbitration,* 6 A.L.R. 4th (1981) 652.

Annotation, *Awarding Attorneys Fees in Connection with Arbitration,* 60 A.L.R. 5th (1998) 669.

Annotation, *Claim of Fraud in Inducement of Contract as Subject to Compulsory Arbitration Clause Contained in Contract,* 11 A.L.R. 4th (1981) 774.

Annotation, *Constitutionality of Arbitration Statutes,* 55 A.L.R.2d (1957) 432.

Annotation, *Construction and Application of 10 (A) (4) of Federal Arbitration Act (9 U.S.C.A. 10 (A) (4)) Providing for Vacating of Arbitration Awards Where Arbitrators Exceed or Imperfectly Execute Powers,* 136 A.L.R. Fed. (1997) 183.

Annotation, *Construction of Provision, in Compromise and Settlement Agreement, for Payment of Costs as Part of Settlement,* 71 A.L.R.3d (1976) 909.

Annotation, *Death of Party to Arbitration Agreement Before Award as Revocation or Termination of Submission,* 63 A.L.R.2d (1959) 754.

Annotation, *Determination of Validity of Arbitration Award Under Requirement that Arbitrators Shall Pass on all Matters Submitted,* 36 A.L.R.3d (1971) 649.

Annotation, *Disqualification of Arbitrator by Court of Stay of Arbitration Proceedings Prior to Award, on Ground of Interest, Bias, Prejudice, Collusion, or Fraud of Arbitrators,* 65 A.L.R.2d (1959) 755.

Annotation, *Liability of Parties to Arbitration for Costs, Fees, and Expenses,* 57 A.L.R.3d (1974) 633.

Annotation, *Modern Status of Rules Respecting Concurrence of all Arbitrators as Condition of Binding Award Under Private Agreement Not Specifying Unanimity,* 83 A.L.R.3d (1978) 996.

Annotation, *Participation in Arbitration Proceedings as Waiver of Objections to Arbitrability Under State Law,* 56 A.L.R. 5th (1998) 757.

Annotation, *Preemption by Federal Arbitration Act (9 U.S.C.A. 1 et seq.) of State Laws Prohibiting or Restricting Formation or Enforcement of Arbitration Agreements,* 108 A.L.R. Fed. 179 (1992).

Annotation, *Setting Aside Arbitration Award on Ground of Interest or Bias of Arbitrators,* 56 A.L.R.3d (1974) 697.

Annotation, *Setting Aside Arbitration Award on Ground of Interest or Bias of Arbitrators-Commercial, Business, or Real Estate Transactions,* 67 A.L.R. 5th (1999) 179.

Annotation, *Setting Aside Arbitration Award on Ground of Interest or Bias of Arbitrators—Insurance Appraisals or Arbitrations,* 63 A.L.R. 5th (1998) 675.

Annotation, *State Court's Power to Consolidate Arbitration Proceedings,* 64 A.L.R.3d (1975) 528.

Annotation, *Statute of Limitations as Bar to Arbitration Under Agreement,* 94 A.L.R.3d (1979) 533.

Annotation, *What Constitutes Corruption, Fraud, or Undue Means in Obtaining Arbitration Award Justifying Avoidance of Award Under State Law,* 22 A.L.R.4th (1983) 366.

CHAPTER 106AT

PROPERTY LAW IN AUSTRIA[1]

Professor David A. Thomas
J. Reuben Clark Law School
Brigham Young University

SYNOPSIS

---

[1] The abbreviations which commonly occur in this chapter include: ABGB (Allgemeines Burgerliches gesetzbuch or General Civil Code), the English translation revised and annotated by Paul L. Baeck; BGBL (Bundesgazetteblatt or Federal Statute Gazette); GBG (Grundbuchgesetz or Land register law); MG (Mietengesetz or Rent/Lease law); LPG (Landpachtgesetz or real estate lease law); KleingartenG (Kleingartengesetz or small-garden law); WEG (Wohnungseigentumsgesetz 1975 or Apartment/Condominium law).

§ 106AT.01   History of Property Law in Austria.

§ 106AT.01(a)   Austrian Peoples in Prehistory.

The earliest known inhabitants in the area of modern Austria were the so-called Danubian Groups of wanderers. These groups gathered in villages consisting of clusters of pile-dwellings near the lakes found abundantly in the Alps. Hunters and other food collectors ventured from the villages up into the mountains, but it was not until the late Bronze and Iron Ages that people started making the mountain areas their homes.

During the middle of the Bronze Age tribes of Celts invaded and dominated the area until Roman armies entered in 15 B.C.[2] The Romans occupied the territory south of the Danube river and built many cities and roads, the remains of which can still be found in Austria today. When Roman rule collapsed in A.D. 476, many wandering tribes of Germans, Asians and Hungarians entered and passed through Austria.

§ 106AT.01(b)   Austrian Peoples in Historic Times.

By the sixth century A.D., the Donau Plateau and the foothills of the Alps were inhabited by Bavarians who probably immigrated from the east. Simultaneously, great movements of Slavic peoples were taking place throughout the land that is now modern Austria and Germany. Late in the eighth century A.D., Austria came under the rule of Charlemagne, but when his death led to the breakup of the Frankish empire, invaders once again asserted themselves, especially the Magyars of Hungary in the early 900's.

The Magyars were conquered by Germany's Otto I in 955, and Austria would remain under the rule of German monarchs for the next several centuries. In 976 Otto I gave control of the Austrian lands to Leopold I, a member of the Babenburg family. The Babenburgs ruled until King Ottokar of Bohemia gained control of the Babenburg duchies. In 1273 Rudolf I, a member of the Habsburg family, was elected the Holy Roman Emperor by the princes of Germany, and though the Habsburg family control would wax and wane through many years, they remained in power until the First World War.

---

[2] Erich Zöllner & Theresa Schüssel, Das Werden Österreichs 15 (1985).

§ 106AT.01(c)   Early Austrian Land Law.

Bavarian land law prevailed in Austria until late in the fourteenth century. Under this essentially feudal system, private property rights held by ordinary people were extremely limited, and most land was used on a communal basis. For example, groups of small villages (Dorfgemeinden) used the surrounding grazing fields and forests collectively. Also, inhabitants shared the responsibility for building and maintaining the wells, roads, and bridges.

Even into the eighteenth century, only a few freeholders existed in a land system that was still dominated by a landed aristocracy:

> Except for a few freeholders (*Freisassen*), whose number was always insignificant, the country was divided into thousands of domains (*Herrschaften*) in which the lord performed all the functions of a sovereign. As a rule there were several villages in such a district, communities which in the main governed only themselves, subject to "custom, privileges, and the provincial constitution."[3]

> [L]andowners [lords] allocated fields to the peasants. Depending on whether land was located within the village community or on the lord's demesne, the fields were called rustic (*rustikal*) or domestic (*domestikal*) . . . Both rustic and domestic fields could either be bought by the peasant or held in usufruct only. But even where a purchase had taken place, the lord retained overlordship (*Obereigentum*) and reversionary right (*Heimfallsrecht*). . ..[4]

Throughout this time, the serfdom that persisted was theoretically mitigated by rules permitting peasants to buy their way out of their feudal obligations.

§ 106AT.02   The First Austrian Civil Code.

Under the Empress Maria Theresa and the influence of Enlightenment philosophies, the development of the first Austrian civil code commenced. The code was to promote the notion that all persons should be permitted to hold and enjoy property, that laws should be stable and certain, and applied consistently throughout the state, and enforced uniformly in the courts.

Austria's first civil code drew heavily from Roman law and from natural law principles popular during the Age of Enlightenment. The first draft of this code was rejected by the Empress because of its excessive length and lack of clarity. Further drafts were then produced during the reigns of Joseph II and Leopold II. Finally, under Francis II a legislative board was set up to complete the drafting process, and in 1811 the Austrian Civil Code (Allgemeines Burgerliches Gesetzbuch fur die Deutschen Erblander, or ABGB) was enacted.[5]

---

[3] Edith M. Link, The Emancipation of the Austrian Peasant 1740–1798 14.

[4] *Id.* at 15.

[5] The ABGB came into force on January 1, 1812.

For the most part, this civil code remains in force today.

§ 106AT.03   The Present Austrian Civil Code.

§ 106AT.03(a)   Modern Validity of the Civil Code.

The Austrian Civil Code has remained in force despite changes of Austrian government during the twentieth century. When Austria's constitution was enacted in 1920, it provided for promulgation of laws outside the constitution through publication of those laws in the Federal Statutes Gazette (BGBL). The ABGB remained in force even during World War II, despite the *Anschluss,* when Austria became part of Germany. After World War II, the Allied powers permitted Austrians to establish a democratic government,[6] and the government re-enacted the constitution and the ABGB in 1947. The constitution also guarantees the right of ownership of property free from the intervention of government.[7]

§ 106AT.03(b)   The Structure of the Austrian Civil Code.

The ABGB (Civil Code of Austria) is divided into an introductory section and three parts. In the introduction the code is declared applicable to all persons, whether individual or corporate. The first part of the ABGB is known as the "rights of persons" and includes the law of marriage, the rights between parents and children, and the law concerning guardianship and curatorship.

The second part of the ABGB is the law of property, divided into two subdivisions, real property rights and personal property rights. Although the majority of real property rights are in fact found in the section which bears its title, many of the rights necessary to conduct a real estate transaction are found throughout the code and ancillary law. Under the sections for personal property rights are found most provisions of general contract and probate laws.

The third part of the ABGB covers rights which are common to the first two parts, such as provisions for sureties and guaranties, and the laws of obligations and provision covering prescription and adverse possession.

§ 106AT.03(c)   Interpretation of the Civil Code.

Under the civil code the principle of plain meaning governs:

> No other interpretation shall be attributed to a particular provision of the law than that which is apparent from the plain meaning of the language employed and from the clear intent of the legislator.[8]

Neither the concept of case law jurisprudence nor the principle of stare

---

[6] The Constitution is known as the Bundes-Verfassungsgesetz or B-VG and was last amended in 1979.

[7] B-VG art. 5.

[8] ABGB art. 6.

decisis are officially recognized under the ABGB:

> If a case can be decided neither from the language nor from the natural sense of the law, similar situations which are determined by reference to the laws and the purpose of related provisions must be taken into consideration. Should the case still remain doubtful, then it must be decided upon the carefully collected and well-considered circumstances in accordance with the natural principles of justice.[9]

> The decisions issued in individual cases and the opinions handed down by the courts in particular litigations never have the force of law; they cannot be extended to other cases or to other persons.[10]

Since the courts are only to render justice in light of the law as promulgated by the legislature, no equitable power exists. Generally, laws which are enacted by the legislature do not have a retroactive effect, unless the legislature explicitly directs a law to affect pending litigation.[11]

§ 106AT.04 Real Property Rights Under the Civil Code.

§ 106AT.04(a) Ownership and Possession of Property.

Austrian law draws a distinction between rights in rem and obligatory rights, a distinction which is based on Roman law. Therefore, the rights which are said to affect the land (in rem) are found in the second part of the code under real rights, whereas the rights concerning property as between persons are found in the other two sections of the code. The code makes a sharp distinction between movable and immovable property.

Rights in property are said to belong to a person without regard to any other certain persons.[12] The ABGB defines real property rights as possession, ownership, pledge, easement, and inheritance.[13] Immovable property is "possessed by setting foot upon, bordering, fencing in, marking or working therein."[14]

An owner who has taken possession of property may protect it by use of suitable force.[15] If an owner believes that the construction of a new building on adjacent land will harm the owner's land, the owner may obtain an injunction, and the court is required under the code to act as fast as is expedient.[16] Other rights protected under the code include rights of ancient

---

[9] ABGB art. 7.

[10] ABGB art. 12.

[11] ABGB art. 8.

[12] ABGB art. 307.

[13] ABGB art. 308.

[14] ABGB art. 312.

[15] ABGB art. 344.

[16] ABGB art. 340.

lights, right of way, access to waterways and highways, and the right to pasture.[17]

Under the code, acquisition of property can occur not only by ordinary conveyance, but also through accretion[18] or through operation of law.[19]

§ 106AT.04(b)   Transfer of Real Property.

Real property is obtained by acquisition of title through the legally prescribed manner of acquisition.[20] In order to transfer land, the seller must have a certified deed of title entered into the land register. If there is only an agreement to sell land, it is enforceable as to the parties involved, but does not impart notice to the world. The ABGB contains a specific provision for an earnest money agreement, which is similar to that commonly used in the United States.[21] Once the deed has been entered into the land register, the document itself is immaterial as to proof of ownership. Therefore, title searches are unknown in Austria.

Land can be transferred only through delivery and acceptance.[22] The delivery of property can be accomplished through a conveyance (commonly referred to as declaration) that shows the name of the acceptor.[23] The conveyance or declaration must then be entered into the land register, which entry is termed intabulation.[24] The instrument to be entered must conform to all applicable legal requirements, such as the requirement that it be notarized.[25] Included in the instrument must be the exact designation of the transferor, the acceptor, the description of the real estate to be transferred, the legal basis of the transfer, the place and date of the instrument in question, and the transferor's express declaration of consent to intabulation (entry in the register) of the acceptor as owner of the property.[26]

All encumbrances recorded in the land register are transferred with the property and remain in force.[27] Transfers of land in rural areas are subject to local government control.

§ 106AT.04(c)   Co-Ownership of Real Property.

Co-ownership is recognized under the ABGB; however, the different

---

[17] ABGB arts. 472 *et seq.*

[18] ABGB arts. 404, 411 *et seq.*

[19] ABGB art. 1342.

[20] ABGB art. 380.

[21] ABGB art. 908.

[22] ABGB art. 425.

[23] ABGB art. 428.

[24] ABGB art. 431.

[25] ABGB art. 432.

[26] ABGB art. 433.

[27] ABGB art. 443.

forms of concurrent ownership have not been codified, but are left to the contracting or transacting parties to decide and describe in detail the form of ownership they desire. This description will be entered into the land registry, and thereby will become official as to all disputes. Concurrent ownership can be created by contract, law, will, or declaration.[28]

§ 106AT.04(d)   Interests in the Land of Another.

Easements can be created by contract and must be entered into the land registry to be enforceable.[29] Mortgages on lands are created by having the mortgagee's name and the sum due entered into the land register.[30] The entry is made by presenting a mortgage deed bearing the mortgagor's signature, execution of judgment, or similar instrument.[31] Priority between mortgages is based on first in time. Default by the mortgagor can result in a forced sale, with any surplus going to the mortgagor. Mortgage interests are assignable under most circumstances.[32]

§ 106AT.04(e)   Prescription and Adverse Possession.

Under the original ABGB, acquisition of land rights through prescription and adverse possession was possible. However, under the present land registry law, no real property rights may be obtained through adverse possession or prescription. The ABGB still recognizes adverse possession of personal property.

§ 106AT.04(f)   Foreign Ownership of Real Property in Austria.

Aliens have essentially the same property rights as Austrian citizens.[33] Also recognized as "persons" who can have rights under Austrian law are foreign governments, foreign corporations, and agricultural organizations.[34] An additional requirement imposed on foreign ownership of land, however, is that it must be registered with the real estate transactions office (*Grundverkehrsbeh/Uorde*), and that office must issue a permit before the transaction may take place. Local government subdivisions in Austria may also impose their own requirements for the transfers of land interests when foreigners are involved.

---

[28] ABGB art. 825.

[29] ABGB art. 472 *et seq.*; specifically enumerated easements can be found at ABGB art. 477.

[30] ABGB arts. 447 *et seq.*

[31] ABGB art. 450.

[32] ABGB arts. 545 *et seq.*

[33] ABGB art. 33. For some rights sought by aliens under Austrian law, the alien must show that the same right is available to an Austrian citizen in the alien's own country.

[34] ABGB art. 26.

§ 106AT.05   The Land Registry Law.

§ 106AT.05(a)   History of the Land Register.

Some form of land register has existed throughout much of Austria's history. The need for uniformity in tax collection procedures led to the earliest form of land registers. In conveyancing, land registers were not used during early medieval times, because the parties simply conducted land transfers between themselves, usually by means of a symbolic exchange before witnesses. In later medieval times a formal transfer (*Auflassung*) before a court, effected through a form of deed or acknowledgement, became common. Beginning in the twelfth century, larger cities developed their own conveyancing and mandatory registration procedures; often the *Auflassung* was combined with an official entry into a register (*Eintragung*). The reception of Roman law threatened, but did not replace, the Germanic tradition as to registration.

In 1871 a national land registry law (*Grundbuchgesetz or GBG*) was promulgated. However, amendments to and commentary on the 1871 law introduced so much complication that a total revision was promulgated in 1955.

§ 106AT.05(b)   The Modern Land Register.[35]

The purpose of the land registry law is to make real property ownership and transfer precise and predictable. The registry gives notice to potential purchasers and creditors, and the state uses the registry for assessing taxes.

The land registry is divided into the main book (*Hauptbuch*) and a deed collection (*Urkundensammlung*). In order to be effectual, all transfers, conveyances, servitudes, and encumbrances must be entered into the main book.[36] Deeds can be entered into the deed collection. The categories of information entered into the main book are strictly limited, but anything that appears on the deed or conveying instrument can be entered into the deed collection. In a conveyancing dispute over facts outside the main book, information from the deed collection may be used. If entries in the main book and deed collection are in conflict, the main book entries are controlling.

Land registry records are maintained for all real estate within Austrian territory, are kept at the district courts, and are freely accessible to the general public. The good faith purchaser is protected against matters not entered in the land register and of which the purchaser has no knowledge. Where multiple good faith conveyances of the same land occur, the party

---

[35] Grundbuchgesetz (GBG, or Land Register Law), BGBl. No. 39/1955. This law was most recently amended in 1979.

[36] GBG § 4.

making the earlier entry in the registry will prevail.[37] The losing party in those circumstances will have an action in contract against the seller. Separate registers for railroads and mining claims are maintained.

The main book of the land register is divided into a property status section (*Gutbestandblatt*), an ownership section (*Eigentumsblatt*), and an encumbrance section (*Lastenblatt*). In the property status section, land parcels are listed according to an assigned number and type, such as residential or agricultural. Certain servitudes are also listed in this section. In the ownership section is information concerning the type of ownership the present possessor has, how the land was conveyed to the present owner, and from whom the property was conveyed. If the transaction is a lease, the terms of the lease will also be entered. The encumbrance section of the main book lists all encumbrances on the land, including rights such as reversionary interests and mortgages.

§ 106AT.05(c)   Notarization of the Transfer.

Before any transaction, encumbrance, or mortgage can be entered into the land register, the documents effecting the transactions must be notarized. A notary public is appointed by the government and functions for life or until the appointment is revoked. Although the notary public is appointed for a specific judicial district, notarial functions can be performed anywhere in Austria.

§ 106AT.06   Property Laws Outside the Civil Code.

§ 106AT.06(a)   Landlord/Tenant Law.

Under Austrian law, the lease between a landlord and a tenant is completely obligatory and is considered a matter of contract law; the landlord is the creditor and the tenant is the debtor. Because the landlord/tenant relationship is obligatory, the landlord has a lien on the tenant's chattels.

Landlord/tenant relationships fall into one of two types:

> If the tenant can use the premises without further work, the law speaks about *Miete*. The most basic and familiar example is the *Miete* of an apartment. If, however, the tenant must do some work to obtain the benefit from the premises for which he pays rent, the legal expression is *Pacht*. This distinction is one of substance because, in certain respects, the mutual rights between landlord and tenant are different if the relation is that of *Miete* rather than that of *Pacht*.[38]

Both *Miete* and *Pacht* are based upon a contract, and under the law they come together under the heading of *Bestandvertrag* (Contract of Granting).

---

[37] ABGB art. 440.

[38] Paul L. Baeck & Hans Kapfer, The General Civil Code of Austria 212 (1972). An example of a *Miete* is a lease for a room, while a lease of a going business would be a *Pacht*.

Austrian landlord/tenant law can be found under the *Mietgesetz* (MG or Lease Law).[39] The first sections of the lease law identify those agreements that are subject to the law.[40] The lease law regulates the rent rates and lists variances and exemptions to the general rules. Under the lease law the lessee is required to return the leased space to the lessor in the same condition as when it was let, subject to reasonable wear and tear.[41]

The assignability of the lease agreement may be restrained or prohibited by the lease agreement, but the lessor may still be required to show good cause for refusal.[42] The lease law explicitly prohibits the landlord from terminating the lease except for "important reasons," such as non-payment of rent.[43] As in most American jurisdictions, the landlord must follow specific procedures to evict a tenant.

The lease law assigns rights and protections to both the lessor and the lessee. For instance, the law imposes a warranty of habitability and lessor duties to pay all taxes on the property, make repairs that are needed, and provide for the essentials of water, light, heat, and sanitation.[44]

Slightly different legal relationships arise in the land lease law[45] and the small-garden law.[46] The land lease law is very similar to the *Mietgesetz*, except that it applies only to unimproved land. The small-garden law has become significant in regulating the massive checkerboards of small leased garden plots found abundantly around large European cities. The law applies to gardens larger than 120 square meters and smaller than 650 square meters and contains restrictions on the terms of the lease contracts for such areas.

§ 106AT.06(b)   Property Rights Between Husband and Wife.

Complete or partial community property is available to couples who make and have notarized an appropriate contractual agreement.[47] Without such an agreement, if a spouse is simply added to the land register as an owner, in the event of divorce, he or she receives one half the value of the property if it is sold.[48]

---

[39] Law of Dec. 7, 1922, BGBL. No. 872, as amended in Law of June 22, 1929, BGBl. No. 210.

[40] Austrian law differentiates between the lease of an apartment, a small garden, and an empty lot.

[41] MG § 18.

[42] MG § 18a.

[43] MG §§ 19 *et seq.*

[44] MG §§ 6 *et seq.*

[45] Landpachtgesetz (LPG), Law of Nov. 26, 1969, BGBL. No. 451.

[46] Law of Dec. 16, 1958, BGBL. No. 6/1959.

[47] ABGB art. 1233.

[48] ABGB art. 1236.

§ 106AT.06(c)   Taxes on Real Property.

§ 106AT.06(c)(1)   Land Transfer Tax (*Grunderwerbsteuer*).[49]

Usually a real property transfer is subject to a 3.5% tax on either the sale price or the determined value of the property. Exemptions apply to certain donative and probate transfers.

§ 106AT.06(c)(2)   Property Tax (*Verm/Uogenssteuer*).[50]

For Austrian residents a property tax of about 1% is assessed against all holdings, whether in Austria or abroad. For non-resident Austrians or for resident aliens, the tax is assessed only against holdings in Austria.

§ 106AT.06(c)(3)   Land Tax (*Grundsteuer*).[51]

This tax is levied by the municipality and varies throughout the country. The tax is paid by the owner of the property.

§ 106AT.06(c)(4)   Land Value Tax (*Bodenwertabgabe*).[52]

This is an annual tax of 1% assessed on unused parcels of land that are worth more than 200,000 Austrian schillings.

------

[49] Law of July 2, 1987, BGBL. No. 309.

[50] Law of July 7, 1954, BGBL. No. 192, amended by, Law of November 24, 1987, BGBL. No. 606.

[51] Law of July 13, 1955, BGBL. No. 149; the current version is the Law of November 10, 1982, BGBL. No. 570.

[52] Law of Dec. 15, 1960, BGBL. No. 285, amended by Law of July 10, 1973, BGBL. No. 383.

CHAPTER 106BR

PROPERTY LAW IN BRAZIL

Professor David A. Thomas
J. Reuben Clark Law School
Bringham Young University

SYNOPSIS

§ 106BR.01   History of Property Law in Brazil.

§ 106BR.01(a)   Discovery and Colonization.

Competition between Portuguese and Spanish explorers in the fifteenth century led to the Treaty of Tordesillas, adopted on June 7, 1494, which limited Spanish rights to territory more than 1,110 miles west of the Cape Verde Islands. Thus confirmed in its rights to explore Africa and the sea routes to India, Portugal sent a fleet under Pedro Alvares Cabral, who was driven far off course and touched the Brazilian coast on April 22, 1500. Cabral claimed the land for Portugal and sent a report to the king.

Portugal granted a brazilwood concession in 1503, and in 1530 sent a fleet to drive out the French and set up settlements and an administrative system. Forced to rely on private interests for colonizing, Portugal in 1533 divided the Brazilian coastline into 15 parallel strips, extending inland as far as the then-uncertain demarcation established by the Treaty of Tordesillas. These huge land grants varied in their north-south dimensions from 90 to 360 miles wide, and were granted as semi-feudal captaincies to twelve private persons, who agreed to colonize, develop and defend their grants. As financial ventures, most of the captaincies eventually failed, but they did succeed in planting permanent colonies on the coast. Further exploration and colonization pushed Brazil's boundaries in all directions and, in the west, well beyond the line of the Tordesillas Treaty.

The proprietary, or donatory, system proved inadequate to the tasks of colonization. The aristocrats received their lands under essentially feudal rights and obligations, including judicial rights, but had inadequate resources to administer their holdings. Consequently, the king established control over the entire colony by establishing a central colonial administration beginning in 1549. The hereditary rights and privileges of the captains were eventually absorbed by royal governors, and new captaincies under the new governance arrangements were created.

When Spain and Portugal united, between 1580 and 1640, the combined parent government pursued a single colonial policy, which was tightly controlled by the central government and its colonial governors and agents. This control was much diminished in the more remote areas, where huge private landholdings were administered as private feudal holdings following the traditions of the early captains. Indeed, because of these feudal origins, a type of feudalism still dominates landholding in the Brazilian backcountry.

In 1736 a reform of colonial governance created a ministry that framed laws for the entire country and appointed and supervised governors. All remaining hereditory captaincies were abolished.

§ 106BR.01(b)   Achieving Independence and Stability.

The notion of independence for Brazil first arose in the late 18th century, and a revolution in Portugal in 1820 gave it decisive impetus. In an essentially peaceful transition, prince Dom Pedro remained in Brazil when his father King John returned to Portugal from Brazilian exile. When the Portuguese Cortes sought to impose the old restrictive controls over Brazil, Dom Pedro was formally proclaimed constitutional emperor of Brazil in 1822. Military leaders revolted in 1889 and established a republic.

In the disorder that spread all over Latin America in the first half of the nineteenth century, following the emergence of independent republics from the former colonies, policies of land distribution planted the seeds of present and future social disorder. The republics distributed huge grants of land to politically prominent persons, resulting in very large estates held by very few persons, and-because of primogeniture, debt, slavery and peonage-the vast majority of the agrarian population in perpetual economic oppression. A property-owning middle class, such as was so vital to prosperity in the northern American nations, simply did not arise.

In more modern times, the Brazilian government has tried several methods of effecting land reform, most importantly taxation of idle land and of the large plantations. These efforts have yielded only modest results.

The first of several modern Brazilian constitutions was promulgated in 1946. In 1985, after periods of military rule, civilians began governing Brazil as a federal republic.

§ 106BR.01(c)   Historical Foundation of Property Rights.

The early colonizing nobles who received the colonial captaincies were awarded title to the land by means of a "donation letter." The property interest thus granted was perpetual and inheritable. Donees were obligated to promote population growth in the territory, defense, good utilization of the natural resources and propagation of the catholic faith. To the humbler colonists the captains gave unproductive land called "Sesmarias," so they can found villages with local administration, including a judicial system. These colonists were exempted from certain taxes.

The captaincies ("Capitanias") or donatory system fell into decline as the captains failed to find adequate resources to carry out their responsibilities, and the captaincies were eventually turned back to royal control. Thereafter the king sought to establish more centralized control over the entire colony.

§ 106BR.02   Basic Principles of the Brazilian Property Law.

§ 106BR.02(a)   Types of Interests in Real Property.

§ 106BR.02(a)(1)   Immovable and Movable Property.

In Brazil, the term *bens imoveis* means immovable property. Under the Brazilian Civil Code (BCC) property is considered either immovable or movable property; property includes intellectual property (which is considered movable). Under article XX of the BCC, immovable property cannot be moved to another place without destroying its substance. On the other hand, movable property can be moved to another place and maintain its substance without damage. This classification is similar to the common-law distinction between real and personal property. Under article 674 of the BCC, property rights arise through emphyteusis, servitude, usufruct, use, habitation, chattel mortgage, antichresis and mortgage, all described in the following paragraphs.

§ 106BR.02(a)(2)   Rights that Arise or May Be Created.

§ 106BR.02(a)(2)(i)   Emphyteusis.

As stated in article 678 of the BCC, emphyteusis is an interest in the real property in which the owner of a non-productive parcel of land can sell rights in the land to another, who pays an annual rent to the seller. Under a contract of emphyteusis, while the seller lives, the grantee is required to pay rent.

§ 106BR.02(a)(2)(ii)   Servitudes.

According to article 695 of the BCC, servitudes are restrictions imposed on the use of the land, often by governments or utilities companies seeking to acquire rights. A common example would be an electric power company acquiring servitudes upon lands in order to place its cables. Governments acquire servitudes to construct and improve water systems, railroads, highways and streets. Various types of uses maintained for ten to fifteen years may give rise to a prescriptive right in the servitude use. According to the Public Registration Act (Law No. 6.015 of Dec. 13, 1973), servitudes much be registered.

As any other real property right, servitudes must be registered in the Official Notary as prescribed by the Public Registration Act (law No. 6.015 of December 31, 1973).

§ 106BR.02(a)(2)(iii)   Usufruct.

When a landowner separates rights of enjoyment from the other rights associated with ownership of real property, a usufruct arises. A usufruct right can be separated and transferred to another without the property owner losing the other rights that have been retained.

As stated in article 713 of the BCC, the person who receives the land has the right to enjoy its facilities and fruits. One who receives a right of usufruct may retain and enjoy and own the produce of the land for the period of that right. At the end of the usufruct period, the holder of that right must return the property in essentially the same condition in which it was received, natural deterioration and wear and tear excepted. Usufructs are transferable.

The usufruct is often granted for the period of the recipient's life. It is common for parents while living to divide the property among their children, reserving for themselves the usufruct during their lives and avoiding disputes among heirs after their death.

§ 106BR.02(a)(2)(iv)   Use.

Use is similar to the usufruct, except that the use was intended to help a person and the person's family with property rights that would provide for their personal necessities, usually without rent or other payment, as described under Habitation, below. Article 745 of the BCC establishes that the rules regarding usufruct are applicable to the use. The use is today rare because its function is fulfilled by the usufruct.

§ 106BR.02(a)(2)(v)   Habitation.

The habitation is a variant of the use in which a person receives land for a family dwelling and has no obligation to pay rent to the landowner. Article 748 of the BCC sets forth that rules governing the usufruct are applicable to the habitation. As with the use generally, this property right is today not common.

§ 106BR.02(a)(2)(vi)   Mortgage.

A mortgage is a property right by which the owner gives to the creditor a security interest in the immovable property. Under the BCC mortgages may be either voluntary or legal. The voluntary mortgage is entered into voluntarily by the debtor in favor of the creditor. The legal mortgage, under article 827 of the BCC, is imposed by a court in favor of a party with an interest in the property, such as a divorced former spouse, children of parents in the process of divorce, and a governmental entity with a claim for property taxes.

As with any other interest over immovable property, the mortgage must be registered under the Public Registration Act (Law No. 6.015 of December 31, 1973) as either a voluntary or a legal mortgage.

The creditor under a legal mortgage has two options to recover payment of the debt. One option is to wait until someone buys the property at a public auction. If there are no buyers, the other option is to take the property itself. Of course, in the case of deficiences, where the value of the property is not enough to cover the debt, the creditor may seek further recovery in the debtor's other property.

The sale of the property at a public auction is not the only way a debtor may be freed from the obligation. According to article 849 of the BCC, the mortgage also is extinguished by destruction of the property, by the retiring of the obligation, by the creditor forgiving the debt, and by the statute of limitations.

Mortgages created prior to 1997 are governed by prior law, according to which the borrower holds legal title to the property. Mortgages created after 1997 are governed by Law 9514, whereby a trustee holds title with fiduciary duty to the borrower. The law was changed to avoid judicial foreclosure, which could last as long as seven years. Under the new law, lenders can foreclose in six months to one year. Operations under the new law drastically reduce the cost of mortgages to financial institutions.

§ 106BR.02(b)   Acquiring and Securing Real Property Rights.

§ 106BR.02(b)(1).   Registration of the Transfer Title in the Official Notary.

The real property interests can be transferred only by registering the title with an Official Notary. Movable (or personal) property interests are transferred by actual or symbolic delivery to the transferee (*traditio*). The BCC, under articles 531 through 535, establishes the basic requirements and what kind of acts are subject to registration in the Official Notary. In addition, the Public Registration Act gives a detailed description of the process itself.

Under articles 531 and 532 of the BCC are provisions governing registration of titles regarding a real property interest created by act *inter vivos* and *causa mortis*, by judicial decisions in division (partition) actions and by *inventarios e partilhas*.

Among the *inter vivos* acts is the sale contract; no special form is required for a valid contract to sell a property interest. The contract may be a private or public instrument, but both have to be registered in order to transfer the property. The greatest advantage of the public instrument over the private is that the former only can be invalidated under severe conditions and substantial proof. The private instrument, if not signed by two witnesses, who confer an execution power to it, can be easily avoided.

See John C. Martin, "Bringing Dead Capital to Life: International Mandates for Land Titling in Brazil, 31 *B.C. Int'l & Comp. L. Rev.* 121–136 (2008).

§ 106BR.02(b)(2).   Accession.

Under article 530, II of the BCC, property may be acquired by accession, which is the incorporation of movable property into immovable property, by either natural or artificial forces. According to article 536 of the BCC, accession can occur in five different ways: island formation, *aluviao*, *avulsao*, *abandono do alveo* and construction of facilities and plantation.

The first four ways of accession are no longer regulated by the BCC. Their provisions are stipulated in the Water Code (Law No. 23.643 of July 10, 1934), which brings together all laws regulating riparian and prior appropriate rights over water and over land contiguous to waters.

§ 106BR.02(b)(3).   Prescription.

The property obtained by prescription is property a person occupies or uses without interruption over a period of time as prescribed by law, after which the person is considered the owner of the property or property right.

Prescription is governed by articles 550 through 553 of the BCC and many other laws, including some Constitutional provisions.

Prescription of land is normally accomplished after the passage of twenty years without interruption and opposition. Under the "Statute of the City" enacted in 2001, an individual or family may obtain title to urban land of up to 250 square meters upon meeting certain conditions. They must use the property as their residence for five years without interruption or opposition, and they must not own any other land. A person may gain title to urban land through this means only once. (Sec. V Art. 10 of statute)

To obtain title to rural land by this means, the family or individual must still reside on the land for five years without interruption or opposition, but they must also make the land productive in some way. The land can be up to 50 hectares (about 125 acres) in size. The limitation to one use of usurpation per person does not apply to rural land, nor does the requirement that the individual not own any other land. A shorter period may apply in special circumstances, such as five years for acquiring rights to up to 300 square meters of land in towns. Also it is necessary to bring an action to declare the possessor the legitimate owner of the land and the decision of this action is registered with the Official Notary.

Article 183, Section 3 of the Brazilian Constitution prohibits the prescription of public lands.

§ 106BR.02(b)(4).   Succession.

Succession means transmitting property from a deceased person to the person's spouse and descendents.

Until the Brazilian Constitution of 1988, there was a difference between legitimate and illegitimate children, but after the Constitution of 1988, there can be no distinction among the children, who are all considered legitimate under the law.

Before 1988, there was also difficulty in dealing with a couple who had formed a union without marriage. Under the old laws, unmarried women suffered severe prejudice regarding the division of the assets because frequently the men who lived with them were married and had many children. Even if an unmarried woman decided to litigate in court to obtain part of the assets, conservative courts did not recognize her rights. Since 1988, some of that problem has been alleviated, but some laws still favor the married woman over the unmarried woman living with the married man.

As yet, no marital and property rights have been conferred on a survivor companion from a homosexual union.

Normally, the surviving spouse is entitled to receive 50% of all assets of the *de cujus,* and the other 50% of the assets has to be divided among the descendants in equal parts. This partition of the property is made only after all debts are paid. If the assets are insufficient to pay all debts, the creditors of the deceased person cannot sue the spouse or descendants for the debts.

It is necessary for a judicial decision to affirm the distribution of assets in order for those interests to be registered. When the survivors agree with the manner of the distribution of the assets, the judicial decree is easy to obtain, but when there is disagreement about division, the court, according to its best judgment, has to determine the distribution. All of these matters can be settled by testament, but use of testaments is not yet widespread in Brazil.

§ 106BR.03   Landlord/Tenant Law.

The relationship between landlords and tenants of urban property is regulated under the Lease Act (Law No. 8.245 of October 18, 1991). Other laws regulate leases of rural properties, hotels, apartment-hotels, and commercial property.

As with any contract under Brazilian Law, the contract of lease has to have, according to article 82 of the BCC, a capable agent to sign the contract, a lawful and possible object, and—if required by the law—the prescribed form.

§ 106BR.03(a)   Formation of a Lease Contract.

The lease contract is formed between landlord and tenant with the simple manifestation of willingness to enter into the contract. No specific form is required, and the contract may be either oral or in writing. The contract must include information concerning the property covered by the lease and the consideration to be paid.

§ 106BR.03(b)   Duties, Responsibilities and Liabilities of the Lessee.

The lessee is responsible to conserve the lease property and to pay the lease consideration in the amount and due time accorded. The lessee also has the duty to permit the landlord to inspect the lease property.

§ 106BR.03(c)   Responsibilities of the Landlord.

The landlord has the responsibility to permit the lessee to use the lease property without opposition and ensure that the property is safe.

§ 106BR.04   Taxation.

Real property transfer taxes may be imposed on property transactions. This tax is a state tax, regulated entirely by each individual state. Under these state laws any acquisition of property or of a property right is taxed at a rate which varies from 0.5% to 4%. The tax is to be paid by the party acquiring the property or property right.

Property taxes are assessed by municipality. Taxes are different for urban and rural land. Each municipality with a population of 20,000 or more must create a master plan with an urban zone boundary (*delimitacao da zona urbana*), separating the urban land from the rural. For urban property tax purposes, land is assessed according to the value of the land plus the value of the building, not taking into account income derived from tenants or other sources.

For rural property tax, only the value of the land itself is assessed, and the value of any buildings is ignored.

§ 106BR.05 Land Use Law.

The government has a duty to expropriate rural property that is not performing its social function. Two types of rural land that cannot be expropriated: small and medium sized rural property, if the owner does not own any other property; and productive property. If the government expropriates rural land and grants that land to a private party, that party cannot sell or lease the land to another party for a period of ten years.

For urban land, the municipal government can penalize landowners of unbuilt, unused, or underused land. The Brazilian Constitution mandates that all municipalities of over 20,000 people must have a master plan. To avoid the designation of "underused," land must be used according to the municipality's master plan. Penalties for landowners of unbuilt, unused, or underused land include compulsory subdivision or construction, increased property taxes (to a maximum of 15% of the value of the property), or expropriation. Expropriation is a last resort and can be used by the municipality only seven years after giving notice to the landowner.

Municipalities retain the right to expropriate urban or rural land for public need.

§ 106-D.06 Bibliography.

Colby, Kevin E. "Brazil and the MST: Land Reform and Human Rights," 16 *N.Y. Int'l L. Rev.* 1 (Summer, 2003).

Martin, John C. "Bringing Dead Capital to Life: International Mandates for Land Titling in Brazil," 31 *B.C. Int'l & Comp. L. Rev.* 121 (Winter, 2008).

Mitchell, Kristen. "Market-Assisted Land Reform in Brazil: A New Approach to Address an Old Problem," 22 *N.Y.L. Sch. J. Int'l & Comp. L.* 557 (2003).

Pindell, Ngai. "Finding a Right to the City: Exploring Property and Community in Brazil and in the United States," 39 *Vand. J. Transnat'l L.* 435 (March 2006).

Valenta, Lisa. "Disconnect: The 1988 Brazilian Constitution, Customary International Law, and Indigenous Land Rights in Northern Brazil," 38 *Tex. Int'l L.J.* 643 (2003).

Wise, Judith. "Hunger and Thieves: Anticipating the Impact of WTO Subsidies Reform on Land and Survival in Brazil," 31 *Am. Ind.an L. Rev.* 531 (2006-2007).

CHAPTER 106CA

PROPERTY LAW IN CANADA

Professor David A. Thomas
J. Reuben Clark Law School
Brigham Young University

SYNOPSIS

§ 106CA.01   Brief History of Canada.

§ 106CA.01(a)   Prehistory of Human Occupation in Canada.

Canada's prehistory of human occupation, it is believed, commenced upon the receding of the last ice age, between 15,000 and 7,000 years ago. The peoples who thinly inhabited the land all across Canada were unspecialized in culture, relying for subsistence on hunting, gathering and fishing. About 4,000 years ago the ancestors of people now generally known as Eskimos migrated into the Arctic coastlands. Cultural and economic advances and differentiation among these native peoples had occurred by the time Europeans first began arriving to explore and settle.

§ 106CA.01(b)   Historical Human Occupation in Canada.

Norse Viking settlements appeared on Canada's east coast about 1,000, A.D., but were eventually abandoned, and to some extent forgotten. Europeans searching for rich fishing waters probably produced contact with the eastern coastline of Canada in the mid-1400's, and John Cabot's exploratory visits began in 1497. In 1534 and 1535, Jacques Cartier sailed deep into the St. Lawrence estuary and claimed a vast area for France. In 1583, an English expedition asserted a claim in Newfoundland. French exploration under Champlain extended deep into the interior beginning in 1615.

§ 106CA.01(c)   Establishing British Dominance in Canada.

When the War of Spanish Succession ended under the Treaty of Utrecht in 1713, the British by the treaty terms were able to take control of vast areas of Canada, including Nova Scotia, Newfoundland and Hudson's Bay. A few years later a series of conflicts broke out between British and French interests in Canada, and the Treaty of Paris in 1763 conferred on the British control over virtually all of French Canada. Quebec was governed under British law from 1763 to 1774, and then thereafter was permitted its own governing officials and to apply French civil law.

§ 106CA.01(d)   Beginning of Canadian Independence.

With the Constitutional Act of 1791, England gave Canada a representative parliamentary government, that was nevertheless criticized for a too strong executive and a lack of democracy. The English and French colonies experienced a series of conflicts, and the various Canadian colonies were legislatively united in 1840. Further study and reform produced a confederation known as the Dominion of Canada in 1867. The terms of the dominion were embodied in the British North America Act, also laying the foundation for the current constitution, through the Constitution Act of 1867 and the Constitution Act of 1982. The 1982 act also formalized a bringing "home" of the Canadian Constitution, so that amendments were not subject to the approval of the British monarch. This removed the last traces of colonial control.

§ 106CA.02   Canada's Two Legal Systems.

Most of Canada is under a common law system, both a general common law and a common law in each province with slight local differences. This is a result of the colonies having "received" the English common law at different dates, and then having independently developed their common law and legislation from the reception date on.

In the province of Quebec, the civil law governs private law. This civil law is based on the Napoleonic Code, which was drawn from the Code of Justinian issued in the late stages of the Roman Empire. General Canadian public law, including constitutional and criminal law prevail in Quebec as elsewhere in Canada. General Canadian law also prevails in those subject areas that were assigned by constitution to the federal government, such as bankruptcy and negotiable instruments.

Substantive law in Quebec is found in the Civil Code of Quebec, which was first published in 1866, and was updated in 1994.

§ 106CA.03   Division of Power Under the Constitution.

The Canadian Constitution divides legislative power between the federal government and the provinces. The subject areas under this division are known as "heads of power." Thirty heads of power are assigned exclusively to the federal government under Section 91 of the Constitution Act. Section 92 assigns 15 heads of power, including property and civil rights in the province.[1]

During the 19th century, Canadian provinces and territories enacted married women's property acts, permitting married women to hold title to property independent of their husbands. In the 20th century, hold married couples' residences in joint tenancy became common. Rules of primogeniture disappeared throughout the country. Beginning with Alberta and Saskatchewan in the early 20th century, the common-law provinces enacted so-called testators' family maintenance or dependants' relief legislation, permitting a will to be set aside if insufficient provision was made for surviving spouse and dependants. A rule of fairness also prevails in dividing marital assets upon dissolution of the marriage.

Recording of land documents differs somewhat among the provinces. A deed registration system, in which land titles are established a chain of predecessors in title, is used in the Atlantic provinces and southern Ontario. The four western provinces and northern Ontario use a land titles or Torrens system, with only the validity of the immediately preceding title at issue.

§ 106CA.04   Property Law in the Provinces.

As ordained in the Constitution, property law is largely left to provincial legislation and decisions. Below are brief discussions of property law in Alberta, as representative of a typical common-law province, and property law in Quebec, the singular and important example of property law in a civil law province.

---

[1] Constitution Act, 1867, § 92(13).

§ 106CA.04(a)   Property Law in a Common Law Province: Alberta.

§ 106CA.04(a)(1)   Estates in Land.

Canadian law generally recognizes the estates of fee simple and life estate. Fee tail has been abolished everywhere but Manitoba.[2] A conveyance is presumed to convey a fee simple interest. Tenancy by the entirety is not recognized, but is considered joint tenancy.[3] The Rule in Shelley's Case does not apply, because it is not compatible the Torrens system of title registration. Condominium ownership in Alberta is governed by legislation.[4]

Rights of dower,[5] except with respect to homestead rights,[6] and curtesy are abolished in Alberta;[7] a surviving spouse obtains a life estate in the real and personal property of the decedent spouse.[8]

Adverse possession may occur, and is based on a ten-year period of occupancy, with tacking permitted.[9]

When land is held in concurrent tenancy, such as joint tenancy or tenancy in common, any co-owner may apply to the court for a partition order.[10]

The common law rule against perpetuities is in force, except as governed by the Perpetuities Act.[11]

§ 106CA.04(a)(2)   Leasehold Estates.

The usual common law rules regarding landlords and tenants are in effect, except as modified by several statutory enactments.[12] The statute of frauds requires that leases for more than three years should be in writing, subject to the usual exceptions to the statute.

§ 106CA.04(a)(3)   Descent and Distribution.

Descent and distribution of decedents' estates are governed by rules found in the Intestate Succession Act.

§ 106CA.04(a)(4).   Mortgages.

Mortgages may be the forms of common law mortgage, equitable

---

[2] Revised Statutes of Alberta, 2000 (hereinafter RSA 2000), c. L-7, § 9.

[3] *Id.* at L-7, Part 1.

[4] Condominium Ownership Act, RSA 2000, c. C-22.

[5] *Id.* at c. L-7, § 3).

[6] *Id.* at c. D-15.

[7] *Id.* at c. L-7, § 4.

[8] *Id.* at §§ 18, 23.

[9] Limitations Act, RSA 2000, c. L-12, §§ 2-2; Land Title Act, RSA 2000, c. L-4, § 74.

[10] RSA 2000, c. L-7, §§ 15, 27.

[11] Perpetuities Act, RSA 2000, c. P-5, § 2.

[12] Land Titles Act, RSA 2000, c. L-4; Mobile Home Sites Tenancies Act, RSA 2000, c. M-20; Residential Tenancies Act, RSA 2000, c. R-17.1.

mortgage, or, most commonly, the statutory mortgage, described as a registered charge against lands in statutory form under the Land Titles System. The mortgagor remains in possession and retains the title.[13] The Land Titles Act provides various standard forms.

§ 106CA.04(a)(5)   Taxation.

Various levels and entities of local government are authorized to impose land taxes.[14]

§ 106CA.04(a)(6)   Environment.

The provincial minister of the Environment has broad powers under the Environmental Protection and Enhancement Act.[15]

All mines, minerals and public lands in the province belong to the provincial government, except those already alienated or leased. The Environmental Protection and Enhancement Act may require may require remediation of land used in mining, exploring or similar activities, with a standard that the land must be returneed to equivalent land capability.

§ 106CA.04(b)   Property Law in the Civil Law Province of Quebec.

§ 106CA.04(b)(1)   Estates and Ownership Rights in Land.

Land in Quebec is held by an owner in "free tenure," or as independently of the government as possible. The basic provisions of property law pertaining to individual persons are contained in the Quebec Civil Code. The Code embodies the two basic principles that there is a right of private ownership in land that land should be able to circulate freely. Legislation other than the code regulates public interests in land.

Under the Quebec civil law, property is considered immoveable or movable. Immoveable property consists of land, appurtenance, and rights in land. Rights in land generally are subject to recording in the land titles registration system. Rights of ownership can be ownership itself, a right in the land consisting of some prerogative or privilege, and a creditor's right to take and sell the property in satisfaction of a debt.

Ownership is considered unitary, so most forms of joint ownership are not recognized, with exceptions for condominiums[16] and some types of ownership by married persons. Less than full rights of ownership can be rights of usufruct (possessing and using the property of another for a specific period) and emphyteusis, essentially a long-term lease in land (usually 10–100

---

[13] Land Title Act, RSA 2000, c. L-4, § 114.

[14] RSA 2000, c. M-26, § 353.

[15] *Id.* at c. E-12.

[16] Divided Co-Ownership of Immovables, Civil Code of Quebec (hereinafter CCQ), §§ 1038–1109.

years).[17] Quebec law also recognizes "real servitudes," whereby one owner of land has rights of use or control in the land of another.[18] Creditors' rights are known as privileges or "hypothec," essentially equivalent to a mortgage in a common-law jurisdiction.

The equivalent of adverse possession in Quebec is called acquisitive prescription. The possession of immovable property must be peaceful, continuous, public and unequivocal for a period of ten years.[19]

Under some circumstances, land may be held in undivided co-ownership, which is similar to concurrent tenancies in common-law jurisdictions.[20]

The customary civil law rules regarding perpetuities are in effect in Quebec.[21] Private or social trusts may be perpetual. The duration of personal trusts is limited to two ranks of beneficiaries of fruits and revenues and one rank of capital beneficiaries whose eligibility to receive comes into existence within 100 years of the trust's creation.

§ 106CA.04(b)(2).   Leasehold Estates.

The Civil Code of Quebec contains detailed rules for all leases, and additional rules for leases of dwellings.[22]

§ 106CA.04(b)(3)   Descent and Distribution.

The Civil Code of Quebec governs the intestate succession[23] and testate succession.[24]

§ 106CA.04(b)(4)   Hypothecs on Immovables (similar to Mortgages).

Hypothecs on immovables are similar to mortgages in common-law jurisdictions, and are governed in detail by the Civil Code of Quebec.[25]

§ 106CA.04(b)(5)   Taxation.

Various levels and entities of local government are authorized to impose land taxes under authority of the Revised Statutes of Quebec.[26]

---

[17] CCQ, §§ 1119, 1195–1211).

[18] CCQ, §§ 1119, 1177–1194.

[19] CCQ, §§ 922, 2918.

[20] CCQ, §§ 1010, 1012–1037.

[21] CCQ, §§ 1271–1273.

[22] CCQ, §§ 1851–2000.

[23] CCQ, §§ 427, 523s, 585, 625, 638, 653, 662–666, 670–679, 682–684, 688, 696, 749, 867–870.

[24] CCQ, §§ 707–711.

[25] CCQ, §§ 2644, 2681, 2693–2695, 2801, 2934–3075.

[26] *See, e.g.,* An Act Respecting Municipal Taxation, Revised Statutes of Quebec (hereinafter RSQ), c. F-2.1.

§ 106CA.04(b)(6)   Environment.

Protection of the environment is governed by the provisions of the Environment Quality Act.[27] Mining rights in the public land are administered under by the Minister of Natural Resources under provisions of the Mining Act.[28] Additional regulating provisions are in the Quebec Mining Companies Act[29] and the Mining Duties Act.[30]

---

[27] RSQ, c. Q-2.

[28] Arts. 3–4, RSQ, c. M-13.1.

[29] RSQ, c. C-47.

[30] RSQ, c. D-15.

CHAPTER 106CH

PROPERTY LAW IN SWITZERLAND

Professor David A. Thomas
J. Reuben Clark Law School
Brigham Young University

SYNOPSIS

§ 106CH.01   History of Property Law in Switzerland.

§ 106CH.01(a)   Swiss Peoples in Prehistory.

Human habitation of the area that is now modern Switzerland goes back at least as far as the most recent ice age. Primitive peoples were forced to live in higher elevations because of glaciers in the valleys, and archaeological and anthropological evidence reveals groups of such prehistoric people living in caves.[1] As the glaciers receded, some of the people moved to the valleys and richly forested areas, often founding small communities on the shores of lakes.

In the centuries before the dominance of Rome, numerous tribes wandered into and out of Switzerland, but the most important of these were tribes of Celts. Around 400 B.C. many groups of Celts are known to have crossed the Alps and settled in Switzerland. It is uncertain when the Celts and Romans first encountered each other in Switzerland, but by 15 B.C., Rome had completed its military occupation of Switzerland.[2]

Following the breakup of the Roman Empire, inhabitants of Switzerland experienced incursions from many wandering tribes, including tribes from Italy and Germany, and some of these settled to become part of the ethnic base for the Swiss people. Beginning in the sixth century A.D., and for three centuries thereafter, most of Swiss territory was included in the domains of Frankish rulers, and thereafter numerous small principalities in Switzerland owed allegiance to the Kingdom of Burgundy or the Holy Roman Empire.

The Swiss Confederation, which continues in governance to this day, arose first in 1291, when the peoples of three valleys, the Uri, Schwyz, and Unterwalden, declared an alliance of states independent of local and foreign lords. This alliance, which styled itself the "Ewiges Bundnis," or eternal alliance, was successful in turning back the assaults of the unhappy overlords and kings, usually by means of battles in which Swiss peasant soldiery triumphed over the medieval military aristocracy.

Although Swiss communities were theoretically independent, in fact the Swiss people shared fully in Europe's feudal history:

> Freemen who were landless offered their services to a powerful neighbor in return for shelter, support, and protection. Known to the Romans as a *patrocinium*, this practice survived through the Middle Ages. An adverse result was the loss of status as a freeman and reduction to that of serf.

> If he were a small landowner and poor, living in fear of losing all to his oppressors, he could surrender his land to a powerful neighbor — usually a noble, able to resist any and all marauders and, because of his political, social, and military prestige, virtually immune from oppression by others.

---

[1] James Murray Luck, A History of Switzerland 1 (1985).

[2] *Id.* at 4.

Transfer of ownership of one's land under this arrangement was originally not irrevocable. The title was transferred for a stated number of years or a lifetime. In return, the donor gained protection from the lord to whom he became a vassal. Use of land continued to be his and he was freed of the hazards and obligations that stemmed from ownership. The arrangement was known as *precarium* tenure.[3]

As was typical throughout medieval Europe, members of the aristocracy and higher officials of the church became great feudal landholders. Even during the hegemony of feudalism, more regions of Switzerland joined the confederation that had been founded late in the thirteenth century. These regions were known then and now as cantons, and between the sixteenth and early nineteenth centuries the total number of confederated cantons rose to thirteen. Although technically subject to the rule of the Holy Roman Emperor, the cantons in reality functioned as nearly autonomous states. With the Peace of Westphalia in 1648, following the Thirty Years' War, the major European powers accepted the confederation as independent of any foreign ruler.

In early 1798, Napoleon conquered most of Switzerland and founded the Helvetica Republic. With Napolean's fall Switzerland regained its independence and, in 1815, reconstituted the federation under the Congress of Vienna. Switzerland's neutrality was guaranteed through the Second Peace of Paris in the same year.

Until 1848 the cantons maintained their unity as they had ever done, through multilateral agreements and treaties concluded by individual cantons. In 1848 the governments of the cantons attempted to create a new constitution modeled roughly after the United States Constitution. This constitution was rewritten in 1874, and this 1874 version remains in force today.

§ 106CH.01(b)   Development of a Civil Code and Code of Obligations.

The basic law of Switzerland has roots in both Roman and Germanic law. The Germanic legal tradition can be traced back to a series of so-called "Barbarian Laws" compiled in Europe's Dark Ages beginning in the fifth and sixth centuries A.D.

Early in the fifth century A.D., the Germanic tribes of Visigoths, Burgundians and Franks, who had been mercenaries of Rome, established their independence from the Empire and introduced Germanic legal customs and institutions into Gaul and surrounding areas. Written codes of laws began to appear, often containing separate provisions for the Germanic inhabitants and for the Roman citizens living in the tribal territories.

The Visigothic laws, and more particularly the Code of Euric, are believed

---

[3] *Id.* at 15.

to have directly or indirectly influenced most Germanic law codes thereafter. The Code of Euric, from circa A.D. 476, shows some Roman influence. The Lex Romana Visigothorum was promulgated by the Visigothic king Alaric II in A.D. 506 to govern Romans living in Visigothic territories. This collection is also known as the Breviarium Alaricianum (Breviary of Alaric). The Leges Visigothorum is a collection of laws that had been issued by Euric's successors, applying to both Gothic and Hispano-Roman subjects. The collection was promulgated in A.D. 654, and replaced the Lex Romana Visigothorum.

Euric's code seems to have been the immediate source for the early codes of both the Salian Franks[4] and the Burgundians,[5] and the Bavarian[6] and Lombard[7] codes also show Visigothic influence. Another early Frankish code, the Lex Ribuaria,[8] was based on the Salian code, and it in turn influenced the codes of the continental Angles and Saxons of the Carolingian Age.

The best known of these early Germanic codes—indeed the oldest Germanic code that is completely preserved—is the Lex Salica, which has been described as "primarily a penal law . . . concerned with the redress of crimes (murder, theft, mutilation, exploitation of women) by monetary means."[9] The Lex Salica and the other early codes consist of both individual "statutes" and precedential judicial sentences ("Weisthuemer"), but they do not refer to most customs of daily living, such as occupancy of land, personal property, commercial dealings, inheritance, family relationships, and class privilege. The only references to land law in the Lex Salica are provisions requiring money payment for damage to agricultural fields,[10] blocking the way of another,[11] and improper fencing and enclosing.[12]

Several of these Germanic law codes specifically influenced the Swiss:

> The most widely used of the Germanic codes were the Leges Alemannorum—first the Pactus Alemannorum of about 580 which was, in effect, agreed to by the inhabitants, and then the Lex Alemannorum of

---

[4] The Code of the Salian Franks, or Lex Salica, is attributed to Clovis, A.D. 481–511.

[5] The Burgundian Code was compiled between A.D. 483 and 532. The Lex Romana Burgundionum was issued ca. A.D. 500, for application to Roman citizens living in the Burgundian kingdom.

[6] The Lex Baiuvariorum is dated from about 744–748, A.D.

[7] The Leges Langobardorum were promulgated between 643 and 755, A.D.

[8] The Lex Ribuaria is believed to have been promulgated after 596, A.D., for the Ripuarian or western Franks.

[9] Laws of the Alamans and Bavarians 19 (Theodore John Rivers trans. 1977).

[10] Title 9.

[11] Title 31.

[12] Title 34.

about 720, a more formal collection of laws. Of secondary influence were the later Frankish codes, the Lex Burgundium of about 500 and the Lex Romana Curiensis of about 750. These collections of Germanic law prevailed throughout the Alpine regions except in the west, where the Romansch population continued to apply a version of Roman law along with Germanic law.[13]

During this period, the cantons were varied in which laws they accepted and applied. Even after Napolean's invasion and occupation had introduced the Swiss to outside influences and to the attractions of codification, the cantons continued to act independently in determining which laws or codes to adopt. Some cantons looked to the French Code Civil, while others modeled their codes after Austrian laws, and yet others made a fresh start.

With the adoption of the constitution, and its revision in 1874, one of the exclusive powers granted to the federal government under the Constitution of 1874 was the administration of the law of obligations. The Swiss Code of Obligations was enacted in 1881. The Swiss Civil Code, prepared by the renowned legal scholar Eugen Huber, was enacted in 1907, went into force in 1912, and incorporated the Code of Obligations as part 5. The Code of Obligations retains its own unique numbering system.

§ 106CH.02   The Fundamental Law of Modern Switzerland.

Modern Switzerland is a republican federation consisting of 26 cantons and half-cantons governed by a federal constitution.[14] In order to amend the constitution a majority of the popular vote of a majority of cantons must assent. Half cantons have less representation than full cantons in the legislature.

All the cantons are equally autonomous. Each canton has a republican government consisting of executive, legislative, and judicial branches. In their judicial branches, the justices of the supreme court are elected by the legislature and have a tenure only as long as the legislature permits.

Federal law is superior to cantonal law.[15] As in the Tenth Amendment of the U.S. Constitution, any power not enumerated by the Swiss Federal Constitution is left to the cantons.[16] Generally, newer laws prevail over conflicting prior laws. There is no established judicial rule of stare decisis, but prior decisions, especially those of the Swiss equivalent of the Supreme

---

[13] 2 Thomas H. Reynolds and Arturo A. Flores, Foreign Law: Current Sources of Codes and Legislation , Switzerland, § 1 (1991).

[14] The Federal Constitution of Switzerland came into force on May 29, 1874.

[15] Federal Constitution, art. 6, § 2.

[16] Cost. Fed. art. 3. Although very similar to the United States version, the cantons have in fact retained more significant areas of potential legislative activity.

Court,[17] are given much weight. In resolving conflicts between laws, usually the more specific law governs a general law. The constitutional Court, whose primary purpose is to interpret the constitution, issues decisions which are binding throughout Switzerland.

For the most part, the laws which regulate property are the federal constitution, the Civil Code, and the Code of Obligations. For matters not covered by any of those sources, a judge will look to customary law.[18] The judges in Switzerland also rely heavily on the writings of legal scholars in reaching decision on matters that lie outside the Codes. Occasionally, the Swiss High Court announces decisions that impact on fundamental property rights. These may be in cases concerning zoning restrictions and expropriation under the federal constitution, as well as on matters governed by customary law. For example, an owner of a private forest must care for the timber, and because the total number of trees in Switzerland may not be diminished, must either receive permission to fell trees or must plant replacement trees.[19]

§ 106CH.02(a)   The General Structure of the Civil Code.

The Civil Code consists of four parts and the Code of Obligations. The four parts of the code are (1) the Law of Persons, (2) Family Law, (3) Inheritance Law, and (4) the Law of Property (Sachenrecht).

§ 106CH.02(b)   Multilingual Interpretations of the Civil Code.

All the laws of Switzerland are issued in all three official languages.[20] In considering a case based on the Civil Code the court must first decide which translation best reflects the legislative intent. Theoretically, all three official language versions are authentic and should have equal force at law, but sometimes the court prefers a language version other than the language in which the text of the law was originally drafted and enacted.

§ 106CH.03   Real Property Rights Under the Civil Code.

§ 106CH.03(a)   Ownership and Possession of Property.

Rights in the ownership of property are recognized under the federal constitution, and private property cannot be abolished.[21] If private land is

---

[17] The Swiss Supreme Court and many of the cantons' highest courts publish many of their decisions.

[18] Cc art. 1.

[19] Entscheidungen des Bundesgerichts 104 Ib 221, 106 Ib 136.

[20] The three official languages of Switzerland are German, French, and Italian. The fourth language spoken in Switzerland, Romansch, is recognized as an "official" language of Switzerland, but is not recognized as official under the law.

[21] Swiss Constitution art. 22.

taken by the government, compensation is required.[22] These broad rights have recently come under restriction; agricultural land may not be resold for a period of ten years, and non-agricultural land may not be resold for a period of five years.[23]

Under the Civil Code, ownership of property includes the right to use and dispose of the land.[24] Enjoyment of these rights, however, may not interfere with another's use and enjoyment of land. Actual freedom of use is also restricted by zoning laws and by license requirements for the construction of improvements on land. The exact zoning requirements are left to each canton. However, the federal government has imposed a duty upon every canton to establish some sort of zoning regulation and administration.

§ 106CH.03(b)   Transfer of Real Property.

Laws governing the transfer of land are found in both the Code of Obligations and the Civil Code. The original conveyance is governed by the Code of Obligations,[25] and the subsequent transfer of land and entry of the transaction into the land register are covered by the Civil Code. Swiss law distinguishes between the sale of land and the transfer of land.

The sale of land is accomplished through a contract of sale, and the contract provisions must conform to strict rules. The price and description of the land must be specific, so the transaction can be entered into the land register with the utmost accuracy. The contract must be notarized, again as an aid to the authenticity and accuracy of the land register.[26] Real property transfers are not complete until the notarized deed is entered in the land register.

All sales contracts, including those for real property, include implied warranties. One implied warranty assures that the item to be sold is fit for the particular purpose for which it is sold. Seller representations in connection with the transaction are considered express, and enforceable warranties.[27] The seller also warrants that the measurements which are in the contract, and which will subsequently be entered into the land register, are correct.[28] A five-year statute of limitations applies to claims of defects. The Code of

---

[22] *Id.*

[23] Code of Obligations art. 218, as amended in Federal Decree of Oct. 6, 1989.

[24] Cc art. 641.

[25] Contracts for the sale of land are governed by the Code of Obligations arts. 216-221. Article 221 declares that all Code of Obligations provisions applicable to sales (arts. 187-215) are also applicable to sales of real property.

[26] Code of Obligations art. 216.

[27] *Id.* at art. 197.

[28] *Id.* at art. 219.

Obligations also provides that risk of loss shifts to the buyer when the buyer takes possession.[29]

Earnest money is also known under Swiss law. Under the Civil Code, earnest money is considered a source of evidence that the contract has been entered into. If the contract is not fulfilled by the buyer, the seller must refund the money. If the money is to be forfeited by the buyer in the event of failure to purchase, then the contract of sale must explicitly declare the earnest money as subject to forfeiture and also the circumstances under which forfeiture may occur.

Interests in real property can also be acquired through a judgment or inheritance. In the case of a judgment, an order would be issued to have the land register amended. If acquisition occurs by inheritance, the new owner announced in the will must request that the land register be amended.

§ 106CH.03(c)   Co-Ownership of Real Property.

Under the Civil Code common ownership (Miteigentum/copropriete) is available.[30] The division of the interests can be in any form desired by the parties, as long as it can be entered into the land register, and the concurrent interests must be entered into the land register to be effective. Property can also be owned in a community of ownership under a partnership or other structure.[31] Co-ownership may also occur in condominium form,[32] and is considered a form of quasi-ownership under the Civil Code. Such interests are fully recognized and alienable under the laws governing the land register.

The law of the canton, (which can vary widely) in which the property is located, determines how the common areas must be administered.

§ 106CH.03(d)   Interests in the Land of Another.

One may obtain an interest in the land of another through the acquisition of a mortgage (Grundpfandverschreibung, Hypotheque) or mortgage note (Schuldbrief, Cedules hypothecaires), the difference being that mortgage notes are negotiable instruments issued in the name of the bearer.[33] The debt which the mortgage secures may be present, future, or contingent.

In order to be valid and effective, both types of mortgage interests must be entered into the land register. In order to be entered, the real estate interests must be described with specificity and the amount of the mortgage must be stated in Swiss francs.

In most cases, any encumbrance upon the property must be entered into

---

[29] *Id.* at art. 220.

[30] Cc art. 651.

[31] *Id.*

[32] *Id.* at arts. 712a *et seq.*

[33] Cc arts. 793-874.

the land register to be binding upon a subsequent purchaser.

Servitudes can either run with the land or be applicable only as between specific persons. Also on this point, specificity is required in the land register entry.

§ 106CH.03(e)   Prescription and Adverse Possession.

Prescription and adverse possession of personal property are possible under Swiss law. However, because the land register imparts notice to all the world, prescription and adverse possession do not apply to real property interests.

§ 106CH.03(f)   Rules Relating to Perpetuities.

A testator may designate the party to receive a reversionary interest when an interest less than full ownership is to be transferred upon death, but this is the limit of the power of testamentary disposition of land. A usufruct interest in favor of an entity may not endure for more than 100 years.

§ 106CH.03(g)   Foreign Ownership of Swiss Land.

Any investment in real estate in Switzerland by an alien requires that the purchaser have a license.[34] In order to obtain a license to own property, the alien individual or business entity must follow both the federal and cantonal requirements for the license. No restrictions apply to aliens who have lived in Switzerland for at least ten years.[35]

Vacation homes, apartments, and condominiums may only be purchased inside certain areas, and the number which may be sold to aliens is subject to quotas under federal supervision and allotted yearly to the cantons. An alien who does not follow the laws concerning acquisition by aliens will not only be prohibited from ever owning real property in Switzerland, but may be subject to criminal prosecution, which may include a fine, imprisonment, or both.

§ 106CH.03(h)   The Land Register Law.

Similar to many countries with roots in Germanic law, the real property law of Switzerland protects the good faith acquisition of land. The Civil Code states that the purchaser in good faith should be able to exercise confidence in the entries of the Land Register.[36] Nevertheless, an entry in the land register is only valid if the underlying transaction is legal.[37]

The land register is a collection of survey maps divided into parcels. Only one half of the country has been surveyed, and therefore in the unsurveyed

---

[34] *See* Federal Statute on Acquisition of Real Property by Nonresidents of Dec. 16, 1983.

[35] This requirement is only five years for persons who are citizens of most EC countries.

[36] Cc art. 973.

[37] *Id.* at art. 974.

portions cantonal and customary law govern. The land register is technically open to all, but because of the propensity of foreign governments to use Switzerland for investment, mainly due to its banking secrecy laws, there is now a bureaucracy which must be confronted in order to see the land register.

§ 106CH.03(i)   Notarization of the Transfer.

All contracts for the sale of property must be properly notarized in order to be valid and effective. Notaries are subject to strict regulation administered by the cantons. Therefore, a notary's authority only extends to the boundaries of the canton in which the notary resides.

§ 106CH.04   Real Property Rights Under the Code of Obligations: Landlord/Tenant Law.

Landlord/tenant law in Switzerland is strictly a contractual matter and thus the law covering leases is found in the Code of Obligations.[38] However, this area of the law has also received much legislative attention, by both federal and cantonal legislatures, mostly in matters of lessee rights and rent control. The tenant is protected in the habitability of the premises, as well as in the procedures the landlord must follow in order to evict the tenant. The cantonal laws covering rent control are typically very restrictive.

The Code of Obligations also ensures that unless otherwise stipulated there is an implied right to sublease. Lessees wishing to ensure their continued occupancy even after sale by the landlord can have such an agreement entered into the land register.

§ 106CH.05   Other Swiss Real Property Laws.

§ 106CH.05(a)   Property Rights Between Husband and Wife.

Spouses are free to arrange their property interests by contract in any way they please. In the event they do not have a legally binding contract, then Civil Code provisions apply. All property and income received by either spouse become part of the community property;[39] property that one spouse owned prior to marriage or received after dissolution of the marriage is not community property. Also, property that is solely for the use of one spouse part of the community property.[40] Upon dissolution of the marriage, that property which constitutes the community property is divided in half for distribution to the former spouses.

§ 106CH.05(b)   Taxes on Real Property.

§ 106CH.05(b)(1)   Land Transfer Tax.

A land transfer tax is levied by each canton and therefore varies. A two

---

[38] Code of Obligations arts. 253-274.

[39] Cc arts. 221-246.

[40] Cc arts. 196-220.

percent tax on the purchase price or market value of the real property transferred would be typical.

§ 106CH.05(b)(2)   Property Tax.

Some cantons also levy a property tax similar to that found in most states in the United States.

CHAPTER 106CL

PROPERTY LAW IN CHILE

Professor David A. Thomas
J. Reuben Clark Law School
Brigham Young University

SYNOPSIS

§ 106CL.01   Brief History of Property Law in Chile.

The area now known as Chile was taken over by Spanish *conquistadores* beginning in 1535, and Santiago, the present capital, was founded by Pedro de Valdivia in 1541. The feudal system of 16th century Spain was then transplanted to Chile. Under that feudal system, succession by primogeniture prevailed, so younger brothers frequently sought their fortunes in the New World campaigns of conquest. If they were successful and became land-owners, they usually organized their estates with a town at the center and the natives as the peasant work force:

> This system became known as the *encomienda* system under which the settlers who came after the *conquistadors* obtained land grants from the Crown. These estates often included one or more Indian communities whose inhabitants were legally "commended," or entrusted, by the Crown

to the Protection of the Spanish landowner. The Amerindians were forced to work a specified number of days each week and to perform other tasks on the estate, while the landowner was required to "civilize" the Indians and convert them to Christianity.[1]

After 1542, the duration of the *encomienda* was by law limited to three generations of landowners. In addition to the *encomienda*, land was distributed by inheritance, as a military prize, by grant from the Crown, and by assignment upon the founding or enlarging of a village or town.

During the colonial era, some of Spain's land management practices were adopted by the colonies, but not all. When registers of mortgages were mandated for Spain in 1539 and again in 1713, this system was not accepted in the New World colonies. A different mortgage registration scheme of 1768 was accepted by the governing colonial council in 1768.

In modern times, land reform has been the main theme of Chilean property law. A conservative land reform scheme was enacted in 1962, but it directly affected only a small portion of the land. A new land reform effort between 1964 and 1969 similarly fell far short of its projected extent. After 1970, frustration with the slow pace of reform and worsening economy led to some land seizures by peasants, which seizures were not resisted by the government.

§ 106CL.02   Forms of Property Ownership.

§ 106CL.02(a)   Generally.

The Chilean Constitution guarantees all persons equal rights, including the right to property.[2] Therefore, at the constitutional level there are no restrictions on the ownership of property. This even applies to foreigners, who may own property in Chile virtually without restriction. Owners may not have their property taken by public authority except for the public good.[3] Concurrent ownership is recognized, and tenants in common may dispose of their shares without the consent of the other tenants in common.[4]

§ 106CL.02(b)   Prescription.

Real property interests may be obtained by prescription, after a time (usually five years for real property and two years for personal property) of uninterrupted possession for the required period of time. Prescription does not run against a recorded title, unless the prescriptive title is also recorded. The prescriptive period is suspended during periods of legal disability (including against married women) and as between spouses. Real property

---

[1] *The Legal System of Chile, in* 10 Modern Legal Systems Cyclopedia § 1.2(C) (Kenneth Robert Redden & Linda L. Schlueter eds. 1991).

[2] Chilean Constitution of 1980, *Capitulo* III, art. 19, para. 24.

[3] *Id.*

[4] *Id.* Codigo Civil, art. 1812.

interests can also be acquired by extraordinary prescription, based on uninterrupted possession for ten years; in such case no title need be shown and there is no suspension on behalf of incapacitated persons.

§ 106CL.02(c)   Community Property.

Generally, all property acquired during the marriage becomes part of the community, except gifts of real property, which remain part of the recipient's estate.

§ 106CL.02(d)   Mortgages.

In general, mortgages may be placed only on real property and real estate rights. Personal property such as machinery, pictures, and statuary may be included in mortgages on realty when the personal property forms a part of the realty. Agrarian pledges may cover animals and their products, machinery and tools, seeds, crops, fruits, and lumber. Such pledges must appear in a public instrument and be recorded in a special registry in the office of the real property registrar.

§ 106CL.02(e)   Mines and Minerals.

The state is considered the owner of all mineral and fossil substances, even if private parties own the surface rights. Private persons may obtain concessions to extract the mineral resources in accordance with the mining code. Such concessions are transferable, mortgageable and irrevocable and are regulated by the same civil laws that regulate real estate and fixed assets. Taxes on mineral concessions are assessed at an annual rate per hectare. If the tax is not paid, the concession is offered at public auction, at which each bidder must deposit the amount of unpaid tax. The owner of the mining concession is not allowed to bid, but may avoid the sale by paying double the amount of tax. Any such sale does not include the mining buildings and accessories, unless the former owner fails to remove them within one year.

§ 106CL.03   Real Property Transactions.

Transfers of rights in immovable property are not perfected or effective until such writing is properly recorded or filed for record in a public registry. Trusts as known in common law jurisdictions are not known in Chilean law, but the freedom of contract that exists in Chile makes it possible to structure real property relationships substantially similar to those of a trust.

§ 106CL.03(a)   Deeds.

All transfers of title to real estate must be by public instrument and must contain a true statement of the consideration involved. The tax on the transfer must be paid at the time the document is executed before the notary, or, if executed in a foreign country, at the time it is authenticated in Chile. Deeds must be recorded in the registries of property. Both grantor and grantee must sign the deed and both must therefore be present before the notary at the same time. An absent party must be represented by an attorney in fact. The original deed, if executed in Chile, must remain in the files of the Chilean notary who gives to either party a certified copy, which has the effect of an original in courts of law. If the deed is executed abroad, it must be authenticated by a Chilean consul or diplomatic agent.

§ 106CL.03(b)   Sales of Real Property.

In sales of real property, the seller usually is obligated to deliver title and provide warranty of title;[5] the buyer is required to pay the price and to register the transaction.[6]

Sales of real property must be recorded. In the absence of an agreement to the contrary, the vendor warrants the thing sold and the title thereto; and in any case the vendor is liable for hidden defects in the thing sold if known to the vendor and not called to the buyer's attention. In private sales of real property rescission may be asked within four years by the vendor, if it is found that the price received is less than one-half the just value of the property, and by the buyer if the value is less than one-half the price paid. A sales contract between spouses not permanently divorced and between father or mother and children is void.[7]

§ 106CL.03(c)   Real Property Records.

The following documents must be recorded in the registry of properties:

documents conveying or declaring the ownership of real estate and real rights;

documents constituting, conveying, modifying or renouncing rights of usufruct, mortgage and certain other rights in real estate; and

judgments declaring the ownership of real property or the definitive possession of the property of absent persons.

Other documents relating to real property or real property rights, such as leases or attachments, may be recorded so as to constitute notice to third parties.

In Chile, recordation is necessary to acquire, modify, transfer, or extinguish rights in immovable property.[8] Documents filed for record are checked for external formalities and checked against previously recorded instruments affecting the same property.[9] Recorders must also verify that the person who appears as vendor or mortgagor in the filed document has the power to grant that particular interest according to previous recordings. The recorder must check the appropriate entry indicating the source from which the grantor

---

[5] *Id.* art. 1824.

[6] *Id.* art. 1871.

[7] *Id.* art. 1796.

[8] *Id.* arts. 670, 686.

[9] *Id.* art. 13.

received title. If the grantor is not the prior recorded grantee, the document is denied the privilege of recordation until the irregularity is cleared up.[10]

A recorder in Chile is law trained,[11] and may be personally liable for errors in recording and for issuing an erroneous certification of registry.[12]

§ 106CL.03(d)   Registration.

The basic priority principle for Chilean and all Latin American registry systems is that priority goes to the first to record, regardless of when the deed is executed and possession is delivered to the purchaser.[13]

Real property interests, including easements, leases and deeds, must be registered if they are to be perfected.[14] These interests are registered in the land register, kept by the *Conservador* of Real Property, and transferred by registration. But entries in the land register do not create rights, since neither the validity and efficacy of the registered rights nor the factual description of the real property are warranted. Registration of ownership merely proves and guarantees possession. Legislation dealing with registration of title to real estate contains a comprehensive set of requirements for the entries of the land records, and recorders are given the authority to suspend or refuse the recordation of instruments that do not comply with those statutory provisions.

§ 106CL.04   Taxation of Real Property.

Chilean real property is subject to national and municipal territorial taxes based on assessed value of the property. Also imposed are assessments for street lighting, street paving and certain other municipal services. Value assessments are made every five to ten years, but may be adjusted annually. Certain properties of low value are exempt. An additional real estate tax is imposed at a flat 7% rate, except tax rates on agricultural land may vary from 4% to 10%.

§ 106CL.05   Foreign Ownership of Chilean Real Property.

Property in Chile may be acquired without restrictions by foreigners, except that Peruvians may not obtain land in the frontier zones.

---

[10] *Id.* arts. 14, 80.

[11] *Id.* art. 7.

[12] *Id.* arts. 96-97.

[13] *Id.* arts. 14, 66.

[14] *Id.* art. 1801.

CHAPTER 106CN

PROPERTY LAW IN THE PEOPLE'S REPUBLIC OF CHINA

Professor David A. Thomas
J. Reuben Clark Law School
Brigham Young University

SYNOPSIS

§ 106CN.01   History.

Before the collapse of the last Chinese Empire in 1911, every acre of land in China was held by the Emperor. The Emperor himself was the sole owner of the land in the true sense of the word. In order to achieve effective control of the land, the Emperor usually divided the land into districts, provinces or prefectures and granted them to his immediate relatives and warriors as awards; those grantees usually held immediately by the Emperor in socage or military service. The grantees then assigned the rights to use the land, and delegated the duties to render military, pecuniary, agricultural and construction services to loyal followers. Assignments and delegations took place at every level until they reached the level of actual possession, held by so-called landlords and villein tenants. This system was kept alive for hundreds and even thousands of years, more by the political administration than by any form of legislation. Governors and ministers served both administrative and judicial functions. Occasionally, the Emperor would send a roving commissioner to hear some complaints; however, land issues were seldom encountered because so little protection was accorded villein rights.

Between the years of 1911 and 1949, China witnessed dramatic changes in land ownership. The Emperor abdicated, and many people declared absolute ownership of the land in their possession. However, soon the warlords began taking the place of the Emperor in their local regions. For mutual support and benefit, the warlords let the claimants draft claims and deeds. No more than two copies were allowed to be executed, one held by the claimant and one by the warlords. The warlords were committed to providing the villeins with security and stability, while in return the villein claimants, subordinated themselves and agreed to render military and pecuniary services. These widely varied arrangements prevailed until Jiang Qieshek secured full power nationwide, when the management of land became uniform again. Jiang's government relied on taxes as the major source of revenue, so for the first time in Chinese history people could obtain fee simple absolute in land without subordinating their vested interest to various overlords. Conveyance of land through land sale contract, execution of deed and probate of wills was no longer a novelty.

When Mao Zedong came to power in 1949, he started a land-ownership revolution from the bottom of the social hierarchy. Only the people who were actually farming the land could claim ownership or an interest in the land.[1] However, before this reform had proceeded very far, political considerations took over; landholders were made to surrender their owner-ship to the nearest municipal authority that had centralized management and control.[2] Farmers still farmed the land, but their return was based upon the hours they worked on the farm and on their involvement in political activities more than on their legal interest in the land. When there was a big harvest, they surrendered most of it to the government. The community then made a distribution of the rest to all its members. During years of natural disasters, the community could apply on behalf of its people for relief and even some government aid. The whole system was built upon the theory that every parcel of land as well as all the natural resources belonged to the public or a community as a whole. It was assumed that the government could better judge the people's needs, and that it was more appropriate to let the

---

[1] Land Ownership Reformation Law, enacted in 1950, and the Constitutional Law, passed in 1954, enabled farmers to claim full and absolute ownership of land. They were allowed to sell, rent or put a lien on their land. Huang, Frank Xianfeng. "The Path of Clarity: Development of Property Rights in China." 17 *Colum. J. Asian L.* 191 (Spring 2004).

[2] The Draft of Amendment of the Rules and Regulations Concerning the Work of the People's Community in the Countryside explicitly authorized state ownership and collective community ownership of land. Private ownership of land was eliminated from the constitution. The draft was published in September 1962.

government hold the wealth and distribute or redistribute it as it saw fit. As people lost their incentive to take care of the land much waste occurred.

More recently, Deng Xiaoping moved the landholding arrangements back toward self-governance and more private ownership. The land itself is still state-owned, but farmers have been given the right to exclusive use of the parcels of land assigned to them. Transfer or conveyance of land is in reality an assignment of the right to use land.

In contrast to holdings of farmland, the history of residential ownership in China did not go through so many changes. Even during the time of Mao, people from the country were allowed to build their own houses within certain zones. They paid a nominal fee every year of occupancy. Failure to pay the fee could result in forfeiture of the dwelling to the state or reconveyance to the community. However, since the fee was very nominal, defaults rarely occurred.

Some political considerations interfered with residential landholding. During the late 1980s and early 1990s, the government would send people to confiscate or tear down the house if the householders violated the one-child family planning policy and there were no other effective means to punish or deter them. In cities where most of the houses and apartment buildings are built and owned by the state or factories or institutions, tenants are more or less tenants for life.

As part of the outcome of the first Opium War, China ceded Hong Kong island to the British by the Treaty of Nanking in 1842; additional territory was ceded in 1860 and 1898, with the British interest being characterized as a 99-year lease. Accordingly, in 1997 Hong Kong was turned over to the People's Republic of China, which committed to keeping Hong Kong law essentially unchanged for several decades. Hong Kong law is an amalgam of old Chinese law and custom, the English common law system as modified by the Hong Kong legislature, and the Basic Law imposed by the communist Chinese government after the handover, which Basic Law leaves most aspects of Hong Kong law and economy unchanged.

§ 106CN.02   Types of Real Property Interests.

§ 106CN.02(a)   Real Property Interests Under the Constitution.

According to the latest Constitution of the People's Republic of China enacted during the Fifth National Conference of the National People's Congress held in 1982, all of the land in the cities is owned by the state:

> Except for the land that is owned by the state in pursuit of specific regulations, all of the land in the country and the outskirts of the cities is owned collectively by communities.

The land used for building houses and for the assigned family agricultural plots is owned collectively by communities.

By use of eminent domain power the state may take over any land in the public interest.

No institution or individual is allowed to intrude on and occupy land or engage in sale, renting or any other form of land transfer in violation of law.

Every institution or individual must use the land reasonably:[3]

> Except for those stipulated by law to be owned collectively by communities, all of the mineral resources, waters, forests, mountains ridges, prairies, uncultivated land, sea banks and other natural resources are owned by the state, that is, owned by the people as a whole.
>
> No institution or individual is allowed to usurp any means to encroach upon or damage the natural resources.[4]

§ 106CN.02(b)   Real Property Interests Under Recent Legislation and Regulations.

Until 2007, several documents have regulated real property interests in China. These will probably now be affected, to one degree or another, by a new basic property law, part of the Chinese Civil Code, enacted by the National People's Congress in March, 2007, and effective October 1, 2007. The new law contains 247 articles and decrees that "the property of the state, the collective, the individual and other obligees is protected by law, and no units or individuals may infringe upon it." Thus, both state property and individual property are to be given equal protection under Chinese law; this is seen as an improvement in protections for private property. The law prohibits various forms of illegal possession, looting, sharing, withholding, and destroying state property, and adds to agricultural lands protections from seizure. When property owned by collectives, whether agricultural or residential, is subject to compulsory takings, compensation must be paid.

About ten other important documents regulate real property interests held by persons or institutions. According to the Rules Regarding the Management of Land, the right to use the land owned by the state or collectively by communities may be transferred with compensation.[5]

This "does not include subterranean resources, trovers buried and found underneath the land or public utilities."[6]

Qualified "companies, corporations or any other forms of organizations and individuals residing inside or outside the territory of the People's Republic of China, may acquire the right to use of the land for land

---

[3] Constitutional Law of the People's Republic of China, art. 10, ch. 1; Collection of Laws of the People's Republic of China, 5 (1989).

[4] *Id.* at p. 5, art. 9.

[5] The Rules Regarding the Management of Land, art. II, ch. 1. The Rules were enacted on June 25, 1986, during the 16th Conference of the Standing Committee of the 6th National People's Congress, and were later amended and went into effect on December 29, 1988.

[6] *Temporary Regulations Regarding Sales and Transfers of the Right to Use State-Owned Land in Cities and Townships of the People's Republic of China,* art. 2, ch. 1, published on May 19th, 1990 by the State Department.

development, utilization and management if they apply in accordance with the other articles of this regulation."[7]

"The tenants who acquired the right to use of the land, may transfer, assign or incur a lien on the right, or use it for any other economic activities during the terms of their contract with the state."[8]

"Maximum terms for special use of land:

(1)   70 years for residential uses;

(2)   50 years for industrial uses;

(3)   50 years for the use of or for education, science and technology, culture, health and sports;

(4)   40 years for the use of commercial, tourist and recreational activities;

(5)   50 years for comprehensive or any other unlisted types of uses."[9]

"Every institution and individual engaging in the actual use of the land is under an obligation to maintain the land in a sound condition and commit it to reasonable uses."[10] These rights are essentially to be continued under the new basic property law, under the loosely translated title of right of use in land for construction. This is considered analogous to a civil law usufructory right, rather than as a form of ownership. Under the new law, as under the prior law, these rights are subject to termination for failure to complete the construction, and generally may be renewed upon expiration.[11] The new law provides for basic protection of lawfully created property rights.[12]

The prior Chinese law is described as loosely recognizing easements and other rules governing relationships of adjoining and nearby landowners.

"The right of easement, interests in water, drainage, interests in air and sunlight of neighboring real estate owners or real estate interest claimers are decided upon the principle of fairness and promotion of production and maintenance. People who commit nuisance or waste that causes damages to their neighbors must be enjoined and pay for the damages."[13] The new basic law of property straightforwardly defines an easement interest.[14]

---

[7] *Id.* art. 3.

[8] *Id.* art. 4.

[9] *Id.* art. 12, ch. 2.

[10] *Id.* art. 7, ch. 2.

[11] Chinese Civil Code, Ch. XIV, Art. 149.

[12] Chinese Civil Code, Ch. XIV, Art. 66.

[13] The General Provisions of the Civil Law of the People's Republic of China, art. 83, ch. 85 (1986).

[14] Chinese Civil Code, Ch. XIV, Art. 156–169. which is normally to be created by the

§ 106CN.02(c)   Real Property Interests in Houses.

In the General Provisions of the Civil Law of the People's Republic of China, houses are classified as personal property. People may obtain full and absolute ownership of them.[15]

A person may transfer ownership of houses by will. In case a person dies intestate or fails to dispose of property properly, the property will descend to the decedent's heirs or escheat to the state.

People residing in cities and townships may apply for permission to build or expand their own houses, within certain zoning restrictions, provided that they have genuine housing needs and have obtained approval from either their work unit or the local residential committee. The construction must not take more than 20 square meters for each legitimate resident. Thus the size of permissible construction is dependent upon the number of people in the household. Within a month after the construction is completed, the applicant may submit the construction permission and construction drafts for review and verification and obtain a certificate of ownership from officials concerned.[16]

The policies and rules with regard to house construction and ownership in the countryside have been comparatively consistent. It is easier to apply for a parcel of land to build a house for oneself and would-be-married children. There is no limit of 20 square meters per person. The amount of land one can get depends on the area one resides in as well as the density of the population of one's community. Thus, in general, the communities have more latitude in deciding the amount of land they want to use for residential construction.

§ 106CN.03   Creation, Transfer, and Termination of Real Property Interests.

§ 106CN.03(a)   In Cities and Townships.

"There are three ways the state may use to transfer possession and the use of land:

(1)   negotiation;

(2)   bidding;

(3)   auction."[17]

---

state in state lands. It is unclear whether the holder of a land use right is authorized to create an easement in the land held under the right.

[15] The General Provisions of the Civil Law of the People's Republic of China were enacted by the 4th National Conference of the National People's Congress on April 12, 1986. Some of the articles relating to real property interests were amended and updated by later regulations, such as the Law of the Management of Land.

[16] Procedures for the Control of Building of Residential Houses by Individuals in Cities and Townships, arts. 2, 3, 5 (1983).

[17] *Id.* art. 13, ch. 2.

"Full amount of the contract price must be paid within 60 days after the land use sales contract . . . is signed. The state may declare rescission of the contract and request compensation for damages if the purchaser fails to pay within the time limit or to pay in full."[18]

"If the state fails to provide the land offered under the contract, the purchaser may rescind the contract and request for pecuniary damages."[19]

"After paying off the full contract price, the purchaser may register with qualified government agencies and obtain a certificate of right to use the land."[20]

"Before a purchaser may change his committed use of the land, he must first get approval from the government agencies, sign his signature on the amended contract and register for the new use of land."[21]

An assignment contract should be executed before a party transfers the right to use the land for compensation, exchange or as a gift. All of the rights and obligations specified in the original contract are assumed to be transferred to the transferee. Failure of a transferee to adhere to the original terms and committed uses will result in the forfeiture of the assignment. The fixtures attached to the land transfer with the right to use the land. Registration of the change of title is required before a party may claim full ownership. If the assignment contract price is much lower than the market price, the state has the first right of refusal.[22]

A lease contract should be executed before a holder of the right to use the land leases the land. The lessee should commit to the same terms and obligations as under the original sales contract.[23]

A lien or a mortgage may be placed upon a holder's right to use the land. All parties involved should sign the contract. In case an obligor fails to honor all the obligations and declares dissolution or bankruptcy, the obligee may become a holder of the right to use the land. Registration is required for the change of title.[24]

The right to use the land automatically terminates upon the expiration of provisions of the sales contract. Fixtures attached to the land escheat to the

---

[18] *Id.* art. 14.

[19] *Id.* art. 15.

[20] *Id.* art. 16.

[21] *Id.* art. 18.

[22] *Id.* arts. 19, 20, 21, 23, 25 and 26, ch. 3.

[23] *Id.* arts. 28-30, ch. 4.

[24] *Id.* arts. 32–38, ch. 5. *See Gregory M. Stein, "Mortgage Law in China: Comparing Theory and Practice," 72 Missouri L. Rev. 1315 (Fall, 2007).* The new basic property law largely continues prior mortgage law and practices. Chinese Civil Code, Ch. XIV, Arts, 186, 192, 194.

state without compensation. Certificate of the right to use the land must be returned to the agencies. In case a holder applies to extend or renew the contract, a new contract must be signed, the contract price must be paid and registration be made again.[25]

The right to use land may be revoked and a certificate may be cancelled if a holder falls into the following categories:

(1) the institution is dissolved or moved;

(2) without approval from the original grantor, the holder lets the land sit idle for 2 consecutive years;

(3) the holder fails to adhere to the approved uses;

(4) the public roads, railroads, airports or mines are declared to be abandoned.[26]

§ 106CN.03(b)   In the Countryside.

The transfer of the right to use land in the countryside is similar to the transfer of land in cities and townships. Rights and obligations are stipulated, contracts are signed and reconveyance is subject to tight scrutiny. However, as the land in the countryside is generally owned collectively by communities, and it is more often than not used for agricultural, fishing and mining purposes, it is much easier to procure an extension or a renewal of the original contract.[27]

Disputes over the ownership and right to use of land are heard and settled by the people's government at various levels.[28]

§ 106CN.03(c)   Registration and Conveyance of Real Property Interests in Houses.

House owners must register with the local housing and management committee and obtain a certificate of ownership or title after investigation and verification are completed. The same administrative procedures occur when there is a transfer of title or the present condition of the house is changed.[29]

Sales of privately owned houses are closed in the office of the local housing and management committee. The seller must produce a certificate of title and personal identification card, while the buyer must submit a testimonial paper proving intent to purchase the described house. An officer

---

[25] *Id.* arts. 39–42, ch. 6.

[26] *Id.* art. 19, ch. 3.

[27] Procedural Provisions Regarding the Implementation of the Rules of the Management of Land (1991).

[28] *Id.* ch. 2.

[29] Chapter 2, Regulations on the Management of Privately-Owned Housing in Cities (published on December 17th, 1983).

then cancels the certificate of title held by the seller and issues a new one for the buyer.[30]

An owner-lessor who sells the house while there is an outstanding lease contract must notify the lessee 3 months before completion of the sale and the lessee has the first right of refusal to purchase the house.[31]

A lease contract must be executed and filed with the local housing and management committee. No deposit is allowed to be taken. Assignment of a lease contract must be accepted by the lessor. The obligation of maintenance is on the lessor.[32]

A sales contract is invalid if the seller has no title to the house. It may also be void if the seller fails to acquire consent from other joint tenants or tenants in common. However, the sale will be valid if the buyer is a bona fide purchaser for value and the joint tenants or tenants in common have knowledge of the sale and fail to raise objections in a timely manner to the sale.[33] With most Chinese urban housing units in the form of apartments in multi unit buildings, it is important that the new basic property law defines the occupants' interests. The unit owner has exclusive ownership of the unit and a form of common ownership of the non exclusive areas, which are left largely undefined.[34] Governance by a type of owners' associations is provided for in the new law, with control shared by local government and the owners.[35] Meanwhile, rural property rights have not been integrated fully into the new Chinese property law.[36]

§ 106CN.04   Restrictions on Ownership of Property by Foreigners.

Foreign investors may obtain the right to use land in the same way as most of the Chinese do, except for two additional restrictions:

(1)   The foreign investors must incorporate in China or they may join with a Chinese corporation through joint venture;

(2)   the foreign investors must engage in comprehensive development or cultivation of the land, and their proposals or feasibility studies are subject to approval and review of related government agen-

---

[30] *Id.* ch. 3.

[31] *Id.* ch. 3.

[32] *Id.* ch. 4.

[33] Opinions of the Supreme People's Court on Matters Concerning the Implementation of the Civil Affairs Policies and Civil Laws, § 6 (1984).

[34] Chinese Civil Code, Ch. XIV, Arts. 70, 72.

[35] Chinese Civil Code, Ch. XIV, Arts. 75, 83.

[36] *See* Benjamin W. James, Expanding the Gap: How the Rural Property System Exacerbates Chinas Urban Rural Gap, 20 Colum. J. Asian L. 451 (2007).

cies.[37]

Foreigners may acquire full ownership of houses in China as may other Chinese. They, however, have to abide by the strict recording and registration rules. In case transfer of title and production of documents are made in a foreign country, related documents must be notarized by the foreign ministry or its diplomatic corps and authenticated by the Chinese diplomatic corps.[38]

§ 106CN.05   Bibliography.

James, Benjamin W. "Expanding the Gap: How the Rural Property System Exacerbates China's Urban Rural Gap," 20 *Colum. J. Asian L.* 451 (Spring 2007).

Liaw, H. Ray. "Women's Land Rights in Rural China: Transforming Existing Laws into a Source of Property Rights," 17 *Pac. Rim L. & Pol'y J.* 237 (January, 2008).

Liu, Chenglin. "The Chinese Takings Law from a Comparative Perspective," 26 *Wash. U. J.L. & Pol'y* 301 (2008).

Rosato Stevens, Margo. "Peasant Land Tenure Security in China's Transitional Economy," 26 *B.U. Int'l L.J.* 97 (Spring 2008).

Stein, Gregory M. "Mortgage Law in China: Comparing Theory and Practice," 72 *Missouri L. Rev.* 1318 (2007).

Zhang, Mo. "From Public to Private: The Newly Enacted Chinese Property Law and the Protection of Property Rights in China," 5 *Berkeley Bus. L.J.* 317 (Fall 2008).

---

[37] Temporary Provisions Concerning Comprehensive Development of Land by Foreign Investors (1990).

[38] Provisions of the Ministry of Urban and Rural Construction and Environmental Protection on the Management of Housing Owned by Foreigners (1984).

CHAPTER 106DE

PROPERTY LAW IN GERMANY[1]

Professor David A. Thomas
J. Reuben Clark Law School
Brigham Young University

SYNOPSIS

---

[1] Abbreviations occurring in this chapter include: GG for Grundgesetz (Basic Law or Constitution), BGB for *B/Uurgerliches Gesetzbuch* (Civil Code of FRG); BGBl for *Bundesgesetzblatt* (Federal Statutes Gazette); FRG for former Federal Republic of Germany; GDR for former German Democratic Republic; RGBl for *Reichsgesetzblatt* (Precursor of the BGBl).

§ 106DE.01   Germanic Peoples in Prehistory.

During the first two millennia, B.C., peoples of Germanic culture were concentrated in the area between the estuaries of the Weser and Oder rivers. A change in climate, about 800 B.C., forced Germanic tribes southward into Celtic territory and eastward into the area between the Oder and Vistula rivers. Persisting population pressures forced Germanic tribes into further conflicts with the Celts, culminating, in the 3rd century B.C., in complete victory for the Germanic tribes occupying the area known now as central and eastern Germany.

By this time the Germanic tribes consisted of three main groups: the northern group eventually became the Norwegians, Danes and Swedes; the eastern group, occupying lands between the Oder and Vistula rivers, emerged as the Goths, Vandals, Burgundians, and Lombards; and the western group consisted of tribes inhabiting the areas of Jutland, Schleswig-Holstein and north central Germany. As the Romans advanced along the Rhine during the 2nd century B.C., some of the western tribes became partially Romanized or at least exposed to Roman culture.

§ 106DE.02   Germanic Landholding Customs According to Roman Observers.

As a result of his military activity in western Europe during the 1st century B.C., Julius Caesar recorded a few observations about the Germanic tribes he encountered. The Germanic people appeared to rely mostly on flocks and herds as their form of wealth. They held their flocks and herds privately, while their land was held in communal ownership. Differences in wealth between individual German families were not large, and such differences were inhibited by the practice of reallocating parcels of land to different kindreds or clans annually.[2]

By the time the Roman Tacitus recorded his information about early Germanic tribes, early in the 2nd century A.D., some changes in the land customs had occurred, or else the customs were different from the Germanic peoples described by Julius Caesar.[3] The amounts and locations of the annual land distributions were influenced by social standing, and were made to individual persons rather than to kindred groups. Wealth disparities widened as certain persons were able to accumulate wealth faster. It has been hypothesized that this change occurred after the Germanic tribes were exposed to Roman goods and the Roman monetary system, which stimulated their desire for private property; the land allocation system was then modified to favor private holdings and production.[4]

Seven of the 46 chapters in Tacitus' Germania describe the laws and legal customs of ancient Germans, with the comment on landholding as follows:

> Land proportioned to the number of inhabitants is occupied by the whole community in turn, and afterwards divided among them according to rank. A wide expanse of plains makes the partition easy. They till fresh fields every year, and they have still more land than enough; with the richness and extent of their soil, they do not laboriously exert themselves in planting orchards, inclosing meadows, and watering gardens.[5]

While landholding appears to have been regulated, there is no indication that any system of estates in land was recognized.

On succession, Tacitus reported the following:

> . . .[E]very man's own children are his heirs and successors, and there are no wills. Should there be no issue, the next in succession to the property are his brothers and his uncles on either side. The more relatives he has, the more numerous his connections, the more honoured is his old age; nor are there any advantages in childlessness.[6]

Although Tacitus did not mention what sort of property was subject to succession, presumably heirs inherited only items of personal property.

§ 106DE.03 The *Leges Barbarorum*, or Barbarian Laws, of the Germanic Peoples.

As the Roman Empire disintegrated and surrendered its western provinces

---

[2] Julius Caesar, De Bello Gallico 6.22.

[3] The Roman Tacitus is the single best source of information on ancient Germanic social and legal customs, but some consider his credibility compromised by his manifest anti-Roman and pro-German moralizing. Also, it is unlikely that he ever directly observed any Germans in their native habitat. *See* Cornelius Tacitus, De Originie et Situ Germanorum xix (John G. C. Anderson ed. 1938) (editor's introduction).

[4] 7 E. A. Thompson, The Early Germans (1965).

[5] *Id.* at ch. 26.

[6] *Id.* at ch. 20.

to Germanic invaders, an official collection of imperial statutes gathered under Theodosius II, the Theodosian Code, was issued by consent of the emperor Valentinian III in A.D. 438. This code may have influenced various Germanic rulers who issued their own law codes in the decades that followed. These collections of laws exhibit varying degrees of influence from Roman and Christian sources, and some were intended to apply different legal rules to Germanic and Roman people living in the same area. These laws of the barbarians, or *Leges Barbarorum*, are summarized below.

The Visigothic laws, and more particularly the Code of Euric, are believed to have directly or indirectly influenced most Germanic law codes thereafter. The Code of Euric, from ca. A.D. 476, shows some Roman influence. The *Lex Romana Visigothorum* was promulgated by the Visigothic king Alaric II in A.D. 506, to govern Romans living in Visigothic territories. This collection is also known as the *Breviarium Alaricianum* (Breviary of Alaric). The *Leges Visigothorum* is a collection of laws that had been issued by Euric's successors, applying to both Gothic and Hispano-Roman subjects. The collection was promulgated in A.D. 654, and replaced the *Lex Romana Visigothorum*.

Euric's code seems to have been the immediate source for the early codes of both the Salian Franks[7] and the Burgundians,[8] and the Bavarian[9] and Lombard[10] codes also show Visigothic influence. Another early Frankish code, the *Lex Ribuaria*,[11] was based on the Salian Code, and it in turn influenced the codes of the continental Angles and Saxons of the Carolingian age.

The best known of these early Germanic codes—indeed the oldest Germanic code that is completely preserved—is the *Lex Salica*, which has been described as "primarily a penal law. . .concerned with the redress of crimes (murder, theft, mutilation, exploitation of women) by monetary means."[12] The *Lex Salica* and the other early codes consist of both individual "statutes" and precedential judicial sentences ("*Weisthuemer*"), but they do not refer to most customs of daily living, such as occupancy of land, personal property, commercial dealings, inheritance, family relationships, and class privilege. The only references to land law in the *Lex Salica*

---

[7] The Code of the Salian Franks, or Lex Salica, is attributed to Clovis, 481-511, A.D.

[8] The Burgundian Code was compiled between 483 and 532, A.D. The Lex Romana Burgundionum was issued ca. A.D. 500, for application to Roman citizens living in the Burgundian kingdom.

[9] The Lex Baiuvariorum is dated from about A.D. 744-748.

[10] The Leges Langobardorum was promulgated between A.D. 643 and A.D. 755.

[11] The Lex Ribuaria is believed to have been promulgated after A.D. 596, for the Ripuarian or western Franks.

[12] Laws of the Alamans and Bavarians 19 (Theodore John Rivers trans. 1977).

are provisions requiring money payment for damage to agricultural fields,[13] blocking the way of another,[14] and improper fencing and enclosing.[15]

§ 106DE.04   The Empire of Charles the Great and the Growth of Feudalism.

For most Europeans, little changed as rule passed from the Merovingian to the Carolingian dynasty. As emperor, Charles the Great followed the Frankish custom under which he considered property and revenues of the empire as his family property. Compensation to his principal supporters, servants and counselors was paid by gifts of land, usually with requirements of military service attached. However, upon the death of Charlemagne, Germanic society suffered a relapse:

> The decades that followed Charles's death witnessed the rapid disintegration of the Empire he had created. Empire and papacy alike became immersed in an abyss of anarchy and barbaric lawlessness. The governing principles of society were the law of force on the one hand and the need for protection on the other. In the course of the ninth century the State lost all contact with the urban tradition and became completely agrarian. The life of the feudal nobility was spent in warfare and private feuds. From their strongholds the feudal lords terrorized peaceful villagers and passing travelers.[16]

Despite the lawlessness of the aristocracy, the disintegration of a strong monarchy meant that the people could turn only to local feudal lords for protection; thus society became increasingly feudalized in the 9th century A.D. Land grants under such circumstances became increasingly hereditary, and through subinfeudation a hierarchy of vassalage eventually developed. These feudal landholding arrangements, either on lands of the monarch or of a member of the aristocracy, have been described as follows:

> The land was divided into estates which were self-sufficient units. . .In the center of each estate was located the Maierhof, surrounded by the huts of the peasants, each of whom had a small strip of land attached to his dwelling. . .Part of the arable land that surrounded the village was set aside for the exclusive use of the king or lord. What remained was parceled out among the peasant tenants. The fields were divided into three parts (three-fallow system, *Dreifelderwirtschaft*), one of which was used for the planting of the summer crop, the second for the winter crop, while the third part would lie fallow. . . The cultivation of the fields was a communal and coDEperative enterprise, although each peasant harvested the crop from his own strips of land.
>
>   . . .The lord gave the peasant protection, furnished the land, built a mill

---

[13] Title 9.

[14] Title 31.

[15] Title 34.

[16] 1 Kurt F. Reinhardt, Germany: 2000 Years 44 (1961).

and a village church, and administered justice in the territory that he had learned to consider his own, either by inheritance or by special grant. The peasant in turn, enjoyed the security that went with the hereditary right to the possession of his strip of land, he took his share of the agricultural produce, and returned the privileges extended to him by making certain payments and rendering certain services to the lord, exactments whose extent and nature were determined by custom. Theoretically still a serf, the peasant of the Carolingian period had actually become a tenant, and although still unfree, this peasant tenant, being exempt from the burden of military and court service, was envied by many a small freeholder.[17]

In post-Carolingian Europe, eventually a dynasty of Saxon monarchs, beginning in A.D. 919, ruled over a smaller empire consisting mostly of German territory. Once order was restored and population growth resumed, additional land was sought through conquest and colonization of territory among Slavs and Hungarians to the east and southeast, and later into the north. For many of the peasants, answering a plea for colonists in the east meant becoming a free tenant. The general disappearance of serfdom resulted from a shift of economic conditions.

§ 106DE.05   Introduction of Roman Law During the Middle Ages.

During the Middle Ages, re-discovery of the documents of classical civilization, including descriptions of Roman law, was influential in German legal history. As the central power of the German-based Holy Roman Empire declined, and that of individual principalities increased, there was no common system of German courts or private law. Exposure to principles of Roman law led in 1495 to the *Reichskam-mergerichtsordnung* adopting, or receiving, Roman law as the basis of decisions in imperial courts, in the absence or aid of local laws. Germanic local laws had by this time also assumed some written form in the *Sachsenspiegel* (1221–1227) and the *Schwabenspiegel* (1275). Subsequent city laws, such as in Nuremberg and Frankfurt, were modified to include elements of the received Roman law.

§ 106DE.06   The Movement Toward Codification and Enactment of the Civil Code (BGB).

Impetus toward codification grew slowly, and culminated only in codes for certain areas, such as Bavaria in 1756 and the Prussian states in 1794. The Napoleanic rule in German territory was too brief to produce a legal code, and the political reaction thereafter delayed comprehensive codification until German unification under Bismarck's leadership. Commercial law had been unified in the German states as early as 1848 and 1861 and certain imperial laws on courts, procedure and bankruptcy had become effective in 1879. Finally, on January 1, 1900, a comprehensive code of private law went

---

[17] *Id.* at 49-50; Draeger, Tonya R. "Property as a Fundamental Right in the United States and Germany: A Comparison of Takings Jurisprudence," 14 Transnat'l Law. 363 (Fall 2001).

into effect in the form of the Civil Code, or *B/Uurgerliches Gesetzbuch*.

§ 106DE.07   Sources of Property Law After Promulgation of the Civil Code (BGB).

§ 106DE.07(a)   The Continuing Validity of the BGB.

The *B/Uurgerliches Gesetzbuch* or Civil Code (hereafter referred to by its familiar designation BGB) has remained essentially in effect since its promulgation, through World War I, the Weimar Republic, the National Socialist era and World War II, the creation of the Federal Republic of Germany and adoption of its *Grundgesetz*, Basic Law, and now in a unified Germany.

Upon the creation of the modern German state after World War II, the *Grundgesetz*, or Basic Law, which would be viewed by an American as Germany's constitution, was promulgated. The *Grundgesetz* protects the ownership and inheritability of land holdings:

(1)   Property and the right of inheritance are guaranteed. Their content and limits shall be determined by the laws.

(2)   Property imposes duties. Its use should also serve the public weal.[18]

Other legal protections of property rights previously in force in Germany are adopted by the *Grundgesetz* to the extent they were not in conflict with the *Grundgesetz*:

(1)   Law in force before the first meeting of the *Bundestag* shall remain in force in so far as it does not conflict with this Basic Law.[19]

Thus the BGB remains in force after adoption of the *Grundgesetz*. With the reunification of the Federal Republic and the German Democratic Republic, or the absorption of the latter by the former, the BGB has been given even wider application.

The judiciary[20] also plays a limited role in fashioning German property law. If an issue before a court is not governed by a statutory provision or available interpretation, the court may provide the interpretation, often derived by analogy from other areas of the law. The courts are guided by the principles in the Swiss Civil Code, which direct the judge in such a situation to rely on customary law or on a rule that the judge would enact if in the position of a legislator.[21]

---

[18] GG art. 14(1) and (2).

[19] *Id.* at art. 123(1).

[20] The activities of the judiciary "shall be bound by law and justice." GG art. 20, § 3.

[21] Norbert Horn et al., German Private and Commercial Law 61 (1982); Crosswhite, Anastasia B. "Women and Land: Aristocratic Ownership of Property in Early Modern England," 77 N.Y.U. L. Rev. 1119 (October, 2002).

§ 106DE.07(b)   Organization of the BGB Property Law Provisions.

The BGB consists of five books, including the introductory general part (*Allgemeiner Teil*), the law of obligations, the law of things (property), family law and the law of succession. In the law of property, a major distinction is drawn between movable and immovable property.

Almost all German land law is contained within the BGB. Some supplemental legal regulation is found in a few ancillary laws and in the Ordinance on the Land Register. Although federal law controls most aspects of property law, the regional and municipal governments (*Kreisen*) administer this law and control local zoning ordinances and pre-emption rights.

§ 106DE.08   Property Law Under the BGB.

§ 106DE.08(a)   Types of Property Interests.

§ 106DE.08(a)(1)   Ownership.

Among the basic rights enumerated in the *Grundgesetz* are guarantees of the rights of property and inheritance[22] and the inviolability of the home.[23] The concept of ownership is set forth in the BGB:

> The owner of a thing may, in so far as the law or the rights of third parties permit, deal with the thing as he pleases and exclude others from interfering with it in any way.[24]

Thus defined, ownership most closely resembles the fee simple absolute interest known in American property law. As stated in the BGB, German ownership interests are explicitly subject to the requirements that ownership activities be legal and not interfere with the rights of third parties.

The kinds of ownership rights or interests one can create in property are limited to those types of rights or interests specifically authorized by law. Only authorized interests may be recorded, and, with certain exceptions, only recorded interests are valid and enforceable. The exceptions are interests that arise out of the law of obligations, security titles and inchoate ownership. Also, occasionally, social developments create pressure to recognize new property interests, which may be authorized by laws other than the original BGB. For instance, a landowner may now allow another to build on the owner's land,[25] and ownership rights in one floor of a multi-level building may be granted.[26]

---

[22] GG art. 14(1).

[23] *Id.* at art. 13.

[24] BGB § 903.

[25] This is permitted under the *Erbbaurecht* (Heritable Building Rights Ordinance). The right to build may not be granted for a period longer than 99 years and, of course, is usually granted for shorter periods of time.

[26] This is permitted under the *Wohnungseigentumsgesetz* (Residential Property Law).

German law makes no distinction between legal and equitable or beneficial ownership of property, and for the most part does not recognize less than absolute interests, such as future interests. By way of exception, recognition is accorded leasehold interests with statutory limits. Owners have the right to press a legal claim against any party that acts adversely to the owner's interests[27] and to demand possession from a wrongful possessor.[28] Under the BGB, an owner has a claim against any other party who acts adversely to the owner's interest.[29] Likewise, the owner can demand possession from a wrongful possessor.[30]

Only ownership in defined things is recognized. Thus, one cannot convey "all the land that I own"; a specific description would be necessary for an effective conveyance.

German law recognizes both joint ownership (*Bruchteilgemein-schaft*) and tenancy in common (*Gesamthandsgesellschaft*). To be valid and effective, such coDEwnership must be entered with specificity into the land register.[31]

Under Article IX the American-German Treaty of Friendship of 1954, reciprocal rights to acquire, hold, and dispose of real and personal property are guaranteed to German and American citizens. Foreigners who own property in Germany are protected against uncompensated taking by the government.

§ 106DE.08(a)(2)   Possession.

Possession is not recognized as a right, but as a factual circumstance that may give rise to rights:

> Possession is regarded not as a right in itself, but as physical relation to a thing, namely the exercise of factual control over it, and is protected by the BGB against invasion and infringement by third parties, regardless of the possessor's title.[32]

The importance accorded possession under German property law means that even a possessor who is not the owner may have certain direct rights of action, such as the right of a tenant to take action directly against one who disturbs the tenant's possession, rather than acting through the landlord.

§ 106DE.08(a)(3)   Interests in the Land of Another.

The BGB recognizes certain interests that one may hold in the land of

---

[27] BGB § 823, § 1.

[28] *Id.* at § 985.

[29] *Id.* at § 823, § 1.

[30] *Id.* at § 985.

[31] *Id.* at §§ 1008–1011.

[32] Norbert Horn, et al., German Private and Commercial Law 171 (1982).

another, including servitudes,[33] encumbrances,[34] and personal servitudes.[35] Among the recognized servitudes are profits, *usufrucht*,[36] licenses, and rights of way. Recognized encumbrances include restrictive building covenants, easements, and mortgages.

German law recognizes security interests in land (real or land securities (*Realkredit*), under the *Grundpfandrechte*) as arising from mortgages (*Hypothek*)[37] and rent obligations (*Grundschuld*).[38] The beneficiary under any real security may seek a remedy against the burdened land, usually by means of a forced auction which is regulated by statute:[39]

> Mortgage and rent charge differ in that the validity of mortgage depends on the legal status of the secured debt, while rent charge does not, but the two forms have grown so alike that in practice they are virtually interchangeable.[40]

§ 106DE.08(a)(4)   Protection of Property Interests.

Under German law, the owner of property has an absolute right to exclude all others from the property, as long as the owner remains within the legal limits of other applicable laws. Self-help in the protection of real property is an absolute right which remains available to the modern German property owner. However, self-help may only be applied when the owner has been dispossessed.[41] Many actions in tort exist for the protection of rights of ownership.[42] The owner is constrained by reasonableness and applicable regulation under public, planning, and environmental laws.

§ 106DE.08(b)   Acquisition and Delivery of Property.

Ownership of land can only be acquired through a contract of sale[43] and an obligation under the principle of abstraction. In principle, the contract of sale and the obligation, or *Auflassung*, are seen as strictly separate, or abstracted. This distinction has generated many artificial complications and now most real property transfers combine everything into one document.

---

[33] BGB §§ 1018–1029.

[34] *Id.* at §§ 1105–1112.

[35] *Id.* at §§ 1090–1093.

[36] *Id.* at § 1030 (*Niessbrauch*).

[37] *Id.* at § 1113 *et seq.*

[38] *Id.* at § 1191 *et seq.*

[39] *Gesetz Uber die Zwangsversteigerung* und *Zwangverwaltung*, promulgated 20 May 1898, RGBl, 773.

[40] Norbert Horn et al., German Private and Commercial Law 184 (1982).

[41] BGB § 985.

[42] These include actions against trespass, nuisance, and the threat of intrusion. *See Id.* at §§ 906, 1004.

[43] BGB § 313.

§ 106DE.08(b)(1)   The Principle of Abstraction.

Somewhat similar to the earnest money agreement, a real property transaction under German law is achieved by means of a contract and then a subsequent performance:

> The principle of abstraction, which has been known to cause problems even to German students, lays down that, while contract and transfer are connected in the sense that the latter is performance of the former and that the former constitutes a justification or causa for the latter, they are nevertheless to be treated as separate or abstract even though they often constitute a single unit in legal reality.[44]

§ 106DE.08(b)(2)   The Contract of Sale.

The contract for the sale of land must be notarized.[45] If the documents memorializing the sale are an offer and acceptance, then both documents must be notarized. However, in the event that a notary is not utilized, the sale will become binding when it is entered into the land register.

§ 106DE.08(b)(3)   Transfer (*Auflassung*).

The transfer, or obligation, as it is often termed, consists of the actual performance of the contract of sale, the payment of monies and the entry of new ownership in the land register. Pursuant to the BGB, the transfer (*Auflassung*) must be declared in the presence of both parties.[46] If an agent represents a party, the agent must be authenticated or certified.[47] Where the transfer occurs as a result of a judgment of a court, the parties' presence is not necessary. Although the transfer is distinct from the contract, in common practice a single document constitutes both a contract of sale and a transfer. Unless the transaction in question comes under one of several exemptions, a tax on the transaction will be applicable. The transaction will not be binding until entered into the land registry.[48]

§ 106DE.08(b)(4)   Notarization of the Contract and the Transfer.

Regardless of what kind of transaction occurs, the transfer must be notarized.[49] If the land is improved, or is land available for development, then under the Federal Building Law[50] local authorities may have a public right of pre-emption, and a declaration of intent not to exercise pre-emption rights must be made before the transfer can take place. For agricultural and

---

[44] Norbert Horn, et al., German Private and Commercial Law 69 (1982).

[45] BGB § 313.

[46] *Id.* at § 925.

[47] *Grundbuchordnung* § 29.

[48] BGB § 873.

[49] *Id.* at § 313.

[50] *Bundesbaugesetz,* Law of 23 June 1960, BGBl I, 341.

forest land, a similar process must be followed under the Law of Dealings on Land.[51]

§ 106DE.08(b)(5)   Prescription and Adverse Possession.

While acquisition of movable property by prescription is possible under the BGB,[52] no acquisition of real property interests through adverse possession or prescription can occur because of the requirement that every interest in land must be recorded.

§ 106DE.09   The Ordinance on the Land Register.

The land register was established as an aid to certainty in matters of land ownership.[53] Absolute rights as to defined things are made public, and clearly ascertainable to the public at large, through the registration system. Land registration is especially significant because so-called equitable remedies are not recognized by German courts. The local municipal court has jurisdiction over all the land in its district.

§ 106DE.09(a)   Land Register Requirements.

Only those dispositions of land which have either been entered or cancelled are eligible for recording in the land register. Either entry or cancellation can be altered by a judgment of the court or by consent of all parties. No entry is necessary for rights which transfer by operation of law, such as the law of succession, although the successor is advised to apply for correction of the register.

The Land Registry is not a register of deeds; in fact, deeds do not exist under German law. It is a register of titles showing the current legal disposition of real property. The land register reflects rights which affect the described property directly, but not necessarily matters which affect only the owner, such as personal judgments. Public charges or obligations of the owner are not entered.

The land register is divided into three sections. Part I is a register of the current owner of the property and lists in an abbreviated form encumbrances which may be on the land. Part II lists in detail the information concerning the encumbrances. Part III lists security interests which affect the land. By analysis of all three parts of the land register, the prospective purchaser or creditor can see a complete picture of the current status of the property in question. All supposed encumbrances or security interests in property which are not registered property are afforded no legal significance. In the event that a creditor finds that a security interest is improperly recorded, the

---

[51] *Grundstucksverkehrsgesetz.*

[52] BGB § 937.

[53] *Grundbuchordnung* of 24 March 1897, RGBl 139, as promulgated on 5 August 1935, RGBl I, 1073.

creditor has a cause of action to require the debtor owner to correct the mistake. But if the land has been sold or otherwise conveyed, the offended creditor has only a cause of action for unjust enrichment against the debtor.

§ 106DE.09(b)   Priority Under the Land Register.

Priority under the land register is usually given by the date of entry, subject to modification by agreement of the parties.

§ 106DE.09(c)   Bona Fide Purchasers.

German property law is especially sensitive to the protection of the principle of good faith. Thus one who takes possession without knowledge of extenuating rights takes that property with absolute rights, free of any encumbrances.[54] Only that knowledge which can come through the Land Register is imputed to the purchaser.

If one loses property due to the negligence or fraud of another, the remedy rests on the rules of unjust enrichment.[55] The harmed party never has recourse against the person who acted in reliance on the land register without notice.

§ 106DE.10   Ancillary Real Property Laws.

While the BGB addresses most of the issues associated with absolute ownership of land, it has little provision for other real property interests. Such provisions have been added by so-called ancillary legislation, which has also become an integral part of German property law.

§ 106DE.10(a)   Heritable Building Rights Law (*Erbbaurecht*).

Building rights under German law are constrained by rigid zoning laws which direct where and how any building may be constructed. Under the BGB only the absolute owner of real property was allowed to build upon it. This changed as modern commercial and social pressures led to the promulgation of the Heritable Building Rights Law.[56] This law permits a heritable building right to be held by one other than the owner for periods of up to 99 years, although most such interests are for shorter periods. The owner receives an annual payment during the life of the right. Upon expiration of the period, the land reverts to the owner, who then must pay for the improvements. During the term of the heritable building right, the holder of the right is considered the owner.

§ 106DE.10(b)   The Law of Home Ownership.[57]

This enactment made possible the ownership of a single story of a

---

[54] BGB § 892.

[55] *Id.* at § 816.

[56] *Erbbaurecht, Verordnung* of 15 January 1919.

[57] *Gesetz uber das Wohnungseigentum* und *das Dauerwohnrecht* of 15 March 1951, BGBl I, 175.

building.[58] The possessors of such rights are considered special owners of their respective floors or apartments, as coDEwners of the entire parcel of land, and as co-responsible for common areas of the building. Such a form of real property ownership is used widely in modern Germany as a means of making property interests available to persons otherwise unable to afford absolute ownership.

§ 106DE.10(c)   Obligatory Rights Relating to Land.

The BGB does not direct its attention to the creation of obligatory rights as they pertain to land. However, through analogy from other areas of the law, scholars and the judicial system have been able to identify certain principles which are made applicable to interests in land.

Under the legal rules relating to suretyship, identical to those found in American jurisprudence, a valid written surety instrument obligates the surety to the extent of all the surety's assets, including real property interests.[59]

Under the BGB, when a person purchases property on credit, the vendor retains all ownership until the purchase price has been paid in full.[60] Many purchasers, however, want some recognition and protection of property rights before they have paid the sum in full. German law now recognizes inchoate ownership.[61] "It is treated as a real right of an independent variety, 'like ownership, only less.'"[62]

§ 106DE.10(d)   Homesteads.

Homesteads can be created under German law[63] when land is expropriated and granted to a person by one of the states (*Laender*), municipalities, or certain private or public corporations. Such a real property holding is entered into the Land Register; however the possessor is restricted in alienation and security rights.

§ 106DE.10(e)   Property Rights of Married Couples.

Although women are guaranteed rights equal to those of men under the German Basic Law,[64] additional equal rights legislation has also been enacted.[65] Property acquired by a married couple is considered within the

---

[58] The drafters of the BGB had expressly excluded such a possibility for fear of disorder and conflict.

[59] BGB § 765 *et seq.*

[60] *Id.* at § 455.

[61] BGHZ 20, 88.

[62] Norbert Horn, et al., German Private and Commercial Law 183 (1982).

[63] *Verordnung* of 10 May 1920, as amended.

[64] GG 3, ¶2; art. 117.

[65] *Gleichberechtigungsgesetz* of 18 June 1957 (BGB1 1957 I 609), amending the BGB.

"community of acquisition," similar to American community property.[66] Married persons' property rights are governed by Book Four of the BGB, dealing with *Familienrecht* (the law of families).

§ 106DE.10(f)   Landlord/Tenant Law.

The basic provisions governing the relationship of landlords and tenants are found in Book Two of the BGB on contract law. The tenant is guaranteed possession and quiet enjoyment, and has a right of action against either the landlord or the disturbing tenant if the quiet enjoyment is disturbed.[67] The tenant in possession has the rights of ownership associated with possession; most remedies for the breach of such rights are found in German tort law. Although the BGB is silent as to rights and responsibilities in common areas, local ordinances provide some remedies for tenants. The landlord/tenant contract is usually standardized (*Deutscher Einheitsmietvertrag*), and some local governments have made the use of this contract form mandatory.

§ 106DE.10(g)   Taxes on Real Property.

All real property holdings are taxable under the capital tax that is assessed against all assets (*Vermogenssteuer*). The percentage of tax is different for corporations and individuals, and many exceptions apply. A separate real property tax may be levied based upon special value (*Einheitswert*).

A tax of up to 7 percent may be levied when land is transferred if none of a host of exceptions apply, and this tax must be paid before the transfer may be recorded in The Land Registry. A capital gains tax may also be applicable to the transfer of real property, if the transaction is not part of the vendor's normal business and the transfer is viewed as speculative.

§ 106DE.11   Effects of Reunification on German Property Law.

On October 3, 1990, the Federal Republic of Germany (FRG) and the German Democratic Republic (GDR) were unified as one country. Under Article 23 of the Basic Law[68] all of the GDR came under the Basic Law of the Federal Republic of Germany, and hence under the BGB as of the date of accession. The Unification Treaty restated the applicability of these laws and also included stipulations for reprivations and restitution of confiscated property.

The legal systems of the FRG and the GDR could not have been more different prior to reunification. While the Federal Republic's laws found their origin in the civil and Germanic law traditions surrounded by a capitalistic society, the German Democratic system was centrally located within a

---

[66] BGB § 1363 *et seq.*

[67] *Id.* at § 535.

[68] GG art. 23 states in pertinent part: "[T]his Basic Law shall apply in the territory of the Laender of [twelve named Laender]. In other parts of Germany it shall be put into force on their accession."

confining communist system. Only personal use of real property was possible in the East, not ownership. Property in the GDR was classified as coDEperative property, people's property, and property of citizens' social organizations. The state exercised great rights of pre-emption, offering only symbolic compensation for acts of confiscation.

§ 106DE.11(a)   The Current Status of Reprivation and Restitution.

The Unification Treaty provides that confiscated properties are to be returned upon demand. In the event that such a return is impossible, then compensation is required under the Basic Law. In practical terms, much of the property confiscated has been put to public use and will be judged impossible to return.

Millions of Germans will be affected by the resolution of these problems, and it will probably take several decades to resolve them. Under the Unification Treaty, confiscations which occurred between 1945 and 1949 are not to be returned to the prior owner. Instead, parliament will arrive at a compensation which is expected to be far below true market value, thus generating even more controversy.

§ 106DE.11(b)   The Activities of the *Treuhandanstalt*.

The reorganization and privatization of properties within the GDR began under the communist government on July 1, 1990. The administration of this program has now fallen fully upon the government of the reunified FRG, which relies on its *Treuhandanstalt* (trustee administration) to conduct affairs much like the government bodies that have dealt with the American savings and loan association liquidations.

The difficulties of the *Treuhand* administration have combined with the problems of restitution for confiscated properties to somewhat hinder the assimilation of the new federal states of the East into the mainstream of German economic life. The consequence of all this turmoil for real property ownership is that as long as the contested title is expressed upon The Land Register, the alienation of these properties will be restricted, since prospective buyers will be aware of potential future complications.

CHAPTER 106DK

PROPERTY LAW IN DENMARK

Professor David A. Thomas
J. Reuben Clark Law School
Brigham Young University

SYNOPSIS

§ 106DK.01   Brief History of Danish Law.

§ 106DK.01(a)   Customary Law in Denmark.

Denmark, like the other Scandinavian countries, differs from other European nations in that its legal system does not rest upon a foundation of Roman law.[1] Thus, comprehensive legal codes, such as those promulgated by France and Germany, are not a part of Danish law and jurisprudence. Nor has Denmark followed the pattern of the United Kingdom and the United

---

[1] Ditlev Tamm, *A Survey of Danish Legal History, in* Danish Law: A General Survey 21 (Hans Gammeltoft-Hansen et al., eds. 1982).

States in developing an extensive common law based on judicial decisions. Instead, much of Danish Law is based on custom. In this respect Denmark falls somewhere between Sweden, which gives less weight to custom than Denmark, and Norway, whose jurisprudence relies even more on custom.[2]

The heavy reliance on customary law in Denmark has produced a jurisprudence that is especially national in character. The outside influences that most affect the Danish legal system are those from Sweden and Norway, along with some English and American developments.

§ 106DK.01(b)   Provincial Laws.

The oldest known sources of Danish written law are the so-called provincial laws of the 12th and 13th centuries.[3] During this period the distinct but similar customary laws of the three areas known as Zealand, Scania and Jutland were reduced to writing. These provincial laws revealed an agricultural economy in a social structure based on kinship, but gradually adjusting to the presence of a powerful church and king. A passage from the preamble of the Jutland provincial law opens with the simplistic declaration that "The law shall be honest and just, bearable in accordance with the customs of the country. . .."[4] In addition to invoking the customary law, the provincial laws also enjoined loyalty to the monarch.

The Jutland code, one of the sets of provincial laws, was drafted in 1240. Together with the "Laws of Thord" it was ratified in 1326 by the Danish king and the Council of State and made the law of all of Denmark. By this time the Jutland code contained some canon law.[5]

During the late 13th century, the Danish monarchy grew weaker, leading to the issuance in 1282 of the "recheche," a document similar in significance to the British Magna Carta of 1215. The "recheche" further limited royal prerogatives by requiring that an annual assembly be called to debate the state of the realm.[6] When the Protestant Reformation reached Denmark, with its ideology that public authority rested on a divine foundation, the power of the monarchy grew relatively stronger, and the canon law element in Danish law receded. Royal legislation increased, so that by the mid-16th century, Denmark even attempted to promulgate a code.[7]

§ 106DK.01(c)   The Danish Code.

The conditions for the Danish Code had emerged by 1660, when the

---

[2] Lester Bernhardt Orfield, The Growth of Scandinavian Law 14 (1953).

[3] Ditlev Tamm, *A Survey of Danish Legal History, in* Danish Law: A General Survey 21 (Hans Gammeltoft-Hansen et al., eds. 1982).

[4] *Id.* at 22.

[5] Lester Bernhardt Orfield, The Growth of Scandinavian Law 15 (1953).

[6] Ditlev Tamm, *A Survey of Danish Legal History, in* Danish Law: A General Survey 23 (Hans Gammeltoft-Hansen, et al., eds. 1982).

[7] *Id.* at 24.

Danish monarchy had gained the support of the clergy and the middle class, and had become an absolute monarchy. This "divine-right" absolutism was given a constitutional foundation by the Royal Act of 1665. Thereafter, in 1683, a legal code, published as the *Danish Code of King Christian V*, abolished all previous royal statutes and provincial laws; however, the provisions of the Danish Code itself were largely drawn from the provincial laws, although some Roman law concepts were added in the 18th century, and some German legal theory notions entered into the Code in the 19th century. In general, however, the Code was not based on any coherent notion of legal theory, and contained jurisprudential inconsistencies.[8] The Code has since been supplanted in piecemeal fashion by legislation and today can no longer be considered the foundation of Danish law.[9]

§ 106DK.01(d)   Emergence of Legal Theory in Denmark.

The possibility for indigenous development of legal theory in Denmark arose with the founding of the University of Copenhagen in 1479, but a formal legal examination was not introduced until 1736. Passing the examination did not become a qualification for a judgeship or higher level public administration position until 1821.

At first, the Danish legal education curriculum was based on natural law and Roman law, and Danish law was sometimes included beginning late in the 16th century. This approach to Danish jurisprudence was greatly altered early in the 19th century by the work of the great Danish legal scientist Anders Sandoe Orsted. He favored a historical approach to the law that removed natural law as an authoritative source. Orsted's activities as a drafter of legislation and as a legal philosopher were influenced somewhat by foreign law; he combined his familiarity with foreign law, foreign judicial practice, and a comprehensive knowledge of Danish law to create a system of Danish law which was much more coherent than those previously known. Orsted was instrumental in turning away a proposal to replace the Danish Code, because he feared suddenly abrogating law developed through centuries on the basis of people's characteristics, their customs and familiar conditions.

Orsted did not produce a comprehensive and systematic exposition of Danish law, but he laid the intellectual foundation for Danish legal scientists to do so in later years.

§ 106DK.01(e)   Danish Law in the 19th and 20th Centuries.

A parliamentary form of government was established in Denmark by the

---

[8] Danske Komite for Sammanlignende Retsforskning, Danish and Norwegian Law: A General Survey 10-11 (1963).

[9] Ditlev Tamm, *A Survey of Danish Legal History, in* Danish Law: A General Survey 26 (Hans Gammeltoft-Hansen et al., eds. 1982).

Danish Constitution of June 5, 1849, and various items of comprehensive legislation followed. Also, in the mid-1800's, the idea of a Nordic federation gained support and eventually led to a number of laws adopted uniformly by Denmark, Sweden and Norway. These acts covered such topics as sales of goods, contracts, commissions, commercial agency, commercial travellers, hiring, purchasing, insurance contracts, promissory notes, marriage, property ownership relations of spouses, and capacity and guardianship. The progress of common legislation was optimistically summarized a generation ago:

> In the field of family law there are greater differences between the various Nordic acts than in the field of the law of property and contracts, although it has been possible to demonstrate uniformity in the principles of family legislation at least until recent years.

> Nordic legal cooperation has also resulted in provisions regarding the implementation of bankruptcy, etc.

> Nordic legal cooperation is still being continued, and in the field of civil law, it has resulted, in later years, in new rules on marriage as well as in legislation on adoption, succession, one's right to one's name, and a number of acts regarding intellectual property, such as acts on copyright, trade marks, and patents. A proposal regarding common Nordic rules on extinction and vindication of personal property is still under debate, but does not appear likely to be adopted. A proposal regarding legislation in the field of torts has been adopted in Norway, Sweden, and Finland, but not yet in Denmark.[10]

§ 106DK.02   Danish Real Property Law.

§ 106DK.02(a)   General Principles.

As in other continental European legal systems, Danish law is divided into the law of things and the law of claims. The law of things deals with rights of disposal in such things as real property, personal property, uses and easements. The law of claims covers transfer of rights and specific contractual rights such as tenancy. Mortgages and pledges are an entirely separate branch of jurisprudence. Property rights are protected by the Danish Constitution:

> The right of property shall be inviolable. No person shall be ordered to surrender his property except where required by the public interest. It can be done only as provided by statute and against full compensation.[11]

> Where the public interest requires that a person surrenders his personal or real property for public use, he should be fully compensated by the treasury.[12]

---

[10] *Id.* at 35.

[11] Constitution of Denmark, § 73.

[12] *Id.* at § 105.

The property rights thus protected include all private proprietary rights, including uses, mortgages and claims.[13] The somewhat absolute wording of the constitutional provisions is, in practice, mitigated by the levy of taxes and by "general limitations" on property rights which subject them to various types of governmental regulation. Such limitations appeared even in the 19th century, by means of laws such as the Nature Preservation Act, the Town Planning Act and the Building Regulation Act. A 20th century example is the 1949 Agricultural Holdings Act. The most severe regulatory limitations have resulted from urban planning in the 20th century.

§ 106DK.02(a)(1)   Impact of Urbanization.

The small size of Denmark and the density of its population have resulted in elaborate regulatory schemes governing land use.[14] Generally, no construction can be started without prior approval from municipal authority, except for some farm houses. Permission is again required before the finished buildings may then be used. Detailed regulations apply to such areas as sewage, insulation, and water, as well as various aspects of town planning. Easements may not be created without local council approval.[15] In relations between adjoining landowners, although regulatory legislation has an impact, rights and duties are still defined principally by judicial decisions.[16]

§ 106DK.02(a)(2)   Impact of Environmental Regulation.

Private property rights in Denmark have also been significantly affected by environmental regulation. The Nature Conservation Act and the Environmental Protection Act form the core of the Danish conservation efforts. The Nature Conservation Act is intended to protect the landscape, waterways, lakes, and forests, while the Environmental Protection Act deals with noxious emissions and general protection of the ecological structure. Certain activities which pose an environmental threat are identified by the environmental ministry, and anyone proposing to conduct such an activity must obtain prior ministry approval. Approval, once granted, is usually secure from revocation, but the whole process tends to encourage voluntary compliance.

Subsurface rights are subject to an unusual legal arrangement, as a result of environmental concerns. Subsurface mineral resources that can usefully be extracted, but were not discovered until after February 23, 1932, are owned by the state. Commercially exploitable resources identified prior to

---

[13] Danske Komite for Sammanlignende Retsforskning, Danish and Norwegian Law: A General Survey 131 (1963).

[14] Jesper Berning, *Property Law, in* Danish Law: A General Survey 180 (Hans Gammeltoft-Hansen et al., eds. 1982).

[15] *Id.* at 180–181.

[16] Danske Komite for Sammanlignende Retsforskning, Danish and Norwegian Law: A General Survey 136 (1963).

that date were subject to private ownership. The result of this ownership is that the government owns most of the oil and natural gas reserves.

Even as to those resources subject to private ownership, limitations are imposed. Prior government authorization is required prior to extraction, and restoration of the site is required when extraction is completed.[17]

§ 106DK.02(b)   Transfers of Real Property Interests.

The Danish law governing transfers of real property is preoccupied with the rights of third parties, or, viewed another way, with protecting the rights of the parties to the transfer from challenges by third parties. Most Danish real property transfers are transfers by agreement or transfers of execution by levying creditors.

§ 106DK.02(b)(1)   Transfers by Agreement and Registration.

Transfers of real property may be based on contract or a money claim entitling the creditor to levy execution. The transfer can be made only by one rightfully entitled to dispose of the property. The most important aspect of real property transfers lies in the registration requirements.[18]

Under Denmark's land registration system, all parcels of land are registered and entered as numbered parcels on charts maintained by the Minister of Agriculture. All information pertaining to any individual parcel of land is kept together. The system of recording or registering is considered a judicial function and is administered at the local level, where each "county" maintains a land registry. Difficulties in registration, including a refusal by the local official to perform a registration, may be pursued in the courts.

A right in real estate must be registered in order to enjoy legal protection.[19] An unregistered right is extinguished when the holder of a competing right registers the right in good faith. Good faith means that the holder is unaware of unregistered rights and this ignorance is not due to gross negligence. It is not required that value have been given to acquire the right; a right that is obtained by gift and registered enjoys the full protection of registration. Only rights derived from rights already registered can be registered. If one acquires a right based on a right not previously registered, protection can be obtained only by registering both transfers.

Under Danish registration procedure, upon receipt of the real property transfer document from an applicant, which document must include the applicant's name and address, it is entered in an "application book." Application entries are made chronologically, and legal rights related to

---

[17] *Id.* at 181–183.

[18] Transfers of chattel ownership are evidenced by possession rather than registration, and easements are not included in the registration protections.

[19] Danish Land Registration Act, § 1.

application are determined by the date the application is received and entered by the Land Registry. Entries will be accepted only if the document is properly signed and a copy is attached.

Property interests are sometimes not subject to extinguishment by non-registration, such as when the competing right is based on forgery, false certification, incapacity or violent duress. In these circumstances, the holder of the conflicting interest will not succeed even if acting in good faith; however, the state awards the good faith holder an indemnity.

Some rights do not require registration, such as leases,[20] assignments of registered mortgages, taxes or rates levied on real property and prescriptive rights acquired before the Land Registration Act in 1927 (provided that their prescriptive period of twenty years had lapsed prior to that date).

§ 106DK.02(b)(2)   Transfers by Prescription.

Property interests may be acquired by prescription following possession for twenty years. The statutory foundation for prescription is in the 1683 Danish Code of King Christian V.[21] When real property interests were transferred by oral ceremonies at periodic meetings among community elders, the passing away and failing memories of such witnesses gave rise to the rules of prescription as a means of providing protection for old titles. Fulfillment of the twenty-year requirement must be proven by the user; it is not necessary to prove that the use or occupancy was adverse to the owner's interest; however, the use must have been visible or otherwise apparent.

§ 106DK.02(b)(3)   Transfers by Inheritance.

Although some transfers of property at death are achieved by operation of legislation and by will, most transfers are by intestate succession. This is the most common practice in Denmark.[22] Intestate succession is regulated by the Inheritance Act. Adopted and illegitimate children generally enjoy the same rights as natural and legitimate issue.

The will in Danish law is one of the few documents which is subject to rules of form.[23] A testator must be 18 years old or married, and the document must be in writing and must be signed or confirmed before either a notary public or two witnesses.

§ 106DK.02(b)(4)   Regulations on the Sale of Real Property.

With a few exceptions, undivided property can usually be sold without

---

[20] However, pre-payments of rent longer than six months must be registered in order to gain protection from extinction. *Id.*

[21] §§ 5-5-1, 5-5-3.

[22] Jorgen Norgaard, *The Law of Inheritance, in* Danish Law: A General Survey 97 (Hans Gammeltoft-Hansen et al., eds. 1982).

[23] *Id.* at 107.

restriction. Among the exceptions is a rule that no single person can acquire more than two farms other than by marriage or inheritance. Also, a farm can only be purchased by a natural person who lives on the premises and farms as a principal activity. Foreigners seeking to acquire Danish real estate must first obtain permission from the Ministry of Justice, subject to current European Community law.[24] In some circumstances, principally in areas zoned for urban development and when lots of over 6,000 square meters are being offered, the real estate must be first offered to the public before it can be sold privately. For land in some recreational areas, the public, rather than the designated purchaser, has the right to enter into the purchase contract.

§ 106DK.02(c)   Landlord and Tenant Law.

Traditionally, apartments could only be rented, and not owned. However, in recent years apartment ownership has become possible. Protection for renters in the form of restrictions on rights of termination by the landlord, and rent controls, have been in place since the 1930's.

§ 106DK.02(d)   Ownership of Danish Land by Foreigners.

Subject to current requirements of the European Community, foreigners must obtain permission from the Ministry of Justice before they can acquire real estate in Denmark. For the purpose of this requirement, a foreigner is a non-resident of Denmark.

---

[24] Jesper Berning, *Property Law, in* Danish Law: A General Survey 184 (Hans Gammeltoft-Hansen et al., eds. 1982).

CHAPTER 106EG

PROPERTY LAW IN EGYPT

Professor David A. Thomas
J. Reuben Clark Law School
Brigham Young University

SYNOPSIS

§ 106EG.01   History.

§ 106EG.01(a)   Traditional Islamic Roots.

"The development of the law of real property in Egypt is essentially a development from a traditional law, mostly Islamic in character, to a modern law, mostly defined in Western terms, but still retaining some of the characteristics of the traditional system."[1] This characterization of property law in Egypt also reflects contemporary Egyptian life, where Islamic tradition is intertwined with the Western practices.

The traditional Islamic system of land tenure is a product of the classical Islamic law known as "the *Shari'a*," as well as administrative or "*qanun* law."[2]

> [Although] Muslim jurists did not develop a cohesive theory of property rights, they did develop certain basic principles. According to the classical jurists, a thing in order to be owned must have the following attributes: it must have some value; must be capable of ownership; and its use must be permitted.[3]

Islamic law dictated which things were not qualified to be owned.[4]

Scattered throughout the *Shari'a*, especially in the sections dealing with contracts, acquisition of property, and state revenue, are various statements of principles which, when brought together, sketch an outline system of land tenure:

---

[1] Farhat J. Ziadeh, *Law of Property in Egypt: Real Rights,* 26 Am. J. Comp. L. 239 (1978).

[2] *Id.*

[3] Herbert J. Liebesney, The Law of the Near and Middle East 223 (1975).

[4] *Id.* For example, wine and pork are forbidden under the Islamic Code and were therefore forbidden for ownership. However, jurists were divided as to whether non-Muslims could own forbidden things.

> According to this system land holdings are basically of three types: holdings of private property held in full ownership, holdings of *waqf* lands, i.e. lands held in perpetuity with the income devoted for the upkeep of a charity or the family of the constitutor of the *waqf* and holdings of state-owned lands with various conditions of tenure.[5]

The first two types mentioned above were dealt with extensively in the *Shari'a*; however, the third category, though arguably the most important in terms of revenue and production, was dealt with only passingly. As a result, the state regulated state-owned lands through the *qanun* or administrative law.[6]

> The *Shari'a* was regarded by all, including the jurists, as a divinely ordained code of morality designed to shape a virtuous community on earth and prepare human beings for the hereafter. To enforce it was the responsibility, indeed the raison d'etre, of the state, and to transgress against it a sin as much as a crime.[7]

§ 106EG.01(b)   Original Types of Land Tenure Contemplated by the Shari'a.

§ 106EG.01(b)(1)   Taxable Private Holdings.

In early Islamic centuries classification of real property was not based on ownership rights as much as on the amount of tax the state could obtain, based on the amount of revenue generated by the land.[8] Lands were classified as either *ushri* or *kharaji*, depending on the type of tax paid.

The *ushri* (tithe) was a religious tax paid by the absolute owner of cultivated land as part of almsgiving (*zakat*). Usually, the tax amounted to approximately one-tenth of the produce of the land.[9] The *ushri* landholder acquired this status by converting to Islam, if the landholder was a member of an Arabian tribe or if the land was included as spoils of war acquired by the invading Moslem soldiers.

The *kharaj* was the tax levied on the non-Muslim landholders. It is not known if these lands were held in *mulk* (full ownership); however, the tax came to be viewed as a rent or tribute.[10] The tax levied on the *kharaj* holder could be as high as one-half of the produce.[11]

---

[5] Farhat J. Ziadeh, Property Law in the Arab World 1 (1979).

[6] *Id.*

[7] Abraham Marcus, *Real Property and Society in the Premodern Middle East: A Case Study, in* Property Social Structure and Law in the Modern Middle East 109 (Ann Elizabeth Mayer ed. 1985).

[8] Farhat J. Ziadeh, *Law of Property in Egypt: Real Rights,* 26 Am. J. Comp. L. 238 (1978).

[9] Farhat J. Ziadeh, Property Law in the Arab World 2 (1979).

[10] Farhat J. Ziadeh, *Law of Property in Egypt: Real Rights,* 26 Am. J. Comp. L. 241 (1978).

[11] Farhat J. Ziadeh, Property Law in the Arab World 2 (1979).

§ 106EG.01(b)(2)   State-Owned Holdings.

Lands that were neither *ushri* or *kharaj* were part of the state domain. The state held the lands in full ownership and was clearly the proprietor. When conquered by the state, these lands were conveyed or conceded as an *iqta'tamlik* (a concession of full ownership) or an *iqta'istighlal* (a concession of the right to use property, with title remaining vested in the state). The latter form in later centuries became the "feudal system" of the Islamic empire. *Mawat* or "dead lands" were those lands deemed to be ownerless and uncultivated (normally stretches of desert); however, jurists held that ownership of *mawat* lands was nevertheless vested in the state.[12]

§ 106EG.01(b)(3)   *Waqf* Landholdings.

Waqf lands were in a class of their own, because of their unique characteristics of inalienability and perpetuity of title.[13] "The title (*raqabah*) was immobilized forever and the usufruct was to be used for the support of a charitable organization or a family (with a reversion to charity in the case of extinction of the family)."[14]

Waqf lands were not to be leased for long periods of time, and because of this restriction, improvement on the land was deterred rather than encouraged. In the centuries that followed, however, legal devices were created to circumvent the restriction and bring about long-term leases. These leases in Egypt were most commonly known as "*ijaratayn, hikr* or *khuluw.*"[15]

Contrary to the laws established in the *Shari'a*, "in later centuries the state allowed the holders of its concessions to constitute their interests in *waqf.*" The *Shari'a* permits only *mulk* lands to become *waqf*. Holders of concessions did not have title to dedicate in perpetuity and as such their *waqfs* were termed "untrue" or "unsound."[16]

Kharaji lands were later assimilated into the state domain category, where the state gradually succeeded to possession of those lands possibly through escheat or confiscation, but more likely by the introduction of tax farming and assignments of the land to pay state debts. Subsequently, a feudal system was established where the *kharaji* lands were assigned to the "feudal lords."[17]

---

[12] Farhat J. Ziadeh, *Law of Property in Egypt: Real Rights,* 26 Am. J. Comp. L. 241 (1978).

[13] Farhat J. Ziadeh, Property Law in the Arab World 2 (1979).

[14] Farhat J. Ziadeh, *Law of Property in Egypt: Real Rights,* 26 Am. J. Comp. L. 242 (1978).

[15] Farhat J. Ziadeh, Property Law in the Arab World 3 (1979).

[16] *Id.*

[17] Farhat J. Ziadeh, *Law of Property in Egypt: Real Rights,* 26 Am. J. Comp. L. 242 (1978).

§ 106EG.01(c)   Pre-19th Century Historical Developments.

The feudal system was in full force by the time the Mamluks came to power in the thirteenth century. Under the Mamluk system,

> all state-domain lands held by private individuals were subject to the disposition of the state. Also, just as *kharaji* lands had been assimilated into the state domain, much former *mulk* land and even *waqf* land, was taken over by the state and regulated as state domain under *qanun* law.[18]

These lands were then distributed to mainly military fief holders as concessions and the state allowed a form of *waqf* (*rizqah ahbasiyah*) on the usufruct of these state lands.[19]

The Ottomans ruled over Egypt beginning in 1517, adding their own modifications to the feudal system of land tenure. Changes included abolishing the Mamluk fiefs and re-establishing tax farms from the land that had reverted to state domain. The tax farmers were given the right to collect taxes from the *kharaj* and retain the portion over that which they were required to pay the state.[20] The tax-farmers were granted land for their personal use, and eventually they acquired rights to the land similar to those of the fiefs in Mamluk times.[21] "Those rights included a life interest in the tax farm with the power to alienate, mortgage, or lease that interest," and their children were given priority to succeed to the rights at the death of the tax-farmer. The tax-farmers were even granted certain justiciable powers over the peasants working on their land.[22] In theory these lands were state lands, although their form of land tenure was different.

This system of land tenure continued into the nineteenth century, at which time there were three forms of property holdings: private property (*mulk*), *waqfs* and state lands. The *mulk* lands were limited to the urban areas and agricultural lands were almost entirely state-held lands (directly through the royal domain or through state farms). However, private property holdings and state lands became more and more difficult to distinguish, because of the expanding property rights of state landholders.[23]

§ 106EG.01(d)   Influences from the 19th Century to the Modern Civil Code.

§ 106EG.01(d)(1)   Muhammad Ali to Ismali.

Muhammad Ali was appointed governor in 1805 by the ruling Ottoman

---

[18] *Id.*

[19] *Id.*

[20] *Id.*

[21] *Id.* at 243.

[22] Farhat J. Ziadeh, Property Law in the Arab World 3 (1979).

[23] Farhat J. Ziadeh, *Law of Property in Egypt: Real Rights,* 26 Am. J. Comp. L. 243 (1978).

Empire. When he came to power, his main objective in the area of land tenure was to reassert the diminished state rights in state land. Immediately tax-farms were abolished and replaced with a burdensome direct tax system, within which even the lands granted to tax-farmers for their private use were subject to tax. Former tax exempt lands such as the *rizqah ahbasiyah* were made subject to the tax and other property holdings were confiscated, leaving former landholders with only a life estate. "By destroying the privileged position of the nobility, Muhammad Ali laid the ground for the later development of extensive private property holdings by the peasantry."[24]

In 1829 Muhammed Ali began redistribution of the land by granting uncultivated land (not included in the cadaster).[25] These lands eventually became indistinguishable from private property and by the mid-1800's under Said private property holdings were significantly increased.[26]

Three important decrees followed that increased individual interests in property. First, the Decree of Ismail (1863-79) allowed *kharaj* landholders to dispose of property at will, previously allowed only with *mulk* lands. Second, the Muqabalh Law of 1871 allowed *kharaj* owners to purchase the fee simple ownership of their land. Third, the Decree of 1896 finally abolished all distinctions between *kharaj* and *mulk* lands, declaring both as "lands of full ownership."[27]

§ 106EG.01(d)(2)   Ottoman Charter of 1841.

The Ottoman Charter of 1841 gave Egypt the right to enact its own land law, rather than adhere to Ottoman law. As a result of the Charter, Egypt never adopted the Ottoman Land Law of 1858 or the Majallah, the Ottoman Civil Code.[28]

§ 106EG.01(d)(3)   Mixed and National Courts.

The Mixed Courts were created in 1876 "to protect foreign interests and the promulgation of the Mixed Civil Code to be used in those courts, based on the Napoleonic Code."[29] The National Courts were created in 1882 to protect and promulgate the National Civil Code and national interests.[30] Both were based on the Napoleonic Code, probably a remnant of the 1798 Napoleonic invasion.

However, there still remained a considerable amount of Islamic law,

---

[24] *Id.*

[25] The cadaster was a public register of land ownership used in assessing taxes. *Id.* at 244.

[26] *Id.*

[27] *Id.*

[28] *Id.*

[29] *Id.* at 245.

[30] *Id.*

because of the unique nature of Egyptian land tenure, which could not be covered by a non-Islamic code. In 1889 Mixed Courts were ordered to apply all Egyptian laws pertaining to lands, embankments and canals. The *Shari'a* Courts, however, still had jurisdiction over all matters involving the *waqf*.[31]

Among the codes' greatest contributions to Egyptian property law was organization, "by clearly defining property rights and means of acquiring and disposing of those rights." Another contribution was the distinction between the private and public domain of state-owned lands, which later under the 1948 council of the state proved to be important.[32]

§ 106EG.02   The New Civil Code.

§ 106EG.02(a)   Introduction.

On October 15, 1949, the new civil code was adopted.[33] This new Egyptian Civil Code was drafted by an Egyptian jurist and a French jurist and superseded all previous codes. The new civil code is a combination of the *Shari'a*, the old codes, jurisprudence from Egyptian courts, and a variety of modern civil codes from twenty European, Asian, African and American nations.

> Fortunately for the drafters of the Code, there had been so much consolidation of real property laws in previous reform measures that their work consisted primarily of revising the law relating to only one form of land tenure, private ownership. State lands and *waqf* lands, the two other categories of land holdings, were regulated by provisions of the Code in a manner consistent with other provisions of civil law. The later abolition of the family *waqf* and the restrictions on land ownership effected after the Revolution of 1952 affected property rights, but for the most part the provisions of the Civil Code continue in force today.[34]

§ 106EG.02(b)   Aspects of Real Property.

§ 106EG.02(b)(1)   Ownership of Real Property.

§ 106EG.02(b)(1)(i)   Rights of Ownership.

Article 802 of the new Civil Code defines ownership as the exclusive right to use, enjoy and dispose of a thing.[35] When adopting the Code, the Senate required that the whole Code be consistent with the "social function" doctrine of ownership, although this is not made explicit in the Code. This means that an owner is protected in rights ownership, as long as those rights

---

[31] *Id.*

[32] *Id.*

[33] *Id.*

[34] *Id.*

[35] *Id.* at 250.

do not conflict with a public interest or with a worthy special interest.[36]

Article 803 provides that ownership of land "includes that which lies above and below the surface of the land to the extent that it can be beneficially used by the owner."[37] However, the state may use the airspace and the land below the surface as a matter of public interest, if that use does not damage the property. An owner can be deprived of property only as prescribed by law and with restitution.[38]

§ 106EG.02(b)(1)(ii)   Restrictions on Ownership.

The first restriction on ownership is a general prohibition against abuse of rights.[39] Article 807 states:

> (1) The owner must not exercise his rights in an excessive manner detrimental to his neighbor's property.

> (2) The neighbor has no right of action against his neighbor for the usual unavoidable inconveniences from neighborhood, but he may claim the suppression of such inconveniences if they exceed the usual limits, taking in consideration . . . custom, the nature of properties, their respective situations and the use for which they are intended.

Two other restrictions are embodied in the principles of ancient lights and privacy, which are particularly important in Islamic countries, and rules on the free alienability of land.[40] As to ancient lights and privacy, Article 819 does not allow a neighbor to have a direct view into his neighbor's property unless the view is of a distance of more than one meter (barring a prescriptive right, in which case the neighbor cannot build within one meter distance). If it is not a direct view, then the view must be of a distance of at least half a meter. A light shaft must be built above the normal height of a person and must be for only air and light and not for a view into a neighbor's property (Article 821).

As to alienability, it may be restricted if a contract or will contains a clause stipulating the inalienability of property, but such a clause will only be valid if based on a legitimate reason and limited to a reasonable duration.[41] Legitimate reason is deemed to mean the protection of a lawful interest of a party to the will or contract and a reasonable duration is the duration of the life of any of the parties.[42]

§ 106EG.02(b)(1)(iii)   Joint Ownership.

Article 825 of the Civil Code defines joint ownership as follows: "When

---

[36] *Id.*

[37] *Id.* at 251.

[38] *Id.*

[39] Farhat J. Ziadeh, Property Law in the Arab World 27 (1979).

[40] *Id.* at 28.

[41] *Id.* at 29.

[42] *Id.*

two or more persons are owners of the same thing, but their respective shares are not divided, they are co-owners and, in the absence of proof to the contrary, their shares are deemed equal."

The joint owner has rights limited to the share, although the right may affect the entire property. The joint owner has rights of use of the entire property and of its fruits, but is limited by the rights of the other joint owners.

Article 826 provides that the joint owner may alienate the share as long as it does not cause damage to the other joint owners.

Special types of joint ownership include obligatory joint ownership, family joint ownership, and joint ownership of stories in a building. Obligatory joint ownership is when "the co-owners of a property held in common cannot demand its partition if it follows from the use to which the property is intended that it should always remain in common (Article 850)."

Family joint ownership was derived from Swiss and Italian law. This joint ownership may be created through an agreement limited to fifteen years, with flexibility as to withdrawal of any of the co-owners with six months notice. The purpose of such a joint ownership is to limit it to family members who may have a common interest in property.[43]

Islamic law is the major contributor to the law governing joint ownership in stories of a building.

> The Code delineates the parts of a building which are owned in common under a joint ownership agreement and stipulates the rights of the co-owners in the jointly-owned premises. The Code outlines the obligation of the owner of a lower story to make repairs of the lower story to prevent higher stories from falling (Art. 859). In the case of the building falling the owner of the lower story is bound to rebuild his story, and the Code provides remedies for his failing to do so (Art. 860).[44]

§ 106EG.02(b)(2)   Acquisition of Real Property.

§ 106EG.02(b)(2)(i)   Appropriation.

Article 874 of the Code states:

> If . . . an Egyptian cultivates or plants uncultivated land or builds thereon, he becomes forthwith owner of the part cultivated, planted, or built on, even without the authority of the state, but he loses his ownership by non-use for five consecutive years during the first fifteen years following his acquisition of ownership.

A 1958 amendment limited the reclamation areas and a 1964 amendment imposed a requirement of state authority. Under the Land Reform Act, some

---

[43] *Id.* at 31-33.

[44] Farhat J. Ziadeh, *Law of Property in Egypt: Real Rights,* 26 Am. J. Comp. L. 252 (1978).

of the *mawat* lands that could be irrigated through subterranean waters were sold rather than acquired through improvement. These lands were subject to several conditions.

§ 106EG.02(b)(2)(ii)   Succession.

The laws of inheritance in the Code are completely governed by the *Shari'a*. All outstanding debts must be settled prior to any distribution to heirs.[45] In practice, this means that:

> (1) the property is subject to the real rights of the estate's creditors, which are akin to the rights of a mortgage;

> (2) the heirs may dispose of the property if they register their rights of inheritance with the proper government bureau, but such disposal is subject to the rights of creditors; and

> (3) the registration of the rights of the creditors renders those rights effective as against third parties.[46]

§ 106EG.02(b)(2)(iii)   Accession.

Accession is the joining of two distinct properties without an agreement between the owners.[47] This occurs when an owner of land acquires materials that are not part of the land, but to remove them would cause serious damage. The owner who acquires by accession must pay the value of the materials plus indemnification, if indemnity is due (Art. 923). If a landowner in good faith builds accidently on a neighbor's land, a court may rule for the transfer of that land to the builder as long as adequate compensation is paid (Art. 928).[48]

Accession by natural forces, such as shifting of river banks, usually does not change ownership.[49]

§ 106EG.02(b)(2)(iv)   Contract.

Transfer of property by contract is the most common type of transfer, other than by inheritance.[50]

> While the code stipulates that ownership of movables and immovables may be transferred by contract (Art. 932), it also provides that real rights

---

[45] *Id.* at 253.

[46] *Id.* at 253-54.

[47] *Id.* at 254.

[48] *Id.*

[49] Art. 918: Alluvium deposited by a river belongs to the adjoining owner. Art. 919: Land uncovered by the sea belongs to the state. Art. 920: Retreat or flooding of water does not change ownership boundaries of land. Art. 921 changed by Law No. 100 of 1964, which states that lands uncovered by a river and islands that form in a channel belong to the state.

[50] Farhat J. Ziadeh, *Law of Property in Egypt: Real Rights,* 26 Am. J. Comp. L. 254 (1978).

over immovable property, including ownership, are not transferred between parties or as regards third parties unless the law regulating the publication of real rights (*al shahr alaqari*) is observed (Art. 934).[51]

Ownership is considered to have been transferred at the time of contract only if the registration has already occurred.[52] Registration has been traditionally filed under the names of the parties; however, a 1964 law creates a system of registration based on plots of land, with implementation depending on a new cadastral survey.

§ 106EG.02(b)(2)(v)   Preemption.

Article 935 defines preemption as "one's right to substitute himself in place of the purchaser in certain sales of immovable property, subject to certain conditions." The Civil Code's provisions of preemption are based on a combination of the two different laws in the Mixed and National Codes. The preemption doctrine was retained in the new Civil Code, despite great opposition, because it was considered historically significant.[53] However, the doctrine was severely restricted.[54]

§ 106EG.02(b)(2)(vi)   Possession.

The new Civil Code attempted to define possession, but it was defeated by the senate and therefore there is no definition of possession in the Code. Possession includes acquisition, transfer, and loss. There is no adverse possession.[55]

Possession can be transferred in two ways: (1) By the effect of law, as with an heir and; (2) as a means of disposal, such as contract or bequest.[56] "Possession ceases when the possessor abandons actual control over the

---

[51] *Id.* at 254-55.

[52] *Id.* at 255.

[53] *Id.*

[54] The right of preemption may be exercised by the following, listed in preferential order: (1) the bare owner; (2) the co-owner in common; (3) the usufructuary; (4) in the case of a *hikr*; (5) the neighboring owner in some cases, as when a servitude exists, buildings are upon the land, or if the land is on both sides of the property and at least half the value of the land has been sold.

A person may not exercise a preemptive right if: (1) the sale is by public auction; (2) the sale is made to relatives; (3) the property sold is for religious purposes or to be annexed to property already for that purpose.

The Code requires that the preemptor notify both the purchaser and the vendor of intentions to preempt (Arts. 940-491), notify within a strict time limit (Art. 943), and deposit the full sale price of the property with the court of the district in which the property is situated, prior to any action towards preemption (Art. 942).

[55] Farhat J. Ziadeh, Property Law in the Arab World 51 (1979).

[56] *Id.*

right or when he loses it any other way."[57]

§ 106EG.02(b)(3)   Types of Interests in Real Property.

§ 106EG.02(b)(3)(i)   Usufruct.

The Egyptian Code does not define usufruct. The right of usufruct is a real right for the use and exploitation of a thing that belongs to another.[58] Usufruct is a right attached to the land and terminates at the death of the usufructuary.[59] "In Egypt, . . . ownership of a right of usufruct is uncommon because the right does not arise by operation of law between spouses or between parents and children and only rarely does a person give a right of usufruct to another by contract or will."[60] Article 985 of the Civil Code provides that ". . . a usufruct may be bequeathed to successive persons only if they are alive at the time of the bequest . . . [and may include] a child en ventre."

Article 993 provides that if the usufruct terminates before the harvest period, because of an expired term or the death of the usufructuary, the period is extended to ripening of the crops.

Articles 987–995 provide for extinction of the right as a result of non-use over a period of fifteen years; they also regulate the uses of the property, the liability of the usufructuary for normal expenses, and repairs to maintain the property.

§ 106EG.02(b)(3)(ii)   *Hikr.*

"*Hikr* is a lease whose duration is longer than that of an ordinary lease and creates a right in the lessor."[61] Egypt has recognized long leases on *waqf* property for modest rents. The lessee can exploit the land and repair it extensively in exchange for the rent paid.[62]

The Code relies on Islamic law to establish the rules regulating *hikrs*. Article 999 limits the duration of the *hikrs* to sixty years. Article 1012 established that all *hikrs* must be on lands recognized as *waqfs*. Article 936(d) provides for the extinction of the *hikr* through preemption either by the holder of the *hikr* or the owner of the property. Article 1000 provides that a ". . . *hikr* can only be concluded with the permission of a judge upon a showing of expediency." Article 1001 provides that ". . . the grantee of a *hikr*, having a real interest, may dispose of it and transmit it by inheritance."

---

[57] *Id.* at 52.

[58] *Id.* at 61.

[59] *Id.*

[60] Farhat J. Ziadeh, *Law of Property in Egypt: Real Rights,* 26 Am. J. Comp. L. 260 (1978).

[61] *Id.* at 261.

[62] *Id.*

Article 1002 establishes that improvements made on the *hikr* belong to the grantee. Article 1004 provides that a *hikr* cannot be concluded for less than the rent given for similar lands. Finally, Article 1011 establishes that if the *hikr* is not used in thirty-three years it reverts to the status of a *waqf.*

Two types of *hikr* are recognized: (1) "two rents" (*ijaratayn*) and (2) *khuluw al-intifa.* Under the first, the *hikr* is paid under two rents. The first rent is a lump sum for the value of the building and the second is an annual payment related to the value of the land. The second type of *hikr* is "a contract by which a *waqf* leases property for an indefinite period of time for a fixed rent."[63] *Hikrs* have little significance in the modern era, especially after a 1952 law abolishing *waqfs.*

§ 106EG.02(b)(3)(iii)   Servitudes.

Article 1015 of the Egyptian Civil Code defines servitude "as a right which limits a property owner's enjoyment of his land and which exists for the benefit of land belonging to another person." Servitudes contain three elements: the dominant tenement, the servient tenement and the benefit which the servient tenement provides for the dominant tenement.[64]

Servitudes survive transfers, are transmitted to the dominant owner, and continue to burden the servient tenement. According to Article 1015 of the Civil Code a servitude may be imposed upon state property, provided that it is not incompatible with the use for which such property is intended.[65]

Servitudes are created by contract or prescription, when there is a discernible object indicating the existence of the servitude. If the servitude is not apparent or visible, it cannot be obtained through a prescription. According to the Civil Code, a prescription may also be created by specification (*takhsis*) of the original owner of the land.[66] "A specification is created when the owner of two separate properties places a visible marker between the two properties, thereby creating a dominant-servient relation-ship between them, which would indicate the existence of a servitude if the two properties belonged to different owners."[67]

Extinction of a servitude occurs after fifteen years of non-use, unless created for the benefit of a *waqf,* in which case the period is thirty-three years. A servitude may also end if it is no longer useful or its burden is disproportionately greater than its benefit. However, if the burden outweighs the benefit, compensation may be required for the forfeiture of the

---

[63] *Id.* at 261-262.

[64] *Id.* at 263.

[65] *Id.*

[66] *Id.*

[67] *Id.* at 263-264.

servitude.[68]

§ 106EG.02(b)(4)   Real Securities.

§ 106EG.02(b)(4)(i)   Mortgage.

The Code defines mortgage as ". . . a contract by which a creditor acquires a real right over an immovable pledged to the payment of his debt, by which he obtains preference over ordinary creditors and secured creditors following a rank to proceeds from a sale of the immovable. A right to the proceeds from a sale of the immovable obtains to the creditor even if the debtor has sold the pledged property to a third person."[69]

According to Article 1041, a mortgage is indivisible, and if the heirs inherit mortgaged property, it continues to be mortgaged for the entire outstanding debt. Article 1031 requires that the mortgage only be constituted through a *rasmi* (authentic or official document). A mortgage ranks solely from the date of its registration, regardless of whether it secures a conditional, future or contingent debt.

§ 106EG.02(b)(4)(ii)   Judgment Charge.

A judgment charge, which differs from a mortgage in its mode of acquisition, may, if obtained in good faith by a creditor, be imposed on immovable property of the debtor as security for a claim. If the debtor dies, a creditor cannot obtain a judgment charge.[70]

§ 106EG.02(b)(4)(iii)   Pledge.

Article 1096 of the Egyptian Civil Code defines the pledge as ". . . a contract by which a person undertakes, as security for his debt or the debt of a third person, to give possession of property (or a real right in property) to a creditor or a person chosen by both parties to take possession in place of the creditor." Possession is retained until the debt is paid; however, in the event of default the right or pledge may be sold to satisfy the debt.

§ 106EG.02(b)(4)(iv)   Privileged Right.

Article 1130 of the Egyptian Civil Code defines the privileged right as a preference accorded to a particular right because of its quality. The commentary of the Code explains that it is the right itself which is privileged, and not the creditor holding the right, and that law determines which rights are to be privileged, as well as how privileged rights are to be ranked.

Three reasons for according preferences are: (1) expenses incurred for the

---

[68] *Id.* at 264.

[69] Article 1030 of the Egyptian Civil Code.

[70] Farhat J. Ziadeh, *Law of Property in Egypt: Real Rights,* 26 Am. J. Comp. L. 266 (1978).

common good by a creditor benefit all creditors and should therefore have preference (legal proceedings for the sale and preservation of property are privileged against that property); (2) a public policy argument that taxes and duties are privileged, only preempted by legal proceedings; (3) movables for their repair and preservation are secured by a privileged right against the movable.[71]

> The general rules relating to privileges are similar to those governing pledges and mortgages. A privilege cannot exist against a good-faith holder of a movable (Art. 1133). A privileged right against immovable property is subject to the same rules as mortgages, to the extent that such rules are compatible with that type of privilege right (Art. 1134). Finally, privileges are extinguished by the operation of the same rules which extinguish mortgages and pledges (Art. 1136).[72]

§ 106EG.02(b)(5)   Leases.

§ 106EG.02(b)(5)(i)   Introduction.

General provisions of the Civil Code deal with the elements of a lease, the effects of a lease, the assignment of a lease and sublease, the termination of a lease and the death or insolvency of the lessee.[73] The Code places responsibility on the lessor to enable the lessee to enjoy the leased property.

> The principal obligations of the lessor to the lessee under the new code are the obligations to: (1) deliver the leased property and its accessories, (2) maintain the leased property in the same state it was at the time of delivery, (3) abstain from doing anything which may disturb the lessee in his enjoyment of the leased property and warrant against any disturbance or damage based on a lawful claim by any other lessee or any successor in title of the lessor, and (4) warrant against all defects which prevent or appreciably diminish the enjoyment of all property (Arts. 564, 567, 571, 576).[74]

§ 106EG.02(b)(5)(ii)   Agricultural Leases.

The Code addresses agricultural leases; however, they have since been modified and supplemented by the provisions in the Agrarian Reform Law of 1952. The Civil Code deals with cattle and agricultural fixtures on the land, defines the agricultural year, establishes use and maintenance of a land's fertility, prevents the lessee from destroying crop or seed, protects the lessee's right to harvest, and requires the lessee to allow the succeeding lessee to prepare the land for sowing.

The Reform Act established rent ceilings, the length of time a lease could

---

[71] *Id.* at 268.

[72] Ziadeh, p. 269.

[73] *Id.* at 248.

[74] *Id.*

run (which was later extended), and required that valid leases be in writing. The Reform Act also limited agricultural leases only to those who worked the land themselves.

§ 106EG.02(b)(5)(iii)   Waqf Lease.

The *waqf* lease, prior to the new Civil Code, was always placed under Islamic courts' jurisdiction and never categorized with normal leases, except under the National Code. Articles 628–634 of the Civil Code adopted provisions from Islamic law to protect the *waqf* lease. According to the Code:

> The *nazir* (guardian) of the *waqf* property has the right to let property, but a beneficiary of a *waqf* has no such right unless the constitutor of the *waqf* specifically grants it to him or unless the *nazir* or a judge authorizes him to exercise it. . . . The *nazir*, with certain exceptions, may not lease *waqf* property for more than three years, and leases of *waqf* property made for grossly inadequate consideration are invalid.[75]

§ 106EG.02(b)(6)   Landlord/Tenant Law.

In the past, landlord/tenant law had been governed by a lease contract with no restrictions. With practically the entire population living on about three percent of the total land of Egypt, population density and congestion have forced more clear-cut regulation of landlord/tenant law. The state has also stepped in on this previously "free relationship between owners and tenants," because of the need to keep social balance and political stability in a country where much recent change has keenly affected the housing market.[76]

In recent years there has been a migration to Cairo, raising demand for housing and at the same time increasing rents ten to fifteen times within three years.[77] Previous laws controlling rents had left investors and landlords bitter, and many now sell their separate units (*tamlik*) in the free market even before construction is complete.[78] In 1977, the government tried to limit the sale of *tamlik* in order to increase the availability of rental flats, but investors found ways to avoid the restricting law.[79] As a result there has been an increase of "informal housing" and of the practice of paying "key money"[80]

---

[75] *Id.* at 249.

[76] Milad M. Hanna, *Real Estate Rights in Urban Egypt: The Changing Sociopolitical Winds, in* Property Social Structure in the Modern Middle East 189 (Ann Elizabeth Mayer ed., 1985).

[77] *Id.* at 200.

[78] *Id.* at 204.

[79] *Id.* at 205.

[80] *Id.* at 207.

to obtain a rent-controlled flat.[81]

§ 106EG.03   Recent Changes in Egyptian Property Law.

§ 106EG.03(a)   Agricultural Reforms.

Many changes occurred under Nasser's "revolutionary regime"; among them were:

> those relative to the reclamation of land, the ownership of land formed by the action of water, the abolition of private *waqfs* and the placing of lands of charitable *waqfs* and of the private domain of the state beyond the pale of acquisitive prescription, and the virtual elimination of *hikr*. All these changes were predicated upon the Agrarian Reform Law of 1952 (no. 178) and the philosophy on which it was based.[82]

The Agrarian Reform Law brought about sweeping land ownership reform and targeted large landowners by limiting the amount of land a person could own to 200 acres. Gradually, this ownership area has been expanded. The Agrarian Reform Law also limited the minimum period of leases to three years, although this, too, was later extended. Leases were required to be in writing.[83]

§ 106EG.03(b)   Foreign Ownership of Land.

Nasser's Administration attacked foreign ownership of Egyptian land, either by severely restricting or banning it outright.[84] In 1963, land owned by foreigners was expropriated. However, when Sadat came to power, a policy of allowing foreigners to own land was re-introduced. "He promised repatriation and guaranteed both foreign and domestic investors that their properties would not be expropriated. Sadat has also given $10 million in compensation to Americans whose holdings were confiscated by Nasser in 1961."[85]

However, the move towards allowing foreigners to own property has been slow. In 1978, foreigners were not allowed to own property worth more than 1,000 Egyptian pounds. This is a sore subject, particularly with non-Egyptian Arabs who would like to purchase land in Egypt.[86]

---

[81] *Id.* at 206-7.

[82] Farhat J. Ziadeh, *Law of Property in Egypt: Real Rights,* 26 Am. J. Comp. L. 271 (1978).

[83] *Id.* at 270.

[84] David F.Forte, *Egyptian Land Law: An Evaluation,* 26 Am. J. Comp. L. 276 (1978).

[85] *Id.* at 276.

[86] *Id.* at 277.

CHAPTER 106EU

PROPERTY LAWS IN THE EUROPEAN UNION AND THEIR IMPACT ON MEMBER STATES

Professor David A. Thomas
J. Reuben Clark Law School
Bringham Young University[1]

SYNOPSIS

§ 106EU.01   The Structure and Governance of the European Union.

§ 106EU.02   The Council of Europe and Property Law.

§ 106EU.03   The European Union and Property Law.

§ 106EU.03(a)   Principal Property Laws and Regulations of the European Union.

§ 106EU.03(b)   Property Case Law of the European Court of Justice.

§ 106EU.01   The Structure and Governance of the European Union.

In 1951, six European countries signed the Treaty of Paris and thereby formed the European Coal & Steel Community (ECSC).[2] This treaty sought to create a common market for raw materials that are often used to make weapons. The theory was that a common community would be less likely to go to war with itself. The success of this treaty led to the Treaty of Rome in 1957.[3] With this document the European Economic Community (EEC) was born and remains the basis of the European Union (EU). In 1987, the Treaty of Rome was amended by the Single European Act which created more economic and social uniformity among the Member States.[4] The most significant treaty for the establishment of the EU as central governing entity

---

[1] Samuel Smith, Esq., contributed significantly to the research and writing of this section.

[2] Treaty Instituting the European Coal and Steel Community, Apr. 18, 1951, 261 U.N.T.S. 140.

[3] Treaty Establishing the European Economic Community, Mar. 25, 1957, 298 U.N.T.S. 11.

[4] Single European Act, June 29, 1987, O.J. (L 169) 1 (1987), 2 C.M.L.R. 741 (1987) (amending Treaty Establishing the European Economic Community).

was the Maastricht Treaty on European Union, signed in 1993.[5] Here, the Treaty of Rome was furthered amended to advance the economic purposes of the European community and clarify certain points of conflict.

In 1997, the EU again convened to sign another amendment to the Treaty on European Union.[6] This was done to prepare the EU economic changes, provision for threats to security and public health and crime.[7] The Treaty of Amsterdam directed the EU to have another conference where further changes would be made to the Treaty on European Union. In 2001, the Treaty on European Union was again amended in Nice to prepare for enlargement of the EU.[8] It included changes in voting structures and increased cooperation among the member states. To this date no further treaties have been signed by the Member States. However, in May of 2004 ten new Member States were admitted into the EU.

The four essential organs that make up the EU are the European Council of Ministers (Council), the European Commission (Commission), the European Parliament (EP) and the European Court of Justice (ECJ). Each of these organs works in cooperation with the others in order to achieve the goals set out in the Treaties on the European Union.

The Council consists of representatives from governments of the Member States, and has the primary legislative power within the EU. Its acts are binding upon the Member States. The four different types of legislation that the Council can enact are Regulations, Directives, Decisions and Recommendation or Opinions. The Regulations are directly operative within each of the Member States and do not require any further legislation by them. The Directives are binding objectives given to the Member States but allow each Member State the freedom to implement the measures according to national policies. Decisions are binding upon those to whom they are addressed. Finally, Recommendation or Opinions are persuasive ideas but are not binding. Council Presidents are in office for six months at a time and the presidency rotates among the Member States. The powers of the Council are checked by the Commission who has the sole power to initiate legislation.[9]

The Commission is the executive organ of the EU, with primary responsibility to propose legislative measures, ensure that legislation is

---

[5] Treaty on European Union, Feb. 7, 1992, O.J. (C 224) 1 (1992) (amending Treaty Establishing the European Economic Community, as amended by Single European Act) [hereinafter Maastricht Treaty].

[6] Treaty of Amsterdam Amending the Treaty on European Union, the Treaties Establishing the European Communities and Certain Related Acts, Oct. 2, 1997, O.J. (C 340) 1 (1997).

[7] *Id.*

[8] Treaty of Nice Amending the Treaty on European Union, The Treaties Establishing the European Communities and Certain Related Acts, Feb. 26, 2001, O.J. (C 80) 1 (2001).

[9] *See* Council's Website available at atue.eu.int/en/summ.htm.

followed, and prosecute when proper legislative procedures are not followed. It consists of twenty commissioners from each of the Member States. These commissioners are appointed for five years by common agreement among the Member States. The Commission is able to act quickly because there are limited checks on its authority; however, it is not accountable to the people.[10] Instead, accountability rests on the European Parliament (EP).

With 626 members, the EP represents the entire populace of the Member States of the EU. It is designed to express the political sentiments of the various constituencies throughout Europe. Representatives or MEPs are elected directly by the people and serve five-year terms. EP has the power to censure the Commission, and has a limited veto power over legislation. In the latest version of the Treaty on the European Union the EP was given what is called "co-decision procedure." This basically requires legislation to pass through the EP before it can be made into EU law.[11] For the EU to ultimately enforce all of the laws that could potentially be created by all of these organizations it is necessary to have a supreme court that settles disputes concerning the treaties and legislative materials of the EU.

That court is the European Court of Justice (ECJ), which is the ultimate authority for resolving legal disputes within the realm of EU law.[12] It handles legal actions against both EU institutions and Member States. Its fifteen judges serve six-year terms. Article 177 of the Treaty on the European Union (Treaty) details its jurisdiction and competency. Decisions from the ECJ include interpretations of the Treaty on the validity of EU institutions and resolution of disputes of law that implicate the Treaty.[13] In addition to the ECJ there is a lower level court called the Court of First Instances with limited jurisdiction. These decisions may be appealed to the ECJ. Additionally, the Advocate General can deliver opinions concerning legal issues, which opinions are not binding upon the parties.

The main aim of the EU was once the unification of a common market but recently it has become more concerned with social affairs, equality and fundamental humans rights. These fields of law have traditionally been left to the Member States but more and more the EU is treading into areas such as property law and creating EU common law.

In addition to the organization that has become known as the European Union, another group is the Council of Europe, presently consisting of 45 member nations.

---

[10] *See* Commission's Website available at ateuropa.eu.int/comm/index_en.htm.

[11] *Available at* europa.eu.int/eur-lex/en/about/abc/.

[12] Treaty on European Union, Feb. 7 1992, Title VI, Art. 35, O.J. (C 224) (1992) [hereinafter Treaty].

[13] *See generally id.*

§ 106EU.02   The Council of Europe and Property Law.

"European Community" is a term that includes the European Union and the member countries of the Council of Europe. Therefore the property laws and regulations within the European Community include Treaties of the EU, Regulations from the EU, case law from the ECJ, as well as Treaties of the CoE and case law from the ECHR.

The most significant legal document within the Council of Europe is the Convention for the Protection of Human Rights and Fundamental Freedoms.[14] As the name implies, fundamental freedoms and human rights are protected by governments who are signatories to this document. With regard to property, Protocol 1, Article 1 of the Convention provides:[15]

Protection of property

> Every natural or legal person is entitled to the peaceful enjoyment of his possessions. No one shall be deprived of his possessions except in the public interest and subject to the conditions provided for by law and by the general principles of international law.

> The preceding provisions shall not, however, in any way impair the right of a State to enforce such laws as it deems necessary to control the use of property in accordance with the general interest or to secure the payment of taxes or other contributions or penalties.[16]

The objective of this article has been clarified in the following statement: "By recognizing that everyone has the right to the peaceful enjoyment of his possessions, Article 1 (P1-1) is in substance guaranteeing the right of property. This is the clear impression left by the words 'possessions' and 'use of property.' "[17] The terms "right to property" and "right of property" were used to describe the subject matter of draft documents that were forerunners to this article.[18] Another policy behind this article is to guard against arbitrary confiscation of property.[19] Three distinct rules are embodied in the Article:

The first rule, in the first sentence of the first paragraph, states, "every. . .person is entitled to the peaceful enjoyment of his possession."[20] This is a general rule that "enunciates the principle of the peaceful

---

[14] *Id.*

[15] *Id.* at Protocol 1, Art. 1. [hereinafter P1-1] This protocol was added to the Convention in 1952 as an addition to the fundamental rights which were outlined in the original document.

[16] *Id.*

[17] Marckx v. Belgium, A31 Eur.Ct.H.R. (1979) at para. 63.

[18] *Id.*

[19] James v. U.K., 3/1984 Eur.Ct.H.R. (1986) at para. 42.

[20] *P1-1.*

enjoyment of property."[21] The second rule, in the second sentence of the first paragraph, states, "[n]o one shall be deprived of his possessions," subject to certain conditions.[22] This rule covers deprivation of possessions unless there is sufficient justification based on the stated conditions.[23] The third rule, found in the second paragraph, "recognizes that the States are entitled, among other things, to control the use of property in accordance with the general interest, by enforcing such laws as they deem necessary for th[at] purpose."[24] The three rules are interwoven.[25]

The ECHR follows a two-step analysis in determining whether a Member State has violated these rules.[26] This analysis first determines whether there is an interference with a property right and then whether this interference was justified; if the interference is not justified then a violation has occurred.[27]

According to the first step in the analysis,[28] an interference occurs when national laws, permits, or decrees significantly reduce the possibility of property use or the very substance of its ownership.[29] If a right to property becomes "precarious and defeasible" then an interference has occurred.[30] In the case of *Sporrong and Lonnroth v. Sweden*,[31] the government issued expropriation permits on properties in a section of Stockholm in order to prepare for the construction of a highway outlet from the city center.[32] Later the government issued prohibitions on construction for these same properties, which kept the owners from building and even selling their land for market value.[33] The ECHR found that this amounted to an interference under the first test of P1-1. Similarly, in France there is a law requiring landowners to join an association which will allow the general public to use their land to hunt.[34] Landowners who wished to exclude hunters from their land were denied this property right and brought a P1-1 claim in the

---

[21] Sporrong and Lonnroth v. Sweden, 7151/75; 7152/75 Eur.Ct.H.R. (1982) at para. 61.

[22] *P1-1.*

[23] Sporrong, at para. 61.

[24] *Id.*

[25] *Id.* at para. 38.

[26] *See generally id.*

[27] *Id.* at para 57.

[28] *Id.* at para. 58.

[29] *Id.* at para. 60.

[30] *Id.*

[31] *Id.* at 1.

[32] *Id.*

[33] *Id.*

[34] Chassagnou v. France, 25088/94 Eur.Ct.H.R. (1999) at para. 13.

ECHR.[35] The court found that the right to exclude is a fundamental property right.[36] Therefore, the French hunting law was found to be an interference under P1-1. In another case, the British government seized some coins that were illegally imported into England.[37] Here the ECHR found that by seizing the coins an interference with a property right had occurred, however, the court quickly moved to the second prong in order to determine whether this interference constituted a violation of the P1-1 rules.[38]

Once an interference has been identified then one must ask whether the interference is justified. An interference is justified if it achieves "a 'fair balance' between the demands of the general interest of the community and the requirements of the protection of the individual's fundamental rights."[39] Whether a "fair balance" has been achieved depends upon two factors: the legitimacy of the interference's aim and the proportionality between the aim sought and means employed.[40] In testing for a fair balance the court recognizes that the Member States enjoy a wide "margin of appreciation" in choosing which policies will best suit their needs.[41]

A legitimate aim is one which confers a direct benefit on the general public interest.[42] In *James v. the United Kingdom*, landowners brought a P1-1 claim against the government because of a law which compelled the landowners to sell their land to long-term leaseholders who met certain requirements.[43] The law was enacted in order to reform real property laws that lead to social injustices.[44] The court found that since the legislation promoted the public interest and enhanced social justice within the community it was a legitimate aim.[45] In *Chassgnou v. France*, the court also found that the hunting law served the legitimate purpose of regulating hunting and encouraging rational management of wildlife.[46] In sum, a legitimate aim can be reached by any bona fide social, economic or political policies that seek to benefit the public interest.[47]

Finally, there must be "a reasonable relationship of proportionality

---

[35] *Id.*

[36] *Id.* at para. 74.

[37] Agosi v. U.K., 9118/80 Eur.Ct.H.R. (1986).

[38] *Id.* at para. 49–50.

[39] Chassagnou, at para. 75.

[40] *Id.* at paras. 76 & 80; *See also* James, at para. 50.

[41] *Id.* at para. 75; Sporrong, at para. 69; Agosi, at para. 52; James, at para. 46.

[42] *See* James, at para. 47.

[43] *Id.*

[44] *Id.* at § C.

[45] *Id.* at para. 41.

[46] Chassagnou, at para. 79.

[47] James, at para. 45.

between the means employed and the aim sought to be realized."[48] In *Sporrong*, this proportionality was expressed as a balancing test.[49] The balance is between the property owner's right to "peaceful enjoyment" and the public interests.[50] When the burden on the property owner is proportional to the benefit enjoyed by the public then a fair balance has been reached.[51] In *Chassagnou*, the hunting law "upset the fair balance" between the property owners' rights and the general public's interests because the property owners were compelled to allow hunters onto their property allegedly without a significant benefit to the general public, since other hunting lands were available.[52] In *Sporrong*, the court found that the expropriation permits and prohibitions on construction on useful land were out of balance with the rights of the property owners since no actual benefit ever inured to the general public and no measures were taken to remedy the situation.[53]

The objective of Article 1 of Protocol 1 is to protect property owners from arbitrary interference with their property and to enable full enjoyment of the property.[54] These goals are often achieved through legal reforms that come about because of the decisions rendered by the ECHR. Member States are given a wide margin of discretion, or appreciation, to determine what is in their public's best interest. However, often the means employed by the Member States infringe upon guaranteed property rights.[55] In these cases the Community law intrudes into areas traditionally left to the competency of the Member States.

The policy behind the Convention is to unify Europe along the lines of fundamental human rights. By agreeing to a single standard, which is the Convention, the Member States are able to gradually discard those property laws which do not conform and thus achieve greater unity until each one has substantially similar property laws.

§ 106EU.03　The European Union and Property Law.

§ 106EU.03(a)　Principal Property Laws and Regulations of the European Union.

The most important legal document in the EU is the Treaty on European Union (Treaty) with its various amendments and revisions. This is the

---

[48] *Id*. at para. 50.

[49] Sporrong, at para. 73.

[50] *Id*.

[51] *Id*.

[52] Chassangou, at para. at 85.

[53] Sporrong, at para. 72–73.

[54] *P1-1*.

[55] *See* James; Sporrong; Chassangou.

document that gives life to the EU through a complex organization of institutions, Foreign Ministers, Commissioners, Members of Parliament and a "Supreme" court (aka. The European Court of Justice). As set forth in the Maastricht Treaty, the objectives of the EU are to promote economic and social progress, achieve sustainable development, strengthen and protect the rights of citizens of the Member States, develop the Union into an area of security and freedom and create a common market.[56] In order to achieve these objectives the Council of Ministers has legislative power to enact regulations which Member States incorporate into their domestic laws.[57] Often these regulations impact the property laws of the Member States.[58] In addition, the Treaty provides in Article 6 that

> The Union is founded on the principles of liberty, democracy, respect for human rights and fundamental freedoms, and the rule of law, principles which are common to the Member States.

> The Union shall respect fundamental rights, as guaranteed by the European Convention for the Protection of Human Rights and Fundamental Freedoms signed in Rome on 4 November 1950 and as they result from the constitutional traditions common to the Member States, as general principles of Community law.[59]

Embodied in Article 6 are the guarantees found in the Convention such as the right to "peaceful enjoyment" of one's property and possessions.[60] The legislative regulations produced by the Council must take into account these fundamental Community policies toward property. To secure this fundamental right to property the European Court of Justice (ECJ) hears cases where the Council Regulations come into conflict with the Convention and thereby create common property law in the European Community.

§ 106EU.03(b)   Property Case Law of the European Court of Justice.

"In all Member States, numerous legislative measures have given concrete expression to [the] social function of the right to property. Thus in all the Member States there is legislation on agriculture and forestry, water supply, protection of the environment and town and country planning."[61] These national measures restrict the use of property and infringe upon the full use of property, but do so for the public interest without creating a

---

[56] *See Maastricht Treaty*, cited *supra* note 5 at Art. 2.

[57] *Id.* at Art. 7.

[58] *See, e.g.*, Council Directive 93/53/EEC, O.J. 1993 L 175; *see also* Case C-20/00, Booker v. Scottish Ministers, [2003] E.C.R. I-7411 (analyzing the validity of Council Regulation 93/53/EEC).

[59] *Maastricht Treaty*, at Art. 6.

[60] *P1-1.*

[61] Case 44/79, Hauer v. Land Rheinland-Pfalz, [1979] E.C.R. 3727, at para. 20.

disproportionate burden on any one individual.

The fundamental rights analysis concerns whether Council Regulations are violations of property rights. Member States incorporate Council Regulations into their domestic laws, domestic laws among the Member States become more similar and unified, and thus help achieve the goal of the EU. The ECJ decides whether these laws are valid according to the Convention for countries which are members of the CoE and according both Convention and Treaty for countries who are members of the EU.

In the case of *Hauer v. Land Rheinland-Pfalz*, the plaintiff had applied for a permit allowing her to plant a vineyard on her property.[62] The application was denied under German law due to the unsuitability of the land. The plaintiff appealed the decision. While the appeal was pending, the Community through the Council adopted Regulation No. 1162/76 which prohibits Member States from issuing new vineyard permits for a period of three years.[63] The purpose of the Regulation was to re-establish a market for wine and stop overproduction within the Member States.[64] The court of appeals in Germany held that the land was suitable for a vineyard; however, it could not grant the planting permits due to the prohibition in Regulation No. 1162/76. Therefore, this case was brought to the ECJ in order to decide whether the Council Regulation infringed upon fundamental property rights and property rights guaranteed by the German Constitution.[65]

The court first pointed out that there was no deprivation of property under Protocol 1, Article 1 of the Convention.[66] However, the court did find an interference with a property due to the control which the regulation imposed on the landowner's right to plant.[67] The court determined that the interference was justified as a remedy for overproduction of wine. Since the aim focused on a benefit to the public, and no one party was disproportionately burdened, the Regulation was justified.[68] It is interesting to note that in this case the German government was ready to issue a planting permit to the plaintiff but because of the Council Regulation was unable to do so.[69]

In the case of *Wachauf v. Bundesamt fur Ernaehrung und Forstwirtschaft*,[70] Council Regulation 857/84[71] dealing with milk produc-

---

[62] *Id.* at para. 1.

[63] *Id.* at paras. 2–3.

[64] *Id.* at para. 8.

[65] *Id.* at para. 5.

[66] *Id.* at para. 19.

[67] *Id.*

[68] *Id.* at para. 30.

[69] *Id.* at para. 3.

[70] Case 5/88, Wachauf v. Bundesamt fur enrahrung und Forstwirtschaft, [1989] E.C.R. 2609.

tion quotas was called into question. The aim of the regulation was to curb growth of milk production by fixing quotas, or reference quantities, on individual holdings and attaching a levy when milk quotas are exceeded.[72] The plaintiff was a tenant farmer, who through his own labors, had earned the rights to produce milk based on the reference quantities set forth in the regulation. Upon the expiration of the lease, the tenant sought compensation because he was going to definitively cease to produce milk and therefore give up his property rights.[73] The court made it clear that the property right of milk production is a right that runs with the land.[74] However, the court stated "that the Community legislature intended that at the end of the lease the reference quantity should in principle return to the lessor who retakes possession of the holding, subject, however, to the Member States' power to allocate all or part of the reference quantity to the departing lessee."[75] This rule could have the effect of precluding the lessee from benefiting from the system of compensation inherent in the regulation because the lessor can refuse to consent to compensation.[76]

The court declared that it would be unacceptable for a farmer who has earned production rights to lose those unused rights upon the expiration of the lease.[77] Therefore the court stated that "community rules which, upon the expiry of the lease, had the effect of depriving the lessee, without compensation, of the fruits of his labor and of his investments in the tenanted holding would be incompatible with the requirements of the protection of fundamental rights in the Community legal order."[78] And these requirements also bind the Member States "when they implement Community rules, the Member States must, as far as possible, apply those rules in accordance with those requirements."[79]

The Council Regulation was upheld because the Member States had a sufficient margin of appreciation to allow for compensation to lessee like the plaintiff and therefore, it did not infringe upon those protected fundamental property rights.[80] However, in order to conform to this holding the Member States would have to alter their domestic property laws in a way that would

---

[71] Council Regulation No. 857/84, O.J 1984 L90.

[72] Case C-2/92, The Queen v. Ministry of Agriculture, Fisheries and Food, [1993] E.C.R. I-955, at para. 2.

[73] *See* Wachauf, at para. 2.

[74] *See id.* at paras. 13–14.

[75] *Id.*

[76] *Id.* at para. 16.

[77] *Id.*

[78] *Id.* at para. 19.

[79] *Id.*

[80] *Id.* at para. 21.

provide compensation to or otherwise protect the property right of tenant farmers in the future.[81] Along these same lines other cases have held that "it cannot be left to the national authorities and courts to determine the substantive content of [] fundamental [property] right[s]. It is possible and to be expected that they should have a certain discretion with regard to the detailed formulation of the rules to protect the interests of tenants but it must ultimately be the Court of Justice which lays down the limits on that discretion, a not altogether easy task."

Again, it is clear that the EU has taken steps to unify the European Community by outlining the goals that each Member State should accomplish in the area of property law. On the other hand there are only two areas in which the ECJ may truly intrude into national legislation: "first, where the national legislation implements Community rules, and secondly, but more indirectly, in cases where a Treaty provision derogating from the principle of freedom of movement is relied on by a Member State in order to justify a restriction on freedom of movement stemming from that Member State's legislation."[82]

The EU institutions and their courts must be careful to allow Member States to resolve concerns of fundamental rights, mainly because each one knows better what their citizens' needs are.[83] The institutions of the EU are set up in order to achieve greater economic unity and secure common freedoms but not to legislate in areas of law traditionally left to the Member States. This is a very delicate and fine line, walked by both the Member States and the EU.

---

[81] *See* The Queen, at para. 16.

[82] *Id.* at para. 31.

[83] *Id.* at para. 33.

CHAPTER 106FR

PROPERTY LAW IN FRANCE

Professor David A. Thomas
J. Reuben Clark Law School
Brigham Young University

SYNOPSIS

§ 106FR.01   History of Property Law in France.

§ 106FR.01(a)   Introduction.

The historical development of French property flows from two distinct cultural streams. One stream, issuing from the south, is the sophisticated written law introduced by the Romans. The other stream emanated from the north with the vigorous and varied customary law of the Celtic and Germanic peoples. The migrations of the latter inevitably confronted the conquering advances of the former to give French law its vitality. French law has also been influenced by canon law, especially as applied by specialized courts during the Middle Ages.[1]

§ 106FR.01(b)   Landholding Before the Romans.

When Julius Caesar invaded Gaul in the 1st century B.C., he found a land without specific boundaries, occupied in large part by nomadic Celtic tribes. These tribes travelled and settled where they pleased in the land and sometimes they resumed migrations even before beginning true settlements. Caesar describes land distribution and landholding customs among some of the Celtic tribes that he encountered:

> None of them [members of the tribe] possesses any settled amount of land of his own; and none of them has any enclosed fields; but each year the chiefs and the magistrates distribute the land to the families and to the male relatives . . . The following year they are compelled to trade places.[2]

Tacitus, another contemporary Roman observer, describing Germanic customs of the same era, told of an "en bloc" ownership by the Germanic community, the extent of which was determined by the number of cultivators. He also described a system of repartition and crop rotation among the members of the community, based at least partially on social rank.[3]

As to other landholding customs among the Gauls, they were probably similar to those of contemporary British Celts, to some of whom they were related and with whom they communicated often. Where farming was practiced, the most common pattern for the British Celts was the cultivation of small rectangular fields marked off by low banks of earth or rocks or some similarly conspicuous boundary. Such land, along with grazing land, was held by family groups, so that clusters of fields would have been worked by

---

[1] Jean Brissaud, A History of French Private Law ix, 317 (Rapelje Howell trans., 2d French ed. 1968).

[2] Julius Caesar, The Gallic War 347 (Edwards trans. 1979).

[3] Jean Brissaud, A History of French Private Law 32, 33 (Rapelje Howell trans., 2d French ed., 1968).

farmers connected through blood ties. The rights to use these fields would quite likely have been passed on to kinship descendants.[4]

§ 106FR.01(c) Landholding During and After Roman Rule.

After Gaul became a province of Rome, its lands were considered as belonging to the Roman people or to the Emperor. Although varied landholding arrangements were introduced, a typical form of ownership was a lease to a private persons under a revocable tenure known as a *precarium* in consideration of the payment of tax.[5] Roman concepts of land were disseminated throughout Gaul through distribution of land to discharged legionary veterans and through the growth of Roman cities and commerce.

The eventual enfeeblement of Roman public authority in Gaul strengthened the power of the great private landholding proprietors. Pressure from invading barbarians and weakened imperial military forces required the fortifying of many towns and prompted great landholders to set themselves as feudal lords in the 5th century A.D. These magnates became independent of local public authorities such as municipal magistrates and maintained private militias and their own tribunals; they exercised authority over the inhabitants of their estates and collected the equivalent of taxes from them.[6]

Early in the 5th century A.D., the Germanic tribes of Visigoths, Burgundians and Franks, who had been mercenaries of Rome, established their independence from the Empire and introduced Germanic legal customs and institutions into Gaul. Written codes of laws began to appear, often containing separate provisions for the Germanic inhabitants and for the Roman citizens living in the tribal territories.

The Visigothic laws, and more particularly the Code of Euric, are believed to have directly or indirectly influenced most Germanic law codes thereafter. The Code of Euric, from ca. A.D. 476, shows some Roman influence. The Lex Romana Visigothorum was promulgated by the Visigothic King Alaric II in A.D. 506, to govern Romans living in Visigothic territories. This collection is also known as the Breviarium Alaricianum (Breviary of Alaric). The Leges Visigothorum is a collection of laws that had been issued by Euric's successors, applying to both Gothic and Hispano-Roman subjects. The collection was promulgated in A.D. 654, and replaced the Lex Romana Visigothorum.

Euric's code seems to have been the immediate source for the early codes of both the Salian Franks[7] and the Burgundians,[8] and the Bavarian[9] and

---

[4] *See* § 2.03, *supra.*

[5] Jean Brissaud, A History of French Public Law 53 (James W. Garner trans. 1915).

[6] *Id.* at 56.

[7] The Code of the Salian Franks, or Lex Salica, is attributed to Clovis, A.D. 481-511.

[8] The Burgundian Code was compiled between A.D. 483 and 532. The Lex Romana

Lombard[10] codes also show Visigothic influence. Another early Frankish code, the Lex Ribuaria,[11] was based on the Salian code, and it in turn influenced the codes of the continental Angles and Saxons of the Carolingian Age.

The best known of these early Germanic codes—indeed the oldest Germanic code that is completely preserved—is the Lex Salica, which as been described as "primarily a penal law . . . concerned with the redress of crimes (murder, theft, mutilation, exploitation of women) by monetary means."[12] The Lex Salica and the other early codes consist of both individual "statutes" and precedential judicial sentences ("Weisthuemer"), but they do not refer to most customs of daily living, such as occupancy of land, personal property, commercial dealings, inheritance, family relationships, and class privilege. The only references to land law in the Lex Salica are provisions requiring money payment for damage to agricultural fields,[13] blocking the way of another,[14] and improper fencing and enclosing.[15]

Under these Germanic tribal rulers, what had been Roman public lands passed to the Germanic chieftains, who kept part and distributed the rest to their principal followers. Some tribes established themselves as guests on the lands of wealthy Romans, at first sharing only the revenue and produce of the lands, but later claiming a share of ownership and title.[16]

§ 106FR.01(d)   The Emergence of Feudalism.

During these Dark Ages, when the Merovingian Dynasty passed from the scene and the Carolingian Dynasty emerged, the evolution of landholding patterns into forms of feudalism continued uninterrupted. For most people in France, these feudal arrangements only gradually emerged and changed in response to changes in social conditions. In the 9th century A.D., the emperor Charles the Great followed the Frankish custom under which he considered property and revenues of the empire as his family property. Compensation to his principal supporters, servants and counselors was paid by gifts of land, usually with requirements of military service attached.

Burgundionum was issued circa A.D. 500 for application to Roman citizens living in the Burgundian kingdom.

[9] The Lex Baiuvariorum is dated from about A.D. 744-48.

[10] The Leges Langobardorum were promulgated between A.D. 643 and 755.

[11] The Lex Ribuaria is believed to have been promulgated after A.D. 596 for the Ripuarian or western Franks.

[12] 5 Laws of the Alamans and Bavarians 19 (Theodore John Rivers, trans. 1977).

[13] Title 9.

[14] Title 31.

[15] Title 34.

[16] *Id.* at 61-62.

However, upon the death of Charlemagne, Germanic society suffered a relapse:

> The decades that followed Charles's death witnessed the rapid disintegration of the Empire he had created. Empire and papacy alike became immersed in an abyss of anarchy and barbaric lawlessness. The governing principles of society were the law of force on the one hand and the need for protection on the other. In the course of the ninth century the State lost all contact with the urban tradition and became completely agrarian. The life of the feudal nobility was spent in warfare and private feuds. From their strongholds the feudal lords terrorized peaceful villagers and passing travelers.[17]

Despite the lawlessness of the aristrocracy, the disintegration of a strong monarchy meant that the people could turn only to local feudal lords for protection; thus society became increasingly feudalized in the 9th century A.D. Land grants under such circumstances became increasingly hereditary and through subinfeudation a hierarchy of vassalage eventually developed. These feudal landholding arrangements, either on lands of the monarch or of a member of the aristocracy, have been described as follows:

> The land was divided into estates which were self-sufficient units . . . In the center of each estate was located the lord's domain, surrounded by the huts of the peasants, each of whom had a small strip of land attached to his dwelling . . . Part of the arable land that surrounded the village was set aside for the exclusive use of the king or lord. What remained was parceled out among the peasant tenants. The fields were divided into three parts, one of which was used for the planting of the summer crop, the second for the winter crop, while the third part would lie fallow.. . . The cultivation of the fields was a communal and co-operative enterprise, although each peasant harvested the crop from his own strips of land.

> *   *   *

> The lord gave the peasant protection, furnished the land, built a mill and a village church, and administered justice in the territory that he had learned to consider his own, either by inheritance or by special grant. The peasant in turn, enjoyed the security that went with the hereditary right to the possession of his strip of land, he took his share of the agricultural produce, and returned the privileges extended to him by making certain payments and rendering certain services to the lord, exactments whose extent and nature were determined by custom. Theoretically still a serf, the peasant of the Carolingian period had actually become a tenant, and although still unfree, this peasant tenant, being exempt from the burden of military and court service, was envied by many a small freeholder.[18]

The great domains of the Frankish period were divided into farms, with a

---

[17] 1 Kurt F. Reinhardt, Germany: 2000 Years 44 (1961).

[18] *Id.* at 49-50.

portion reserved for the owner, and the rest granted to tributary cultivators, who had to pay quit-rents to the lord and perform various duties on the lord's land. The uncultivated lands, such as pastures and woods, were left for common use by all the cultivators of the domain.[19]

In summary, during the feudal era in France the property relationships to be found on a typical great domain consisted of:

1. The lord's manor and land which he kept to be worked by slaves, servants and tenants.

2. Lands held subject to servile tenures by "coloni," "lites," and slaves. The "coloni" were perhaps less bound to the soil than the slaves, but their burdens were quite heavy. Those burdens included dues (among which were taxes collected by hearth or head, field rent paid in kind, fees for the use of property belonging to the lord, and supplies or money for the army) and services (plowing and manual labor on the lord's domain).[20]

3. Lands held by free tenure or by a tenure at will, subject to quit rents, annual rents, and similar compulsory dues. The tenancy at will (précaire) was used especially in the case of lands belonging to the Church. The folk law seems to have merged the Roman "precarium" with the Roman lease, fusing the two into a Frankish institution. The "précaire" was sometimes revocable, sometimes temporary in duration, sometimes for life, and sometimes perpetual and hereditary. Regardless of the durations of such "precarious" tenure, the tenant or grantee owed an annual charge in money or in kind to the grantor; this was sometimes a rent charge, and at other times was purely nominal.[21]

4. Benefices or lands held by tenure in exchange for military service to the grantor. The benefices eventually became hereditary and were thus transformed into fiefs.

The "précaire" and the "bénéfice" differed in that the précaire was economic in character and the bénéfice was political.[22]

The alod, or freehold, was land held in free and full ownership and was therefore outside the feudal system.[23] It was not subject to feudal dues, nor charges for its dues, nor transmission fees. Under French feudalism, the alod

---

[19] Experts have disagreed over whether these arrangements were simply extensions of practices from ancient times, but with new subservience to powerful lords for security purposes, or a novel creation stimulated by conditions of the times, or a natural byproduct of the Roman landholding practices for wealthy owners, or resulted from the combined influences. *See* Jean Brissaud, A History of French Private Law 43 (Rapelje Howell trans., 2d French ed. 1968).

[20] *Id.* at 137.

[21] Jean Brissaud, A History of French Public Law 144-145 (James W. Garner trans. 1915).

[22] *Id.* at 142, 247.

[23] *Id.* at 247.

was partially absorbed into the system as a form of landholding similar to a fief or copyhold, especially if the holder of the alod needed the protection of the seignior, or lord. In parts of France still governed by custom, all land was presumed to be non-allodial fief or copyhold until shown otherwise; in other parts land was considered allodial unless shown otherwise. The seigniors, who still had the right to administer justice even on allodial land, took advantage of the confusion and began treating some allodial lands as fiefs.[24] The Edict of August 1692 abolished the noble freehold while leaving the villein alod undisturbed, but even by 1789 the question of rights over the alod was still not resolved.[25]

As the French monarchy grew stronger, the king eventually claimed universal lordship over any land not owned by the seigniors. This resulted in fees being owed to the king in case of sale or alienation.

In the north of France, a system of social organization and landholding known as the Germanic March arose. The Germanic March consisted of the village (including dwellings with their yards and gardens), arable lands divided into parcels available for private ownership, and common areas open to use by all inhabitants.[26] This arrangement began to break down in the 15th century, and during the 16th and 17th centuries, the lords frequently used violence or the invention of false titles to secure the rights in the commons, wasteland and unoccupied areas in these communities. A typical tactic would be to press a false claim of community indebtedness, which claim would be withdrawn if the commons areas would be sold to the claimant at bargain prices.[27]

§ 106FR.01(e)   The Influence of Canon Law.

Through canon law the Church in France sought to reduce violence by removing the right or practice of violent self-help. Under canon law, if a party sought to take possession by force from a third party who was withholding the property, the attacker forfeited all rights to that property.[28] In place of self-help through force, legal actions for possession were introduced.

§ 106FR.01(f)   Conflict Between Monarchy and Aristocracy over Rights of Commons.

In the 16th and 17th centuries, the monarchy and the aristocracy, with the

---

[24] *Id.* at 292-93.

[25] Jean Brissaud, A History of French Private Law 293 (Rapelje Howell trans., 2d French ed. 1968).

[26] *Id.* at 35; Jean Brissaud, A History of French Public Law 246-47 (James W. Garner trans. 1915).

[27] Jean Brissaud, A History of French Private Law 46-47 (Rapelje Howell trans., 2d French ed., 1915).

[28] *Id.* at 317.

peasants caught in between, found themselves feuding over rights of commons. The nobles regarded rights of commons as having been created by the lords, because they arose at a time when the peasants were incapable of land ownership. Therefore, rights of commons, having been created by the lords, could also be modified by the lords.

Based on this rationale, the lords began exercising triage, or confiscation of one-third of the commons areas. Triage was exercised in the 17th century by the Lords, who claimed that while they had abandoned ownership to the inhabitants, they had not abandoned use. Up to one-third of such common areas as had been earlier surrendered without rent or quit-rent reserved could be taken back by the lord, who nevertheless had to leave enough to meet the needs of the local populace. Alternatively in the 18th century, lords exercised the so-called right of restriction, by which they took up to two-thirds of the commons area, with the one-third being left to the people, in which full ownership was acknowledged.

The monarchy and its supporters, on the other hand, maintained that rights of commons had existed before feudalism, that the lands therefore belonged to the monarch, and that the lords had received their fiefs only on the condition that they preserved for the people the commons rights.[29]

§ 106FR.01(g)   The Impact of the French Revolution.

Claims to the commons by both the aristocracy and the monarchy were abolished under the law introduced during the French Revolution. The Declaration of April 13-20, 1791, stated that: "the right . . . of appropriating waste and abandoned or barren and devastated lands, uncultivated or unoccupied possessions, desert lands, common passageways and waste lands for public pastures shall no longer exist for the benefit of the former lords." Triage was abolished, and communes were able to gain back some of the lands they had lost to seignorial encroachments. The revolutionaries also tried to change the right of commons into private ownership, but had to call an end to this program because of the abuses and inequities that resulted.[30]

The domains of the crown, of the clergy, and of the émigrés (nobles who had fled the fury of the revolutionaries) passed into the hands of small proprietors. The revolutionaries reestablished ownership according to principles of Roman property law and put into the channels of trade the property of the clergy and of the crown.[31]

Napoleon promulgated the Napoleonic Civil Code of 1804, and the legislation contained in that code is still today the basis of French civil law. Book II and Book III of the code deal with things and the different modes

---

[29] *Id.* at 23.

[30] *Id.* at 48-50.

[31] Jean Brissaud, A History of French Public Law 549 (James W. Garner trans. 1915).

of ownership and the different ways of acquiring ownership. The Napoleonic Codes transformed and modernized French law through the synthesis of the diverse influences of Roman law, customary law, canon law, revolutionary ideology, legislation from the monarchy and the personal ideas of Napoleon.

There has not been a revision of the Code since its inception; however, the Constitution of 4 October 1958 confers on the legislature jurisdiction over all matters concerning succession and gifts. It also lets the legislature define the fundamental principles of ownership and of real rights and obligations; the details of these matters are left to government regulations.

§ 106FR.02 Acquisition of Real Property.

§ 106FR.02(a) The Nature of Real Property.

French law distinguishes between two types of property: movables (roughly equivalent to personal property) and immovables (roughly equivalent to real property). According to the French Civil Code, property is immovable by its nature or by its purpose or because of the object to which it is attached.[32] Thus, objects furnished by the landowner (even including seed and animals employed in cultivation) to the tenant farmer or sharecropper for the use and development of the land are immovables by purpose as are such movables affixed by plaster, lime or cement.[33] Usufruct (rights of enjoyment) of immovables, servitudes or easements, and causes of action to recover immovables are all considered immovables,[34] as are real property mortgages and certain other liens.

§ 106FR.02(b) How Real Property Is Acquired.

§ 106FR.02(b)(1) Accession.

Accession refers to land or property which is joined with and incorporated into real property.[35] For example, by means of accession pavement constructed by the German army during the Second World War was found to be part of the property held by a private landowner, who has thus been held responsible for damage caused to a third party by the pavement's collapse.[36] The same principle of accession also applies to land acquired through acts of nature, such as alluvial lands.

§ 106FR.02(b)(2) Succession.

Succession is the passage of property from the decedent to the survivors,

---

[32] C. civ. 516 (Dalloz).

[33] *Id.* at 525.

[34] *Id.* at 526.

[35] C. civ. 551.

[36] 1973 Bull. Civ. II, No. 306.

without regard to the nature or the origin of the property.[37] In France, children inherit from their ascendants (ancestors) without regard to gender or primogeniture, or whether they are the issue of different marriages. They also inherit in equal portions and per capita, when they are all of the first degree and inheriting in their own right; they inherit per stirpes, when some or all of them are taking by representation.[38] If the decedent leaves no posterity, and has no brother or sister, the succession is divided in half between the ascendants on the mother's side and those on the father's side. The closest relative on a particular side receives the entire half assigned to his or her part of the family.[39] In this the French law both resembles and differs from the 6 Uniform Probate Code6 found in several American states, which provides for equal distribution on both sides of the family, but allows for distribution by representation on each side.[40] The illegitimate child has the same rights as a legitimate child under French law, and is entitled to inherit as if he or she were legitimate, as are the child's ascendants.[41]

§ 106FR.02(b)(3)   Prescription.

Prescription is the acquisition of title by adverse possession. In order to prescribe, possession must be continuous and uninterrupted, peaceful, public, unequivocal, and under a claim of ownership. For prescription to be awarded, judges must find that possession included material acts characteristic of such possession. In these cases, the judges themselves have the authority to decide whether or not an act is characteristic of possession.[42]

Peaceful possession includes a lack of physical or moral violence, during both the inception and duration of the possession.[43] The limitation period for prescription is 30 years, unless the adverse possessor has apparent title and acts in good faith, in which case the period is reduced. Good faith is always presumed; according to Article 2268 of the Civil Code, the person alleging bad faith must prove it. If there is no showing of bad faith, the limitation period is reduced to 10 years, if the true owner lives in the jurisdiction of the Court of Appeals where the land is situated, and 20 years if the owner lives in another jurisdiction.[44] Possession periods may be tacked.[45]

---

[37] C. civ. 732 (Dalloz).

[38] *Id.* at 745.

[39] *Id.* at 746.

[40] 6 Uniform Probate Code § 2-103(4)6.

[41] C. civ. 757, 758 (Dalloz).

[42] *Id.* at 2229; 1972 Bull. Civ. III, No. 101.

[43] 1969 Bull. Civ. III, No. 348.

[44] C. civ. 2262, 2265 (Dalloz).

[45] *Id.* at 2235.

§ 106FR.02(b)(4)   Contract.

Every creation or transfer of a real property interest by contract must be by notarial act registered upon the Register of Real Estate Mortgages. This includes deeds of sale, deeds of gift, contracts creating rights of usufruct or servitudes, long term leases, attachment liens, and contracts creating or dissolving tenancy in common and condominiums.

§ 106FR.02(b)(5)   Sale.

A sale is final between parties as soon as agreement is reached as to the thing and the price, even if delivery has not yet taken place or the price has not been paid.[46] Under French law, a promise of sale is equivalent to a sale when the parties agree as to property and price.[47] However, a promise to sell real estate is void if not stated in a notarized writing or private act registered at the tax registry office within ten days after acceptance by the buyer. If the promise to sell was made with payment of a deposit, either party may withdraw, but must pay a penalty. If the withdrawing party is the party that made the deposit, that party forfeits the deposit upon withdrawing; if the withdrawing party is the party that received the deposit, that party must return double the amount of the deposit upon withdrawal.[48]

Sellers of property must set forth clearly the obligation they are assuming. An obscure or ambiguous statement will be construed against the seller.[49] A seller's two main obligations are to deliver and warrant the property being sold.[50] The delivery obligation is fulfilled when the seller hands over the keys of the building or delivers the documents of title to the buyer.[51] The seller also warrants the peaceful enjoyment of the property and the absence of hidden faults or latent defects.[52] The parties may, by contract, add to or subtract from this legal obligation.[53] However, sellers may not escape liability for problems caused by themselves.[54] If the purchaser is dispossessed through a breach of warranty, the seller must refund the purchase price, reimburse any income the purchaser had to turn over to the dispossessing party and expenses incurred by both the buyer and the dispossessor, and must pay any other damages as well as contract costs. This

---

[46] *Id.* at 1583.

[47] *Id.* at 1589.

[48] *Id.* at 1590.

[49] *Id.* at 1602.

[50] *Id.* at 1603.

[51] *Id.* at 1605.

[52] *Id.* at 1625.

[53] *Id.* at 1627.

[54] *Id.* at 1628.

warranty also applies to anyone to whom the buyer subsequently sells the property.[55]

The buyer's main obligation is to deliver the price agreed upon.[56]

§ 106FR.03   Types of Interests in Real Property.

§ 106FR.03(a)   Ownership.

Ownership under French law is defined by Article 544 of the Civil Code as the right to enjoy and dispose of things in the most absolute manner, provided the use is not prohibited by statute or regulation. Ownership of the soil carries with it ownership of what is above and beneath it. Thus, the owner may excavate as much as desired, and draw from the earth all the products beneath the property, unless prohibited in some manner by law or regulation relating to mines, or by police laws and regulation. The owner is also entitled to build and construct whatever desired, as long as some aspect of that activity is not prohibited by the exceptions contained in the Title of Servitudes or Burdens on Land.[57]

§ 106FR.03(b)   Usufruct.

Usufruct is the right to enjoy property owned by another, in the same way an owner would, but on the condition of preserving the substance of the property.[58] It is analogous to a life estate in that it gives the right to a person to use and enjoy the property while another remains vested with the underlying title. The usufruct may be created either by operation of law or by gift or sale.[59] Unless exempted by the instrument creating the usufruct, the usufructuary (one who benefits from the usufruct) must often give security to ensure that the rights will be enjoyed prudently, without damage to the property.[60] However, the usufructuary takes things as they are, and is required to prepare an inventory of the movables and a description of the immovables before entering into their enjoyment.[61] The usufructuary is obligated only to maintain the property. All major repairs, unless arising from lack of maintenance, are chargeable to the owner,[62] but neither the owner nor the usufructuary is required to rebuild structures deteriorating from old age. The usufructuary may enjoy the fruits of existing mines on the

---

[55] P. Dupont Delestraint, Droit Civil, Principaux Contrats 27 (3d ed. 1973).

[56] C. civ. 1759 (Dalloz).

[57] *Id.* at 552.

[58] *Id.* at 578.

[59] *Id.* at 579.

[60] *Id.* at 601.

[61] *Id.* at 600.

[62] *Id.* at 605.

property, but may not open up new mines, and is not entitled to keep any treasure found on the property.[63]

The usufruct may be extinguished through the death of the usufructuary, the expiration of the time for which it was granted, the consolidation in the same person of the rights of ownership and usufruct, the non-use of the usufruct for thirty years, or the total loss of the property that the estate was based on.[64] A usufruct may also end because the usufructuary abuses the property through neglect or damage.[65] This particular feature of the usufruct indicates that in France, as well as in the United States, waste actions can be maintained in order to preserve the rights of the reversionary owner of the property. France, however, allows creditors of the usufructuary to intervene in litigation, to protect their rights, and to offer to repair the damage and give security for the future preservation of the property. Depending on the seriousness of the circumstances, judges may either extinguish the usufruct completely, or permit the owner to reenter the property under condition of paying the usufructuary (or assigns) a fixed sum until the time when the usufruct would have terminated.[66]

§ 106FR.03(c)   Servitudes.

Servitudes are burdens imposed upon one property for the use and benefit of a property belonging to another owner.[67] These burdens are both prohibitory and prescriptive: French law seems to have incorporated the American concepts of easements, real covenants and equitable servitudes, as well as zoning and preventive nuisance law, into its laws governing servitudes. French servitudes, generally, arise from the natural location of the premises, or from obligations imposed by law, or from agreements between the owners.[68] An example of a servitude arising from the location of the properties occurs when one of the properties is situated on higher ground than the other: the owner of the lower ground cannot build an obstruction that will prevent naturally occurring run-off water from passing through the lower property; conversely, the owner of the higher property cannot use the property in a way that exacerbates the effects of run-off on the lower property.[69] This example is similar to regulation of land use by nuisance law in the United States.

Servitudes established by law must have some public, community or

---

[63] *Id.* at 598.

[64] *Id.* at 617.

[65] *Id.* at 618.

[66] *Id.*

[67] *Id.* at 637.

[68] *Id.* at 639.

[69] *Id.* at 640.

private benefit.[70] Typical of these are servitudes to facilitate the construction or repair of roads and other public or community works.[71] An interesting example of a servitude established by law is the right of property owners in cities to require neighbors to participate in the construction and repair of fences separating houses, yards and gardens.[72] Likewise, all property owners are required to build roofs in such a manner that rain water can only drain on the owner's property or on public property; the water may not be directed to the neighbor's property.[73] An owner of landlocked land is entitled to a right-of-way, but must pay an indemnity proportionate to the damage caused by use of the neighbor's property.[74]

According to Article 686 of the Civil Code, landowners may establish whatever servitudes they desire on their land, or in favor of their land; however, these servitudes run with the land and may not be based on a mere personal promise to another. In a recent case it was held that a doctor could not sell property while reserving the right to object to the creation of another medical office in the building he was selling, because the covenant did not relate to the building itself.[75]

Continuous and open (apparent from visible exterior works) servitudes are acquired by document of title or by possession for 30 years.[76] Continuous but hidden servitudes and intermittent servitudes may only be established by documents of title.[77] However, witnesses or presumptions may serve to present needed additional evidence if the instrument of title alone is somehow insufficient to establish proof of the servitude.[78] The establishment of a servitude presumes the grant of everything necessary for its use; thus, a servitude to draw water from the well of another necessarily implies a right of way to the well.[79]

§ 106FR.03(d)   Tenancy in Common.

Tenancy in common exists when several persons are concurrent owners of a specific tract, usually obtained simultaneously by succession or gift. Each tenant in common is entitled to use and enjoy the object of the tenancy, as long as use is for normal purposes and in a manner compatible with the

---

[70] *Id.* at 649.

[71] *Id.* at 650.

[72] *Id.* at 663.

[73] *Id.* at 681.

[74] *Id.* at 682.

[75] *Id.* at 686, Comment 5.

[76] *Id.* at 690.

[77] *Id.* at 691.

[78] 1965 Bull. Civ. I, No. 483.

[79] C. civ. 696 (Dalloz).

rights of the other tenants. If one of the tenants uses the property exclusively, that tenant must pay consideration to the other tenants.[80]

Administration and disposition of the common tenancy requires the consent of all of the tenants, but they may delegate to one or several of them general administrative powers. Special authority is required for actions that do not relate to the normal administration of the tenancy, as well as the renewing and the cancellation of leases.[81] However, if a tenant acts without the consent of co-tenants in selling part of the property, the sale will still be valid.[82] Revenues from the common tenancy go to its increase, absent an agreement to divide them. Each tenant has a right to these benefits and makes good the losses incurred through the tenancy in proportion to the tenant's respective interest in it.[83] Each tenant is also entitled to an annual share of the revenues, less expenses.[84]

Article 815 of the Civil Code provides that any tenant may ask for partition at any time, unless either contract or law prevents it. For example, if a tenant requests it, a tribunal may delay partition for up to two years, if the immediate partition would diminish the value of the asset. Interestingly, French law protects farming families by preventing the partition of farmland at the death of the landowner under certain conditions; the spouse (if she is a co-owner) or minor children can actually request the delay of partition for a maximum of five years. This delay may be renewed until the spouse dies or the youngest child reaches the age of majority.[85] An agreement not to partition may not exceed five years in duration, although it is renewable at the end of the five-year period.[86]

The concept of joint tenancy, as it is known in the United States, does not exist under French law.

§ 106FR.03(e)   Condominium.

Ownership of condominium shares, in French law, gives the right to use the property and, at dissolution, to receive a predetermined part of the company's real estate holding.

§ 106FR.03(f)   Mortgage.

A mortgage is a right over immovables encumbered for the performance of an obligation, which right follows those immovables into whatever hands

---

[80] *Id.* at 815-9.

[81] *Id.* at 815-8.

[82] 1987, Bull. Civ. I, No. 197.

[83] C. civ. 815-10 (Dalloz).

[84] *Id.* at 815-11.

[85] *Id.* at 815-1.

[86] *Id.* at 1873-3.

they pass.[87] Mortgages are either legal, judicial or conventional; they exist solely in those cases and forms authorized by law.[88] Such cases, however, include only immovable property and immovable accessories which are in commerce, as well as their usufruct.[89]

A legal mortgage is created by law. By way of examples, legal mortgages can arise in the following circumstances, creating rights in the parties indicated:

> Spouses, over the property owned by the other spouse;
>
> Minors, or adults under guardianship, over the property of the guardian or the legal administrator;
>
> The State and local and regional governments of France, over the property of some administrators.

A judicial mortgage, on the other hand, arises in favor of a person who obtains a judgment, such as by means of a debt, or of back taxes, for instance (similar to a judgment lien in the United States).

The conventional mortgage, other than the legal or judicial mortgage, may be granted only by one who has the capacity to alienate the property. The possibility of rescission, if any, and any conditions upon the ownership are handed down with the mortgage.[90] A husband cannot, for example, mortgage the family dwelling without the consent of his spouse; although his obligation remains the same, the mortgage is simply not valid. Article 215 of the Civil Code states that the spouse who did not consent to the mortgage has the right to demand its annulment.

In the past the conventional mortgage was bound by very strict procedural rules. It could only be granted by an instrument executed in authentic form in the presence of two notaries, or before a notary and two witnesses. This requirement has since been repealed, but a valid mortgage still requires a description of the specific nature and location of the immovables encumbered; such provisions may not be supplied later to cure a defect in the instrument.[91] Furthermore, and perhaps with the same goal of protecting the mortgagor against imprudence, after-acquired property may not be mortgaged. However, if a debtor does not own sufficient property to secure the debt, the debtor may consent that particular items of subsequently acquired property items be specifically encumbered upon their acquisition.[92]

Article 2134 of the Civil Code governs the priorities among creditors and mortgagors:

---

[87] *Id.* at 2114.

[88] *Id.* at 2115, 2116.

[89] *Id.* at 2118.

[90] *Id.* at 2124, 2135.

[91] *Id.* at 2129.

[92] *Id.* at 2130.

> As among the creditors, a mortgage, whether legal, judicial or conventional, ranks only from the date of inscription by the creditor in the mortgage register in the form and manner prescribed by law . . .

> The order of priority among creditors with liens or mortgages and the holders of negotiable liens, insofar as the latter encumber property deemed to be immovable, is determined by the dates when the respective documents of title were published . . .

The French statute governing recording is thus the equivalent of a race statute: whoever records first, wins.

§ 106FR.04   Landlord/Tenant Law.

§ 106FR.04(a)   Formation of a Lease Contract.

Under French law, a lease may be either written or oral. However, rules for oral leases applied to rural land differ from the rules applied to leases of houses.[93] A person leasing in France would be well-advised in any case to prepare the lease in writing, because if an oral lease has not been fully performed and one of the parties denies its existence, proof from witnesses may not be received at all.[94] If the dispute concerns price, the rule of "buyer beware" applies. The lessor's evidence will be presumed correct, unless the lessee demands an appraisal by experts; if the appraisal exceeds the price the lessee declared, then the lessee is also liable for the expense of the experts.

§ 106FR.04(b)   Duties, Responsibilities and Liabilities of the Lessee.

A lessee has an obligation to furnish the dwelling with enough furniture; otherwise the lessee may be evicted at the landlord's discretion, unless the lessee gives to the lessor adequate security for the rent.[95] The lessee must use the property as a good administrator would[96] and for the purpose for which it was intended.[97] The lessee is also required to pay rent. In case of a dispute as to the amount of rent, the lessee must still pay rent, unless a court judgment intervenes in the lessee's favor.[98]

Article 1754 of the Civil Code designates the specific repairs for which the tenant is responsible (unless a contrary clause is part of the contract):

> To fireplaces, back-plates, sides and tops of mantelpieces;

> To replastering the base of walls of apartments and other places of abode to the height of one meter;

---

[93] *Id.* at 1714.

[94] *Id.* at 1715.

[95] *Id.* at 1752.

[96] "Bon pere de famille" is the expression used in the French Code, which means wise head of the family.

[97] *Id.* at 1728.

[98] 1969 Bull. Civ. III, No. 285.

To panes of glass, unless they have been broken by hail or other extraordinary accidents . . .

To doors, casements, windows, partitions or shutters of shops, hinges, bolts and locks.

The main concern seems to be with ordinary wear-and-tear where it occurs most frequently, such as at the bottom of the walls, and with the prevention of fires and break-ins. The next section of the Civil Code states that none of these repairs are even chargeable to the tenant if they are needed only because of decay or "act of God."[99] Furthermore, if the tenant must make repairs that the landlord should have made, the tenant may deduct those repair expenses from rent.[100]

In case of fire, the tenant is automatically assumed to be responsible and liable, unless the tenant can prove either that the fire was an "act of God," or occurred because of some other circumstance beyond the control of the tenant, or was communicated from an adjoining house.[101]

§ 106FR.04(c)   Responsibilities of the Landlord.

The landlord is obligated to deliver the premises in good repair and to maintain them in good repair for the duration of the lease (with the exceptions mentioned above).[102] Under the covenant of quiet enjoyment, the landlord is also responsible for hidden defects, but only if these actually prevent the use of the premises and were unknown to the renter at the time the lease was signed.[103] This implied covenant of quiet enjoyment also prohibits renting the premises to another party or materially modifying the premises.[104]

§ 106FR.04(d)   Government Intervention in the Rental Market.

Since 1948, the French government has rather heavily regulated the rental market in the heavily populated and rapidly expanding population areas. Among the protections now afforded some renters in those areas are rent ceilings, as well as assurance that as long as they fulfill their obligations under the rent contract (especially paying rent) they may not be ejected at the expiration of the rent contract. Renters may be displaced at the end of a contract if the owner has decided to build or has decided to inhabit the premises. However, even in these cases, requirements of notice and justification by the landlord are sometimes imposed.

---

[99] *Id.* at 1755.

[100] 1985 Bull. Civ. V, No. 89.

[101] C. civ. 1733 (Dalloz).

[102] *Id.* at 1720.

[103] P. Dupont Delestraint, Droit Civil, Principaux Contrats 48 (3d ed. 1973).

[104] *Id.*

CHAPTER 106GB

PROPERTY LAW IN GREAT BRITAIN (ENGLAND AND WALES)

Professor David A. Thomas
J. Reuben Clark Law School
Brigham Young University

SYNOPSIS

§ 106GB.01   History.

Various forms of property ownership were recognized among the inhabitants of the British Isles well before the earliest manifestations of the present legal system began to form. Whoever the earliest prehistoric inhabitants of Britain were, they had been subsumed within the waves of Celtic invaders who had arrived in the later centuries of the pre-Christian era. By the time of Julius Caesar's first reconnaissance probe on the British Isles in 55 B.C., the earlier Celtic peoples were living in what archaeologists describe as a Late Bronze Age civilization, and the more recent Celtic invaders had introduced Iron Age characteristics. In their relationship to the land, it has been said that Britain's

> people lived either in isolated farms or in hut-villages, situated for the most part on the gravel of river-banks or the light upland soils such as the chalk downs or oolite plateaux, which by that time had been to a great extent cleared of their native scrub; each settlement was surrounded by small fields, tilled either with a foot plough. . .or else at best with a light ox-drawn plough which scratched the soil without turning the sod; the dead were burnt and their ashes, preserved in urns, buried in regular cemeteries. Thus the land was inhabited by a stable and industrious peasant population, living by agriculture and the keeping of live stock, augmented no doubt by hunting and fishing.[1]

The most recently arrived Celtic invaders, specifically the Belgae, also followed the practice of marking the boundaries of the territories under their dominance by means of a continuous rampart and ditch.[2]

Caesar followed his reconnaissance with an invasion the following year, in 54 B.C., but the conquest was not completed and Romans then became preoccupied with events closer to Rome. Not until the reign of Claudius, in A.D. 43, did the Romans return and, by conquest, gain the better part of Britain. Even this wholesale political change did not alter the Celtic customs of landholding, except in the few urban areas that became so thoroughly romanized that Roman law was applied, especially as between Roman citizens. For a few, the rise of Roman Britain meant that isolated farms became villas, and substantial farm houses replaced Iron Age dwellings,[3] but for perhaps 85% of the British population "their pre-Roman lifestyles survived into and through the Roman occupation."[4]

With the increase of barbarian aggressions throughout the Roman Empire in the 5th century A.D., the Roman legions were withdrawn from Britain. The Romano-Britons eventually succumbed to the persistent attacks and invasions from Angles, Saxons and Jutes, crossing over from north Germany and the Danish peninsula.

---

[1] R. G. Collingwood & J. N. L. Myres, Roman Britain and the English Settlements 20 (1937).

[2] *Id.* at 28.

[3] Peter Salway, Roman Britain 234-235 (Oxford, 1981).

[4] David A. Thomas, *The Disappearance of Roman Law from Dark Age Britain*, B.Y.U. L. Rev. 563, 583.

These Germanic invaders had different land-holding customs. From earliest times, as agriculture became more prominent among them, chieftains had made distributions of land annually to kindred groups. Eventually, the distributions were made to individuals, some of whom began to accumulate wealth. These customs underwent substantial change when the invasions of Britain enabled whole tribes to leave their Germanic homelands and settle anew:

> The passage of time and opportunities for conquest produced quite different land distribution practices among the early Anglo-Saxons in Britain. Land freshly conquered or pioneered by Anglo-Saxon settlers was divided by lot, with a number of tracts kept in reserve as commons or as defensive buffers. Holdings assigned to individual warriors who became settlers were permanent, not subject to the annual reallocations practiced by their ancestors.. . . Apart from contributing to physical survival, holding an individual portion of land was a prerequisite for sharing in the use and product of the commons, for voting in public assemblies, and for going to court. Ownership of land therefore signified both freedom and franchise.[5]

As kingship developed among the Anglo-Saxons in Britain, the kings took over large tracts of subjugated land, granting substantial portions to their chief warrior companions. Most of such land was actually worked by peasants, and most of the land was eventually impressed with obligations of military service, bridge construction, fortress maintenance, taxation and other labor projects. When land was conveyed, the grantee held only for life, unless special permission was obtained to pass the holding to a descendant. Written documents called charters came into use for granting lands to the church, so that such land came to be called "bookland." Those who held bookland often had rights of alienation or devise, but other granted lands, called "laenland" or "loan land," could be alienated or inherited only with the lord's permission or charter. The large tracts of land not held as bookland or loan land were held as "folk land," a term of uncertain meaning, but probably subject to certain customary rights based on occupancy.

As the watershed event of the Norman Conquest neared, probably most Anglo-Saxon land was occupied under some sort of manorial economy. Within the manorial system typical over much of England, the lord of the manor held the land, but it was actually worked and occupied by peasants who owed services and rents to the lord, and in addition were in some form of personal servitude to the lord, in return for rights to occupy and till their plots of land. Personally free peasant farmers were more numerous in the eastern and northern areas of England, where Viking invaders of the ninth and tenth centuries A.D., had been most dominant.

After the Norman Conquest, which commenced in A.D. 1066, the

---

[5] David A. Thomas, *Anglo-Saxon Antecedents of the Common Law,* Per Author 1985 B.Y.U. L. Rev. 453, 467.

landholding arrangements among the peasants were left intact, but most English lands changed lords. Within two decades after the Conquest began, the 4,000–5,000 English lords who held land before the Conquest had been replaced by 1,400–1,500 Norman lords. The Norman feudal customs, those customs establishing the conditions under which land was held, began to replace their English counterparts, creating greater emphasis on the military obligations of chief tenants and bringing about greater uniformity in the landholding practices overall. Inheritability, the most important attribute of property, had become widely recognized by the beginning of the twelfth century.

Along with inheritability, other important property rights, such as alienability and devisability, achieved increasing acceptance during the Middle Ages. The persistent impulse on the part of some to render land freely alienable so its inherent market value could be realized, was countered by others who sought to limit the ability of descendants to transfer away portions of great family holdings. Various forms of landholding, called estates in land, were recognized by the courts, but then often came to be restricted or even abolished by royal decree or statute. The various kinds of estates, with their individual attributes or incidents, together formed a complex and highly technical system of property rights.

Once the legal rules governing those property interests formed and stabilized, the rules tended to become rigid, resulting in occasional injustices for property owners whose situations had not been anticipated by the rules. For such, the monarch was prepared to dispense individual justice, but not necessarily in conformance with the "common law" rules, the rules emanating from the law common to all of England. These alternative rules came to be known as equity, because their purpose was to do justice and equity in cases not covered adequately by common law rules. Thus equity decrees produced a second set of property rules, parallel to and often in concurrent jurisdiction with common law rules, which rules further complicated property rights in England.

Because land was considered the ultimate form of wealth, the most affluent and ambitious persons in England sought to accumulate as much as possible with the broadest incidents or rights. Property holding was closely associated with social status, so that not only the size of landholdings, but also the type of ownership—the particular kind of estate by which one held property—correlated closely with one's social class. Persons who were not bound in some way to the land under a manorial economy were considered free, and the property interests they typically held were called freeholds. Conversely, the peasants or serfs typically owed such heavy duties of labor service and farm produce to their feudal lords, that they were considered not free to leave the land, and the forms of property holding typical for this class were labeled as non-freeholds or unfree tenures. Medieval serfs usually held land by arrangements akin to the modern leasehold, a right to occupy the land for a period of time in consideration of services or produce paid to the landlord. These property interests, or tenures, retain even in England today the labels of freehold or unfree, even though the social status distinctions are no longer relevant.

As England emerged from feudalism, the feudal obligations of military service or other kinds of service given in return for landholding also became irrelevant. Eventually the legal and equitable rules were adjusted to enable landholders more easily to obtain the money value of property by conveying various kinds of interests in the property, practices that were less acceptable in a feudal society which relied on well-known landholders to loyally perform their service obligations. Yet some of the old elements of property law with feudal origins and complexities lingered on, only reluctantly responsive to changes in economy and society.

To boldly achieve a system of general property law fit for modern society, the English Parliament culminated an extensive period of law reform by enactment of the Property Acts of 1925, consisting of several statutory components: the unrepealed portions of earlier reform acts, especially of the Law of Property Act of 1922[6] and the Law of Property (Amendment) Act of 1924;[7] the Settled Land Act of 1925;[8] the Trustee Act of 1925;[9] the Law of Property Act of 1925;[10] the Land Registration Act of 1925;[11] the Land Charges Act of 1925;[12] and the Administration of Estates Act of 1925.[13] Since 1925, specific areas of property law have also been subject to reform statutes, including, among others, the Perpetuities and Accumulations Act,[14] the Law of Property (Joint Tenants) Act,[15] the Matrimonial Homes Act,[16] the Leasehold Reform Act,[17] another Law of Property Act,[18] the Charging Orders Act,[19] and the Limitation Act.[20] Particularly during the twentieth century, English land law reforms have been characterized by increasing

---

[6] 12 & 13 Geo. 5, c. 16; Law of Property (Amendment) Act, 15 & 16 Geo. 5, c. 5.

[7] 15 & 16 Geo. 5, c. 5.

[8] 15 & 16 Geo. 5, c. 18.

[9] 15 & 16 Geo. 5, c. 19.

[10] 15 & 16 Geo. 5, c. 20.

[11] 15 & 16 Geo. 5, c. 21.

[12] 15 & 16 Geo. 5, c. 22, later replaced by the Land Charges Act of 1972, c. 61.

[13] 15 & 16 Geo. 5, c. 23.

[14] 1964, c. 55.

[15] 1964, c. 63.

[16] 1967, c. 75.

[17] 1967, c. 88.

[18] 1969, c. 59.

[19] 1979, c. 53.

[20] 1980, c. 24.

governmental regulation to achieve public benefits or protections at the expense of purely private interests in land.

§ 106GB.02   Types of Real Property Interests.

§ 106GB.02(a)   Legal Estates in Real Property.

As a result of the 1925 property acts, English law recognizes only two types of legal estates, an estate being an interest in land of defined duration.[21] These estates recognized in law are the fee simple absolute in possession and the term of years absolute. Apart from these estates and the legal property interests described in § 106GB.02(b) *infra,* all other estates, interests, and charges relating to land are treated as equitable interests.

§ 106GB.02(a)(1)   Fee Simple Absolute in Possession.

The fee simple absolute is the form of land ownership with the maximum cognizable interests associated with land ownership, and the ownership is potentially infinite in duration; as an "in possession" interest, the fee simple absolute is a presently possessory interest rather than an interest that will become possessory at some time in the future.

§ 106GB.02(a)(2)   Term of Years Absolute.

The term of years absolute means any right to possess land for a period of fixed and certain duration, even for less than a year, and can include periodic tenancies. It need not be a presently possessory interest, and can be created to commence at some time in the future less than 21 years from the time the lease was created.

§ 106GB.02(a)(3)   Concurrent Ownership of Legal Estates.

If a conveyance is made to multiple tenants in common directly or to multiple trustees, the number of concurrent owners is limited to four.[22] The limitation of concurrent ownership to four owners is not so explicit as to joint tenants, but is so treated under English law.[23]

§ 106GB.02(b)   Legal Interests in the Land of Another.

English law also recognizes five types of legal estates that constitute interests in the land of another.

§ 106GB.02(b)(1)   Easement, Right, or Privilege in Land, Equivalent in Duration to a Legal Estate.

Easements, rights or privileges in land equivalent in duration to a legal estate, include the right to use the land of another in a certain way, or to prevent a certain use of the land of another, or to take something from the

---

[21] David J. Hayton, Megarry's Manual of the Law of Real Property 28 (1982).

[22] Law of Property Act of 1925, sec. 34.

[23] David J. Hayton, Megarry's Manual of the Law of Real Property 310 (1982).

land of another, typically called easements and profits. They are considered legal interests if their specified duration is similar to one of the two legal estates, either perpetual or limited to a fixed and certain time.

§ 106GB.02(b)(2)   A Rentcharge in Possession Imposed on Land, Either Perpetual or for a Term of Years Absolute.

A rentcharge is a right to periodic payment of a sum of money imposed as a burden on land. For a rentcharge to be a legal interest, the party obligated to pay must be in possession of the property, even if the charge itself commences at a future date; further, the duration of the rentcharge must be a duration similar to one of the two legal estates, either perpetual or limited to a fixed and certain time. Since 1977, severe restrictions have been placed on the creation of new rentcharges.

§ 106GB.02(b)(3)   A Charge by Way of Legal Mortgage.

The legal mortgage is created either by conveying a term of years absolute subject to being defeated by redemption, or by a deed creating a charge by way of legal mortgage. This is an interest in land, given as security for the repayment of a debt, and which is extinguished upon full repayment. If default occurs, the mortgagee has certain rights in the land which may be employed to obtain satisfaction of the debt.

§ 106GB.02(b)(4)   Charges on Land That Are not Created by an Instrument.

These encumbrances consist of obligations similar to the now abolished land taxes and tithe rentcharges. Land taxes were abolished in 1963 and tithe rentcharges were abolished in 1936. The charges considered to be legal interests consist of periodic payments burdening the land by operation of law.

§ 106GB.02(b)(5)   A Right of Entry Connected with a Term of Years Absolute or with a Rentcharge.

A typical right of entry considered to be a legal interest is the landlord's right to enter premises under a legal term of years absolute if the tenant fails to pay the rent or observe other covenants of the term.

§ 106GB.02(c)   Equitable Interests in Land.

All interests in land other than those described above are considered equitable interests. This means, for instance, that a life estate or a fee tail is no longer a legal estate, but can exist within the framework of a trust. So if the legal estate in fee simple is vested in a trustee, then the beneficial or equitable interests defined by the trust instrument can take the form of a life estate or a fee tail or numerous variants of those interests. Other interests that are no longer legal in nature but are still recognized as equitable interests are restrictive covenants and other interests under trust.

The basic distinction between legal and equitable interests is that a purchaser who buys property without notice of an adverse legal right is bound by the right (so the present holder is protected), while a purchaser who buys without notice of an equitable interest takes free of the equitable interest (so the present holder is not protected from a bona fide purchaser). The important changes in property law made in 1925 were intended to reduce the number of legal estates and interests and thus protect purchasers, and also to protect holders of equitable interests.

Holders of equitable interests are protected by the ability to register their interests of a commercial (economic) nature under the Land Charges Act of 1925. Registration of the equitable interest confers notice on all, and any potential purchaser is bound by such notice. Indeed, if no registration of the equitable interest has occurred, the purchaser is not bound even if actual notice has occurred by some other means. Certain equitable interests not specifically covered by the Land Charges Act are still subject to the old doctrine of constructive notice. Apart from equitable interests registrable under the Land Charges Act, only the now severely limited legal estates and legal interests in the land of another can be registered for title purposes under the Land Registration Act of 1925.

§ 106GB.02(d)   Land Ownership by Aliens.

Since 1914 aliens have been permitted generally to hold and acquire land in the same ways as British citizens.[24]

§ 106GB.03   Conveyancing.

Closely connected with the procedures for conveying real property are the legal rules for registering land titles and for conducting transactions in unregistered land titles. By the term registration is meant a system of certified titles guaranteed by the government, which replaces the routine of making a separate investigation of the state of the title each time a transaction occurs involving that title. In other words, an examination of the register is substituted for the search that traditionally involves review of the abstract of the deed and of encumbrances on the title, and inspection of the property. It is estimated that about 75% of current conveyancing activity in England and Wales concerns registered land. Whether land is registered or unregistered, conveyances usually begin with preliminary negotiations and inquiries, the creation of a draft contract, and the execution of a formal contract, and culminates with carrying out the terms of the contract by exchange of consideration and title documents on the completion day agreed upon by the parties.

In this section, the basic outline of the registration law is described, followed by a summary of contract procedure for the sale of land, and

---

[24] Status of Aliens Act, 4 & 5 Geo. 5, c. 17, s. 17 (1914).

descriptions of conveyancing procedure after the contract is executed for registered and unregistered title, respectively.

§ 106GB.03(a)   Creation of a Contract.

In the typical case where a fee simple interest is being sold for money, the parties will enter into a contract before the transaction actually occurs. Even before entering into the contract, the purchaser should conduct a preliminary examination of title and inspection of the property. If items seem to be not entirely in order, a form called Inquiries before Contract will be prepared to note such items and then sent to the vendor. A search of local land charges (public encumbrances) should be made, and an inquiry of the pertinent local authority is made by a standard form to learn of encumbrances that are not registrable. These contract procedures are typical whether the land to be conveyed is registered or unregistered.

§ 106GB.03(b)   Registration of Land.

Some areas of England and Wales have been designated as compulsory areas, within which registration of title is required if the proposed convey-ance results from the sale of a fee simple or from the creation or assignment of certain leases. For other transactions in the compulsory areas, registration is optional. The constantly expanding compulsory areas are concentrated in urban regions, so that they now cover about half the area and three-fourths the population of England and Wales. Outside the compulsory areas, applications to register now will not be accepted in all but a limited class of cases and where certain public housing units are sold to tenants. In a conveyance of registered land, the legal interest does not pass to the purchaser until the purchaser is registered as the new proprietor of the title.

§ 106GB.03(c)   Registration of Land Charges.

The Land Charges Act of 1925 and its successor, the Land Charges Act of 1972, greatly increased the types of rights that can be registered and thus protected against purchasers without notice. If an interest is properly registered, the registration constitutes notice to all persons for all purposes. The types of interests entitled to be registered are land charges (generally, equitable interests that are of value because of their effect on another's land),[25] pending actions (both an ordinary *lis pendens* and actions in bankruptcy),[26] writs and orders affecting land,[27] and deeds of arrangement (similar to receiverships).[28] The land charges category is the most compre-hensive type of registrable interest. This consists of charges (that is, interests or encumbrances) imposed on land by statute; certain legal mortgages; an

---

[25] Land Charges Act of 1972, §§ 2–4.

[26] Land Charges Act of 1972, § 5.

[27] Land Charges Act of 1972, § 6.

[28] Land Charges Act of 1972, § 7.

obligation owed to a tenant for life or statutory owner for discharging death duties or other liabilities; general equitable charges (such as an unpaid vendor's lien); a contract to convey or create a legal estate (including purchase options and pre-emptive rights); death duties, restrictive covenants, and certain equitable easements; certain annuities; and a spouse's right to enter and occupy a house owned by the other spouse.

§ 106GB.03(d)   Conveyance of Registered Title.

When parties have entered into a contract for the sale of registered land, the vendor gives the purchaser authorization to make a search of the Land Register, which is otherwise not open to public inspection.[29] The vendor also provides copies or abstracts of documents noted on the register, such as those that impose encumbrances on the land. If any unfavorable or unexpected entries appear in the register, the parties conduct a process of inquiries or "requisitions" and responses to achieve satisfaction of the contract terms. If this process is completed successfully, the purchaser fills in a draft transfer form, with any appropriate special clauses, and sends the form to the vendor for approval. Upon approval, a clean copy is prepared by the purchaser and sent to the vendor for execution. A few days before the day fixed for completion or closing, another search, called an official search, of the register is conducted to learn of any new entries. Following the official search, a priority period begins, now 30 days, within which the register is closed to certain new entries and the transaction must be completed:[30]

> Before expiry of the priority period afforded by the official search certificate, [the purchaser] will attend upon [the vendor] to receive the duly executed transfer and the land certificate in return for [the purchaser's] banker's draft for the moneys due under [the vendor's] completion statement. Unlike the unregistered land position, the legal title does not pass until [the purchaser] has lodged his application to register the transfer with the appropriate District Land Registry, and [the purchaser] must ensure that this is done before expiry of the priority period afforded by the official search certificate.[31]

§ 106GB.03(e)   Conveyance of Unregistered Title.

When parties have entered into a contract for the conveyance of unregistered title, the vendor delivers to the purchaser an abstract of title. The abstract begins with a document in the chain of title that constitutes a

---

[29] Land Registration Act of 1925, §§ 112, 112A.

[30] The official search certificate protects the purchaser against entries of certain interests made in the thirty working days following the day of the certificate, referred to as the priority period. Such entries made during the period are subordinated, or "postponed," to the purchaser's interest if the purchaser's application of registration is received at the appropriate registry before expiration of the priority period.

[31] David J. Hayton, Megarry's Manual of the Law of Real Property 156 (1982).

good "root of title," which is now required to be only 15 years old or more,[32] and summarizes the documents and events that have affected the title subsequent to the root of title.[33] For encumbrances or transactions subsequent to the root of title, the Land Charges Register must be searched. As an alternative to the abstract, an epitome may be prepared, which summarizes the essential facts in the chain of title and provides photocopies of the supporting documents.

If the abstract or epitome raises questions on the part of the purchaser, further information may be requested of the vendor by a series of written questions or requirements for corrective action called "requisitions on title." The vendor answers the requisitions and the parties go through further requisitions and answers until appropriate and mutually satisfactory terms for the transaction are worked out.

The purchaser then prepares a draft conveyance (deed)[34] on a standard form and sends the form to the vendor for approval. When any amendments by either party are included and approved, a new, formal copy is prepared by the purchaser and sent to the vendor for signature. The parties then determine a day for completion or closing, and shortly before then the purchaser conducts an official search of the land charges register. A search certificate is issued, which begins the priority period, within which new entries of certain interests are subordinated or "postponed," until the expiration of 30 working days. The completion should occur before the priority period expires.

At the completion, the vendor delivers the title deeds[35] and the signed conveyance to the purchaser,[36] who pays the purchase price. A completion statement will have been previously prepared to show the exact amount due after apportioning rates (taxes) and other charges to the date of completion. The purchaser would thereafter typically submit an application to register the conveyance with the Land Registry.

---

[32] Law of Property Act of 1969, § 23.

[33] A root of title document is one that (1) deals with the entire legal and equitable interest, (2) accurately and adequately describes the property, (3) shows nothing to cast doubt on the title, and (4) is at least fifteen years old.

[34] A conveyance of a legal estate must be by deed. Law of Property Act of 1925, § 52(1).

[35] The vendor may retain title deeds that relate to additional land of the vendor, that create a trust which continues in existence, or that relate to the appointment or discharge of trustees. As to any retained deeds, the vendor must provide the purchaser with an acknowledgement of the purchaser's right to have the deeds produced, plus an undertaking for their safekeeping. Law of Property Act of 1925, § 64.

[36] The purchaser will sign the conveyance only if it contains some obligation that the purchaser must observe toward the vendor, such as conformity to restrictive covenants.

CHAPTER 106IN

PROPERTY LAW IN INDIA

Professor David A. Thomas
J. Reuben Clark Law School
Brigham Young University

SYNOPSIS

§ 106IN.01   Brief History of India.

§ 106IN.01(a)   Prehistory of India.

The earliest written documents from what is present-day India date from approximately 1500, B.C. All information about India prior to that time, therefore, shall be treated in this chapter as the prehistory of India.

Such evidence of India's prehistory shows that from as early as 30,000 through 4,000, B.C., hunter-gatherer peoples living in Stone Age conditions inhabited parts of India.[1] By 7000, B.C., pastoral and agricultural communities had come into existence. The earliest known civilization in India is called the Harappan civilization, named for some of its ruins first discovered in a place called Haripah in northwest India. The origin of this culture is unknown; the time of its entry into India, if indeed it was not indigenous to India, is unknown. Scholars believe the cultural had acquired some urban characteristics by 2600, B.C.[2] "Harrapan cities were trading and craft production centers, set within the mixed economies—farming, herding, hunting and gathering—of the wider Indus region and dependent on these surrounding economies for food and raw materials . . . . Workshops in larger Harrapan towns and sometimes even whole settlements existed for the craft production of traded items."[3] Some of these cities and smaller settlements may have been planned communities.[4] This society was contemporary with nearby Mesopotamian and Egyptian societies, but, in contrast, apparently had no written texts, monuments or large statues.

§ 106IN.01(b)   The Early History of India.

By 1800, B.C., the Harappan civilization had mysteriously disappeared, its communities either abandoned or occupied by peoples with a different culture. A few generations after this disappearance, peoples now referred to as Indo-Aryans gradually migrated from areas of modern Iran and Afghanistan into the Punjab region of northwest India. With its Reg-Veda and numerous other ancient hymns, and its Sanskrit language, this nomadic, pastoral and warrior Aryan culture achieved a distinct identity.[5] Even though much of Sanskrit writing remains unintelliglble, it still marks the beginning of India's historical period. With iron-age technology, by the early centuries of the post-Christian era this "Sanskrit-based Aryan culture in which competing Hindu, Buddhist, and Jaina religions vied for dominance had spread its cultural hegemony through all settled regions of the subcontinent."[6] This led to a second Indian urbanization that developed from 600 to 300, B.C.

In this period, population grew and cities emerged, both in the plains and along trade routes. It was a time of vigorous religious development and "volatile and competitive" political life.[7] By 327, A.D., armies of Alexander the Great had penetrated into Indian territory, and after his death in 323,

---

[1] Judith E. Walsh, *A Brief History of India* 6 (2004).

[2] *Id.*

[3] *Id.* at 9.

[4] *Id.* at 11.

[5] *Id.* at 13, 17–18.

[6] *Id.* at 20.

[7] *Id.* at 33.

A.D., a Seleucid dynasty founded by one of his generals continued in power for about a century. Elsewhere in India, one of the greatest emperors, Ashoka, reigned from c. 268-233, B.C., and created an enormous empire, judging from his widespread edicts inscribed in rocks and pillars. Trade between the Roman empire and the eastern and western coasts of India continued between the first century, B.C., and the seventh century, A.D. A series of regional tributary political systems was stabilized during the so-called Gupta dynasty, c. 320–550, A.D. "By the seventh century elites who identified with a Sanskrit-based, Aryan culture dominated atll regions of the Indian subcontinent."[8]

In the seventh century, A.D., Islamic armies invaded India and in various degrees maintained a dominance in India until the 18th century. During the 16th and 17th centuries, the Portuguese, Dutch, English and French established trade with India and engaged in a variety of conflicts and struggles to maintain and expand those trading interests. During the middle of the 18th century the French and English trading companies engaged in open warfare for control of the Indian trade, with the English emerging supreme. The ruling British East India Company came under governmental regulation beginning with a series of laws in 1773, and by 1833 the company controlled most of India. Indeed, England's "Charter Act of 1833 abolished the East India Company's commercial functions, opening all of Asia to private trade and ending the company's existence as a commercial body. It left the company's government structures in place, however, as a bureaucratic shell through which Parliament would continue to govern India."[9] In 1858, after having survived serious native revolts, the British abolished the East India Company and placed India directly under the rule of the British Crown. Queen Victoria became empress of India in 1876. One-third of India was ruled by almost 600 "Princely States" under British supervision.

A nationalist movement for Indian independence from England was led by Mohandas Gandhi from 1920 to 1948. In 1947, India became independent from Great Britain, and a Dominion of the Commonwealth, and east and west Pakistan were partitioned from India. India became a republic in 1950.

§ 106IN.02   Governmental and Legal Foundations for Property Law in Modern India.

A new Indian Constitution, one of the longest and most detailed written constitutions in the world, became law in 1950. The Constitution's preamble guaranteed to all citizens the rights of justice, liberty, equality and fraternity. It created the Republic of India as a national government, which was also a federation of regional state governments. "The union government is divided into three distinct, but not entirely separate, branches: the executive,

---

[8] *Id.* at 58.

[9] *Id.* at 104.

legislative, and judicial. The executive leadership is drawn from and is responsible to the legislative body. The Constitution provides for a judiciary that is free from executive or legislative interference in its deliberations."[10]

Statutes, customary law and case law are also sources of law in India. The statutes are enacted by the national Parliament, by state legislatures and by union territory legislatures. Despite this federal diversity, the India court system is a "single integrated system of courts to administer both the union and the state laws."[11]

Fundamental rights in India are defined in Articles 12–35 of the Constitution. Originally Article 9(1) included the fundamental rights to acquire, hold and dispose of property among those fundamental rights, but that particular provision fell victim to a lengthy controversy over judicial review in India.[12] The controversy centered on Article 31 of the Constitution, providing that no person could be deprived of property except by authority of law and only for compensation. These provisions as written interfered with Indian attempts at land reform.

Land reform in India long remained at the "level predetermined by the British Indian Tenancy Acts,"[13] which secured rights of peasants holding directly from their landlords. Many of the rural poor were unprotected.

> Of course, there were ceilings on landholdings imposed by legislation and there was the prohibition of subletting of land. But in the absence of a proper record of rights, breaches of the law were hard to prove and this type of legislation remained a mere eyewash.[14]

Resistance to land reform ultimately rested on the constitutional guarantees of property rights, and the Indian courts accepted these arguments. This led to constitutional amendments severely limiting the courts' powers of judicial review, including judicial review rights over even constitutional amendments. After many constitutional amendments, many judicial decisions, and significant political upheavals, judicial review over whether even constitutional amendments conformed to the basic structure of the constitution was mostly restored, but property rights were removed from the category of fundamental rights and now is classed as an ordinary right.

Now the Constitution of India simply regulates the government's acqui-

---

[10] Chun-Chi Young, "The Legal System of the Republic of India," in 9 Linda L. Schlueter (ed.), *Modern Legal Systems Cyclopedia* 9.80.16 (2001).

[11] Price Waterhouse, *Doing Business in India* 4 (1989).

[12] Ruediger Wolfram and Rainer Grote (gen. eds.), "India," VIII *Constitutions of the Countries of the World* 11–15 (2006); P. P. Pandit, "Constitutional Protections of Property in India," in *Some Aspects of Indian Law Today* 15–24 (1964); Lalit Bhasin, *The Law of Land Acquisition in India* (Sao Paulo Conference on the Law of the World, 1981).

[13] Hermann Kulke and Dietmar Rothermund, *A History of India* 317 (1986).

[14] *Id.* at 318.

sition or extinguishment of estate or rights therein,[15] and proclaims, "No person shall be deprived of his property save by authority of law."[16] Articles 294–296 deal, respectively, with "Succession to property, assets, rights, liabilities and obligations in certain cases," "Succession to property, assets, rights, liabilities and obligations in other cases," and "Property accruing by escheat or lapse or as *Bona Vacantia*."

Under Article 39(b), the government is directed to ensure "that the ownership and control of the material resources of the community are so distributed as best to subserve the common good."

§ 106IN.03   Basic Indian Property Law.

Basic Indian property law is extensively a product of statutory enactment. The principal laws and rules on selected property topics are described below.

§ 106IN.03(a)   Estates in Land.

Under India property law, the term immovable property includes essentially all that is meant by real property in English law. Despite this civil law terminology, Indian property law still rests on a foundation of English law, including the estates of fee simple and life estate well-recognized in English law.

§ 106IN.03(b)   Concurrent Estates.

The concurrent estates of tenancy in common and joint tenancy are recognized in India. The tenancy in common is presumed if the nature of the concurrent estate is not specified.

§ 106IN.03(c)   Leaseholds.

A registered instrument is required for a lease of immoveable property for a term exceeding one year or for a year-to-year term. Leases for other terms can be created by oral agreement and transfer of possession. Permission of tax authorities may be required for leases above a certain value.

§ 106IN.03(d)   Gifts.

All gifts of immoveable property must be made by registered instrument.

§ 106IN.03(e)   Succession.

Among the significant property topics regulated by major statutory enactments are several succession statutes. The Indian Succession Act of 1952 governs intestate succession for Parsis (professing the Zoroastrian religion), Indian Christians, Jews and others. The Hindu Succession Act of 1956 governs intestate succession among Hindus. Muslim succession,

---

[15] Constitution of India, Article 31A.

[16] Constitution of India, Article 300A.

testate and intestate, is governed by Sunni and Shia doctrines.[17]

§ 106IN.03(f)   Wills.

As mentioned above, a variety of statutory and customary approaches to testate and intestate succession are set forth in several Indian succession laws, mostly corresponding to one's professed religion. The Indian Succession Act of 1925 governs wills, and these laws as they relate to formalities are closely patterned after the English model.

§ 106IN.03(g)   Real Estate Transactions.

Real property in India is generally included in the statutory references to immoveable property. The Transfer of Property Act governs conveyances of property to living persons, such term including a company, association or body of individuals, whether or not incorporated. Actual conveyances of immoveable property interest over a certain value can be made only by registered instrument; other transfers can be made by delivery. Real estate contracts do not create interests in the property.

These rules also apply to mortgages. In certain large cities, equitable mortgages on immoveable property are created by the debtor delivering documents of title to the creditor for the purposes of securing the loan.

Other transactions involving the conduct of the parties or operation of law, but not delivery of title documents, where property is made security for payment of money, are called legal charges.

The Industrial Policy (1991) invites and regulates foreign investment, including foreign direct investment in virtually all sectors.

§ 106IN.03(h)   Special Rules.

Conveyances of immoveable property to charitable trusts, or of agricultural property to one who will not use the property for agriculture require prior approval from appropriate government officials. Also, agricultural lands are subject to laws limiting the amount of such land that may be held.

§ 106IN.03(i)   Title Registration.

The Indian Registration Act governs registration of documents of transfer. No registration should occur unless the proper authorities have certified that arrangements have been made to satisfy all existing liabilities relating to the property.

§ 106IN.03(j)   Stamps.

Transactional documents must bear the appropriate stamps, as determined by federal and state law and according to varying rates, under authority of the Indian Stamp Act of 1899. Stamp duty is to be paid on all documents that

---

[17] Chun-Chi Young, "The Legal System of the Republic of India," in 9 Linda L. Schlueter (ed.), *Modern Legal Systems Cyclopedia* 9.80.34–35 (2001).

are registered, and averages 12–13%, a relatively high rate. Efforts to avoid registration are often intended to avoid paying the stamp tax.

§ 106IN.03(k)   Taxation.

§ 106IN.03(k)(1)   Estate Tax.

The estate tax was abolished in India with respect to deaths occurring after March 16, 1985. Income tax is subject to special rules and rates for residential rental income (house property).

§ 106IN.03(k)(2)   Wealth Tax.

The Wealth Tax Act of 1957 imposed an annual tax, similar to a property tax, on 1% of the value of various kinds of property above a certain value, including buildings and appurtenant lands used for residential or commercial purposes, urban land, and land held for investment.

§ 106IN.03(l)   Environmental Regulation.

Environmental regulation and protection in India is a vast subject with an enormous amount of statutory detail. It suffices, for purposes of this chapter, to list below the principal governing statutes, to illustrate the scope and diversity of environmental regulation:[18]

The Atomic Energy Act of 1962

The Delegated Legislation Provisions Act (Amendment, 2004) (delegating much regulation authority to the states)

The Environmental Protection Act of 1986

The Factories Act of 1948

The Forest Conservation Act of 1980

The Indian Forest Act of 1927

The Insecticides Act of 1968

The National Environment Policy 2004

The National Environment Tribunal Act (1995)

The Public Liability Insurance Act (1991) (relating to hazardous materials)

The Water Prevention and Control of Pollution Act of 1974

The Water Prevention and Control of Pollution Cess Act of 1977

The Wildlife Protection Act of 1974

---

[18] *See also,* Aditya Shankar and Saptak Sanyal, "Property Rights and Sustainable Development in India," 22 *Colum. J. Asian L.* 235–257 (2009).

CHAPTER 106JP

PROPERTY LAW IN JAPAN

Professor David A. Thomas
J. Reuben Clark Law School
Brigham Young University

SYNOPSIS

§ 106JP.01   Brief History of Japanese Property Law.

Before the 7th century A.D., Japanese law was unwritten and dealt mostly with rituals of ancestor worship and the relationships of clans and families. Only in some of the laws now governing the imperial household may be found any remnants of this prehistoric law.

When Chinese influence reached Japan by way of Korea during the 7th century, the accompanying priests helped create a new moral structure in Japan. This same moral structure still forms the basis of Japanese social ethics. The result of this new influence for development of law was the Taiho Code of A.D. 701, which was based on Chinese law. The Taiho Code did not draw a clear line between morality and law or between private law and public law — its aim was to preserve moral order and harmony in human relationships. In this code much attention was given to the form of government, the hierarchy of offices, and the discipline of officials and subjects. Most of the legal rules, therefore, would be described today as "public law." The few rules of private law dealt mostly with family and succession matters. Some family regulations were in the nature of public law, because order in the family was considered essential to harmonious world order.

With the weakening of central authority, a feudal system developed in the 12th century and persisted until the 19th century. During the feudal period, the government was ruled by a succession of military houses and the old, formal Chinese laws were modified to fit feudal conditions, and later to accommodate the military government that was controlled by a single dynasty for the final three hundred years of the period. Separate sets of laws and traditions governed the Imperial Court, warriors, commoners, and outcasts. The ownership of land was at first restricted to the warrior classes, but merchants gradually overcame this handicap and gained a substantial economic position. Law, for the most part, consisted of private instructions and regulations for officials, and were rarely or only partially publicized.

In 1868 the ruling Tokugawa family was overthrown by opposition clans, which then established government controls in the Emperor Meiji. This was followed by the re-establishment of a strong central government, the abolition of the feudal regime, and the abandonment of the policy of isolation which had secluded Japan from the rest of the world for three hundred years.

Meanwhile, a second wave of foreign influence had commenced with the coming of the "black ships" under the American Commodore Perry in 1853. This resulted in opening the country to trade and shipping and the adoption of Western technology. New laws were adopted to accommodate a society changing from agricultural and feudal to industrial and commercial. New laws enabled Japan to obtain better trade treaties and also reduce foreign extra-territorial privileges.

The new laws were based, principally, on the continental European legal system. The commercial code, the bankruptcy law and the code of civil procedure were derived from the counterpart German codes; the criminal code and the code of criminal procedure were influenced by their French counterparts.

The first Japanese Civil Code compilation commission was formed in 1875, but the entire Civil Code was not enacted until 1898. The delay was caused by uncertainty about how to frame laws dealing satisfactorily with family and succession. Eventually a two-part code was adopted, one part containing the general provisions based mostly on continental European law, and the other with provisions on family and succession, drawn largely from traditional law and custom. This two-part code was still in force when Western occupation commenced at the end of World War II.

With the inception of that occupation, law in Japan came under increased influence of Anglo-Saxon legal ideas. The revision of the Civil Code in 1947, under the direction of occupation authorities, essentially completed the transition of Japanese civil law to European law.

The new post-war constitution included principles regarding marriage and family, which thus once again became matters of public law. The adoption of this new constitution on January 1, 1948, also hastened the revision of the Civil Code, which was already underway. The new Civil Code was created by a committee consisting of ministerial officials, judges, scholars, lawyers, journalists, and representatives of both houses of the Diet. Women were also included on the committee. This committee worked with occupation lawyers to articulate reforms that were carried out under the military occupation. With the exception of one article, the revision of the Civil Code dealt almost exclusively with family law, Books 4 and 5 of the old civil code. The property laws of Book 2 were generally not the subject of revision.

§ 106JP.02   Property Interests Recognized in Japan.

§ 106JP.02(a)   General Concepts.

Land and things fixed to land are considered immovables. Things are considered fixed to the land if they are closely attached, such as buildings and fixtures, or form a body with the land, such as water and minerals. Rights in real property are known as real rights. Real rights may be created by intention of the parties coupled with delivery or registration.[1]

§ 106JP.02(b)   Possessory Rights.

Japanese law distinguishes between:

  legal possession and natural possession;

  possession by just title and possession by unjust title;

  possession in good faith and possession in bad faith;

  defective possession and non-defective possession;

  faulty possession and faultless possession; and

  continuous possession and non-continuous possession.

Possessory rights are acquired by holding things with the intention of so doing on one's own account,[2] or are acquired through a representative.[3]

§ 106JP.02(c)   Ownership.

"An owner has the right of freely using, receiving profits of, and disposing of the thing owned within the restrictions of laws and ordinances."[4] "The ownership of land, within the restrictions of laws and ordinances, extends above and under the surface."[5]

§ 106JP.02(c)(1)   Civil Code Provisions Relating to Various Aspects of Land Ownership.

§ 106JP.02(c)(1)(i)   Limits on Ownership of Buildings.

1.   When several persons each own a portion of a building divided into parts, the parts in common use of the building and its accessories are presumed to be jointly owned by them.

2.   The expenses of repairing and other charges for the parts in

---

[1] 1 Annotated Civil Code of Japan, art. 176 (J. E. de Becker trans. 1979) (hereafter "Civil Code").

[2] *Id.* art. 180. Scott, Geoffrey R. "The Cultural Property Laws of Japan: Social, Political, and Legal Influences." 12 Pac. Rim L. & Pol'y J. 315 (March, 2003); West, Mark D. "Losers: Recovering Lost Property in Japan and the United States." 37 Law & Soc'y Rev. 369 (June, 2003).

[3] *Id.* art. 182.

[4] *Id.* art. 206.

[5] *Id.* art. 207.

common use are shared proportionately according to the value of the portion owned by each.[6]

§ 106JP.02(c)(1)(ii)   Restrictions Between Adjacent Owners.

§ 106JP.02(c)(1)(ii)(a)   Right of Using Adjacent Land.

a. The owner of land can demand the use of adjacent land within the limits necessary for constructing or repairing fences and walls or buildings on or near the boundary, but cannot enter the dwelling house of an adjacent owner unless with the latter's consent.

b. In the case of the preceding paragraph, the adjacent owner who has sustained damages, can claim compensation.[7]

§ 106JP.02(c)(1)(ii)(b)   Right of Thoroughfare.

a. When a piece of land is surrounded by other land and so has no passage to the public road, the owner of such land may pass over the surrounding land in order to reach the public road.

b. The same applies when there is no outward passage except by pond, marsh, river, canal, or sea or ocean, or when there is a considerable difference in height between the land and the public road on account of a cliff or bank.[8]

c. In the case of the preceding article the place and method of passage must be so chosen as to meet the needs of the person who is entitled to the right of passage and yet cause as little damage as possible to the surrounding land. The person who has the right of passage may construct a road when it is necessary.[9]

d. The person who is entitled to the right of passage must pay just compensation for any injury caused to the land passed over, but the compensation can be paid annually.[10]

e. When in consequence of partition, a plot of land comes into being which has no passage to the public road, the owner of such piece of land may pass to the public road only through the piece of land owned by the other co-partitioners. In this case the owner need not pay any compensation.

f. The provisions of the preceding paragraph apply correspondingly when the owner of a piece of land has assigned a part thereof.[11]

---

[6] *Id.* art. 208.

[7] *Id.* art. 209.

[8] *Id.* art. 210.

[9] *Id.* art. 211.

[10] *Id.* art. 212.

[11] *Id.* art. 213.

§ 106JP.02(c)(1)(ii)(c)   Rights with Respect to Running Water.

a. The owner of land cannot prevent water from naturally flowing in from adjacent land.[12]

b. When the course of water is obstructed upon a lower piece of land by accident, the owner of the higher land may, at the owner, own expense, construct works necessary for its drainage.

c. The owner of the lower piece of land is under no obligation to facilitate the outflow of water.[13]

d. When works relating to a water course constructed "A" piece of land for collecting, draining, or conducting water, cause or may cause damage to "B" piece of land, the owner of "B" can cause the owner of "A" to make repairs or drain off the water or construct preventative works if necessary.[14]

e. In the case of the preceding two articles, when there is a special custom with regard to the incidence of expenses, such custom is followed.[15]

f. The owner of land cannot construct roofs or other structures which cause rain water to fall directly upon adjacent land.[16]

g. The owner of the bed of a canal or other water course cannot change the course of water or the width of the bed when the land on the opposite shore belongs to another person.

h. When the land on both shores belongs to the owner of the bed of the watercourse, the owner can change the course of water or the width, but the water must be restored to its natural course at its lower mouth.[17]

i. The owner of higher land may conduct water through lower land for the purpose of draining land under water (marsh land) or of discharging superfluous water in household, agricultural or industrial use until it reaches a public highway, a public stream, or a drain, but the owner must so select the place and method as to cause the least possible damage to the lower land.[18]

---

[12] *Id.* art. 214.

[13] *Id.* art. 215.

[14] *Id.* art. 216.

[15] *Id.* art. 217.

[16] *Id.* art. 218.

[17] *Id.* art. 219.

[18] *Id.* art. 220.

§ 106JP.02(c)(1)(ii)(d)   Right of Using Adjacent Works.

a.   The owner of land can, for the purpose of conducting the water on the land, use the works constructed by the owner of a higher parcel of land.

b.   In the case of the preceding paragraph, a person who uses the works of another person must bear the expenses of their construction and preservation in proportion to the benefit derived therefrom.[19]

§ 106JP.02(c)(1)(ii)(e)   Right of Using the Opposite Shore.

The owner of the bed of a watercourse may, when it is necessary to construct a dam, rest the dam on the opposite shore, but must pay compensation for any damages which may arise in consequence. The owner of the opposite shore who owns apart of the bed of water may use the dam but must bear a share of the expenses in accordance with the provisions of the preceding article.[20]

§ 106JP.02(c)(1)(ii)(f)   Territorial Boundary Rights.

a.   The owner of land may, by sharing expenses with the owner of the adjacent land, construct a thing indicating the boundary, notwithstanding the non-consent of the other party.[21]

b.   The expenses of constructing and preserving the boundary marks are to be borne in equal shares by adjacent owners, but the expenses of measurement (survey) are to be borne in shares proportionate to the extent of the area of each parcel of land.[22]

§ 106JP.02(c)(1)(ii)(g)   Rights of Fencing.

a.   When two buildings belonging to different owners are separated by unoccupied land, either owner can construct a fence on the boundary line at the common expense of both owners.

b.   When the parties concerned cannot come to an agreement, the fence of the preceding article shall be wood or bamboo and six feet in height [so as to avoid an unreasonably expensive material used in construction].[23]

c.   The expenses of constructing and preserving the fence are to be borne in equal shares by the adjacent owners.[24]

d.   One of the adjacent owners may construct a fence of a better

---

[19] *Id.* art. 221.

[20] *Id.* art. 222.

[21] *Id.* art. 223.

[22] *Id.* art. 224.

[23] *Id.* art. 225.

[24] *Id.* art. 226.

material or of a greater height than fixed in paragraph 2 of article 225, but must bear the consequent increase of expense.[25]

e.   When there is a custom differing from the provisions of the preceding three articles, such custom is to be followed.[26]

§ 106JP.02(c)(1)(ii)(h)   Rights of Mutual Ownership.

a.   The boundary marks, fences, walls and ditches constructed on the boundary line are presumed to belong in common to the adjacent owners.[27]

b.   The provisions of the preceding article do not apply to a wall which stands on a boundary line and which forms a part of one of the buildings.

c.   The same rule applies to that part of the wall between two buildings of unequal height which rises above (overtops) the lower building, but this does not apply to walls built for the prevention of fire.[28]

§ 106JP.02(c)(1)(ii)(i)   Right of Improving Fences and Walls.

a.   One of the adjacent owners may increase the height of the wall jointly owned, notwithstanding the non-consent of the other owner; but if the wall cannot support the strain of the superstructure that owner must strengthen or re-construct the wall and pay the entire expense. The additional part of the wall increased in height in accordance with the preceding paragraph is exclusively owned by the person who has constructed it.[29]

b.   In case of the preceding article, the adjacent owner who has suffered damage can demand compensation.[30]

§ 106JP.02(c)(1)(ii)(j)   Right of Cutting Trees.

When the branches of trees and bamboos on adjacent land encroach over the boundary line, the owner of such trees and bamboos can be required to top off the branches. When the roots of trees and bamboos on adjacent land encroach across the boundary line they can be cut off.[31]

§ 106JP.02(c)(1)(ii)(k)   Restrictions Relating to Works on Boundary Lines.

a.   In constructing a building, a distance of at least eighteen inches

---

[25] *Id.* art. 227.

[26] *Id.* art. 228.

[27] *Id.* art. 229.

[28] *Id.* art. 230.

[29] *Id.* art. 231.

[30] *Id.* art. 232.

[31] *Id.* art. 233.

must be left from the boundary line.

b.   When any person is about to construct a building contrary to the provisions of the preceding paragraph, the owner of the adjacent land may require the person to abandon or modify the construction; but after one year has elapsed from the commencement of the construction, or after the building is finished, only compensation for damages can be demanded.[32]

c.   Any person who constructs at a distance of less than three feet from the boundary line a window or a veranda which overlooks the grounds of another person must attach a screen thereto.

d.   The distance of the preceding paragraph is measured from that point of the window or veranda which is nearest to the adjacent land in a straight line to the boundary line.[33]

e.   When there are customs different from the provisions above such customs are to be followed.[34]

f.   In digging a well, a cistern, a cesspool, or a receptacle for manure, a distance of at least six feet must be left from the boundary line and in digging a pond, a cellar or a water-closet vault, at least three feet.

g.   In laying waterpipes under ground or digging ditches, a distance of at least one half of its depth must be left from the boundary line, but it need not exceed three feet.[35]

h.   When the works of the preceding article are made in the neighborhood of a boundary line, necessary precautions must be taken in order to prevent the collapse of earth and sand or the infiltration of water or filthy liquids.[36]

§ 106JP.02(c)(2)　Acquisition of Ownership.

Ownerless immovables belong to the state,[37] but the owner of an immovable acquires the ownership of a thing that has been attached to the immovable property as its accessory, "but this does not affect the right of another person who has attached the thing by virtue of a title."[38] Ownership rights in both movables and immovables may be acquired by prescription, possession, partition, transfer and succession.

---

[32] *Id.* art. 234.

[33] *Id.* art. 235.

[34] *Id.* art. 236.

[35] *Id.* art. 237.

[36] *Id.* art. 238.

[37] *Id.* art. 239.

[38] *Id.* art. 242.

§ 106JP.02(c)(3)   Concurrent Ownership.

Japanese law recognizes a form of concurrent ownership called "co-proprietorship," which can arise from contract, succession, legacy, marital relationship, or accident (such as confusion of property). The principal Civil Code rules relating to the rights of co-owners are as follows:

§ 106JP.02(c)(3)(i)   Ownership by a Joint Owner.

Each joint owner may use, in proportion that owner's share, the whole of the common property. [The common object must be so used as not to interfere with the joint use of the other participants.][39]

§ 106JP.02(c)(3)(ii)   Presumption of the Shares of Joint Owners.

In case of doubt, the shares of the different joint owners are presumed to be equal.[40]

§ 106JP.02(c)(3)(iii)   Alteration of Common Property.

None of the joint owners may make any alteration to the common property without the consent of the other joint owners.[41]

§ 106JP.02(c)(3)(iv)   Management and Preservation of Common Property.

Matters relating to the management of common property are, except in the case of the preceding article, decided by a vote of the majority, each joint owner having the number of votes proportionate to the value of such owner's share, but acts of preservation may be done by either of the joint owners.[42]

§ 106JP.02(c)(3)(v)   Expenses of Management of Common Property.

a.   Each joint owner is bound to pay the expenses of management and the other charges of the common property in proportion to such owner's share.

b.   If the obligations of the preceding paragraph are not performed within one year, the other joint owners can acquire the share of the party in default upon payment of suitable compensation.[43]

§ 106JP.02(c)(3)(vi)   Obligations Among Joint Owners.

An obligation which one of the joint owners possesses with regard to the

---

[39] *Id.* art. 249.

[40] *Id.* art. 250.

[41] *Id.* art. 251.

[42] *Id.* art. 252.

[43] *Id.* art. 253.

common property against another joint owner may also be exercised against the latter's singular successor.[44]

§ 106JP.02(c)(3)(vii)   Effect of Joint Ownership.

When one of the joint owners renounces such owner's share or dies without an heir, the share reverts to the other joint owners.[45]

§ 106JP.02(c)(3)(viii)   Partition of Common Property.

a.   Each joint owner can at any time demand the partition of the common property, but a contract may be concluded not to partition it for a period not exceeding five years.

b.   Such contract can be renewed, but the renewal time must not exceed five years.[46]

c.   This does not apply to common property mentioned in Articles 208 [where building is owned in parts] and 209 [in cases of boundary marks and other common property constructed on the boundary line].[47]

§ 106JP.02(c)(3)(ix)   Commonage and Iriai-ken.

Commonage is a type of customary rural servitude by which the inhabitants of certain villages have rights to cut grass and timber and to conduct water into their fields, and to use a forest or plain in common. *Iriai-ken* is a form of joint ownership based on the customs of each locality. Japanese law permits persons with rights of commonage or *iriai-ken* to obtain partition of their separate portions under some circumstances.[48]

§ 106JP.02(d)   Superficies.

Superficies is the right to use the land of another for support of things—such as structures, trees, and bamboos—which the user, called the superficiary, owns.[49] It is considered a real right, a highly valuable right in rem, similar to a lease, and with some features of ownership. It is enforceable against third persons. Superficies is similar to the German heritable building right. In case the period of time for duration of a superficies has not been fixed by the act of creation, the superficiary can at any time renounce the right, if there is no special custom. But when a rent is to be paid, either one years previous notice must be given or rent for one

---

[44] *Id.* art. 254.

[45] *Id.* art. 255.

[46] *Id.* art. 256.

[47] *Id.* art. 257.

[48] *Id.* arts. 258-263.

[49] *Id.* art. 265.

year paid, in order to renounce.[50] Upon termination of the superficies, the superficiary can remove the structures or trees and bamboos upon restoring the land to its original state. However, if the landowner gives notice of intent to purchase them and offers to pay their current value, the superficiary may not unreasonably refuse the offer.[51]

§ 106JP.02(e)   *Emphyteusis.*

Emphyteusis is common among Japanese peasants and is a kind of permanent tenancy. With a duration of 20 to 50 years,[52] it enables poor farmers to rent the land of others and gain a livelihood by farming. An *emphyteusis* is a real right by which the land of another person can be used in consideration of paying a rent and is exercised for the purpose of agriculture or stock-farming.[53]

An *emphyteuta* has the right of possessing the land, and may transfer the right, unless prohibited by the act of creation, or in violation of the right of the landowner.[54] An *emphyteuta* owns the fruits produced on the land at their separation.

An *emphyteuta* must maintain the land in its original state and cannot make alterations to the land that cause permanent damage.[55] The *emphyteuta's* obligation to pay rent is so firm that no rebate is possible even after damage to the land or loss of farming revenue caused by irresistible force.[56] Bankruptcy or two years delinquency in rent payment can cause termination of the *emphyteusis.*[57]

§ 106JP.02(f)   Servitudes.

A servitude is a real right, to use the land of another person for the benefit of one's own land.[58] Servitudes are distinguished as pertaining to arable land and building land, as positive and negative, as continuous and discontinuous, and as apparent (visible) and non-apparent. Servitudes may be acquired by prescription.[59] If a servitude involves use of structures on the servient land, the servient land owner may also use the structures, if there is no interference

---

[50] *Id.* art. 268.

[51] *Id.* art. 269.

[52] *Id.* art. 278.

[53] *Id.* art. 270.

[54] *Id.* arts. 272-273.

[55] *Id.* art. 271.

[56] *Id.* arts. 274-275.

[57] *Id.* art. 276.

[58] *Id.* art. 281.

[59] *Id.* art. 283.

with the servitude use.[60]

§ 106JP.02(g)   Preferential Rights.

"A preferential right is a special right of obtaining performance in preference to all others, which right is given by the law to holders of certain obligations for their protection."[61]

"1. A preferential right may be exercised against money or other things which the debtor receives in consequence of the sale, letting, extinction, or damage of its subject; but the privileged creditor must seize (attach) the money or other thing previous to the payment or delivery thereof. 2. The same applies with regard to considerations for real rights created by the debtor in the subject of the preferential right."[62] The holder of the preferential right may exercise the right against the whole thing retained until performance of the whole of the obligation.[63]

A general preferential right is one by virtue of which any movable or immovable property among properties of the debtor may be seized and the performance of the obligation obtained therefrom.[64] The preferential right for hiring or letting of immovables exists in the movables of the hirer with regard to the rent of the immovables and other obligations of the hirer arising from the relation of hiring.[65]

A preferential right in immovables arises with regard to expenses for the preservation of immovables, for work done upon immovables, and for the purchase price and accrued interest for immovables.[66] Preferential rights also exist for obligations of leases of land, for assigned or sublet leases, in liquidations of leased property, and for money received as security for rent.[67]

§ 106JP.02(h)   Liens.

"1. A lien is a right which the possessor of a thing has of retaining such thing until the performance of the obligation is obtained when the possessor has an obligation in the possessor's favor arising on account of the thing possessed. 2. The conditions of a lien are that: a. A thing belonging to another person be possessed; b. that possession has not been obtained by an illegal act; c. that the obligation is one which arises on account of the thing possessed; d. that the performance of the obligation is due. 3. The lien-holder

---

[60] *Id.* art. 288.

[61] *Id.* art. 303.

[62] *Id.* art. 304.

[63] *Id.* art. 305.

[64] *Id.* art. 306.

[65] *Id.* art. 312.

[66] *Id.* arts. 326-328.

[67] *Id.* arts. 315-316.

may exercise the right against the whole thing retained until performance of the whole of the obligation."[68]

A lien-holder may reap the fruits of the thing retained and appropriate them to the performance of the obligation in preference to other creditors.[69]

The debtor may demand the extinction of the lien upon depositing appropriate security.[70]

§ 106JP.02(i)   Pledges.

A pledge is a class of credit against things. A pledgee/creditor has the right of possessing the thing received from the debtor or a third person as security for an obligation and subsequently of obtaining the performance of the obligation out of the thing, by selling the thing or demanding the sale by auction, in preference to the creditors.[71] Pledge is not a real right which has independent and separate existence like ownership, superficies or *emphyteusis*, but is an accessory real right which exists for the purpose of securing the obligation which is its principal; therefore, when there is no principal obligation there is no pledge which secures it, and when the principal obligation is extinguished the accessory pledge is likewise extinguished. Pledge differs from mortgage in that the pledgee must possess the thing which has been received as a security from the debtor or a third person, and the pledgor or creator therefore cannot, be allowed to possess the thing pledged.

§ 106JP.02(j)   Mortgages.

A mortgage is an accessory real right in an immovable that is in the possession of another person. The mortgage is indivisible and has a preferential right and the right of pursuit. A mortgage has no effect on the rights of third persons unless it is registered. A superficies and an *emphyteusis* can also be made the subject of a mortgage, although most leases cannot be mortgaged.[72]

§ 106JP.03   Restrictions on Ownership of Property by Foreigners.

Foreigners and foreign corporations may acquire, possess, and sell land in Japan, as a general rule. The Alien Land Law of Japan provides that Japan may apply reciprocal restrictions if the home country of the alien restricts land ownership by Japanese nationals; but the Japanese-American Treaty of Friendship, Commerce, and Navigation provides for mutual "national treatment" of Japanese nationals in the United States and United States nationals in Japan.

---

[68] *Id.* art. 296.

[69] *Id.* art. 297.

[70] *Id.* art. 301.

[71] *Id.* art. 342.

[72] *Id.* art. 369.

§ 106JP.04   Land Tax.

Japan imposes a recordation tax on land sales at the rate of 5% of the value listed in the fixed assets register. A stamp tax is also imposed on documents used to evidence the establishment, transfer, or change of a property right. Fixed assets are appraised by a city appraiser and the appraised value is listed in the land register, building register, or supplemental building register. On this appraisal is based a fixed assets tax of 1.4% annually, payable in four installments, with an exemption of Y20,000 for land and Y30,000 for houses. Ownership for the purposes of this tax is determined on the 1st day of each year. There is also a city tax, which varies as to city. In Tokyo, the city tax is 0.1% of the appraised value. One who acquires an interest in an immovable must report the transaction for tax purposes, or be subject to a penalty for failure to report. The tax applies to the purchase, new construction, addition, remodelling, or gift of immovable property. In the case of an acquisition, the tax is 3% of the value as listed in the fixed assets register. Transactions under Y10,000 for land, or Y100,000 for new construction of a building, or Y50,000 for purchase of a building, are exempted from this tax. For additions or remodeling, the tax is 3% of the increased value, amounts under Y100,000 being exempted. If one buys land for construction of a dwelling and within one year builds a new dwelling upon that land, the price of the land is taxed at 3% of the value over Y600,000.

The land tax is levied on and collected from the persons who are registered in the Land Register as owners at the commencement of the period when the tax becomes due. In cases where the land is subject to a pledge of any duration or a superficies exceeding 100 years, the tax is levied on any person registered as pledgee or superficiary in the Land Register. Foreigners are taxed for land the same way as Japanese landowners.

CHAPTER 106KE

PROPERTY LAW IN KENYA

Professor David A. Thomas
J. Reuben Clark Law School
Brigham Young University

SYNOPSIS

§ 106KE.01   Historical Background: From Colonial to Independent Status.

Although the British entered East Africa in the area that is now Kenya about the middle of the 19th century, Germany was the first to take official colonial action, by declaring the region a protectorate in 1885. In 1886, England and Germany entered into an agreement permitting England to annex from the protectorate an area including modern Kenya. A second agreement in 1890 more clearly defined the boundaries of the respective territories. Thereafter England assigned certain administrative duties to the Imperial British East Africa Company, but in 1895 declared a protectorate directly over East Africa. In 1920, the British annexed Kenya as a colony, known as the Colony and Protectorate of Kenya.[1]

British administration of Kenya as a colony gradually moved Kenya toward independence. Following a constitutional conference and a new constitution, general elections were held in 1963, the same year Kenya was granted powers of internal self-government. On December 12, 1963, the country officially became a member of the Commonwealth of Nations, and on December 12, 1964, Kenya became a Republic with a president as head of state.[2] This progression from a colony to an independent nation has had profound effect on the land law of Kenya.

§ 106KE.02   Historical Development of Land Law in Kenya.

Land law in Kenya is diverse and complex, clearly the product of the area's history as a land of native settlement and foreign colonization:

> The Land Law of Kenya is a history of its development from customary law to modern statute law. But, this development and the advent of independence has brought its problems. There are in Kenya, two systems of substantive law, three systems of conveyancing and five systems of registration. . . There are, in fact, twenty-nine statutes to say nothing of subsidiary legislation, embracing the subject of land law in Kenya, either specifically applied or of general application. The substance of the Land Law of Kenya is bulky and complex and finding its whereabouts more difficult still.[3]

In a very general sense, customary law governs the land relationships among the native Africans, while modern statutory law governs land

---

[1] Charles Mwalimu, The Kenyan Legal System: An Overview 3-5 (1988); *see* T. Jackson, *The Legal System of Kenya, in* 6 Modern Legal Systems Cyclopedia 6.260.5 (Kenneth R. Redden ed. 1990).

[2] Charles Mwalimu, The Kenyan Legal System: An Overview 11-12 (1988).

[3] T. Jackson, *The Legal System of Kenya, in* 6 Modern Legal Systems Cyclopedia 6.260.12-.13 (Kenneth R. Redden ed. 1990).

relationships among those who came as colonists. This section will discuss the substance of customary law and its present state. This will be followed by a history of modern statutory law.

§ 106KE.02(a)   Customary Land Law.

§ 106KE.02(a)(1)   General Summary of Customary Land Law.

Within the native lands, the substantive land law is based on customary law and varies from tribe to tribe. However, some generalizations may be made. Land in east Africa was traditionally held communally, controlled either by the clan or by the elders of the clan. According to the native perspective, the clan did not actually "own" the land; rather, God owned the land, and the elders were designated trustees to administer and manage the land for the benefit of the clan.

§ 106KE.02(a)(1)(i)   Land Rights Among the Bantu.

In practice, the enjoyment of land rights among the Bantu was typical:

> The basis of Bantu land tenure was that the individual had inheritable rights as a *user* of his arable lands; but with regard to grazing lands, forest, and salt licks, he shared with the clan or tribe the beneficial use of such natural sources or wealth that had come into the possession of the tribe either by conquest or by original occupation. This does not imply individual ownership of fields, nor individual rights to misuse land. Ownership, insofar as there was such a concept, was usually vested in the ancestor spirits who played a very real part in the life of the African and who symbolized his community past, present, and future. Every clan member had the right to claim support from the clan land, either through the "shifting agriculture" based on individual shambas, or among pastoral tribes through the unrestricted individual right to run stock on what was regarded as communal land; but this right was more a preemptive, possessory right than one of property. Sale was normally unthinkable, if not forbidden.[4]

§ 106KE.02(a)(1)(ii)   Land Rights Among the Gikuyu.

Even though most landholding under customary law was communal,[5] some tribes did recognize forms of individual ownership of land. For example, some land of the Gikuyu tribe could be held by an individual tribe member

> for an indefinite period, under a developed and workable customary law. He had the following rights therein or therefrom. He could lease it to another, the rental given by the *mohoi* or *mothami* (tenant) to his landlord

---

[4] Ann P. Munro, *Land Law in Kenya, in* Africa and Law: Developing Legal Systems in African Commonwealth Nations 76-77 (Thomas W. Hutchinson ed. 1968).

[5] Krisham M. Maini, Land Law in East Africa 22 (1967) (*see also* on p. 17 of this work a table summarizing the methods of acquiring title, rights and interest in land of six Kenya tribes).

being a gourd of beer whenever he brewed it, and the performance of certain small services; he could sell or mortgage the land or the trees which grew on it; when he died, the land passed in accordance with the customary law of succession; he might evict trespassers, or grant an easement to his neighbor so that he might pass, with or without cattle, across his land; he could define the boundaries by setting fixed markers, such as a line of trees or lillies. . .. The methods by which the Mugikuyu became a proprietor of land were four, viz., by hunting right, sale, inheritance and exchange.[6]

If the member decided to sell the land, the clan had the first option to purchase. Despite these customs, large portions of Gikuyu land were not subject to individual ownership rights.[7]

§ 106KE.02(a)(1)(iii)   Land Rights Among the Gusii.

Customary law of the tribes has also changed with the times, as illustrated by the Gusii of western Kenya. Initially, the Gusii had no controllers or spokesmen to manage their affairs at the tribal level. The father or grandfather of each family was the central authority. The tribe maintained coherence through a mutual loyalty or solidarity based on the notion that tribal members were all descended from a common ancestor.[8] The Gusii were constantly to more productive lands, and land was readily available. Consequently, no central authority was needed for allotment of the land. Customs for land distribution and management developed as required with each relocation; when conflicts arose between clans, the Gusii clans would fight among themselves for control of land, according to recognized Gusii customs.

These patterns changed as good lands became scarce. Beginning in the 1920's, Gusii families, traditionally located on scattered plots, had to consolidate their holdings and defend against encroachments by other tribes.[9] Clans were no longer able to expand into unclaimed land, but had to look within their own traditional territories to meet their land needs.

After the period of consolidation, individual land rights came to be recognized when a structure was built on the land. If a hut were constructed, for instance, the land immediately surrounding it would be claimed as an individual holding. To expand the individual holdings, a family member would be sent to build another hut nearby. Through this process, legal and social concepts of estate ownership had developed by the late 1940's.[10]

---

[6] *Id.* at 3.

[7] *Id.* at 4 (also noting that principles of individual ownership were more predominant in the Kiambu area).

[8] Phillip Mayer & Iona Mayer, *Land Law in the Making, in* African Law: Adaption and Development 51-52 (Hilda Kuper ed. 1956).

[9] *Id.* at 54.

[10] *Id.* at 65.

Within ten years after the consolidation of landholdings had occurred, the Gusii territory had been divided into estates with recognized boundaries. Enforcement of these boundaries was primarily according to the strength of each group.

Within the clan's landholdings lived dwellers, those who had settled in clan territory, but did not belong to the clan by way of descent. Among the dwellers, land could never be permanently alienated, but use rights could be temporarily transferred. In order to obtain rights to build on the land, the dweller would have to obtain permission through some distant relative. If land were available and permission obtained, the dweller could have rights in land on much the same basis as could a regular clan member.[11]

As illustrated by the Gusii, many tribes in Kenya introduced individual ownership of land between the 1920's and the 1950's, but were forced to rely on their customary law, rather than on the statutory law that was by then available and applicable to non-tribal lands. This resort to uncoordinated development of customary law has led to chaos in Kenyan land law by customary right.

In summary, the Gusii people developed lines of segmentation that were drawn around patrimonial and territorial interests. This was based on the principle that every corporate group of lineage type, every family, and every individual was entitled to portions that were ideally all equal, scaled to average needs. Enforcement of these lines was primarily by fighting and a rudimentary legal process.[12]

§ 106KE.02(b) British Colonial Approach to Land Law.

§ 106KE.02(b)(1) For Native Lands.

British colonial policy required that the native inhabitants manage their land under one system of law, i.e., their own customary law, and that the European settlers abide by the rules of a separate system. At bottom the separation enabled the European settlers, who were conspicuously in the minority, to retain power over colonial affairs by ostensibly constitutional and legal means.[13] While Africans tried to work out landholding under a maze of varied and fluid customary rules, British land rights were governed by statutory law resembling the common law in England. The British also determined that the best way to preserve native land rights was to create reserves or special areas for natives, where they could remain isolated and insulated from the effects of European settlement.[14] Within those areas,

---

[11] *Id.* at 74.

[12] Mayer, *supra* note 19, at 77.

[13] Ann P. Munro, *Land Law in Kenya, in* Africa and Law: Developing Legal Systems in African Commonwealth Nations 76-77 (Thomas W. Hutchinson, ed. 1968).

[14] *Id.* at 81.

however, the colonial government offered little protection for native land rights.

The earliest colonial legislation regarding native land in Kenya was the Crown Lands Ordinance of 1902, which allowed the Commissioner to grant leases of Crown lands consisting in part of native lands or villages, so long as the natives were not in actual occupation.[15] This act was repealed in 1915 and replaced by the Government Lands Act, which was intended to promote European settlement in the Kenyan highlands and to maintain racial segregation. The Act gave the colonial government the power to vest in the Crown any Crown lands[16] reserved for the benefit of an African tribe, thus making the Africans, in effect, tenants at will of the colonial government. As to lands held under customary law, the natives had to claim rights of protection from the government, and tribes could not assert rights of ownership or alienate land.[17]

The Native Lands Trust Ordinance enacted in 1930 enlarged the protection of native land rights by setting aside certain areas of state land as permanent reserves for the benefit of the African tribes.[18] However, the protection of native land rights became somewhat illusory because of provisions allowing incursions into African areas for certain public purposes, such as exploiting gold discoveries, which began in 1933.[19]

Another attempt at improving protection for native land rights was the Native Lands Trust Ordinance Act of 1938. This act and other legislation were intended to prevent interference with native land rights from the Kenya legislature. Even though heavily amended, the basic provisions of this Act remain in effect today as the Trust Land Act.[20] Even this legislation, however, did little to recognize and preserve African land claims under customary law,[21] and to the contrary, formally extinguished all native rights

---

[15] Krishan M. Maini, Land Law in East Africa 22 (1967).

[16] Crown land includes all lands occupied by the African tribes of Kenya and all lands reserved for the use of the members of any African tribe, except the land in the special areas.

[17] Krishan M. Maini, Land Law in East Africa 26-27 (1967). Under the act, special reserves were established for the natives. However, the Governor was granted power to abolish those reserves, if the land was no longer required for the use and enjoyment of the tribes. Additionally, the act set up special settlement areas for the settlement of the natives. However, as with the reserves, the Governor could abolish these areas also. Furthermore, land in these special areas could not be registered.

[18] The act is now repealed.

[19] *Id.* at 35-36.

[20] *Id.* at 36. The Trust Land Act presently allows for the setting aside of Trust land, and preserves the existing African land rights recognized under the customary law of a tribe, as long as they are not contrary to any statutory law.

[21] *Id.*

in lands outside the boundaries of the native areas.[22]

In 1959, the colonial government enacted legislation allowing for the registration of consolidated tribal land designated as "special areas," and for the acquisition of individual native titles to these lands. This new legislation was the Native Lands Registration Ordinance of 1959, soon renamed the Land Registration (Special Areas) Act. This act has since been repealed and its provisions re-enacted in both the Registered Land Act, which covers registration matters, and the Land Adjudication Act, which includes the land adjudication and consolidation provisions.[23]

The result of these provisions was that natives were able to register land. Under the provisions of the Land Adjudication Act, original titles to land were obtained through the process of land consolidation, or converting several fragmented pieces of native land into a contiguous, unified holding, which improves the productivity of the land. When land was ready for consolidation, the rights of each individual tribal member were determined according to customary law, and the consolidated holding was then registered in the name of the new owner. Former owners of portions of the consolidated parcel were compensated by an allocation of an equivalent parcel of other land, to which they obtained legal title.[24]

§ 106KE.02(b)(2)   For Non-Native Lands.

The basic territorial land law for non-Africans was the Indian Transfer of Property Act of 1882, along with local ordinances. Based on the contemporary English common law of real property, the act provided for freehold estates and individual leaseholds in areas specifically set aside for European occupation.[25] These basic legal rules are still in effect, and in matters not covered by the act, rules of English law are applicable. In addition to the Indian Transfer of Property Act, provisions of the Indian Transfer of Property Act also apply. Together, these acts govern all transactions in land not governed by customary law, and land registered under the Registered Land Act.[26]

Other statutes and regulations provide additional detailed legal rules for European land rights in Kenya:

---

[22] Ann P. Munro, *Land Law in Kenya, in* Africa and Law: Developing Legal Systems in African Commonwealth Nations 82 (Thomas W. Hutchinson ed. 1968).

[23] Krishan M. Maini, Land Law in East Africa 37 (1967). The Land Consolidation Act provides for the ascertainment of rights and interests in, and for the consolidation of, land in the special areas (Trust Land); the Land Adjudication Act provides for the ascertainment and recording of rights and interests in Trust land where the Land Consolidation Act does not apply.

[24] *Id.* at 37-41.

[25] Ann P. Munro, *Land Law in Africa, in* Africa and Law: Developing Legal Systems in African Commonwealth Nations 78-79 (Thomas W. Hutchinson ed. 1968).

[26] Krishan M. Maini, Land Law in East Africa 42-43 (1967).

Rights to parcels of land in private occupation were first recognized by the East Africa Land Regulations of 1897, under which certificates of occupancy for terms of twenty-one years were issued in respect of such rights. By virtue of the East Africa (Land Acquisition) Order, 1901, the Government received its authority to alienate parcels of land. The East Africa Land Regulations of 1897 had in fact replaced the land regulation of the Imperial East Africa Company, which had published them in 1897. The regulations of 1897 in their turn were repealed by the Crown Lands Ordinance 1902.[27]

The Crown Lands Ordinance of 1902 provided for alienation of land by way of sales of freehold; purchasers were required to mark their land. The Government Lands Act of 1915 repealed the Crown Lands Ordinance and introduced a system for registration of deeds, provided authority for the Commissioner to execute conveyances for the occupation of Crown lands on behalf of the Governor, and allowed for disposal of state land within townships. The act also allowed the Commissioner of Lands to grant leases of town plots for any term not exceeding ninety-nine years, and leases on agricultural lands for up to 999 years.[28]

Along with the Government Lands Act, the Registration of Documents Act, passed in 1897, instituted a country-wide system for registration of deeds.[29] Also, the Land Titles Act of 1908 provided for adjudicating claims and for registering titles.[30] Under the Land Titles Act, a claimant may be awarded a certificate of title from the Recorder of Titles. This certificate is conclusive evidence against all persons (including the government) that the person is the owner of the land. However, once a certificate of ownership is given by the Recorder of Titles, it must be registered or else it is void.

The Registration of Titles Act of 1920 ended the applicability of Land Titles Act provisions for lands coming within the jurisdiction of the Registration of Titles Act. This act also permitted or required transfer of titles from registers created under the Government Lands Act, the Land Titles Act and the Registration of Documents Act, whereupon those registers would close.[31]

Apart from titles registered under the Registered Land Act, most land titles in Kenya are registered under the Registration of Titles Act. Registration under the Government Lands Act has been almost eliminated by this act,

---

[27] *Id.* at 21.

[28] *Id.* at 28.

[29] The act required registration of all documents conferring any right, title, or interest to be registered, except for documents registrable under the Registration of Titles Act, the Government Lands Act, or the Registered Land Act.

[30] *Id.* at 23.

[31] *Id.* at 26.

but since conversion under this act is voluntary, some titles remain in the old registry.[32]

The Registered Land Act of 1963 was intended to unify land law in Kenya and eventually all registrations are to be under this Act.[33]

The 1963 Act uses predominantly English terms to describe customary interests in land and makes accommodation for certain features of customary law. For aspects of land law not covered by the Act, English law is used.[34]

When it became effective, the 1963 Act automatically applied to all land to which the Land Registration (Special Areas) Act had applied, which was generally all land in the former special areas which had been consolidated and in the settlement scheme areas. As for the areas to which the Government Lands Act, the Registration of Titles Act and the Land Titles Act now apply, the 1963 Act will eventually apply to these areas on a district by district basis.[35] Also, as land is consolidated under the Land Adjudication Act, and titles consolidated or other land are given to persons affected by the consolidations, those title registrations are also recorded under the 1963 Act.[36]

The effect of registration under the 1963 Registered Land Act is to establish one of two forms of estate or interest in land, modeled after the English 1925 Law of Property Act.[37] The system is a registration of title, and registration, rather than possession of the deed, proves title.

§ 106KE.03   Summary of Current Statutory Land Law in Kenya.

The welter of various tribal customary law for land is matched by a swarm of statutes and regulations, many of which are intended to expand or contract in their applicability over a period of time:

> All the land in Kenya is divided into two categories: (a) Special Areas, basically Trust Land (including the old Native Land Units) and private freehold, totaling 50,000 square miles of territory; and (b) Crown Lands, that is, special reserves, alienated and unalienated land, and private freehold, constituting the remaining 174,000 square miles of territory.
>
> The Special Areas are governed by two laws: (a) the Trust Land Act (formerly the Native Lands Trust Ordinance, 1939), which defines the Special Areas and provides for agricultural and township plot leases of up to thirty-three years. . .; and (b) the Land Registration (Special Areas) Act which was enacted as the Native Lands Registration Ordinance No. 27 of

---

[32] *Id.* at 34.

[33] *Id.* at 163.

[34] *Id.* at 163.

[35] *Id.* at 164.

[36] *Id.* at 41.

[37] *Id.* at 174.

1959, and which provides for the ascertainment of rights and interests in land, the consolidation of land holdings, and the registration of land titles in these areas. In addition, it provides for the control over subsequent transactions involving such land through the Land Control (Special Areas) Regulations, 1961, which replaced the Land Control (Native Lands) Ordinance No. 28 of 1959.

The Crown Lands are governed principally by three laws. First, the Crown Lands Act, which provides for 999-year leases for agricultural land. . . The English form of conveyancing was introduced to Kenya through its predecessor, the Crown Lands Ordinance, 1915. The second law governing the Crown Lands is the Registration of Titles Act, which was enacted in 1919 and which has provided a Torrens-type title registration system for all land outside the Special Areas. The third law governing Crown Lands is the Land Titles Act which was enacted in 1908 and which provides for the certification and registration of titles or interests in immovable property within certain prescribed coastal areas.

*   *   *

The Registered Land Act No. 25 of 1963 came into force on August 16, 1963. The provisions of this act. . . are intended to obliterate the distinction between Special Areas and Crown Lands by providing a single system of land-titled registration and land transfer. This system will gradually be extended to cover all land previously covered by other laws.[38]

The Registered Land Act of 1963 repeals the Indian Transfer of Property Act of 1882 and has superseded part of the Land Registration (Special Areas) Act. What was left of the latter act was renamed the Land Adjudication Act, and it allows for converting African interests into freehold statutory estates, which then can be registered.

Thus, in the Special Areas, tenures and interests under customary law are being investigated and recorded (after consolidation and adjudication) under the Land Adjudication Act, and then registered under the Registered Land Act. Crown Land is also registered and subject to the conveyancing provisions set forth in the Registered Land Act.[39]

§ 106KE.04   Types of Real Property Interests.

The Kenya property statutes use the word "proprietorship" rather that the word "ownership." Under the Registration of Titles Act, the word "proprietor" means a person or corporation registered under the Act as the owner of land or as a lessee from the government. Under the Registered Land Act, "proprietor" is defined as: (a) in relation to land or a lease, the person named in the register as the proprietor thereof; and (b) in relation to a charge of land

---

[38] Ann P. Munro, *Land Law in Kenya, in* Africa and Law: Developing Legal Systems in African Commonwealth Nations 100-101 (Thomas W. Hutchinson ed. 1968).

[39] *Id.* at 102.

or a lease, the person named in the register of the land or lease as the person in whose favor the charge is made.

§ 106KE.04(a)   Freehold Estates.

Under the Registered Land Act of 1963, the registration of a person as the proprietor of land vests in that person the absolute ownership of that land.[40] Some concern had been raised, because the now repealed Land Registration (Special Areas) Act declared that the effect of registration of the freehold estate was to vest the fee simple, and the use of that term has special connotations in England. However, the Registered Land Act of 1963 refers to absolute ownership rather than fee simple. Other statutes still refer to the so-called "fee simple" estate; these include, for instance, the Land Titles Act,[41] the Government Lands Act,[42] and the Registration of Titles Act.[43]

Under the Registered Land Act of 1963, the proprietor with an absolute ownership obtains rights that cannot be defeated except as provided by the Act, and the land is held free from all other interests and claims.[44]

§ 106KE.04(b)   Leasehold Estates.

Under the Registered Land Act of 1963, a proprietor of land may lease the land to any person for a definite term, or for the life of the lessor or of the lessee or for a period which, though indefinite, may be determined by the lessor or the lessee.[45] The act also allows for periodic tenancies, but they may not be registered.[46]

Any lease for a period exceeding two years or for the life of the lessor or the lessee must be registered and must be in the prescribed form.[47] The Act also allows a lease to be made for a period to commence on a future date, not being later than twenty-one years from the date on which the lease is executed, if it is registered. A lease to commence more than twenty-one years in the future, or upon the fulfillment of a condition that may occur more than twenty-one years in the future, is void.[48]

Leases from the government to private persons are not provided for under the Government Lands Act but are authorized under the Indian Transfer of

---

[40] Registered Land Act, § 27.

[41] Land Titles Act § 20(2)(a).

[42] Government Lands Act § 3.

[43] Registration of Titles Act § 3 (providing that the person named as proprietor of the land is the absolute and indefeasible owner) and Form B(2) (indicating that the grant is in fee).

[44] Registered Land Act § 28.

[45] *Id.* at § 45.

[46] *Id.* at § 46.

[47] *Id.* at § 47.

[48] *Id.* at § 51.

Property Act. This Act also provides statutory forms for registration of written leases which are for a period exceeding one year.

The Registration of Titles Act contains a provision for the creation of a lease for a term exceeding twelve months by presenting for registration a lease in the prescribed form.[49] Such a lease must be registered to be valid, but a lease for a term not exceeding twelve months is valid even if not registered.[50]

§ 106KE.04(c)   Concurrent Ownership.

The Registered Land Act of 1963 provides for concurrent ownership and partition, both for joint proprietors and proprietors in common. These are recognized as forms of legal, but not equitable, ownership. Co-ownership is limited to five proprietors unless otherwise permitted by the Minister.[51]

No joint proprietor is entitled to any separate share in the land, and dispositions of the land may be made only by all joint proprietors. When one joint proprietor dies, that interest vests in the surviving proprietor or proprietors jointly. Severance of the joint proprietorship is accomplished by completing the correct form and registering the joint proprietors as proprietors in common.[52]

Each proprietor in common is entitled to an undivided share in the whole, and on the death of a proprietor in common, the decedent's share is administered as part of the decedent's estate. A proprietor in common may not deal with the undivided share in favor of any person other than another proprietor in common, except with the consent of the remaining proprietors. Such consent may not unreasonably be withheld.[53] Partition of land owned in common may be made by any one or more of the proprietors, or any person in whose favor an order has been made for an undivided share in the land.[54]

§ 106KE.04(d)   Interests in the Land of Another.

The Kenyan statutory law on easements, profits, licenses and restrictive agreements has been summarized as follows:

> No provision is made in respect of easements, *profits-a-prendre*, licenses, and restrictive covenants in the Government Lands Act, Land Titles Act, Registration of Titles Act or the Indian Transfer of Property Act. Questions concerning the said rights arise not infrequently and it is difficult to comprehend why this important aspect of rights in land was not included

---

[49] *Id.* at § 40.

[50] *Id.* at § 41.

[51] *Id.* at § 101.

[52] *Id.* at § 102.

[53] *Id.* at § 103.

[54] *Id.* at § 104.

in the said enactments. The framers of the Registered Land Act were aware of the shortcoming in the law and thought fit to make provision in respect of the said rights in the act as these are matters which are best covered by registration.[55]

§ 106KE.04(d)(1)   Easements.

An easement is defined as the right attached to a parcel of land which allows the proprietor of the parcel either to use the land of another in a particular manner or to restrict its use to a particular extent, but does not include a profit.[56] The proprietor of land or of a lease may grant an easement over the land to the proprietor or lessee of other land for the benefit of that other land by an instrument in the prescribed form, or by a grant or reservation in either an instrument of transfer or in a lease.[57]

§ 106KE.04(d)(2)   Profits.

A profit is defined as the right to go on the land of another and take a particular substance from that land, whether of the soil or the products of the soil.[58] A profit may be granted by the proprietor of land or of a lease by an instrument in the prescribed form. The instrument must indicate whether it is to be enjoyed in gross or as appurtenant to other land, and whether it is to be enjoyed by the grantee exclusively or in common with the grantor. To complete the grant, it must be registered as an encumbrance, and the instrument must be filed.[59]

§ 106KE.04(d)(3)   Licenses.

A license is not qualified for registration under the Act, but a licensee's interest may still be protected by lodging a caution.[60]

§ 106KE.04(d)(4)   Restrictive Agreements.

Any restrictive agreement must be registered to be binding on the proprietor of the land burdened by it or on a subsequent acquirer of the land. A restrictive agreement is an agreement by which one proprietor agrees to restrict construction or other use and enjoyment of the land for the benefit of the proprietor of other land. When the agreement is contained in an instrument other than a charge or a lease, the Registrar notes the restrictive agreement in the encumbrances section of the register.[61] The restrictive

---

[55] Krishan M. Maini, Land Law in East Africa 245-246 (1967).

[56] Registered Land Act § 3.

[57] *Id.* at § 94.

[58] *Id.* at § 3.

[59] *Id.* at § 96.

[60] *Id.* at § 100.

[61] *Id.* at § 95.

agreement is also effective as to successors in title. Racially restrictive agreements are void.[62]

§ 106KE.04(d)(5)   Mortgages.

Although mortgages are governed by the Government Lands Act and charges are governed by the Registration of Titles Act, various substantive elements of mortgage law are still found in the 1882 Indian Transfer of Property Act. Under the Government Lands Act, a mortgage or charge must be created by an instrument in writing and registered.[63] The act also recognizes equitable mortgages by deposit of documents of title in Forms A and B of the Schedule to the Act.

The Registration of Titles Act provides for statutory charges when land is intended to be charged or made security in favor of any person by having the proprietor or lessee execute a statutory form, which must then be registered.[64] When registered, the property is subject to the same security and to the same powers and remedies on the part of the chargee as if it were under legal mortgage.[65] The Act also allows for a charge to be created by deposit of documents of title to land, and evidenced by a prescribed instrument.[66]

Under the Registered Land Act, a proprietor may charge the land, lease or charge to secure the payment of an existing or future or contingent debt or other money or money's worth or the fulfillment of a condition by an instrument in the prescribed form.[67] The form must specify the date for repayment, and if no date is specified it shall be deemed to be repayable three months after service of demand in writing by the chargee. The charge is completed by registration as an encumbrance. The charge does not operate as a transfer, but has effect only as security.[68] The Act also lists the agreements implied in a charge.

Charged land may be redeemed after paying the principal and interest on the date specified in the charge. The charged land nay be redeemed before this time by paying the interest on the principle secured up to that date. If payment is late, the land may still be redeemed by giving three month's notice or paying three months' interest in lieu thereof.[69] The act makes no provision for the creation of an equitable mortgage or charge by deposit of title deed. Thus, it appears that equitable charges and mortgages cannot be created.

---

[62] *Id.*

[63] Government Lands Act § 100.

[64] Registration of Titles Act § 46.

[65] *Id.*

[66] *Id.*, Form U in the First Schedule.

[67] Registration of Land Act § 65.

[68] *Id.*

[69] *Id.* at § 72.

§ 106KE.05 How Land Ownership Originates.

Ownership of land in east Africa arises in two ways: the first is through an initial allotment from the state; the second and more common way is through inheritance by which the heir claims the land under customary law. To gain recognition of ownership from the state, the land must be entered on the register. Thus, the person will submit evidence of the claim of ownership to the state, which may accept or reject the claim. If accepted, the land is entered or "brought on" to the register and the claimant is registered as proprietor. Normally, a freehold estate is granted.[70]

§ 106KE.05(a)   Registration.

Two systems of land registration prevail in Kenya, one for registration of deeds and one for registration of titles. Under the system for registration of deeds, the deed or other document dealing with land rather than the title is registered. If a purchaser wants to insure that the proprietor has good root of title, a search should be made through all the recorded documents concerning the land. Such a search protects a purchaser only against unregistered documents, but it does not reveal whether any of the registered conveyances or assignments are valid, because the documents are not inspected when received. Thus the search does not guarantee title.

In Kenya, a system of deed registration was introduced by the East African Registration Regulations in 1901 and is now known as the Registration of Documents Act. It provides that all documents conferring or extinguishing any right, title or interest shall be registered.[71] Such a document is to be filed for registration within two months of the transaction and must describe the land.[72] The system now has nearly been superseded by the registration of title system.[73]

The registration of title system title is assured by the state, which is responsible for maintaining a compiled register which is conclusive evidence of title. Conveyancing is facilitated by eliminating the need to investigate the title to a good root and the need to examine documents to establish their validity.[74]

Registration of title is governed by several statutes in Kenya. When land is registered under the Registered Land Act, the person named as proprietor of land is declared the absolute and indefeasible owner. The title is then

---

[70] Krishan M. Maini, Land Law in East Africa 208 (1967).

[71] Registration of Documents Act § 4.

[72] *Id.* at §§ 8-9.

[73] Under the 1915 Government Lands Act a system of deed registration is also used, but it is very similar to a registration of titles system, because a deed is not accepted for registration unless it appears valid, and the deeds are noted in the register.

[74] Maini, *supra* note 6, at 134.

indefeasible, subject only to overriding interests stated in the Act. Although older statutes in Kenya, such as the Government Lands Act and the Registration of Titles Act, also provide for registration of titles, the Registered Land Act is intended to unify all of these provisions in one statute for the future.

§ 106KE.05(b)   Conveyancing.

§ 106KE.05(b)(1)   Under the Government Lands Act.

Under the Government Lands Act, no evidence of sale or other transfer *inter vivos* of land is receivable in a civil court, unless the sale or transfer is effected by an instrument in writing that has been properly registered.[75] No statutory form of transfer is prescribed by the Act; however, any proprietor of either the fee or the lease may transfer the interest to another through the use of a deed in accordance with the English form of conveyancing, executed by both the transferor and transferee. The deed follows the pattern of private conveyancing by reciting first the root of the title and then subsequent changes in ownership.

§ 106KE.05(b)(2)   Under the Registration of Titles Act.

Under the Registration of Titles Act, a proprietor is defined as a person or corporation registered under the Act as the owner of land or a lessee from the government.[76] A proprietor is issued land through a grant which is defined as any conveyance, agreement for sale, lease or license for a period exceeding three years, made by and on behalf of the government, and includes a certificate of title:[77]

> The certificate of title issued by the registrar to any purchaser of land upon a transfer or transmission by the proprietor thereof shall be taken by all courts as conclusive evidence that the person named therein as proprietor of the land is the absolute and indefeasible owner thereof, subject to the encumbrances, easements, restrictions and conditions contained therein or endorsed thereon, and the title of such proprietor shall not be subject to challenge, except on the ground of fraud or misrepresentation to which he is proved to be party.[78]

The word "land" also includes an estate for a term of years.

Transfers of land or rights of way or other easements are also provided for by having the registered proprietor execute a statutory form. The form describes the land, refers to the grant or certificate of title, and contains an accurate statement of the land and easement, or the easement, intended to be transferred or created, and a memorandum of all leases, charges and other

---

[75] Government Lands Act § 100.

[76] Registration of Titles Act § 2.

[77] *Id.*

[78] *Id.* at § 23(1).

encumbrances to which the land may be subject, and of all rights-of-way, easements and privileges intended to be transferred.[79] Statutory forms are also provided for transfer of land and leases. The effective words of transfer are "hereby transfer all my right, title and interest in the said piece of land."[80] A transferor may also transfer only part of the land by issuing a certificate of title for only the transferred part.

§ 106KE.05(b)(3)   Under the Registered Land Act.

Under the Registered Land Act, a proprietor is defined as follows: in relation to land or a lease, the person named in the register as the proprietor thereof; and in relation to a charge of land or of a lease, the person named in the register of the land or lease as the person in whose favor the charge is made.[81]

The nature of a proprietor's title is either absolute (freehold) or leasehold, but the Act does not use the word freehold. If absolute, the proprietor may apply for and receive a land certificate, and, if a leasehold, a certificate of lease may be granted if the estate is for a period exceeding twenty-five years.

A proprietor may transfer the land, lease or charge to any person, with or without consideration, by an instrument in the prescribed form. Registration of the transferee as proprietor of the land, lease or charge and filing the instrument completes the transfer.[82] A transfer may not be expressed to take effect on the happening of an event or the fulfillment of any condition.[83]

Land may also be transferred subject to a charge or to a lease.[84]

§ 106KE.06   Taxation of Real Property.

Some property is subject to local taxation, but the amounts are not a significant portion of a person's overall tax burden. Before 1985, a capital gains tax could be levied on the sale of a private residence if the seller had not lived in the house continuously for at least three years prior to the transfer; however, the capital gains tax was suspended in June 1985.

§ 106KE.07   Ownership of Real Property by Foreigners.

The legal status of aliens is governed by the Kenya Constitution and by various statutes. The principal pertinent laws are the Kenyan Citizenship Act of 1963, the Immigration Act of 1967, and the Aliens Restriction Act of

---

[79] *Id.* at § 34.

[80] *Id.*, Form F of First Schedule.

[81] Registered Land Act § 3.

[82] *Id.* at § 85.

[83] *Id.* at § 87.

[84] *Id.* at §§ 90-93.

1973. These laws affect aliens in matters of citizenship, immigration and property ownership.[85]

In Kenya's 1979 Constitution an alien is defined in Arts. 87-98 as any person who is not a citizen of Kenya either by birth or naturalization. Article 75 of the Constitution guarantees the right to own property without interference from the Kenyan government, but for aliens, this guarentee is subject to certain restrictions in the statutes and as described in the following comment:

> Section 3 of the Alien Restriction Act of 1973 empowers the Minister responsible for internal security to impose an order or other restriction prohibiting aliens from engaging in any activity he specifies. These orders, however, are to be imposed only when there is a state of war between Kenya and another country, during a state of emergency, and when there is an actual or perceived imminent danger to the welfare of the country. The Foreign Investment Protection Act of 1964, however, protects alien businesses and enterprises from government compulsory acquisition, unless such compulsory expropriation is for state purposes carried out under Article 75 of the Kenyan Constitution. In case of compulsory acquisition by the state, the alien is entitled to full and prompt compensation as required by this article of the Kenyan Constitution.

Under the Land Control Act of 1967 all transactions in land are void unless carried out with the consent of the Land Control Board of the area. Section 9 of this law therefore provides that:

> In deciding whether to grant or refuse consent in respect of a controlled transaction, the Land Control Board shall. . . refuse consent in any case in which the land or share is to be disposed of by way of sale, transfer, lease, exchange or partition to a person who is not a citizen of Kenya. . ..

The President of Kenya, however, can exempt any land transaction or any person from all the provisions of this law via publication of a notice in the government gazette. Aliens may also benefit from § 3 of the Government Lands Act of 1915, which enables the President of Kenya to alienate land for any purpose.[86]

---

[85] Charles Mwalimu, The Kenyan Legal System: An Overview 55 (1988).

[86] *Id.* at 55-56.

CHAPTER 106KR

PROPERTY LAW IN SOUTH KOREA

Professor David A. Thomas
J. Reuben Clark Law School
Brigham Young University

SYNOPSIS

§ 106KR.01   Brief History of the Republic of Korea.

Tungusic people from central Asia, a branch of the Mongoloid race, may have begun inhabiting the Korean peninsula between 10,000 and 5,000 years ago. Various legends tell of Tungusic people invading from China. When a military figure named Wiman took control of northwestern Korea in 194, B.C., Korea's recorded history began. Chinese invaders conquered that area in 108, B.C. A Korean ruler emerged in another part of the peninsula in about

100, A.D., and Koreans took over the Chinese-dominated areas in 313, A.D.

Thereafter, various kingdoms and federations rose and fell for several centuries throughout the peninsula. In 1392, A.D., the Yi dynasty established a dominance that lasted until the Japanese annexed Korea in 1910.

Japanese power over Korea resulted directly from Japan's victory over Russia in the Russo-Japanese War of 1904–1905. Japan ordered the Korean army to be disbanded in 1907 and then annexed Korea to Japan in 1910. From then until World War II, various nationalist groups sought to oppose the Japanese hegemony, but could not unite their efforts.

Although the Soviet Union had agreed to a four-power trusteeship over Korea when World War II ended, it reneged and the result was that Japanese forces surrendered to Americans south of the 38th parallel of north latitude, and to the Russians north of the 38th parallel. Soon thereafter, all Japanese in Korea returned to Japan. The Soviets blocked and obstructed all attempts at uniting the two Koreas. A U.N.-supervised election took place in the south on May 10, 1948, and the new Republic of Korea National Assembly promulgated a democratic constitution on July 17, 1948. On August 15, 1948, American military commanders transferred sovereign authority to the Koreans, who inaugurated Syngman Rhee as president.

On June 25, 1950, north Korean armies launched a massive military invasion of south Korea, in an attempt to unify the two Koreas by force. The Korean War ended by armistice and the establishment of a demilitarized zone neat the 38th parallel in July, 1953.

During the ensuing decades turbulent relations with the north and fractious internal politics have led to various governmental changes and seemingly not impeded remarkable economic growth. The First Republic founded in 1948 has now evolved into the current Sixth Republic.

§ 106KR.02   Governmental and Legal Foundations for Property Law in Modern Korea.

In April, 1948, the U.S. military governors in Korea promulgated the "Ordinance of the Rights of the Korean People," containing many rights similar to the American Bill of Rights, including a prohibition of deprivation of property without due process of law. Some of these probably influenced the 1948 Constitution. That Constitution "largely lost its relevance" with the outbreak of the Korean War.[1] Following the war and the unsettled domestic political situation, the Constitution was amended several times and with some fundamental substantive changes resulting. Two articles of the current Constitution relate directly to property rights. Article 16 declares, "All citizens shall be free from intrusion into their place of residence. In case of

---

[1] Rainer Grote, "Republic of Korea: Introductory Note," in Ruediger Wolfram and Rainer Grote (gen. eds.), VIII *Constitutions of the Countries of the World* 5 (2006);

search or seizure in a residence, a warrant issued by a judge upon request of a prosecutor shall be presented." Article 23 addresses property rights:

(1)   The right of property of all citizens shall be guaranteed. The contents and limitations thereof shall be determined by statute.

(2)   The exercise of property rights shall conform to the public welfare.

(3)   Expropriation, use or restriction of private property from public necessity and compensation therefor shall be governed by statute. In such a case, just compensation shall be paid.

In Article 59, "Types and rates of taxes shall be determined by statute."

"Most of the substantive law in the Republic of Korea is contained in the Civil Code, originally promulgated in 1958. The Civil Code is divided into five 'books'.. . . Book II, 'Real Rights,' deal with property, . . . and Book V, 'Succession,' covers succession in family headship as well as succession to property."[2]

§ 106KR.03   Basic South Korean Property Law.

§ 106KR.03(a)   Estates in Land.

The Civil Code provides for the following forms of ownership:[3]

Ownership (fee simple)

Possession, superior to parties without rights

Superficies, which are rights in another's land while owning structures or trees on that land

Easements

Deposit lease (the right to use and take profits from the land of another)

Commonage, based on old customs of use of a forest or plain in common.[4]

§ 106KR.03(a)(1)   Adverse Possession.

A person may obtain ownership through adverse possession by possessing real property peacefully and openly, with intent to own, for 20 years or more, and by making registration thereof.[5]

§ 106KR.03(a)(2)   Condominium Ownership.

Separate ownership of individual units in a multiple-unit structure is

---

[2] Margaret O. Steinbeck, "Legal System of the Republic of Korea (South Korea)," in 2A Kenneth Robert Redden (ed.), *Modern Legal Systems Cyclopedia* 2A.10.33–34 (1991).

[3] Civil Code of Korea (hereafter CC) § 185.

[4] CC §§ 192, 211, 279, 291, 302, 303.

[5] CC § 245.

recognized. Unit owners have tenancies in common interests in common areas.[6]

§ 106KR.03(a)(3)   Concurrent Estates.

Tenancy in common with the usual incidents is recognized by the Korean Civil Code.[7]

§ 106KR.03(b)   Leaseholds.

A lease is not considered a property right.[8] A lease can be recorded only with the consent of the owner. One who holds a recorded building on leased land can maintain that lease against persons who acquire title to the land.[9]

§ 106KR.03(c)   Foreign Ownership of Land.

Foreigners are not permitted to buy land, and face some difficulties in attempting to purchase a house. A foreign company with foreign investments may own property and land necessary for the performance of its business activities, if approved by the Economic Planning Board. Under the Alien Land Act, enterprises with 50 percent or more foreign equity ownership are required to obtain approval from the Minister of Home Affairs for ownership of land except for land designated by the Government for special purposes.[10]

§ 106KR.03(d)   Gifts.

Property acquired by gift is subject to a gift tax. The gift tax in Korea is payable by residents who acquire property by gift and by nonresidents who acquire Korean property by gift. Rates range from 10% to 50%.[11]

§ 106KR.03(e)   Succession.

The rules of descent and distribution for real property are set forth in the Civil Code.[12] Korea does not recognize dower or curtesy rights.

§ 106KR.03(f)   Wills.

Persons 17 years of age and older may make valid wills,[13] and the Civil Code provides forms and formalities for various kinds of wills.[14]

§ 106KR.03(g)   Real Estate Transactions.

Transfer of real property is accomplished by agreement of the parties and

---

[6] *See*, Law Relating to the Ownership and Management of Multiple-Unit Buildings.

[7] CC §§ 262–264.

[8] CC § 621; Law of Protection of Lease of House 1.

[9] CC § 622.

[10] Margaret O. Steinbeck, "Legal System of the Republic of Korea (South Korea)," in 2A Kenneth Robert Redden (ed.), *Modern Legal Systems Cyclopedia* 2A.10.18 (1991).

[11] *See*, Inheritance Tax and Gift Tax Law.

[12] CC §§ 1000, 1001.

[13] CC § 1063.

[14] CC §§ 1066–1070.

upon registration.[15] Registration is required for creation or transfer of real rights in immovable property, including ownership, superficies, servitudes, deposit leases, and mortgages.

Korea has no statute of frauds, but does require a writing for such items as wills and articles of incorporation.[16]

Two types of security liens recognized in the Civil Code are the possessory lien and the mortgage.[17] A mortgage is defined in the Civil Code as an encumbrance on a specific item of property whereby the creditor obtains a preferential position in order to satisfy the obligation out of proceeds realized from the sale of the property; the encumbrance occurs without transferring ownership or possession.[18] Priority among multiple mortgages on the same property is determined by the order of registration.[19] No lien rights similar to mechanics' liens are recognized.

§ 106KR.03(h)   Title Registration.

As mentioned above, registration is required for creation or transfer of real rights in immovable property, including ownership, superficies, servitudes, deposit leases, and mortgages.

§ 106KR.03(i)   Stamps.

A stamp tax is one of the national taxes that may be imposed by national legislation.

§ 106KR.03(j)   Taxation.

"Types and rates of taxes shall be determined by statute."[20] National taxes in Korea are imposed by the national legislature, and local taxes are imposed by local authorities.Korean national law provides for income, value added, gift and inheritance taxes, among others.[21] Local taxes that may relate to real property include acquisition tax, registration, inhabitant tax, property tax, composite land tax, city planning tax, community facility tax, area development tax, among others.

Inheritance tax in Korea is payable by residents who acquire property by inheritance and by nonresidents who acquire Korean property by inheritance. Rates range from 10% to 50%.[22]

---

[15] CC § 186.

[16] CC §§ 1068–1069; Commercial Code 229.

[17] CC §§ 320, 356).

[18] CC § 356.

[19] Real Property Registration Law 5.

[20] Art. 59, Constitution of Korea.

[21] *See*, Income Tax Law; Inheritance Tax and Gift Tax Law.

[22] *See*, Inheritance Tax and Gift Tax Law.

§ 106KR.03(k)   Environmental Regulation.

Korea has numerous laws to regulate and protect the environment. Included among them are the following:

Basic Environmental Policy Act and Its Enforcement Decree

Act on Environment, Traffic and Disaster, etc. Impact Assessment

Liability for Environment Improvement Expenses Act

Environment Dispute Mediation Act

Natural Environment Preservation Act

Noise and Vibration Regulation Act

Water Environment Preservation Act

Noxious Chemical Substance Control Act

Atmospheric Environment Preservation Act

Odor Prevention and Sea Pollution Prevent Act and Its Enforcement Decree

Wastes Management Act

Soil Environment Preservation Act

Drinking Water Control Act

Law Relating to Transboundary Movements of Waste and Its Disposal

Indoor Air Quality Control in Public Facilities Act

Act Relating to Promotion of Economy and Reutilization of Resources

CHAPTER 106KZ

PROPERTY LAW OF THE REPUBLIC OF KAZAKHSTAN

John JA Burke
Professor of Law, Faculty of Law,
Kazakhstan Institute of Management,
Economics and Strategic Research

Roman Nurpeissov
Associate, Salans Almaty,
Kazakhstan

SYNOPSIS

§ 106KZ.01   Overview of Real Property Law in Kazakhstan.

During the Soviet period, land in the Republic of Kazakhstan [RK] belonged unconditionally to the State.[1] The State exercised sole ownership of land during the first years of Kazakhstan's independence, following the Soviet Union's disintegration. The 1993 Constitution provided that land, its soil, water, flora and fauna, and other natural resources are owned *exclusively* by the State.[2] The 1993 Constitution, however, marginally relaxed the state's control: it allowed non-state actors to possess land on behalf of the State in certain instances.[3] The 1995 Constitution further relaxed the State's hold on land: it eliminated the word "exclusively" from the clause on State ownership of land, and added a sentence providing that the land "may also be privately owned under the terms and conditions set forth in the law."[4]

On January 24, 2001, the RK adopted the Law on Land (the "Land Law"). The main features of the Land Law included: (1) the establishment of limits on the size of land plots granted to private parties, (2) introduction of restrictions applying to foreigners, and (3) reduction of the duration of long-term land use from 99 years to 49 years.

---

[1] Konstitutsiya (Osnovnoi Zakon) Kazakhskoi Sovetskoi Sotsialisticheskoi Respubliki ot 20 aprelya 1978 goda [Constitution (the Primary Law) of the Kazakh Soviet Socialist Republic dated April 20, 1978], art. 11. This article states in pertinent part that the land, its subsoil, water, and forests shall belong exclusively to the state.

[2] Konstitutsiya Respubliki Kazakhstan ot 28 yanvarya 1993 goda [Constitution of the Republic of Kazakhstan dated January 28, 1993], art. 46. (emphasis added).

[3] *Id.*

[4] Konstitutsiya Respubliki Kazakhstan ot 30.08.1995 [Constitution of the Republic of Kazakhstan dated Aug. 30, 1995, with amendments and additions as of May 21, 2007], art. 6.3.

On June 20, 2003, the new Land Code, predicated upon the legal status of the Land Law, was adopted ("Land Code"). Under the Land Code, the sale and leasing of buildings by and to private commercial entities is permitted, and is generally free from excessive State regulation.[5] The State's participation in private transactions involving land and buildings primarily is limited to title registration[6] and levying of taxes.[7]

Under the Land Code, an owner may (1) possess, (2) use, and (3) alienate (sell, and otherwise dispose of) its land plot.[8] The owners of buildings [improved property] on the land enjoy rights identical to the owner of the land under the Civil Code.[9] The right to own the land arises from: (1) a grant, (2) transfer or (3) inheritance, including succession resulting from a legal entity's reorganization.[10]

§ 106KZ.02 Forms of Ownership of Real Property.

Under Kazakhstan law, the term "real estate" (or, as it is commonly called "immovable property") includes, *inter alia*, land and buildings. The law treats land and buildings as separate objects of real property. The mechanisms for acquiring ownership rights to such objects are summarized below.

§ 106KZ.02(a) Buildings.

Generally, buildings or other structures located on land may be bought, inherited, bartered, or received as gifts. Any transfer of ownership rights necessitates State registration. An owner of a building under construction cannot transfer the unfinished building as immovable property before it has been registered with the pertinent State authority. The unfinished building, however, may be transferred as movable [personal] property instead. Such a transfer does not require State registration.

From a practical standpoint, transfers of real property involve the risk of a third party's challenge, based on, for instance, the seller's voidable title.

---

[5] *See*, Zemel'nyi Kodeks Respubliki Kazakhstan [Land Code of the Republic of Kazakstan], Ch. 2 (the "Land Code").

[6] *See generally*, Zakon Respubliki Kazakhstan O Gosudarstvennoi Registratsii Prave na Nedvizhimoe Imushestvo i Sdelok s nim [Law of the Republic of Kazakhstan On State Registration of Rights to Immovable Property and Transactions with it] (the "Law on Reg'n of Immovable Property").

[7] *See generally*, Kodeks Respubliki Kazakhstan O Nalogah i Drugih Obyazatel'nyh Platezhah v Byudzhet (Nalogovyi Kodeks) [Code of the Republic of Kazakhstan On Taxes and Other Obligatory Payments to the Budget (the "Tax Code")], ch. 53–56 for the land tax, and ch. 57–58 for property tax.

[8] Land Code, art. 21.

[9] Grazhdanskiy Kodeks Respubliki Kazakhstan [Civil Code of the Republic of Kazakhstan] (the "Civ. Code"), art. 188.2.

[10] Land Code, art. 22.

The "good faith purchaser" provisions of the Civil Code[11] provide some protection against this risk. Generally, pursuant to such provisions, a purchaser will (subject to certain exceptions) qualify as a *bona fide* purchaser of the object of purchase so long as that purchaser neither knew nor should have known that the seller's rights to the property were not properly acquired. Purchasers of real estate also may obtain title insurance to protect themselves from potential future claims of third parties.

§ 106KZ.02(b)   Land Plots.

Under the Land Code, a land plot can be held under: (a) private or State ownership;[12] (b) a right for temporary land use (lease) for consideration;[13] (c) a right of permanent land use;[14] (d) a right of temporary free of charge land use;[15] (e) a right of secondary land use (sublease);[16] and, (f) service land allotment (the right of temporary land use of a plot of land granted by the State to certain categories of civil servants free of charge).[17] In addition, third parties may enjoy easement rights over a land plot under a right of limited use of another's land plot (servitude).[18]

Under the Civil Code,[19] any items of material value found underneath the soil (treasure) shall be divided equally between the land owner and the individual who found them unless agreed upon otherwise. If the land owner did not consent to his land being excavated in search of hidden treasure, then any such treasure found belongs solely to the land owner.[20] If the items constituting the "discovered treasure" also have historic and cultural value, they are transferred to the State while the finder and owner of land are entitled to monetary remuneration in the amount of fifty percent of the value of the discovered items.[21]

§ 106KZ.02(b)(1)   Land Occupied by Buildings.

Under the Land Code, the holder of title to a building is also entitled to ownership or lease of the land plot occupied by such building,[22] except for specific cases envisaged by the RK Land Code. Therefore, if a buyer has

---

[11] Civ. Code, art. 261.

[12] Land Code, art. 3.

[13] *Id.* art. 35.

[14] *Id.* art. 34.

[15] *Id.* art 36.

[16] *Id.* art. 38.

[17] *Id.* art. 41.

[18] *Id.* Ch. 7.

[19] Civ. Code, art. 247.

[20] *Id.*

[21] *Id.*

[22] Land Code, art. 52.1.

acquired title to a building located on a State-owned land plot, such buyer shall have the exclusive right to lease or purchase such underlying land from the State owner. Any privately owned land plot containing improved real property may be sold to a third party only as an indivisible whole constituting the land and improved property (unless the building is owned by such third party).

§ 106KZ.03   Title, Registration and Insurance.

§ 106KZ.03(a)   Technical inspection.

Surveying of a land plot by an authorized governmental agency is a prerequisite for any real estate transaction. Once the land plot survey is completed, the land plot is recorded in the State Legal Cadastre and is assigned a cadastre serial number.[23]

Completed buildings are also subject to technical inspection. Immediately following the commissioning of the building by the relevant authority, the owner arranges, at its own expense, for preparation of a "technical passport," that is, governmental approval of the completed works, of the building by the technical inventory authorities. Buildings must have technical passports as a prerequisite for title to the completed building being registered.

§ 106KZ.03(b)   State Registration.

Under RK law, State registration is required to transfer title to a purchaser of real estate, (a land plot and/or improved property), and to transfer the underlying agreement.[24] Title is conveyed from the seller to the purchaser upon State registration.

A lease/sublease and/or easement concluded for a period of one year or more, and mortgage agreements in relation to real estate, are subject to state registration. An agreement for a lease, mortgage or easement is deemed concluded only upon State registration and is deemed null and void in the absence of such registration.[25] Title to real property, as well as any encumbrance (lease or mortgage), is registered in the State Legal Cadastre maintained by the Kazakhstan Ministry of Justice and its territorial (local) offices.

Real estate may be the subject of a sale or lease/mortgage agreement, only if the seller's/lessor's rights have been previously registered in the State Legal Cadastre. State registration is certified by a special registration endorsement on the document indicating the substance of the transaction (for example, a sale-purchase agreement, lease agreement, or mortgage agreement).

---

[23] *Id.* art. 152–54.

[24] Law on Reg'n of Immovable Property, art. 4.1.

[25] *Id.*, art 4 & 5.

§ 106KZ.04   Forms of Leases And Restrictions on Basic Terms.

Lease rights to real estate are acquired by virtue of a written real estate lease agreement. The parties are free to establish any term of lease, though the right to temporary land use for consideration may either be short-term (up to 5 years) or long-term (from 5 to 49 years).[26] Therefore, when the State acts as a landlord, the duration of the lease cannot exceed 49 years. In instances where land is in private ownership, there is no limitation as to the duration of the lease.

A valid lease agreement must be executed as a single document signed by the authorized representatives of the parties, and include certain material terms with respect to the real property in question. For example, a lease agreement must provide information with respect to the identity, exact location, type of permitted use and cadastre number of the property and the rent amount payable under the lease. Notarization of real property lease agreements is not required. A lease agreement of a building concluded for a period one year or more is subject to State registration[27] and is considered valid only from the moment of registration.

§ 106KZ.04(a)   Land Leases.

Both the Civil Code[28] and the Land Code[29] govern land leases. Some of the Codes' provisions on landlord-tenant law are mandatory and the parties may not modify those rules in their agreement. Such mandatory provisions usually concern unilateral termination rights of landlords under State land lease contracts, maximum lease terms and currency requirements.

§ 106KZ.04(a)(1)   Termination.

A lease may be terminated prior to its stated term upon the occurrence of circumstances specifically provided for in the lease agreement. If the lease term is not specified, either party may terminate the lease upon three months' prior notice, unless another period is stipulated in the lease agreement.[30] In accordance with applicable law, a lease agreement may be terminated by the court upon a claim of either party in the event of a material breach of the other party's obligations. Extra-judicial unilateral termination is possible only if specifically stipulated in the lease agreement.

§ 106KZ.04(a)(2)   Renewability.

Under general rules governing leases, all tenants have a right of first refusal to renew the lease agreement, unless the agreement provides

---

[26] Land Code, art.35.

[27] Law on Reg'n of Immovable Property, art. 4.4.

[28] Civ. Code, Ch. 29.

[29] Land Code, Ch. 4.

[30] Civ. Code, art. 545.2.

otherwise.[31] Furthermore, owners of real estate situated on a plot of land are entitled by statute to rights of use to the land on which such real estate is located.[32]

§ 106KZ.04(a)(3)   Assignment, Sublease and Mortgage.

Unless otherwise provided by the land lease agreement, an assignment, sublease or mortgage of rights and obligations under land leases with State authorities does not require the prior consent of the other party. The sublease of a land plot (or its part) shall be based on a sublease contract and is subject to notification to the relevant authority at the place of the land plot location.[33]

§ 106KZ.04(b)   Commercial Leases.

The legal framework regulating commercial leases in the RK stipulates a number of mandatory provisions of law that cannot be varied by contract. Some of the more important mandatory rules are discussed below.

§ 106KZ.04(b)(1)   Recovery of Operating Expenses; Taxes.

The lease agreement determines operating costs chargeable to tenants. Each taxpayer, however, is obliged to pay its own taxes.[34] This provision is usually interpreted by the tax authorities so as to include not only the physical act of paying the tax, but also bearing of the tax burden. Expenses in connection with current repairs, made by the tenant with a view to preserve and maintain the real estate object and not compensated by the landlord according to the contract of lease, shall be deducted from the tax base.

§ 106KZ.04(b)(2)   Remedies in the Event of Breach.

The landlord may terminate the lease through judicial proceedings in the event of a tenant's breach of the lease agreement, only if the landlord has served a prior "cure" notice to the tenant and given the tenant a reasonable time to cure the breach.[35] The lease agreement may not waive the landlord's statutory right. Likewise, the tenant may terminate the lease through judicial proceedings in the event of the landlord's breach of certain duties described in the Civil Code (*e.g.* to undertake a major maintenance of the leased property).[36] Notably, the tenant is not obliged to serve a "cure" notice upon the landlord, and thus the latter is not provided with any grace period to cure the breach.

---

[31] *Id.*, art. 557.

[32] Land Code, art. 37.

[33] *Id.*, art. 38.

[34] Tax Code, art. 26.

[35] Civ. Code, art. 556.

[36] *Id.*

In case of early termination that accords with the lease agreement, damages are payable if stipulated in the lease agreement. Should a lease agreement be terminated by a court decision due to the material breach of a party, the claimant may be awarded damages for breach of contract. The law requires the non-defaulting party to mitigate its damages in order to have a valid claim for compensation of lost profit from the other party.[37]

§ 106KZ.04(b)(3)   Casualty/Condemnation.

The landlord is responsible for any defects in the leased property which prevent the tenant, in part or in full, from using the leased property.[38] Arguably, a casualty or condemnation affecting the leased premises could be construed as a "defect" in the lease property. In the event of such defects, the tenant has an option at law to:

(a)   demand that the landlord cure those defects at no cost to the tenant;

(b)   reduce the rent accordingly;

(c)   withhold the amount of expenses incurred in curing the defects from the rent, upon advance notice to the landlord; or

(d)   demand early termination of the lease.[39]

If the landlord has been notified by the tenant of the tenant's claim or its intention to cure the defects of the leased property at the landlord's expense, then the landlord has an option either to substitute promptly another similar property free from defects for the leased property, or to cure the defects itself at its cost.[40] The tenant is free to accept or reject the substitute offered by the landlord. The law does not identify what would be a "similar (or analogous) property". Such substitute presumably must be capable of performing similar functions or achieving similar results as the original leased property would have performed or achieved had it been free from defects. Given that the acceptance of the substitute is the tenant's right, it follows that it is the tenant who determines the "similarity" of the substitute, and its suitability for his needs. If the rent is insufficient to cover the tenant's damages resulting from defects in the leased property, the tenant has a claim against the landlord for that part of the damages not covered by rent.[41]

§ 106KZ.04(b)(4)   Ownership of Tenant's Improvements.

The law distinguishes between two types of improvements: detachable and non-detachable. Non-detachable improvements are those that may not be detached without damage to the property. Any detachable improvements

---

[37] *Id.*, art. 350.4.

[38] *Id.*, art. 548.1.

[39] *Id.*

[40] *Id.*, art. 548.2.

[41] *Id.*, art. 548.3.

the tenant makes at his own expense remain his property, unless otherwise provided in the lease agreement.[42] The tenant's non-detachable improvements are made at its own expense, and with the prior consent of the landlord, shall remain on the premises upon termination of the lease, but the tenant shall be entitled to compensation for the value of the improvements made, unless the lease agreement stipulates otherwise.[43] The value of improvements is established at the date of termination. If the tenant makes non-detachable improvements without the landlord's consent, the landlord is under no obligation to pay any compensation to the tenant.[44]

§ 106KZ.04(b)(5)   Tenant's Right to Sublease.

A tenant may transfer his rights and obligations under the lease agreement to a third party, or pledge his lease rights, or contribute the lease rights to the charter capital of a company, but in each case only with the landlord's prior consent.[45] In all the aforementioned cases, other than transfer of lease, the tenant remains primarily liable to the landlord under the lease agreement.

§ 106KZ.05   Mortgage of Real Estate, Enforceability and Foreclosure.

§ 106KZ.05(a)   Mortgage Agreements.

The mortgage of real estate is widely used in the RK to secure loans. The main law governing mortgages is the Law "On Mortgages of Immovable Property" ("Mortgage Law") enacted in December 1995.

A mortgage agreement enters into force as of the date of its State registration, and it is not necessary to notarize the mortgage agreement.[46] Registration of creditor's rights as a mortgagee provides protection against the debtor's disposing of the mortgaged assets in bad faith without the creditor's knowledge.

§ 106KZ.05(b)   Validity and Enforceability of Mortgages.

§ 106KZ.05(b)(1)   Enforceability of Mortgages, Existence of Non-Contractual Mortgages.

In the vast majority of cases, a mortgage over real estate arises as a result of a mortgage contract. In some instances, however, a non-contractual mortgage (pledge) can be created automatically as a matter of law. Examples of situations where this may arise are as follows:

    (a)   if a recipient of an annuity transfers a land plot or some other

---

[42] Civ. Code, art. 555.1.

[43] *Id.*, art. 555.2.

[44] *Id.*, art. 555.3.

[45] *Id.*, art. 551.

[46] Mortgage Law, art. 6.2 & 6.3.

immovable property to the payee of the annuity, the payments are automatically secured by pledge rights to the property;

(b) unless otherwise provided by law or agreement, if the owner of a land plot mortgages it, the mortgage will extend to all buildings belonging to the mortgagor, located or being developed on the applicable land plot;

The above mortgages do not require the consent of the mortgagor, who is usually a debtor under a claim to be secured. The law requires that such non-contractual mortgages be registered simultaneously with the debtor's title.

§ 106KZ.05(b)(2)   Priority of claims.

Mandatory rules govern priority among creditors upon the distribution of proceeds from foreclosure (sale of mortgaged real estate). The following claims have priority over those secured by a contractual mortgage:

- enforcement costs;

- personal injury claims;

- salary and severance pay claims, and other labor and personal service-related claims;

Since this order of priority results from mandatory legal rules, lenders cannot contractually improve their position of priority (seniority) with the borrower.

§ 106KZ.05(c)   Enforcement and Foreclosure Mechanism.

§ 106KZ.05(c)(1)   Who May Foreclose and Which Remedies May Be Exercised.

A mortgage creditor may act to foreclose on the mortgage. If a debtor is insolvent, any creditor may file a bankruptcy petition that potentially may lead to bankruptcy foreclosure proceedings.

§ 106KZ.05(c)(2)   Bankruptcy vs. Enforcement of Mortgage.

Enforcement mechanisms are regulated by the Civil Code (for collection proceedings) and the Law "On Bankruptcy" dated January 21, 1997 No. 67-I (for enforcement through bankruptcy proceedings). The creditor holding rights under a mortgage may elect either to foreclose on the mortgage or to file a bankruptcy petition against the debtor (other circumstances permitting). Since it is impossible to conduct collection proceedings and bankruptcy proceedings simultaneously, a creditor must choose between the two types of proceedings.

In collection proceedings, and so long as the debtor is solvent, the mortgage creditor obtains the proceeds of the sale of the mortgaged asset in the first place provided that there are no other creditors pursuing their claims through collection proceedings. If, however, there are multiple creditors (and, therefore, more than one 'enforcement writ') and the assets are insufficient to meet all creditors' claims, the proceeds are distributed in the following order:

- enforcement costs;
- personal injury claims;
- copyright claims;
- claims secured by mortgage;
- tax and fiscal claims;
- all other claims.

Lower ranking claims are satisfied only after higher ranking claims have been reimbursed in full. In the event that the funds are insufficient to reimburse all of the equally ranking creditors, then the funds are distributed pro rata to the size of their claims. The same principle applies to bankruptcy proceedings.

However, if during collection proceedings and before relevant assets are ordered to be sold, a bankruptcy proceeding with respect to the debtor is initiated, the collection proceeding is suspended (akin to an automatic stay). The mortgage creditor would have a similar third ranking priority in both types of proceedings. As a result, even if the collection proceeding is suspended because of the bankruptcy proceeding, the mortgage creditor may participate in the bankruptcy proceeding. The creditor secured by mortgage must file his claim in bankruptcy proceeding no later than two months following the moment that the notice of bankruptcy proceeding is published.

Bankruptcy proceedings usually involve several creditors. Therefore, they are routinely regulated, and thus likely to take more time, as opposed to collection proceedings.

Under RK law, parties may not agree that real property becomes the property of the mortgage creditor in case of default by the creditor, that is, for example, in case of insolvency of the creditor.

§ 106KZ.05(c)(3)   Non-Judicial Foreclosure.

Non-judicial foreclosure over real estate is possible if such option is clearly envisaged in the mortgage agreement. Non-judicial foreclosure is prohibited when: (i) the mortgage agreement requires third party consent; (ii) mortgaged property has significant historical, artistic, or other cultural value for society, or (iii) the mortgaged property is real estate that is common property, and one of the proprietors does not give written approval for the settlement of the pledgeholder's (pledgee's) claims

§ 106KZ.05(c)(4)   Requirements For Exercising Remedies; Enforcement Timeframe; Sensitivities and Restrictions.

The procedure for enforcing creditors' rights in collection proceedings is the same regardless of whether the claims are secured or unsecured: only the priority of the creditors to the proceeds collected is different.

Collection proceedings generally entail the following steps:
- obtaining an enforceable decision;
- obtaining a writ of enforcement;
- instructing the court bailiff to take a specified collection measure and payment of his fees;
- the court bailiff's execution of the requested collection measure and notification to the debtor;
- collection.

Remedies are not restricted to monetary damages. For example, in the event of a payment default, a creditor may enforce a termination clause permitting acceleration of the loan.

§ 106KZ.06   Zoning.

Zoning designation of a land plot is important. If the purchased land is intended to be used for purposes other than its existing zoning designation, the buyer must change such designation to adapt it to the intended purposes. Zoning designation is changed upon application to the local municipality, provided that such change does not contravene the zoning regulations effective within a given municipality.

Under the Law on Architectural, Town Planning and Construction Activity in the RK (the "Town Planning Law") dated July 16, 2001, urban territories are divided into various zones with appropriate construction rules for different zones.

§ 106KZ.07   Eminent Domain.

Articles 84–88 of the Land Code regulate the area of eminent domain. Article 84 of the Land Code states that a land plot may be (1) judicially taken from the owner (2) for the State's purposes (3) if there is no other means for satisfying the State's needs, (4) provided that the owner of the land plot is compensated appropriately. The state may request the landlord to sell his property only when public interest is involved: the construction of roads, defense needs, building of new neighborhoods and districts and etc.[47]

§ 106KZ.08   Restrictions on Foreign Ownership.

Foreign individuals or legal entities cannot hold *a right of permanent land use* of a land plot. A "foreign" legal entity under RK law is an entity incorporated under the laws of a foreign country that derives its formal existence from that foreign incorporation. Accordingly, a foreign company establishing a wholly owned Kazakh subsidiary, such as a Limited Liability

---

[47] Land Code, art. 84.2.

Partnership or a Joint Stock Company, is exempt from the restriction prohibiting foreign ownership of land and entitled to hold a right of permanent land use of a land plot.

Therefore, foreign legal entities that have established a wholly owned company in the RK are permitted to *own and lease land* in Kazakhstan. They also may enter into construction (including reconstruction) contracts and utilities agreements. However, foreign legal entities may not own land plots intended for agricultural purposes and forestry. These restrictions do not apply to Kazakhstan legal entities with foreign capital.

In addition, a foreign individual that obtains the status of a permanent resident of the RK may purchase land and improved property primarily for the purpose of individual residence. A foreign individual, with or without permanent residence, cannot own agricultural or forestry land. However, the State may impose restrictions on the duration and use of that property.

§ 106KZ.09   Taxes.

The following chart summarizes the two types of taxes directly affecting owners of real estate:

Type of tax	Tax base	Tax rate
Property tax (for individuals)	An average annual residual value of real property calculated through a certain formula	Rate varies depending on the value of real property
Property tax (for legal entities)	An average annual residual value of real property or related immovable property according to accounting data	Legal entities pay property tax at the rate of 1.5 percent of the tax base.
Land Tax	Area of the land plot	Rate varies depending on the category, designation, and quality of land, *e.g.* rate of tax on land in Almaty that is not occupied by housing facilities is KZT 28.95 per square meter. The land occupied by housing facilities is taxed at the rate of KZT 0.96 per square meter.

§ 106KZ.10   Ownership of Subsoil Use Rights.

1. The Republic of Kazakhstan has significant oil and gas reserves, as well as major deposits of minerals, including but not limited to, uranium, gold, zinc, copper, lead, coal, nickel, and aluminum bauxite. The extractive industries account for approximately 60% of exports and constitute the main applications of foreign direct investment. The legislative base for subsoil use

is critical to rights of ownership and use of resources below the ground surface. The legal framework is the Law of the Republic of Kazakhstan as of January 27, 1996 No 2828 on Subsoil and Subsoil Use them (amended and supplemented as of 07/07/2006) [The Subsoil Law].[48]

2. The Constitution of the Republic of Kazakhstan provides in Section I, Article 6(3) that the State owns all land and all natural resources.[49] Secondary legislation hence establishes private ownership of land and natural resources and allocates the right of ownership over subsoil use, with the State retaining substantial authority over grants of concession. Special regulations apply to private ownership of subsoil intended to meet governmental needs in strategic and scarce types of mineral raw materials; to ensure national security, preserve environment, and protect population; or conserve subsoil portions to save mineral stocks for the future generations.

3. The term "Subsoil" is defined as "part of the earth's crust underneath the topsoil, or in the case of its absence, underneath the earth's surface and the bottom of seas, lakes, rivers and other reservoirs which extends up to the depths accessible for performing subsoil use operations with account of scientific and technological advance".[50] The term "subsoil use right" is, "a right to possess and use subsoil within the contractual territory which is granted to subsoil users in accordance with this Law".[51]

4. A "subsoil user" is an individual or juridical entity [domestic or foreign] that acquires a right to perform operations upon the subsoil, for personal or commercial purposes. Subsoil use rights comprise the right to possess and the right to use the subsoil within the terms of a State grant. Article 10 of the Subsoil Law delineates subsoil use rights by providing that "The right to use subsoil shall be granted to perform the following operations":

1. Governmental geological research of subsoil;

2. Exploration;

3. Extraction;

4. Combined exploration and extraction; or

5. Construction and/or maintaining of underground facilities not related to exploration and/or extraction.

Subsoil use holders are divided into two classes: (1) holders of a permanent right to use the land and its subsoil, including the right of alienability, and

---

[48] The Law of the Republic of Kazakhstan as of January 27, 1996 No. 2828 On subsoil and subsoil use (amended and supplemented as of 07/07/2006) [Subsoil Law]. The Law contains 10 parts and 76 Articles.

[49] The Constitution of the Republic of Kazakhstan (Date needed; Official citation).

[50] Article 1(28), Subsoil Law.

[51] Article 1(38), Subsoil Law.

(2) holders of a temporary right to use the land and its subsoil.[52]

5. Subsoil use rights arise from allocation by the State, transfer from another subsoil user, or succession in title [*e.g.*, company holding subsoil use right is reorganized or acquired in a merger].[53] With certain exceptions for "bargain-based contracts", a holder acquires subsoil use rights by entering into a contract with the competent State authority, that is, the Ministry of Energy and Mineral Resources [MEMR].[54] The MEMR conducts open or restricted tenders advertised in the mass media regarding acquisition of rights in a subsoil plot.[55] The winner of the tender selected by the Tender Board is obliged to enter into a contract with the MEMR.[56]

6. The MEMR uses standardized contracts for granting ownership of the right governing subsoil use: (1) product separation contracts, (2) concession contracts, and (3) work or service contracts.[57] The State and the contractor establish terms by mutual consent provided they are consistent with the laws of Kazakhstan. Major contractual issues are: taxation, forfeit for failure to observe contractual norms, compliance with Kazakhstan content [*e.g.*, requirement to retain Kazakhstan labor and formula to set wages], the conditions of exploration and extraction, duration of the contract, and its territorial scope.[58] The MEMR monitors compliance of the holder with its contract obligations. In the event of contractual violation, the MEMR has the competence to require correction of the violation.[59] In the event the holder fails to correct the contractual violation, the MEMR has the authority to invalidate the contract under the terms of the Subsoil Law.[60]

7. Subsoil users have the following statutory rights:[61]

1. Independence to exercise subsoil rights based on the contract;

2. Use the products of activity, including mineral raw materials;

3. Construct necessary industrial and social facilities on the allocated territory and, by agreement, to use common facilities or telecommunications on or outside the contractual territory;

4. Negotiate prolongation of the contract within the framework of

---

[52] Article 11, Subsoil Law.

[53] Article 12(1)(1)(2) and (3), Subsoil Law.

[54] Article 13(1), Subsoil Law.

[55] Articles 41-1 to 41-7, Subsoil Law.

[56] Article 41-7(8), Subsoil Law.

[57] Article 42(1), Subsoil Law.

[58] Articles 42, 42-1 and 43-1, Subsoil Law.

[59] *See generally*, Part 2 of the Subsoil Law, Articles 7 & 8.

[60] Articles 45, 45-1 & 45-2, Subsoil Law.

[61] Article 62, Subsoil Law.

Kazakhstan law;

5.   Hire subcontractors;

6.   Transfer wholly or partially rights of ownership in subsoil use to another party provided the transfer is consistent with the Law on Subsoil and subsoil use; and

7.   Terminate activities by conforming to Kazakhstan legislation

Excepting for the State pre-emptive right, the rights of the subsoil user are protected under the law and are insulated from the retroactive application of subsequent legislation.[62]

8. Subsoil users are obliged by the Subsoil Law: (1) to protect the environment, human life and health, (2) to exploit the subsoil efficiently, (3) to preserve natural landscapes and geomorphic structures, (4) to avoid risks capable of leading to soil degradation, and (5) to maintain the natural state of waters.[63] Subsoil users also must apply rational and complex measures to effectuate the contract.[64] Violations of mandatory rules subject the subsoil user to liability established by Kazakhstan law.[65]

9. The State retains a pre-emptive right in the event of any intended alienation by a subsoil user of its license, participation rights in the subsoil user, or transfer of its rights to an entity that influences its decision-making.[66] The pre-emptive right shall not be exercised on terms less favorable than those offered by competing purchasers. The purpose of the pre-emptive right is to block shareholders' pre-emptive rights and to prevent off-shore transactions designed to dispose of subsoil use rights in Kazakhstan.[67]

10. In addition, the State retains the right to require a subsoil user to renegotiate the terms of its contract when the State deems that the deposit is of "strategic importance", and that its use constitutes a "material alteration" to Kazakhstan's economic interests or a threat to its national security.[68] Refusal to renegotiate may result in suspension or termination of the contract.

11. Disputes are settled according to the dispute settlement provisions of the

---

[62] *Id.*

[63] *See generally*, Parts 6 & 7, Articles 47 & 54, Subsoil Law.

[64] Article 63, Subsoil Law.

[65] *E.g.*, Articles 45 (Contract declared invalid); 45-1 (Suspension of Contract); 45-2 (Amendment and Cancellation of Contract); and Article 71-1, Subsoil Law.

[66] Article 71, Subsoil Law.

[67] *Id.* Note that the concept of "material alteration" is defined neither in the Law nor in judicial decisions.

[68] Subsoil Law, amendment of 24 October 2007 signed by President Nursultan Nazarbayev.

contract. Article 71-1 requires parties to enter into negotiations to settle a dispute prior to proceeding to litigation or international arbitration.

CHAPTER 106MX

PROPERTY LAW IN MEXICO

Professor David A. Thomas
J. Reuben Clark Law School
Brigham Young University

SYNOPSIS

§ 106MX.01   History of Property Law in Mexico.

The region of Mexico was inhabited perhaps as long as 15,000 to 20,000 years ago. It seems likely that even 10,000 years ago a wetter climate supported more abundant vegetation and animal life than at present. Even larger animals, such as mammoths, elephants, buffalos, antelopes and horses were able to sustain themselves. The earliest people may have immigrated along with and hunted some of the larger animals. The people who inhabited this area apparently lived in groups with a certain hierarchy and order.

Between 7,000 and 5,000 B.C., the inhabitants of the Mexican central plateau changed their hunting-based economy into a mixed farming and hunting society. Findings from 3,000 B.C. show widespread domestication of animals such as the peacock, *escuincle* (mutt), turkey, and Chihuahua dogs.

This economic pattern was broken in about 2,000 B.C., when maize made its appearance and became the most important food of these ancient settlers. Maize also led to the refining of the textile industry, ceramics, the decorative use of feathers, and other arts as well as the developing of certain sports. With these refined products came specialization, exchange of products, and the rise of non-agricultural classes, such as nobles, priests, merchants, sculptors, and other artisans.

The position of the upper classes was strengthened as warfare yielded slaves, who then made possible the creation of the great architectural monuments left by the Maya, Mixtec, Aztec, Zapotec, Toltec, and Chichemecas civilizations.

Although these great civilizations of ancient Mexico developed out of the surplus created by the prevailing maize agriculture, the primitive agricultural techniques exhausted the soil and forced the people to migrate, leaving fields and cities behind.

The evidence of these ancient cultures shows irrigation systems, religious rituals, and elaborate cities and markets.

The Olmec civilization flourished between the 9th and the 1st centuries B.C., in the area of the Mexican Gulf coast. Thereafter, it decayed and passed many of its features on to the Teotihuacan civilization. The Aztec civilization appeared around the 4th century and came to the Mexican valley from the Yucatan peninsula. The Aztecs transformed their aristocratic government to a monarchy.

As the Aztec empire developed, their real property was governed by public rather than private law. Some land was owned by the monarch as personal property and other lands were used to support the monarch's military leaders for the duration of their services. Some lands held by these noble followers were held for life only and were inalienable.[1]

The Aztecs were divided into clans called *Calpullis*, and families of a clan held land as tenants in common. The tenancy vested if the family remained on the land for two years. The Aztec clan also held lands for community, religious, military, certain public purposes, and for the king's purposes. Some of these lands were used to pay taxes and for other public expenses.

By the time Montezuma II began ruling in 1502, the Aztec empire was in decline:

> The spirit of this emperor was weakened, for he believed in assorted bad

---

[1] Gillermo F. Margadant, An Introduction to Mexican Law 20 (1980).

omens. His enormous empire, comprising perhaps as many as ten million people, was too large for the means of communication available at the time; it lacked the coherence that can only be based in common ideals; and it was generally hated by its subject tribes. Hence, a mere handful of some four hundred and fifty Spaniards were able to conquer where their limited number made it at first appear improbable.[2]

With Cortez's conquest of Mexico in 1520, two great cultural streams converged, the Aztec and the Hispanic. The Hispanic current carried its law, which was *Castilian*, and applied that law to its Latin American empire. New Spain became a new kingdom of the empire. Soon after the Conquest, Indian affairs were handled through a Council of Indies similar to the Council of Castile. However, the supreme power remained in Spain, the economic interests of the New Spain were subordinated to those of her European sovereign, and European Spaniards were privileged relative to New World Spaniards.

The property law of New Spain also reflected the shifting legal currents in Spain and Europe. Very early in New Spain's colonial history, large dynastic landholdings emerged as the *conquistadores* were given huge land grants for the services they had rendered. Economic disparities with the natives were further exacerbated as the Indians were usually required to render services to the governing class. Spaniards' holdings were increased as they purchased or seized adjacent lands.[3]

The Spanish Roman Church also became a large landholder, and so, in the 19th century became a target of reform. In the *Leyes de Reforma* of Benito Juarez it was decreed that "anyone, especially the tenant of a church property, could buy it for a very small price by making a claim or *denuncia*. The claim was necessary since many farms or houses were in the names of priests but were, in fact, Church property."[4]

The reform was mostly ineffective, because the peasants did not have any money to buy lands; or their religious beliefs prevented them from buying church lands. On the other hand, the wealthy class did buy, very cheaply, most of the Church's real property. The result of the reform laws, then, was to impoverish the church and threaten many of its charitable activities on behalf of the landless poor.

Strengthening of large landholders continued under Porfirio Diaz. Many enormous *Latifundios* (large tracts of privately owned lands) were granted, not to Mexican peasants, but to foreign companies or individuals who would hopefully promote progress. Sometimes corrupt politicians took lands

---

[2] Adolph F.A. Bandelier, On the Social Organization and Mode of Government of the Ancient Mexicans 12 (1879).

[3] Alberto Mayagoitia, A Layman's Guide to Mexican Law 13 (1976).

[4] *Id.*

intended for support of the Indians. Many prominent persons took "advantage of the political climate that favored landholders, merchants, and investors to the detriment of the general population."[5]

Such injustices fomented deep discontent among the peasants. Civil unrest eventually resulted in a new constitution in 1917. This constitution not only opened the way for land reform, but also dealt with another abuse, the aggressive acquisition and use of Mexican real property by foreign governments.

The 1917 constitution solved this problem because Mexican law forbade foreigners to own any real estate in Mexico. A non-Mexican seeking to acquire land the acquirer's had to agree not to seek the protection of his or her government. Article 27 of the Constitution proclaims that original ownership of the land and water belongs to the Mexican nation and that dominion over these lands can be conveyed to private individuals. Also, the Mexican nation has the right to limit ownership of private property to protect public interest and to make a just and fair distribution.

The constitution divided and distributed many *Latifundios* to small landowners and peasants. Small landholdings were given protection, and takings for public needs were to fairly compensated.

Now, only Mexicans by birth or naturalization may freely acquire property over lands or waters or obtain concessions to exploit mines. Religious orders and churches of any faith are not allowed to own any type of property in Mexico. Social services or welfare institutions, businesses, or corporations can own only the real estate needed for their purposes. Foreigners cannot buy land within 50 kilometers of the seashore (31 miles) or 100 kilometers (62.5 miles) of the borders with other countries.

Mexico also exerts sovereignty over its natural resources:

> All waters and territorial seas belong to the nation, as do all minerals, salts, ore deposits, natural gas, and petroleum. With respect to all this, the dominion of the nation is inalienable, but the federal government may grant concessions to exploit them to individuals or Mexican corporations that fulfill all the requirements of the law.[6]

§ 106MX.02   Types of Property Interests.

Real property rights under Mexican law include the traditional Roman components of ownership, the *jus disponendi*, the *fructus*, and the *usus*. The *jus disponendi* is the right to dispose of the property by gift, sale, will, or even destruction. The *fructus* is the right to the fruits or income of the property, such as rent, interest, dividends, and crops from land. The *Usus* is the right to enjoy and use the property. These attributes collectively

---

[5] *Id.*

[6] *Id.*

constitute ownership and cannot be separated. However, ownership may be shared.[7]

Under the Mexican Civil Code, the following items are considered real property:

a. Land the buildings attached to it;

b. Plants and trees, so long as these are attached to the ground, and their attached fruits;

c. Everything that is permanently attached to real property;

d. Statues, paintings and reliefs which are permanently affixed to buildings;

e. Pigeon houses, beehives, fish ponds or similar breeding places, when they are part of the farm;

f. Machinery, storage vessels, tools or utensils intended by the owner of the farm for its operation, directly and exclusively;

g. Fertilizers intended for the cultivation of a farm, which are on the land where they are to be used, as well as the seed necessary for the cultivation of the farm;

h. The electrical appliances and accessories attached to the ground or to the buildings on the land, unless there is an agreement to the contrary;

i. Springs, ponds, cisterns and water courses;

j. Breeding stock and work animals;

k. Dams and irrigation works, as well as piers;

l. Rights *in rem* in real property are also considered to be real property;

m. Rolling stock of railroads, telephone and telegraph lines and fixed radio-telegraph stations.[8]

Property rights are secured by the constitution[9] and civil code.[10] Private property may be taken by the government only for public purposes and only with compensation. Property exhibiting characteristics of national culture may be so taken.

In addition to sale, gift and exchange, property may be acquired by adverse possession, either after five years if in good faith, or after 10 years, if in bad faith.[11]

§ 106MX.02(a)   The Usufruct.

A *usufruct* can be created by contract or by operation of law, and it is a temporary right to the use of and fruits of the property. Both the *usus* and

---

[7] James E. Herget & Jorge Camil, An Introduction To The Mexican Legal System 48 (1978).

[8] The Mexican Civil Code art. 750 (hereafter "Civil Code").

[9] Const. art. 27.

[10] Civil Code art. 830.

[11] *Id.* arts. 1151-1157.

fructus are temporarily assigned to the *usufructuary* who also has the power to alienate the *usufruct* to another within some limitations. A limited form of *usufruct* is recognized in the right to use a habitation; this is limited to the temporary use of dwelling, is not alienable, and is analogous both in concept and in social function to the common law life estate and widow's interest.[12]

§ 106MX.02(b)   Servitudes.

The servitude corresponds to the common law easement. A servitude is a burden on the servient tenement and runs with the land, as does an easement under the common law. The servitude is commonly used for drainage, canals, aqueducts, pipelines, rights of way, and utility lines.[13]

§ 106MX.02(c)   Security Interests.

The chattel mortgage is not recognized, but the ordinary mortgage is very common in Mexico. Livestock, farm machinery, crops, and other agricultural items may be covered by the mortgage lien as fixtures. Other special provisions exist for maritime shipping and commercial aviation. A mortgage may be conveyed in favor of a third party by endorsing the negotiable instrument, without notice to the mortgagor. The security interests of mortgages include the natural accessions to the mortgaged property, improvements made by the owner, movable objects permanently incorporated into the property by the owner, new buildings built by the owner, and additions to mortgaged buildings.[14]

In Mexico it is necessary to distinguish between the civil pledge and the commercial pledge. Under the commercial pledge, the creditor or third party must be given actual possession of the property. Under the civil pledge, constructive possession suffices.

The conditional sale contract is another common security in Mexico, either as a sale subject to rescission (*venta sujeta a clausula rescisoria*), or a sale with title reserved (*venta con reserva de dominio*). The trust (*fideicomiso*) is used for complicated land development transactions. The lender or principal creditor in such a transaction is prohibited from acting as trustee. To secure the interest of a foreign lender with a trust requires a permit from the central bank.

§ 106MX.03   Co-Ownership.

Co-ownership is common in Mexico, but no right of survivorship is recognized. Each co-owner has right to require a partition of the property.[15]

---

[12] *Id.* arts. 980-1048.

[13] *Id.* arts. 1057-1134.

[14] *Id.* arts. 2893-2943.

[15] *Id.* arts. 938-979.

§ 106MX.04   Transfer of Ownership.

The voluntary transfer of land in Mexico may be accomplished by sale, donation or devise. Involuntary transfers are achieved by judicial orders, by inheritance, and by prescription. Transactions are required to be formalized through a notary and by recordation in the public registry (*registro publico*).[16]

§ 106MX.05   The Recording System.

Under Mexico's recording system, an instrument which creates, extinguishes, modifies, or otherwise affects rights *in rem* in inmovables may be recorded. The documents recorded are documents executed by a notary, by judges, and by administrative judges. This recording law is based on the principles of publicity, legality, specification, priority, and sequence.[17]

§ 106MX.05(a)   Publicity.

If an instrument transfers an interest to another party, then it is normally effective even if it is not recorded. But to be effective against third parties, the instrument needs to be properly recorded. In Mexico a person is not considered a third party if he or she has notice of the transaction or did not act in good faith.

§ 106MX.05(b)   Legality.

The registrar may refuse to record any type of document which is not legally valid. For example, the registry determines from the records whether the grantor has the power to convey the property, whether the parties to the instrument have the legal capacity to act, whether the instrument complies with external formalities, and whether the property is properly defined.

§ 106MX.05(c)   Specification.

Specification means that the conveyance has be specific as to the nature of the obligation, type of ownership, amount of lien, and individual parcels.

§ 106MX.05(d)   Priority.

Priority is the familiar "first in time, first in right." The first instrument to be recorded will prevail against other conveyances. If a registrar refuses to record an instrument because of invalidity, the registrar must nevertheless enter a preventive inscription on the record to preserve the priority of the instrument, in case it should later be determined that the instrument is recordable.

§ 106MX.05(e)   Sequence.

A party seeking to record an instrument must indicate the source of the

---

[16] Juan F. Moreno, "Closing the Deal: Buying Residential Land in Mexico's 'Restricted Zone,'" 38 Ariz. Att'y 30 (March, 2002).

[17] *Id.* arts. 2999-3074.

grantor's title. This requirement links the instrument chronologically to show the source of each grantor's interest. However, the Mexican Supreme Court has interpreted this law to mean that when two parties are asserting ownership based upon a record title, the first to be recorded (principle of priority) does not necessarily prevail. Rather, the chain of title must be traced back to the earliest recording from a common grantor or, if no common grantor appears, then the priority principle applies.

§ 106MX.06   Wills and Intestate Succession.

Property may be devised through either of two types of wills, ordinary and special wills. Ordinary wills are classified as public open, public closed, and holographic wills. Public open wills are executed before the notary and three witnesses with the full panoply of formalities—signatures, readings aloud, certification, and the enrollment in the notary's records. Public closed wills are privately executed. A public closed will is signed by the executor, sealed in an envelope, and presented to the notary. The notary certifies then the will before witnesses and testators, makes an entry of protocol, and gives the will to the testator. A holographic will is a will written entirely by the hand of the testator. Formalities such as sealing wax and fingerprints are required. This type of will must be deposited in the general archives of the notarial office to be effective. Special wills include private, military, maritime, and foreign wills. Upon intestate succession the title to property vests immediately in the heirs, each of whom has the right to partition or to purchase other heirs' shares.[18]

§ 106MX.07   Leases.

Under Mexican leases, the lessor is the sole "owner," and the lessee does not acquire a property interest in the premises. Residential leases may not exceed ten years, commercial leases are limited to 15 years, and industrial leases are limited to 20 years. Low income property leases may be extended indefinitely. Leases with rent above a certain amount must be in writing and leases for rural property must be in the form of public documents. Leasehold rights may not be transferred without the consent of the lessor.[19]

§ 106MX.08   Ownership of Mexican Property by Foreigners.

Immigrants to Mexico may own Mexican real property after obtaining a permit to buy land. Non-residents and tourists may not purchase Mexican land. Indirect ownership by means of a trust is permissible, especially of recreational property in the resort areas. Such properties may also be leased or rented to others by the trust foreign beneficiary.

§ 106MX.09   Taxation of Property.

Under the Mexican national law, a federal stamp tax is imposed on

---

[18] *Id.* arts. 1281-1791.

[19] *Id.* arts. 2398-2496.

transactions required to be in writing, including sales and leases of real property located in Mexico. City taxes are also usually imposed on rental income.

CHAPTER 106PH

PROPERTY LAW IN THE PHILIPPINES

Professor David A. Thomas
J. Reuben Clark Law School
Brigham Young University

SYNOPSIS

§ 106PH.01   Brief History of the Philippines.

§ 106PH.01(a)   Prehistory of the Philippines.

Fossils of early humans in the Philippines resemble specimens also found in Java and China. Most Filipinos are descended from people who came from Taiwan or people who migrated along the peninsulas of southeast Asia and through the islands of Indonesia. The first immigrants by sea probably came about 11,000 B.C. Various subsequent migrating groups introduced a series of advancing levels of economy and culture. Both prehistoric and historic migrations have produced a fantastic variety of ethnic groups in the Philippines, with at least 45 distinct ethnic groups. Speakers of Cebuano and Tagalog are the two largest language groups. These two groups, considered the Filipino language, are with English, the official languages of the Philippines.

§ 106PH.01(b)   The Early History of the Philippines.

Filipinos for centuries lived in independent communities under customary, unwritten rules or laws. Researches have found evidence of at least two written law codes, dating from the 13th and 15th centuries, A.D. The customary laws dealt with property rights, among many other subjects.[1]

When Ferdinand Magellan landed in the Philippines in 1521, even though he was killed there, the way was opened for introduction of Spanish rule over the Filipino archipelago. From that time until Philippine independence in 1898, Spanish laws and codes prevailed in the Philippines.

§ 106PH.01(c)   Summary of Modern Filipino Legal History.

Later in that same year, in December, 1898, the Treaty of Paris terminating the Spanish-American War provided for Spain to cede the Philippines to the United States. "Upon the establishment of American sovereignty, the political laws of the Philippines were totally abrogated and Spanish laws, customs and rights of property inconsistent with the U.S. Constitution and with American principles and institutions were superseded."[2]

The Americans established a Commonwealth government intended to prepare for Philippine independence, and the Filipinos adopted their own Constitution in 1935. Later that year they elected their first executive and legislative officials.

From December, 1941, when the Japanese invaded the Philippines to open World War II there, until 1944, the Japanese occupied the Philippines and even produced a constitution in 1943. A Commonwealth government in exile returned to power in 1945, and the Philippine Republic was inaugurated on July 4, 1946. Filipinos ratified a new Constitution in 1973.

The new Constitution introduced a parliamentary system with merged executive and legislative powers. The prime minister became the chief

---

[1] Myrna S. Feliciano, "The Legal System of the Philippines," in 9 Linda L. Schlueter (ed.), *Modern Legal Systems Cyclopedia* 9.290.5 (2001).

[2] *Id.* at 9.290.6.

executive and the president became head of state, a largely symbolic and ceremonial office. However, by a series of parliamentary maneuvers and constitutional amendments, this system was never implemented. Instead, it was changed into a modified presidential/parliamentary system. The president declared the inauguration of the Fourth Republic in 1981. The electorate ratified a new Constitution on Feb. 2, 1987. It establishes three branches of government and a bill of rights similar to those in the United States.

§ 106PH.02 Governmental and Legal Foundations for Property Law in the Modern Philippines.

The Constitution of 1986 contains basic provisions protecting property rights. "No person shall be deprived of life, liberty, or property without due process of law, nor shall any person be denied the equal protection of the law."[3] "The right of the people to be secure in their persons, houses, papers, and effects against unreasonable searches and seizures of whatever nature and for any purpose shall be inviolable . . . ."[4] "The liberty of abode and of changing the same within the limits prescribed by law shall not be impaired except upon lawful order of the court."[5] "Private property shall not be taken for public use without just compensation."[6]

Contemporary Filipino law is drawn partly from Spanish law and partly from the law of the United States, thus being a mixed civil law and common law system. Many Codes modeled on civil law codes are in effect, as are statutes modeled on U.S. statutes. U.S. case law is cited and considered persuasive.

Of the 26 codes in force today, the codes relating to property are the Civil Code, the Code of Agrarian Reforms, the National Building Code, the Forestry Reform Code, the Real Property Tax Code, the Water Code, and the Philippine Environment Code.

The Civil Code, adopted in 1950, replaced the Spanish Civil Code of 1889. Two of its four books are Property and Different Modes of Acquiring Ownership. The Code of Agrarian Reforms embodies the basic land reform rules and has been controversial.

§ 106PH.03 Basic Filipino Property Law.

Property described as immovable property in Philippine law is similar to real property in a common law system, although the concept of immovable property is broader.[7] The principal laws and rules on selected property topics

---

[3] Art. III, Sec. 1.

[4] Art. III, Sec. 2.

[5] Art. III, Sec. 6.

[6] Art. III, Sec. 9.

[7] Civil Code of the Philippines (hereafter CC), Art. 415.

are briefly described below.

§ 106PH.03(a)   Estates in Land.

Under Philippine property law, the term immovable property includes much of what is meant by real property in a common law system. Immovables include, among other things: lands, buildings, roads and structures of all kinds attached to the soil; trees, plants, and growing fruits while they are attached to the land; everything fixed or attached to an immovable; and "contracts for public works, and servitudes and other real rights over immovable property."[8] This covers essentially all that is meant by real property in Anglo-American common law.

The Civil Code declares that "Ownership may be exercised over things and rights."[9] The enumerated ownership rights include:

Right to enjoy and dispose of a thing, including a right of action to recover it.[10]

Right to exclude.[11]

Right to enclose or fence.[12]

The owner may not use the thing "in such a manner as to injure the rights of a third person,"[13] may not prohibit interference that is "necessary to avert an imminent danger and . . . threatened danger . . . ."[14] "No person shall be deprived of his property except by competent authority and for public use and always upon payment of just compensation."[15]

"The owner of a parcel of land is the owner of its surface and of everything under it . . . ."[16] "Hidden treasure belongs to the owner of the land, building, or other property on which it is found."[17]

The owner of property also owns the natural fruits, the industrial fruits and the civil fruits, e.g., rents.[18]

"Whatever is built, planted or sown on the land of another and the

---

[8] *Id.*

[9] CC Art. 427.

[10] CC Art. 428.

[11] CC Art. 429.

[12] CC Art. 430.

[13] CC Art. 431.

[14] CC Art. 432.

[15] CC Art. 435.

[16] CC Art. 437.

[17] CC Art. 438.

[18] CC Art. 441.

improvements or repairs made thereon, belong to the owner of the land,"[19] subject to exceptions specified in the code.[20]

One who holds a legal or equitable title to or interest in the real property may bring a quiet title action.[21] Dower and curtesy interests are not recognized.

Another form of the property right traditional in civil law jurisdictions is the usufruct. In the Philippines, "Usufruct gives a right to enjoy the property of another with the obligation of preserving its form and substance, unless the title constituting it or the law otherwise provides."[22] Servitudes are covered in Articles 613–693 and nuisance in Articles 694–707 of the Civil Code.

Philippine law also recognizes the concept of the family home: "The family home is the dwelling house where a person and his family reside, and the land on which it is situated. If constituted as herein provided, the family home shall be exempt from execution, forced sale or attachment, except as provided in Articles 232 and 243."[23]

§ 106PH.03(b)   Foreign Ownership of Land.

Under the general rule, only Filipino citizens, or entities owned at least 60% by Filipinos, are entitled to acquire land in the Philippines. Numerous exceptions relating to married couples and dual citizens and other special circumstances also apply.[24] Foreign nationals and corporation may enter into long-term leases, for up to 50 years, renewable for up to 25 years.

§ 106PH.03(c)   Concurrent Estates.

The Civil Code recognizes and regulates co-ownership.[25] The Code makes detailed provisions for rights of partition, and does not recognize a right of survivorship. Specific co-ownership provisions are made for owners of different stories of a house.[26]

§ 106PH.03(d)   Leaseholds.

Leases of terms for one year or longer are required to be in writing, subject to exceptions. Leases of things for more than 99 years are not valid.[27]

---

[19] CC Art. 445.

[20] CC Arts. 446–465.

[21] CC Arts. 476–481.

[22] CC Art. 562. Usufructs are governed by Arts. 562–612 of the Civil Code.

[23] CC Art. 223.

[24] Batas Pambansa 185; Republic Act 8179.

[25] CC Arts. 484–501.

[26] CC Art. 490.

[27] CC Art. 1643.

Leases may be recorded in the Registry of Property,[28] and if unrecorded, are not binding on third persons.[29] A lessee does not have a right to assign without the lessor's consent,[30] but does have a right to sublet with the lessor's consent, unless the lease agreement provides otherwise.[31] The Civil Code contains detailed provision for regulation of leaseholds.[32]

§ 106PH.03(e) Succession.

Detailed rules of succession are provided in the Civil Code[33] and also in Art. 190 of Executive Order 209. Intestate succession is covered by Arts. 960 to 1014 of the Civil Code.

§ 106PH.03(f) Wills.

The Civil Code also governs formalities and other requirements for wills.[34] Persons under 18 are not authorized to make a will.[35] Wills must be in writing and executed in a language or dialect known to the testator.[36]

§ 106PH.03(g) Real Estate Transactions.

A contract of mortgage may be applied to immovables and alienable real rights in connection with immovables.[37] "In addition to the requisites stated in Article 2085, it is indispensable, in order that a mortgage may be validly constituted, that the document in which it appears be recorded in the Registry of Property. If the instrument is not recorded, the mortgage is nevertheless binding between the parties."[38]

"The form, extent and consequences of a mortgage, both as to its constitution, modification and extinguishment, and as to other matters not included in this Chapter, shall be governed by the provisions of the Mortgage Law and of the Land Registration Law."[39]

By contract of antichresis, a creditor acquires the right to receive the fruits of an immovable of his debtor, and to apply them to the payment of the

---

[28] CC Art. 1648.

[29] CC Art. 1646.

[30] CC Art. 1649.

[31] CC Art. 1650.

[32] CC Arts. 1642–1688.

[33] CC Arts. 774–1105.

[34] CC Arts. 783–959.

[35] CC Art. 797.

[36] CC Art. 804.

[37] CC Art. 2124.

[38] CC Art. 2125.

[39] CC Art. 2131. The basic mortgage provisions are in Arts. 2124–2131 of the Civil Code.

interest, if owing, and thereafter to the principal of the debt.[40]

§ 106PH.03(h)   Special Rules.

"Mining claims and rights and other matters concerning minerals and mineral lands are governed by special laws.[41]

§ 106PH.03(i)   Title Registration.

"The Registry of Property has for its object the inscription or annotation of acts and contracts relating to ownership and other rights over immovable property."[42] "For determining what titles are subject to inscription or annotation, as well as the form, effects, and cancellation of inscriptions and annotations, the manner of keeping the books in the Registry, and the value of the entries contained in special books, the provisions of the Mortgage Law, the Land Registration Act, and other special laws shall govern."[43] The Philippine registration system is a Torrens system.

§ 106PH.03(j)   Stamps.

Document stamp taxes are required for documents, instruments, loan agreements, acceptances, assignments, sales and transfers of obligations.[44]

§ 106PH.03(k)   Taxation.

§ 106PH.03(k)(1)   Estate Tax.

A graduated estate tax is imposed nationwide, payable within six months of the decedent's death, when the estate tax returns are due.[45]

§ 106PH.03(k)(2)   Property Tax.

Real estate taxes are also imposed, with different rates from region to region and city to city.[46]

§ 106PH.03(l)   Environmental Regulation.

The Department of Environment and Natural Resources is the chief government agency responsible for protecting, conserving, managing, developing and exploring the environment and natural resources. The principal laws enacted or decreed for these purposes are:

National Pollution Control Decree of 1976[47]

---

[40] CC Art. 2132.

[41] CC Art. 519.

[42] CC Art. 708.

[43] CC Art. 711.

[44] Republic Act 9243.

[45] Republic Act 8424.

[46] Republic Act 5447.

[47] Presidential Decree (hereafter PD) 984.

Prevention, Control and Abatement of Air Pollution Decree[48]

Marine and Pollution Decree of 1976[49]

Environmental Impact Statement System [50]

Toxic Substances and Hazardous and Nuclear Waste Control Act of 1990 [51]

National Integrated Protected Areas Systems Act[52]

Philippine Clean Air Act of 1999[53]

Ecological Solid Waste Management Act of 2000[54]

---

[48] PD 1181.

[49] PD 979.

[50] PD 1586.

[51] Republic Act 6969.

[52] Republic Act 7586.

[53] Republic Act 8749.

[54] Republic Act 9003.

CHAPTER 106PL

PROPERTY LAW IN POLAND

C. David DeBenedetti[1]
DeBenedetti Majewski Szczesniak
Kancelaria Prawnicza Sp. K.
Saski Crescent, ul. Królewska 16
00-103 Warsaw Poland

SYNOPSIS

---

[1] New York Attorney/Partner Not admitted in Poland.

§ 106PL.01   Historical Background of Polish Property Law.

§ 106PL.01(a)   Property Law in the Middle Ages.

The Polish legal system in the Middle Ages was based on a feudal monarchy (*patrimonium*), which was characterized by the belief that the country was the private property of its monarch.

In the Middle Ages in Poland, there were four classes of people who varied in their rights and obligations: peasants, middle class, knighthood/nobility and clergy.

In most cases, the right to property was granted to nobility and clergy by the monarch. In addition, the land was acquired by virtue of acquisitive prescription, acquisition of land belonging to no-one, or transfer of ownership. The transfer of ownership required the presence of a clerk from a local court, transferor and transferee, the neighbors and other witnesses. The transfer of ownership had to be registered in the land books, otherwise it was null and void.

In the Middle Ages in Poland, the ownership of real property depended on membership in a particular social class. The largest and also the poorest social group—the peasants—did not own property, but were obliged to perform many duties as a result of their serfdom.

§ 106PL.01(b)   Property Law in the 19th Century.

§ 106PL.01(b)(1)   Partitions Times (1795–1918).

In 1795, Poland disappeared from the political map of Europe when its territory was divided between Russia, Prussia and Austro-Hungary. Before it regained independence, the former Polish lands were governed by three separate legal systems. The most important legal acts regulating the civil relationships were: volume X of the Rules of the Russian Empire (*Zwód Praw Cesarstwa Rosyjskiego*) of 1832, the Prussian BGB of 1896 and the Austrian ABGB of 1811.

On the annexed territories, property law was regulated by some statutes *e.g.*, the statute on the privileges and mortgages (1818, 1825). Following the introduction of this statute, the land and mortgage register became an important tool in establishing the existence of mortgages securing the repayment of loans. Land and mortgage registers became widely respected and had a significant impact on economic relations.

§ 106PL.01(b)(2)   Napoleonic Era-Temporary Reemergence of Poland.

In 1807, the Kingdom of Warsaw was established, although it was under the domination of Napoleonic France.

By virtue of the constitution of the Kingdom of Warsaw, Napoleon's Civil Code of 1804 was introduced into the territory of the Kingdom of Warsaw. Napoleon's Civil Code was based on the principles of Roman and natural law and provided for the distinction of main property rights (such as ownership, usufruct, easement) and dependent property rights (pledge, mortgage), as well as between ownership and possession. According to Napoleon's Civil Code, the transfer of ownership did not require the transfer of possession, and acquisitive prescription required at least 10 years of uninterrupted possession.

§ 106PL.01(c)   Regaining Independence in the First Half of the 20th Century.

Initially, after Poland regained independence in 1918, the legislation of the three annexing countries (i.e., the laws of Russia, Germany, and Austro-Hungary) applied.

In 1919, a codification committee was appointed and began work on the unification of the main areas of law, including civil law and civil procedure. Fundamental legal principles were agreed upon: ownership was considered as the center of the legal system and the inviolability of ownership was recognized by the Constitution, although some exceptions were allowed. Expropriation was accepted only for high social usefulness, for consideration and only in accordance with law.

Since 1933, the transfer of ownership of real property must be accomplished by means of a notarial deed.

§ 106PL.01(c)(1)   World War II.

During World War II, Poland was first divided between Nazi Germany and the USSR. Further, Western Poland was annexed directly into the Third Reich and became subject to German law. The area under German control not annexed directly into the Third Reich became subject to the so-called General Government /Generalne Gubernatorstwo/ (GG). In practice, the law in the GG was adopted almost exclusively by the General Governor. Polish law, which applied earlier, was preserved only to a minor extent.

In the areas annexed by the USSR, Soviet authorities introduced "revolutionary social and legal order," which was based on liquidation of private ownership, forced expropriation of landowners and nationalization of industry, banks and mines.

§ 106PL.01(c)(2)   Polish People's Republic (PRL).

§ 106PL.01(c)(2)(i)   Influence of Soviet Union.

In the period between the end of the World War II and the first free elections in 1989, Poland was strongly influenced by the law and philosophy of the Soviet Union.

§ 106PL.01(c)(2)(ii)   Expropriation and Nationalization.

Political and ideological premises caused the post-war authorities to specifically regulate the legal status of the properties located within the area of Warsaw. In compliance with the provisions of the decree of October 26, 1945 on Ownership and Usufruct of Land within the Area of Warsaw (Journal of Laws No. 50, item 279, as amended; hereinafter the Decree), the title to all land within the area of the capital city was transferred to the capital city of Warsaw, while the existing owners were granted rights to hold land in perpetual tenancy.

Pursuant to the Act of January 3, 1946 on the Takeover of the Fundamental Sectors of the National Economy by the State, the Peoples Republic of Poland acquired the ownership (without compensation or for minor compensation) of, *inter alia,* industrial, mining, communications, banking and insurance enterprises.

§ 106PL.01(c)(2)(iii)   Civil Code 1964.

The Civil Code was adopted in 1964, above all, due to the need to unify Polish civil law and modernize existing provisions. Before the effective date of the Civil Code, civil-law relations were governed by a number of rather inconsistent legal acts.

The adopted Civil Code referred to, for instance, so-called socialist ownership, which was vested in the state and social organizations of working people. The state property could not be acquired by acquisitive prescription. For ideological and political reasons, the title to land or other state-owned properties could not be transferred to private individuals.

§ 106PL.02　Current Laws Regarding Real Property in Poland.

The first open elections which took place in 1989 led to a series of reforms, which culminated in Poland joining the European Union in 2004, but in fact, this process of reform has still been occurring to date.

Real property law in Poland is governed by several legal acts, and is best described by starting with the most fundamental issues (right to own private property), then basic principles (right to transfer property), and finally particular provisions (zoning, development, etc.) Such fundamental principles are stipulated in the Constitution,[2] basic principles are addressed in the Polish Civil Code,[3] and several other legal acts[4] provide the many detailed provisions.

§ 106PL.02(a)　The Constitution of the Republic of Poland.

The Polish Constitution is the supreme law of the country, and provisions regarding real property are contained in the key chapters[5] of the Constitution. Those chapters also deal with the protection of the democratic system of elections and civil rights. The most important principles refer to the protection by the state of the right to ownership and inheritance.[6] According to the Polish Constitution, the right of ownership can be restricted only by a law passed by the Parliament, and only insofar as it does not violate the nature/essence of the ownership right itself.[7] In the Constitution, the term property right has broad meaning, referring both to movables and immovables. Under the Constitution, expropriation[8] can be conducted legally, only if it serves public purpose and for fair compensation.

§ 106PL.02(a)(1)　Civil Code.

The Polish Civil Code regulates basic terms and concepts regarding property law, such as ownership,[9] co-ownership,[10] movable and immovable property, and protection of ownership rights. These are mandatory provisions of the Civil Code and cannot be regulated otherwise in any contract between particular parties.

---

[2] Constitution of the Republic of Poland dated April 2,1997 (Journal of Laws of 1997, No. 78, item 483), available in English at http://www.trybunal.gov.pl/index2.htm.

[3] Act of April 23, 1964 Civil Code (Journal of Laws of 1964, No. 16, item 93 as amended).

[4] *E.g,* Act on Planning and Spatial Development, Act on Land and Mortgage Registers and Mortgages, Act on Protection of Rights of Occupants, Housing Resources of Municipalities and Changes to the Civil Code, Act on Taxes and Local Fees, Private International Law.

[5] Chapter I and II of the Constitution of the Republic of Poland of April 2, 1997.

[6] Art. 21 § 1 of the Constitution of the Republic of Poland of April 2, 1997.

[7] Art. 64 § 3 of the Constitution of the Republic of Poland of April 2, 1997.

[8] Art. 21 § 2 of the Constitution of the Republic of Poland of April 2, 1997.

[9] Article 140 of the Polish Civil Code.

[10] Article 195 of the Polish Civil Code.

§ 106PL.02(a)(2)   Property Laws Not Contained in the Civil Code.

In addition to the provisions of the Civil Code, there are detailed statutory regulations referring to the right to a cooperative flat, the land and mortgage register, and construction law, to name a few.

Private International Law determines the law that governs international personal and property relations within the scope of civil, family, and labor law.[11] According to its provisions, the law chosen by the parties, provided that this law is connected with the obligations, may govern the contractual relations of these parties.[12] However, the legal status of real estate and any rights or obligations related thereto, shall be governed by the law of the state in which that real estate is located.[13]

Regarding taxation and tax residence, as an example, according to the Treaty on the Avoidance of Double Taxation executed between Poland and the United States of America,[14] if any person sells, exchanges a real property, or performs any other transaction with relation to that property, which is situated on the territory of the other party of the agreement,[15] the income such party obtains from that transaction is subject to taxation in both the country where such person has place of residence or registered office and in the country where the real estate is located.[16] Thus, the sale of property in Poland is subject to tax in Poland and the jurisdiction of Polish law.

§ 106PL.02(b)   Real Property Under the Civil Code.

§ 106PL.02(b)(1)   Co-Ownership of Real Property.

The Polish Civil Code provides for two types of co-ownership:[17] joint co-ownership and fractional co-ownership. As opposed to fractional ownership, joint co-ownership[18] is combined with certain legal relationships

---

[11] Art. 1 of the Act of November 12, 1965 Private International Law (Journal of Laws of 1965, No. 46, item 290).

[12] Art. 25 § 1 of the Act of November 12, 1965, Private International Law.

[13] Art. 25 § 2 of the Act of November 12, 1965, Private International Law.

[14] Agreement between the Government of the People's Republic of Poland and the Government of the United States of America dated October 8, 1974 on the Avoidance of Double Taxation and Prevention of Fiscal Evasion with Respect to Taxes on Income (Journal of Laws of 1976, No. 31, item178).

[15] Art. 7 of the Agreement between the Government of the People's Republic of Poland and the Government of the United States of America dated October 8,1974 on Avoidance of Double Taxation and Prevention of Fiscal Evasion with Respect to Taxes on Income.

[16] Art. 14 of the Agreement between the Government of the People's Republic of Poland and the Government of the United States of America dated October 8,1974 on Avoidance of Double Taxation and Prevention of Fiscal Evasion with Respect to Taxes on Income.

[17] Article 196 § 1 of the Polish Civil Code.

[18] Article 196 § 2 of the Polish Civil Code.

(marital joint co-ownership, civil law partnership). Fractional co-ownership means that at least two persons have fractional proprietary rights in one property. In the case of fractional co-ownership, each of the co-owners is entitled to dispose of his/her/its right.[19] However, in order to dispose of the co-owned property as well as to perform acts beyond the ordinary management of that property (including encumbering it with a mortgage, extensive renovation), the consent of all co-owners is required.[20]

In certain cases it is difficult to obtain the consent from all of the co-owners for particular action. The Polish Civil Code provides that in such cases the co-owners having at least 50% of the shares in the property are entitled to apply to the court for such consent.[21]

§ 106PL.02(b)(2)   Ownership and Possession.

Ownership is the fullest legal form of the use of a property under Polish law. The owner may, within the limits specified by statutory law and the principles of community life and to the exclusion of other persons, use a property in accordance with the socio-economic purpose of his right.[22] In particular, the owner may derive benefits and other income from that property and dispose of that property.[23]

The term "Land ownership" includes not only the proprietary rights to the surface, but also to the space above and below that surface.[24]

Polish law provides for some limitation of an owner's rights. For instance, the owner of a property, in exercise of his right, should abstain from acts that would excessively disturb the use of neighboring properties.[25] Although the owner has the right to build on his/her/its land, he/she/it should not carry out construction works in a manner threatening the neighboring properties with a loss of subjacent or lateral support.[26]

The Polish Civil Code distinguishes between ownership and possession.[27] Contrary to ownership, possession is not a legal but factual status, *i.e.*, the possessor is a factual holder of the property (although the possessor may have a legal title to the property, *e.g.*, lease or usufruct agreement).[28]

---

[19] Article 198 of the Polish Civil Code.

[20] Article 199 of the Polish Civil Code.

[21] Article 199 of the Polish Civil Code.

[22] Article 140 of the Polish Civil Code.

[23] Article 140 of the Polish Civil Code.

[24] Article 143 of the Polish Civil Code.

[25] Article 144 of the Polish Civil Code.

[26] Article 147 of the Polish Civil Code.

[27] Article 336 of the Polish Civil Code.

[28] Article 336 of the Polish Civil Code.

Nevertheless, both possession[29] and ownership[30] are legally protected.

§ 106PL.02(b)(3)   Transfer of Ownership.

In Poland, there are 3 ways of obtaining legal title to the property: acquisition, inheritance and acquisitive prescription (hostile possession).

The purchase of real property is governed by special rules. A sale agreement relating to the property must be executed in the form of a notarial deed.[31] In practice, usually preliminary sale agreements are executed.[32] The Polish Civil Code does not stipulate the form of preliminary sale agreements but the buyer's interest is best secured if such preliminary sale agreement is also executed in the form of a notarial deed. In such case, if the seller refuses to execute the final sale agreement, the buyer may demand the issuance of a court decision (forcing specific performance).[33]

Prior to the purchase of real property, the buyer should verify the entries and annotations in the land and mortgage register in order to make sure that the seller is the owner of that property and that there are no encumbrances on it.

The Polish Civil Code stipulates that inheritance shall be governed by the applicable legal provisions on inheritance which are in force at the moment of the death of the decedent.[34] In Poland there are two ways of inheriting: by virtue of a testament[35] or by virtue of statutory provisions.[36] Special provisions apply to the inheritance of agricultural land, depending on the date of the death of the decedent.[37]

Acquisitive prescription (hostile possession) means acquisition of ownership by extended possession and it is a legal tool that provides for the possibility of eliminating the discrepancies between the actual situation and the legal status of ownership. According to the Polish Civil Code, a possessor of a real estate who is not an owner (or co-owner) shall acquire the ownership of that real estate if he/she/it possesses that real estate uninterruptedly for at least 20 years as an autonomous possessor in good faith.[38] If the possessor is acting in bad faith, the uninterrupted possession of the real

---

[29] Article 344 of the Polish Civil Code.

[30] Article 222 of the Polish Civil Code.

[31] Article 158 in conjunction with 73 § 2 of the Polish Civil Code.

[32] Article 389 of the Polish Civil Code.

[33] Article 64 of the Polish Civil Code.

[34] Art. LI. of the Act dated April 23, 1964 Provisions Introducing Civil Code (Journal of Laws of 1964, no. 16, Item 94).

[35] Article 941 of the Polish Civil Code.

[36] Article 931 of the Polish Civil Code.

[37] Articles 1058–1088 of the Polish Civil Code.

[38] Article 172 § 1 of the Polish Civil Code.

estate must last for at least 30 years before the possessor acquires the right of ownership.[39]

§ 106PL.02(b)(4)   Limited Property Rights.

Contrary to the right of ownership, limited property rights ensure only limited rights towards a property. The catalogue of such rights is listed in the Polish Civil Code.[40] All limited property rights, except for a Pledge,[41] may be established over a real estate. The economic purpose of the establishment of limited property rights may be various: mortgage and pledges are used as a security for claims (mostly credits), whereas the right to a cooperative flat is established for residential purposes. Usufruct may constitute a basis for production activity or ensure usage of real estate for particular periods during the year (timesharing is a form of usufruct).

Limited property rights are established by an agreement,[42] court decision, administrative decision, or acquisitive prescription.

Limited property rights, with a few exceptions, may be transferred from one party to another.

§ 106PL.02(b)(4)(i)   Usufruct.

According to the Polish Civil Code, usufruct is a legal form of using another party's property in a way similar to its owner.[43] The user is entitled to use a property and take profit from it. Usufruct is non-transferable.[44]

Timesharing[45] is one of the forms of the usufruct. Timesharing is created by an agreement between an entrepreneur and a natural person for at least a 3-year period. Timesharing enables use of a specified apartment or house of another in a particular period of each calendar year in exchange for payment.

§ 106PL.02(b)(4)(ii)   Easement.

An easement is a limited property right encumbering one's property on behalf of the owner of another real estate or a specific person.[46] As a result, the performance of the rights of the owner of the encumbered real estate is

---

[39] Article 172 § 2 of the Polish Civil Code.

[40] Article 244 of the Polish Civil Code.

[41] Article 306 of the Polish Civil Code.

[42] According to Article 245 of the Polish Civil Code, legal provisions regulating the transfer of ownership apply accordingly to the establishment of limited property rights.

[43] Article 252 of the Polish Civil Code.

[44] Article 254 of the Polish Civil Code.

[45] Art. 1. of the Act dated July 13, 2000 on Protection of Acquirers of the Right to Use Buildings or Residential Premises in the Prescribed Time in Any Year and Changes of Acts: Civil Code and Code of Offences and Act on Land and Mortgage Registers and Mortgage. (Journal of Laws of 2000, No. 74, item 855).

[46] Article 285 § 1 of the Polish Civil Code.

limited (in most cases due to the fact that the owner of the dominant real estate is entitled to use the encumbered property within the designated scope).[47]

An easement is established by virtue of an agreement between the owner of the property, which is to be encumbered, and the beneficiary of the easement, or by the virtue of a court verdict, administrative decision or as a result of acquisitive prescription.[48]

Among various easements, the Polish Civil Code provides for the transmission easement[49] (słuzebnosc przesyłu). The transmission easement enables the transmission companies to use someone else's property in order to maintain the transmission facilities (electricity transmission lines, gas pipelines, water connections).

§ 106PL.02(b)(4)(iii)   Mortgage.

In Poland a mortgage is a key form used in order to secure cash receivables. A mortgage can only be established over real estate.[50] Detailed stipulations governing mortgage are included in the Land and Mortgage Register and Mortgages Act.

In Poland mortgages may be established in an agreement (voluntary mortgage)[51] or by a court decision (forced mortgage or judicial mortgage).[52] Contrary to a voluntary mortgage, which in practice is used to secure bank credit, forced mortgage is established without the approval of the owner, and sometimes against the owner's will. Mortgage becomes valid, binding and enforceable security upon final registration by an appropriate court in the relevant land and mortgage register.[53]

§ 106PL.02(b)(4)(iv)   Perpetual Usufruct.

Land owned by the State Treasury or local community or their subsidiaries which is located within the administrative borders of towns, or lands situated outside these borders but included in the master plan of a town and designated to serve its economic needs, may be let for perpetual usufruct[54] to natural and legal persons for 99 years.[55] In exceptional circumstances, the perpetual usufruct may be created for a period not shorter than 40 years.

---

[47] Article 285 § 1 of the Polish Civil Code.

[48] Article 292 § 1 of the Polish Civil Code.

[49] Article 305 § 1 of the Polish Civil Code.

[50] Art. 65 of the Act of July 6, 1982 on Land and Mortgage Register and Mortgage.

[51] Art. 65 of the Act of July 6, 1982 on Land and Mortgage Register and Mortgage.

[52] Art. 109 of the Act of July 6, 1982 on Land and Mortgage Register and Mortgage.

[53] Art. 67 of the Act of July 6, 1982 on Land and Mortgage Register and Mortgage.

[54] Article 232 of the Polish Civil Code.

[55] Article 236 of the Polish Civil Code.

Perpetual usufruct is established against payment.[56]

The perpetual usufructuary is obliged to exercise his/her/its rights in accordance with the agreement on perpetual usufruct.[57] The agreement on perpetual usufruct provides, inter alia, for designated usage of the property, permitted constructions, method of calculating the value of any buildings erected by a perpetual usufructuary and the fee for perpetual usufruct.[58]

According to the Polish Civil Code, the perpetual usufructuary is the owner of any buildings and other structures located on the land which is the subject of perpetual usufruct.[59] However, upon the termination of perpetual usufruct, the ownership of these buildings is transferred to the owner of the land for a consideration specified in the agreement on perpetual usufruct.[60]

A contract for perpetual usufruct shall be concluded in the form of a notarial deed. The transfer of perpetual usufruct also requires a notarial deed.[61]

§ 106PL.02(c)   Land and Mortgage Register.

The land and mortgage register is an official register kept in the district courts[62] which defines the legal status of a particular real estate.[63] In Poland, the land and mortgage registers include the description of a real estate and ownership thereof, entries of limited property rights and claims of third persons.[64]

The main purpose of the land and mortgage register is to ensure safety of transfer of ownership. The registration of entry in the land and mortgage registers has its legal consequences: it is deemed that the right disclosed in the land and mortgage registers is registered in accordance with the actual legal status,[65] and a right deleted from the land and mortgage register does not exist.[66]

The principle of priority provides that the rights registered in the land and mortgage registers have priority over those which have not been regis-

---

[56] Article 238 of the Polish Civil Code.

[57] Article 233 of the Polish Civil Code.

[58] Article 239 of the Polish Civil Code.

[59] Article 235 of the Polish Civil Code.

[60] Article 239 of the Polish Civil Code.

[61] Article 234 of the Polish Civil Code.

[62] Art. 23 of the Act of July 6, 1982 on Land and Mortgage Register and Mortgage. (Journal of Laws of 2001, no. 124, item 136).

[63] Art. 1 of the Act of July 6, 1982 on Land and Mortgage Register and Mortgage.

[64] Art. 16 of the Act of July 6, 1982 on Land and Mortgage Register and Mortgage.

[65] Art. 3 § 1 of the Act of July 6, 1982 on Land and Mortgage Register and Mortgage.

[66] Art. 3 § 2 of the Act of July 6, 1982 on Land and Mortgage Register and Mortgage.

tered.[67] Moreover, the priority of limited property rights registered in the land and mortgage registers depends on the date of the registration (the sooner, the higher priority).[68]

§ 106PL.02(d)   Lease and Tenancy (*Dzierzawa*).

§ 106PL.02(d)(1)   Basic Principles of Lease and Tenancy.

Under Polish law, there are two agreements allowing use of another's property in consideration for payment of rent: lease and tenancy.

Under a lease agreement the lessor undertakes to give the lessee a *res* for a specified or unspecified period of time, whereas the lessee undertakes to pay the lessor the agreed rent.[69] Under a tenancy agreement, the lessee is not only entitled to use the property, but also to benefit from it.[70] Therefore, the most common subject of the lease is a residential or office space, whereas a farm, agricultural land, plant or enterprise are the typical subject of tenancy agreements.

§ 106PL.02(d)(1)(i)   Lease Between Entrepreneurs.

According to the Polish Civil Code,[71] a lease agreement concluded by entrepreneurs[72] for a period exceeding 30 years, will, upon the lapse of 30 years, be considered as if it was concluded for an indefinite period of time, and therefore be easily terminated by virtue of a termination notice.

§ 106PL.02(d)(1)(ii)   Eviction.

If any person occupies the real property without any legal title (*e.g.*, the lease agreement expired or was terminated as a result of lessee's failure to pay the rent), the owner may demand the eviction of such person.[73] Eviction is performed by a court bailiff[74] according to special procedure. Currently, no eviction can be performed, if no substitute premises are provided for the evicted person. In case of entrepreneurs, eviction procedure is regulated in

---

[67] Art. 11 of the Act of July 6, 1982 on Land and Mortgage Register and Mortgage.

[68] Art. 12 of the Act of July 6, 1982 on Land and Mortgage Register and Mortgage.

[69] Article 659 of the Polish Civil Code.

[70] Article 693 of the Polish Civil Code.

[71] Article 661 § 2 of the Polish Civil Code.

[72] In Poland an entrepreneur is any entity registered in the register of entrepreneurs of the National Court Register or sole entrepreneur conducting business activity under his own name, registered in the register of entrepreneurs kept by an administrative officer of a commune, mayor or president of a town.

[73] Article 13 of the Act of June 21, 2005 on Protection of Rights of Occupants, Housing Resources of Municipalities and changes to the Civil Code. (Journal of Laws of 2005, No. 31, item 266).

[74] Article 14 of the Act of June 21, 2005 on Protection of Rights of Occupants, Housing Resources of Municipalities and changes to the Civil Code. (Journal of Laws of 2005, No. 31, item 266).

the Polish Civil Code.[75] There is no requirement for providing substitute premises for an evicted entrepreneur.

§ 106PL.02(e)   Foreign Ownership of Real Property in Poland.

§ 106PL.02(e)(1)   Limited Acquisition of Real Property By Foreigners.

The acquisition of real property by foreigners is regulated by the Act on the Acquisition of Real Estates by Foreign Persons.[76] Foreigners[77] must first obtain permission of the Minister of Interior and Administration, to purchase property or shares in a commercial company with a registered office in Poland, which is the owner or a holder of a perpetual usufruct of property in Poland.[78]

§ 106PL.02(e)(2)   Permits.

Permission by the Minister of Interior and Administration is granted in the form of an administrative decision, only if there is no probability of a threat to the defense or national security or interruption to public order.[79] Upon applying for permission, a foreigner must prove his/her/its link to the Republic of Poland. Circumstances confirming a foreigner's contact with the Republic of Poland may include,[80] in particular: possessing Polish nationality or Polish origin; celebrating marriage with a citizen of the Republic of Poland; possessing a permit to reside for a definite time or to settle; possessing membership of a managing body of entrepreneurs previously mentioned; conducting business of agricultural activities on the territory of the Republic of Poland in compliance with the provisions of Polish legislation.

Since Poland's accession to the European Union (May 1, 2004) the above mentioned rules do not apply to foreigners from the territory of the European Economic Area.[81] However, there are some exceptions. For instance, the purchasing of agricultural real property by foreigners from the territory of

---

[75] Article 222 of the Polish Civil Code.

[76] The Act dated March 24, 1920 on Acquisition of Real Estates by Foreigners (Dz. U. 2004, Nr 167, poz. 1758).

[77] In this Act, a foreigner shall mean: a natural person not possessing Polish citizenship; a legal person having its seat abroad; a company not being a legal person, of persons previously mentioned, having its seat abroad, established in compliance with the legislation of foreign states; a legal person and a commercial partnership not being a legal person, having its seat on the territory of the Republic of Poland, controlled directly or indirectly by persons or companies previously mentioned.

[78] Art. 1 of the Act dated March 24, 1920 on Acquisition of Real Estates by Foreigners.

[79] Art. 1a of the Act dated March 24, 1920 on Acquisition of Real Estates by Foreigners.

[80] Art. 1a § 2 of the Act dated March 24, 1920 on Acquisition of Real Estates by Foreigners.

[81] Art. 8 § 2 U of the Act dated March 24, 1920 on Acquisition of Real Estates by

the European Economic Area requires a permit within 12 years following the accession of Poland to the European Union.[82] Finally, it is not necessary to receive the permission from the Minister of Internal Affairs and Administration for acquisition of a separate living accommodation within the meaning of the Act on the Ownership of Premises.[83]

§ 106PL.02(f)   Investing in Real Property in Poland.

§ 106PL.02(f)(1)   Local Spatial Development Plan.

The Local Spatial Development Plan is a fundamental act passed by the local commune[84] in order to establish the functions of the land and planned investments.[85] A Local Spatial Development Plan includes mandatory principles of sustainable territorial and economic development, functional zoning and indication of areas for housing and other direct investments; general proposals for technical infrastructure systems; the location of main roads and other technical networks; and the most important preservation areas due to their economic, natural, and cultural value.[86]

Local Spatial Development Plans do not cover the whole territory of Poland. If such a plan has been adopted for the property to be developed, the design and construction works must be performed in strict compliance with the terms and conditions set out in the plan.[87] If there is no Local Spatial Development Plan for the area where the investment is planned (which happens frequently), Zoning Decisions must be obtained.[88]

§ 106PL.02(f)(2)   Zoning Decisions.

If no Local Spatial Development Plan has been adopted for the particular area, it is necessary to obtain a zoning decision to proceed with the investment/construction works.

A zoning decision is an administrative decision granted by the village administrator, mayor or president of a city[89] (depending on the size of the commune) upon a request of any person (there are no objections to issue this

---

Foreigners. European Economic Area-consist of all European Union members states and Norway, Iceland and Liechtenstein.

[82] Art. 8 § 2 of the Act dated March 24, 1920 on Acquisition of Real Estates by Foreigners.

[83] Article 2 of the Act dated June 24, 1994 on the Ownership of Premises (Journal of Laws, of 2000, No 80, item 903).

[84] Art. 3 of the Act dated March 24,1920 on Acquisition of Real Estates by Foreigners (Journal of Laws of 2003, No. 80, item 717).

[85] Art. 15 § 2 of the Act dated March 27, 2003 on Planning and Spatial Development.

[86] Art. 15 § 2 of the Act dated March 27, 2003 on Planning and Spatial Development.

[87] Article 81 § 1 of Polish Construction Law.

[88] Art. 60 of the Act dated March 27, 2003 on Planning and Spatial Development.

[89] Art. 60 of the Act dated March 27, 2003 on Planning and Spatial Development.

decision to a number of different applicants at the same time).[90]

A zoning decision specifies the type of allowed investment, parameters of such investment and the site including the whole infrastructure.[91] Moreover, a zoning decision provides for the following steps, opinions, agreements and conditions that must be fulfilled by the investor (*e.g.*, the permission for cutting down trees, agreement with the conservation officer).[92]

§ 106PL.02(f)(3)   Building Permit.

In Poland, most construction works can begin only upon the issuance of a final building permit.[93] In some cases the mere notification of the envisaged construction works is sufficient (this applies to some small construction works and renovations).[94]

A building permit is a decision issued by a local mayor (president of a town)[95] in an administrative procedure to which the investor and the owners of the properties located within the planned investment's interference zone are parties. The building permit authorizes the commencement or continuation of a specified building or performance of particular construction works other than the construction of an object. A building permit expires if the construction works are not initiated within 3 years or a break in the works exceeds 3 years.[96]

§ 106PL.02(f)(3)(i)   Permit To Use Constructed Premises.

This permit is an administrative decision allowing for the use of a building and is issued by a local construction supervision inspector after the performance of an inspection of that building.[97] Inspection is performed in order to establish whether the construction was carried out in compliance with the construction designs and other construction law regulations such as fire risks, sanitary and environmental issues.[98]

---

[90] Art. 63 of the Act dated March 27, 2003 on Planning and Spatial Development.

[91] Art. 64 in conjunction with Art. 54 of the Act dated March 27, 2003 on Planning and Spatial Development.

[92] Art. 64 in conjunction with Art. 54 of the Act dated March 27, 2003 on Planning and Spatial Development.

[93] Art. 28 i 39 of the Act of July 7, 1994 r. Polish Construction Law (Journal of Laws of 2006, No. 156, item 1118).

[94] Article 30 of Polish Construction Law.

[95] Article 82 § 2 of Polish Construction Law.

[96] Article 37 of Polish Construction Law.

[97] Article 55 of Polish Construction Law.

[98] Article 59a of Polish Construction Law.

§ 106PL.02(g)   Taxes and Fees on Real Property.

§ 106PL.02(g)(1)   Civil Law Transactions Tax (Known as "PCC").

The tax on civil law transactions is imposed on the contracts of sale or exchange of things and property rights.[99] This tax applies to transactions of sale of the property, perpetual usufruct, and the co-operative members' right to an apartment. In transaction of sale a buyer is obliged to pay the tax.[100] The tax base and rate differ depending on the type of contract concluded. For instance, in the case of a contract of sale the tax base is the market value of the property and the tax rate amounts to 2% of this value.[101] The tax is payable within 14 days of the date of the execution of the contract at the bank account of the relevant tax office.[102]

§ 106PL.02(g)(2)   Value Added Tax.

In some cases, the sale of real estate may be subject to Value Added Tax (VAT). The obligation to pay VAT depends on the identity of the seller, the frequency of real estate sales and the parameters of the property.

There are huge differences between VAT and civil transaction tax: if VAT is paid in conjunction with a particular transaction, no civil transaction tax is due.

§ 106PL.02(g)(3)   Perpetual Usufruct Fee.

By virtue of contract, the perpetual usufructuary is obliged to pay an initial fee amounting to 25% of the value of the land and an annual fee of 0.3%–3% of the estimated value of the land, depending on the purpose of the perpetual usufruct.[103] The fee may be lowered by a competent body in some specific cases, for instance in relation to some non-profit organizations or cultural and educational associations.

§ 106PL.02(g)(4)   Property Tax.

Property tax in Poland is one of the local taxes[104] and is collected by the village administrator, mayor or president of a city (depending on the size of the commune).[105] It is paid annually by the owner of property or perpetual

---

[99] Art. 1 of the Act of September 9,2000 on Tax on Civil Law Transactions (Journal of Laws of. 2007, No. 68, item 450).

[100] Art. 4 of the Act of September 9,2000 on Tax on Civil Law Transactions.

[101] Art. 7 § 1 of the Act of September 9,2000 on Tax on Civil Law Transactions.

[102] Art. 10 of the Act of September 9,2000 on Tax on Civil Law Transactions.

[103] Art. 72 of the Act dated August 21, 1997 on Real Estate Management (Journal of Laws of 2004, No. 261, item 2603).

[104] Art. 1 of the Act dated January 12, 1991 on Taxes and Local Fees (Journal of Laws of 2006 No 121, item 844).

[105] Art. 1c of the Act dated January 12, 1991 on Taxes and Local Fees.

usufructuary[106] in the amount that depends on the size of the property.[107] The tax is calculated regardless of the property's market value. Each commune council specifies by resolution the rate of the property tax for estates situated within its boundaries.[108] However, the tax rate cannot exceed the limit set in the statute.[109]

§ 106PL.02(g)(5)   Fee for the Exclusion from Agricultural Production.

Under Polish law,[110] construction works cannot be commenced[111] on arable land comprising organic or forest land other than that owned by the State Treasury, without the consent of the Minister of the Agriculture or Minister of the Environment, expressed in the form of an administrative decision.[112] The consent for the exclusion of the land from agricultural production entails the payment of one-off and annual fees,[113] the value of which depends on the type of soil.[114]

§ 106PL.03   Bibliography.

A. Karnicka-Kawczyńska, J. Kawczyński, Współwłasnoś jako szczególna forma własności. Problematyka i wzory pism/Co-ownership as a particular form of ownership. Issues and Legal forms, Lexis Nexis 2004.

H. Witczak, Wygaśnicie uytkowania wieczystego/ Expiry of the perpetual usufruct, Lexis Nexis 2005.

S. Rudnicki, Komentarz do kodeksu cywilnego; ksiga druga; własnoś i inne prawa rzeczowe/ Commentary to the Civil Code, Book II, ownership and other property rights, Lexis Nexis 2005.

S. Rudnicki, Ustawa o ksiegach wieczystych i hipotece; Przepisy o postpowaniu w sprawach wieczysto ksiegowych, Komentarz / Commentary to the land and mortgage register Act, and provisions regulating registry procedure, Lexis Nexis 2005. T. Dybowski (red.), autorzy: P. Machnikowski, R. Mikosz, A. Stelmachowski, System prawa prywatnego; Tom 3. Prawo rzeczowe,/ System of private law, Book III, Property law, C.H. BECK 2003.

E. Gniewek (red.), autorzy: A. Cisek, E. Gniewek, J. Gołaczyński, R. Mikosz, J. Pisuliński, K. Zaradkiewicz, System prawa prywatnego; Tom 4, Prawo rzeczowe/ System of private law, Book IV, Property law, C.H. BECK 2005. J.Kawecka-Pysz, Nabywanie nieruchomości przez cudzoziemców/ Acquisition

---

[106] Art. 3 § 1 of the Act dated January 12, 1991 on Taxes and Local Fees.

[107] Art. 4 § 1 of the Act dated January 12, 1991 on Taxes and Local Fees.

[108] Art. 5 § 1 of the Act dated January 12, 1991 on Taxes and Local Fees.

[109] Art. 5 § 1 i § 2 of the Act dated January 12, 1991 on Taxes and Local Fees.

[110] Act on Protection of Agricultural and Forest Land (Journal of Laws of 2004 No. 121, Item 1266).

[111] Article 3 of the Act on Protection of Agricultural and Forest Land.

[112] Article 7 of the Act on Protection of Agricultural and Forest Land.

[113] Article 12 § 1 of the Act on Protection of Agricultural and Forest Land.

[114] Article 12 § 7 of the Act on Protection of Agricultural and Forest Land.

of Real Property by Foreigners, Zakamycze 2004.

G. Bieniek i S. Rudnicki, Nieruchomosci; problematyka prawna/ Real Estate, legal issues, Lexis Nexis 2005.

E. Gniewek (red.); autorzy: B. Burian, A. Cisek, W. Dubis, E. Gniewek, J. Gołaczyński, J. Kremis, P. Machnikowski, J. Nadler, J. Strzebińczyk, K. Zagrobelny, Kodeks cywilny, Tom I; Komentarz do art. 1–534/ Commentary to articles 1–534 of the Civil Code, Book I C.H. BECK 2004.

K. Pietrzykowski (red.); autorzy: Z. Banaszczyk, A. Brzozowski, J. Mojak, M. Pazdan, L. Ogiegło, J. Pietrzykowski, W. Popiołek, M. Safjan, E. Skowrońska-Bocian, J. Szachułowicz, K. Zaradkiewicz, K. Zawada, Kodeks cywilny; Tom I; Komentarz do art. 1–449/ Commentary to articles 1–449 of the Civil Code, Book I, C.H. BECK 2005.

Z. Truszkiewicz, Uzytkowanie wieczyste/Perpetual usufruct, Zakamycze 2004.

J. Ignatowicz, K. Stefaniuk, Prawo rzeczowe/Property law, Lexis Nexis 2005.

J. Bardach, B. Leśnodorski, M. Pietrzak, Historia ustroju i prawa polskiego/ History of the political system, and Polish law, Lexis Nexis 2001.

CHAPTER 106RO

REAL PROPERTY LAW IN ROMANIA

Nicholas Hammond
Hammond, Bogaru & Associates
Romania

SYNOPSIS

§ 106RO.01   History of Property Law in Romania.

§ 106RO.01(a)   Property in the Era of Geto Dacians; Property in Dacia When It Was A Roman Province.

The presence and stability of Geto Dacians on the Romanian territory since the second millennium B.C. has been mentioned by historical sources.

During the existence of the Geto Dacian state (until year 106 A.D.) there are mentioned two types of property, and these referred to the private lands of the aristocracy and the lands of the territorial community of the free peasants who possessed the land as a collective, a form of commonly held property. However, they exercised individual rights of possession over the arable land.

With the extension of slave-owning relationships, disparity of wealth and great private property developed.[1]

The collective property of the territorial community in the main referred not only to the land but also to slaves and cattle. The land of the community was divided within lots and was given to individuals or families for their use for a period of one (1) year. In the following year the parcels of land were redistributed within the community by the drawing of lots.

Therefore, in the Geto-Dacian State Era within the territorial community the land was collectively possessed but there existed signs that private property was developing.

When Dacia became a Roman province, after the military confrontations between the Dacians and Romans between 85 and 106 A.D. there were at the same time two forms of property: a) provincial/rustic property and b) the

---

[1] Strabon, VII, 3, 12.

Roman property called the "proprietate quiritara".

Ownership over the provincial property was exercised by the free local residents from the province.

According to an ancient rule the conquered land became the property of the Roman state known as the "ager publicus," but in reality the land ownership was retained by the local population.

The councillors of those times considered that the locals from the provinces had a right of possession and usufruct over the land. When a provincial local died, the land could be transferred to his heirs. Also, the land could be transferred between living persons by simple transfer.

§ 106RO.01(b)   Property Ownership During the Medieval Period.

The Medieval Era refers to the period of the Romanian history between the ancient era of Dacia and the modern era.

Land played an important role in the Medieval Era for the agricultural communities, as agriculture was the main work of such communities.

In order to work the land the communities had a common ownership right over the land that they worked on and this was referred to as the "joint property domain." For this purpose the community's members had a common right of use over the entire joint property domain. Sometimes, with the community's approval, parts of the joint property domain could be individually and personally used under the supervision and control of the community.

The ground from where there was extracted silver, gold or iron ores was considered to be under common ownership.

Property in Medieval Era referred to a personal ownership over the land based on an individual's work for the maintenance and development of land, which represented part of the joint property domain.

The first parcels of land to be detached from the joint property domain were the parcels of land on which a community's members has established their house and the yard.

The same process happened with fields by delimitation plots of land and which in this way were permanently distributed to the respective families.

§ 106RO.01(c)   Changes to the Old Norms During Early Feudalism.

The period of Early Feudalism corresponded with the period where in the Carpathians region during the tenth to thirteenth Century there were formed the so called "countries" as political state organizations.

Although the maintenance of the territorial communities during the earlier feudalism was determined by the old juridical norms which were observed, there could be created new norms and old ones could be modified.

Due to the development of agricultural tools and the extension of agricultural land there can be identified a development of private property. Many of the lands were valued by the families who were trying to take these properties out of the common regime.

Therefore instead of the norm which prohibited a member of the community from transferring any part of the territory of the community there emerged a norm which permitted the transfer of a land to the relatives of the transferor and the other members of the community had preference right to buy the land.

§ 106RO.01(d)   Property Ownership During the Era of "Moldova and Tara Romaneasca".

In Moldova and Tara Romaneasca the feudal society reached maturity with full state independency. Although there was Ottoman domination, the "law of the country" represented the main juridical source.

A main characteristic of the developed feudalism was the existence of more types of property ownership as follows:

   a.   *The great feudal property* was formed when the territorial community started to disappear.

   b.   *The property of the territorial community* started to have new characteristics similar to private property and consisting of the local household and agricultural lots. The forests, the pastures and waters remained the property of the state.

   c.   *The property of the free peasants*, which consisted of their household, the agricultural land that they worked, tools and cattle. This type of property disappeared as it was taken by the feudal owner.

   d.   *The property of the craftsmen*, which was exercised by them over their workshops and their work tools.

   e.   *The property of the slaves*, referring to their shelters.

§ 106RO.02   Property Legislation Before the Communist Era.

§ 106RO.02(a)   Agrarian Reform Under the Romanian rule of Alexandru Ioan Cuza.

During the revolution of 1848 and during and after the Unification of the Romanian countries from 24th January 1859, the peasants acquired the right to receive ownership over the lands that they were using and occupying.

On 14th August 1846 the Land Law[2] was adopted, according to which "The villagers are and remain the landlords of the lands they have already possessed in a surface established according to this law".

After adoption of the Land Law, most of the lands became the property of

---

[2] Land Law, art. 1.

the peasants who occupied such lands depending of their economic status, and depending on the number of cattle they owned.

As a result of this law the peasants obtained recognition of rights over the lands by converting their right of use over the land to ownership over the same land.

§ 106RO.01(b)   The First Romanian Civil Code.

Under Alexandru Ioan Cuza and considering that the previous existing civil norms at that time were no longer applicable with respect to their content and form, the first Romanian Civil Code came into force on 1st December 1865. The Romanian Civil Code was inspired by the provisions of the French Civil Code adopted during Napoleonic period.

Although there have been several attempts to modify the Code during the years 1940, 1971 and 2004 the Romanian Civil Code adopted under Alexandru Ioan Cuza has remained substantially unmodified.

A chapter regarding property was allocated in the Romanian Civil Code and special attention was given to the main attributes of the property. The Code also mentioned the differences between the various forms of the possession of goods.

The first Romanian Civil Code stipulated provisions with regard to the goods that husband brought within the marriage, the principle of the freedom for a husband to choose between the separation of goods regime, the community of goods and the dowry regime.[3]

The Code provided that the property could be transferred by deeds concluded between persons or by inheritance.

§ 106RO.01(c)   The Romanian Constitution in 1866.

When the reign of Alexandru Ioan Cuza ended and the German prince Carol de Hohenzollern—Sigmaringen became the successor to the Romanian throne, the country created a fundamental law.

In July 1866 the First Constitution of Romania was adopted. This fundamental law was structured on eight titles with chapters and sections. Under this fundamental law, property was declared sacred and inviolable.

After the extension of the national territory of Romania in 1918 a new constitution was adopted on 29th March 1923.

During the Communist period the Constitution of 1923 was modified in 1948, 1952 and 1965. After the revolution in 1989 a new constitution was adopted in 1991 and the current constitution was subsequently adopted.

The current Constitution of Romania came into force on 29th October 2003 and it was adopted on the basis of a national referendum.

---

[3] Civil Code, art. 1223, 1224, 1260, 1287.

According to the current Constitution of Romania private property is guaranteed and protected by law.

§ 106RO.03   Land/Property Holding During the Communist Era.

The appointment of Government of Petru Groza on 6th March 1945 represented the installation of the communism regime in Romania.

Beginning March 23, 1945, the Land Reform law expropriated agricultural lands with a surface bigger than fifty hectares. In total one million four hundred sixty eight thousand nine hundred forty six hectares were expropriated, of which one million one hundred and nine thousand five hundred sixty two hectares were distributed to the families of peasants.

The land reform in 1945 aimed to abolish the great landed properties and families. According to the Land Law 187 dated 1945 regarding the application of the land reform, all the expropriated properties became the property of the state without payment of any compensation.

The major principles of land ownership and property were set forth in the Romanian Constitution from 1952 issued under the Communists as follows:

Article 6: "The foundation of the socialist social economic formation is the socialist property over the production resources and which have the form of either the state property (joint property of the people), or in the form of the cooperative-collectivist property (the property of the collective agricultural households or the property of the cooperative organizations)"

Article 8: "The land in the Republic Romania belongs to those who work".

Article 9: ". . . The peasants, members of the collective households have a personal use of the plot of land besides their house and personal household on that land . . . -in accordance with the collective agricultural household".

Article 12: "The private property right of the citizens of the Republic Romania over their incomes and savings arising out of their work, incomes over the house and the auxiliary household, over the objects of domestic and personal use as well as the right of inheritance over the citizens' private property are to be protected by law."

§ 106RO.04   Legal Remedies in Relation To Property Against the Abuses Committed in the Communist Era.

During and after the communist period when expropriations and confiscation of properties by the state were specific to that regime, the Romanian legislation referred to laws as a means of acquisition and reacquisition of property.

Land Law 18 dated 1991 is one example of the applicable post communist property legislation in Romania by which there "is established the private property right over the lands that are in the patrimony of the agricultural cooperatives by reconstitution or constitution of the property right."[4]

Land Law 18 refers to and is applicable to those persons who brought land to the agricultural cooperatives. Also subject to this law are the persons from whom the land was taken in any way by the Communist regime and the heirs of such persons.

Law 10 dated 2001 establishes the juridical regime for buildings abusively taken over by the state between 6th March 1945 and 22nd December 1989, the communist era. This law provided the legal conditions for the restitution of such buildings to those entitled to receive them either in kind or through compensation.

Currently in Romanian there are thousands of applications and pending court trials based on these two laws.

§ 106RO.05   Private Ownership Rights.

The Romanian Civil Code defines at article 480 the ownership right as "the right that entitles someone to exclusively enjoy and dispose of an asset, within the limits determined by law." The ownership right comprises three attributes: possession, use and disposal.

Currently,[5] the Parliament is adopting a new Civil Code, but until the date when it enters into force (this being subject to a further regulation) the provisions of the current Civil Code on property rights remains fully applicable.

§ 106RO.05(a)   The Legal Limitations on the Rights of Ownership.

The legal limitations on ownership rights are to be seen in relation to: a) the exercise by the state of the disposal of state assets (assets of public interest or use are not subject to private disposal); b) the relationship of neighborhood properties (i.e. there are specific obligations that have to be respected by the owners of adjoining properties); c) the use of the subsoil of land for works of general interest (the state public authority may use the subsoil of any real estate property, provided that the owner of the property is indemnified against all damages or prejudices caused to the soil).

Private property is protected equally by law, irrespective of the holder. All possessions and belongings acquired by legal means can not be confiscated; the ownership is presumed to have been acquired under legal conditions.

According to article 44 of the Constitution "no property can be expropriated unless there is a cause of public interest and after payment of compensation."

---

[4] Land Law no 18 /1991, art. 8.

[5] 2010.

§ 106RO.05(b)   The Acquisition of Lands By Foreign Citizens.

The acquisition of lands by foreign citizens is regulated by the Law 312/2005.[6]

The citizen of an EU member state, stateless citizens domiciled in a member state or in Romania, as well as the legal persons incorporated in accordance with the legislation of an EU member state, may acquire the ownership right over land for second homes under the same conditions established for Romanian legal and natural persons.

Foreign citizens, stateless citizens and legal persons of a third state may acquire ownership over lands under the conditions provided by the international treaties, based on reciprocity.

Foreign citizens, stateless citizens and legal persons of a third state can not acquire ownership over lands in conditions more favorable than the ones applicable to a citizen of a member state and to a legal person incorporated according to the legislation of a member state.

§ 106RO.06   Public Ownership Rights.

The public ownership right is the ownership right of the State or its territorial administrative units over the assets that, by their nature or by an express legal provision, are deemed to be of public use and utility. Under article 136 (3) of the Constitution the following assets are made the exclusive object of public ownership: any resources of the subsoil, the national air space, the ways of communication, the waters with potential use as suppliers of energy, the beaches, the territorial sea, and the natural resources of the economic zone and the continental shelf.

§ 106RO.06(a)   The Public Administration Right.

Public property assets may be entrusted by administrative acts to autonomous administrative bodies as well as to central and local entities. These entities are entitled to have their own patrimony, to accomplish their own objectives and to participate in all matters in accordance with their legal capacity. An important qualification is that the holders of such administrative rights do not have the right of disposal over the goods and assets entrusted to them.

§ 106RO.06(b)   The Concession of Public Property.

A concession granted by an authority holding public property assets is by way of a concession contract in which an authority or public institution (the "Grantor") transfers to another person (the "Grantee") for a determined period not exceeding forty nine (49) years, the right and the obligation to carry on an activity or public service of national/local interest, on its own

---

[6] Published in the Official Gazette Part 1, no. 1008/14th November 2005 and entered into force on 1st January 2007.

risk and responsibility and to pay the agreed royalty.

The Grantor may be a ministry or other specialized institutions of public administration. The Grantee may be any legal or natural person, irrespective of citizenship or nationality, except for a public legal person.

The procedure to grant the concession contract is provided by Government Emergency Ordinance no. 54/2006[7] regarding the regime of the concession contracts for the public assets, and by the Government Emergency Ordinance no. 34/2006[8] regarding the assignment of the public procurement contracts, of the public works and services concession contracts. Such procedure can be by auction or by direct negotiation. The principles governing these procedures refer to transparency, equal treatment, non-discrimination and free competition. The main criterion of assigning the contract is the price, but there are also other elements to be considered, such as the economic and financial capacity of the Grantee, environmental protection, and specific conditions given the nature of the asset that is subject of the concession.

The holder of a concession right does not have a right of disposal over the asset which is the object of a concession contract.

§ 106RO.06(c) The Renting of Public Property.

The renting contract will contain clauses referring to the exploitation of the specific assets. The renting is always perfected following a public auction as mentioned by article 15 of the Law 213/1998.[9]

§ 106RO.07 The Forms of Property Rights.

As a general rule the right over property is unconditional and unequivocal and can belong to one or more owners. The ownership of an asset or a number of assets may be vested in several owners.

There are cases when a property right can be acquired through a contract concluded in breach of the conditions of capacity required by law for a valid transfer (i.e. conclusion of a contract by a party who is under a disability which is subsequently confirmed).

§ 106RO.07(a) Conditional Ownership Provided By the Will of the Parties.

A property may be transferred by a contract, conditional upon the non-occurrence of an event so that if the event occurs then the transfer is not effective. The property right transferred under such condition is characterized by the fact it is uncertain. If the condition occurs the transferee will return the asset to the transferor. If the condition is not accomplished, the

---

[7] Published in the Official Gazzete Part I, no. 569/30th June 2006.

[8] Published in the Official Gazzete Part I, no. 418/15th May 2006.

[9] Published in the Official Gazzete Part I, no. 488/24th November 1998.

right of the transferee of ownership is retroactively included in the transferee's patrimony.

§ 106RO.07(b)   Conditional Ownership by Law.

The Civil Code makes specific references to transfers which are revocable in certain circumstances proscribed by law.

Any donation concluded between spouses is revocable. The donor spouse is entitled to revoke the donation at any time without justification and the property right transferred to the donee spouse is uncertain depending on the decision of the donor spouse.

Other examples are gifts (deemed as current donations, with insignificant economic value) by persons having no direct relatives at the moment the gift is transmitted and which are likely to be revoked by law if the donor will have direct descendents.

§ 106RO.07(c)   Voidable Ownership.

If a property right is acquired by a voidable contract the ownership right is voidable at the option of the purchaser within three years from the date of signing the contract. The contract can be confirmed by the person who is entitled to invoke the void nature of the contract. Such confirmation may be express or implied within the legal time limits. By the express or implied act the property right of the acquirer is retroactively consolidated.

§ 106RO.07(d)   Common Ownership.

Common ownership exists when one or more persons exercise simultaneously the ownership rights over an asset or group of assets.

§ 106RO.07(d)(1)   Temporary co-ownership.

Normally, temporary co-ownership arises as a consequence of a succession, when a decedent leaves several heirs, each of whom is entitled to a share of the assets or rights in the estate. Temporary co-ownership may also result from the agreement of the parties or from co-possession.

Co-owners do not have an exclusive right over a specific asset. Each co-owner is entitled to use of the asset on the condition that the right of the other co-owners is not violated and the nature of the asset is not affected. The legal acts relating to the asset require the agreement of all the co-owners. In exceptional cases a co-owner can act without the consent of the other co-owners if it can be shown that the act was necessary for the preservation of the asset.

Temporary co-ownership is terminated by the division of the assets according to law. Also a co-owner can become an exclusive owner by purchase, succession or by other legal means.

§ 106RO.07(d)(2)   Perpetual/Forced Co-Ownership.

Imposed co-ownership affects goods that by their nature or designation are to be used by several parties. The goods constituting such co-ownership are ancillary goods and rights.

The Civil Code mentions the following cases of such co-ownership: co-ownership over the common parts of the buildings with flats designed as dwellings, co-ownership over the things necessary for the use of two adjoining premises, co-ownership over common divisions and enclosures (partition walls, fences), co-ownership over the things deemed as family goods (documents, pictures or paintings).

§ 106RO.07(d)(3)   Joint Ownership.

Joint ownership pertains to an asset that belongs to all joint-owners; there is no allocated part of the asset.

The Civil Code regulates the joint ownership of spouses. All goods acquired by the spouses during their marriage are deemed as goods in joint ownership, even if the property contract indicated only one spouse, the purchase was carried out using the assets of one spouse only, or the good may have been acquired during the period when the spouses were separated. Spouses cannot conclude conventions by which the joint ownership due to marriage is circumvented.

There is a presumption that the spouse who exercises ownership rights over the common assets is considered to have the consent of the other spouse and that he/she is mandated to represent the other. This relates even to business assets. Joint ownership ceases once the marriage is terminated.

§ 106RO.08   Acquisition of Property.

§ 106RO.08(a)   Acquisition by Law.

The Civil Code makes reference to the acquisition of property rights by an individual by donation or gift, a purchaser for value in good faith (Article 485), co-ownership (article 597 and 598); and rights of ownership acquired by adverse possession(art 1909).

§ 106RO.08(b)   Acquisition by Order of a Judge.

The ownership property can arise as a result of a judge's order confirming such right. In practice, there have been orders in matters such as the expropriation of land for public utility, or in cases where the signature of one of the parties to a transfer contract is required, the parties previously undertaking such an obligation by a pre-sale agreement.

§ 106RO.08(c)   Acquisition by Contract.

In contracts for the transfer of rights in or over property, the transfer arises at the moment both parties agree and sign the contract, even if the actual possession of the asset does not occur immediately, such as where the payment of the price is not paid immediately. In order for there to be a transfer of ownership by simple agreement several conditions must be accomplished. The asset must be the property of the transferor; the asset must exist at the moment of signature; the asset must be defined; and there is no provision in law or contract that postpones the transfer of ownership to a subsequent date.

By Law 247/2006[10] lands with or without buildings can only be transferred or acquired by either sale or gift by a document executed in authenticated form. In other cases the contract is void.

§ 106RO.08(d)   Acquisition by Administrative Contract.

The administrative deed is as legal contract and conveys real rights such as property rights.

The following administrative acts create or transmit real rights: a) the decisions of the local commissions by the application of Law no. 18/1991 (Land Law) by the reconstruction constitution of private ownership rights over agricultural or forest lands; b) orders issued by a prefect by which are reconstructed or constituted the private ownership over agricultural lands in accordance with Law no. 18/1991; c) decisions of the Government or public administrative authorities regarding administration right over public assets by autonomous administrations, central and local entities.

§ 106RO.08(e)   Acquisition by Delivery.

The Civil Code article 644 refers to the delivery of goods, as distinct from real estate, as a means of the acquisition of property. Such cases are for example a gift or the handing over of bearer bonds where the property right is transferred at the moment the bond is handed over.

§ 106RO.08(f)   Acquisition by Incorporation.

Ownership rights may be acquired by the incorporation of good into another good by either natural force (i.e. formation of an island) or artificial force (i.e. constructions, plantations).

§ 106RO.08(g)   Acquisition by Succession.

By succession, the patrimony of a deceased person is transmitted to his/her heirs. Heirs are persons who survived the deceased and who have the capacity to inherit. The civil code stipulates two types of succession: legal and testamentary succession.

§ 106RO.08(h)   Acquisition by Prescription.

Prescription is a way of acquiring the property by exercising possession over real estate for the period of time provided by law. This period of time is thirty (30) years when the possessor does not hold a property contract and ten (10) years when the possessor holds a contract and the act of possession is made in good faith. Assets which are public property are not subject to prescription. In respect of the movables, these are acquired by the simple act

---

[10] Published in the Official Gazzete Part I, no. 201/03rd March 2006.

of good-faith possession, no time limit being imposed.

§ 106RO.09   The Cadastre and Real Estate Publicity.

On the basis of the Law 7/1996[11] there are organized the cadastre and real estate publicity offices (Land Registry). Their responsibility is to register the cadastral documentation and the claims related to the land book registration.

The land book registrations have a limited role–to make the rights registered known to third parties. The rights that are acquired take effect at the date the respective contract is concluded, the land book registration recording such rights.

The real estate publicity office by its representatives will issue to the rightful person (who lodged a claim in this respect) the resolution of land book registration and the land book excerpt of information.

The registration is not a guarantee of title.

---

[11] Published in the Official Gazzete Part I, no. 653/22nd July 2005.

CHAPTER 106RU

PROPERTY LAW IN RUSSIA

Professor David A. Thomas
J. Reuben Clark Law School
Brigham Young University[*1]

SYNOPSIS

---

[*] Bryant Bair, J.D., Brigham Young University Law School, 2008, assisted significantly with researching and writing this section of Chapter 106, especially in Russian language materials.

§ 106RU.01   Historical Background of Russian Land Law

§ 106RU.01(a)   From Serfdom to Emerging Democracy.

Russia was one of the last great nations to emerge from medieval patterns of landholding. This is indicated by the well-known fact that serfdom in Russia was not formally and legally abolished until 1861, and, of course, the transition to more modern types of property ownership required much time thereafter. In Russia of 1861, over 20 million of the 60 million Russians lived in a form of serfdom, working the land but not owning it, and subject to numerous other personal restrictions and impositions from the approximately 100,000 owners of the land they occupied. The legislation abolishing serfdom also conferred on the liberated serfs rights to purchase the land from the landowners. These owners, however, typically overvalued the land sold, and the sale transactions often left the former serfs heavily in debt or in some other form of economic bondage little different from their former status as serfs.[1]

Land rights of the owning class were also uncertain during this period, with confiscations frequently occurring.[2]

Thus, the land law reforms begun in the 1860s were largely ineffective, and those millions who had been poor, landless, and in some form of subjugation to wealthy landowners were still so when the communist revolution occurred in 1917.

---

[1] William P. Kratzke, "Russia's New Land Code: A Two Percent Solution," 12 *Minn. J. Global Trade* 109, 112–113 (2003).

[2] Lee A. Farrow, *Between Clan and Crown: The Struggle to Define Noble Property in Imperial Russia* 158 (2004).

§ 106RU.01(b)   Russian Land Law and Landholding During the Communist Era.

Surprisingly, in the early years of Lenin's rule following the communist takeover of Russia in 1917, some forms of private land ownership were tolerated. When the Second All-Russia Congress of Soviets decreed the state as owner of all land and income-producing assets, it was applied to lands owned by the Tsar, the nobility and the church, while lands owned by peasants were exempted. The Second All-Russia Congress of Soviets issued a decree that established the state as owner of all land and income-producing assets.[3] This decree socialized all of the land that belonged to the Tsar, the nobility and the Church while exempting the land owned by the peasants.[4] Even most of this land came under state control following Lenin's nationalization initiative beginning in 1922.[5] This initiative was legitimized in the 1924 Soviet Constitution authorizing the state "to establish general principles of exploitation and use of the earth, as well as those of the sub-soil, the forests, and the waters of the territories of the Union."[6] The decree of 1922 and the 1924 Constitution established the legal regime of state-owned land, but in fact most land remained at the time in private ownership, especially in provincial areas not yet fully affected by the communist revolution.

Toleration of land in private ownership swiftly ended when Lenin died in 1924 and Josef Stalin seized control of the state.[7] Stalin had become party General Secretary in 1922 and, after consolidating his power upon Lenin's death, imposed a draconian collectivization program in the early 1930s. Under this program, the state acted, often with violence, to seize both land and assets of the landowning peasants, called Kulaks, creating large, collective agricultural operations, and integrating agriculture into nationwide economic planning.[8] The process evicted and dispossessed over five million Kulaks from their villages and caused the deaths of up to 11 million

---

[3] *Fundamentals of Legislation in the USSR and the Union Republics* 10 (Progress Publishers 1968, Murad Saifulin and Yuri Sdobnokov, trans., 1974).

[4] Stephen B. Butler and Sheila O'Leary, "Survey of the Emerging Land Law of the Russian Federation," 1 *Parker Sch. J.E. Eur. L.* 541–542 (1994).

[5] Stephen B. Butler and Sheila O'Leary, "Survey of the Emerging Land Law of the Russian Federation," 1 *Parker Sch. J.E. Eur. L.* 542–543 (1994).

[6] Konstitutsiia SSSR (1924) [Konst. SSSR] art. 1(m). Later versions of the constitution published in 1936 and 1977 also contained similar language, continuing state control of property. Stephen B. Butler and Sheila O'Leary, "Survey of the Emerging Land Law of the Russian Federation," 1 *Parker Sch. J.E. Eur. L.* 543 (1994).

[7] Martin Malia, *The Soviet Tragedy: A History of Socialism in Russia 1917–1991* 154, 169 (The Free Press, 1994).

[8] University of Leyden, *Soviet Law After Stalin: Part I* 162 (A.W. Sijthoff-Leyden, 1977).

peasants in the resulting famine.[9] Collectivization was basically complete by the mid-1930s and resulted in most agricultural lands coming under actual state ownership and control.[10]

§ 106RU.01(c)   Characteristics of Landholding During the Communist Era.

Legal regulation of Soviet landholding emerged and evolved only gradually, impeded by the recovery from the ravages of World War II and the preoccupation with the Cold War. Use rights in land were granted to state organizations, collectives and to individual citizens. The 1968 Fundamentals of Legislation of the USSR and the Union Republics declares the principle of state ownership of land, methods for distributing land, types of land tenure, and the rights and duties of land users.[11] The *Fundamentals* also set forth provisions for a strict zoning of land into three categories: agricultural land[12], land in urban areas or other populated localities,[13] land of industry, including non-agricultural land,[14] state forests,[15] state waters,[16] and state reserve land.[17]

The general principles for land ownership set forth in Section I may be briefly described as follows:

Article 7: Provides for land use by "collective farms, state farms and other agricultural government, co-operative and non-government enterprises, organizations and institutions; industrial transport and other non-agricultural government, co-operative and non-government enterprises, organizations and institutions; citizens of the USSR."

Article 8: Allots land to these entities free of charge.

---

[9] Martin Malia, *The Soviet Tragedy: A History of Socialism in Russia 1917-1991* 196-198 (The Free Press, 1994).

[10] University of Leyden, *Soviet Law After Stalin: Part I* 162 (A.W. Sijthoff-Leyden, 1977).

[11] *Fundamentals of Legislation in the USSR and the Union Republics*, Sec. I (Progress Publishers 1968, Murad Saifulin and Yuri Sdobnokov, trans., 1974).

[12] *Fundamentals of Legislation in the USSR and the Union Republics*, Sec. II (Progress Publishers 1968, Murad Saifulin and Yuri Sdobnokov, trans., 1974).

[13] *Fundamentals of Legislation in the USSR and the Union Republics*, Sec. III (Progress Publishers 1968, Murad Saifulin and Yuri Sdobnokov, trans., 1974).

[14] *Fundamentals of Legislation in the USSR and the Union Republics*, Sec. IV (Progress Publishers 1968, Murad Saifulin and Yuri Sdobnokov, trans., 1974).

[15] *Fundamentals of Legislation in the USSR and the Union Republics*, Sec. V (Progress Publishers 1968, Murad Saifulin and Yuri Sdobnokov, trans., 1974).

[16] *Fundamentals of Legislation in the USSR and the Union Republics*, Sec. VI (Progress Publishers 1968, Murad Saifulin and Yuri Sdobnokov, trans., 1974).

[17] *Fundamentals of Legislation in the USSR and the Union Republics*, Sec. VII (Progress Publishers 1968, Murad Saifulin and Yuri Sdobnokov, trans., 1974).

Article 9: Authorizes land tenure either for a specified term or for unlimited time. Land allotted to collective farms is assigned permanently or for an unlimited time. Other land can be granted for a short term of up to three years or a long term of between three and ten years. The term can be extended if required for production.

Article 11: Limits a user's right to uses compatible with the designated type of land. Land uses includes building a dwelling and other structures, planting crops and trees, using meadows and pastures, using common minerals, peat and water resources. A right to be compensated for losses to the land is also established. Duties imposed on the land user include a duty to not interfere with neighbor's use of his land. The restoration of allotments of land used in strip mining or any other activity that changes the land must be accomplished during the course of work, or if this is impossible, within one year of completion. The restoration must return the lands to "a condition making them suitable for agriculture, forestries or fisheries" in accordance with the designated type of land.

Article 13: Declares the responsibility for improving soil and protecting land from erosion is shared equally between the land users and the government.

Articles 14 and 15: Describes how permanent or temporary tenure may be terminated for a variety of reasons. In the cases of organizations, enterprises, and institutions the termination may occur if the plot is no longer needed by the organization or if the organization becomes defunct. The tenure of a citizen may be voluntarily released or be terminated when all members of the family move to another location or all members of the family die. (If a citizen attempts to sell, mortgage or otherwise transfer ownership of the land, the person may be stripped of tenure. Additionally, failure to fulfill duties outlined in the law will also result in confiscation of the land.[18] Tenure for both organizations and persons can be terminated at the expiration of the term, because of state need, or the non-development of the plot of land for 2 years.

Articles 18 and 19: Although the land is state owned, a compensation system is in effect for damages or losses caused by the withdrawal of a plot of land for state use, not caused by the user's conduct. If the plot is non-agricultural and is withdrawn, the compensation would be paid by the enterprise or organization that was subsequently allotted the plot of land. If the land withdrawn is agricultural, the organization would be required to additionally compensate for loss of agricultural production. As we will see later, this concept has carried on to modern Russian law.

---

[18] *Fundamentals of Legislation in the USSR and the Union Republics*, Sec. I, Art. 50 (Progress Publishers 1968, Murad Saifulin and Yuri Sdobnokov, trans., 1974).

§ 106RU.01(c)(1)   Regulation of Agricultural Land.

The following articles of Section II of the 1968 *Fundamentals of Legislation* pertain to regulation of agricultural land:

Article 23: Collective farms, government organizations, and citizens can be granted agricultural land for unlimited (permanent) use while other enterprises are limited to temporary use. Users of agricultural land have duties imposed upon them in addition to those outlined in Article 11 of Section I. Land users are required to employ the most efficient methods of farming. They were also required to develop irrigation systems, ensure proper drainage and to treat soils with "lime and gypsum."

Articles 24–26: Members of collectives and select other groups are allowed to hold small "household" plots of land for their family use. These plots are allotted first to the collective and then doled out to the households in the collective for their use. The members of collectives are entitled to these plots while workers on state farms and other organizations do not necessarily have such a right. The possession of a plot of land is retained when the user is called to active military service, begins a course of study, or holds an elective office.

§ 106RU.01(c)(2)   Regulation of Lands of Populated Localities.

Section III of the *Fundamentals of Legislation* governs all land within the boundaries of cities, townships, and populated rural locations. Control and planning regarding this land is delegated to the Union Republics with the exception of "land used by railway, water, air and pipe-line transport and by the mining industry. . . ."[19] Land within the city limits that is used by collectives is exempt from the planning process and is allotted to the collective permanently.[20]

§ 106RU.02   Land Legislation of the Post-Soviet Era.

The demise of the government of the Soviet Union did not signal an immediate and total change in land rights. Commentators have noted that, in this period of transition from state control of land to a freer market system, change has been slow and every reform has been contested. The politicians elected to the Duma and to local offices are often the same people who held power under the communist system, and they typically resist the transition to private land ownership.[21] Nevertheless, the period has seen rapid changes in property law, many changes introduced by legislation and executive decrees, as described below.

---

[19] *Fundamentals of Legislation in the USSR and the Union Republics*, Sec. III, Arts. 30-31 (Progress Publishers 1968, Murad Saifulin and Yuri Sdobnokov, trans., 1974).

[20] *Fundamentals of Legislation in the USSR and the Union Republics*, Sec. III, Art. 32 (Progress Publishers 1968, Murad Saifulin and Yuri Sdobnokov, trans., 1974).

[21] William P. Kratzke, "Russia's New Land Code: A Two Percent Solution," 12 *Minn. J. Global Trade* 109, 116-118 (2003).

§ 106RU.02(a)   The Land Reform Law of 1990.

This was the first of legislative reforms of land law in the post-Soviet era and provides for private ownership of land.[22] This reform, however, did not establish a market for land and the state remained the only entity that could buy land from citizens.[23] Additional restrictions on the alienability of land were also included in the law.[24]

§ 106RU.02(b)   The Law on Peasant Holding.

This law directed the reorganization of the state collective farms into a form of private enterprise.[25] Members of the collectives also gained an interest in land. The interest could be an ownership interest or the newly created life-long inheritable possession or a right of permanent use. These interests in land were not alienable because the law still did not provide a market structure for the exchange of land.[26]

§ 106RU.02(c)   Land Code of 1991.

This code represents a comprehensive attempt to update Russian property law, and it sets forth many details about incidents of land ownership. The Code zones land according to its purpose and use, and establishes standards for the sale of land, the payment of the price of land, and leasing. It restricts ownership of different types of land to certain types of land interests; foreign entities are limited to long-term leases.[27]

§ 106RU.02(d)   1993 Constitution of the Russian Federation.

The 1993 Constitution's main effect on property law is to integrate and reconcile the old and new property laws. Article 9 declares the basic regulatory scheme for land in Russia:

(1) Land and other natural resources shall be utilized and protected in the Russian Federation as the basis of life and activity of the people living in the corresponding territories

(2) Land and other natural resources may be in private, state, municipal, and other forms of ownership.

---

[22] William P. Kratzke, "Russia's New Land Code: A Two Percent Solution," 12 *Minn. J. Global Trade* 109, 118 (2003).

[23] *Fundamentals of Legislation in the USSR and the Union Republics*, Sec. I, Art. 32 (Progress Publishers 1968, Murad Saifulin and Yuri Sdobnokov, trans., 1974).

[24] For instance, land can be seized by the government if it is not being used for its designated purpose or is being used only inefficiently.

[25] William P. Kratzke, "Russia's New Land Code: A Two Percent Solution," 12 *Minn. J. Global Trade* 109, 117 (2003).

[26] *Fundamentals of Legislation in the USSR and the Union Republics*, Sec. I, Art. 32 (Progress Publishers 1968, Murad Saifulin and Yuri Sdobnokov, trans., 1974).

[27] Grazhdanskii Kodeks [GK] [Civil Code] Article 257 (Rus.).

This Constitution also provides for private ownership and alienation of land.[28]

§ 106RU.02(e)   Civil Code of 1994.

This code effectively replaces the patchwork of legislation that preceded it with a homogeneous body of law. In combining the laws of the former Soviet Union with the laws passed since its fall, it creates a consistent body of law.[29]

§ 106RU.03   Current Laws Regarding Property in Russia.

Land law in Russia today is governed by the 1993 Constitution, the Land Code of the Russian Federation,[30] and several Presidential Decrees. The 1993 Constitution states in article 9 that "recognition and equal protection shall be given to private, state, municipal, and other forms of ownership."[31] More specifically, the Constitution states that "[land] and other natural resources may be in private, state, municipal and other forms of ownership."[32] The Civil Code of the Russian Federation establishes the alienability of land[33] and the rights of citizens and judicial persons to own land. The several modes of possession established by the constitution are discussed in the Land Code, and include State,[34] Federal,[35] Regional,[36] and Municipal.[37] The reforms set forth in the Land Code apply only to urban and dacha (country home) properties, but not to agricultural and forestry land.

§ 106RU.03(a)   Acquisition of Property.

Property rights may be acquired by finding, manufacture, purchase, acquisitive prescription (adverse possession), and inheritance.[38] The finders concept is codified in Article 227 of the Civil Code. The finder of an item must return the item to the owner, if the owner is known. Otherwise the finder must report the find to the police or to other local government authority. The owner may recover for loss or damage to the found item only if the loss or damage occurred intentionally or due to gross negligence.

---

[28] Konstitutsiia Rossiiskio Federatsii]Konst. RF] [Constitution] Article 10.

[29] William P. Kratzke, "Russia's New Land Code: A Two Percent Solution," 12 *Minn. J. Global Trade* 109, 120 (2003).

[30] Zemelnyi Kodeks [ZK] [Land Code] (Russ.).

[31] Zemelnyi Kodeks [ZK] [Land Code] (Russ.) Art. 9(1).

[32] Zemelnyi Kodeks [ZK] [Land Code] (Russ.) Art. 9(2).

[33] Zemelnyi Kodeks [ZK] [Land Code] (Russ.) Arts. 209 and 260.

[34] Zemelnyi Kodeks [ZK] [Land Code] (Russ.) Art. 16.

[35] Zemelnyi Kodeks [ZK] [Land Code] (Russ.) Art. 17.

[36] Zemelnyi Kodeks [ZK] [Land Code] (Russ.) Art. 18.

[37] Zemelnyi Kodeks [ZK] [Land Code] (Russ.) Art. 19.

[38] Civil Code Ch. 14.

§ 106RU.03(a)(1)　Finding.

The regulations for establishing ownership in the finder are set out in Article 228. The statute of limitations is six months, after which the finder may claim ownership. If the finder declines to take ownership of the found item, the ownership is vested in the municipality in which it was found.

Buried or concealed treasure is governed by Article 233. The ownership of the treasure is vested in equal shares in the finder and the owner of the land on which it was found. If the finder, without permission, was present on the land or digging the treasure vests entirely in the owner of the land. If the treasure is of historical or cultural value the item is subject to transfer to the state. The finder and landowner are entitled to 50% of the value of the treasure in equal shares, unless the finder was unauthorized, in which case the owner receives the entire 50% share.

The Civil Code includes language establishing finders rules for neglected animals,[39] articles that have no owner,[40] and abandoned property.[41]

§ 106RU.03(a)(2)　Manufacture or Construction.

If a person creates goods from material of which the person had legal ownership, the ownership of the newly created item is vested in the person.[42] The construction of immovable property on land owned by the builder does not immediately vest ownership in the builder, but rather vests when the property is registered with the state. If a person builds immovable property on land owned by another, ownership does not vest in the builder.[43] The arbitrary building is subject to demolition at the expense of the builder and the builder holds no rights to make any transaction relating to the property. Arbitrary structures include those built without government authorization or in violation of code. If the arbitrary structure is built on the land of another, the builder may keep the property and gain ownership rights if the builder acquires title to the property on which it was built.

§ 106RU.03(a)(3)　Conversion.

If a person converts materials owned by another to a new manufactured product, the ownership of that new product rests in the owner of the materials from which it was made.[44] The owner of the materials must compensate the converter for the value of the conversion, unless the

---

[39] Civil Code Art. 230.

[40] Civil Code Art. 225.

[41] Civil Code Art. 226.

[42] Civil Code Art. 218.

[43] Civil Code Art. 222.

[44] Civil Code Art. 220(1).

conversion was made in bad faith;[45] in case of bad faith, the owner of the materials has a right to the materials and an award of damages for any losses sustained.[46]

§ 106RU.03(a)(4)   Acquisitive Prescription.

This is ownership acquired similarly to adverse possession in common law jurisdictions. The statute of limitations established in the Civil Code is 15 years for immovable property and 5 years for other property.[47] Property must be held in good faith, openly, and uninterruptedly.[48] Ownership does not vest until the acquirer registers the immovable property with the State after 15 years of possession. The possessor has the right to protect the property against all claimants except the actual owner. A prescriptive possessor may join the possessory times of successive possessors if there was no break in possession.

§ 106RU.03(b)   Termination of Property Rights.

§ 106RU.03(b)(1)   Renunciation of Right of Ownership (Abandonment).

An owner of property may renounce his status as owner and effectively abandon the property.[49] Intent need not be declared, but may be manifest by specific actions that indicate an intent to abandon the property. Abandonment does not relieve the owner of duties, such as paying taxes and responsibility for condition of the land, until the property is acquired by another.

§ 106RU.03(b)(2)   Confiscation.

The Civil Code allows for the confiscation of property as punishment or sanction for the commission of certain crimes or other breaches of the law.[50] The government is not required to pay any compensation for the taking. The criminal code lists the violations of law that allow for the confiscation of property.

§ 106RU.03(b)(3)   Withdrawal of Land (Eminent Domain).

The right of the government to withdraw a plot of land for public use is similar to the doctrine of eminent domain as understood in the United States. The government entity seeking must show in court that the purpose for which the plot is withdrawn cannot be achieved without the withdrawal.[51]

---

[45] Civil Code Art. 220(2).

[46] Civil Code Art. 220(3).

[47] Civil Code Art. 234.

[48] Civil Code Art. 234(1).

[49] Civil Code Art. 236.

[50] Civil Code Art. 243.

[51] Civil Code Art. 239.

The land must be purchased by the state in order to compensate the property owner. In similar action, the government can requisition property during natural disasters and other extraordinary circumstances.[52] In these cases, the government must compensate the owner for the property or for the use of the property. The owner may also sue for the return of the property at the end of the situation that gave rise to the taking if the property. The owner may contest the award received for use of the property in court if unsatisfied with the amount provided.

§ 106RU.03(b)(4)   Levying Execution on the Property for the Owner's Obligations.

In the event a landowner is unable to meet debt obligations, a creditor may sue in court for property owned by the debtor to satisfy the debt.[53]

§ 106RU.03(c)   Types of Ownership Entities.

§ 106RU.03(c)(1)   Common Ownership.

Russian law recognizes only two types of concurrent ownership. Participatory ownership is roughly analogous to a tenancy in common under Anglo-American law.[54] Joint ownership is similar to a joint tenancy.[55] The Civil Code also recognizes a mode of concurrent ownership known as the (Farmer's) Economy, a type of unincorporated cooperative farm.[56]

§ 106RU.03(c)(1)(i)   Participatory Ownership.

Property held in participatory ownership is held in equal shares or as determined by agreement of the parties and, if not established by agreement.[57] If one participant contributes to the property financially, that participant's share of the property is increased an equivalent amount.[58] If the improvement is divisible and not attached to the property, ownership of the improvement vests in the improving participant.[59] Participants are required to contribute to any taxes, upkeep or maintenance of the property in order to maintain their participatory share.[60] Participants may transfer their shares,[61] but other participants have a right of first refusal,[62] unless the share is subject

---

[52] Civil Code Art. 242.

[53] Civil Code Art. 237.

[54] Civil Code Arts. 245-252.

[55] Civil Code Arts. 253-255.

[56] Civil Code Arts. 257-259.

[57] Civil Code Art. 245(1).

[58] Civil Code Art. 245(3).

[59] Civil Code Art. 245(3).

[60] Civil Code Art. 249.

[61] Civil Code Art. 246.

[62] Civil Code Art. 250.

to levying execution.[63] Participants may partition their property, either by agreement or by court action.[64]

§ 106RU.03(c)(1)(ii)   Joint Ownership.

The rules for joint ownership are basically the same as those of participatory ownership.[65] The property is held in common with equal rights to use and all of the owners may transact business related to the property without the consent of the other parties. Division or partition of the property requires a determination of the participatory share each owner possesses. No right of survivorship is recognized: if one joint owner dies, a determination will be made to set the participatory share of the deceased. This participatory share is then available as part of decedent's estate to be passed on to heirs.[66]

§ 106RU.03(c)(1)(iii)   Peasant (Or Farmer's) Economy.

This type of ownership is the successor to the collective farm and the Peasant Land Holding, and allows for members of a collective farm to hold their land, livestock, equipment, and other assets in joint ownership.[67] Because the assets are held in joint ownership, the shares of the participants are presumptively equal.[68] This form also provides for the produce of the farm to be common property of the entire group, subject to division by agreement.[69] A single person withdrawing from the group cannot force the partition of the whole economy, but rather is given a monetary award.[70] The Code also provides for a cooperative formed on the base of a peasant economy.[71]

§ 106RU.03(c)(2)   Marital Property.

Under Russian marital property law, all property acquired by spouses during marriage is presumptively held in joint ownership.[72] Property that a spouse owned before the marriage remains in individual ownership, unless the property is improved or otherwise significantly increased in value with marital assets, in which case the property is converted into marital property.[73] The improvements must be significant in nature for this to have

---

[63] Civil Code Art. 255.

[64] Civil Code Art. 252.

[65] Civil Code Art. 256.

[66] Civil Code Art. 1150.

[67] Civil Code Art. 257.

[68] Civil Code Art. 258.

[69] Civil Code Art. 257.

[70] Civil Code Art. 258.

[71] Civil Code Art. 259.

[72] Civil Code Art. 256.

[73] Civil Code Art. 256(2).

effect.[74] Foreclosure on obligations entered into separately by one spouse can reach the participatory share of the property that the spouse would have been entitled to if the joint property was partitioned under article 252 of the Civil Code.[75] Upon the death of one spouse, the deceased spouse's participatory share is then eligible to be inherited by that spouse's heirs.[76]

Upon dissolution of the marriage, property that is considered joint property may be divided by agreement of the spouses or, failing in this, by the courts.[77] If the division is to be made in court, the spouses' participatory shares are presumptively equal unless otherwise provided for in contract.[78] Besides property owned by the spouses before marriage, any property obtained after separation and cessation of conjugal relations, property acquired exclusively for children, and personal use items obtained during the marriage are exempted from division.[79]

Judges, when dividing marital property, are allowed to vary from the presumptively equal concept in cases when an unequal division would better serve the interests of the children involved. If one spouse squandered marital assets to the detriment of the family, he or she may find be assigned a smaller share of the property. Tied to the participatory share of common property assigned to each spouse, common debt is distributed in proportion to the participatory share assigned.[80]

The Russian Family Code sets forth a complex system of spousal support,[81] child support,[82] parental support,[83] and other familial support.[84] The law spells out in fairly specific detail who owes what support to whom; however, the judges exercise discretion in determining specific amounts, usually based on the financial and family situations of the payer and the recipient.[85]

§ 106RU.03(d)   Types of Ownership Interests.

Current Russian Property law recognizes five types of ownership interests in land: ownership, inheritable life-long possession, permanent use, lease,

---

[74] Civil Code Art. 256(2).

[75] Civil Code Art. 256(3) and (4).

[76] Civil Code Art. 1150.

[77] Family Code Art. 38.

[78] Family Code Art. 39(1).

[79] Family Code Art. 38.

[80] Family Code Art. 39(2).

[81] Family Code Arts. 89, 90, 92.

[82] Family Code Arts. 80, 81, 83-86.

[83] Family Code Arts. 87, 88, 97.

[84] Family Code Arts. 93-96.

[85] Family Code Art. 98.

and easement. The Land Code defines five different terms in relation to interests in land:

Owners of plots of land—possess plots of land under a right of ownership.

Users of land—possess and use plots of land by the right of permanent (infinite) use or by the right of free use for a term.

Tenants—possess and use state owned plots of land by a right of lifetime inheritable possession.

Lessees of plots of land—possess and use private or state owned plots of land under a lease or sub-lease.

Holders of Easements—possess a limited right to use another's plot of land.[86]

§ 106RU.03(d)(1)   Ownership.

Ownership is the most full form of property ownership recognized in Russia today. This form of ownership was firmly established by the Constitution of the Russian Federation in 1993.[87] The constitution provided that a citizen may alienate an interest in land to another without using the state as an intermediary.[88] The citizen may also create interests in land in another in the form of a lease[89] or mortgage on the land.

Land ownership includes rights to the surface, water located within the boundaries of the plot, forests located on the plot, rights to the airspace above the plot and rights to everything located under the plot.[90] Exercise of these rights is subject to the all other laws of use and zoning and must not infringe on the rights of other land owners.[91]

Owners of land have the right to build on their land, subject to the designation assigned to that land.[92] Unless provided for in contract or law, the landowner acquires ownership of the immovable property. Ownership in property built on the owner's land also automatically vests in the owner.[93]

§ 106RU.03(d)(1)(i)   Inheritable Life Long Possession.

Inheritable life long possession is an interest in land that is no longer possible to acquire under the current code.[94] Those who held such interests

---

[86] Land Code Art. 5.

[87] Constitution, Art. 9.

[88] Civil Code Art. 209.

[89] Civil Code Art. 260.

[90] Civil Code Art. 261.

[91] Civil Code Art. 261(3).

[92] Civil Code Art. 263.

[93] Civil Code Art. 263.

[94] Land Code Art. 21.

at the time the law was enacted are allowed to retain those interests but rights of alienability are limited. Tenants possess full use rights, including the right to build on the land and to rent the land to another, but the only method for transferring the property is through inheritance.[95] Citizens are allowed to convert their life-long inheritable use into a clear title to the property once without additional cost.[96]

§ 106RU.03(d)(1)(ii)   Permanent Use.

The right of permanent use may arise in one of two ways; either the right is granted from a state agency that is authorized to grant plots of land in such a way[97] or it arises when an individual, who does not own the land, owns a building situated on that land.[98] Those whose interest is in an entire plot of land may only act within the limits of the law and of the act that granted him the use of the land. Unless otherwise provided for, the user of land may use the land according to that act to build or install immovable property on the premises. Users of land may only grant fixed-term use of the land to others and may not collect compensation for this use.[99] If a legal entity is reorganized the right of permanent land use is passed to the new legal entity.[100]

Owners of immovable property situated on land that they do not own gain a right of permanent use to the land on which the building or other immovable property is located.[101] If ownership to the immovable property is transferred the right of permanent use is transferred with it. If the land user loses the right to permanent use, the rights of the owner of the immovable property may be determined in an agreement with the owner of the land. Absent an agreement, the issue may be decided in court. The decision of the court can fall into one of three categories. First, the owner may demand the immovable property be removed and the land restored to its previous state. Second, if the building cannot be demolished for reasons of law or the building clearly is valued more than the land on which it stands, the court can allow the owner of the building to acquire the land or the landowner to acquire the building. Third, the court may stipulate conditions on which the land is to be used.[102]

§ 106RU.03(d)(1)(iii)   Lease.

Leases are the least restricted interests in land, in terms of who may

---

[95] Land Code Art. 21.

[96] Land Code Art. 21.

[97] Civil Code Art. 268.

[98] Civil Code Art. 271.

[99] Civil Code Art. 270.

[100] Civil Code Art. 268.

[101] Civil Code Art. 271.

[102] Civil Code Art. 272.

possess the interest. Foreign citizens and legal entities are allowed to hold leases as long as the property does not have a state interest and is not of historical importance.[103] Those who own the buildings located on a plot of land are given a preferential right to lease or acquire the land.[104] A lessee also has a preferential right to a new lease at the expiration of the term of the lessee's lease.[105] If the land is to be leased from a private individual, the terms of the lease are set out in contract and the price is negotiated between the parties. If the lease is from the state, the amount of payment for the lease is figured by a set formula.[106]

The lessee is allowed to sublease the property to another without consent, if notice is given to the owner. This right may be altered by contract.[107] The code does not provide for the lease to be assigned or all rights and duties of the lease transferred.

§ 106RU.03(d)(1)(iv)   Easements.

The Land Code authorizes creation of both public and private easements.[108] The owner of the encumbered property may demand compensation from the easement holder for the use.[109]

A public easement is described as a "legal act of a . . . government body in the cases when it is required for ensuring interests of the state, local government or local public without plots of land being taken."[110] The following situations give rise to public easements: right of way; use for public utilities; use in drainage works; use of water; passage of cattle; hunting, fishing, and gather plants; prospecting and research; and free access to a coastline.[111]

The easement imposed must be the least burdensome for the plot of land to which it attaches and may be either permanent or temporary.[112] If the easement makes use of the land by the landowner impossible, a court may require the governmental easement holder to purchase the land or to grant another plot of land of commensurate value. If the inconvenience caused by the public easement is significant, but not so severe to make use of the land

---

[103] Land Code Art. 22. Law also appears to prohibit leasing of agricultural land to foreign citizens or entities).

[104] Land Code Art. 35.

[105] Land Code Art. 22.

[106] Land Code Art. 22.

[107] Land Code Art. 22(6).

[108] Land Code Art. 23.

[109] Land Code Art. 23(6).

[110] Land Code Art. 23(2).

[111] Land Code Art. 23(3).

[112] Land Code Art. 23(4) and (5).

impossible, then the landowner may seek payment for the loss of use.[113] As with all interests in land, an easement is subject to state registration.[114]

§ 106RU.03(e)   Land Registration.

Transactions relating to real property are registered with the government. In Russia, all interests in land and immovable property are subject to mandatory state registration, to include ownership rights, leases and sub-leases greater than one year, mortgages and trusts.[115] Because private ownership of land is relatively new, the registration requirement is also new. Only interests obtained after the registration law was passed in 2001 are required to be registered.[116] Property interests in Russia are assigned a unique number in a national system of registration.[117]

The responsibility to ensure clear title through a records search is greatly simplified by the centralized registration system. Instead of an attorney or title search agent filing through the county records or even compiling their own set of land records, all that is required to obtain an extract showing the title to the land is to present an identity card to the Single State Register of Rights.[118] One weakness of this system is that the registration law has been in effect less than a decade.

§ 106RU.03(f)   Zoning.

The zoning system in the Russian Federation is similar to that of the former Soviet Union, including virtually the same categories.[119] The zoning system is more comprehensive and restrictive than zoning laws in the United States. Zoning of Russian property also deals with the alienability of certain types of property.[120]

---

[113] Land Code Art. 23(7).

[114] Land Code Art. 23(9).

[115] Federal Law of the Russian Federation on the State Registration of Rights to Real Estate and of Transactions with It 2001, Art. 4.

[116] Federal Law of the Russian Federation on the State Registration of Rights to Real Estate and of Transactions with It 2001, Art. 4.

[117] Federal Law of the Russian Federation on the State Registration of Rights to Real Estate and of Transactions with It 2001, Art. 1.

[118] Federal Law of the Russian Federation on the State Registration of Rights to Real Estate and of Transactions with It 2001, Art. 7.

[119] Land Code Chs. XIV-XVIII.

[120] Land Code Art. 95.

TABLE OF CASES

[References are to sections]

C

[References are to sections]

D

E

[References are to sections]

[References are to sections]

[References are to sections]

N

[References are to sections]

[References are to sections]

TABLE OF CASES

[References are to sections]

[References are to sections]

Y

Z

INDEX

[References are to sections.]

I-1

[References are to sections.]

[References are to sections.]

[References are to sections.]

[References are to sections.]

EGYPT—Cont.
State-owned holdings under Shari'a law
. . . 106EG.01(b)(2)
Succession; acquisition and delivery of property
. . . 106EG.02(b)(2)(ii)
Taxable private holdings under Shari'a law
. . . 106EG.01(b)(1)
Transfers of real property (See subhead: Acquisition of real property)
Types of interests in real property
Hikr . . . 106EG.02(b)(3)(ii)
Original types of land tenure (See subhead: Historical background in Shari'a law)
Servitudes . . . 106EG.02(b)(3)(iii)
Usufruct . . . 106EG.02(b)(3)(i)
Usufruct . . . 106EG.02(b)(3)(i)
Waqf
Landholdings . . . 106EG.01(b)(3)
Lease . . . 106EG.02(b)(5)(iii)

EMINENT DOMAIN
Kazakhstan . . . 106KZ.07
Russia . . . 106RU.03(b)(3)

EMPHYTEUSIS
Brazil; definition . . . 106BR.02(a)(2)(i)
Canada; civil law in Quebec
. . . 106CA.04(b)(1)
Japan; recognized property interests
. . . 106JP.02(e)

ENGLISH LAW
Great Britain, property law in (See GREAT BRITAIN)

ENVIRONMENTAL CONSIDERATIONS
Canada
Most provinces . . . 106CA.04(a)(6)
Quebec . . . 106CA.04(b)(6)
Denmark . . . 106DK.02(a)(2)
India . . . 106IN.03(l)
Korea . . . 106KR.03(k)
Philippines . . . 106PH.03(l)

EQUIPMENT TRUST CERTIFICATES
Federal securities regulation, transactions subject to . . . 103.03(a)(7)

ESTATE TAX
India . . . 106IN.03(k)(1)
Philippines . . . 106PH.03(k)(1)

EUROPEAN UNION (EU)
Governance of . . . 106EU.01
Historical background . . . 106EU.01
Property law
Generally . . . 106EU.02
Case law . . . 106EU.03(b)
Convention for the Protection of Human Rights and Fundamental Freedoms
. . . 106EU.02
European Court of Justice
. . . 106EU.03(b)
Treaty on European Unions
. . . 106EU.03(a)

EUROPEAN UNION (EU)—Cont.
Structure of . . . 106EU.01

EVICTION
Poland . . . 106PL.02(d)(1)(ii)

EVIDENCE
Evidences of indebtedness; transactions subject to federal securities regulation
. . . 103.03(a)(2)

EXPROPRIATION OF LAND
Brazil . . . 106BR.05
Poland
Constitution, expropriation under
. . . 106PL.02(a)
Post-World War II period, expropriation and nationalization in
. . . 106PL.01(c)(2)(ii)
Romania . . . 106RO.05(a)

F

FEE SIMPLE ABSOLUTE
Great Britain; fee simple absolute in possession
. . . 106GB.02(a)(1)

FENCES
Japan; rights of fencing
. . . 106JP.02(c)(1)(ii)(g); 106JP.02(c)(1)(ii)(i)

FEUDALISM
France, emergence of feudalism in
. . . 106FR.01(d)
Germany, growth of feudalism in
. . . 106DE.04
Romania . . . 106RO.01(c)

FIDUCIARIES
Mortgages, banker or broker liability for aggressive . . . 104.02(d)
Promissory notes; fiduciary duty contrasted with duty to counsel . . . 104.02(d)

FIXED RATE MORTGAGES
Adjustable rate mortgages (ARMs) and, choosing between . . . 104.03(d)
Five year fixed note, adjustable thereafter
. . . 104.03(e)
Risks of making . . . 104.03(c)(1)

FLORIDA
Mortgages
Prepayment of . . . 104.05(c)
Usury law exemption for corporate borrowers . . . 104.03(f)(6)
Securities brokers and dealers, regulation of
. . . 103.08(j)
Usury law exemption for corporate borrowers
. . . 104.03(f)(6)

FORECLOSURES
Grace period on late charges, stay of foreclosure during . . . 104.06(c)
Kazakhstan (See KAZAKHSTAN, subhead: Foreclosure)

[References are to sections.]

[References are to sections.]

J

[References are to sections.]

[References are to sections.]

[References are to sections.]

[References are to sections.]

[References are to sections.]

[References are to sections.]

[References are to sections.]

[References are to sections.]

[References are to sections.]

[References are to sections.]

S

SALES AND TRANSFERS OF PROPERTY

SAVINGS BANKS

SECURITIES REGULATION

[References are to sections.]

[References are to sections.]

[References are to sections.]

[References are to sections.]

THOMPSON ON REAL PROPERTY

THIRD THOMAS EDITION

2022 Cumulative Supplement

Volume 13

Place in pocket of bound volume and recycle previous supplement.

QUESTIONS ABOUT THIS PUBLICATION?

For questions about the **Editorial Content** appearing in these volumes or reprint permission, please call:

Jessie Carnevale, Esq. at 212.229.4942
Email: .... jessica.carnevale@lexisnexis.com
Outside the United States and Canada, please call . . . . (973) 820-2000

For assistance with replacement pages, shipments, billing or other customer service matters, please call:

Customer Services Department at . . . . (800) 833-9844
Outside the United States and Canada, please call . . . . (518) 487-3385
Fax Number . . . . (800) 828-8341
Customer Service Website . . . . http://www.lexisnexis.com/custserv/

For information on other Matthew Bender publications, please call

Your account manager or . . . . (800) 223-1940
Outside the United States and Canada, please call . . . . (937) 247-0293

Library of Congress Card Number: 98-85590

ISBN: Fifteen Volume Set 978-1-5583-4156-2 (print)

Cite this publication as:

13 THOMPSON ON REAL PROPERTY, SECOND THOMAS EDITION (David A. Thomas, ed. LexisNexis)

Editorial Office
230 Park Ave., 7th Floor, New York, NY 10169 (800) 543-6862
www.lexisnexis.com

MATTHEW●BENDER

CHAPTER 103

FEDERAL AND STATE SECURITIES REGULATION OF REAL ESTATE TRANSACTIONS

§ 103.02 Brief History of Federal Securities Regulation.

Page 4: Replace footnote 1 with the following:

[1] The Transportation Act of 1920, 41 Stat. 456, 66 Cong. Ch. 91 (Feb. 28, 1920) was referred to as the Esch—Cummins Act. Title III of this Act was repealed in 1926 by the Railway Labor Act, Pub. Law No. 69-257, 44 Stat. 577 (May 20, 1926).

§ 103.03 Real Estate Transactions Subject to Federal Securities Regulation.

§ 103.03(a) Definitions of Securities in Various Real Estate Transactions.

Page 9: Add to footnote 19:

[19] Salameh v. Tarsadia Hotel, 726 F.3d 1124 (9th Cir. 2013) (The court stated that substance governs, not the name or label or form, when determining whether a real estate transaction is a security. The plaintiffs had purchased condominium units in a hotel and had subsequently signed a rental-management agreement. The court held that the plaintiffs had not adequately alleged facts showing that they were offered the real-estate and rental-management contracts as a package. The plaintiffs also failed to allege facts showing that they were induced to buy the condominiums by the rental-management agreement. The court affirmed the dismissal on the pleadings of a putative class action.), *cert. denied*, 571 U.S. 1201 (2014). *See also* Alexander D. Selig, *A Practitioner's Guide to When Real Estate Becomes a Security*, 9 Elon L. Rev. 391, 419–24 (2017) (discussing Salameh v. Tarsadia Hotel and concluding that the Ninth Circuit missed an opportunity to properly apply the Howey test and provide guidance to real estate practitioners.).

§ 103.03(a)(1) Notes.

Page 10: Add to footnote 24:

[24] *See generally* People v. Black, 8 Cal. App. 5th 889 (2017) (This case involved a criminal prosecution under Cal. Corp. Code, §§ 25401, 25540, subd. (b), for false statements in the offer or sale of a security. The court found that the promissory notes offered by the defendant in exchange for an investment in a real estate development scheme were not securities because the investment was a one-to-one transaction, there was no prospectus or indication that the arrangement could have been traded publicly, the agreement bound the defendant's separate property for payment of the notes, and the agreement provided for repayment regardless of whether the deal succeeded.); Roumen Manolov, *Are All Promissory Notes Securities Under Missouri Law?* 68 J. Mo. B. 332 (Nov./Dec. 2012).

§ 103.03(a)(4) Oil, Gas and Other Mineral Rights.

Page 12: The cite for footnote 35 should be 15 U.S.C. § 77b(a)(1).

§ 103.03(a)(5)   Investment Contracts.

Page 13: Add to footnote 41:

[41] *See also* Foxfield Villa Assocs., LLC v. Robben, 967 F.3d 1082, 1090–1100 (10th Cir. 2020) (discussing the Howey test), *cert. denied*, 209 L. Ed. 2d 128 (2021); Living Benefits Asset Mgmt., L.L.C. v. Kestrel Aircraft Co. (*In re* Living Benefits Asset Mgmt., L.L.C.), 916 F.3d 528 (5th Cir. 2019) (discussing the Howey test).

Page 13: Add to footnote 43:

[43] Bamert v. Pulte Home Corp., 445 Fed. Appx. 256 (11th Cir. 2011) (purchase agreement alone did not constitute the transactions as investment contracts, but other circumstances may have constituted the arrangements as investment contracts).

§ 103.03(a)(7)   Equipment Trust Certificates.

Page 16: The cite in footnote 60 should be 15 U.S.C. § 77b(a)(4).

§ 103.03(b)   Real Estate Securities and Transactions Subject to Federal Securities Regulation.

Page 16: Add to footnote 62:

[62] San Francisco Residence Club, Inc. v. Amado, 773 F. Supp. 2d 822 (N.D. Cal. 2011) (real estate investment adviser and developers were subject to the requirements of the Securities Act); United States SEC v. Bravata, 763 F. Supp. 2d 891 (E.D. Mich. 2011) (civil enforcement action by Securities and Exchange Commission against a real estate investment firm); Bradley v. Miller, 96 F. Supp. 3d 753 (S.D. Ohio 2015) (action against a real estate securities Ponzi scheme).

Page 17: Delete COMPUTER-ASSISTED RESEARCH

§ 103.04   How to Comply with Federal Securities Regulation Requirements for Real Estate Transactions.

§ 103.04(a)   Registration of Securities in Real Estate Transactions.

§ 103.04(a)(5)   Summaries of Forms Most Frequently Used in Securities Filings for Real Estate Transactions.

§ 103.04(a)(5)(i)   Summary of Form S-1, Registration Statement Under the Securities Act of 1933.

Page 20: Add a footnote to the sentence that ends in "are contained in 17 C.F.R. Sections 229.10 to .915:

[77.1] The SEC publishes Industry Guides. One of these Guides pertains to the preparation of registration statements relating to interests in real estate limited partnerships. *See* 17 C.F.R. § 229.801(e); Guide 5 found at https://www.sec.gov/files/industryguides.pdf (visited May 23, 2022).

§ 103.04(a)(7)   Registration Exemptions and Alternative Offering Procedures for Real Estate Transactions.

§ 103.04(a)(7)(ii)   Intrastate Issues as Exempted Securities.

Page 27: Add to footnote 106:

[106] The SEC amended Rule 147 and promulgated a new Rule 147A (17 C.F.R. § 230.147A) effective April 20, 2017. The Rule 147 amendments and the new Rule 147A seek to modernize and update the exemption that allows companies to raise money from investors who are located within one state without having to register those securities with the SEC. *See generally* Julius J. Brecht, *New Dance for an Old Shoe—Revised Rule 147 & New Rule 147A*, 41 AK Bar Rag 16 (Summer 2017); Heath DeJean and Dasha Hodge, *Raising Capital for Cheap(er): An Overview of Common Securities Registration Exemptions*, 57 Houston Lawyer 28 (Nov./Dec. 2019).

Page 28: Delete COMPUTER-ASSISTED RESEARCH

§ 103.04(a)(7)(iii)   Small Issues as Exempted Securities (Regulation A).

Page 29: Delete COMPUTER-ASSISTED RESEARCH

§ 103.04(a)(7)(iv)   Certain Fractional Oil and Gas Issues as Exempted Securities (Regulation B).

Page 29: Add to footnote 120:

[120] This Regulation B is no longer a valid exemption. This regulation was enacted in 1963. In 1996, the Task Force on Disclosure Simplification recommended that it be deleted.

Page 30: Delete COMPUTER-ASSISTED RESEARCH

§ 103.04(a)(7)(v)   Transactions by a Non-Issuer as Exempted Transactions.

Page 30: Add to footnote 128:

[128] *See generally* John F. Griffee, IV, *Guide to Structuring Resales of Restricted Securities Held by Control and Non-Control Holders Under Federal and Arkansas Law*, 38 U. Ark. Little Rock L. Rev. 1 (2015).

Page 31: Add to footnote 135:

[135] 17 C.F.R. § 230.144(h)(1) (2021) states in part, "If the amount of securities to be sold in reliance upon this rule during any period of three months exceeds 5,000 shares or other units or has an aggregate sale price in excess of $ 50,000, three copies of a notice on Form 144 (§ 239.144 of this chapter) shall be filed with the Commission."

Page 31: Delete COMPUTER-ASSISTED RESEARCH

§ 103.04(a)(7)(vi)   Private Offerings as Exempted Transactions (Regulation D).

Page 31: In footnote 136, the section number should be 77d(a)(2).

Page 32: Add to footnote 137:

[137] Regulation D is found at 17 C.F.R. § 230.500 *et seq.* (2021). *See generally* Christopher R. Zimmerman, Note, *Accredited Investors: A Need for Increased Protection in Private Offerings*, 114 Nw. U.L. Rev. 507 (2019).

Page 33: Add to footnote 145:

[145] 17 C.F.R. § 230.504 was substantially amended effective January 20, 2017. *See* 81 Fed. Reg. 83494 (Nov. 21, 2016).

Page 33: Add to footnote 146:

[146] 17 C.F.R. § 230.505 was removed effective on May 22, 2017. *See* 81 Fed. Reg. 83494 (Nov. 21, 2016).

Page 33: Delete COMPUTER-ASSISTED RESEARCH

§ 103.04(a)(7)(vii)   Large Sales of Real Estate Mortgage Notes as Exempted Transactions.

Page 33: Add to footnote 150:

[150] This exemption was deleted in 2010 by the Dodd-Frank Wall Street Reform and Consumer Protection Act.

§ 103.04(a)(7)(viii)   Sales to Accredited Investors as Exempted Transactions.

Page 34: In footnote 154, the cite should be 15 U.S.C. § 77d(d).

Page 34: Add to footnote 155:

[155] Regulation D, "Rules Governing the Limited Offer and Sale of Securities Without Registration Under the Securities Act of 1933" is found at 17 C.F.R. §§ 230.500 to 230.508 (2021). The definition of an accredited investor is found in 17 C.F.R. § 230.501(a) (2021). Rule 506(c) allows an exemption from registration if the purchasers of securities in the offering are accredited investors and the company takes reasonable steps to verify that the investors are accredited investors. *See* 17 C.F.R. § 230.506(c) (2021). *See generally* Blake W. Delaplane, *Red, Yellow, or Green Light? Assessing the Past, Present, and Future Implications of the Accredited Investor Definition in Exempt Securities Offerings*, 14 Va. L. & Bus. Rev. 329 (2020); Syed Haq, *Revisiting the Accredited Investor Standard*, 5 Mich. Bus. & Entrepreneurial L. Rev. 59 (2015); Ilon Oliveira, Comment, *Regulation of Rule 506 Private Placements: The Teetering Balance Between Investor Protection and Capital Formation*, 45 Golden Gate U.L. Rev. 287 (2015); Jason A. Tiemeier, Note, *Striking a Balance Between Protecting Investors and Promoting Small Business: The New Rule 506, Accredited Investor Standards, and the Guidelines of General Solicitation*, 10 Ohio St. Bus. L.J. 101 (2015).

§ 103.04(b)   Penalties for Violations of Registration Requirements.

§ 103.04(b)(3)   Summary of the Anti-Fraud Provisions.

Page 36: Add to footnote 167:

[167] United States SEC v. Bravata, 763 F. Supp. 2d 891 (E.D. Mich. 2011) (SEC civil enforcement action against real estate investment firm and others for unauthorized sale of securities and for operating a Ponzi scheme).

Page 39: Add to footnote 200:

[200] In Cyan, Inc. v. Beaver County Employees Retirement Fund, 200 L. Ed. 2d 332, 342 (2018), the Court stated that 15 U.S.C. § 77v(a)'s "except clause" does not deprive state courts of their jurisdiction to decide class actions brought under the Securities Act of 1933.

Page 39: Delete COMPUTER-ASSISTED RESEARCH

§ 103.05   Federal Regulation of Broker-Dealers in Real Estate Transactions.

§ 103.05(a)   Definitions of Securities Brokers and Dealers.

Page 39: Add to footnote 201:

[201] 15 U.S.C. § 78c(a)(4)(A) (2021) defines a broker while § 78c(a)(4)(B) (2021)

provides an exception from the broker definition for certain enumerated banking activities.

Page 40: Add to footnote 202:

202 The current definition of a dealer found at 15 U.S.C. § 78(c)(a)(5)(A) states: "In general. The term "dealer" means any person engaged in the business of buying and selling securities (not including security-based swaps, other than security-based swaps with or for persons that are not eligible contract participants) for such person's own account through a broker or otherwise."

§ 103.05(c)   Summary of Federal Registration Requirements for Securities Brokers and Dealers.

§ 103.05(c)(2)   Conduct That May Lead to Denial, Suspension or Revocation of Applications and Registrations.

Page 44: Delete COMPUTER-ASSISTED RESEARCH

§ 103.05(f)   Rules for Transactions in Penny Stocks.

Page 46: Add to footnote 272:

272 The Penny Stock Reform Act is currently codified, as amended, at 15 U.S.C. § 78o(h)(3). The term "penny stock" is defined in 17 C.F.R. § 240.3a51-1. *See also* SEC v. Abellan, 674 F. Supp. 2d 1213, 1223 (W.D. Wash. 2009) ("Pursuant to 17 C.F.R. § 240.3a51-1, a penny stock must, inter alia, have a value less than $5 per share, not be a national market stock with a market value of listed securities greater than $50 million for 90 consecutive days, and have tangible net assets of less than $2,000,000.").

§ 103.05(g)   The Requirement of Securities Association Membership.

Page 46: Add a footnote to the sentence that ends in "which has been registered by the SEC." This is the footnote text:

273.1 In 2007, the National Association of Securities Dealers, Inc. merged with the New York Stock Exchange's regulation committee to form the Financial Industry Regulatory Authority, Inc. (FINRA). All securities brokers must be licensed by and registered with FINRA. *See* About FINRA, What We Do, https://www.finra.org/about/what-we-do (visited May 23, 2022). FINRA, promulgates rules to enforce broker-dealer compliance with the Exchange Act and FINRA's rules. *See* Scottsdale Capital Advisors Corp. v. Financial Industry Regulatory Authority, 844 F.3d 414, 417 (4th Cir. 2016), *cert. denied*, 197 L. Ed. 2d 761 (2017). *See generally* Yesenia Cervantes, Note, *"FIN RAH!"* . . . *A Welcome Change: Why the Merger Was Necessary to Preserve U.S. Market Integrity*, 13 Fordham J. Corp. & Fin. L. 829 (2008); Christopher W. Cole, Note, *Financial Industry Regulatory Authority (FINRA): Is the Consolidation of NASD and the Regulatory Arm of NYSE a Bull or A Bear for U.S. Capital Markets?*, 76 UMKC L. Rev. 251 (2007); Jonathan W. Evans and Michael S. Edmiston, *Wall Street's Other Cop*, 43 Los Angeles Lawyer 24 (Oct. 2020).

Page 48: Delete COMPUTER-ASSISTED RESEARCH

§ 103.06   The Complementary Relationship of Federal and State Securities Regulation of Real Estate Transactions.

Page 49: Add to footnote 283:

283 HSH Nordbank AG v UBS AG, 941 N.Y.S.2d 59 (App. Div. 2012) (negligent misrepresentation and punitive damages claims by a bank that participated in a credit swap transaction involving real-estate-backed securities).

§ 103.07   State Regulation of Securities Broker-Dealers in Real Estate Transactions.

Page 50: Add a footnote to the sentence that ends with "in each of the states.":

284.1 *See generally* NNN Durham Office Portfolio 1, LLC v. Highwoods Realty Ltd., 820 S.E.2d 322, 327–28 (N.C. Ct. App. 2018) (discussing secondary liability under the North Carolina Securities Act in a case where summary judgment was granted in favor of seller and a real estate company on the purchasers' secondary liability claims).

§ 103.07(a)   "Syndicate" and "Syndication" Defined.

Page 51: Delete COMPUTER-ASSISTED RESEARCH

§ 103.07(b)   Real Estate Investment Syndications as Securities.

Page 53: Delete COMPUTER-ASSISTED RESEARCH

§ 103.08   Summary of State Registration and Licensing Requirements for Securities Brokers and Dealers.

§ 103.08(a)   Alabama.

Page 53: Add to the Fees information for Alabama:

Effective August 1, 2009, these fees were: $250 for a dealer, $60 for an agent, $250 for an investment adviser and $60 for an investment adviser representative. Effective June 1, 2019 the fees will be: $250 for a dealer, $70 for an agent, $250 for an investment adviser and $70 for an investment adviser representative.

§ 103.08(e)   California.

Page 54: Add to the Statutory reference for California:

Cal. Bus. & Prof. Code § 10153.9 was repealed effective Jan. 1, 2007. *See* Stats. 2006 ch. 278 § 5 (AB 2429).

§ 103.08(g)   Connecticut.

Page 54: Add to the Connecticut fees information:

Pursuant to Conn. Gen. Stat. § 36b-12, effective Dec. 1, 2017, the fees were increased to $340 for a broker-dealer registration or an or investment adviser registration and $125 for an agent or investment adviser agent registration.

§ 103.08(h)   Delaware.

Page 54: Add to the Delaware Fees information:

Pursuant to Del. Code tit. 6, § 73-302, the fees are $300 for a broker-dealer, $65 for an agent, $300 for an investment adviser and $65 for an investment adviser representative.

Page 54: Under the Delaware statutory reference, delete the existing cite and replace it with the following:

• Del. Code tit. 6, §§ 73-301 to 73-306.

§ 103.08(i) District of Columbia.

Page 55: In § 103.08(i), change the D.C. statutory reference to:

D.C. Code §§ 31-5602.01 to 31-5602.11.

§ 103.08(j) Florida.

Page 55: In the Florida fees, change $40 for associated persons to $50 for associated persons.

§ 103.08(k) Georgia.

Page 55: In the Georgia statutory reference, change the cites to: O.C.G.A. §§ 10-5-30 to 10-5-41.

§ 103.08(l) Hawaii.

Page 55: In the Hawaii statutory reference delete the second section symbol.

§ 103.08(m) Idaho.

Page 55: In the fees section for Idaho change the fees to $200 for a broker-dealer and $50 for an agent. Add: $150 for an investment adviser; $30 for an investment adviser representative.

Page 55: In the statutory reference for Idaho, change the cite to: Idaho Code § 30-14-410.

§ 103.08(n) Illinois.

Page 56: In § 103.08(n), change the Illinois statutory reference to:

815 ILCS 5/2.7 to 815 ILCS 5/2.10.

§ 103.08(o) Indiana.

Page 56: In § 103.08(o), change the Indiana statutory cite to:

Ind. Code Ann. §§ 23-19-4-1 to 23-19-4-12.

§ 103.08(p) Iowa.

Page 56: In the Iowa fees, change $30 to $40 for agents.

Page 56: In the Iowa statutory reference change the section numbers to 502.401 to 502.412.

§ 103.08(q) Kansas.

Page 56: In the Kansas fees change the $50 for agents to $100 and add the following: $300 for investment advisers; $100 for investment adviser representatives.

Page 56: In the Kansas statutory reference, delete the current cite and replace it with: Kan. Stat. §§ 17-12a401 to 17-12a412.

§ 103.08(s)   Louisiana.

Page 57: In § 103.08(s), change the Louisiana statutory cite to:
La. Rev. Stat. §§ 51:703 and 51:704.

§ 103.08(t)   Maine.

Page 57: In Maine, replace the fees with the following:

A fee not to exceed $500 for a broker-dealer, a fee not to exceed $200 for an agent, a fee not to exceed $500 for an investment adviser, a fee not to exceed $200 for an investment adviser representative.

Page 57: In Maine, delete the statutory reference and replace it with the following:

Me. Rev. Stat. Ann. tit. 32, §§ 16401 to 16412.

§ 103.08(u)   Maryland.

Page 57: In § 103.08(u), change the Maryland statutory cite to:
Md. Corp. & Ass'ns Code Ann. §§ 11-401 to 11-408.

§ 103.08(v)   Massachusetts.

Page 57: For the Massachusetts fees change them to state:

A fee not to exceed $300 for a broker-dealer, a fee not to exceed $50 for an agent, a fee not to exceed $300 for an investment adviser, a fee not to exceed $50 for an investment adviser representative.

§ 103.08(w)   Michigan.

Page 57: In the Michigan fees section, change the fee for broker-dealers to $300 (before Oct. 1, 2019) and $250 (after Sept. 30, 2019) and $65 for agents (before Oct. 1, 2019) and $30 (after Sept. 30, 2019). and add: $200 for investment advisers (before Oct. 1, 2019) and $150 (after Sept. 30, 2019) and $65 for an investment adviser representative (before Oct. 1, 2019) and $30 (after Sept. 30, 2019).

Page 57: In Michigan's statutory reference, delete the current cite and replace it with the following: Mich. Comp. Laws §§ 451.2401 to 451.2413.

§ 103.08(x)   Minnesota.

Page 58: In § 103.08(x), change the Minnesota statutory reference to:
Minn. Stat. §§ 80A.56 to 80A.67

§ 103.08(y)   Mississippi.

Page 58: In the Mississippi statutory reference, change the section numbers to: 75-71-401 to 75-71-413.

§ 103.08(z)   Missouri.

Page 58: Add to the end of the Missouri section in § 103.08(z):

Statutory reference: Mo. Rev. Stat. §§ 409.4-401 to 409.4-412.

§ 103.08(cc)   Nevada.

Page 59: In Nevada, change the fees to the following: $300 for a broker-dealer, $125 for a sales representative, $300 for an investment adviser, and $110 for an investment adviser representative.

§ 103.08(dd)   New Hampshire.

Page 59: In the New Hampshire fees section, change the fees to: $300 for the initial registration of a broker-dealer and $250 for a renewal; $130 for the initial registration of an agent and $100 for a renewal; $250 for the initial registration of an investment adviser and $200 for a renewal; $125 for the initial registration for an investment adviser representative and $100 for a renewal.

Page 59: In the New Hampshire statutory reference, change the section no. to 421-B:4-410.

§ 103.08(ff)   New Mexico.

Page 59: In the New Mexico fees section, change the $35 to $50 and ADD the following: $300 for an investment adviser; $50 for an investment adviser representative.

Page 59: In the New Mexico statutory reference section change the section numbers to 58-13C-401 to 58-13C-412.

§ 103.08(gg)   New York.

Page 59: Change the New York fees to read as follows: $1,200 for brokers and dealers; $1,200 for issuers for offerings over $500,000 and $300 for issuers for offerings under $500,000; $300 for each broker-dealer's statement filed by a person, firm, association or corporation solely for the purpose of selling or offering for sale from or to the public within or from this state securities consisting of condominiums, shares of cooperative apartment corporations or commercial cooperative corporations, interests in homeowners associations or interests in timeshare projects, plus $15 for each partner, officer, director or principal of any such firm, association or corporation; $150 for salespersons.

§ 103.08(hh)   North Carolina.

Page 60: In the North Carolina fees, change $200 to $300 and change $55 to $125.

§ 103.08(jj)   Ohio.

Page 60: In the Ohio fees section, delete the existing material and replace it with: The fee for each dealer's license, and for each annual renewal is $200. The fee for each salesperson's license, and for each annual renewal is $60. The fee for each investment adviser's license, and for each annual renewal $100. The fee for each investment adviser representative's license, *and for each annual renewal is $35.*

§ 103.08(kk)   Oklahoma.

Page 60: In the Oklahoma fees section, delete the existing material and replace it with: Fees are addressed in Okl. St. tit. 71 § 1-612.

Page 60: In § 103.08(kk), change the Oklahoma statutory reference to: 71 Okl. St. §§ 1-401 to 1-411.

§ 103.08(ll)   Oregon.

Page 60: In the Oregon fees section, delete the existing material and replace it with the following:

Fees: Or. Rev. Stat. § 59.175(10) directs the director to set the fees "in an amount that the director determines is equal as nearly as possible to the national midpoint for similar fees charged by all other state regulatory agencies within the United States responsible for regulating securities."

§ 103.08(mm)   Pennsylvania.

Page 61: In the Pennsylvania fees section, delete the existing material and replace it with the following:

Fees: 70 P.S. § 1-602(d.1) states that an applicant for an initial or renewal license shall pay a filing fee of $350 for a broker-dealer, $80 for an agent, $275 for an investment adviser and $80 for an investment adviser representative.

§ 103.08(nn)   Rhode Island.

Page 61: For the Rhode Island fee section, delete the existing material and replace it with:

Fees: $300 for a broker dealer and $100 for each branch office; $75 for a sales representative; $300 for an investment adviser; and $60 for an investment adviser representative.

§ 103.08(oo)   South Carolina.

Page 61: For the South Carolina fees, change this information to state:

Fees: Pursuant to S.C. Code Ann. § 35-1-410(a), the Commissioner establishes the fees by rule or order.

Page 61: In the South Carolina statutory reference, change the cite to S.C. Code Ann. §§ 35-1-401 to 35-1-412.

§ 103.08(pp)   South Dakota.

Page 61: In the South Dakota fees, add the following: $100 for investment advisers; $50 for investment adviser representatives.

Page 61: In the South Dakota statutory reference, change the cite to: S.D. Codified Laws §§ 47-31B-401 to 47-31B-412.

§ 103.08(qq)   Tennessee.

Page 61: In the Tennessee fees add the following:

$200 for an investment adviser; and $50 for an investment adviser representative.

Page 61: In the Tennessee statutory reference, change the cite to:

Tenn. Code Ann. §§ 48-1-109 & 48-1-110.

§ 103.08(rr)   Texas.

Page 62: In the Texas fees, delete the existing material and replace it with:

Fees: A fee not to exceed $100 for the filing of the original application or a renewal for a dealer or an investment adviser; a fee not to exceed $100 for the filing of an original application or a renewal for an agent or an investment adviser representative.

Page 62: In § 103.08(rr), change the Texas statutory reference to:

Tex. Rev. Civ. Stat. Art. 581-12, *et seq.*

§ 103.08(ss)   Utah.

Page 62: In the Utah fees, delete the present material and replace it with:

Utah Code Ann. § 61-1-18.4 addresses fees but does not specify amounts.

Page 62: In the Utah statutory reference change the section numbers with 61-1-3 & 61-1-4.

§ 103.08(tt)   Vermont.

Page 62: Delete the current Vermont fees material and replace it with: Pursuant to 9 Vt. Stat. Ann. § 5410, the fees are:

$300 for a broker-dealer, $120 per branch office, $90 for an agent, $300 for an investment adviser, $120 per branch office, and $80 for an investment adviser representative.

Page 62: Delete the current material in the Vermont statutory reference and replace it with: 9 Vt. Stat. Ann. §§ 5401 to 5404.

§ 103.08(uu)   Virginia.

Page 62: In the Virginia fees, delete "$30 for agents, initial and renewal" and add:

a fee of not less than $30 nor more than $50 for an agent, initial or renewal; $200 for an investment adviser, initial or renewal; a fee of not less than $30 nor more than $50 for an investment adviser representative, initial or renewal.

§ 103.08(vv)   Washington.

Page 62: In the Washington fees section, delete the existing material and replace it with:

Pursuant to Rev. Code Wash. § 21.20.340(6) and (7), effective June 7, 2018, the fees are: $150 for the original registration of a broker-dealer or investment adviser and $75 for annual renewals; $40 for the original registration of an agent or investment adviser representative an $20 for annual renewal.

Page 62: In § 103.08(vv), change the Washington statutory reference to:

Rev. Code Wash. §§ 21.20.040 to 21.20.135

§ 103.08(ww)   West Virginia.

Page 63: In the West Virginia fees section, delete the existing material and replace it with:

$300 for broker-dealer and the agent of an issuer initial or renewal registration; $66 for an agent; $200 for an investment adviser; and $75 for each investment adviser representative.

§ 103.08(xx)   Wisconsin.

Page 63: In the Wisconsin fees section delete the existing material and replace it with:

Pursuant to Wis. Stat. § 551.614(2), the fees generally are $200 for both the initial registration and renewal of broker-dealers and investment advisers; $80 for an agent representing a broker-dealer or issuer or an investment adviser representative.

Page 63: In § 103.08(xx), change the Wisconsin statutory reference to:

Wis. Stat. §§ 551.401 to 551.412.

§ 103.08(yy)   Wyoming.

Page 63: In the Wyoming fees, change $35 to $45 and add the following:

$250 for an investment adviser; $45 for an investment adviser representative.

Page 63: In Wyoming statutory reference, delete the existing cite and replace it with:

Wyo. Stat. Stat. §§ 17-4-401 to 17-4-412.

Page 94: Add new section § 103.10 Bibliography. after end of Appendix 4 Form S-11.:

§ 103.10   Bibliography.

Books

Fabozzi, Frank J. and John N. Dunlevy, Real Estate-Backed Securities (John Wiley & Sons, Inc. 2001).

Levine, Mark Lee and Philip Feigin, *Real Estate Securities: Syndicating Real Estate* (Professional Publications & Education, Inc. 2020).

Sommer, A.A., Jr., *Federal Securities Act of 1933* (Matthew Bender).

Sommer, A.A., Jr., *Federal Securities Exchange Act of 1934* (Matthew Bender).

Articles

Affleck, Michael P., Note, "Shares of Water Stock in Utah: Personal Property or Real Estate?" 21 *Utah L. Rev.* 211 (2021).

Al-Alami, Leen, "Business Roundtable v. SEC: Rising Judicial Mistrust and the Onset of a New Era in Judicial Review of Securities Regulation," 15 *U. Pa. J. Bus. L.* 541 (2013).

"Annual Review of Federal Securities Regulation," 70 *Bus. Law.* 835 (2015).

Behar, Rachel, Note, "EB-5 Visa Regulation and Controversy: How an Immigration-Securities Hybrid Visa Has Been Used to Fund Real Estate Ventures," 2 *Cardozo J. Int'l & Comp. L.* 184 (2018).

Berdejo, Carlos, "Small Investments, Big Losses: The States' Role In Protecting Local Investors From Securities Fraud," 92 *Wash. L. Rev.* 567 (2016).

Booth, Samantha, "Here Comes the Sun: How Securities Regulations Cast a Shadow on the Growth of Community Solar in the United States," 61 *UCLA L. Rev.* 760 (2014).

Bratton, William W. and Adam J. Levitin, "A Tale of Two Markets: Regulation and Innovation in Post-Crisis Mortgage and Structured Finance Markets," 20 *U. Ill. L. Rev.* 47 (2020).

Brecht, Julius J., "New Dance for an Old Shoe—Revised Rule 147 & New Rule 147A," 41 *AK Bar Rag* 16 (Summer 2017).

Brockmeyer, Neal, H., "Regulation of Securities Offerings in California: Is It Time for a Change After a Century of Merit Regulation?" 54 *Loy. L.A. L. Rev.* 1 (2020).

Brummer, Chris, "Disruptive Technology and Securities Regulation," 84 *Fordham L. Rev.* 977 (2015).

Campbell, Rutheford B., Jr., "The Role of Blue Sky Laws After NSMIA and the JOBS Act," 66 *Duke L.J.* 605 (2016).

Chrisman, Rodney D., "Toward a Christian Worldview of Securities Regulation," 9 *Liberty U. L. Rev.* 467 (2015).

Cowan, Robert K., "Time for Plan(et) B? Why Securities Litigation Is a Misguided Attempt at Regulating Climate Change," 33 *Geo. Envtl. L. Rev.* 333 (2021).

Cox, James D., "Iterative Regulation of Securities Markets After Business Roundtable: A Principles-Based Approach," 78 *Law & Contemp. Probs.* 25 (2015).

Chung, Christine Sgarlata, "The Devil You Know: A Survey Examining How Retail Investors Seek Out & Use Financial Information and Investment Advice," 37 *Rev. Banking & Fin. L.* 653 (2018).

Culpepper, Clinton, "Establishing an Executive Agreement to Permit Regulation A Securities and Avoid the Fraudulent Activities Associated with Their Secondary Transfers," 31 *Rev. Litig.* 661 (Summer 2012).

DeJean, Heath and Dasha Hodge, "Raising Capital for Cheap(er): An Overview of Common Securities Registration Exemptions," 57 *Houston Lawyer* 28 (Nov./Dec. 2019).

Delaplane, Blake W., "Red, Yellow, or Green Light? Assessing the Past, Present, and Future Implications of the Accredited Investor Definition in Exempt Securities Offerings," 14 *Va. L. & Bus. Rev.* 329 (2020).

Eldar, Ofer & Andrew Verstein, "The Enduring Distinction Between Business Entities and Security Interests," 92 *S. Cal. L. Rev.* 213 (2019).

Evans, Jonathan W. and Michael S. Edmiston, "Wall Street's Other Cop," 43 *Los Angeles Lawyer* 24 (Oct. 2020).

Fedderke, Johannes W., "Do Conservative Justices Favor Wall Street? Ideology and the Supreme Court's Securities Regulation Decisions," 67 *Fla. L. Rev.* 1211 (2015).

Griffee, John F., IV, "Guide to Structuring Resales of Restricted Securities Held by Control and Non-Control Holders Under Federal and Arkansas Law," 38 *U. Ark. Little Rock L. Rev.* 1 (2015).

Haq, Syed, "Revisiting the Accredited Investor Standard," 5 *Mich. Bus. & Entrepreneurial L. Rev.* 59 (2015).

Hunt, Thomas D., "Securitization of Our Nation's Forests: Legal and Practical Implications of the Timber REIT Phenomenon," 34 *J. Tax'n Inv.* 47 (2017).

Jennings, Andrew K., "State Securities Enforcement," 47 *B.Y.U.L. Rev.* 67 (2021).

Lee, Yoon-Ho Alex, "The Efficiency Criterion for Securities Regulation: Investor Welfare or Total Surplus?" 57 *Ariz. L. Rev.* 85 (2015).

Manolov, Roumen, "Are All Promissory Notes Securities Under Missouri Law?" 68 *J. Mo. B.* 332 (December, 2012).

Martin, Jena, "Changing the Rules of the Game: Beyond a Disclosure Framework for Securities Regulation," 118 *W. Va. L. Rev.* 59 (2015).

Molk, Peter, "Protecting LLC Owners While Preserving LLC Flexibility," 51 *U.C. Davis L. Rev.* 2129 (2018).

North, Erik, "The Language of Loans: Distilling Real Estate Financing Jargon into Everyday Plain English Is the True Sign of Expert Conversance, i.e., 'Know Your Audience'," 41 *Los Angeles Lawyer* 32 (Jan. 2019).

Oliveira, Ilon, Comment, "Regulation of Rule 506 Private Placements: The Teetering Balance Between Investor Protection and Capital Formation," 45 *Golden Gate U.L. Rev.* 287 (2015).

Pino, Laurence J. and Sean M. Southard, "Turnkey Real Estate Investments as Securities," 95 *Fla. Bar J.* 29 (Jul./Aug. 2021).

Rotunda, Joseph J., and Mogey Lovelle, "From Stocks and Bonds Through Betting on Death the Applicability of Securities Laws and the Regulation of New and Creative Investments," 59 *The Advoc. (Texas)* 58 (Summer, 2012).

"Securities Regulation—Consent Decrees—Second Circuit Clarifies That a Court's Review of an SEC Settlement Should Focus on Procedural Propriety.—SEC v. Citigroup Global Markets, Inc., 752 F.3d 285 (2d Cir. 2014)." 128 *Harv. L. Rev.* 1288 (2015).

"Securities Regulation—Dodd-Frank Wall Street Reform and Consumer Protection Act—SEC Finalizes Regulations Requiring Companies to Disclose Pay Ratio Between the CEO and Meian Employee.—Pay Ratio Disclosure, 80

Fed. Reg. 50, 104 (Aug. 18, 2015) (to be Codified at 17 C.F.R. Pts. 229, 240, 249)," 129 *Harv. L. Rev.* 1144 (2016).

Selig, Alexander D., "A Practitioner's Guide to When Real Estate Becomes a Security," 9 *Elon L. Rev.* 391 (2017).

Shobe, Gladriel, "The Substance over Form Doctrine and the UP-C," 38 *Va. Tax Rev.* 249 (2018).

Simkovic, Michael, "Competition and Crisis in Mortgage Securitization," 88 *Ind. L.J.* 213 (Winter, 2013).

Spaulding, Arthur O., Jr., Karen D. Dennison, and Robert S. Freedman, "Federal and State Regulation of Timeshares and Fractional Interests," 36 *Probate & Property* 49 (May/June 2022).

Tiemeier, Jason A., Note, "Striking a Balance Between Protecting Investors and Promoting Small Business: The New Rule 506, Accredited Investor Standards, and the Guidelines of General Solicitation," 10 *Ohio St. Bus. L.J.* 101 (2015).

Tucker, Devon, Note & Comment, "Not All Securitizations Are Equal: Risk Retention for Commercial Mortgage-Backed Securitization in an Era of Deregulation," 23 N.C. Banking Inst. 295 (2019).

Zimmerman, Christopher R., Note, *Accredited Investors: A Need for Increased Protection in Private Offerings*, 114 Nw. U.L. Rev. 507 (2019).

CHAPTER 104

THE PROMISSORY NOTE IN REAL ESTATE TRANSACTIONS

§ 104.01   Note Formalities.

§ 104.01(a)   The Difference Between the Note and the Deed of Trust.

Page 99: Add a footnote to the phrase "deeds of trust":

[1.1] *See* Tennessee State Bank v. Mashek, 616 S.W.3d 777, 794–95 (Tenn. Ct. App. 2020) (A deed of trust secures a debt with real property. The debt is typically evidenced by a promissory note that is a negotiable instrument governed by Uniform Commercial Code Article 3. Deeds of trust are not, in and of themselves, negotiable instruments.); Centrum Financial Services, Inc. v. Union Bank, NA, 406 P.3d 1192, 1197 (Wash. Ct. App. 2017) (A statutory deed of trust is a three-party transaction. The borrower is the grantor of the deed of trust. The lender is the beneficiary. The trustee holds title in trust for the lender as security for a loan.).

Page 99: Add a footnote to the second sentence of the second paragraph of subsection 104.01(a):

[1.2] *See, e.g.,* OneWest Bank, FSB v. Erickson, 367 P.3d 1063, 1078 n. 14 (Wash. 2016).

Page 99: Add to footnote 2:

[2] DuPree v. Sun Trust Bank, 699 S.E.2d 846 (Ga. App. 2010) (lender could sue on the note without being required to foreclose on the collateral).

Page 100: Add to footnote 5:

[5] *See also* West Sunset 2050 Trust v. Nationstar Mortg., LLC, 420 P.3d 1032, 1036 (Nev. 2018) (To have standing to foreclose, the current beneficiary of the deed of trust and the current holder of the promissory note must be the same.); HSBC Bank USA v. Wiles, 468 P.3d 922, 925 (N.M. Ct. App. 2020) (The foreclosing party must demonstrate that when it filed its foreclosure action, it either (1) had physical possession of the promissory note indorsed to it or indorsed in blank or (2) received the note with the right to enforcement, as required by the Uniform Commercial Code.).

Page 100: Add at the end of footnote 6:

[6] ; State ex rel. U. S. Bank N.A. v. McGraw, 769 S.E.2d 476 (W. Va. 2015) (an assignment of a trust deed securing the payment of a promissory note for the purchase of real property is not required under state law to be recorded).

Page 100: Add to footnote 7:

[7] Estes v. McKinney, 354 S.W.3d 144 (Ky. App. 2011) (payment on note discharged the debt under the doctrine of accord and satisfaction).

§ 104.01(b)   Contents of the Note and the Deed of Trust.

Page 100: Add as the final paragraph of subsection 104.01(b):

Promissory notes are contracts that are construed using the rules of contract construction.[8.1] A lender has the right to sue on the note rather than pursuing a foreclosure of the mortgage or deed of trust.[8.2] An action on the note is an in personam action while a foreclosure is an in rem action.[8.3] The note holder can also pursue both remedies at the same time, but will be entitled to only one recovery.

[8.1] *See, e.g.*, FV-I, Inc. v. Kallevig, 392 P.3d 1248, 1256 (Kan. 2017); JPMorgan Chase & Co. v. Casarano, 963 N.E.2d 108, 111 (Mass. Ct. App. 2012); Dovi Interests, Ltd. v. Somerset Point Ltd. P'ship, 2003 Ohio App. LEXIS 3537, *8; Stacey Properties v. Wixen, 766 P.2d 1080 (Utah Ct. App. 1988).

[8.2] *See* Competition Marine of MS, Inc. v. Whitney Bank, 220 So. 3d 1019, 1022 (Miss. Ct. App. 2017).

[8.3] *See* Competition Marine of MS, Inc. v. Whitney Bank, 220 So. 3d 1019, 1022 (Miss. Ct. App. 2017).

§ 104.02   How Much to Borrow.

§ 104.02(a)   Underwriting Standards; Qualifying the Borrower.

Page 103: Add to footnote 21:

[21] *See* Patricia A. Mccoy & Susan M. Wachter, *Why the Ability-to-Repay Rule Is Vital to Financial Stability*, 108 Geo. L.J. 649 (2020) (Professors McCoy and Watcher discuss the risks of lax mortgage underwriting and assert that an ability-to-repay rule will help prevent poorly underwritten loans from creating another bubble in housing prices and the risk of financial collapse.).

§ 104.02(a)(2)   Filing False Loan Applications.

Page 105: Add to footnote 24:

[24] CoreLogic® reported that through the second quarter of 2020, an estimated one in 164 mortgage applications, or 0.6% of applications, contained indications of fraud, compared with the reported one in 123 mortgages, or 0.8% in the second quarter of 2019. Press Release, "CoreLogic Reports A 26.3% Year-Over-Year Decrease in Mortgage Fraud Risk in Second Quarter of 2020" (Oct. 28, 2020). *See generally* Matthew A. Edwards, *The Concept and Federal Crime of Mortgage Fraud*, 57 Am. Crim. L. Rev. 57, 62–69 (2020) (discussing the relaxation of underwriting criteria and the increase in "liar's loans").

Page 105: Add to footnote 26:

[26] Since there is no specific "mortgage fraud" statute in the U.S. Code, federal prosecutors rely on other provisions such as: 18 U.S.C. § 371 (conspiracy to defraud the U.S.); 18 U.S.C. § 1341 (mail fraud); 18 U.SC. § 1343 (wire fraud); 18 U.S.C. § 1344 (bank fraud); 18 U.S.C. § 1349 (conspiracy to commit mail, wire, or bank fraud); and 18 U.S.C. § 1956(a) (money laundering). *See* Daniel B. Mestaz, *Building a Mortgage Fraud Defense*, 47 AZ Attorney 18, 21–22 (Jan. 2011).

§ 104.02(c)   Where Homebuyers Go for Financing.

Page 112: Change "basic" to "basis."

§ 104.02(d)   Is There Mortgage Broker or Lender Liability for Aggressive Loans? Fiduciary Duty Contrasted with Duty to Counsel.

Page 115: Add to footnote 40:

[40] *See generally* Tracie R. Porter, *The Field Between Lions and Zebras . . . Evening the Playing Field Between Lenders and Borrowers: Conflicts of Interest and Legal Obligations in the Residential Mortgage Transaction*, 30 Quinnipiac L. Rev. 623 (2012) (Professor Porter discusses the problems caused by a lender's lack of any legal obligation to its borrowers. She proposes combining fiduciary law with suitability in a manner to force lenders and borrowers to behave responsibly in residential mortgage transactions.).

§ 104.03   The Rate of Interest and Monthly Payment Levels.

§ 104.03(c)   Fixed vs. Adjustable Rate Mortgages (F.R.M.s vs. A.R.M.s).

§ 104.03(c)(1)   The Rationale for A.R.M.s.

Page 120: Add to footnote 47:

[47] *See generally* Todd Zywicki, *The Behavioral Law and Economics of Fixed-Rate Mortgages (and Other Just-So Stories)*, 21 S. Ct. Econ. Rev. 157, 209–11 (2013) (discussing teaser rates).

§ 104.03(c)(2)   Truth-in-Lending.

Page 121: Change "fo" to "of."

[49] of

Page 121: Change "fo" to "of."

of

Page 121: Add the missing "t" to "statute."

statute

Page 121: Add to the end of the first paragraph of subsection 104.03(c)(2):

Effective July 21, 2011, the rule-making authority under the Truth in Lending Act was transferred to the Consumer Financial Protection Bureau.[49.1] Under the Bureau's authority, the Truth in Lending regulation referred to as "Regulation Z," is found at 12 C.F.R. Part 1026.

[49.1] *See* 12 U.S.C. § 5581.

Page 121: Add to footnote 51:

[51] ; U.S. Bank Nat'l Ass'n v. Dumas, 144 So. 3d 29, 38–39 (La.App. 1 Cir. 2014) (the Truth-in-Lending Act did not prohibit the bank from enforcing a promissory note and mortgage by executory process).

§ 104.03(c)(3)   Computing the Rate; Choosing the Index.

Page 123: Add to footnote 60:

[60] Pursuant to the Dodd-Frank Wall Street Reform and Consumer Protection Act, the Office of Thrift Supervision (OTS) ceased to exist. *See* Pub. Law No. 111-203, § 312, 124 Stat. 1376, 1521 (July 21, 2010). OTS merged with the Office of the Comptroller of the Currency on July 21, 2011. See https://www.occ.treas.gov/news-events/newsroom/news-issuances-by-year/ots-issuances/index-ots-issuances.html (visited May 26, 2021).

Page 123: Add to footnote 61:

[61] *See generally* Christopher J. Click, Note & Comment, *Death of a Benchmark: The Fall of LIBOR and the Rise of Alternative Rates in the United Kingdom and United States*, 22 N.C. Banking Inst. 283 (2018); Gary A. Goodman and Alice F. Yurke, *The Death of LIBOR and the Afterlife*, 34 Probate & Property 9 (Jan./Feb. 2020); Michael R. Koblenz, Kenneth M. Labbate, and Carrie C. Turner, *LIBOR: Everything You Ever Wanted to Know But Were Afraid to Ask*, 6 J. Bus. Entrepreneurship & L. 281 (2013); Alec Foote Mitchell, Note, *LIBOR: The World's Most Important Headache*, 105 Minn. L. Rev. 1485 (2021); John Michael Neubert, Note, *LIBOR Phaseout: Litigation Is Coming*, 10 Mich. Bus. & Entrepreneurial L. Rev. 113 (2020).

§ 104.03(f)   Usury Laws.

§ 104.03(f)(3)   The Federal Preemption of State Usury Laws.

Page 133: In footnote 75, change 1735-5 to 1735f-7a. There is no parenthesis in this section number.

Page 133: In footnote 76, change 1735-5 to 1735f-7a. There is no parenthesis in this section number.

§ 104.03(f)(4)   The Four Elements Necessary to Establish Usury Under State Law.

§ 104.03(f)(4)(ii)   What Is "Interest"?

Page 141: Add the missing "s" to result.

§ 104.03(f)(6)   The Corporate Borrower Exemption.

Page 146: Add to footnote 112: 12 C.F.R. § 7.7310 was removed and redesignated as 12 C.F.R. § 7.4001.

§ 104.05 Prepayment.

§ 104.05(b) Why Lenders Care About Prepayments.

§ 104.05(b)(5) Keeping the Premium and Avoiding the Discount Caused by Rate Fluctuations.

Page 154: Add as the second sentence of subsection 104.05(b)(5):

Some commercial lenders use lock-out provisions which prevent a borrower's prepayment of the loan for a certain term.[135.1]

[135.1] *See* BKCAP, LLC v. Captec Franchise Trust 2000–1, 2011 U.S. Dist. LEXIS 80557, *7 (N.D. Ind.); Adam J. Levitin and Susan M. Wachter, *The Commercial Real Estate Bubble*, 3 Harv. Bus. L. Rev. 83, 91 (2013).

§ 104.05(c) Prepayment: A Right or a Privilege.

Page 158: Add to the end of footnote 152:

[152] (1983).

Page 158: Add to the end of footnote 153:

[153] (1984).

Page 158: Delete the second section number of 234.37(b).

§ 104.05(d) Prepayment Charges: Is the Sky the Limit?

§ 104.05(d)(6) Yield Maintenance Fees.

Page 164: Add to footnote 166:

[166] *See* River East Plaza, L.L.C. v. Variable Annuity Life Ins. Co., 498 F.3d 718 (7th Cir. 2007) (upholding a yield maintenance prepayment clause). *See generally* Megan W. Murray, Note, *Prepayment Premiums: Contracting for Future Financial Stability in the Commercial Lending Market*, 96 Iowa L. Rev. 1037 (2011).

§ 104.06 Late Payments.

§ 104.06(d) Acceleration on Default.

Page 172: Add to footnote 189:

[189] *See generally* Eric A. Zacks & Dustin A. Zacks, *No Brakes: Loan Acceleration and Diminishing Foreclosure Defenses*, 18 Wake Forest J. Bus. & Intell. Prop. L. 389 (2018).

§ 104.08 Restrictions on the Borrower's Right to Assign or Borrow.

§ 104.08(a) Due-on-Sale.

§ 104.08(a)(1) The Difference Between Due-on-Sale Clauses and Prohibitions Against Sale.

Page 177: Delete the case number in footnote 222 and replace the LEXIS cite with: 80 S.W.3d 601

§ 104.08(a)(5)　Why Due-on-Sale Clauses Are Optional, Not Automatic.

Page 179: Remove the extra "n" in alienate.

[228] alienate

§ 104.10　Secondary Markets and Negotiability.

§ 104.10(b)　Negotiability.

§ 104.10(b)(1)　The Implications of Negotiability.

Page 196: Add a footnote to the second sentence of subsection 104.10(b)(1):

[263.1] *Cf.* Kalnoki v. First American Trustee Servicing Solutions, LLC, 8 Cal. App. 5th 23, 48 (2017) (A borrower must anticipate that a promissory note might be transferred to another creditor since it is a negotiable instrument.).

Page 210: Add a new subsection 104.10(b)(7):

§ 104.10(b)(7)　Financial Technology Firms (Fintech).

Financial technology firms (fintech firms) engage in fintech lending which has been referred to as "online marketplace lending" and defined as "lending through digital platforms that often collect and base lending decisions on nontraditional data sources."[314] Underwriting by fintech lenders "is typically automated and may employ nontraditional credit algorithms."[315] Fintech lenders use electronic note or e-notes rather than the traditional paper promissory note. Such e-notes are secured by a mortgage or deed of trust when the loan is secured by real estate. Should such a loan go into default, the fintech lender can pursue foreclosure in the same manner as the traditional mortgage lender. A borrower's complaints based on the fact that an e-note was used should not affect the foreclosure process.[316] Traditional mortgage lenders are also using e-notes. The use of e-notes has expedited the lending process and the sale of these loans to secondary mortgage market entities.

[314] Vincent DiLorenzo, *Fintech Lending: A Study of Expectations Versus Market Outcomes*, 38 Rev. Banking & Fin. L. 725, 726 (2019). *See generally* Christopher K. Odinet, *Predatory Fintech and the Politics of Banking*, 106 Iowa L. Rev. 1739 (2021); Christopher K. Odinet, *Securitizing Digital Debts*, 52 Ariz. St. L.J. 477 (2020).

[315] *Id.*

[316] *See, e.g.*, Rivera v. Wells Fargo Bank, N.A., 189 So. 3d 323, 329 (Fla. Dist. Ct. App. 2016) (foreclosure action was based on an electronic note (e-note) executed by the borrowers).

§ 104.11　Bibliography.

Books

Page 210: Add to Books:

Floyd, Michael D., *Mastering Negotiable Instruments (UCC Articles 3 and 4) and Other Payment Systems* (Carolina Academic Press 2nd ed. 2017).

Gerding, Erik, ed., *Negotiable Instruments Under the U.C.C.* (Matthew Bender).

Huggard, John P., *Negotiable Instruments Law: A Detailed Explanation of Article 3 of the Uniform Commercial Code* (Carolina Academic Press 2019).

Veltri, Stephen C., *The ABCs of the UCC: Article 3: Negotiable Instruments and Article 4: Bank Deposits and Collections and Other Modern Payment Systems* (American Bar Association 3d ed. 2015).

Articles

Page 210: Add to Articles:

Banich, Terence G., "Bank Did Not Have Standing to Foreclose Mortgage Because It Did Not Demonstrate When It Took Possession of Borrower's Promissory Note," 131 *Banking L.J.* 637 (July/August, 2014).

Baumeister, Heather M., Note, "Old Dogs Won't Adopt New Tricks, But Continue to Befuddle Their Own: New York's Antiquated UCC Article 3 and the Ambiguity of Assignment Requirements in Mortgage Foreclosure Actions," 82 *Alb. L. Rev.* 267 (2018/2019).

Brummer, Chris and Yesha Yadav, "Fintech and the Innovation Trilemma," 107 *Geo. L.J.* 235 (2019).

Carson, Darren R., "Internal Revenue Code Section 453: 'Monetizing' The Tax Deferred Installment Sale of Farmland and Farm Commodities," 52 *Creighton L. Rev.* 153 (2019).

Click, Christopher J. Click, Note & Comment, "Death of a Benchmark: The Fall of LIBOR and the Rise of Alternative Rates in the United Kingdom and United States," 22 *N.C. Banking Inst.* 283 (2018).

DiLorenzo, Vincent, "Fintech Lending: A Study of Expectations Versus Market Outcomes," 38 *Rev. Banking & Fin. L.* 725 (2019).

Goodman, Gary A. and Alice F. Yurke, "The Death of LIBOR and the Afterlife," 34 *Probate & Property* 9 (Jan./Feb. 2020).

Harrell, Alvin C., "Update on Promissory Notes, Checks, Bank Deposits and Collections," 68 *Consumer Fin. L.Q. Rep.* 130 (2014).

Heekin, M. Mark, "Modernizing Mortgage Foreclosure Law: A Call for Transparency and an End to the Payment Rule," 33 *Quinnipiac L. Rev.* 165 (2014).

Heekin, M. Mark, "A National Mortgage Notes Registry: America's Immense Need for Transparency and Certainty in Mortgage Ownership and the Right to Foreclose," 17 *J. Bus. & Sec. L.* 67 (2016).

Hunt, John Patrick, "Should the Mortgage Follow the Note?," 75 *Ohio St. L.J.* 155 (2014).

Koblenz, Michael R., Kenneth M. Labbate, and Carrie C. Turner, "LIBOR: Everything You Ever Wanted to Know But Were Afraid to Ask," 6 *J. Bus. Entrepreneurship & L.* 281 (2013).

Levitin, Adam J. & Susan M. Wachter, "The Commercial Real Estate Bubble," 3 *Harv. Bus. L. Rev.* 83, 91 (2013).

Magnuson, William, "Regulating Fintech," 71 *Vand. L. Rev.* 1167 (2018).

Manolov, Roumen, "Are All Promissory Notes Securities Under Missouri Law?" 68 *J. Mo. B.* 332 (December, 2012).

Mestaz, Daniel B., "Building a Mortgage Fraud Defense," 47 *AZ Attorney* 18 (Jan. 2011).

Mitchell, Alec Foote, Note, "LIBOR: The World's Most Important Headache," 105 *Minn. L. Rev.* 1485 (2021).

Murphy, J. Parker, Student Article, "More Sense Than Money: National Charter Option for Fintech Firms Is the Right Choice," 18 *N.C. J.L. & Tech. On.* 359 (2017).

Murray, Megan W., Note, "Prepayment Premiums: Contracting for Future Financial Stability in the Commercial Lending Market," 96 *Iowa L. Rev.* 1037 (2011).

Neubert, John Michael, Note, "LIBOR Phaseout: Litigation Is Coming," 10 *Mich. Bus. & Entrepreneurial L. Rev.* 113 (2020).

Odinet, Christopher K., "Predatory Fintech and the Politics of Banking," 106 *Iowa L. Rev.* 1739 (2021).

Odinet, Christopher K., "Securitizing Digital Debts," 52 *Ariz. St. L.J.* 477 (2020).

Oppenheim, Roy D. and Jacquelyn K. Trask-Rahn, "The Emperor's New Clothes: How the Judicial System and the Housing-Mortgage Market Have Turned a Blind Eye to the Destruction of the Negotiability of Mortgage Promissory Notes," 6 *Wm. & Mary Bus. L. Rev.* 557 (2015).

"Sale of Land Purchasers' Promissory Notes to Investors—Notes Secured by Mortgage—Sale of 'Securities,' " *Fed. Sec. L. Rep.* ¶ 21,183.325 (CCH, 2015).

"Sale of Land Purchasers' Promissory Notes to Investors—Notes Secured by Mortgages—Sale of 'Securities,' " *Fed. Sec. L. Rep.* ¶ 1071.545 (CCH, 2016).

Schneider, Stephanie, Note, "Deceleration: Slowing Down to Determine an Accelerated Loan's Post Dismissal Status," 49 *N.M.L. Rev.* 149 (2019).

"Selling Promissory Notes Secured by Real Estate," *Fed. Sec. L. Rep.* ¶ 25,009.17 (CCH, 2016).

Wayte, Alan, "Promissory Note Sample," SS047 ALI-ABA 43 (April 14–15, 2011).

Weinstein, Morgan L., "The Non-Uniform Commercial Code: The Creeping, Problematic Application of Article 9 to Determine Outcomes in Foreclosure Cases," 14 *U.N.H. L. Rev.* 267 (2016).

Whaley, Douglas J., "Mortgage Foreclosures, Promissory Notes, and the Uniform Commercial Code," 39 *W. St. U. L. Rev.* 313 (Spring, 2012).

Willenzik, Davis S., "Louisiana Future Advance Mortgages: A 20-Year Retrospective," 75 *La. L. Rev.* 613 (2015).

Zacks, Eric A. & Dustin A. Zacks, "No Brakes: Loan Acceleration and Diminishing Foreclosure Defenses," 18 *Wake Forest J. Bus. & Intell. Prop. L.* 389 (2018).

Annotations

Page 210: Add to Annotations:

Annotation, Admissibility of Oral or Extrinsic Evidence on Question of Liability on Bill of Exchange, Promissory Note, or Other Contract Where Signature Is Followed by Word or Abbreviation Which May be Either Descriptive or Indicative of Contracting Character, 113 A.L.R. 1364.

CHAPTER 105

ALTERNATIVE DISPUTE RESOLUTION IN REAL PROPERTY MATTERS

§ 105.01 Introduction.

Page 214: Delete "COMPUTER-ASSISTED RESEARCH"

§ 105.02 Devices for Settling Claims or Shortening Litigation.

§ 105.02(b) Mini-Trial.

Page 215: Add to footnote 1:

[1] *See* Ind. R. Alternative Disp. Resol. 4.1 *et seq.* (mini-trial procedures); Minn. Gen. R. Prac. 114.02 (Subsection 8 classifies a mini-trial as a hybrid process and defines this term. It states in part, "A forum in which each party and their counsel present its position before a selected representative for each party, a neutral third party, or both, to develop a basis for settlement negotiations."); Tex. Civ. Prac. & Rem. Code § 154.024 ("Mini-Trial"); Michael Morrison, James Wren and Chris Galeczka, *Expedited Civil Actions in Texas and the U.S.: A Survey of State Procedures and a Guide to Implementing Texas's New Expedited Actions Process*, 65 Baylor L. Rev. 824 (2013).

Page 215: Delete "COMPUTER-ASSISTED RESEARCH"

§ 105.02(c) Summary Jury Trial.

Page 215: Add to footnote 3:

[3] *See generally* Bert I. Huang, *Trial by Preview*, 113 Colum. L. Rev. 1323 (2013); Nino Monea, *Summary Jury Trials: How They Work and How They Can Work for You*, 97 MI Bar Jnl. 16 (Feb. 2018); Nino Monea, *The Administrative Power: How State Courts Can Expand Access to Justice*, 53 Gonz. L. Rev. 207, 244–49 (2018); Andrew S. Pollis, *Busting up the Pretrial Industry*, 85 Fordham L. Rev. 2097, 2110–14 (2017); J.J. Prescott and Kathryn E. Spier, *A Comprehensive Theory of Civil Settlement*, 91 N.Y.U.L. Rev. 59 (2016) (The authors include their empirical study using data from New York's Summary Jury Trial Program.).

Page 215: Delete "COMPUTER-ASSISTED RESEARCH"

§ 105.02(d) Accord and Satisfaction.

Page 216: Delete "COMPUTER-ASSISTED RESEARCH"

§ 105.02(e) Compromise and Settlement.

Page 217: Delete "COMPUTER-ASSISTED RESEARCH"

§ 105.02(f) Novation and Release.

Page 217: Delete "COMPUTER-ASSISTED RESEARCH"

§ 105.03 Arbitration.

§ 105.03(b)   The Common Law of Arbitration.

Page 218: Add at the end of footnote 17:[17]

Page 218: Delete "COMPUTER-ASSISTED RESEARCH"

[17] ; Wilczewski v. Charter West National Bank, 861 N.W.2d 700 (Neb. 2015) (the appeal provision of the state's arbitration statute did not apply to an order denying a motion to compel arbitration that was not a final, appealable order).

§ 105.03(c)   Statutory Modification of Arbitration Law.

Page 219: Add a footnote to the last sentence of the second paragraph of subsection 105.03(c):

[22.1] The Uniform Law Commission (ULC) revised the Uniform Arbitration Act in 2000. According to the ULC, this Act has been enacted in Alaska, Arizona, Arkansas, Colorado, Connecticut, the District of Columbia, Florida, Hawaii, Kansas, Michigan, Minnesota, Nevada, New Jersey, New Mexico, North Carolina, North Dakota, Oklahoma, Oregon, Pennsylvania, Utah, Washington and West Virginia.

Page 219: Add to footnote 23:

[23] Gustavus, L.L.C. v. Eagle Invests., 2012 Ohio App. LEXIS 1229 (the arbitration clause in the real estate purchase and sale agreement did not violate public policy).

Page 219: Add to footnote 25:

[25] ; Cape Romain Contractor, Inc. v. Wando E., LLC, 747 S.E.2d 461 (S. C. 2013) (a subcontractor's attempt to foreclose a mechanics' lien was subject to arbitration under the Federal Arbitration Act).

§ 105.03(d)   Requirements, Scope and Effect of Arbitration Agreements.

Page 219: Add to footnote 26:

[26] ; Zephyr Haven Health and Rehab Center, Inc. v. Estate of Clukey, 133 So. 3d 1230 (Fla. Dist. Ct. App. 2014) (a person holding a durable power of attorney had authority to agree to arbitration). *See also* Hayslip v. U.S. Home Corp., 276 So. 3d 109 (Fla. Dist. Ct. App. 2019) (A valid agreement to arbitrate was found in the property's special warranty deed. The fact that the buyer did not sign the deed did not invalidate this agreement. The arbitration clause was a restrictive covenant running with the land. The original buyers knew of the clause. Fla. Stat. § 689.01 did not require that the buyers sign the deed in order to be bound by it.). *See generally* David K. Taylor and Jeffrey N. Brown, *Arbitration and Other Forms of ADR in Real Estate Deals: The Process, Drafting Considerations, and Making ADR Provisions Work*, 28 Probate & Property 57 (March/April 2014).

Page 220: Add to footnote 30:

[30] Day v. CTA, Inc., 324 P.3d 1205 (Mont. 2014) (arbitration clause in property owner's contract for various services was not oppressive, unconscionable or against public policy, and was thus enforceable against owners).

Page 221: Add to footnote 31:

[31] Lemon Drop Properties, LLC v. Pass Marianne, LLC, 73 So. 3d 1131 (Miss. 2011) (a real estate agent had the right to compel arbitration under the terms of the purchase agreement).

Page 221: Add to footnote 32:

[32] Noble Real Estate, Inc. v. Seder, 101 So. 3d 197 (Miss. Ct. App. 2012) (the arbitration clause in the real estate purchase agreement was limited claims brought against the builder in its capacity as the listing broker). Jahanbein v. Ndidi Condominium Unit Owners Association, Inc., 85 A.3d 824 (D.C. 2014) (condominium association sued for breach of fiduciary duty; claim was subject to arbitration, but the condominium bylaws did not create an enforceable agreement to arbitrate a dispute between two unit owners); MSO, LLC v. DeSimone, 94 A.3d 1189 (Conn. 2014) (considered whether landlord waived the right to enforce the arbitration clause); Derose v. Jason Robert's, Inc., 216 A.3d 699, 714 (Conn. App. Ct. 2019) ("The scope of arbitration, including the delineation of the issues to be decided, is determined and limited by the parties' submission to arbitration.").

Page 221: Add at the end of footnote 36:

[36] ; First Weber Group, Inc. v. Synergy Real Estate Group, LLC, 860 N.W.2d 498 (Wis. 2015) (real estate agency action to compel arbitration of dispute with another real estate agency).

Page 222: Delete "COMPUTER-ASSISTED RESEARCH"

§ 105.03(e)   The Arbitration Award.

§ 105.03(e)(1)   Technical Requirements.

Page 223: Delete "COMPUTER-ASSISTED RESEARCH"

§ 105.03(e)(2)   Enforcement of the Award.

Page 223: Add to footnote 49:

[49] *See also* Seneca Nation of Indians v. New York, 420 F. Supp. 3d 89, 101 (W.D.N.Y. 2019) (Arbitration awards are not self-enforcing. Judicial orders give awards force and effect.), *aff'd*, 988 F.3d 618) 2d Cir. 2021).

Page 224: Add to footnote 52:

[52] 5 Bros., Inc. v. D.C.M. of N.Y., LLC, 998 N.Y.S.2d 192 (App. Div. 2014) (parties barred from relitigating claims decided as part of the arbitrator's determination).

Page 224: Delete "COMPUTER-ASSISTED RESEARCH"

§ 105.03(e)(3)   Impeachment or Vacation of the Award.

Page 225: Add to footnote 55:

[55] Strausser Enterprises, Inc. v. Segal and Morel, Inc., 89 A.3d 292 (Pa. Super. Ct. 2014) (the arbitration panel left unresolved one of the party's claims, and was not a final award for purposes of common law, and thus the trial court lacked authority to confirm the decision as an award).

Page 225: Delete "COMPUTER-ASSISTED RESEARCH"

§ 105.03(f)   Compulsory Arbitration.

Page 225: Add a footnote to the first sentence of subsection 105.03(f):

[57.1] *See* Ariz. Rev. Stat. § 12-133 (permitting the superior court to require arbitration in cases in which the amount in controversy does not exceed $65,000). *See generally* D. Greg Sakall & Julie A. Pack, *Short Trials: An Appropriate Replacement for Compulsory Arbitration in Arizona?*, 59 Ariz. L. Rev. 485 (2017).

Page 225: Add to footnote 58:

[58] Geographic Expeditions, Inc. v. Estate of Lhotka, 599 F.3d 1102 (9th Cir. 2010)

(compulsory arbitration regarding contracts to provide guided expedition services).

Page 226: Add to footnote 59:

⁵⁹ Garcia v. Huerta, 340 S.W.3d 864 (Tex. App. 2011, *pet. denied*) (action regarding order compelling arbitration of a borrower's claims against a real estate agent).

Page 226: Delete "COMPUTER-ASSISTED RESEARCH"

§ 105.03(g)   Real Property Issues Amenable to Arbitration.

Page 227: Delete "COMPUTER-ASSISTED RESEARCH"

§ 105.03(h)   Evaluation of Arbitration as an Alternative to Litigation.

Page 227: Delete "COMPUTER-ASSISTED RESEARCH"

Page 227: Add a new subsection 105.03(i).

§ 105.03(i)   Federal Arbitration Act.

The Federal Arbitration Act (FAA or the Act) is codified at 9 U.S.C. §§ 1 to 16. This Act was enacted in response to judicial hostility to arbitration agreements.[69.1] The reach of this Act is expansive and coincides with that of the Commerce Clause.[69.2]

The FAA applies to agreements to arbitrate which are in a written maritime contract or a contract involving interstate commerce.[69.3] Arbitration is a matter of consent.[69.4] Section 2 is the primary substantive provision of the Act. This section states:

> A written provision in any maritime transaction or a contract evidencing a transaction involving commerce to settle by arbitration a controversy thereafter arising out of such contract or transaction, or the refusal to perform the whole or any part thereof, or an agreement in writing to submit to arbitration an existing controversy arising out of such a contract, transaction, or refusal, shall be valid, irrevocable, and enforceable, save upon such grounds as exist at law or in equity for the revocation of any contract.[69.5]

Section 2 reflects a "liberal federal policy favoring arbitration"[69.6] and the "fundamental principle that arbitration is a matter of contract."[69.7]

Under FAA § 4, a party may ask the court to compel an arbitration proceeding agreed upon in the parties' agreement. However, the U.S. Supreme Court had held that a federal court may not have jurisdiction to decide such a request since the FAA authorization of a petition does not itself create jurisdiction. Instead, a federal court must have an independent jurisdictional basis to resolve the matter.[69.7.1] In addressing this jurisdictional issue, the Court found that FAA § 4 instructs a federal court to "look through" the petition to the parties' "underlying substantive controversy" even though that controversy is not before the court. When the underlying dispute falls within the court's jurisdiction, then the court may rule on the petition to compel regardless of whether the petition alone could establish the court's jurisdiction.[69.7.2] However, this "look through" approach does not apply to requests to confirm or vacate arbitral awards under the FAA's §§ 9 and 10.[69.7.3]

Under the Act, courts must place arbitration agreements on "equal footing with other contracts" and enforce arbitration agreements according to their terms.[69.8] A state court cannot decide that the basic provisions of a contract are fair enough to be enforceable, but then refuse to enforce an arbitration agreement in that contract.[69.9]

The last clause of § 2 permits arbitration agreements to be invalidated by "generally applicable contract defenses, such as fraud, duress, or unconscionability," but not by defenses that apply only to arbitration or that derive their meaning from the fact that an agreement to arbitrate is at issue.[69.10] This clause has been referred to as the "saving clause."[69.11] While the saving clause preserves general contract defenses, it does not preserve state-law rules that obstruct accomplishment of the FAA's objectives.[69.12] The U.S. Supreme Court has found that when state law prohibits the arbitration of a particular type of claim, the conflicting rule is displaced by the FAA.[69.13]

Under § 2, there are two types of challenges to an arbitration agreement. First, a party can challenge the validity of the arbitration agreement. Second, a party can challenge the underlying contract on a ground that affects the entire contract such as fraudulent inducement.[69.14] Arbitration agreements are not to be avoided by allowing one party to ignore the contract and resort to the courts.[69.15]

The Act provides these mechanisms for enforcing arbitration awards: a judicial decree confirming an award,[69.16] an order vacating an award,[69.17] or an order modifying or correcting it.[69.18]

Though most arbitration agreements appear in traditional bilateral written contracts signed by all parties, an arbitration agreement may validly appear in documents not requiring the signature of all parties.[69.19] Examples of such documents include corporate charters and bylaws and the governing documents of common interest communities.

[69.1] Hall Street Associates, L. L. C. v. Mattel, Inc., 552 U.S. 576, 581 (2008); Allied-Bruce Terminix Cos. v. Dobson, 513 U.S. 265, 274 (1995).

[69.2] Allied-Bruce Terminix Cos. v. Dobson, 513 U.S. 265, 270 (1995).

[69.3] See, e.g., Stone & Webster, Inc. v. Baker Process, Inc., 210 F. Supp. 2d 1177, 1181 (S.D. Cal. 2002).

[69.4] Stolt-Nielsen S. A. v. AnimalFeeds Int'l Corp., 559 U.S. 662, 684 (2010).

[69.5] 9 U.S.C. § 2. See Moses H. Cone Memorial Hospital v. Mercury Constr. Corp., 460 U.S. 1, 24 (1983); Taylor v. Extendicare Health Facilities, Inc., 147 A.3d 490, 493 (Pa. 2016), cert. denied, 197 L. Ed. 2d 555 (2017).

[69.6] Moses H. Cone Memorial Hospital v. Mercury Constr. Corp., 460 U.S. 1, 24 (1983). See also Southland Corp. v. Keating, 465 U.S. 1, 10 (1983) ("In enacting § 2 of the federal Act, Congress declared a national policy favoring arbitration and withdrew the power of the states to require a judicial forum for the resolution of claims which the contracting parties agreed to resolve by arbitration.").

69.7 Rent-A-Center, West, Inc. v. Jackson, 561 U.S. 63, 67 (2010).

69.7.1 *See* Badgerow v. Walters, 212 L. Ed. 2d 355, 361 (2022).

69.7.2 *Id.*, quoting Vaden v. Discover Bank, 556 U. S. 49, 62 (2009).

69.7.3 *Id.*

69.8 AT&T Mobility LLC v. Concepcion, 563 U.S. 333, 339 (2011). *See* United States Home Corp. v. Ballesteros Trust, 415 P.3d 32, 40 (Nev. 2018) (Under the FAA, a state must place arbitration provisions on the same footing as other contractual provisions.); Taylor v. Extendicare Health Facilities, Inc., 147 A.3d 490, 503 (Pa. 2016) (States may not decline to enforce arbitration agreements solely because they are arbitration agreements.),*cert. denied*, 197 L. Ed. 2d 555 (2017).

69.9 Doctor's Assocs. v. Casarotto, 517 U.S. 681, 687 (1996); Allied-Bruce Terminix Cos. v. Dobson, 513 U.S. 265, 281 (1995). *See* United States Home Corp. v. Ballesteros Trust, 415 P.3d 32, 40 (Nev. 2018).

69.10 AT&T Mobility LLC v. Concepcion, 563 U.S. 333, 339 (2011).

69.11 *Id.*

69.12 AT&T Mobility LLC v. Concepcion, 563 U.S. 333, 352 (2011). The Court held the FAA preempts the rule espoused by the Supreme Court of California in *Discover Bank v. Superior Court*, 36 Cal. 4th 148, 30 Cal. Rptr. 3d 76, 113 P. 3d 1100 (2005). The *Discover Bank* rule classified most collective-arbitration waivers in consumer contracts as unconscionable.

69.13 AT&T Mobility LLC v. Concepcion, 563 U.S. 333, 341 (2011).

69.14 Rent-A-Center, West, Inc. v. Jackson, 561 U.S. 63, 70 (2010).

69.15 Southland Corp. v. Keating, 465 U.S. 1, 7 (1983).

69.16 9 U.S.C. § 9.

69.17 9 U.S.C. § 10.

69.18 9 U.S.C. § 11.

69.19 *See, e.g.*, Pinnacle Museum Tower Assn. v. Pinnacle Market Development (US), LLC, 282 P.3d 1217, 1221 (Cal. 2012); Hayslip v. U.S. Home Corp., 276 So. 3d 109 (Fla. Dist. Ct. App. 2019); United States Home Corp. v. Ballesteros Trust, 415 P.3d 32, 36 (Nev. 2018).

§ 105.04　Conciliation.

Page 228: Delete "COMPUTER-ASSISTED RESEARCH"

§ 105.05　Negotiation and Mediation.

Page 228: Add to footnote 75:

75 Anderson Property Management, LLC v. H. Anthony Miller, Jr., LLC, 943 N.E.2d 1286 (Ind. Ct. App. 2011) (mediation preceding vendor action against the purchaser); *In re* Allen, 343 S.W.3d 513 (Tex. App. 2011) (mediator in this case was authorized to decide specified issues).

Page 229: Delete "COMPUTER-ASSISTED RESEARCH"

§ 105.06   Consensual References; Factfinders.

Page 229: Delete "COMPUTER-ASSISTED RESEARCH"

§ 105.07   Ombudsman.

Page 229: Add to footnote 79:

[79] Ariz. Rev. Stat. § 41-1312 was repealed effective Jan. 1, 2011. In 2019, Or. Rev. Stat. § 446.543 was renumbered as Or. Rev. Stat. § 456.403. Utah Code Ann. 63-34-13 was renumbered in 2006. The Utah Property Rights Ombudsman Act is codified at Utah Code Ann. § 13-43-101 *et seq.*

Page 230: Add to footnote 80:

[80] *Cf.* Wildflower Int'l, Ltd. v. United States, 105 Fed. Cl. 362, 379–380 (2012). Federal Acquisition Regulation 16.505(a)(10) limits protests. The only recourse for a would-be protestor of a task or delivery order valued at less than $10 million whose protest does not concern the scope of the underlying contract is to make a complaint to the contract ombudsman, who is tasked with ensuring that all contractors are afforded a fair opportunity to be considered for the task or delivery order. The Court does not view the ombudsman procedures for complaints as comparable to an administrative or judicial review of protests.

Page 230: Delete "COMPUTER-ASSISTED RESEARCH"

§ 105.08   Bibliography.

Books

Page 230: Add to Books:

AAA Handbook on Arbitration Practice (JurisNet, LLC 2d ed. 2016).

AAA Handbook on Commercial Arbitration (JurisNet, LLC 3d ed. 2016).

AAA Handbook on Construction Arbitration and ADR (JurisNet, LLC 3d ed. 2016).

Andrews, Neil, *Arbitration and Contract Law: Common Law Perspectives* (Springer 2016).

Blankley, Kristen M. and Maureen A. Weston, *Understanding Alternative Dispute Resolution* (Carolina Academic Press 2017).

Feeley, Kelly M. and James A. Sheehan, *Mastering Alternative Dispute Resolution* (Carolina Academic Press 2015).

Gaitis, James M., A. Holt Gwyn, Laura A. Kaster and John J. McCauley, *The College of Commercial Arbitrators Guide to Best Practices in Commercial Arbitration* (JurisNet, LLC 4th ed. 2017).

Georgakopoulos, Alexia, *The Mediation Handbook: Research, Theory, and Practice* (Routledge 2017).

Martinez-Fraga, Pedro J., *The American Influence on International Commercial Arbitration: Doctrinal Developments and Discovery Methods* (Cambridge University Press 2d Ed. 2020).

Palmer, Michael and Simon Robert, *Dispute Processes: ADR and the Primary Forms of Decision-Making* (Cambridge University Press 3d ed. 2020).

Zwier, Paul J. and Thomas F. Guernsey, *NITA Advanced Negotiation and*

Mediation Theory and Practice (LEXISNEXIS / National Institute for Trial Advocacy 2d ed. 2015).

Articles

Page 230: Add to Articles:

Adcock, Eric S., "Federal Privilege In The Ombudsman's Process," 8 *Charleston L. Rev.* 1 (2013).

Baaij, Cornelis J.W., "A Case of Mistaken Identity: Questioning the U.S. Supreme Court's Contract Theory of Arbitration," 14 *Va. L. & Bus. Rev.* 121 (2020).

Billemont, Jean, "Arbitration of Real Estate Disputes under French Law," 20 *IBA Arb. News* 70 (Sept. 2015).

Bookman, Pamela K., "The Arbitration-Litigation Paradox," 72 *Vand. L. Rev.* 1119 (2019).

Bryant, Graham K. and Kristopher R. McClellan, "The Disappearing Civil Trial: Implications for the Future of Law Practice," 30 *Regent U.L. Rev.* 287 (2017–2018).

Cataldo, Craig E., Note, "Delegating the Administration of Justice: The Need to Update the Federal Arbitration Act," 52 *Suffolk U. L. Rev.* 37 (2019).

Chang, Lou, "Mediation, Its Roots, And Its Future In A Post-Pandemic World," 24 *Hawaii B.J.* 4 (Sept. 2020).

Cohen, Amy J., "The Rise and Fall and Rise Again of Informal Justice and the Death of ADR," 54 *Conn. L. Rev.* 197 (2022).

del Prado, Fabio Nunez, "The Fallacy of Consent: Should Arbitration Be a Creature of Contract?" 35 *Emory Int'l L. Rev.* 219 (2021).

Drahozal, Christopher R., "Arbitration and Rule Production," 72 *Case W. Res.* 91 (2021).

Farkas, Brian, "Arbitration at the Supreme Court: The FAA from RBG to ACB," 42 *Cardozo L. Rev.* 2927 (2021).

Frankel, Richard, "Corporate Hostility to Arbitration," 50 *Seton Hall L. Rev.* 707 (2020).

Gabrieli, Amos, Nourit Zimerman & Michal Alberstein, "Authority-Based Mediation," 20 *Cardozo J. Conflict Resol.* 2 (Fall 2018).

Garcia, Julian Cardenas, "The Era of Petroleum Arbitration Mega Cases," 35 *Hous. J. Int'l L.* 537 (2013).

Halper, Adam J. with Donna Erez Navot, "Make Online Mediation Work for You and Your Clients," 45 *Westchester B. J.* 91 (Fall 2020).

Hensler, Deborah R. and Damira Khatam, "Re-Inventing Arbitration: How Expanding the Scope of Arbitration Is Re-Shaping its Form and Blurring the Line Between Private and Public Adjudication," 18 *Nev. L.J.* 381 (2018).

Horton, David, "Arbitration about Arbitration," 70 *Stan. L. Rev.* 363 (2018).

Horton, David, "Infinite Arbitration Clauses," 168 *U. Pa. L. Rev.* 633 (2020).

Huang, Bert I., "Trial by Preview," 113 *Colum. L. Rev.* 1323 (2013).

Isaac, Kendall D., "The Organizational Ombudsman's Quest for Privileged Communications," 32 *Hofstra Lab. & Emp.* L.J. 31 (2014).

Kessler, Amalia D., "Deciding Against Conciliation: The Nineteenth-Century Rejection of a European Transplant and the Rise of a Distinctively American Ideal of Adversarial Adjudication," 10 *Theoretical Inq. L.* 423 (2009).

Kisiel, Edwin, "The War on Trees: How to Diffuse Neighborly Feuds over View Rights," 35 *J. Envtl. L. & Litig.* 145 (2020).

Lande, John and Peter W. Benner, "Why and How Businesses Use Planned Early Dispute Resolution," 13 *U. St. Thomas L.J.* 248 (2017).

Leake, Timothy, Note, "Arbitration Waiver and Prejudice," 119 *Mich. L. Rev.* 397 (2020).

Leslie, Christopher R., "Conspiracy to Arbitrate," 96 *N.C.L. Rev.* 381 (2018).

Lewis, John Bruce & Dustin M. Dow, "Searching for Clarity Amid Confusion: An Examination of the Standards for Determining Waiver and Revival of the Right to Arbitrate," 67 *Kan. L. Rev.* 327 (2018).

Monea Nino, "Summary Jury Trials: How They Work and How They Can Work for You," 97 *MI Bar Jnl.* 16 (Feb. 2018).

Monea, Nino, "The Administrative Power: How State Courts Can Expand Access to Justice," 53 *Gonz. L. Rev.* 207 (2018).

Moroni, Gina, Comment, "Mediating Farm Nuisance: Comparing New Jersey, Missouri, and Iowa Right to Farm Laws and How They Utilize Mediation Techniques," 2018 *J. Disp. Resol.* 299 (2017–2018).

Morrison, Michael, James Wren, and Chris Galeczka, "Expedited Civil Actions in Texas and the U.S.: A Survey of State Procedures and a Guide to Implementing Texas's New Expedited Actions Process," 65 *Baylor L. Rev.* 824 (2013).

Noll, David L., "Arbitration Conflicts," 103 *Minn. L. Rev.* 666 (2018).

Noll, David L., "Regulating Arbitration," 105 *Calif. L. Rev.* 985 (2017).

Plass, Stephen A., "Federal Arbitration Law and the Preservation of Legal Remedies," 90 *Temp. L. Rev.* 213 (2018).

Pollis, Andrew S. "Busting up the Pretrial Industry," 85 *Fordham L. Rev.* 2097 (2017).

Prescott, J.J. and Kathryn E. Spier, "A Comprehensive Theory of Civil Settlement," 91 *N.Y.U.L. Rev.* 59 (2016).

Press, Sharon, "Mortgage Foreclosure Mediation in Florida—Implementation Challenges for an Institutionalized Program," 11 *Nev. L.J.* 306 (Spring 2011).

Resnik, Judith, "Lawyers' Ethics Beyond the Vanishing Trial: Unrepresented Claimants, De Facto Aggregations, Arbitration Mandates, and Privatized Processes," 85 *Fordham L. Rev.* 1899 (2017).

Roberge, Jean-Francois & Dorcas Quek Anderson, "Judicial Mediation: From Debates to Renewal," 19 *Cardozo J. Conflict Resol.* 613 (2018).

Sakall, D. Greg & Julie A. Pack, "Short Trials: An Appropriate Replacement for Compulsory Arbitration in Arizona?" 59 *Ariz. L. Rev.* 485 (2017).

Soleimani, Charlene, Note, "New York's Attempts to Regulate Airbnb (and Other Home-Sharing Platforms) Have Hit a Roadblock and, in the Process, Have Inadvertently Hurt Landlords: How Alternate Dispute Resolution Can Come to the Rescue," 21 *Cardozo J. Conflict Resol.* 771 (2020).

Spanheimer, Ryan, Comment, "Justification for Creating an Ombudsman Privilege in Today's Society," 96 *Marq. L. Rev.* 659 (2012).

Stipanowich, Thomas J., "Arbitration, Mediation, and Mixed Modes: Seeking Workable Solutions and Common Ground on Med-Arb, Arb-Med, and Settlement-Oriented Activities by Arbitrators," 26 *Harv. Negotiation L. Rev.* 265 (2021).

Stipanowich, Thomas J. and Véronique Fraser, "Exploring the Interplay Between Mediation, Evaluation and Arbitration in Commercial Cases," 40 *Fordham Int'l L.J.* 839 (2017).

Szalai, Imre S., The Failure of Legal Ethics to Address the Abuses of Forced Arbitration, 24 *Harv. Negotiation L. Rev.* 128 (2018).

Tanz, Jill S. and Martha K. McClintock, "The Physiologic Stress Response During Mediation," 32 *Ohio St. J. on Disp. Resol.* 29 (2017).

Taylor, David K., and Jeffrey N. Brown, "Arbitration and Other Forms of ADR in Real Estate Deals: The Process, Drafting Considerations, and Making ADR Provisions Work," 28 *Prob. & Prop.* 57 (March/April, 2014).

Tokarz, Karen, Samuel Hoff Stragand, Michael Geigerman and Wolf Smith, "New Directions in Domestic and International Dispute Resolution: Addressing the Eviction Crisis and Housing Instability Through Mediation," 63 Wash. U. J.L. & Pol'y 243 (2020).

Van Soye, Scott C., "Illusory Ethics: Legal Barriers to an Ombudsman's Compliance with Accepted Ethical Standards," 8 *Pepp. Disp. Resol. L.J.* 117 (2007).

Waldman, Ellen, "How Mediation Contributes to the 'Justice Gap' and Possible Technological Fixes," 88 *Fordham L. Rev.* 2425 (2020).

Ware, Stephen J., "The Centrist Case for Enforcing Adhesive Arbitration Agreements," 23 *Harv. Negotiation L. Rev.* 29 (2017).

Welsh, Nancy A., "Bringing Transparency and Accountability (with a Dash of Competition) to Court-Connected Dispute Resolution," 88 *Fordham L. Rev.* 2449 (2020).

Willis, Brian C. "Resolving Disputes by Expert Determination: What Happens When Parties Select Appraisers, Accountants, or Other Technical Experts to Decide Disputes," 91 *Fla. Bar J.* 35 (July/Aug. 2017).

Wissler, Roselle L. and Art Hinshaw, "The Initial Mediation Session: An Empirical Examination," 27 *Harv. Negotiation L. Rev.* 1 (2021).

Yarn, Douglas. "The Death of ADR: A Cautionary Tale of Isomorphism Through Institutionalization." 108 *Penn St. L. Rev.* 929 (2003).

Annotations

Page 236: Add to Annotations:

Annotation, *Enforcement of Arbitration Agreement Contained in Real Estate Contract by or Against Nonsignatory Under State Law*, 10 A.L.R.6th 669.

CHAPTER 106AT

PROPERTY LAW IN AUSTRIA

§ 106AT.05   The Land Registry Law.

§ 106AT.05(c)   Notarization of the Transfer.

Pag 245: Add a footnote to the first sentence of subsection 106AT.05(c):

37.1 *See* Jonathan Goldsmith, *Opinion: State of the Union: One for the textbooks*, LS Gaz, 27 Mar, 14 (27 March 2017). Mr. Goldsmith discusses a judgment from the Court of Justice of the European Union in Piringer (Case C-342/15) which he described as part of "the long-running war between lawyers and notaries." Ms. Piringer owned half of a property in Austria. She sought to register in the Austrian land registry an intention to sell her interest. A Czech lawyer certified that she had signed the official form before him. In the Czech Republic, this act would have been valid. But Austrian law requires that the form be authenticated by a court or notary. The Czech lawyer was neither. Mr. Goldsmith stated:

> [T]he court found that the authentication of a signature by a Czech lawyer is not comparable to that of an Austrian notary, because even in the Czech Republic a Czech lawyer's authentication does not constitute a public instrument. . . . If the Czech signature were to be recognised in Austria for the purposes of entry in the land register, and so considered equivalent to a notary's authentication, it would have to acquire the value of a public instrument—and would have a different strength in Austria than in the Czech Republic where it originated.

This case was a victory for notaries.

§ 106AT.06   Property Laws Outside the Civil Code.

§ 106AT.06(c)   Taxes on Real Property.

§ 106AT.06(c)(4)   Land Value Tax (*Bodenwertabgabe*).

Page 247: Add to the text of subsection 106AT.06(c)(4) after the first and only sentence:

This annual tax is currently 1% on undeveloped land that is eligible for construction purposes and whose unit value is more than € 14,600.[53]

[53] *See* https://www.bmf.gv.at/themen/steuern/immobilien-grundstuecke/grundbesitzabgaben-einheitsbewertung/bodenwertabgabe.html (visited May 23, 2022).

CHAPTER 106BR

PROPERTY LAW IN BRAZIL

§ 106BR.01   History of Property Law in Brazil.

§ 106BR.01(b)   Achieving Independence and Stability.

Page 251: Change Portugual to Portugal.

Portugal

§ 106BR.02   Basic Principles of the Brazilian Property Law.

§ 106BR.02(a)   Types of Interests in Real Property.

§ 106BR.02(a)(2)   Rights that Arise or May Be Created.

§ 106BR.02(a)(2)(i)   Emphyteusis.

Page 252: Add a footnote to the first sentence of subsection 106BR.02(a)(2)(i):

0.1 *See generally* Thomas T. Ankersen & Thomas Ruppert, *Tierra y Libertad: The Social Function Doctrine and Land Reform in Latin America,* 19 Tul. Envtl. L.J. 69, 86–87 (2006).

§ 106BR.02(a)(2)(vi)   Mortgage.

Page 253: Change the word deficiences to deficiencies.

deficiencies

§ 106BR.02(b)   Acquiring and Securing Real Property Rights.

§ 106BR.02(b)(4).   Succession.

Page 255: Change the word descendents to descendants.

descendants

§ 106BR.04   Taxation.

Page 256: Add a footnote to the third sentence of subsection 106BR.04:

2 The tax rate currently ranges from 2% to 6% of the economic value of the transaction. *See* Lex Mundi Brazil Business Guide XIX.3 (2019). Oceanfront land is subject to laudemeo or a marine tax at the rate of 5% of the land's value, not including the value of buildings.

§ 106BR.06   Bibliography.

Page 257: Change "§ 106-D.06" to "§ 106BR.06"

Books

Page 257: Add to Bibliography:

Abbud, André, Daniel Levy and Rafael Francisco Alves, *The Brazilian Arbitration Act: A Case Law Guide* (Kluwer Law International 2019).

Benvindo, Juliano Zaiden, *The Rule of Law in Brazil: The Legal Construction of Inequality* (Hart Publishing 2022).

Deffenti, Fabiano & Welber Barral, *Introduction to Brazilian Law*, ch. 5 "Property Law" (Kluwer Law International 2d ed. 2016).

Fazio, Silvia, *Brazilian Commercial Law: A Practical Guide* (Kluwer Law International 2d ed. 2015).

Rogoff, Adam C., Richard F. Broude and Daniel M. Glosband, *Collier International Business Insolvency Guide* ch. 16, Brazil (Matthew Bender).

Articles

Page 257: Add to Articles:

Aguiar, Rayane, Jody M. Endres, Caroline Taylor and Samuel Evans, "Public Conservation Policies on Private Land: A Case Study of the Brazilian Forest Code and Implications for the Agro-Industry Sector," 34 *Pace Envtl. L. Rev.* 325 (2017).

Ankersen, Thomas T. & Thomas Ruppert, "Tierra y Libertad: The Social Function Doctrine and Land Reform in Latin America," 19 *Tul. Envtl. L.J.* 69 (2006).

Ball, Jessica, "A Step in the Wrong Direction: Increasing Restrictions on Foreign Rural Land Acquisition in Brazil," 35 *Fordham Int'l L.J.* 1743 (2012).

Benjamin, Antonio Herman, "Water Justice: The Case of Brazil," 48 *ELR* 10211 (2018).

Bennett, Elizabeth, "Animal Agriculture Laws on the Chopping Block: Comparing United States and Brazil," 31 *Pace Envtl. L. Rev.* 531 (2014).

Bryner, Nicholas S., Public Interests and Private Land: The Ecological Function of Property in Brazil, 34 *Va. Envtl. L.J.* 122 (2016).

Colby, Kevin E. "Brazil and the MST: Land Reform and Human Rights," 16 *N.Y. Int'l L. Rev.* 1 (2003).

Corbella-Valea, Montserrat, "Indirect Expropriation and Resource Nationalism in Brazil's Mining Industry," 46 *U. Miami Inter-Am. L. Rev.* 61 (2014).

Daibert, Arlindo, "Rainforests and Regulation: New Directions in Brazilian Environmental Law and Legal Institutions: Historical Views on Environment and Environmental Law in Brazil," 40 *Geo. Wash. Int'l L. Rev.* 779 (2009).

Dalton, Taylor Reeves, "Rights for the Landless: Comparing Approaches to Historical Injustice in Brazil and South Africa," 44 *Colum. Human Rights L. Rev.* 171 (2012).

Dolin, Gregory and Irina D. Manta, "Parallel State," 38 *Cardozo L. Rev.* 2083 (2017).

Engle, Karen and Lucas Lixinski, "Quilombo Land Rights, Brazilian Constitutionalism, and Racial Capitalism," 54 *Vand. J. Transnat'l L.* 831 (2021).

Evensen, Krista, Note, "Preventing a Favela Whitewashing: How a Tax Code Revision Can Mitigate the Danger of Bare Title Rights to Rio De Janeiro's Slum Residents," 19 *U. Ill. L. Rev.* 773 (2019).

Goldstein, Anna, Note, "Dirty Business: Accountability For Harmful Pesticide Use In Brazil," 3 *Cardozo Int'l & Comp. L. Rev.* 1265 (2020).

Intrator, Jessica, "From Squatter to Settler: Applying the Lessons of Nineteenth Century U.S. Public Land Policy to Twenty-first Century Land Struggles in Brazil," 38 *Ecology L.Q.* 179 (2011).

Kaufhardt, Sara, Note, "Impunity for Burning the Earth's Lungs: The Legality of Deforestation Under International Law and the Quest to Preserve the World's Biodiversity," 59 Colum. J. Transnat'l L. 469 (2021).

Klafehn, Ruslan, Student Article, "Burning Down the House: Do Brazil's Forest Management Policies Violate the No-Harm Rule Under The CBD and Customary International Law?" 35 *Am. U. Int'l L. Rev.* 941 (2020).

Luiz, Fernando Vieira, "Designing a Court-Annexed Mediation Program for Civil

Cases in Brazil: Challenges and Opportunities," 15 *Pepp. Disp. Resol. L.J.* 1 (2015).

Pargendler, Mariana, "Politics in the Origins: The Making of Corporate Law in Nineteenth-Century Brazil," 60 *Am. J. Comp. L.* 805 (2012).

Pargendler, Mariana and Bruno Salama, "Law and Economics in the Civil Law World: The Case of Brazilian Courts," 90 *Tul. L. Rev.* 439 (2015).

Perez, Richard, Note/Comment, "Deforestation of the Brazilian Amazon Under Jair Bolsonaro's Reign: A Growing Ecological Disaster and How It May Be Reduced," 52 *U. Miami Inter-Am. L. Rev.* 195 (2021).

Rosenn, Keith S., "Federalism in Brazil, 43 *Duq. L. Rev.* 577 (2005).

Sampaio, Rômulo S. R., "Affordable Housing Policies in Brazil," 4 *J. Comp. Urb. L. & Pol'y* 424 (2020).

Thaher, Nael H., Helen Hambly Odame & Victoria Henson-Apollonio, "A Case Study of Management of IPRs in Soybean Biotechnology: Evidence from Brazil and a Successful Coexistence in Canada and USA," 26 *Drake J. Agric. L.* 203 (2021).

Thimmayya, Ned, Note, "A Pioneering Statute in a Hostile Landscape: Brazil's Article 225 and Its Success in Protecting Biodiversity," 37 *Brooklyn J. Int'l L.* 713 (2012).

CHAPTER 106CA

PROPERTY LAW IN CANADA

§ 106CA.03   Division of Power Under the Constitution.

Page 261: Add to footnote 1:

[1] Watson, Blake A., "The Impact of the American Doctrine of Discovery on Native Land Rights I Australia, Canada, and New Zealand," 34 *Seattle U. L. Rev.* 507 (2011).

Hamill, Sarah E., "Private Rights to Public Property: The Evolution of Common Property in Canada," 58 *McGill L.J.* 365 (2012).

Kong, Hoi, "Sustainability and Land Use Regulation in Canada: An Instrument Choice Perspective," 13 *Vt. J. Envtl. L.* 553 (2012).

Watson, Blake A., "The Impact of the American Doctrine of Discovery on Native Land Rights in Australia, Canada, and New Zealand," 34 *Seattle U. L. Rev.* 507 (2011).

§ 106CA.04   Property Law in the Provinces.

§ 106CA.04(a)   Property Law in a Common Law Province: Alberta.

§ 106CA.04(a)(6)   Environment.

Page 263: Change returneed to returned.

Page 263: Delete the second "may require."

Page 265: Add at end of chapter:

§ 106CA.05   Bibliography.

Books

Alcantara, Christopher, *Negotiating the Deal: Comprehensive Land Claims Agreements in Canada* (University of Toronto Press 2013).

Benson, Marjorie Lynne, Marie-Ann Bowden & Dwight Newman, *Understanding Property: A Guide to Canada's Property Law* (Carswell Legal Publications 2d ed. 2008).

Chambers, Lori, *Married Women and the Law of Property in Victorian Ontario* (University of Toronto Press 1997).

Cuming, Ronald C.C., *Overview of Saskatchewan Real Property Law* (Regina: Office of the Queen's Printer 2016).

Long, John S., *Treaty No. 9: Making the Agreement to Share the Land in Far Northern Ontario in 1905* (McGill-Queen's University Press 2010).

McCallum, Margaret E. and Alan M. Sinclair, *An Introduction to Real Property Law* (LexisNexis Canada 7th ed. 2017).

Rogoff, Adam C., Richard F. Broude and Daniel M. Glosband, *Collier International Business Insolvency Guide* ch. 17, Canada (Matthew Bender).

Sinclair, Alan M. & Margaret E. McCallum, *An Introduction to Real Property Law* (LexisNexis Canada 6th ed. 2012).

Taylor, Greg, *Law of the Land: The Advent of the Torrens System in Canada* (University of Toronto Press 2008).

Ziff, Bruce H., *Principles of Property Law* (Carswell 7th ed. 2018).

Articles

Adkins, Sam, Bryn Gray, Kimberly Macnab and Gordon Nettleton, "Calculating the Incalculable: Principles for Compensating Impacts to Aboriginal Title," 54 *Alberta L. Rev.* 351 (2016).

Blair, Chase, "Indigenous Sacred Sites & Lands: Pursuing Preservation Through Colonial Constitutional Frameworks," 25 *Appeal* 73 (2020).

Borrows, John, "Indigenous Legal Traditions in Canada," 19 *Wash. U.J.L.& Pol'y* 167, 176 (2005).

Bowden, Marie-Ann, "Book Review: The Law of the Land: The Advent of the Torrens System in Canada, Greg Taylor (Toronto: University Of Toronto Press, 2008)," 47 *Alberta L. Rev.* 1051 (2010).

Braul, Wally, "The Changing Regulatory Scheme in Northeast British Columbia," 49 *Alberta L. Rev.* 369 (2012).

Brock, Jason and Jim Phillips, "The Commercial Lease: Property or Contract?" 38 *Alberta L. Rev.* 989 (2001).

Charles, Bill, "The Story of Law Reform in Nova Scotia: A Perilous Enterprise," 40 *Dalhousie L.J.* 339 (2017).

Charlton, Guy, "The Law of Native American Hunting, Fishing and Gathering Rights Outside of Reservation Boundaries in the United States and Canada," 39 *Can.-U.S. L.J.* 68 (2015).

Cuming, Ronald C.C., "Mortgage Obligation Deficiency Recovery," 81 *Sask. L. Rev.* 113 (2018).

Cuming, Ronald C.C., "Protecting the 'Castle': The Saskatchewan Home Exemption," 82 *Sask. L. Rev.* 1 (2019).

Curran, Deborah, "Leaks in the System: Environmental Flows, Aboriginal Rights, and the Modernization Imperative for Water Law in British Columbia," 50 *U.B.C. L. Rev.* 233 (2017).

Donovan, Brian, "Common Law Origins of Aboriginal Entitlements to Land," 29 *Man. L.J.* 289 (2003).

Drouillard, Michael, "A Critique of the British Columbia Residential Real Estate Brokerage Industry's Use of Dual Agency," 16 *Appeal* 84 (2011).

Duke, Katie, "Ownership of Rainwater and the Legality of Rainwater Harvesting in British Columbia," 19 *Appeal* 21 (2014).

Essert, Christopher, "The Office of Ownership," 63 *Univ. of Toronto L.J.* 418 (2013).

Flanagan, Tom & Christopher Alcantara, "Individual Property Rights on Canadian Indian Reserves: A Review of the Jurisprudence," 42 *Alberta L. Rev.* 1019 (2005).

Foote, Nathaniel L., "Not In My Backyard: Unconventional Gas Development and Local Land Use in Pennsylvania and Alberta, Canada," 3 *Penn. St. J. L. & Int'l Aff.* 235 (February, 2015).

Gordon, Scott R., Howard A. Gorman & Gunnar Benediktsson, "May You Litigate in Interesting Times: Specific Performance, Mitigation, and Valuation Issues in a Rising (or Falling) Market," 56 *Alberta L. Rev.* 367 (2018).

Grabin, Sari, "Lessons for Indigenous Property Reform: From Membership to Ownership On Nisga'a Lands," 47 *U.B.C. L. Rev.* 399 (2014).

Grinlinton, David, "The Continuing Relevance of Common Law Property Rights and Remedies in Addressing Environmental Challenges," 62 *McGill L.J.* 633 (2017).

Hamill, Sarah E., "Common Law Property Theory and Jurisprudence in Canada," 40 *Queen's L.J.* 679 (Spring, 2015).

Handlarski, Ryan, "Canada's Wonderlands: Can a Convicted Sex Offender Subject to a Section 161(1)(A) Order Legally Enter an Amusement Park?" 54 *U.B.C. L. Rev.* 629 (2021).

Hanna, Alan, "Going Circular: Indigenous Legal Research Methodology as Legal Practice," 65 *McGill L.J.* 671 (2020).

Harris, Douglas C., "Condominium and the City: The Rise of Property in Vancouver," 36 *Law & Soc. Inquiry* 694 (2011).

Harris, Douglas C., "Property And Sovereignty: An Indian Reserve and a Canadian City," 50 *U.B.C. L. Rev.* 321 (2017).

Harris, Douglas C. and May Au, "Title Registration and the Abolition of Notice in British Columbia," 47 *U.B.C. L. Rev.* 535 (2014).

Irvine, John, "A House Divided: Access to Partition and Sale under the Laws of Ontario and Manitoba," 35 *Man. L.J.* 217 (2011).

Judge, Elizabeth F. & Tenille E. Brown, "Pokémorials: Placing Norms in Augmented Reality," 50 *U.B.C. L. Rev.* 970 (2017).

Katz, Larissa, "The Moral Paradox of Adverse Possession: Sovereignty and Revolution in Property Law," 55 *McGill L.J.* 47 (2010).

Lavoie, Malcom, "Why Restrain Alienation of Indigenous Lands?" 49 *U.B.C. L. Rev.* 997 (2016).

Lavoie, Malcolm and Moira Lavoie, "Land Regime Choice in Close-Knit Communities: The Case of the First Nations Land Management Act," 54 *Osgoode Hall L.J.* 559 (2017).

Leew, Edward A. & Zeke Purves-Smith, "Operators' and Processors' Liens: Priority, Enforcement, and Practical Considerations," 47 *Alberta L. Rev.* 297 (2010).

Leslie, Jason, "The Philosopher and the Developer: Pluralist Moral Theory and the Law of Condominium," 54 *Osgoode Hall L.J.* 511 (2017).

Lewinsohn-Zamir, Daphna, "The Importance of Being Earnest: Two Notions of Internalization," 65 *U. Toronto L.J.* 37 (2015).

Lifshitz, Yael R., "Rethinking Original Ownership," 66 *Univ. of Toronto L.J.* 513 (2016).

Lubetsky, Michael H., "Adding Epicycles: The Inconsistent Use Test in Adverse Possession Law," 47 *Osgoode Hall L.J.* 497 (2009).

Lund, Anna, "Elaborate Imaginings: Rethinking Environmental Obligations in Canadian Insolvency Law," 71 *Univ. of Toronto L.J.* 301 (2021).

Lund, Anna Jane, "Tenant Protections in Mobile Home Park Closures," 53 *U.B.C. L. Rev.* 759 (2021).

MacDonald, Alexander and Nicholas Crosbie, "The Land Tenure System in the Newfoundland and Labrador Offshore Regulatory Regime: Review, Analysis and Current Issues," 37 *Dalhousie L.J.* 1 (2014).

McNeil, Kent, "Aboriginal Rights and Indigenous Governance: Identifying the Holders of Rights and Authority," 57 *Osgoode Hall L.J.* 127 (2020).

McNeil, Kent and Joshua Nichols, "Exclusive Occupation and Joint Aboriginal Title," 48 *U.B.C. L. Rev.* 821 (2015).

Macneill, C. Mark, "Inuit Nunangat Regional Overlaps: Reciprocal Harvesting & Wildlife Management Agreements," 9 *American Indian L.J.* 291 (2021).

Metcalf, Cherie, "Property Law Culture: Public Law, Private Preferences and the Psychology of Expropriation," 39 *Queen's L.J.* 685 (2020).

Metcalf, Cherie, "Public Law, Private Preferences and the Psychology of Expropriation," 39 *Queen's L.J.* 685 (2014).

Melnuychuk, Katherine, "One Click Away: The Prospect of Electronic Wills in Saskatchewan," 77 *Sask. L. Rev.* 27 (2014).

Ruru, Jacinta, Comment, "Finding Solutions for the Legislative Gaps in Determining Rights to the Family Home on Colonially Defined Indigenous Lands," 41 *U.B.C. L. Rev.* 315 (2008).

Sanderson, Douglas, "The Residue of Imperium: Property and Sovereignty on Indigenous Lands," 68 *Univ. of Toronto L.J.* 319 (2018).

Sanderson, Douglas (Amo Binashii) and Amitpal C. Singh, "Why Is Aboriginal Title Property if It Looks Like Sovereignty?" 34 *Can. J.L. & Juris.* 417 (2021).

Seidler, Reagan, "The Law of Haunted Houses: A Comment on Stigmatized Properties Following Wang v. Shao," 54 *U.B.C. L. Rev.* 455 (2021).

Sinel, Zoe, "De-Ciphering Self-Help," 67 *Univ. of Toronto* L.J. 31 (2017).

Thomson, Patrick A., "Book Note: Review of Saskatchewan Real Property Law, by Ronald C.C. Cuming. Regina: Office of the Queen's Printer, 2016. 278pp., $ 60.00 pb.," 80 Sask. L. Rev. 311 (2017).

Stacey, Jocelyn, "The Deliberative Dimensions of Modern Environmental Assessment Law," 43 *Dalhousie L.J.* 865 (2020).

Warrier, Vivek, Luke Morrison, Ashley White and Stephen Buffalo, "Indigenous Ownership of Natural Resource Projects: A Framework for Partnership and Economic Development," 59 *Alberta L. Rev.* 393 (2021).

Wilkins, Kerry, "The Road Not Taken: Reserving Lands for Exclusive Indigenous Use and Occupation," 53 U.B.C. L. Rev. 881 (2021).

Woods, Una, "Protection for Owners under the Law on Adverse Possession: An Inconsistent Use Test or a Qualified Veto System?" 57 *Osgoode Hall L.J.* 342 (2020).

Young, Raymond E., "Canadian Law of Constructive Expropriation," 68 *Sask. L. Rev.* 345 (2005).

Ziff, Bruce, "Death to Semelhago!" 39 *Dalhousie L.J.* 1 (2016).

CHAPTER 106CH

PROPERTY LAW IN SWITZERLAND

§ 106CH.01   History of Property Law in Switzerland.

§ 106CH.01(a)   Swiss Peoples in Prehistory.

Page 269: Correct the spelling of the name to:

Napoléon's

§ 106CH.01(b)   Development of a Civil Code and Code of Obligations.

Page 271: Correct the spelling of the name to:

Napoléon's

§ 106CH.03   Real Property Rights Under the Civil Code.

§ 106CH.03(a)   Ownership and Possession of Property.

Page 272: Add to footnote 21:

[21] *See generally* Georg von Segesser, Property and Trust Law in Switzerland (Wolters Kluwer 2016). *See generally* David Wallace Wilson and Caroline López Nagai, *Country Report: Switzerland,* 18 Colum. J. Eur. L. Online 26 (2012) (summary overview of the substantive Swiss provisions applicable to trusts).

Page 273: Add a footnote to the sentence ending in "improvements on land."

24.1 *Cf.* Andrew T. Hayashi & Richard M. Hynes, *Protectionist Property Taxes*, 106 Iowa L. Rev. 1091, 1111 (2021). "In 2012, Switzerland effectively prohibited the construction of second homes in certain regions."

§ 106CH.03(g)   Foreign Ownership of Swiss Land.

Page 275: Add as the final paragraph of subsection 106CH.03(g):

Since 2002, European Union nationals residing in Switzerland can freely acquire Swiss property.[35.1]

35.1 David Wallace Wilson and Caroline López Nagai, *Country Report: Switzerland*, 18 Colum. J. Eur. L. Online 26, 32 (2012). The authors also report that European Union nationals "no longer require a so called 'Lex Koller' authorization, contrary to non-resident foreigners who are still submitted to a preliminary administrative authorization in order to become owners of a Swiss property." (footnote omitted).

§ 106CH.03(h)   The Land Register Law.

Page 276: Add a footnote to the phrase "banking secrecy laws,":

37.1 *See* Taylor Ball, Note, *International Tax Compliance Agreements and Swiss Bank Privacy Law: A Model Protecting a Principled History*, 48 Geo. Wash. Int'l L. Rev. 233 (2015); Ray Flores, Note, *Lifting Bank Secrecy: A Comparative Look at the Philippines, Switzerland, and Global Transparency*, 14 Wash. U. Global Stud. L. Rev. 779 (2015); Jane G. Song, Comment, *The End of Secret Swiss Accounts?: The Impact of the U.S. Foreign Account Tax Compliance Act (FATCA) on Switzerland's Status as a Haven for Offshore Accounts*, 35 NW J. Int'l L. & Bus. 687 (2015). *See generally* Marialuisa Taddia, *Switzerland Feel the Bern*, LS Gaz, 11 Sep, 21 (11 September 2017) (stating in part, "Switzerland's reputation as a haven for offshore banking suffered from the US crackdown on tax evasion that deployed secret Swiss accounts. The 2008 UBS scandal, and the subsequent $780m settlement a year later between the world's biggest private bank and the US Department of Justice (DoJ), led US prosecutors to investigate other Swiss banks for allegedly aiding tax evasion.").

§ 106CH.03(i)   Notarization of the Transfer.

Page 276: Add a footnote to the third and final sentence in subsection 106CH.03(i):

37.2 *See generally* Peter Soskin, Note, *Protecting Title in Continental Europe and the United States—Restriction of a Market*, 7 Hastings Bus. L.J. 411, 423 (2011) ("Some countries consider registration and other related fees a separate cost of the transaction, with registry fees varying from about a quarter of a percent of the value of the transaction in Switzerland, to up to eleven percent in Italy. . . . Switzerland's notary fees are on the lower end, averaging less than ten percent of the transaction costs.").

§ 106CH.05   Other Swiss Real Property Laws.

§ 106CH.05(a)   Property Rights Between Husband and Wife.

Page 276: Add to footnote 39:

39 *See generally* Dorian Kessler, *Economic Gender Equality and the Decline of Alimony in Switzerland*, 17 J. Empirical Legal Stud. 493 (2020).

CHAPTER 106CL
PROPERTY LAW IN CHILE

SYNOPSIS

Page 279: Add a new section after § 106CL.05:

§ 106CL.06 Bibliography.

§ 106CL.01   Brief History of Property Law in Chile.

Page 280: Add to footnote 1:

[1] Mirow, M. C., "Origins of the Social Function of Property in Chile," 80 *Fordham L. Rev.* 1183 (December, 2011).

§ 106CL.03   Real Property Transactions.

§ 106CL.03(b)   Sales of Real Property.

Page 282: Add a footnote to the first sentence of the second paragraph of subsection 106CL.03(b):

See Lex Mundi Chile Business Guide 7.3 which states: "In the case of a real estate, in order to enter into a valid contract, the purchase agreement must be executed by means of a public deed granted before a Notary Public. Although the purchase agreement may be valid, the real estate property has not been transferred yet. In order to do so, the real estate must be registered under the purchaser's name in a public registry."

§ 106CL.05   Foreign Ownership of Chilean Real Property.

Page 283: Add a footnote to the only sentence in subsection 106CL.05:

[14.1] *See* Lex Mundi Chile Business Guide 7.3. This restriction also applies to nationals of Bolivia and Argentina.

Page 283: Add a new section after § 106CL.06 Bibliography. after end of § 106CL.05:

§ 106CL.06   Bibliography.

Books

Chirgwin, Andrés, *Doing Business in Chile* (The British-Chilean Chamber of Commerce 2d ed. Kindle ed. 2014).

Couso, J., A. Coddou, D. Lovera & M. Guilof, *Constitutional Law in Chile* (Kluwer Law International 2013).

Di Giminiani, Piergiorgio, *Sentient Lands: Indigeneity, Property, and Political Imagination in Neoliberal Chile* (University of Arizona Press 2018).

Donoso, Guillermo, ed., *Water Policy in Chile* (Springer International Publishing AG 2018).

Murphy, Edward, *For a Proper Home: Housing Rights in the Margins of Urban Chile, 1960–2010* (University of Pittsburgh Press 2015).

Ruiz-Tagle, Pablo, *Five Republics and One Tradition: A History of Constitutionalism in Chile 1810–2020* (Cambridge University Press 2021).

Articles

Davis, Annie Rischard, Comment, "The Cultural Property Conundrum: The Case for a Nationalistic Approach and Repatriation of the Moai to the Rapa Nui," 44 *Am. Indian L. Rev.* 333 (2020).

De Cuenca, Monserrat Madariaga Gómez, "Is Chile building good climate governance? Reflections on the drafting process of the climate change framework law," *ELR* 23 1 (40) 1 March 2021.

Hurtado, Hugo, "The U.S. and Chile Tax Treaty and Its Impact on Foreign Direct Investment," 13 *Fla. Tax Rev.* 41 (2012).

Lazo, Rodrigo Polanco, "Legal Framework of Foreign Investment in Chile," 18 *Law & Bus. Rev. Am.* 203 (2012).

Long, Jerrold A., Shana Hirsch and Jason Walters, "Chile, the Biobio, and the Future of the Columbia River Basin," 53 Transp. L. J. 239 (2017).

Mantilla, Yuri, "Indigenous Peoples' Diplomacy, Mediation, and Conciliation as a Response to the I.C.J. Decision in the Obligation to Negotiate Access to the Pacific Ocean Case," 51 *Cal. W. Int'l L.J.* 29 (2020).

McCawley, Diego Gil, "Law and Inclusive Urban Development: Lessons from Chile's Enabling Markets Housing Policy Regime," 67 *Am. J. Comp. L.* 587 (2019).

McCawley, Diego Gil, "The Political Economy of Land Use Governance in Santiago, Chile and Its Implications for Class-Based Segregation," 47 *Urb. Law.* 119 (2015).

Miller, Robert J., Lisa LeSage, and Sebastian Lopez Escarcena, "The International Law of Discovery, Indigenous Peoples, and Chile," 89 *Neb. L. Rev.* 819 (2011).

Mirow, M.C., "The Social Function of Property at Work in Latin America: Origins of the Social Function of Property in Chile," 80 *Fordham L. Rev.* 1183 (2011).

Poindexter, Georgette Chapman and Wendy Vargas-Cartaya, "En Ruta Hacia El Desarrollo: The Emerging Secondary Mortgage Market in Latin America," 34 *Geo. Wash. Int'l L. Rev.* 257 (2002).

Ramos, Claudia B. Alonso, "Derecho a la Vivienda: El Fenómeno Tras el Fenómeno," 90 *Rev. Jur. U.P.R.* 833 (2021).

CHAPTER 106CN

PROPERTY LAW IN THE PEOPLE'S REPUBLIC OF CHINA

§ 106CN.01   History.

Page 286: Add to footnote 1:

[1] *See* John W. Head, *Great Legal Traditions: Civil Law, Common Law and Chinese Law in Historical and Operational Perspective* (Carolina Academic Press 2011); Chenglin Liu, *Chinese Law in Context* (Carolina Academic Press 2020).

§ 106CN.02   Types of Real Property Interests.

§ 106CN.02(a)   Real Property Interests Under the Constitution.

Page 287: Add a footnote:

[2.1] The Constitution of the People's Republic of China was revised in 1999, 2004 and 2018. As revised, this Constitution states in part:

Article 9 All mineral resources, waters, forests, mountains, grasslands, unreclaimed land, mudflats and other natural resources are owned by the state, that is, by the whole people, except for the forests, mountains, grasslands, unreclaimed land and mudflats that are owned by collectives as prescribed by law.

The state shall ensure the rational use of natural resources and protect rare animals and plants. It is prohibited for any organization or individual to seize or damage natural resources by any means.

Article 10 Land in cities is owned by the state.

Land in rural and suburban areas is owned by collectives except for that which belongs to the state as prescribed by law; housing sites and cropland and hillsides allotted for private use are also owned by collectives.

The state may, in order to meet the demands of the public interest and in accordance with the provisions of law, expropriate or requisition land and furnish compensation.

No organization or individual shall unlawfully transfer land through seizure, sale and purchase, or in any other form. Land-use rights may be transferred in accordance with the provisions of law.

All organizations and individuals using land must use it in an appropriate manner.

Article 13 Citizens' lawful private property is inviolable.

The state shall protect the right of citizens to own and inherit private property in accordance with the provisions of law.

The state may, in order to meet the demands of the public interest and in accordance with the provisions of law, expropriate or requisition citizens' private property and furnish compensation.

See generally Larry Catá Backer, *Chinese Constitutionalism in the "New Era": The Constitution in Emerging Idea and Practice*, 33 Conn. J. Int'l L. 163 (2018); Taisu Zhang & Tom Ginsburg, *China's Turn Toward Law*, 59 Va. J. Int'l L. 313 (2019).

§ 106CN.02(b) Real Property Interests Under Recent Legislation and Regulations.

Page 288: Add a footnote:

[4.1] The current Civil Code of the People's Republic of China was adopted at the Third Session of the Thirteenth National People's Congress on May 28, 2020. Chapter V, titled "Civil-law Rights," contains articles addressing the personal rights of natural persons. Article 114 states in part, "Real rights are the rights to directly and exclusively control a specific thing by the right holder in accordance with law, which consists of the ownership, right to usufruct, and security interests in the property."

Page 289: Add to footnote 12:

[12] *See generally* Lei Chen, The Making of Chinese Condominium Law: A Comparative Perspective with American and South African Condominium Laws (Intersentia 2010); Perry Keller, Obligations and Property Rights in China (Routledge 2012); Gregory M. Stein, Modern Chinese Real Estate Law: Property Development in an Evolving Legal System (Routledge 2012); Shuguang Zhang, The Segmentation, Implementation and Protection of Land Rights in China (World Scientific Publishing Co. 2015); Valerie Jaffee Washburn, *Regular Takings or Regulatory Takings?: Land Expropriation in Rural China*, 20 Pac. Rim L & Pol'y Rev. 71 (2011).

§ 106CN.03 Creation, Transfer, and Termination of Real Property Interests.

§ 106CN.03(c) Registration and Conveyance of Real Property Interests in Houses.

Page 293: Add to the end of subsection 106CN.03(c) as a new paragraph:

On March 1, 2015, the Provisional Regulations on Real Estate Registration became effective. These Regulations establish a nationwide real estate registration system in China.[36.1]

[36.1] Laney Zhang, China: Nationwide Real Estate Registration Rules Entered into Effect, https://www.loc.gov/item/global-legal-monitor/2015-07-07/china-nationwide-real-estate-registration-rules-entered-into-effect/ (visited May 24, 2022).

§ 106CN.05 Bibliography.

Books

Page 294: Add to Books:

Cao, Junjian Albert, *The Chinese Real Estate Market: Development, Regulation and Investment* (Routledge 2015).

Cheuk-Yuet, Ho, *Neo-Socialist Property Rights: The Predicament of Housing*

Ownership in China (Lexington Books 2015).

Liu, Chenglin, *Chinese Law in Context* (Carolina Academic Press 2020).

Ni, Pengfei, Linhua Zou, Guangchun Gao & Xuemei Jiang, *Housing Reform and China's Real Estate Industry: Review and Forecast* (Springer 2019).

Qiao, Shitong, *Chinese Small Property: The Co-Evolution of Law and Social Norms* (Cambridge University Press 2017).

Stein, Gregory M., *Modern Chinese Real Estate Law: Property Development in an Evolving Legal System* (Routledge 2012).

Wei, Wenfeng, *Collective Ownership and Land Distribution in China:—Is Privatization a Solution?* (LAP Lambert Academic Publishing 2019).

Wu, Yi, *Negotiating Rural Land Ownership in Southwest China: State, Village, Family* (University of Hawaii Press 2016).

Zhu, Jieming, *Urban Development in China under the Institution of Land Rights* (Routledge 2019).

Articles

Page 294: Add to Bibliography:

Austin, Daniel A. and Cheng to Lin, "Personal Bankruptcy in the Middle Kingdom: China's Local Pilot Programs and Half of a Bankruptcy System," 95 *Am. Bankr. L.J.* 81 (2021).

Backer, Larry Catá, "Chinese Constitutionalism in the 'New Era': The Constitution in Emerging Idea and Practice," 33 *Conn. J. Int'l L.* 163 (2018).

Beuchel, Matz, "Administration of Agricultural Resources Land and Water Law in China," 8 *Eur. Food & F_ed L. Rev.* 25 (2013).

Brown, Lloyd Andrew, "V.nat's the lender liability risk for soil pollution in the People's Republic of China? An evaluation of China's new Soil Pollution and Control Law in *t*.e light of the USA and UK regimes," *ELR* 21 3 (173) (Sept. 16, 2019).

Chan, Pete C.H., "Do the 'Haves' Come Out Ahead in Chinese Grassroots Cour* ∠ Rural Land Disputes Between Married-Out Women and Village C' ectives, 71 *Hastings L.J.* 1 (2019).

*` .ang, Valerie L., "No Gold Diggers: China's Protection of Individual Property Rights in the New Marital Property Regime," 45 *Geo. Wash. Int'l L. Rev.* 149 (2013).

Chen, Lei, "Land Registration, Property Rights and Institutional Performance in China: Progress Achieved and Challenges Ahead," 44 *Hong Kong L.J.* 841 (2014).

Chen, Lei, "Specific Performance as a Contractual Remedy in Chinese Courts: An Empirical Study," Chin. J. Comp. Law (2019) 7(1): 95–123.

Chen, Lei and Larry A. DiMatteo, "Inefficiency of Specific Performance as a Contractual Remedy in Chinese Courts: An Empirical and Normative Analysis," 40 *NW J. Int'l L. & Bus.* 275 (2020).

Chen, Weitseng, "Arbitrage for Property Rights: How Foreign Investors Create Substitutes for Property Institutions in China," 23 *Wash. Int'l L.J.* 47 (2015).

Chow, Daniel C. K., "Navigating the Minefield of Trade Secrets Protection in

China," 47 *Vand. J. Transnat'l L.* 1007 (2014).

Clarke, Donald, "China's Stealth Urban Land Revolution," 62 *Am. J. Comp. L.* 323 (2014).

Cluxton, David, "The Chicago Convention 1944 in an UNCLOS 1982 World: Maritime Zones, Continental Shelves, Artificial Islands, and Some Other Issues," 41 *U. La Verne L. Rev.* 137 (2020).

Downey, Kiel, "Intellectual Property Rights and Renewable Energy Technology Transfer in China," 9 *S.C. J. Int'l L. & Bus.* 89 (2012).

Drawz, James, Note, "Whose Sea Is It Anyway?: An Analysis of the Permanent Court of Arbitration's South China Sea Arbitration Decision," 12 *Creighton Int'l & Comp. L.J.* 43 (2022).

Han, Simeng, "Chinese Use of Administrative Proceedings to Enforce Intellectual Property Rights: Evaluating and Improving ADR in China," 14 *Cardozo J. Conflict Resol.* 195 (2012).

Head, John W., *Great Legal Traditions: Civil Law, Common Law and Chinese Law in Historical and Operational Perspective* (2011).

Hung, Alvin Hoi-Chun, "Did Exclusion Ignite China's Drive to Compete in Space Station Technology? An Analysis of the Techno-Legal Implications of the Wolf Amendment (2011)," 2022 *U. Ill. J.L. Tech. & Pol'y 119.*

Hyatt, Conor J., Note, "Hong Kong Small House Policy: Modernity, Crisis Morality & Policies for Repair," 4 *Cardozo Int'l & Comp. L. Rev.* 763 (2021).

Jeffery, Michael I., and Xiaobo Zhao, "Developing a National Contaminated Land Liability Scheme in China: The Comprehensive Environmental Response, Compensation, and Liability Act Revisited," 30 *J. Energy & Nat. Resources L.* 423 (2013).

Jiang, Dong, "Home-Based Business Law in China: Is there a Seven-Year Itch?," 25 *J. Transnat'l L. & Pol'y* 101 (2015).

Jiang, Hao, "The Making of a Civil Code in China: Promises and Perils of a New Civil Law," 95 *Tul. L. Rev.* 777 (2021).

Kielsgard, Mark D., and Lei Chen, "The Emergence of Private Property Law in China and Its Impact on Human Rights," 15 *Asian-Pac. L. & Pol'y J.* 94 (2013).

Lan, Gil, "American Legal Realism Goes to China: The China Puzzle and Law Reform," 51 *Am. Bus. L.J.* 365 (2014).

Mao, Wenzheng and Shitong Qiao, "Legal Doctrine and Judicial Review of Eminent Domain in China," 46 *Law & Soc. Inquiry* 826 (2021).

Munzer, Stephen R., "Dam(n) Displacement: Compensation, Resettlement, and Indigeneity," 51 *Cornell Int'l L.J.* 823 (2019).

Parry, Rebecca, Haizheng Zhang and Jiahui Fu, "Personal Insolvency in China: Necessities, Difficulties, and Possibilities," 46 *Brooklyn J. Int'l L.* 517 (2021).

Pritchett, Wendell & Shitong Qiao, "Exclusionary Megacities," 91 *S. Cal. L. Rev.* 467 (2018).

Qioa, Shitong, "Expropriation in the Name of Rights: Transferable Development Rights (TDRs), the Bundle of Sticks and Chinese Politics," 13 *NYU J.L. & Liberty* 1 (2019).

Qiao, Shitong, "Fragmented Laws, Contingent Choices: The Tragicomedy of the

Village Commons in China," 29 *Duke J. Comp. & Int'l L.* 235 (2019).

Qiao, Shitong, "Rights-Weakening Federalism," 102 *Minn. L. Rev.* 1671 (2018).

Qiao, Shitong, "Small Property, Big Market: A Focal Point Explanation," 63 *Am. J. Comp. L.* 197 (2015).

Qiao, Shitong and Frank Upham, "The Evolution of Relational Property Rights: A Case of Chinese Rural Land Reform," 100 Iowa L. Rev. 2479 (2015).

Sitaraman, Ganesh, Morgan Ricks & Christopher Serkin, "Regulation and the Geography of Inequality," 70 *Duke L.J.* 1763 (2021).

Stein, Gregory M., "Private and Public Construction in Modern China," 12 *San Diego Int'l L.J.* 5 (2010).

Stein, Gregory M., "What Will China Do When Land Use Rights Begin to Expire?," 50 *Vand. J. Transnat'l L.* 625 (2017).

Szto, Mary, "Chinese American Property Ownership and Discrimination in Historical Perspective," 25 *J. Transnat'l L. & Pol'y* 33 (2015).

Wang, Alex L., "Explaining Environmental Information Disclosure in China," 44 *Ecology L.Q.* 865 (2018).

Wang, Kai, "Whatever-ism with Chinese Characteristics: China's Nascent Recognition of Private Property Rights and Its Political Ramifications," 6 *E. Asia L. Rev.* 43 (2011).

Washburn, Valerie Jaffee, "Regular Takings or Regulatory Takings?: Land Expropriation in Rural China," 20 *Pac. Rim L. & Pol'y J.* 71 (2011).

Wen, Wei, "Comparative Analysis of Sino-American Contractual Writing Attributes: Underpinnings for China's Future Uniform Civil Code to Mandate Writing for Land Sale Contracts," 16 *S.C. J. Int'l L. & Bus.* 23 (2020).

Wen, Wei, "The Need for Certainty and Written Form in Land Sale Contracts in China: A Legal Reform Recommendation," 3 *Cardozo Int'l & Comp. L. Rev.* 383 (2020).

Zhang, Taisu, "Beyond Information Costs: Preference Formation and the Architecture of Property Law," 12 *J. of Legal Analysis* 1 (2020).

Zhang, Taisu, "Social Hierarchies and the Formation of Customary Property Law in Pre-Industrial China and England," 62 *Am. J. Comp. L.* 171 (2014).

Zhang, Taisu & Tom Ginsburg, "China's Turn Toward Law," 59 *Va. J. Int'l L.* 313 (2019).

Zhao, Yuhong, "Contaminated Land in China—The Legal Regime and Its Weakest Links," 16 *U. Pa. Asian L. Rev.* 150 (2020).

CHAPTER 106DE

PROPERTY LAW IN GERMANY

Page 295: Remove the slash and the first "U" from B/Uurgerliches. This word should be:[1]

§ 106DE.04 The Empire of Charles the Great and the Growth of Feudalism.

[1] *Bürgerliches*

Page 299: "coDEperative" should be "cooperative."

cooperative

§ 106DE.06 The Movement Toward Codification and Enactment of the Civil Code (BGB).

Page 300: Correct the spelling of Napoleonic. The second "a" should be an "o."

Napoleonic

Page 301: Remove the slash and the first "U" from B/Uurgerliches. This word should be:

Bürgerliches

§ 106DE.07 Sources of Property Law After Promulgation of the Civil Code (BGB).

§ 106DE.07(a) The Continuing Validity of the BGB.

Page 301: Remove the slash and the first "U" from B/Uurgerliches. This word should be:

Bürgerliches

Page 301: Add a footnote to the first sentence of subsection 106DE.07(a):

[17.1] *See generally* Michael Mütze, Thomas Senff and Jutta C. Möller, Real Estate Investments in Germany: Transactions and Development (Springer-Verlag 2d ed. 2012).

§ 106DE.08 Property Law Under the BGB.

§ 106DE.08(a) Types of Property Interests.

§ 106DE.08(a)(1) Ownership.

Page 303: I believe coDEwnership should be co-ownership.

co-ownership

§ 106DE.08(a)(4) Protection of Property Interests.

Page 304: Add new footnote 42.1 at the end of last sentence of only paragraph of § 106DE.08(a)(4):

[42.1] Draeger, Tonya R., "Property as a Fundamental Right in the United States and Germany: A Comparison of Takings Jurisprudence," 14 *Transnat'l Law*. 363 (Fall 2001).

§ 106DE.10 Ancillary Real Property Laws.

§ 106DE.10(b) The Law of Home Ownership.

Page 308: I believe coDEwners should be co-owners.

co-owners

Page 310: Add a new section:

§ 106DE.12   Bibliography.

Books

Foster, Nigel & Satish Sule, *German Legal System and Laws* (Oxford University Press 4th ed. 2010).

James, Peter, *Modern Germany: Politics, Society and Culture* (Routledge 2020).

Just, Tobias & Wolfgang Maennig, *Understanding German Real Estate Markets* (Springer 2d ed. 2017).

Kommers, Donald P. & Russell A. Miller, *The Constitutional Jurisprudence of the Federal Republic of Germany* (Duke University Press Books 3d ed. 2012).

McClurg, Andrew J. McClurg, Adem Koyuncu and Luis Eduardo Sprovieri, *Practical Global Tort Litigation: United States, Germany and Argentina* (Carolina Academic Press 2007).

Rogoff, Adam C., Richard F. Broude and Daniel M. Glosband, *Collier International Business Insolvency Guide* ch. 23, Germany (Matthew Bender).

Zekoll, Joachim & Gerhard Wagner, *Introduction to German Law* (Wolters Kluwer 3d ed. 2018).

Articles

Determann, Lothar and Markus Heintzen, "Constitutional Review of Statutes in Germany and the United States Compared," 28 *J. Transnat'l L. & Pol'y* 95 (2018–2019).

Jaggi, Stephan, "Revolutionary Reform in German Constitutional Law," 41 *Hastings Int'l & Comp. L. Rev.* 173 (2018).

Kotzé, Louis J., "Neubauer et al. versus Germany: Planetary Climate Litigation for the Anthropocene?" 22 German Law Journal 1423 (2021).

Krämer-Hoppe, Rike, "The Climate Protection Order of the Federal Constitutional Court of Germany and the North-South Divide," 22 *German Law Journal* 1393 (2021).

Lachner, Constantin M. and Rafael von Heppe, "The Introduction of Real Estate Investment Trusts [REITs] in Germany," 8 *German Law Journal* 133 (2007).

Rehahn, Johannes and Alexander Grimm, "Country Report: Germany," 18 *Colum. J. Eur. L.* 97 (2012).

Schmeilzl, Bernhard, "UK-German probate: process & pitfalls," 172 *NLJ* 7972, p17 (25 March 2022).

Walser, Miles, Note & Comment, "Putting the Brakes on Rent Increases: How the United States Could Implement German Anti-Gentrification Laws Without Running Afoul of the Takings Clause," 36 *Wis. Int'l L.J.* 187 (2018).

Williamson, Richard L., Jr. & Monika Bohm, "Dirty Water: Lessons for Comparative Public Law and International Governance From Wastewater Regulation in the United States and Germany," 43 *ELR* 10237 (2013).

CHAPTER 106DK

PROPERTY LAW IN DENMARK

§ 106DK.01   Brief History of Danish Law.

§ 106DK.01(a)   Customary Law in Denmark.

Page 311: Add to footnote 1:

[1] *See generally* Peter Blume, Legal Method in Danish Law (Djoef Publishing 2011); Peter Munk Christiansen, Jørgen Elklit and Peter Nedergaard, The Oxford Handbook of Danish Politics (Oxford University Press 2020); Ditlev Tamm, The History of Danish Law: Selected Articles and Bibliography (Djoef Publishing 2011); Ditlev Tamm and Helle Vogt, The Danish Medieval Laws: The Laws of Scania, Zealand and Jutland (Routledge 2020).

§ 106DK.02   Danish Real Property Law.

§ 106DK.02(a)   General Principles.

Page 314: Add a footnote to the fourth sentence of subsection 106DK.02(a):

[10.1] *See generally* Jocelyn H. W. C. Chong, Note, *Danish Mortgage Regulations—Structure, Evolution, and Crisis Management*, 9 Wash. U. Global Stud. L. Rev. 371 (2010).

§ 106DK.02(a)(2)   Impact of Environmental Regulation.

Page 315: Add a footnote to the first sentence of subsection 106DK.02(a)(2):

[16.1] *See generally* Ellen Margrethe Basse, Environmental Law in Denmark (Wolters Kluwer 3rd ed. 2020).

CHAPTER 106EG

PROPERTY LAW IN EGYPT

§ 106EG.01   History.

§ 106EG.01(a)   Traditional Islamic Roots.

Page 320: Add to footnote 1:

[1] Nada Moumtaz, God's Property: Islam, Charity and the Modern State (University of California Press 2021); Yehya Ikram Ibrhaim Badr, *Party Autonomy under the Egyptian Arbitration Code: The Freedoms and the Limits*, 28 Willamette J. Int'l L. & Dispute Res. 35 (2021); Ari Z. Bryen, *Review Symposium: Interdisciplinary Readings of Ari Z. Bryen's Violence in Roman Egypt: A Study in Legal Interpretation—Introduction*, 40 *Law & Soc. Inquiry* 783 (2015); Ari Z. Bryen, *The Constitution of Violence Through the Language of Law: Legal Hermeneutics in Second-Century Roman Egypt*, 40 *Law & Soc. Inquiry* 797 (2015). *See generally* J.G. Manning, Land and Power in Ptolemaic Egypt: The Structure of

Land Tenure (Cambridge University Press 2007); Reem A. Meshal, Sharia and the Making of the Modern Egyptian: Islamic Law and Custom in the Courts of Ottoman Cairo (The American University in Cairo Press 2014); Maria Bhatti, *The Role of Shari'a in International Commercial Arbitration*, 36 Wis. Int'l L.J. 46 (2018).

§ 106EG.02   The New Civil Code.

§ 106EG.02(b)   Aspects of Real Property.

§ 106EG.02(b)(2)   Acquisition of Real Property.

§ 106EG.02(b)(2)(iii)   Accession.

Page 328: Add to footnote 49:

[49] *See generally* Jack Hernandez, Student Article, *Changing Tides of the Nile: Analyzing Egypt's Claim to Preserve Its Historical Water Rights*, 50 Denv. J. Int'l L. & Pol'y 39 (2021); Ricarda E. von Meding, *The Grand Ethiopian Renaissance Dam: A Large-Scale Energy Project in Violation of International Law?*, 10 LSU J. of Energy L. & Resources 33 (2022); Salma H. Shitia, Student Article, *Climate Change, Competition, and Conflict Along the River Nile: The Grand Ethiopian Renaissance Dam & Shifting International Water Law*, 32 Fordham Envtl. Law Rev. 537 (2021).

§ 106EG.03   Recent Changes in Egyptian Property Law.

§ 106EG.03(b)   Foreign Ownership of Land.

Page 335: Add as new paragraphs in the text after footnote 86:

Foreigners can own residential property in Egypt under Law No. 230 of 1996. The purchase must be approved by the Council of Ministers. As a general rule, a foreigner is limited to ownership of two real estate properties in Egypt for accommodation purposes of the person and his family. Generally, the area of each property cannot exceed four thousand square meters and cannot be a historical site. An exemption can be granted with respect to the number of properties and the size requirement. Foreigners who own vacant land must build within a five-year period from the date that their ownership became effective.[87]

The ownership of non-residential property is governed by other laws and regulations.

[87] Doing Business in Egypt, Land Ownership Regulations, American Chamber of Commerce in Egypt Inc., http://amcham-egypt.org/dbedtls.asp?sec=2&subsec=8 (visited May 24, 2020).

Page 335: Insert new Chapter 106ES after Chapter 106EG:

CHAPTER 106ES
PROPERTY LAW IN SPAIN

SYNOPSIS

§ 106ES.01   Civil Code and Regional Systems *("Regímenes Forales")*.

The legal system of real property in Spain is the result of a long and rich history based on Roman law, which constitutes the core of the Spanish legal tradition. Law on the Peninsula evolved with the Visigothic invasion at the beginning of the 5th century. This resulted in the entry of Germanic law which coexisted with the law of Hispanic people. The legal unification and territorial application of a sole legal system took place with the promulgation in the 7th century of the *Liber Judiciorum.* In the 13th century this was translated and adapted in Castile, where it was known as *Fuero Juzgo.* The importance of Muslim rule from the 8th century over large parts of the Peninsula and the long period of reconquest, which ended with the taking of Granada in 1492 must also be noted. During this period many kingdoms were set up. These kingdoms were unified under a single crown with the marriage of Isabella of Castile and Ferdinand of Aragon. However the legal institutions of each kingdom did not disappear as a result of the unification of the kingdoms. In some cases, and as a result of subsequent historic events, the regional systems were recognized and maintained as a privilege for the services rendered to the nation.

Given this history anyone who comes into contact for the first time with the Spanish legal system should not be surprised that different private legal systems coexist. Real property law is not only ruled by the Civil Code (CC) and other State legislation, but many regions have their own law in this matter, particularly Aragon, the Balearic Islands, Catalonia, Galicia, the Basque Country and Navarre.

§ 106ES.01(a)   Constitution of 1978.

The Constitution of 1978 created a new territorial organization system. Spain is currently divided into 17 autonomous regions (*Comunidades Autónomas)* and 2 autonomous cities, and each one has its own parliament, executive government and judicial authority with jurisdiction over matters arising in the territory.

Therefore the promulgation of the Constitution and the subsequent development of the so-called State of Autonomous Communities, with the passing of the relevant Statutes of Autonomy (*Estatutos de Autonomía)* by each autonomous region, has resulted in the creation of the different regional legal systems. When considering this structure one must bear in mind that "the main principle of their relationship with State law is not the principle of normative hierarchy, or of succession in time, but the principle of competence in matters, in accordance with the Constitution and the Statutes" (Lacruz Berdejo and others, *"Elementos de Derecho Civil—I Parte General, Vol. I" Ed. Dykinson* (Madrid, 2008).

This chapter presents Spanish real property rights on issues important to the common law, based on the Civil Code and other State regulations.

§ 106ES.02   Rights *In Rem.*

§ 106ES.02(a)   Concept and Classification.

The classic distinction between rights *in rem* and credit rights or rights *in personam* is still commonly used as starting point.

Rights *in rem* are defined as the domination or power of men over things. This domination, or ownership, is protected by the legal system, in principle *erga omnes*. Rights *in rem* can be total or limited. The latter can be classified as enjoyment rights *in rem* (usufruct, easement, use and habitation, emphyteutic, ground rents and surface rights), acquisition rights *in rem* (option, pre-emption and redemption) and guaranty rights *in rem* (mortgage, pledge and *antichresis*).

Ownership is defined in the Civil Code as the right to enjoy and dispose of a thing, without greater limitations than those set forth in the laws. The Code also provides that the owner shall have an action against the holder and the possessor of the property to reclaim it (art. 348 CC).

Limited rights *in rem* involve other people's things, and grant to their holders limited rights and actions to prevent third parties from disturbing the exercise of their right or not recognizing it.

§ 106ES.02(b)   Acquisition of Rights *In Rem*.

Art. 609 of the Civil Code sets forth that "ownership is acquired by occupancy. Ownership and other rights over property are acquired by law, by gift, by testate and intestate succession, and as a result of certain contracts by tradition. They may also be acquired by prescription."

This list of the Civil Code has been criticized but it may be useful to define the different ways to acquire rights *in rem*:

(a) **Occupancy**: property rights capable of appropriation without an owner, such as game or wild fish, hidden treasure and abandoned movable things, are acquired by occupation (art. 610 CC). Therefore occupancy can be used to acquire ownership, not limited rights *in rem*, of movable property, by taking control of a thing with the intent of acquiring it for oneself.

(b) **Discovery of a hidden treasure**: a hidden treasure is defined as the hidden and ignored deposit of money, jewelry or other precious objects, when it is unknown who they legitimately belong to (art. 352 CC). Hidden treasure shall belong to the owner of the land on which it is found. However, when the discovery happens by chance on another's property, or on State property, half shall belong to the discoverer. If the objects discovered should be of interest to science or art, the State may acquire them for their fair value. Payment shall be distributed in accordance with the above provisions (art. 351 CC).

(c) **Finding**: a person who finds a movable thing that is not a treasure must return it to its owner. If the owner is unknown, he must immediately consign it with the mayor of the municipality where it was found. The mayor shall publish the finding on two consecutive Sundays. If the owner does not appear within two years counting from the second publication, the thing found or its value shall be

55

awarded to the person who found it. If the owner should appear in time, he shall be obliged to pay, as an award to the person who found it, approximately 5% of the value of the thing (art. 615 and 616 CC).

(d) **Accession**: ownership of the property shall, pursuant to the right of accession, entitle the owner to everything produced thereby, or naturally or artificially joined or incorporated thereto (art. 353 CC).

(e) **Gift**: a gift is an intentional liberality whereby a person gratuitously disposes of a thing in favor of another person, who accepts it (art. 618 CC).

(f) **Succession** (arts. 657 to 1087 CC): succession takes place pursuant to the will of a person expressed in a testament—testamentary succession—and, where intestate, by operation of law—legal succession. A person who succeeds pursuant to universal title is an heir, and a person who succeeds pursuant to specific title is a legatee.

(g) **Prescription** (arts. 1930 to 1975 CC): ownership of movable property prescribes after three years of uninterrupted good faith possession, or six years without any other condition. Ownership and other rights *in rem* over real property prescribe after ten years' possession for persons resident in Spain, and twenty for those persons not residing in Spain, in good faith and with just title. Ownership and other rights in rem over real property also prescribe as a result of thirty years of uninterrupted possession, without requiring any title or good faith, and without distinction between residents and non-residents, save in case of some easements (art. 1959 CC).

(h) **Delivery** (arts. 1095, 1462 to 1464 CC): the effect of transfer takes place when in the operation of an agreement between the parties, the *tradens* delivers the property with the intent to transfer ownership. Therefore the Spanish system follows the theory of title and manner: the purchaser by means of the agreement or title acquires a credit against the vendor, the right to request the delivery of the thing or right. The acquisition of ownership or a right *in rem* takes place only upon delivery (manner).

§ 106ES.03   Limited Rights *In Rem*.

§ 106ES.03(a)   Usufruct.

Usufruct entitles one to enjoy another's property with the obligation to preserve its form and substance, unless otherwise authorized by the deed pursuant to which it was created, or the law (art. 467 CC).

Usufruct is created by law (for example, usufruct rights of the surviving spouse set forth in the CC), by the will of individuals expressed in acts *inter vivos*, or in a last will and testament and by prescription (art. 468 CC).

§ 106ES.03(b)   Use and Habitation.

Use entitles a person to receive from among the natural, industrial or economic products resulting from a thing belonging to another, those resources that are sufficient for the needs of the holder of the right and his family, even if the latter should increase in size. Habitation entitles a person to occupy in another's house the necessary rooms for himself and the persons in his family (art. 524 CC). These rights are regulated by the title establishing them, and subsidiarily by the CC.

§ 106ES.03(c)   Easement.

An easement is an encumbrance imposed on real property for the benefit of another property belonging to a different owner. The real property in whose favor the easement is constituted is called a dominant tenement; the property subject to it is the servient tenement (art. 530 CC). Easements may also be established for the benefit of one or several persons or a community to whom the encumbered property does not belong (art. 531 CC).

The CC sets forth the following classification of easements:

- continuous or discontinuous, depending on the use.

- apparent or non-apparent, depending on whether they present external signs or indications of their existence. (art. 532 CC).

- positive or negative. A positive easement is that which imposes on the owner of the servient tenement the obligation to allow something to be done or to do it himself, and a negative easement is that which forbids the owner of the servient tenement from doing something which would be lawful if the easement did not exist (art. 533 CC).

- Legal or voluntary, depending on whether the easement is established by law or by the will of the owners.

§ 106ES.03(d)   Ground Rents (*Censos*).

A ground rent is constituted when certain real properties are earmarked for the payment of an annual rent or annuity as remuneration for a capital sum received in cash, or for the full or limited ownership transferred in respect of the same properties (art. 1604 CC).

This is, as mentioned above, a limited right *in rem* on real property which is subject to the encumbrance of paying a rent or annuity. If the owner or person in possession fails to pay, the real property given as a guaranty may be disposed of in order to collect the payment with the proceeds of the sale.

§ 106ES.03(e)   Emphyteutic Ground Rents.

The ground rent is emphyteutic where one person assigns in favor of the other useful ownership of a property, and reserves for himself legal ownership and the right to receive from the emphyteutic lessee an annual pension due to his ownership (art. 1605 CC). The emphyteutic lessee has a right to the produce of the property and any accessions thereof, and shall have the same rights as the owner to any treasures and mines discovered on the property constituting the subject matter of the emphyteutic ground rent (art. 1632 CC). Another distinctive feature is that the emphyteutic lessee may dispose of the emphyteutic property and any accessions *inter vivos* and by last will and testament, except for the rights of the direct owner and subject to the other provisions of the CC.

§ 106ES.03(f)   Surface.

This right is mentioned but not regulated in the CC. It is defined in the Land Act (Royal Legislative Decree 2/2008, of June 20) as a right *in rem*. The right permits the surface lessee to build structures on the slope, projection and subsoil of property of another. The lessee keeps the temporal ownership of the structures built. This right may also be granted on structures already built or on dwellings, premises or privative elements of structures.

For the surface right to be duly incorporated it must be granted in a public deed, and registered in the Property Registry.

The public deed must state the duration of the surface right. The right may not exceed ninety nine years.

The surface right may only be granted by the owner of the land.

The surface right may be subject to consideration. If it is for consideration, it may be payment of a lump sum or a periodic amount, or the allocation of dwellings or premises or lease rights in favor of the owner of the land, or a combination of some of the above. This is notwithstanding the total reversion of the buildings at the end of the term agreed to upon constitution of the surface right.

§ 106ES.03(g)   Option.

An option is the right that the owner of a thing grants to a third party in order to acquire it, paying the agreed price and any other stipulated amounts (DIEZ-PICAZO y GULLÓN, *Sistema de Derecho Civil*, vol. III, Ed. Tecnos). The option agreement may be for consideration or not.

To become effective vis-à-vis third parties the option must be registered in the Property Registry. Art. 14 of the Mortgage Regulation provides that options to purchase agreements or express covenants or stipulations expressly determining this in any other contract subject to registration, may be registered as long as, in addition to the usual requirements for registration, they meet the following requirements:

1. Express agreement between the parties regarding registration.

2. Stipulated price for the acquisition of the property and price agreed for the granting of the option, if any.

3. Term for the exercise of the option, which shall not exceed four years.

Options in leases or other contracts may have a duration greater than 4 years, but shall only be effective between the parties and not vis-à-vis third parties. Unless otherwise agreed to between the parties an option expires upon tacit or legal extension of the lease agreement.

§ 106ES.03(h)   Pre-emption and Redemption.

Pre-emption entitles the rights holder to acquire a thing before a third party for the same price that the latter would be willing to pay.

Redemption entitles the holder thereof to acquire a thing that has been sold, for the same price paid by the third party under the same conditions set forth in the acquisition agreement.

Pre-emption and redemption rights may be established by law (for example, the right of the lessee to acquire the leased property in case of sale—art. 25 Urban Lease Act), but they can also be agreed between the parties.

§ 106ES.03(i)   Mortgage.

A mortgage directly and immediately subjects the property it encumbers, no matter who its possessor is, to the performance of the obligation it was created to secure (art. 1876 CC). Therefore it is a right *in rem* of guaranty, which grants a right to compel the sale of the mortgaged property, and use the resulting price as consideration for the principal obligation that has been secured.

The constitution of a mortgage requires the granting of a public deed and registration in the Property Registry.

Depending on their origin, mortgages can be classified as legal or voluntary. Voluntary mortgages are those agreed between the parties or imposed by the owner of the secured properties, and may only be constituted by those who are able to freely dispose of them or, if they may not, they are authorized by the laws to constitute a mortgage (art. 138 of the Mortgage Law). Legal mortgages are those expressly established by law. This legal provision means that the persons in favor of whom the law grants a legal mortgage have the sole right to request the incorporation of a special mortgage that is sufficient enough to guarantee their right (art. 158 ML).

The general rule is that a mortgage may be constituted to secure any kind of obligation and shall not alter the unlimited personal liability of the debtor set forth under art. 1911 CC (art. 105 ML). However, the public deed of incorporation of the voluntary mortgage may establish that the secured obligation is only covered by the mortgaged properties. If that happens the liability of the debtor and the action of the creditor, by virtue of the mortgage, are limited to the amount of the mortgaged properties, and shall not affect the remaining properties of the debtor (art. 140 ML). In practice and unlike what happens in other countries, the application of the covenant of limitation of liability to the mortgaged properties is not usual. Therefore, in the context of a general fall of real estate prices, it is not surprising that the sale value of the mortgaged real property is less than the secured debt, and therefore the execution of the mortgage does not release the debtor, who shall continue to be personally liable with all its present and future properties for the unpaid part of the debt.

§ 106ES.03(j)   Pledge.

There are two kinds of pledge depending on whether the thing subject to pledge is delivered to the creditor, a third party or not.

A pledge with a change in possession, regulated in the CC, is a right *in rem* guaranty, which grants the right to dispose of the thing pledged and use the resulting amount to pay the credit. Pledge contracts may secure all kinds of obligations, and all movable things that are subject to trade may be pledged, provided that they are capable of being possessed. The correct constitution of a pledge requires, in addition to an agreement by common consent, giving possession of the thing to the creditor or to a third party. No pledge shall be effective against a third party unless the certainty of its date is set forth in a public instrument.

A pledge without change of possession is regulated under the law of Movable Mortgage and Pledge without Displacement (law of December 16, 1954), which establishes a *numerus clausus* of the things capable of being pledged: agricultural fruits, crops, forest products, animals, certain machines, tools and the products from agricultural and farming exploitations, stored merchandises and raw materials and paintings, sculptures, pieces of china, books and any other thing of artistic or historic value. Credits and other rights corresponding to the holders of agreements, licenses, administrative concessions or grants may be subject to pledge without change in possession as long as the law or the relevant constitutive title authorizes their sale to a third party. Credit rights, even future credits, may be subject to pledge without change in possession as long as they are not represented by securities and are not considered as financial instruments for purposes of Royal Decree-law 5/2005, of March 11, of Urgent Reforms to boost Productivity and improve Public Contracting. To be effectively constituted they shall be registered in the Registry of Movable Goods.

§ 106ES.03(k)   *Antichresis.*

Pursuant to *antichresis* the creditor acquires the right to receive the economic benefits of real property belonging to the debtor. The receipts are allocated first to any interest, if due, and subsequently to the principal (art. 1881 CC).

The creditor is obliged to pay any taxes and charges that the property may be subject to, and the necessary expenses for the conservation and repair of the property. He may deduct any amounts spent from the economic benefits produced. If the debtor does not pay the debt in time, the creditor may claim, according to the Civil Procedure Law, the payment of the debt or the sale of the property.

§ 106ES.03(l) Time-Sharing.

Law 42/1998, of December 15, which regulates time-sharing rights in real property used for tourism and tax rules, meant not only the transposition of Directive 94/47/CE, but also the development of a broader internal regulation. The aim was to regulate a new legal concept which was remarkably on the increase in a booming Spanish tourism sector. A new time-sharing right *in rem* was created, which could also be configured as a variant of a seasonal lease.

By virtue of a time-sharing right in real property one is entitled to enjoy, exclusively, during a specific period each year, an accommodation capable of being used independently and which has the appropriate furniture for this purpose, and complementary services.

The yearly period of use may never be less than seven days in a row. The duration of this right may be from three to fifty years.

This right must be granted in a public deed and registered in the Property Registry. The law establishes a minimum content for the agreement (art. 9).

The acquirer of time-sharing rights has a term of ten days from the signature of the agreement to desist at his own discretion without any cost. He may also terminate the agreement within three months if the latter does not contain any of the references or documents required by law, or if the acquirer has not been sufficiently informed. The mentioned terms are also important because any advance payment by the acquirer to the transferor before expiry of these terms is forbidden.

§ 106ES.04 Lease.

Leases are regulated by Law 49/2003, of November 26, regarding Rustic Lease and law 29/1994, of November 24, regarding Urban Lease.

Subsidiarily they are addressed in the Spanish Civil Code (Book IV, Title VI, Chapters I and II—articles 1542 to 1582).

§ 106ES.04(a) Rustic Lease.

Law 49/2003 covers lease agreements on properties to be used for agricultural, ranching and forestry purposes. A specific type of exploitation of a property can also be the object of a lease agreement, as long as the parties expressly state this and attach an inventory to the agreement. It is possible to simultaneously have leases for different types of exploitation of the same property.

Under Law 49/2003 both property and exploitation lease agreements incorporate the right of agricultural production and other rights inherent in the leased property or exploitation.

§ 106ES.04(b)   Urban Lease.

Law 29/1994 covers lease agreements on urban properties and distinguishes two kinds of urban leases:

—Housing lease:

Housing leases are lease agreements on habitable properties to be used as permanent housing by the lessee. It also applies to furniture, store rooms, parking places or any other places leased as an accessory to the property.

Legal dispositions regarding housing leases are aimed at protecting the lessee. Therefore any clause contained in the agreement which modifies the legal dispositions against the interests of the lessee is considered null and void.

The duration of housing leases is negotiated between the parties. However, if the duration of the agreement is less than five years, then it is automatically extended for further one year terms up to a minimum duration of five years. The lessee has the option to terminate the lease with 30 days notice.

By law the lessee must provide a rental deposit equal to at least one month's rent. It is common practice for a lessor to request a rental deposit that is higher or even to ask for a bank guaranty.

—Lease for a use other than housing:

Lease agreements on properties for purposes other than the one described above include seasonal lease agreements and lease of properties to be used for industrial, commercial, professional, recreational, cultural or educational purposes.

The duration of leases for a use other than housing can be freely agreed between the parties.

The lessee must provide a rental deposit equal to at least two monthly rental payments. It is common practice for lessors to request a rental deposit of more than that required by law or to ask for a bank guaranty.

When a business or professional activity is carried out at the leased property, the lessee may sublease the property or assign the lease agreement without the lessor's consent. Unless otherwise agreed by the parties, the lessor is entitled to a ten per cent increase in the rent if there is a partial sublease, and a twenty per cent increase if there is an assignment of the agreement or total sublease of the property. Changes in the person of the lessee as a consequence of merger, transformation or spin-off of the lessee company are not considered as an assignment, but unless otherwise agreed by the parties, the lessor shall be entitled to the rent increase mentioned above.

Unless otherwise agreed between the parties, upon termination of a lease agreement for a property which has served for the previous five years as the site where sales to the public are made, the lessee shall be entitled to compensation from the lessor, as long as the lessee has communicated four months in advance of the termination date its intention not to extend the agreement for at least five more years and for a market rent.

§ 106ES.05 Tax.

This section addresses below the taxes on the different legal transactions involving real property, and on the ownership of rights *in rem*. There are distinctions between investment in properties, the term when ownership thereof is held and, finally, the transfer of properties. This brief section does not discuss the enormous variations in taxes, particularly indirect taxes, established for particular situations and circumstances.

§ 106ES.05(a) Acquisition of Real Properties.

Upon acquisition of a property for consideration, whether monetary or in kind, the purchaser is subject to one of the following indirect taxes, which are exclusive of each other. These are applicable whether the purchaser has its tax residence in Spain or not.

If the seller is a businessperson or a professional and the property is new, Value Added Tax (VAT) is applicable. VAT taxes the entire building process, from the beginning until the end, at one time which is at the moment of transfer by the developer. Further transfers are VAT-free but subject to Transfer Tax and Stamp Duty (*Impuesto sobre Transmisiones Patrimoniales y Actos Jurídicos Documentados-ITPyAJD*). The general rule is for the seller to charge VAT to the purchaser. The applicable VAT is 10% of the value of the property in case of housings, and 21% in case of business premises.

When the transfer is subject to *ITPyAJD*, and has been for consideration, it is generally subject to a tax rate of 7 to 8% of the value of the property (the autonomous regions, the Basque Country and Navarre, may modify it).

On the other hand if the transfer is granted in a public deed, which is normally the case, in addition to VAT it is also subject to a Documented Legal Acts tax at a rate of 0.5% of the value of the property, unless the autonomous regions, the Basque Country or Navarre have ruled otherwise.

Finally, with respect to an acquisition by inheritance or donation of a property, the person receiving the property is subject to the Inheritance and Donation Tax, with a progressive tax rate depending on the value of the acquired property. In these cases no indirect tax is applicable.

§ 106ES.05(b) Ownership of Real Properties.

Any person or entity who is the owner of a property, either rural or urban, is subject to a local tax (from the town hall where the property is located) which accrues yearly. This Real Estate Tax (*Impuesto sobre Bienes*

Immuebles-IBI) is paid by residents and non-residents in Spain, at a rate of approximately 1% of the so-called property value, which is determined by town halls and updated every year.

In addition to *IBI* if the owner of a property is a legal person non-resident in Spain that does not carry out economic activities in Spain, it shall be subject to another yearly tax, the Special Tax on Real Properties of Non Resident Entities (*Gravamen Especial sobre Bienes Inmuebles de Entidades No Residentes*), which amounts to 3% of the property value.

Any income obtained from real properties, for example, due to a lease to a third party, shall be subject to the Income Tax *(Impuesto sobre la Renta de las Personas Físicas-IRPF)*, Company Tax (*Impuesto sobre Sociedades-IS*) or Income Tax for Non Residents *(Impuesto sobre la Renta de No Residentes-IRNR)*.

Furthermore rents obtained from real properties used in an economic activity may be subject, in some cases, to the Tax on Commercial and Professional Activities (*Impuesto sobre Actividades Económicas-IAE*), a local tax.

§ 106ES.05(c)   Transfer of Real Properties.

In the realm of direct taxes, the capital gain resulting from the sale of a property, if any, due to the difference between purchase value and sale value is subject to the *IRPF, IS* or *IRNR*. Regarding *IRPF* the capital gain is subject to a fixed rate of 19% (up to 6.000 €) and 21% for the excess.

If *IS* applies, the capital gain is usually subject to the general rate of 30%, unless the property is subject to the economic activity carried out by the entity and the transfer value is invested again in the acquisition of other elements corresponding to the relevant activity. In this case the tax would be reduced to 18%.

When applying the *IRNR* there is a distinction depending on whether the property is subject or not to a permanent establishment in Spain. If the owner is, the tax shall be the same as the tax under the *IS*. If it is a non-resident without a permanent establishment, the capital gain is subject to a fixed rate of 19%. Furthermore in these cases the purchaser of the property is obliged to withhold and pay to the Public Treasury 3% of the price agreed, as payment on account of *IRNR* corresponding to the non-resident.

Finally, with the transfer of urban properties a local tax also accrues, the so called "Local Capital Gains Tax" (*Plusvalía Municipal*), which taxes the increase in the value of the land where the property is located from the date of its purchase to the date of its transfer.

§ 106ES.06   Bibliography.

Books

Gambino, Silvio, Jorge Lozano Miralles, Fernando Puzzo and Juan José Ruiz,

The Spanish Constitutional System (Eleven International Publishing 2018).

Rogoff, Adam C., Richard F. Broude and Daniel M. Glosband, *Collier International Business Insolvency Guide* ch. 40, Spain (Matthew Bender).

Romani Carlos Fernández de Casadevante, *Legal Implications of Territorial Secession in Spain* (Springer 2022).

Sánchez Arisit, Rafael & Nieves Moralejo Imbernón, *Property and Trust Law in Spain* (Wolters Kluwer Law & Business 3d ed. 2019).

Articles

Behzadi, Emily T., " 'Spain for the Spaniards': An Examination of the Plunder & Polemic Restitution of the Salamanca Papers," 11 *Geo. Mason J. Int'l Com. L.* 1 (2020).

Bosch, Jaume Tarabal, "Will-Substitutes in the U.S. and in Spain," 103 *Iowa L. Rev.* 2294 (2018).

Carreño, Florentino, "Cross-border planning for real estate: Spain," *Trusts & Trustees* (2018) 24 (1): 34.

Christiansen, Eric C., "Forty Years from Fascism: Democratic Constitutionalism and the Spanish Model of National Transformation," 20 *Or. Rev. Int'l L.* 1 (2018).

Estella, Antonio, "Potential Exit from the Eurozone: The Case of Spain," 22 *Ind. J. Global Leg. Stud.* 335 (2015).

Flanzer, David, Note, "A World Class Solution: How Implementing Class Action Lawsuits In Spain Could Help Remedy The Spanish Housing Crisis," 24 *Cardozo J. Int'l & Comp. L.* 631 (2016).

Flint, George Lee, Jr. and Marie Juliet Alfaro, "Secured Transactions History: The Impact of English Smuggling on the Chattel Mortgage Acts in the Spanish Borderlands," 37 *Val. U.L. Rev.* 703 (2003).

Franzese, Christina, Note and Comment, *"Balancing Justice and Peace: A Historical and Hypothetical Exploration of Justice During Spain's Post-Franco Transition from Dictatorship to Democracy,"* 31 Temp. Int'l & Comp. L.J. 497 (2017).

Frering, Gregory, Student Article, *The Olives of Others: The United States' Anti-Dumping and Countervailing Duties on Ripe Olives from Spain*, 36 Am. U. Int'l L. Rev. 651 (2021).

Gurrea-Martínez, Aurelio, "The Low Usage of Bankruptcy Procedures: A Cultural Problem? Lessons from Spain," 27 *U. Miami Int'l & Comp. L. Rev.* 275 (2020).

Hermosa, Pedro Ignacio Botello, Trust in Spain? *Trusts & Trustees* (2020) 26 (10): 950 (1 December 2020).

Narotzky, Susana, "Evidence Struggles: Legality, Legitimacy, and Social Mobilizations in the Catalan Political Conflict," 26 *Ind. J. Global Leg. Stud.* 31 (2019).

Sinclair, Katie, Note, "Blood and Treasure: How Should Courts Address the Legacy of Colonialism When Resolving Ownership Disputes Over Historic Shipwrecks?" 38 *Berkeley J. Int'l L.* 307 (2020).

CHAPTER 106EU

PROPERTY LAWS IN THE EUROPEAN UNION AND THEIR IMPACT ON MEMBER STATES

Professor David A. Thomas J. Reuben Clark Law School Brigham

Page 337: Change Bringham to Brigham. Young University

§ 106EU.01   The Structure and Governance of the European Union.

Page 338: Add a footnote to this sentence:

[8.1] As of May 2022, there are twenty-seven member states in the EU. They are Austria, Belgium, Bulgaria, Croatia, Cyprus, Czechia, Denmark, Estonia, Finland, France, Germany, Greece, Hungary, Ireland, Italy, Latvia, Lithuania, Luxembourg, Malta, Netherlands, Poland, Portugal, Romania, Slovakia, Slovenia, Spain and Sweden *See* https://europa.eu/european-union/about-eu/countries_en (visited May 24, 2022).

Page 338: In footnote 9, replace the URL with:

[9] https://european-union.europa.eu/institutions-law-budget/institutions-and-bodies/institutions-and-bodies-profiles/council-european-union_en (visited May 24, 2022).

Page 339: In footnote 10, replace the URL with:

[10] https://ec.europa.eu/info/index_en (visited May 24, 2022).

Page 339: Replace 626 members with: 705 members as of May 2021.

705 members as of May 2021

Page 339: Add a footnote to the sentence that ends with "populace of the Member States of the EU.":

[10.1] *See* https://www.europarl.europa.eu/about-parliament/en/organisation-and-rules/organisation/members (visited May 24, 2022). This webpage states: "The European Parliament is made up of 705 Members elected in the 27 Member States of the enlarged European Union. Since 1979 MEPs have been elected by direct universal suffrage for a five-year period." An individual can search for his or her member of the European Parliament on this webpage: https://www.europarl.europa.eu/meps/en/home (visited May 24, 2022).

Page 339: In footnote 11, replace the URL with:

[11] https://european-union.europa.eu/institutions-law-budget/law_en (visited May 24, 2022).

Page 339: Add to footnote 12:

[12] The webpage for the Court of Justice of the European Union is at: https://european-union.europa.eu/institutions-law-budget/institutions-and-bodies/institutions-and-bodies-profiles/court-justice-european-union-cjeu_en (visited May 24, 2022). For the Court of Justice, there is one judge from each country plus eleven advocates general. The General

Court has two judges from each country.

§ 106EU.02 The Council of Europe and Property Law.

Page 340: Add after "Council of Europe" but before the period:

(CoE)

Page 342: The name "Chassgnou" should be "Chassagnou."

Chassagnou

Page 347: Add at end of chapter:

§ 106EU.04 Bibliography.

Books

Arnull, Anthony and Damian Chalmers, *The Oxford Handbook of European Union Law* (Oxford University Press 2015).

Butler, Graham and Adam Lazowski, *Shaping EU Law the British Way: UK Advocates General at the Court of Justice of the European Union* (Hart Publishing 2022).

Capeta, Tamara, Iris Goldner Lang and Tamara Perišin, *The Changing European Union: A Critical View on the Role of Law and the Courts* (Hart Publishing 2022).

Dinnage, James D. & John F. Murphy, *Constitutional Law of the European Union; Documentary Supplement 2012* (Carolina Academic Press).

Fiebig, Andre, *EU Business Law* (American Bar Association 2016).

Herzog, Peter, Christian Campbell & Gudrun Zagel, *Smit & Herzog on The Law of the European Union* (Matthew Bender).

Hofmann, Herwig C.H., Gerard C. Rowe and Alexander H. Turk, *Specialized Administrative Law of the European Union: A Sectoral Review* (Oxford University Press 2019).

Horspool, Margot, Matthew Humphreys and Michael Wells-Greco, *European Union Law* (Oxford University Press 10th ed. 2018).

Korah, Valentine, *Competition Law of the European Union* (Matthew Bender).

Lianos, Ioannis, Valentine Korah & Paolo Siciliani, *Competition Law: Analysis, Cases, & Materials* (Oxford University Press 2019).

Rogoff, Adam C., Richard F. Broude and Daniel M. Glosband, *Collier International Business Insolvency Guide* ch. 43, European Union Regulation on Insolvency Proceedings (Matthew Bender).

Articles

Aguirre, Emilie K., "Sickeningly Sweet: Analysis and Solutions For the Adverse Dietary Consequences of European Agricultural Law," 11 *J. Food L. & Pol'y* 252 (2015).

Caviston, Jeffrey, "Protecting Eastern Europe's Farmland in the Era of Eurosceptic Populism: Liberal Solutions to the European Union's Conflict with Its Eastern Members over Foreign Acquisition of Farmland," 26 *Mich. St. Int'l L. Rev.* 537 (2018).

Coffey, Emma, Note, "Cutting Off the EU to Spite Its Face?: How to Promulgate the UK's Contractual Choice of Law Rules to Ensure Stability Post-Brexit," 61 *B.C. L. Rev.* 1447 (2020).

Druzin, Bryan H., "Tipping Points and the Formation of the European Union: Birth, Brexit, and Beyond," 27 *Colum. J. Eur. L.* 68 (2021).

Eddington, Benjamin J.W., Note, "A Poorly Decided Divorce: Brexit's Effect on the European Union and United Kingdom, 41 *Suffolk Transnat'l L. Rev.* 101 (2018).

Epstein, Richard A., "The Role of Exit Rights: What the Theory of the Firm Says about the Conduct of Brexit Negotiations," 39 *Cardozo L. Rev.* 825 (2018).

Eriksen, Christoffer C, "Constraining Administrative Discretion to Facilitate Renewable Energy: Wind Farms as a Challenge for EU Law and the European Commission," 32 *J. Energy & Nat. Resources L.* 273 (Aug. 2014).

Gormley, Laurence W., "Brexit—Nevermind the Whys and Wherefores? Fog in the Channel, Continent Cut Off!," 40 *Fordham Int'l L.J.* 1175 (2017).

Grabowska, Julia, Note, "Forced Evictions: Racial Persecution and Social Exclusion of the Roma Minority in Romania," 56 *Colum. J. Transnat'l L.* 855 (2018).

Griffin, Christine E., Note, "Por Favor, Get Your Bulldozer Away From My Villa: An Analysis of the Nascent European Land Registry Association's Cross-Border Electronic Conveyancing Project," 36 *Suffolk Transnat'l L. Rev.* 89 (2013).

Haddock, Alexis, Note, "EIA Directive Procedural Guarantees as Substantive Individual Rights in IL v. Land Nordrhein-Westfalen," 10 *Mich. J. Envtl. & Admin. L.* 463 (2021).

Hargrove, Benjamin D., "Brexit: A Harbinger of Change for the European Union," 16 *U. St. Thomas L.J.* 111 (2019).

Kenny, Mel, "Descending The Circles of 'Brexit': Toxicity of Future EU-UK Relations and the Road to EU Re-Accession?," 28 *Colum. J. Eur. L.* 36 (2022).

Lee, Maria, "Environmental Pasts and Futures: The European Union and the 'British Way'," *J. Environmental Law* (2019) 31 (3): 559.

Lehavi, Amnon, "Globalizing Property Law: An Institutional Analysis," 50 *Vand. J. Transnat'l L.* 1173 (2017).

McEvoy, Kieran, Anna Bryson, & Amanda Kramer, "The Empire Strikes Back: Brexit, the Irish Peace Process, and the Limitations of Law," 43 *Fordham Int'l L.J.* 609 (2020).

Parikh, Samir D., "Bankruptcy Tourism and the European Union's Corporate Restructuring Quandary: The Cathedral in Another Light," 42 *U. Pa. J. Int'l L.* 205 (2020).

Ramaekers, Eveline, "What Is Property Law?" *Oxford J Legal Studies* (2017) 37 (3): 588.

Slaybaugh, Jason A., Comment, "Garbage Day: Will Italy Finally Take Out Its Trash in the Land of Fires?" 26 *Pac. Rim L. & Pol'y J.* 179 (2017).

Schwarzschild, Maimon, "Complicated—but Not Too Complicated: The Sunset of E.U. Law in the U.K. After Brexit," 39 *Cardozo L. Rev.* 905 (2018).

CHAPTER 106FR

PROPERTY LAW IN FRANCE

§ 106FR.01   History of Property Law in France.

§ 106FR.01(c)   Landholding During and After Roman Rule.

Page 352: Change "as" to "has."

has

§ 106FR.01(d)   The Emergence of Feudalism.

Page 353: Change the spelling of "aristrocracy" to "aristocracy."

aristocracy

Page 366: Add at the end of the chapter:

§ 106FR.05   Bibliography

Books

Bell, John, *Contemporary French Administrative Law* (Cambridge University Press new ed. 2022).

Bell, John, Sophie Boyron and Simon Whittaker, Principles of French Law (Oxford University Press 2d ed. 2008).

Cartwright, John and Simon Whittaker, The Code Napoleon Rewritten: French Contract Law after the 2016 Reforms (Hart Publishing 2017).

Kim, Marie Seong-Hak, *Custom, Law, and Monarchy: A Legal History of Early Modern France* (Oxford University Press 2022).

Kolla, Edward James, Sovereignty, International Law, and the French Revolution (Cambridge University Press 2017).

Rogoff, Adam C., Richard F. Broude and Daniel M. Glosband, *Collier International Business Insolvency Guide* ch. 22, France (Matthew Bender).

Steiner, Eva, French Law: A Comparative Approach (Oxford University Press 2d ed. 2018).

Youngs, Raymond, *English, French & German Comparative Law* (Routledge 3d ed. 2014).

Articles

Billemont, Jean, "Arbitration of Real Estate Disputes under French Law," 20 *IBA Arb. News* 70 (Sept. 2015).

Dow, Steven B. & Louise E. Fontaine, "Acquiring Lawyering Skills in the United States and France: A Comparative Study," 28 *Tul. J. Int'l & Comp. L.* 259 (2020).

Einbinder, Fred, "Mass Torts: Dispute Resolution in France and the United States—The Vioxx and Mediator Cases Compared," 29 *Wash. Int'l L.J.* 575

(2020).

Muenchinger, Nancy E., "French Law: Reforms in Real Property and Estate Law," 59 *RI Bar. Jnl.* 23 (Nov./Dec. 2010).

Rowan, Solène, "The New French Law of Contract," *International and Comparative Law Quarterly* 66, 2017 pp 805–831 (2017).

Snyder, Laura, "Acquiring a Business in France: A Buyer's Guide," 57 *Bus. Law.* 793 (2002).

CHAPTER 106GB

PROPERTY LAW IN GREAT BRITAIN (ENGLAND AND WALES)

SYNOPSIS

Page 367: Add a new section after § 106GB.03(e)

§ 106GB.04 Bibliography.

§ 106GB.01 History.

Page 372: Add new footnote 20.1 at the end of the last sentence of the last paragraph of § 106GB.01:

[20.1] Crosswhite, Anastasia B., "Women and Land: Aristocratic Ownership of Property in Early Modern England," *77 N.Y.U. L. Rev. 1119* (October, 2002).

§ 106GB.02 Types of Real Property Interests.

§ 106GB.02(a) Legal Estates in Real Property.

Page 372: Add to footnote 21:

[21] Simpson, A.W.B., "Constitutionalizing the Right of Property: the U.S., England and Europe," 31 *U. Haw. L. Rev.* 1 (Winter 2008).

§ 106GB.02(d) Land Ownership by Aliens.

Page 374: Add to footnote 24:

[24] ; Daly, William J., "A Comparative Analysis of the New Real Estate Investment Trust Legislation in Germany and the United Kingdom: Will Those Markets Experience the Same Success as the United States?" 17 *Transnat'l L. & Contemp. Probs.* 839 (Fall 2008).

Page 377: Add a new section § 106GB.04 Bibliography. after end of § 106GB.03(e)

§ 106GB.04   Bibliography.

Books

Abbey, Robert and Mark Richards, *A Practical Approach to Conveyancing* (Oxford University Press 22nd ed. 2020).

Abbey, Robert and Mark Richards, *A Practical Approach to Commercial Conveyancing and Property* (Oxford University Press 5th ed. 2016).

Abbey, Robert and Mark Richards, *A Practical Approach to Conveyancing and Property* (Oxford University Press 19th ed. 2017).

Abbey, Robert and Mark Richards, *Property Law 2018–2019* (Oxford University Press 11th ed. 2018).

Arden, Andrew and Andrew Dymond, *Manual of Housing Law* (Legal Action Group 11th ed. 2020).

Badger, Christopher & Stuart Jessop, *A Practical Guide to Environmental Enforcement* (Law Brief Publishing 2021).

Bray, Judith, *Unlocking Land Law* (Routledge 6th ed. 2019).

Burn, Edward and John Cartwright, *Cheshire and Burn's Modern Law of Real Property* (Oxford University Press 18th ed. 2011).

Clarke, Sandra and Sarah Greer, *Land Law Directions* (Oxford University Press 8th ed. 2022).

Cooke, Elizabeth, *Land Law* (Oxford University Press 2d ed. 2012).

Denyer-Green, Barry, *Compulsory Purchase and Compensation* (Routledge 11th ed. 2018).

Dixon, Martin, *Modern Land Law* (Routledge 11th ed. 2018).

Dixon, Martin and Gerwyn LL. H. Griffiths, *Contemporary Perspectives on Property, Equity and Trust Law* (Oxford University Press 2008).

Dwomoh, Elizabeth, *A Practical Guide to the Ending of Assured Shorthold Tenancies* (Law Brief Publishing 2018).

Garner, Simon and Alexandra Frith, *A Practical Approach to Landlord and Tenant* (Oxford University Press 8th ed. 2017).

Garton, Rachel, *A Practical Guide to Residential Service Charges* (Law Brief Publishing 2021).

George, Martin and Antonia Layard, *Thompson's Modern Land Law* (Oxford University Press 2022).

Goodall, Martin H., *The Essential Guide to the Use of Land and Buildings Under the Planning Acts* (Bath Publishing Limited 2017).

Goodall, Martin H., *A Practical Guide to Permitted Changes of Use: under the General Permitted Development Order* (Bath Publishing Limited 3rd ed. 2019).

Hayes, Richard & David Sawtell, *A Practical Guide to the Landlord and Tenant Act 1954: Commercial Tenancies* (Law Brief Publishing 2017).

Hewitsone, Russell, *Residential Conveyancing Practice: A Guide for Support Staff and Paralegals* (The Law Society 2nd ed. 2020).

Laitos, Jan G., *The Right of Nonuse* (Oxford University Press reprint ed. 2013).

Lovegrove, Stephanie, *A Practical Guide to the Law of Unlawful Eviction and Harassment* (Law Brief Publishing 2nd ed. 2020).

McKie, Andrew and Ian Skeate, *A Practical Guide to Running Housing Disrepair and Cavity Wall Claims* (Law Brief Publishing 2nd ed. 2018).

Richardson, Lorraine, *A Practical Guide to Document Signing and Electronic Signatures for Conveyancers* (Law Brief Publishing 2021).

Rogoff, Adam C., Richard F. Broude and Daniel M. Glosband, *Collier International Business Insolvency Guide* ch. 21, England and Wales (Matthew Bender).

Sams, Paul & Rebecca East, *A Practical Guide to New Build Conveyancing* (Law Brief Publishing 2021).

Shapiro, Eric, David Mackmin & Gary Sams, *Modern Methods of Valuation* (Estates Gazette 12th ed. 2019).

Shelton, Mark, *Short-Term Commercial Lets for Lawyers, Agents, Landlords and Tenants—A Practical Guide* (Law Brief Publishing 2021).

Smith, David, *A Practical Guide to the Law of Private Renting in Wales* (Law Brief Publishing 2021).

Stafford, Paul, *A Practical Guide to the Law of Manorial Rights* (Law Brief Publishing 2021).

Tagg, Adrian, *Technical Due Diligence and Building Surveying for Commercial Property* (Routledge 2018).

Thomas, Meryl, *Blackstone's Statutes on Property Law 2017–2018* (Oxford University Press 25th ed. 2017).

Walsh, Emily, *A Guide to Landlord and Tenant Law* (Routledge 2018).

Williams, Greg, *A Practical Guide to TOLATA Claims* (Law Brief Publishing 2019).

Articles

Burns, Fiona, "Adverse Possession and Title-By-Registration Systems in Australia and England," 35 *Melbourne U. L.R.* 773 (2011).

Clough, Benjamin K., Note, "License to Trash? Can Biodiversity Offsetting Adequately Protect England's Natural Habitats and Facilitate Development?," 24 *Transnat'l L. & Contemp. Probs.* 193 (2014).

Cooper, Simon and Emma Lees, "Interests, Powers and Mere Equities in Modern Land Law" *Oxford J Legal Studies* (2017) 37 (2): 435, 1 June 2017.

Holligan, Bonnie, "Narratives of Capital versus Narratives of Community: Conservation Covenants and the Private Regulation of Land Use," *J Environmental Law* (2018) 30 (1): 55.

Lonegrass, Melissa T., "Eliminating Landlord Retaliation in England and Wales—Lessons from the United States," 75 *La. L. Rev.* 1071 (2015).

Mualam, Nir, "Appeal Tribunals in Land Use Planning: Look-Alikes or Different Species? A Comparative Analysis of Oregon, England and Israel," 46 *Urb. Law.* 33 (2014).

Roche, Juanita, "Historiography and the Law of Property Act 1925: The Return of Frankenstein," *The Cambridge Law Journal*, 77 [2018], pp 600–629 (1 November 2018).

Rogers, Christopher, "ELR opinion issue 3 2016: BREXIT: What implications for land use and the natural environment?," *ELR* 18 3 (187) 1 Sept. 2016.

Thomas, David A., "Anglo-American Land Law: Diverging Developments from a Shared History Part I: The Shared History," 34 *Real Prop. Prob. & Tr. J.* 143 (1999).

Thomas, David A., "Anglo-American Land Law: Diverging Developments from a Shared History—Part III How Anglo-American Land Law Diverged after American Colonization and Independence," 34 *Real Prop. Prob. & Tr. J.* 295 (1999).

Thomas, David A., "Anglo-American Land Law: Diverging Developments from a Shared History: Part III: British and American Real Property Law and Practice-A Contemporary Comparison," 34 *Real Prop. Prob. & Tr. J.* 443 (1999).

Walsh, Rachael and Lorna Fox O'Mahony, "Land law, property ideologies and the British-Irish relationship," *CLWR* 47 1 (7) 1 March 2018.

Zhang, Taisu, "Social Hierarchies and the Formation of Customary Property Law in Pre-Industrial China and England," 62 *Am. J. Comp. L.* 171 (2014).

CHAPTER 106IN

PROPERTY LAW IN INDIA

§ 106IN.01   Brief History of India.

§ 106IN.01(b)   The Early History of India.

Page 380: Correct the spelling of unintelliglble to unintelligible.

unintelligible

Page 381: Delete the "t" in "all."

§ 106IN.03   Basic Indian Property Law.

Page 383: Add as the second paragraph of subsection 106IN.03:

Non-residents are not allowed to acquire and own immoveable property in India without the prior permission of the Reserve Bank of India.[16.1] A webpage of the Ministry of External Affairs in response to a question as to whether a foreign national of non-Indian origin outside of India can purchase immoveable property in India, provides the following answer:

> No. A foreign national of non-Indian origin, resident outside India cannot purchase any immovable property in India unless such property is acquired by way of inheritance from a person who was resident in India. However, he/she can acquire or transfer immovable property in India, on lease, not exceeding five years. In such cases, there is no requirement of taking any permission of/ or reporting to the Reserve Bank of India.[16.2]

In response to the question, "Can a foreign national who is a person resident in India purchase immoveable property in India?" the following answer is provided:

> Yes, a foreign national who is a 'person resident in India' within the meaning of Section 2(v) of FEMA,[16.3] 1999 can purchase immovable property in India, but the person concerned would have to obtain the approvals and fulfil the requirements, if any, prescribed by other authorities, such as, the State Government concerned, etc. The onus to prove his/her residential status is on the individual as per the extant FEMA provisions, if required by any authority. However, a foreign national resident in India who is a citizen of Pakistan, Bangladesh, Sri Lanka, Afghanistan, China, Iran, Nepal and Bhutan would require prior approval of the Reserve Bank.[16.4]

This webpage contains additional questions and answers regarding the ownership of real property in India.

[16.1] Lex Mundi India Business Guide 11.1.

[16.2] https://www.mea.gov.in/property-related-matters-of-nri-oci.htm (visited May 23, 2019).

[16.3] FEMA is the Foreign Exchange Management Act.

[16.4] https://www.mea.gov.in/property-related-matters-of-nri-oci.htm (visited May 23, 2019).

Page 385: Add at end of chapter:

§ 106IN.04   Bibliography.

Books

Cullet, Philippe and Sujith Koonan, *Water Law in India* (Oxford University Press 2017).

D'Costa, Anthony P. and Achin Chakraborty, *The Land Question in India: State, Dispossession, and Capitalist Transition* (Oxford University Press 2017).

Devendra, Amitabh, *Hotel Law* (Oxford University Press 2013).

Dong, Shikui, Jayanta Bandyopadhyay & Sanjay Chaturvedi (Editors), *Environmental Sustainability from the Himalayas to the Oceans: Struggles and Innovations in China and India* (Springer International Publishing 2017).

Franceschin, Germano & Francesco Misuraca, *India: Commercial, Customs and Tax Law* (Kluwer Law International 2011).

Fyzee, Asaf & Tahir Mahmood, *Outlines of Muhammadan Law* (Oxford University Press 5th ed. 2009).

Jain, M.P., Justice Jasti Chelameswar and Justice Dama Seshadri Naidu, *M P Jain Indian Constitutional Law* (LexisNexis 8th ed. 2018).

Khosla, Madhav, *India's Founding Moment: The Constitution of a Most Surprising Democracy* (Harvard University Press 2020).

Mittal, J.K., *Indian Legal & Constitutional History* (Allahabad Law Agency 2017).

Narasappa, Harish, *Rule of Law in India: A Quest for Reason* (Oxford University Press 2018).

Naseem, Mohammad, *Energy Law in India* (Kluwer Law International 2011).

Pandey, J.N., *Constitutional Law of India* (Central Law Agency 2020).

Patel, Bimal N. and Ranita Nagar, *Sustainable Development and India* (Oxford University Press 2018).

Rogoff, Adam C., Richard F. Broude and Daniel M. Glosband, *Collier International Business Insolvency Guide* ch. 25, India (Matthew Bender).

Sen, Sarbani, *The Constitution of India* (Oxford University Press 2011).

Serajuddin, Alamgir Muhammad, *Cases on Muslim Law of India, Pakistan, and Bangladesh* (Oxford University Press 2015).

Articles

Ashok, Krithika, Paul T. Babie & John V. Orth, "Balancing Justice Needs and Private Property in Constitutional Takings Provisions: A Comparative Assessment of India, Australia, and the United States," 42 *Fordham Int'l L.J.* 999 (2019).

Badrinarayana, Deepa, "The 'Right' Right to Environmental Protection: What We Can Discern from the American and Indian Constitutional Experience," 43 *Brooklyn J. Int'l L.* 75 (2017).

Balganesh, Shyamkrishna, "Codifying the Common Law of Property in India: Crystallization and Standardization as Strategies of Constraint," 63 *Am. J. Comp. L.* 33 (2015).

Burman, Anirudh, "Making Land Titles in India Marketable: Using Title Insurance as a Viable Alternative to Conclusive Titling," 28 *Wash. Int'l L.J.* 109 (2019).

Good, Michael D. & Pramod K Singh, "Loan to own? Or liquidate? US and Indian distressed debt investing compared," (2018) 10 *JIBFL* 626 (1 November 2018).

Jaiswal, Anjali, Madhura Joshi and Sameer Kwatra, "Climate consequences: If India sneezes," 10 Jindal Global L. Rev. 19 (April 2019).

Mandviwala, Tahere, "Restrictive Covenants and Unlawful Competition in India," 25 No. 2 *Emp. & Indus. Rel. L.* 41 (Sept. 2015).

Mittal, Akaant, "According legal identity to natural resources: approach towards environment protection," 10 *Jindal Global L. Rev.* 7 (April 2019).

Naik, Gayathri D., "The Right to a Clean Environment in India: Gender Perspective," 21 *Vt. J. Envtl. L.* 371 (2019).

Narayanan, Nikhil, "An Introduction to the Key Concepts and Practical Considerations in Indian M&A Transactions for an International Lawyer," 19 *BLI* 101 (May 2018).

Note, *From Domicile to Dominion: India's Settler Colonial Agenda in Kashmir,* 134 Harv. L. Rev. 2530 (2021).

Prasad, Deva and Suchithra Menon, "Indian Forest Rights Legislation: Significance of Recognizing the Legal Pluralism for Indigenous Peoples Rights," *Statute Law Rev.* (2020) 41 (1): 78.

Rossi, Christopher R., *Blood, Water, and the Indus Waters Treaty*, 29 Minn. J. Int'l L. 103 (2020).

Sharafi, Mitra, *Law and Identity in Colonial South Asia: Parsi Legal Culture, 1771–1947* (2014).

Sreejith, S.G., "Dam Jurisprudence of the Supreme Court of India: Situating the Case of Mullaperiyar Dam Dispute," 45 *Hastings Int'l & Comp. L. Rev.* 129 (2022).

Woodard, Jason D., *Racing to Resolution: A Preliminary Study of India's New Bankruptcy Code*, 52 Geo. Wash. Int'l L. Rev. 393 (2020).

Zasloff, Jonathan, "India's Land Title Crisis: The Unanswered Questions," 3 *Jindal Global L. Rev.* 117 (Sept. 2011).

Page 385: Insert new Chapter 106IT after Chapter 106IN:

CHAPTER 106IT

PROPERTY LAW IN ITALY

SYNOPSIS

§ 106IT.01   Constitutional Foundation of Private Property in Italy.

When, at the outset of the postwar reconstruction in the 1940s, the Assembly of Constitutional Framers had to establish the foundations of the newly born Italian Republic, the regulation of property was one of the most heated issues subject to public debate. The Constitutional Assembly, which was elected in the aftermath of a controversial referendum that decided to abolish the monarchy and opted for a republican form of state, was the clear expression of a divide in the society.[1] The Assembly was comprised of three major constituencies: a strong communist and socialist party, a strong Christian-democratic party and a significant liberal party. Each of the three constituencies had a firmly held ideological view on the functions and the regulation that property should have. A liberal tradition had been enshrined in the 1848 Albertine Constitution, which at article 29 provided: *"All properties without exceptions are inviolable. Nonetheless, when the public interest legally ascertained requires it, it might be required to cede all or part of them for a fair indemnity"*. Marxists stressed the need for a reform toward collectivization of property and less extreme, Catholics leaned toward a functional view of property as a means to grant dignity and personal development. To compromise, the framers found a formula that would allow any possible actual future application: from a neo-capitalistic economy to collectivization and echoing the roman tradition of Gaius (*res publicae sunt aut privatae*, Inst., II, par.10) they provided at Article 42 Const.: *"Property is public and private. Economic assets belong to the State, local authorities or citizens. Private Property is recognized and granted by the law which sets the ways by means of which it might be acquired, enjoyed and its limitations in order to assure the social function of it and to make it accessible to everyone. In cases set by the law and for an indemnity, private property may be expropriated for general interest."*

[1] *See generally* Marta Cartabia and Nicola Lupo, The Constitution of Italy: A Contextual Analysis (Hart Publishing 2022).

§ 106IT.02   Property and the 1942 Italian Civil Code.

The Italian Civil Code (ICC) is heavily indebted to the Roman tradition and to the legislative technique of the Code Napoleon, from which it drew the most important norms on property. The Civil Code's framers preferred the technique of wide legal definitions and general concepts given by the Code Napoleon which constituted the most important model from which they took inspiration. The Civil Code comprises six books and property is regulated by the third book (from Article 810 to Article 1171), which is divided into nine subdivisions or "titles." The third book gives a complete regulation of property: it defines what assets might be objects of property and the different kinds of real property rights and interests in the land of others, it provides norms about confining properties, it regulates co-ownership and condominiums, it defines possession and ownership and sets rules on claims and protection of possession and ownership.

§ 106IT.03   Property and the 1942 Civil Code Basic Principles of the Italian Property Law.

In Italy, assets are divided into movable (*"beni mobili"*) and immovable property (*"beni immobili"*), a distinction similar to the common-law concepts of personal and real property. Under article 812 of the Civil Code, the ground, the natural resources, the watercourses, the trees and the buildings or other constructions and in general what is naturally incorporated into the ground are immovable property. All other goods are movable property. Natural energy is considered a movable property.

An important subset of movable property consists of registered movable property (*"beni mobili registrati"*): vehicles and boats are among registered movable property, because they must be registered in a special public registry. Even if such assets are not incorporated into the ground, they are subject to rules on transferability that are similar to those set for immovable property.

§ 106IT.04   State Property in Italy.

Under the Civil Code, the shore, the beaches, the ports, the rivers, the torrents, the lakes and other public waters so defined by special laws as well as buildings and constructions made for national defense are state property (*"demanio pubblico"*). Also, roads, highways, railways, airports, aqueducts, and buildings that are recognized by special laws as of historical interest are State property. State property cannot be sold or be the object of individual property rights and is protected and regulated by the State. Except for State property, property rights on movable or immovable property can arise through transfer from a previous legitimate owner (derivative constitution of right) or through prescription, occupation, or acquisition.

§ 106IT.05   Acquiring Real Property Rights.

Under the Italian Civil Code, except for State property, property rights interests can be acquired in nine different ways: seven of them are defined as "original acquisitions of interests" because the resulting interest do not derive from the property of a previous owner. Original acquisition of rights are: occupation, invention, accession, specification, union, commingling, prescription. Two of them are defined derivative acquisition of rights and they are: transfer by contract and succession.

§ 106IT.06   Occupation and Invention.

By occupation a property interest in movables that do not belong to anybody (*res nullius*) may be acquired. Two conditions are necessary for occupation to be effective: one has to (1) take possession of the immovable (2) with the intention of becoming the owner of the occupied movable. Immovables cannot be effectively occupied because immovables that do not belong to anybody are considered to belong to the State. Under the civil code, movables that do not belong to anybody are: chattels that have been abandoned with the intention of losing the property interest and the catch from fishing. Traditionally wild animals had been considered as if they were not owned by anyone (*"res nullius"*), but a strict regulation of hunting has excluded wild animals (*"ferae naturae"*) from the goods of which one can obtain property by taking possession on it.

Different from movables that do not belong to anybody are movables that have been lost. If someone finds a movable that has been lost (*"invention"*), the finder must return the lost item to the owner if known or, if not, the finder must deliver the lost movable to the relevant office of the local authority where the good has been found. Once one year has passed and the owner has not claimed the lost movable, the finder becomes the owner of the lost item. If the lost movable is claimed, the finder has the right to an indemnity equal to a tenth of the value of the movable. Also, treasures found in the soil may be acquired through invention if they are found by the owner of the soil. If the treasure is found by someone other than the owner of the soil, the finder has to share fifty percent of the value of the treasure with the owner of the soil. However, treasures that have historical, archeological or artistic value belong to the State.

§ 106IT.07   Accession.

A traditional principle provides that property in the most important good may include property on something that is ancillary to it. Through accession, a movable that is incorporated into an immovable may become part of the immovable. For example, if somebody discovers a building on soil of which he is the owner, he becomes the owner of the building as long as it is embedded in the soil. Under the Civil Code, when somebody, who acts in good faith, discovers a building on the land of another, the latter has the right at his option to pay the cost of the works or to pay the increase in value that the land has gained because of the new building. The owner of the land will be entitled to obtain the demolition of the new building at the builder's cost only if the builder acted in bad faith and has constructed the building while he was aware that the land belonged to somebody else. Accession may occur also between two immovables: for example when an upstream piece of land is dragged by a river and joins a downstream piece of land.

§ 106IT.08   Union, Commingling and Specification.

Union (*"unione"*) or commingling (*"commistione"*) occurs when two movables are united or commingled in order to form a different object. In this case, the finished product belongs to the owner of the most important of the commingled properties. If the components of the new object are of equal importance and they cannot be easily separated, the owners of the components become co-owners of the new object. Specification (*"specificazione"*) occurs when somebody uses raw material that belongs to somebody else to create a new finished product: it is the case of the sculptor who uses somebody's else marble. The sculptor becomes the owner of the raw material but he has to pay a fair price for the material he used. As in Anglo-American case law, the Civil Code provides a test similar to the *"disproportionate value"* test if the raw material one used is far more valuable than the finished product. In this event, as it happens in the case of a goldsmith who uses somebody's else gold, the owner of the raw material becomes owner of the finished product but he has to compensate the labor costs.

§ 106IT.09   Possession.

The Italian Civil Code provides protection not only for property rights but also for possession. A traditional definition draws the line between possession and property in that while the former is a "matter of fact," the latter is a "matter of law." Under Article 1140 C.C., possession is the power exercised on something in a way that appears to correspond to the exercise of the right of ownership: as in Anglo-American property law, one may generally be said to have possession of something if he has dominion and control over it. Therefore, the difference between title and possession is the same as between being the owner and behaving like the owner. According to a Latin tradition, possession requires the intention of being the owner (*"animus possidendi"*): therefore if someone holds something on the basis of a contract that recognizes that somebody else owns the good, she will not possess the good. In other words, when the possessor is not the owner himself, possession must be inconsistent with owner's rights and without the owner's consent: holding an article with the owner's consent gives rise to a bailment (*"detenzione"*).

§ 106IT.10   *Bona fide* Purchaser of Movables and Valid Transfer of Property Interest.

Personal property may be acquired through possession: a general rule is usually condensed in the motto "possession counts as title" (*"possesso vale titolo"*). This is a strikingly different approach from what most Anglo-American jurisdictions do with reference to *bona fide* purchasers. In these jurisdictions, "a seller cannot convey better title than that which he holds." The rule "possession counts as title" aims at making trade and transfer of movables easy and safe. Under Article 1153 of the Civil Code, if somebody receives a movable from somebody who is not the actual owner, he acquires nonetheless the ownership of the movable if he was in good faith when he took possession of the good and obtained it through a formally valid title. The acquisition of the property right interest of the *bona fide* purchaser does not depend on the status or qualification of the seller, who could be a layperson or a merchant.

§ 106IT.11   Acquiring and Securing Real Property Rights.

Under Italian law, real property interests can be transferred from a previous owner to another owner only by a contract in writing or by a public instrument made by a notary public, who has to follow certain forms provided by law ("Atto pubblico").[2]

Italy has a recording system ("registri immobiliari") that is able to deal with conflicting claims on the same parcel and differently from what is for example the Autrian system: its recording system has a personal basis. Therefore the search for title has to be done not on the land parcel but rather on the chain of persons who owned the land. In Italy, there is also a public register that is based on parcels of land, the cadaster ("Catasto"): however it has mainly tax purposes. To be recorded in the recording system, the contract has to be notarized by a public notary.

In the Italian recording system, not only real property interests but also claims on property are registered. Italy has adopted what is generally called a "pure race statute": the subsequent purchaser that records before the earlier purchaser is protected whether or not he has actual notice of the earlier conveyance. However, in the event the subsequent purchaser had actual notice of the previous sale, the previous purchaser will be able to claim damages against the seller and the subsequent purchaser.

With reference to real property, a seller cannot convey better title than that which he holds; therefore if somebody buys from a previous owner whose title was invalid, the owner with a valid title might claim his title against the subsequent purchaser who bears the risk of being evicted ("evizione"). However, this strict rule is softened for the subsequent bona fide purchaser who bought on the basis of a formerly valid title that has been registered in the recording system. If the above-mentioned condition occurs, the Civil Code provides a statute of limitations of five years after which the subsequent owner cannot be evicted.

> [2] *See generally* Guido Abate and Giuditta Losa, Real Estate in Italy: Markets, Investment Vehicles and Performance (Routledge 2016); Raul-Angelo Papotti, *Cross-border planning for real estate: Italy*, Trusts & Trustees (2018) 24 (1): 57, 1 January 2018.

§ 106IT.12 Adverse Possession or Acquisitive Prescription ("*Usucapione*").

The principle "possession counts as title" does not apply in relation to real property, when the rule that "a seller cannot convey better title than that which he holds" applies. However, real property might be acquired through the joint occurrence of possession and the passage of time. It may happen that real property is possessed by somebody who does not have a valid title. If such a situation continues uninterrupted for a sufficient period of time, the possessor ends up acquiring a valid title. Whether the possessor is in good faith is not relevant, even though good faith status might affect the length of time required to acquire a valid title.

As in most Anglo-American jurisdictions, in order to result in prescription, possession has to be open (notorious and visible), exclusive, actual and continuous. If possession has been gained by the use of force or violence, the term for prescription starts running once the violence has ended or the possession has become visible and notorious.

As stated above, the length of time for acquiring a valid title on real property varies. To acquire a valid title on real property, possession has to be continuously held for twenty years. However, if the purchaser of the real property acted in good faith and bought the real property from a non-owner on the basis of a formerly valid title that has been filed with the land registry, he will acquire a valid title in ten years. The possessor or a registered movable will have to hold the property for three years.

§ 106IT.13   Other Interests in Real Property.

In Italy, as discussed above, the regulation of property is indebted more to the Roman tradition than to feudalism; this has created a legal framework and an economic structure where unrestricted property is the rule and minor interests in real property are the exceptions. To use concepts that derive from a common-law background, the fee simple (an unrestricted and endless right to a land or real estate, save the application of zoning rules) is the most common form of property rights. However, the Civil Code provides a regulation of six minor interests (or estate) other than property. Minor interests usually coexist and limit the unrestricted use of an estate.

§ 106IT.14   Emphyteusis.

Among minor interests, emphyteusis is the largest in scope: once it used to be very common because it was a way for noblemen to obtain a rent from unused lands, but it has now declined in use, because it has not been favored by the parliament who has introduced rules to redeem the property of lands subject to emhyteusis (law n. 607 of 1966 and 1138 of 1970).

As stated in Article 958 of the ICC, emphyteusis is a perpetual interest in the real property and if a limitation in duration is provided for, emphyteusis has to last at least twenty years. Emphyteusis can be transferred by contract (*inter vivos*) or it can be bequeathed (*mortis causa*).

The holder of a emphyteusis, the emphyteuta, has the same rights to enjoy of the estate of an owner subject to two duties: (1) he has to improve the estate and (2) he has to pay periodic rent. Even though it is an interest more common in the countryside, emphyteusis can be agreed on any kind of real estate.

The emphyteuta may redeem the property on the land by paying an amount equal to the value of fifteen years of capitalized rent. On the other hand, if the emphyteuta does not comply with his duties to improve the land or pay the rent, the owner can judicially obtain the re-assignment of the property.

§ 106IT.15   Servitudes.

According to Article 1027 of the ICC, servitudes are burdens imposed on the use of the land, to the advantage of an adjoining land. Even though servitudes are created mostly to regulate adjoining lands, they have been used to allow passage of aqueducts, electric system, railroads and other public utilities on somebody's else land. Usually the latter are imposed by a public authority with a decision that has the same value of a judgement.

The content of servitudes is heterogeneous. By servitude, a right to pass through a land or a right to draw water from a land to the benefit of another land may be obtained. Servitudes may also have a negative content whereby the owner of a land burdened by a servitude may be prevented from building over a certain height if this impedes the view of an adjoining land that enjoys a view-servitude.

They may arise voluntarily by a contract signed between the owners of two adjoining lands. However, if someone owns land that is surrounded by other lands that prevent access a public road from his parcel, he may obtain a judicial decision that gives rise to a servitude on adjoining land.

Servitudes, like other minor real interests, may be acquired or lost by adverse possession if the servitude is used (or not used) for twenty years.

§ 106IT.16   Usufruct.

When a landowner separates rights of enjoyment, which are given to a life tenant, from the other rights associated with ownership of real property, a usufruct arises. The usufruct is usually given for the duration of a tenant's life; if it is granted to a company it cannot exceed thirty years.

In common law, the most similar estate to usufruct is life estate (or estate for years). A usufruct right can be separated and transferred to another without the property owner losing the other rights that have been retained (he remains what is called a *"naked owner" "nudo proprietario"* as he owns a *"naked property" "nuda proprietà"*). However, the life tenant must preserve the economic value of the asset he holds in usufruct.

As stated in Article 981 of the Italian Civil Code, the life tenant has the right to enjoy its facilities and fruits. Fruits include both natural produce (if the usufruct is on cultivated land) or rents if the estate is rented out.

Costs for maintaining the estate are divided between the life tenant and the owner: all extraordinary costs for repairs are borne by the naked owner whereas the costs for ordinary repairs are borne by the life tenant. The former pays all taxes related to property and the latter pays the taxes related to income from the use of the land.

At the end of the usufruct period, the life tenant must return the property in essentially the same condition in which it was received, natural deterioration and wear and tear excepted. Usufructs are transferable. Usufruct usually arises voluntarily from a contract or a will, but the Civil Code provides for a mandatory usufruct given to the parents on the assets owned by their minor child.

§ 106IT.17   Use and Habitation.

Use is similar to the usufruct, except that the use gives a tenant the right to enjoy fruits of an estate as long as they are necessary to fulfill the tenant's personal and family needs. The habitation is a variant of the use in which a person receives land or real estate for a family dwelling and has no obligation to pay rent to the landowner. Article 1026 of the Italian Civil Code establishes that the rules regarding usufruct are applicable to the use and the habitation. Nowadays, these property rights are not common because usufruct is usually used instead.

§ 106IT.18   Surface Rights.

The right of surface gives the holder the right to build and own a building on (or under) somebody else's soil. The surface right agreed by contract suspends the occurrence of accession. The right of surface might be perpetual or established for years. If its duration is limited, once it expires the accession rules make the building the property of the soil's owner. The surface interest may end by prescription if the building is not constructed within 20 years from the beginning of the right.

§ 106IT.19   Bibliography.

Books

Abate, Guido & Giuditta Losa, *Real Estate in Italy: Markets, Investment Vehicles and Performance* (Routledge 2016).

Cartabia, Marta and Nicola Lupo, *The Constitution of Italy: A Contextual Analysis* (Hart Publishing 2022).

Livingston, Michael A., Pier Giuseppe Monateri & Francesco Parisi, *The Italian Legal System: An Introduction* (Stanford Law Books 2d ed. 2015).

Onida, Valerio, *Constitutional Law in Italy* (Wolters Kluwer 2nd ed. 2019).

Rogoff, Adam C., Richard F. Broude and Daniel M. Glosband, *Collier International Business Insolvency Guide* ch. 28A, Italy (Matthew Bender).

Siclari, D., *Italian Banking and Financial Law: Regulating Activities* (Palgrave Macmillan 2015).

Articles

Alpa, Guido, "The 'Principles of European Contract Law' and the Italian Civil Code: Some Preliminary Remarks," 15 *Tul. Eur. & Civ. L.F.* 81 (2001).

Amore, Giuliana, "Trust of 'after us' in the Italian system and the American trust 'for special needs,' " *Trusts & Trustees* (2020) 26 (3): 246 (1 April 2020).

Caponigri, Felicia, Note, "Who Owns Villa La Pietra? The Story of a Family, their Home, and an American University under Italian Law, 5 *Notre Dame J. Int'l & Comp. L.* 201 (2015).

Cavallini, Cesare and Emanuele Ariano, "Issue Preclusion Out of the U.S. (?) The Evolution of the Italian Doctrine of Res Judicata in Comparative Context," 31 *Ind. Int'l & Comp. L. Rev.* 1 (2021).

Fandl, Kevin J., "Regulatory Policy and Innovation in the Wine Industry: A Comparative Analysis of Old and New World Wine Regulations," 34 *Am. U. Int'l L. Rev.* 279 (2018).

Indovina, Vittorio, "When Mandatory Mediation Meets the Adversarial Legal Culture of Lawyers: An Empirical Study in Italy," 26 *Harv. Negotiation L. Rev.* 69 (2020).

Mazzotta, Francesco G., "Precedents in Italian Law," 9 *MSU-DCL J. Int'l L.* 121 (2000).

Papotti, Raul-Angelo, "Cross-border planning for real estate: Italy," *Trusts & Trustees* (2018) 24 (1): 57 (1 February 2018).

Rosano, Sara and Birgit Kurtz, "Tear Down This Wall? The Destruction of Sanctioned Street Art Under U.S. and Italian Law," 30 *Fordham Intell. Prop. Media & Ent. L.J.* 767 (2020).

Saccardo, Nicola, "Inheritance, estate and gift tax treaties-Italy," *Trusts & Trustees* (2020) 26 (1): 41 (Feb. 21, 2020).

Slaybaugh, Jason A., Comment, "Garbage Day: Will Italy Finally Take Out Its Trash in the Land of Fires?" 26 *Pac. Rim L. & Pol'y J.* 179 (2017).

Turitto, Francesca Romana, "A Primer on Franchising in Italy," 39 *Franchise L.J.* 235 (2019).

CHAPTER 106JP

PROPERTY LAW IN JAPAN

§ 106JP.02   **Property Interests Recognized in Japan.**

   § 106JP.02(c)   **Ownership.**

     § 106JP.02(c)(1)   **Civil Code Provisions Relating to Various Aspects of Land Ownership.**

       § 106JP.02(c)(1)(ii)   **Restrictions Between Adjacent Owners.**

         § 106JP.02(c)(1)(ii)(e)   **Right of Using the Opposite Shore.**

Page 393: Insert a space after the "a" and before "part."

a part

   § 106JP.02(d)   **Superficies.**

Page 397: Change years to year's.

Page 401: Add at end of chapter:

§ 106JP.05   **Bibliography.**

Books

Callicott, J. Baird and James McRae, *Japanese Environmental Philosophy* (Oxford University Press 2017).

Garon, Sheldon, *Molding Japanese Minds: The State in Everyday Life* (Princeton University Press 2021).

Goodman, Carl F., *The Rule of Law in Japan: A Comparative Analysis* (Wolters Kluwer 4th ed. 2017).

Haley, John O., Fundamentals of Transnational Litigation, The United States, Canada, Japan, and The European Union (LexisNexis 2d ed. 2014).

Hardacre, Helen, *et al.*, *Japanese Constitutional Revisionism and Civic Activism* (Lexington Books 2021).

Kitagawa, Zentaro, *Doing Business in Japan* (LexisNexis).

Matsui, Shigenori, *Law and Disaster: Earthquake, Tsunami and Nuclear Meltdown in Japan* (Routledge 2020).

Matsuo, Hiroshi, *Property and Trust Law in Japan* (Wolters Kluwer 2021).

Milhaupt, Curtis, J. Ramseyer and Mark West, *The Japanese Legal System* (Foundation Press 2d ed. 2012).

Minamikata, Satoshi, *Family and Succession Law in Japan* (Wolters Kluwer 2d ed. 2017).

Nishiok, Kazuaki and Yuko Nishitani, *Japanese Private International Law* (Hart Publishing 2021).

Oda, Hiroshi, *Japanese Law* (Oxford University Press 4th ed. 2021).

Wynkoop, Jeff, *Legal Issues in Japanese Real Estate Investment* (SCW Publishing, LLC 2012).

Odell, Graham F., *State Reconstitution in China, Japan and East Africa* (Routledge 2020).

Port, Kenneth L., Gerald Paul McAlinn and Salil Mehra, *Comparative Law: Law and the Process of Law in Japan* (Carolina Academic Press 3d ed. 2015).

Rogoff, Adam C., Richard F. Broude and Daniel M. Glosband, *Collier International Business Insolvency Guide* ch. 29, Japan (Matthew Bender).

Articles

Dreyzin, Gary, Note, "The Next Wave of Climate Change Litigation: Comparing Constitutional Inverse Condemnation Claims in the United States, South Africa, and Japan," 31 *Geo. Envtl. L. Rev.* 183 (2018).

Gibson, Rebecca L., Note & Comment, "Cast Your Fate to the Wind (Turbines): Strengthening Japanese Wind Energy Law and Policy," 9 *Tex. J. Oil Gas & Energy L.* 123 (2014).

Ryan, Trevor, "A Reverse Mortgage over the Family Home as a Panacea for Ageing Societies? Comparative Lessons from Japan," *Int. J. Law Policy Family* (2017) 31 (2): 207 (1 August 2017).

Tamaruya, Masayuki, "Japanese Law and the Global Diffusion of Trust and Fiduciary Law," 103 *Iowa L. Rev.* 2229 (2018).

Tamaruya, Masayuki & Mutsuhiko Yukioka, "The Japanese Law of Fiduciaries from Comparative and Transnational Perspectives," 5 *UC Irvine J. of Intl., Trans. & Comp. L.* 135 (2020).

Wold, Chris, "Japan's Resumption of Commercial Whaling and Its Duty to Cooperate with the International Whaling Commission," 35 *J. Envtl. L. & Litig.* 87 (2020).

Yi, Yujin, "The Status Quo of Racial Discrimination in Japan and the Republic of Korea and the Need to Provide for Anti-Discrimination Laws," 7 *Colum. J. Race & L.* 410 (2017).

CHAPTER 106KE

PROPERTY LAW IN KENYA

§ 106KE.07 Ownership of Real Property by Foreigners.

Page 420: Change guarentee to guarantee.

Page 420: Add at the end of the chapter:

§ 106KE.08 Bibliography.

Books

Cheeseman, Nic, Karuti Kanyinga, and Gabrielle Lynch, *The Oxford Handbook of Kenyan Politics* (Oxford University Press 2020).

Joireman, Sandra R., *Where There is No Government: Enforcing Property Rights in Common Law Africa* (Oxford University Press 2011).

Kameri-Mbote, Patricia, Collins Odote, Celestine Musembi and Murigi Kamande, *Ours by Right: Law, Politics and Realities of Community Property in Kenya* (White Horse Press 2020).

Maxon, Robert M., *Britain and Kenya's Constitutions, 1950–1960* (Cambria Press 2011).

Mey, Brenda Pamela, *Competition Law in Kenya* (Wolters Kluwer 2017).

Onalo, Peter L., *Land Law & Conveyancing in Kenya* (LawAfrica).

Onyango, Gedion and Goran Hyden, *Governing Kenya: Public Policy in Theory and Practice* (Palgrave Macmillan 2021).

Otiso, Wycliffe, *Kenya Investment Law and Policy: Analysis of Bias and Priorities in the Incentive Regime* (VDM Verlag Dr. Müller 2011).

Oyaya, Charles O. and Nana K. Poku, *The Making of the Constitution of Kenya: A Century of Struggle and the Future of Constitutionalism* (Routledge 2018).

The Consolidated Laws of Kenya (LawAfrica).

Articles

Carpenter, Stefan, Elizabeth Baldwin and Daniel H. Cole, "The Polycentric Turn: A Case Study of Kenya's Evolving Legal Regime for Irrigation Waters," 57 *Nat. Resources J.* 101 (2017).

Dorf, Nicholas, "Making an Offer They Can't Refuse: Corporate Investment in Africa and the Divestment of Indigenous Land Rights," 38 *B.C. Int'l & Comp. L. Rev.* 65 (2015).

Hoexter, Cora, "Administrative Justice in Kenya: Learning from South Africa's Mistakes," *Journal of African Law*, 62, 1 (2018), 105–128 (1 February 2018).

Joireman, Sandra Fullerton, "The Evolution of the Common Law: Legal

Development in Kenya and India," 44 *Commonwealth & Comp. Pol.* 190, 192–93 (2006).

Mbaku, John Mukum, "Constitutionalism And Africa's Agenda 2063: How To Build 'The Africa We Want' ", 45 *Brooklyn J. Int'l L.* 537 (2020).

Mujuzi, Jamil Ddamulira, "The Islamic Law of Marriage and Inheritance in Kenya," *Journal of African Law*, 65, 3 (2021), 377–401.

Munoru, G.G.S., "The Development of the Kenya Legal System, Legal Education and Legal Profession," 9 *E. Africa L.J.* 1 (1973).

Nyarango, Archibold Ombongi, "A Jigsaw Puzzle or a Map? The Role of Treaties under Kenya's Constitution," *Journal of African Law*, 62, 1 (2018), 25–50, 1 Feb. 2018.

Sang, Brian, "Trending Towards Greater Eco-Protection in Kenya: Public Interest Environmental Litigation and Its Prospects Within the New Constitutional Order," *Journal of African Law*, 57, 1 (1 April 2013), 29–56.

Soyapi, Caiphas B., "Environmental Protection in Kenya's Environment and Land Court," *J. Environmental Law* (2019) 31 (1): 151 (3 October 2019).

Soyapi, Caiphas B., "Environmental Protection in Kenya's Environment and Land Court," *J. Environmental Law* (2019) 31 (1): 151 (1 March 2019).

Wabwile, Michael, Nyongesa, "The Place of English Law in Kenya," *Oxford University Commonwealth Law Journal*, 3:1, 51–80 (2003).

Wiley, Liz Alden, "The Community Land Act in Kenya Opportunities and Challenges for Communities," *LAND* 1 (2018), https://www.mdpi.com/2073-445X/7/1/12 [https://perma.cc/NEY4-GQJT].

Witchger, Kathryn E., "Equality in Process: Community Land Dispute Resolution Mechanisms in Kenyan Law," 37 *Colum. J. Gender & L.* 68 (2018).

CHAPTER 106KR

PROPERTY LAW IN SOUTH KOREA

SYNOPSIS

Page 421: Add a new section after § 106KR.03(k):

§ 106KR.04 Bibliography.

§ 106KR.03   Basic South Korean Property Law.

§ 106KR.03(j)   Taxation.

Page 425: Insert a space after the period but before Korean.

Page 426: Add a new section § 106KR.04 Bibliography. after § 106KR.03(k) Environmental Regulation.:

§ 106KR.04   Bibliography.

Books

Cho, Kuk, *Litigation in Korea* (Edward Elgar Publishing 2010).

Introduction to Korean Law (Korea Legislation Research Institute 2013).

Kim, Iljoong, Hojun Lee & Ilya Somin, *Eminent Domain: A Comparative Perspective* (Cambridge University Press 2017).

Kim, Jasper S., *Korean Business Law: The Legal Landscape and Beyond* (Carolina Academic Press 2010).

Kim, Joongi, *International Arbitration in Korea* (Oxford University Press 2017).

Kim, Marie Seong-Hak, *Constitutional Transition and the Travail of Judges: The Courts of South Korea* (Cambridge University Press 2019).

Kim, Marie Seong-Hak, *Law and Custom in Korea: Comparative Legal History* (Cambridge University Press 2012).

Mo, Jongryn and David W. Brady, *The Rule of Law in South Korea* (Hoover Institution Press 2010).

Rogoff, Adam C., Richard F. Broude and Daniel M. Glosband, *Collier International Business Insolvency Guide* ch. 30, Korea (Matthew Bender).

Yang, Sung Chul, *The North And South Korean Political Systems: A Comparative Analysis* (Routledge 2021).

Articles

Arner, Douglas W., Charles D. Booth, Paul Lejot & Berry F.C. Hsu, "Property Rights, Collateral, Creditor Rights, and Insolvency in East Asia," 42 *Tex. Int'l L.J.* 515 (2007).

Caylor, Matthew P., Note, "Eminent Domain and Economic Development: The Protection of Property Four Ways," 36 *Ariz. J. Int'l & Comp. Law* 165, 179–81 (2019) (discussing eminent domain in South Korea).

Choi, Jongsok, "How to Develop an International Arbitration Industry in South Korea," 21 *Asian-Pacific L. & Pol'y J.* 1 (2020).

Duong, Alanna T., Note, "Green Growth 1.0 and 2.0: Towards Meaningful Environmental Policy in South Korea," 31 *Ariz. J. Int'l & Comp. Law* 357 (2014).

Jin, Oh Seung, "Overview of Legal Systems in the Asia-Pacific Region: South Korea," SCHOLARSHIP@CORNELL LAW: A DIGITAL REPOSITORY (2004), http://scholarship.law.cornell.edu/lps_lsapr/6 (visited May 29, 2021).

Kim, Jasper, "Anti-Speculation Laws and their Impact on The Real Estate And Financial Markets: The Korean Case," 18 *Colum. J. Asian L.* 47 (2004).

Kim, Jihye, Comment, "The Displaced Residents' Right to Relocation Assistance: Toward an Equitable Urban Redevelopment in South Korea," 19 *Pac. Rim L. & Pol'y J.* 587 (2010).

Kim, Rakhyun E., "Is Ramsar Home Yet? A Critique of South Korean Laws in Light of the Continuing Coastal Wetlands Reclamation," 24 *Colum. J. Asian L.* 437 (2011).

Kwon, Youngjoon and Yong-Shik Lee, "Real Estate in Asia—Policy, Pride & Prejudice: Legal Analysis of Traditional Leasehold in Korea (Chonsegwon) from a Comparative Legal Perspective," 29 *Ariz. J. Int'l & Comp. Law* 263 (2012).

Lee, Grace, Note, "Taming the Beast: Confucianism as the Key to Reforming Korea's Chaebol System for the Common Good," 45 *Fordham Int'l L.J.* 155 (2021).

Park, Seo Jung, Comment, "How South Korea Can Improve Its Carbon Market: The Importance of Economic Incentives and International Cooperation in the Fight Against Climate Change," 35 *Emory Int'l L. Rev.* 485 (2021).

Rhee, Robert J., "The Political Economy of Corporate Law and Governance: American and Korean Rules under Different Endogenous Conditions and Forms of Capitalism," 55 *Wake Forest L. Rev.* 649 (2020).

Yi, Yujin, "The Status Quo of Racial Discrimination in Japan and the Republic of Korea and the Need to Provide for Anti-Discrimination Laws," 7 *Colum. J. Race & L.* 410 (2017).

CHAPTER 106KZ

PROPERTY LAW OF THE REPUBLIC OF KAZAKHSTAN

§ 106KZ.01   Overview of Real Property Law in Kazakhstan.

Page 429: Add to footnote 5:

[5] *See generally* Zhenis Kembayev, Introduction to the Law of Kazakhstan ch. 7, "Property Law" (Kluwer Law International 2012).

Page 443: Add a new section:

§ 106KZ.11   Bibliography.

Books

Butler, William E., *Civil Code of the Republic Kazakhstan* (Wildy, Simmonds & Hill Publishing UK ed. 2008).

Kembayev, Zhenis, *Introduction to the Law of Kazakhstan* (Kluwer Law International 2012).

Lillis, Joanna, *Dark Shadows: Inside the Secret World of Kazakhstan* (I.B. Tauris 2018).

Paterson, John, M. K. Suleimenov & Ilias Bantekas, *Oil and Gas Law in Kazakhstan: National and International Perspectives* (Kluwer Law International 2004).

Wight, Robert and Carole Mitchell, *Vanished Khans and Empty Steppes: A History of Kazakhstan from Pre-History to Post-Independence* (Silk Road Media 2015).

Yerkinbayev, Adlet, Joel Benjamin, Muborak Kambarova and Akmal Abdisamatov, *Corporate Acquisitions and Mergers in Kazakhstan & Uzbekistan* (Kluwer Law Intl. 2019).

Articles

Bantekas, Ilias, "The Rise of Transnational Commercial Courts: The Astana International Financial Centre Court," 33 *Pace Int'l L. Rev.* 1 (2020).

Brown, J. Robert, Jr., "Culture, Chaos and Capitalism: Privatization in Kazakhstan," 19 *U. Pa. J. Int'l Econ. L.* 909 (1998).

Cleveland, Anna Kate, Comment, "How Kazakhstan's Strategy 2050 Affects Its Current International Environmental Obligations Under the Kyoto Protocol," 16 *Wyo. L. Rev.* 99 (2016).

Hanson, Margaret, "Legalized Rent-Seeking: Eminent Domain in Kazakhstan," 50 *Cornell Int'l L.J.* 15 (2017).

Sievers, Eric W., "Transboundary Jurisdiction and Watercourse Law: China, Kazakhstan, and the Irtysh," 37 *Tex. Int'l L.J.* 1 (2002).

Yessengeldin, Bauyrzhan, Zhibek Khussainova, Aigul Kurmanova, Dinara Syzdykova and Azamat Zhanseitov, "Exploitation of Natural Resources in Kazakhstan: Judicial Practice for Foreign Investment," 12 *JEAIL* 169 (2019).

Yeung, Horace, Flora Huang, Zhanyl Bekmurzayeva and Dina Janaidar, "Institutional Development and the Astana International Financial Center in Kazakhstan," 19 *Wash. U. Global Stud. L. Rev.* 53 (2020).

CHAPTER 106MX

PROPERTY LAW IN MEXICO

§ 106MX.01   History of Property Law in Mexico.

Page 448: Add to footnote 5:

[5] Azuela, Antonio, "Property in the Post-Post-Revolution: Notes on the Crisis of the Constitutional Idea of Property in Contemporary Mexico," 89 *Tex. L. Rev.* 1915 (2011).

§ 106MX.02   Types of Property Interests.

Page 449: Add to footnote 7:

[7] ; Azuela, Antonio, "Property in the Post-Post-Revolution: Notes on the Crises of the Constitutional Idea of Property in Contemporary Mexico," 89 *Tex. L. Rev.* 1915 (2011).

Page 453: Add new section § 106MX.10 Bibliography. at the end of the § 106MX.09:

§ 106MX.10   Bibliography.

Books

Castagnola, Andrea and Saul Lopez Noriega, *Judicial Politics in Mexico: The Supreme Court and the Transition to Democracy* (Routledge 2016).

Gallardo, Yurixhi & Patrick Del Duca, Editors, *Mexico and Its Legal System: Lawyers: Essays on the Continuing Evolution* (Carolina Academic Press 2018).

González, José Antonio Márquez, *Family and Succession Law in Mexico*

(Wolters Kluwer Law & Business 2nd ed. 2014).

Hall, Frederick, *The Laws of Mexico: A Compilation and Treatise Relating to Real Property, Mines, Water Rights, Personal Rights, Contracts, and Inheritances* (The Lawbook Exchange, Ltd. 2016).

Marquez, Jose Juan Gonzalez, *Environmental Law in Mexico* (Wolters Kluwer 2d ed. 2017).

Murray, Claudia, Camilla Ween, Yadira Torres-Romero, Yazmin Ramirez, *Real Estate in Central America, Mexico and the Caribbean* (Routledge 2021).

Ortega-Rubio, Alfredo, *Mexican Natural Resources Management and Biodiversity Conservation: Recent Case Studies* (Springer International Publishing AG 2018).

Rogoff, Adam C., Richard F. Broude and Daniel M. Glosband, *Collier International Business Insolvency Guide* ch. 32, Mexico (Matthew Bender).

Rull, Ana Pulido, *Mapping Indigenous Land: Native Land Grants in Colonial New Spain* (University of Oklahoma Press 2020).

Signet, William D., *Introduction to the Mexican Real Estate System* (Carolina Academic Press 2010).

Vargas, Jorge A., *Mexican Law for the American Lawyer* (Carolina Academic Press 2009).

Zamora, Stephen, José Ramón Cossío, Leonel Pereznieto, José Roldán-Xopa and David Lopez, *Mexican Law* (Oxford University Press 2005).

Articles

Baur, Donald C., Heather D. Rally & Miranda M. Jensen, "Cooperative Conservation: Strengthening U.S.-Cuba-Mexico Relations Through Joint Management of Marine Protected Areas in the Gulf of Mexico," 31 *Tul. Envtl. L.J.* 173 (2018).

Brandys, Roy R., Nicholas P. Laurent & Blaire A. Knox, "The US-Mexico Border Wall: A Unique Project with Unique Real Estate Issues," 33 *Probate & Property* 36 (Jan./Feb. 2019).

Caris, Daniel, Note, "Viva la FIBRA-E: An Analysis of Mexico's Response to the Master Limited Partnership," 12 *Tex. J. Oil Gas & Energy L.* 93 (Jan. 2017).

Dehler, Dane J., Note, "Buying Property in Mexico's 'Restricted Zone': The Missed Opportunity that Was the 2013 Beltrones Proposal to Amend Article 27 of the Mexican Constitution," 32 *Ariz. J. Int'l & Comp. Law* 309 (2015).

Halawi, Samir, Note, "Sniffing Out Clandestine Water Pollution in the Tijuana River Valley," 31 *Geo. Envtl. L. Rev.* 785 (2019).

López-Velarde, Alejandro, "New Regulation for the Power Generation and Gas Industries in Mexico: The Possibilities for Foreign Investors," 40 *Energy L. J.* 87 (2019).

Payne, Tylynn R., Comment, "In (Not So) Deep Water: The Texas—New Mexico Water War and the Unworkable Provisions of the Rio Grande Compact," 52 *Tex. Tech L. Rev.* 669 (2020).

Rosenblatt, Michelle and Abril Rodríguez Esparza, "U.S.—Mexico Cross-Border Estate Planning: Planning Techniques from a U.S. and Mexican Perspective," 14 *Tex. Tech. Est. Plan. Com. Prop. L.J.* 121 (2021).

Smith, Kameron B., Comment, "Subsurface Tension: The Conflicting Laws of Texas and New Mexico Over Shared Groundwater and New Mexico's Desire for Regulation," 7 *Tex. A&M L. Rev.* 453 (2020).

Summerfield, Jason N., "The Memphis Sand Aquifer and the Uncertain Jurisprudence Over Groundwater," 50 *U. Mem. L. Rev.* 587 (2020).

Veteto, Jeff, "Foreign Land Ownership on Mexico's Coasts: The Proposed Amendment to Article 27 of the Mexican Constitution," 20 *L. & Bus. Rev. Am.* 325 (Spring, 2014).

CHAPTER 106PH

PROPERTY LAW IN THE PHILIPPINES

§ 106PH.01   Brief History of the Philippines.

§ 106PH.01(b)   The Early History of the Philippines.

Page 456: Change Researches to Researchers.

Page 456: Add to footnote 1:

[1] *See generally* Nicole, CuUnjieng Aboitiz, Asian Place, Filipino Nation: A Global Intellectual History of the Philippine Revolution, 1887–1912 (Columbia University Press (June 16, 2020).

§ 106PH.01(c)   Summary of Modern Filipino Legal History.

Page 456: Add to footnote 2:

[2] *See generally* Raul C. Pangalangan, Philippine Materials in International Law (Brill | Nijhoff 2021); Mark Thompson and Eric Vincent Batalla, Routledge Handbook of the Contemporary Philippines (Routledge 2018).

CHAPTER 106PL

PROPERTY LAW IN POLAND

§ 106PL.02   Current Laws Regarding Real Property in Poland.

§ 106PL.02(a)   The Constitution of the Republic of Poland.

§ 106PL.02(a)(2)   Property Laws Not Contained in the Civil Code.

Page 468: Add to footnote 12:

[12] *See generally* Piotr Machnikowski, Justyna Balcarczyk and Monika Drela, Contract

Law in Poland (Wolters Kluwer 3d ed. 2017).

§ 106PL.03   Bibliography.

Page 480: Add to Bibliography:

Banaszak, Boguslaw, *Constitutional Law in Poland* (Kluwer Law International 2012).

Bień-Kacała, Agnieszka and Anna Młynarska-Sobaczewska, *Constitutional Law in Poland* (Wolters Kluwer 2nd ed. 2021).

Drinóczi, Tímea and Agnieszka Bień-Kacała, *Rule of Law, Common Values, and Illiberal Constitutionalism: Poland and Hungary within the European Union* (Routledge 2020).

Frankowski, Stanislaw J., Editor, in cooperation with Adam Bodner, *Introduction to Polish Law* (Kluwer Law International 2005).

Granat, Miroslaw, *et al.*, *The Constitution of Poland: A Contextual Analysis* (Hart Publishing 2021).

Jasinski, Piotr and Helen Lawton-Smith, *Environmental Regulation in Transforming Economies: The Case of Poland* (Routledge 2018).

Habdas, Magdalena, *Property and Trust Law in Poland* (Wolters Kluwer 2d ed. 2018).

Kowalszyk, Barbara, Rafal Mikowski & Lukasz Mikowski, *Environmental Law in Poland* (Wolters Kluwer 2019).

Lukowski, Jerzy and Hubert Zawadzki, *A Concise History of Poland* (Cambridge University Press 3d ed. 2019).

Mikua, Maciej, *Municipal Magdeburg Law (Ius municipale Magdeburgense) in Late Medieval Poland* (BRILL 2021).

Rogoff, Adam C., Richard F. Broude and Daniel M. Glosband, *Collier International Business Insolvency Guide* ch. 37, Poland (Matthew Bender).

Sadurski, Wojciech, *Poland's Constitutional Breakdown* (Oxford University Press 2019).

Szymczyk, Przemysław, "Are Current Owners and Usufructuaries of Polish Real Estate Nationalized after World War II Entitled to the Status of Parties to Reprivatization Proceedings?" 41 *Loy. L.A. Int'l & Comp. L. Rev.* 409 (2018).

CHAPTER 106RO

REAL PROPERTY LAW IN ROMANIA

§ 106RO.02   Property Legislation Before the Communist Era.

§ 106RO.01(c)   The Romanian Constitution in 1866.

Page 485: Add a footnote at the end of fourth paragraph of section 106RO.01(c):

[3.1] *See generally* Bianca Selejan-Gutan, The Constitution of Romania: A Contextual Analysis (Hart Publishing 2016); Irina Zlatescu, Constitutional Law in Romania (Wolters Kluwer 2d ed. 2017).

§ 106RO.06   Public Ownership Rights.

§ 106RO.06(b)   The Concession of Public Property.

Page 489: Change the spelling of Gazzete to Gazette.

[7] Gazette

Page 489: Change the spelling of Gazzete to Gazette.

[8] Gazette

§ 106RO.06(c)   The Renting of Public Property.

Page 489: Change the spelling of Gazzete to Gazette.

[9] Gazette

§ 106RO.07   The Forms of Property Rights.

§ 106RO.07(b)   Conditional Ownership by Law.

Page 490: Change descendents to descendants.

§ 106RO.08   Acquisition of Property.

§ 106RO.08(c)   Acquisition by Contract.

Page 492: Change the spelling of Gazzete to Gazette.

[10] Gazette

§ 106RO.09   The Cadastre and Real Estate Publicity.

Page 493: Change the spelling of Gazzete to Gazette.

[11] Gazette

Page 493: Add a new section:

§ 106RO.10   Bibliography.

Books

von Bogdandy, Armin & Pál Sonnevend, *Constitutional Crisis in the European Constitutional Area: Theory, Law and Politics in Hungary and Romania* (Nomos Verlagsgesellschaft (2015).

Cartwright, A.L., *The Return of the Peasant: Land Reform in Post-Communist Romania* (Routledge 2017).

Cercel, Cristian, *Romania and the Quest for European Identity* (Routledge 2021).

Csiki, Zsuzsa, Iustinian Captariu, Diana Kioko, Mihai Coada and Ioana Naroasi, Corporate *Acquisitions and Mergers in Romania* (Wolters Kluwer 2d ed. 2019).

Levasseur, Alain A., J. Randall Trahan and David Gruning, *The Legal System of Romania* (Carolina Academic Press 2020).

Marin, Anca Monica, *Assessing PNDL: Romanian Leaders in Quest for State-*

Budget Funds (Springer 2021).

Menyhárd, Attila & Emőd Veress, Editors, *New Civil Codes in Hungary and Romania* (Springer International Publishing AG 2017).

Serban, Mihaela, *Subverting Communism in Romania: Law and Private Property 1945–1965* (Lexington Books 2019).

Sinea, Anca, *Romania as an Energy Actor in the EU* (Routledge 2020).

Stanescu, Catalin Gabriel, *Energy Law Romania* (Wolters Kluwer 2d ed. 2018).

Zlatescu, Irina, *Constitutional Law in Romania* (Wolters Kluwer 2d ed. 2017).

Articles

Grabowski, Julia, Note, "Forced Evictions: Racial Persecution and Social Exclusion of the Roma Minority in Romania," 56 *Colum. J. Transnat'l L.* 855 (2018).

Grygierowska, Karolina, Comment, "When a Home Is Not a House: The Destruction of Romani Personal Property as a Human Rights Violation," 28 *Emory Int'l L. Rev.* 557 (2014).

Leal-Arcas, Rafael, Andrew Filis and Victoria Nalule, "Energy Decentralization and Decarbonization: The Case of Romania and Malta," 60 *Nat. Resources J.* 117 (2020).

Serban, Mihaela, "Regime Change and Property Rights Consciousness in Postcommunist Romania," 43 *Law & Soc. Inquiry* 732 (2018).

CHAPTER 106RU

PROPERTY LAW IN RUSSIA

Page 511: Add at end of chapter:

§ 106RU.04   Bibliography.

Books

Aliberti, Marco & Ksenia Lisitsyna, *Russia's Posture in Space: Prospects for Europe* (Springer International Publishing AG 2019).

Butler, William E., *Civil Code of the Russian Federation* (Oxford University Press 2003).

Butler, William, *Russian Foreign Relations and Investment Law* (Oxford University Press 2006).

Butler, William, *Russian Law* (Oxford University Press 2009).

Butler, William E., *The Russian Legal Practitioner* (Eleven International Publishing 2011).

Krasheninnikov, Pavel, *The 12 Apostles of Russian Law: Lawyers Who Changed Law, State and Society* (Glagoslav Publications B.V. 2019).

Maggs, Peter, Olga Schwartz and William Burnham, *Law and Legal System of the Russian Federation* (Juris Publishing, Inc. 6th ed. 2015).

Muravyeva, Marianna Editor, The Foundations of Russian Law (Hart Publishing 2019).

Rogoff, Adam C., Richard F. Broude and Daniel M. Glosband, *Collier International Business Insolvency Guide* ch. 38, Russia (Matthew Bender).

Shashkova, Anna V., *Study Manual on the Bases of Russian Law* (Cambridge Scholars Publishing 2015).

Shostak, Scott Alexandr, Editor, *Russia Corporate, Financial, and Commercial Law* (American Bar Association 2019).

Vorobieva, Olga, *Private International Law in Russia* (Wolters Kluwer 2d ed. 2015).

Articles

Anisimov, Alexey & Anatoliy Ryzhenkov, "Theory and Practice of Legal Experiments in Land Law: The View from Russia," *Statute Law Rev.* (2018) 39 (2): 155 (1 June 2018).

Garipov, Ruslan, "Indigenous Peoples' Rights in Russian North: Main Challenges and Prospects for Future Development," 23 *Hum. Rts. Br.* 32 (2020).

Hendley, Kathryn, "Do Lawyers Matter in Russia," 2021 *Wis. L. Rev.* 301.

Hendley, Kathryn, "Mobilizing Law in Contemporary Russia: The Evolution of Disputes over Home Repair Projects," 58 *Am. J. Comp. L.* 631 (2010).

Kilborn, Jason J., "Fatal Flaws in Financing Personal Bankruptcy: The Curious Case of Russia in Comparative Context," 94 *Am. Bankr. L.J.* 419 (2020).

Kulkov, Maxim, and Dmitry Vlasov, "Russian Supreme Commercial Court Rules in Favour of Arbitration in a Construction Contract and Related Agreements," 9 No. 3 *Construction L. Int'l* 4 (September, 2014).

Lewinbuk, Katerina P., "True Perestroika or Still Perfunctory: A Decade of Developments in Russian Law Practice Reform," 32 *Fla. J. Int'l L.* 301 (2021).

Lindsay, Ira, "A Troubled Path to Private Property: Agricultural Land Law in Russia," 16 *Colum. J. Eur. L.* 261 (2010).

Mälksoo, Lauri, "International Law and the 2020 Amendments to the Russian Constitution," 115 *A.J.I.L.* 78 (2021).

Sawers, Brian, "Reevaluating the Evidence for Anticommons in Transition Russia," 16 *Colum. J. Eur. L.* 233 (2010).

Sidortsov, Roman & Elena Gavrilina, "When foundation matters: overcoming legal and regulatory barriers to oil and gas well decommissioning in Russia," *J. World Energy Law Bus.* (2018) 11 (3): 209 (1 June 2018).

Page 511: Insert new Chapter 106ZA after Chapter 106RU:

CHAPTER 106ZA
PROPERTY LAW IN SOUTH AFRICA

David John Vlcek
Deneys Reitz Inc
3 Pencarrow Crescent,
Pencarrow Park,
La Lucia Ridge, 4051, South Africa

SYNOPSIS

§ 106ZA.01   History of Property Law in South Africa.

§ 106ZA.01(a)   Colonization.

Prior to the arrival of the Colonialists from Europe, the majority of the indigenous inhabitants of South Africa were nomadic and did not recognize the concept of individual land ownership. The area of land governed by the tribe was owned or vested in the monarch that governed the tribe; alternatively, in the tribe itself.

In 1652, the Dutch East India Company established a settlement at the Cape under Jan van Riebeeck. With their arrival, a very simple system of registration of land began. This early land registration was based on a *placaat* of Charles V of Holland, which was passed in 1529. The *placaat* provided that every sale of immovable property was to occur in the presence of a Judge. A Dutch edict of 1650 also provided that written registers should be kept of all such transactions.

An early issue that arose in the Cape was that there were no Judges present before whom such transactions could take place. As a solution, two members of the *Politieke Raad* were appointed so that deeds could be executed. Title Deeds were executed and registered in this manner until 1828, after which a Registrar of Deeds was formally appointed due to the establishment of a Supreme Court. The office of Registrar of Deeds was established in terms of Ordinance 39 of 1828.

In 1828, the Registrar of Deeds had the additional task of being the Registrar of slaves.

As settlers arrived at the Cape from Europe, they were granted land so that the development of the land could commence and communities could be established. These transfers were called "Grants" and were referred to as such because they described the very first time that a portion of land was transferred to and owned by an individual from the state.

Prior to 1882, no formal land registers were maintained. Grants and Deeds of Transfer were simply numbered and placed in chronological order. Registers recording the history of each portion of land and a system of numbering portions of land for identification purposes did not exist. In addition, there was no Index or Register kept of the owners of the various portions of land. This made ascertaining the identity of the owner of a specific portion of land an incredibly arduous task.

Prior to 1844, Grants and Deeds were drafted by Government officials. In 1844, Advocates were authorized to do so.

In 1859, due to intensifying public dissatisfaction as a result of delays in the Deeds Office at Cape Town, the Government appointed a committee to investigate possible alternative methods of registration and transfer of land. The committee recommended that land registers should be created in which the Grant and subsequent registration history of each portion of land could be recorded. Sadly, only farm registers were opened and portions of land were never properly identified.

Land was not granted to the indigenous people. During this period, land was taken from the indigenous tribes that inhabited the Cape, and as expansion continued inland, this trend continued. This conduct caused great tension between the colonizers and the local tribes, such as the Xhosa and Zulu, which escalated and resulted in well-documented bloodshed.

The discovery of diamonds in the Northern Cape in 1867 and gold in the Witwatersrand area in 1886 changed South Africa forever and resulted in both an economic and population boom in the respective areas.

There was also conflict between the Dutch and British settlers, who initially arrived at the Cape in 1795. This led to the first Anglo-Boer war in 1880, and a second in 1899.

§ 106ZA.01(b)   The Union of South Africa.

On May 31, 1910, the Union of South Africa was established. Four colonies existed in South Africa at the time; namely, the Cape, Natal, the Orange Free State and the Transvaal. The Union was a self-governing authority within the British empire, and negotiations excluded the majority black population and deprived them of more of their land. This led to the formation of the African National Congress (ANC) in 1912.

The Black Land Act 27 of 1913, together with the Natives (Urban Areas) Act 21 of 1923 limited black land ownership to existing tribal territories—a result of which was the calculated separation of the races.

The Union Statute, Act 13 of 1918 was the first legislation passed governing the registration of deeds and the transfer of immovable property within the Union. The Union Statute was repealed and replaced by the Deeds Registries Act 47 of 1937.

This Act sets out the procedure and requirements for acquiring rights to land. The main purpose of the Deeds Registries Act is to regulate administrative aspects of the registration of land and to provide owners with protection and security.

The Deeds Registries Act is a combination and codification of the principles of the transfer of land ownership and the administration thereof in South Africa. The Deeds Registries Act is primarily concerned with the transfer and registration of real rights to immovable property.

§ 106ZA.01(c)   The Apartheid Era.

The National Party (NP) came into power in 1948 when they were successful in the national election. Shortly thereafter, the National Party enacted the policy of separate development of the races, otherwise known as "Apartheid." Apartheid became official government policy.

Under Apartheid, black people were severely restricted to certain occupations, paid far lower wages than other citizens for similar work, and could not vote. Only white people could vote or run for public office. People of Asian-Indian descent and those of mixed race also had very limited political rights.

In 1950, the government promulgated legislation providing for the creation of Bantu nations or "Bantustans." The Group Areas Act 41 of 1950 resulted in the physical separation of the races by creating different residential areas for each of the different race groups, as prescribed by the Act.

This led to "forced removals" of entire communities in circumstances where they were living in the "wrong" areas. The Group Areas Act further prevented black people from purchasing, owning, or leasing property in areas designated for other race groups.

Due to the ongoing oppression, the black majority began to rise up and protest. On March 21, 1960, sixty-nine black protestors were killed by police and government officials at Sharpeville.

South Africa left the commonwealth in 1961 and became a Republic.

In 1964, the Rivonia Trials were held and Nelson Mandela, Walter Sisulu and other ANC activists were sentenced to life imprisonment for Treason due to their opposition to Apartheid.

In 1976, approximately six hundred people were killed in anti-Apartheid protests. During 1977, the United Nations Security Council imposed a mandatory arms embargo against South Africa. On October 19, 1977, several political organizations, including the ANC, and various newspapers, were banned.

During June 1988, approximately two million black South African workers staged a huge strike in defiance of Apartheid laws. Due to ever-increasing national and international pressure, the then President, P W Botha, resigned on August 14, 1989 and was replaced by F W De Klerk.

In 1990, the government lifted its ban on the ANC, PAC and other various political parties. On February 11, 1990, Nelson Mandela was released from prison after serving twenty-seven years.

In 1993, negotiations took place between the relevant role players, in terms of which basic principles for a new democratic Constitution were agreed. During 1993, an interim Constitution was promulgated providing for non-racial, multi-party democracy, the creation and implementation of a Bill of Rights and the end of Apartheid. During 1993, the Interim Constitution came into effect and paved the way for the creation of the Final Constitution.

In April 1994, South Africa held its first non-racial democratic elections, as a result of which Nelson Mandela was inaugurated as the country's first democratically elected President.

§ 106ZA.01(d)   Democracy Begins.

§ 106ZA.01(d)(1)   Constitution Invalidates Race-Related Property Restrictions.

On February 4, 1997, South Africa's Final Constitution came into effect. The Constitution of the Republic of South Africa, Act 108 of 1996, is the supreme law of the Republic of South Africa, and any law or conduct inconsistent with it is therefore invalid. The Bill of Rights contained in Chapter 2 thereof is the cornerstone of democracy in South Africa.

It enshrines the rights of all people in the country and affirms the democratic values of human dignity, equality and freedom.

Section 25(1) of the Final Constitution states that "no one may be deprived of property except in terms of law of general application, and no law may permit arbitrary deprivation of property." Subsection (5) goes on to say that "the state must take reasonable legislative and other measures, within its available resources, to foster conditions which enable citizens to gain access to land on an equitable basis."

Section 25 read with sections 8(1) and 39(2) of the Final Constitution envisages the development of South African property law in terms of the spirit, purport and object of the Bill of Rights.

Section 2 of the Final Constitution has ensured that all of the discriminatory Apartheid laws that are in obvious conflict with Constitutional principles, are now invalid and have been repealed. To this extent, all references to "race" have been removed from all documents registered in the Deeds Registries and every South African citizen, regardless of their race, is free to own, purchase and lease property within the Republic.

§ 106ZA.01(d)(2)   Constitution Provides for Land Redistribution.

Under the new Constitutional dispensation, the previously disadvantaged majority black population who were deprived of their land and forcibly removed from their homes are now afforded the opportunity of regaining the land under what is referred to as "land redistribution."

§ 106ZA.02   An Introduction to South African Property Law.

§ 106ZA.02(a)   The South African Land Registration System.

South Africa's legal system is comprised of both common law and civil law—civil law in the form of legislation and the rules and regulations that inform and give content to the legislation. South African common law is uncodified and is comprised of case law that is influenced by English and Roman-Dutch law, depending on the specific area concerned.

South African property law is primarily based on the ancient principles of Roman law, but some traces of Germanic law can also be identified. Accordingly, many of the rights that one has in and to property in South African law are based on ancient Roman law principles that have survived the test of time and are still widely applicable throughout Europe.

South Africa has one of the most comprehensive and secure land registration systems in the world. Every portion of land in South Africa has been measured and surveyed by a trained and educated land surveyor. The property is then plotted and depicted on a diagram or a general plan which is kept in the Surveyor General's office for the area where the property is situated.

As a result, whenever an individual needs to ascertain the particulars of a specific portion of land, they can simply conduct a search at the Surveyor General's office on that property. The diagram will reflect the boundary lines, size and rights that are registered over or in favor of that portion of land. The deeds registry will not permit a portion of land to be transferred to another individual if a diagram or general plan does not exist for that portion of land.

Under the South African land registration system a person can virtually always ascertain the identity of the owner of a specific portion of land.

Every portion of land is registered in a deeds registry. The deeds registry or deeds office is a public office, state owned and controlled, and its records and the documents kept there are open for inspection by the public. Thus, any individual can inspect the details of a property or its owner.

Whenever a portion of land is transferred, hypothecated, alienated, or granted, a certified copy of the diagram, mentioned above, together with the deed recording the details of the property and the reason for the transfer or hypothecation, is executed and registered at the deeds registry. Once it is executed, the seal and signature of the Registrar of Deeds is placed thereon and it is filed for record purposes at the particular deeds registry.

The financial institutions that grant loans to purchasers to purchase land register bonds over the land in order to record and secure their real rights in and to the said property. This hypothecation is also recorded and registered in the deeds registry and the deed pertaining to the portion of land is endorsed in order to reflect the hypothecation.

The land cannot be transferred or disposed of unless the bond has either been cancelled or the owner has obtained the financial institution's consent to register a further bond over that portion of land. A bond cannot be cancelled unless the bond holder has provided its written consent, in the prescribed form, to do so.

The documents necessary for the transfer, hypothecation, and alienation of land are prepared and drafted by a conveyancer. A conveyancer is an admitted attorney who has passed a practical examination in the law and practice of conveyancing and who has been admitted as a conveyancer by the High Court of South Africa. The conveyancer will appear in the Deeds Registry in order to execute the deeds in the presence of the registrar of deeds.

§ 106ZA.02(b)   The Deeds Registry.

There are nine Deeds Registries in South Africa. They are located in Pretoria, Johannesburg, Bloemfontein, Pietermaritzburg, Cape Town, Vryburg, King Williams Town, Nelspruit and Kimberley.

Each Deeds Registry has a very specific jurisdiction with regards to the position of the land that is to be registered and recorded in it. The person in charge of each Deeds Registry is called the Registrar of Deeds.

The Chief Registrar of Deeds is based in Pretoria and it is the duty of the Chief Registrar of Deeds to ensure uniformity in the procedures and practices of the Deeds Registries and to maintain very high standards for the deeds.

To ensure that the standards do not drop, controllers and examiners are employed by every Deeds Registry to examine and inspect every deed submitted for registration. If a deed does not comply with the requirements of the Deeds Registries Act 47 of 1937, it is rejected and cannot be registered.

§ 106ZA.03   Immovable and Movable Property Defined.

The word "land" is often used as a synonym for immovable property. However, the definition of what comprises immovable property, as set out in section 102 of the Deeds Registries Act 47 of 1937, is wider than simply referring to "land."

Section 102 defines immovable property to include, *inter alia*, land, any registered long lease (a lease for ten years or more), a registered right of leasehold, and a registered right of initial ownership.

Generally speaking, immovable property is land and everything that has acceded to the land by either natural or other (man-made) means and cannot be detached from the land without being materially damaged, altered, or having its very nature completely altered.

The importance of being able to define something as immovable property is that ownership and rights in and to the property can be registered in a Deeds Registry and can be mortgaged by means of a mortgage bond. This provides the owner, lessee, mortgagee, or mortgagor with greater security.

Movable property is property that can be readily moved and relocated from one place to another. Movable property can be attached to immovable property and still remain movable property.

§ 106ZA.04   Acquiring and Securing Real Property Rights.

§ 106ZA.04(a)   Real Rights to Property.

A real right is an absolute right. Real rights are primarily rights that a person has in and to a thing. The thing, or object of the right, is bound to the person. In the case of *Denel (Pty) Ltd v Cape Explosive Works Limited* 1999 (2) SA 419 (T), at page 433J, the court described a real right as "a direct power or absolute control over a thing."

In South African property law, there are various categories and examples of real rights to property. Individuals can have a real right in and to their own property as well as the property of another. When one enjoys a real right with respect to a thing that one does not own, this is referred to as a limited real right.

A real right is a claim or a right that an individual has to a thing against the public at large. Therefore, the holder of a real right can enforce that right against the public at large. For example, ownership is a real right and it offers complete control, by the owner, over that thing.

Section 102 of the Deeds Registries Act 47 of 1937 defines a real right as "including any right which becomes a real right upon registration." South African law does not have a closed list of real rights and new real rights in and to property can develop.

§ 106ZA.04(b)   Securing Real Property Rights.

One secures and protects a real right by registering the right in the Deeds Office. In terms of section 3(1) of the Deeds Registries Act 47 of 1937, the Registrar of Deeds has a duty to register specific real rights as set out in that section.

In the case of *Denel (Pty) Ltd v Cape Explosive Works Limited* 1999 (2) SA 419 (T), at page 438B, the court confirmed that when a real right is established by way of registration of the right in the Deeds Registry, it is "maintainable against the whole world."

§ 106ZA.04(c)   Acquiring Real Property Rights.

In South African property law there is a distinction between original and derivative acquisition of real rights. The original acquisition of a real right is a unilateral act carried out by the person who acquires that real right. The real right is newly created and is not obtained from a predecessor. The real right is thus free from any limitation. Prior to the unilateral action taking place, the real right did not exist. The best example of this would be expropriation by the government.

The derivative acquisition of a real right is a bilateral transaction between the person who is the holder of the real right and the person who wishes to acquire the real right. The person acquiring the real right acquires the right with all of the limitations and blemishes that the real right is subject to. A good example of such a transaction is the purchase and sale of land by way of a written agreement of sale.

§ 106ZA.05   Real Rights in Property.

§ 106ZA.05(a)   Ownership.

Private ownership is universally a highly valued and protected real right.

South African property law, ownership is the real right that potentially confers the most complete or comprehensive control over a thing, which means that the right of ownership entitles owners to do with their property as they see fit, subject to the limitations imposed by public and private law.[1]

In the case of *Gien v Gien* 1979 (2) SA 1113 (T) at page 1120, the court defined ownership as:

> "The right of ownership is the most comprehensive real right that a person can have in respect of a thing. The point of departure is that a person can, in respect of immovable property, do with and on his property as he pleases. This apparently unfettered freedom is however, a half-truth. The absolute power of an owner is limited by the restrictions imposed thereon by the law."

Ownership of immovable property can be derived via a grant, private treaty or sale, prescription or expropriation. Ownership is unlimited in duration and is an independent real right as it is not dependant on or derived from any other right.

Ownership of immovable property in South Africa is effected by way of entering into and concluding a written agreement of sale in terms of the provisions of the Alienation of Land Act 68 of 1981.

A conveyancer then drafts a deed of transfer and transfers the property from the seller to the purchaser by executing and registering the deed in the Deeds Registry. The deed of transfer constitutes the purchaser's title deed to the property. Ownership passes to the purchaser upon registration of transfer.

§ 106ZA.05(b)   Servitudes.

Servitudes are limited real rights in immovable property that are registered and recorded in the Deeds Registry. A servitude entitles the holder thereof to either:

1. The undisturbed use and enjoyment of another person's property; or
2. To demand that another person refrain and desist from exercising certain rights that they have stemming from their right of ownership with respect to their property.

In *Dreyer v Letterstedt's Executors* (1865) 5 Searle 88 at page 99, the court defined a servitude as "a real right to an advantage out of the property of another."

It is the direct relationship of the real right of servitude between the holder thereof and the property over which they hold the servitude that distinguishes it from a personal contractual right with the owner of the property over which they enjoy the servitude.

South African law distinguishes between two different types of servitudes, namely personal and praedial servitudes. A praedial servitude is a servitude between two pieces of land. The servitude is created in favor of the dominant tenement property over the servient tenement property. The servitude confers a real right on the dominant tenement property and creates a burden on the servient tenement property.

The owner of the dominant tenement property is entitled to enforce the servitude over the servient tenement property. The servitude exists with the property and thus transfers from owner to owner and continues to exist despite the property being transferred to a new owner.

A personal servitude is a servitude created in favour of a specific individual to whom it provides the right to the undisturbed use and enjoyment of another's property.

The personal nature of the servitude means that it is not transferable and ceases to exist when the individual in whose favor it was created, dies. Good examples common personal servitudes are *usufructs, usus* and *habitatio*.

Servitudes can be created by the state government by way of a grant over state land, agreement between individuals and owners of land, statute or prescription.

One can also approach the High Court of South Africa to enforce or create a servitude. The court order granted by the High Court will either bring the servitude into existence or compel compliance with an existing servitude.

§ 106ZA.05(c) Mortgage Bonds.

A mortgage bond is a form of hypothecation of immovable property which confers a limited real right to an individual or entity over the property of another with the object of securing payment of a debt or performance of an obligation.[2]

Traditionally, a mortgage bond is a bilateral written agreement concluded between a debtor (traditionally the owner of the property) and a creditor (traditionally a financial institution, such as a bank) in terms of which the creditor obtains a real right over the immovable property of the debtor as security for the fulfilment of the debtor's obligations in terms of the agreement.

A mortgage bond is classified as real security in that if the debtor is unable to meet the obligations in terms of the agreement (*i.e.*: fails to repay the debt), the creditor can demand that the immovable property, being the asset bonded as security, be sold and that the proceeds of the sale are used to satisfy the claim.

A mortgage bond is a written instrument that is signed by both the creditor and the debtor. It is then registered by a conveyancer in a Deeds Registry. A mortgage bond is cancelled by registering and executing a deed, in the prescribed form, in a Deeds Registry. A mortgage bond can only be cancelled with the consent of the creditor.

§ 106ZA.05(d) Lease.

A lease is a bilateral agreement whereby one person or other entity agrees to provide another with the temporary, undisturbed, use and enjoyment of property in return for the payment of rental.

In terms of the provisions of the Formalities with respect to Leases of Land Act, 18 of 1969, a long lease is a lease for a period of no less than ten years, for the length of the natural life of the lessee, or is renewable from time to time at the behest of the lessee indefinitely, which periods, when added together, constitute a period not less than ten years.

In terms of section 1(2)(a) of the Formalities in respect of Leases of Land Act, 18 of 1969, a long lease is not valid for a period of greater than ten years unless it has been registered in the deeds registry against the title deed of the leased property.

. The title deed of the leased property will then be endorsed with an annotation reflecting the fact that a long lease has been entered into in relation to that property. The long lease, once registered, provides the lessee with a limited real right in and to the leased property.

[1] Johannesburg Municipal Council v. Rand Townships Registrar 1910 TPD 1314 at 1319.

Regal v African Superslate (Pty) Ltd 1963 (1) SA 102 (A) at 106 to 107.

Page 91 Silberberg and Schoeman's The Law of Property, Fifth Edition.

[2] Grotius 2 48 1.

Page 357 Silberberg and Schoeman's The Law of Property, Fifth Edition.

§ 106ZA.06   Sectional Title and Shareblock Ownership.

In Roman law, the principle of *superficies solo cedit* provides that an individual who owns land also owns all of the buildings that are situated on the land. There is no differentiation between the land and the immovable structures situated thereon. In terms of the Deeds Registries Act 47 of 1937, land is transferred without any reference to the buildings or structures thereon. This means that prior to legislative enactments, it was impossible for an individual to be the owner of a defined portion of a piece of land or part of a building. With residential property becoming increasingly expensive and rare, the need for apartment blocks to be built and sold was becoming great.

The South African legislature created what is now commonly referred to as "sectional ownership," or the ownership a part of a portion of land or a building. On September 17, 1986, the Sectional Titles Act 95 of 1986 was promulgated. This new Act replaced the earlier 1971 Sectional Titles Act. The new Act was heavily based on the Strata Titles Act 17 of 1961 of New South Wales, Australia.

The Sectional Titles Act 95 of 1986 created a new type or class of property defined as a "unit." The unit can be owned by an individual. The unit comprises of a part of the building or "section" and an undivided share in the common parts of the building or land known as the "common property."

Being the owner of a sectional title unit also means that the individual will automatically become a member of an association of sectional owners. The entire sectional scheme is governed by the association which is called a Body Corporate.

Another form of collective ownership and an alternative to Sectional Title ownership is Share Block ownership. In terms of the Share Blocks Control Act, 59 of 1980, a single entity referred to as a Share Block company either owns or controls an immovable property. Members of the Share Block company acquire personal rights of occupation of specific parts of the property based on their membership in the Share block company.

One becomes a member in the Share Block company by purchasing shares in the company and this in turn provides the company with share capital enabling the company to either purchase property or construct additional structures. The purchase of a share in the Share Block company provides the holder of the share with the right to use and occupy a specific portion of the immovable property.

§ 106ZA.07 Taxation.

The primary form of taxation on the acquisition of immovable property in South Africa is prescribed by the Transfer Duty Act, 40 of 1949. In terms of the Transfer Duty Act, 40 of 1949, transfer duty is payable on the acquisition of immovable property, on the transfer of real rights and on the cancellation of real rights. Transfer duty is a form of government tax and is payable prior to registration taking place in the Deeds Registry. It is payable to the South African Revenue Service.

The amount of transfer duty payable is calculated as a percentage of the total consideration paid for the property. Depending on the purchase price of the property, transfer duty varies between 0% and 8% for individuals, and 10% for juristic persons.

In certain limited cases, Value Added Tax (VAT) can be imposed on the sale of immovable property. The obligation to pay VAT largely depends on the nature and identity of the seller. VAT is charged at the rate of 14% of the purchase price of the property. VAT is a form of government tax and is payable to the South African Revenue Service.

When selling an immovable property that is not one's principle residential property, and if the property is sold for over one million rand more than it was purchased for, Capital Gains Tax might be levied by the South African Revenue Service on the consideration received by the seller from the purchaser.

§ 106ZA.08 Bibliography.

Books

Atuahene, Bernadette, *Want What's Ours: Learning from South Africa's Land Restitution Program* (Oxford University Press 2014).

Badenhorst, P.J., Juanita Magrietha Pienaar & Hanri Mostert, *Silberberg and*

Schoeman's The Law of Property (LexisNexis South Africa).

Brand, Danie, Christopher Gevers and Karthigasen Govender, *South African Constitutional Law in Context: Public Law* (Oxford University Press 2015).

Christie, JO & Allen West, *The Conveyancing Practice Guide* (LexisNexis South Africa).

Eksteen, Riaan, *The Role of the Highest Courts of the United States of America and South Africa, and the European Court of Justice in Foreign Affairs* (T.M.C. Asser Press 2019).

Hornby, Donna, Rosalie Kingwill, Lauren Royston and Ben Cousins, *Untitled—Securing Land Tenure In Urban And Rural South Africa* (University Of Kwazulu-Natal Press 2017).

Juta's Pocket Statutes. "The Constitution of the Republic of South Africa, Second Edition" (Juta and Company (Pty) Ltd. 2004).

Miller, Carey, D.L., *The Acquisition and Protection of Ownership* (Juta Legal and Academic Publishers 1986).

Mostert, Hanri, Anne Pope, Juanita Pienaar, Jeannie van Wyk, Warren Freedman, and Pieter Badenhorst, *Property Law in South Africa* (Oxford University Press 2010).

Nel, H.S., *Jones Conveyancing in South Africa* (Juta 4th ed.1991).

Rogoff, Adam C., Richard F. Broude and Daniel M. Glosband, *Collier International Business Insolvency Guide* ch. 39, South Africa (Matthew Bender).

Stohler, Stephan, *Reconstructing Rights: Courts, Parties, and Equality Rights in India, South Africa, and the United States* (Cambridge University Press 2019).

Van Rensburg, A.D.J. and Treisman, S.H., *The Practitioner's Guide to the Alienation of Land Act* (Butterworths 2d ed. 1984).

Articles

Atuahene, Bernadette, "Dignity Takings and Dignity Restoration: Creating a New Theoretical Framework for Understanding Involuntary Property Loss and the Remedies Required," 41 *Law & Soc. Inquiry* 796 (2016).

Atuahene, Bernadette, "Property Rights & the Demands of Transformation," 31 *Mich. J. Int'l L.* 765 (2010).

Badenhorst, Pieter J., "Priority Disputes Between Holders of Old Order Mineral Rights and Holders of Prospecting Rights or Mining Rights Under the MPRDA in South Africa: Aquila has Landed (Continued)," 32 *Colo. Nat. Res. Energy & Envtl. L. Rev.* 195 (2021).

Belinkie, Sasha Fannie, Note, "South Africa's Land Restitution Challenge: Mining Alternatives from Evolving Mineral Taxation Policies," 48 *Cornell Int'l L.J.* 219 (2015).

Christiansen, Eric C., "Empowerment, Fairness, Integration: South African Answers to the Question of Constitutional Environmental Rights," 32 *Stan. Envtl. L.J.* 215 (2013).

Dreyzin, Gary, "The Next Wave of Climate Change Litigation: Comparing Constitutional Inverse Condemnation Claims in the United States, South Africa, and Japan," 31 *Geo. Envtl. L. Rev.* 183 (2018).

Dube, Felix, "Unlawful Occupiers, Eviction and the National State of Disaster: Considering South Africa's Emergency Legislation and Jurisprudence During COVID-19," *Journal of African Law*, 65, Supplement 2 (2021), 333–346.

Frank, Rashri Baboolal, "Historical Milieu of Tribunals in South Africa: The Role of Church Tribunals," *Ecclesiastical Law Journal*, 23, 67–81 (2021).

Hunter, Justin, "Native Title in Australia and South Africa: A Search for Something that Lasts," 22 *U. Miami Int'l & Comp. L. Rev.* 233 (2015).

Viljoen, Sue-Mari, "The South African Redistribution Imperative: Incongruities in Theory and Practice," *Journal of African Law*, 65, 3 (2021), 403–429.

Wertman, Clarissa A., Note, "There's No Place Like Home: Access to Housing for All South Africans," 40 *Brooklyn J. Int'l L.* 719 (2015).

Zamudio, Jose Vega, Comment, "On the Expropriation Bill of South Africa," 52 *Cal. W. Int'l L.J.* 247 (2021).

Zhu, Weidong, "Enforcing Commercial Judgments between China and South Africa in the Context of BRICS and BRI," *Journal of African Law*, 65, 2 (2021), 179–203.